Social
FOUNDATIONS
AND MULTICULTURAL
PERSPECTIVES IN EDUCATION

PRELIMINARY EDITION

Edited by Pamela Twyman Hoff
and Mohamed Nur-Awaleh

Illinois State University

 cognella™

Bassim Hamadeh, Publisher
Michael Simpson, Vice President of Acquisitions
Christopher Foster, Vice President of Marketing
Jessica Knott, Managing Editor
Stephen Milano, Creative Director
Kevin Fahey, Cognella Marketing Program Manager
Al Grisanti, Acquisitions Editor
Jamie Giganti, Project Editor
Luiz Ferreira, Licensing Associate

First published in the United States of America in 2012 by University Readers, Inc.

Trademark Notice: Product or corporate names may be trademarks or registered trademarks, and are used only for identification and explanation without intent to infringe.

16 15 14 13 12   1 2 3 4 5

Printed in the United States of America

ISBN: 978-1-60927-130-5

www.cognella.com 800.200.3908

Contents

SECTION IV: TEACHING AND LEARNING—A MULTICULTURAL AND GLOBAL APPROACH

Section 1

Introduction: What Is a Social Foundations and Multicultural Perspective?

Highly Qualified Teachers and the Social Foundations of Education

Courses in the social foundations of education are under attack. But if we want to prepare truly professional, high-quality teachers, those courses are essential.

By Richard Neumann

While everyone agrees that students need highly qualified teachers, the debate over what these teachers should know and how they should be prepared continues. However, one area of traditional, university-based teacher preparation has been marginalized in that debate. That area is the social foundations of education.

The social foundations of education commonly are divided into two areas: courses that focus on philosophy, history of education, and sociopolitical aspects of schooling and courses concerned with multiculturalism. Courses in the first group are intended to strengthen prospective teachers' ability to understand why U.S. public schools operate as they do. Among other things, this ability requires knowledge of the social, political, and economic forces that influenced the historical construction of public education generally, as well as particular regional, state, and local conditions of schooling. These courses also encourage teachers to contemplate competing purposes of public education, their first and primary obligation as educators, and a guiding vision for their work.

> *Social foundations courses encourage educators to contemplate their role as transformative intellectuals in the eradication of injustice and advancement of democratic ideals.*

Courses in multiculturalism are intended to provide knowledge about the histories and cultures of different groups and knowledge about how stereotypes are formed and perpetuated. They also attempt to engender in teachers a commitment to equal educational opportunity for all students.

The leading advocate for including the social foundations of education in teacher preparation programs is the Council of Social Foundations in Education (CSFE), formerly known as the Council for Learned Societies in Education (CLSE). The CSFE promotes standards prepared by the CLSE for academic and professional instruction in foundations of education, which the National Council for Accreditation of Teacher Education (NCATE 2007) includes as a requirement for its accreditation of teacher education programs. According to the CLSE, "the purpose of foundations study is to bring these disciplinary resources to bear in developing interpretive, normative, and critical perspectives on education, both inside and outside of schools" (CLSE 2004).

> *The social foundations of education are not on the radar for many policy makers or researchers, although some prominent scholars in the field do recognize them as valuable.*

The standards not only recommend that educators and prospective teachers understand existing conditions of education and their consequences, they encourage contemplation of goals, alternative conceptions of schooling, and possibilities of education: What *should* schools be doing? What structures and processes of schooling best facilitate achieving those goals?

Distinguished education theorists—such as John Dewey, Paulo Freire, Maxine Greene, Michael Apple, and Henry A. Giroux—have argued that public education has an obligation to prepare young people for democratic citizenship and to advance social justice. Social foundations courses often provide prospective teachers with their first exposure to these ideas of social justice and preparing citizens for a democracy.

The CLSE standards do not explicitly identify advancing social justice as the purpose for studying the social foundations of education. But it's implicit in the practical performance measures provided for evaluating professional development and preparation programs in the field: "The educator can assist the examination and development of democratic values that are based on critical study and reflection" (CLSE 2004).

THE CRITICS OF SOCIAL FOUNDATIONS COURSES

Teacher education has been under siege for decades from both within and outside the university (Labaree 2004). A recent major offensive began with George W. Bush's appointment of Rodney Paige as Secretary of Education. In his first annual report to Congress on teacher quality, Paige broadsided schools of teacher education:

> Schools of education and formal teacher training programs are failing to produce the types of highly qualified teachers that the No Child Left Behind Act demands. ... There is little evidence that education school coursework leads to improved student achievement. ... The data show that many states mandate a shocking number of education courses to qualify for certification. ... These burdensome requirements are the Achilles heel of the certification system. They scare off talented individuals while adding little value. Certainly, some of the required courses might be helpful, but scant research exists to justify these mandates. (U.S. Department of Education 2002)

Paige's later reports circumscribed conceptions of "highly qualified teacher" within narrow measures of student achievement, namely standardized test scores. The development of critical, normative, and interpretive perspectives and the ideals of social justice and building democratic character were marginalized and have been largely absent in policy documents concerning teacher preparation. Instead, the discourse is dominated by an instrumentalist view of teaching coupled to an economic utility concept of school goals.

The economic utility narrative defines the goal for teacher education as increased student achievement and narrowing achievement gaps, particularly in literacy and mathematics, in order to provide corporations with a more capable pool of workers. In this narrative, the goal is to provide corporations with a range of capable, cost-efficient workers, which will result in favorable economic conditions for Americans. Public education's primary purpose is human resource development. The economic utility narrative is central to understanding the depreciation of social foundations in policy discourse on teacher preparation and teacher quality.

Dan W. Butin reviewed 10 major education policy documents disseminated between January 2003 and April 2005 and found "an almost complete lack of attention" to social foundations of education. The documents were prepared by the Progressive Policy Institute, Achieve Inc. and the National Governors Association, National Council on Teacher Quality, National Collaborative on Diversity in the Teaching Force, American Association of State Colleges and Universities, Educational Testing Service, Teaching Commission, Education Commission of the States, and the National Commission on Teaching and America's Future. Six of the policy documents made no reference to knowledge and skills associated with social foundations of education; three included only passing reference. All of the policy documents used "achievement gaps" to justify change in teacher preparation, and none of them cited a need to better prepare democratic citizens or advance social justice (Butin 2005).

Many policy documents on teacher quality issued after Butin's review reiterate the theme of increasing student achievement for economic benefits. For example, *Teaching at Risk: Progress and Potholes*, the final report of the Teaching Commission, in a section titled "What's at Stake," argued:

> A fiercely competitive global information economy, powered as never before by innovation and intellect, demands that America's young people be well educated. It is not only their potential that hangs in the balance; it is the nation's economic future. (Teaching Commission 2006: 12)

Indeed, the No Child Left Behind Act, the signature education policy achievement of the Bush Administration, does not mention democratic citizenship.

Critics of teacher education can find support for their arguments in studies by prominent leaders and researchers in the field. For example, in *Educating School Teachers*, by Arthur E. Levine, former president of Teachers College Columbia University, assails the condition of teacher preparation and seemingly dismisses courses in the social foundations of education and even

Several influential conservative groups want to eliminate social justice from preservice teacher education.

instructional methods as largely irrelevant: "The content of the curriculum is too often a grab bag of courses, ranging across the various subfields of teacher education from methods to the philosophy and history of education, rather than the focused preparation needed for real classrooms" (2006: 107).

It is interesting to note that two of the exemplary teacher education programs identified in Levine's study, the STEP program at Stanford University and Alverno College in Milwaukee, Wisconsin, both include courses in the social foundations of education. In addition, the *Conceptual Framework* of Teachers College maintains that teaching is an "ethical and political act." In the faculty's view: "the educators and scholars that have shaped Teachers College's philosophy believed that education could enlighten democracy, challenge and transform social inequities, and help to build a more humane and just society. ... We see teachers as moral actors whose job is to facilitate the growth and development of other human beings ... and as such, as participants in a larger struggle for social justice" (Teachers College Accreditation Team 2003: 26).

> *The economic utility narrative is central to understanding the depreciation of social foundations in policy discourse on teacher preparation and teacher quality.*

Critics of teacher education also can find support for their arguments in the American Educational Research Association (AERA) report, *Studying Teacher Education*, the most comprehensive review of research on the field. However, according to the AERA report, "the body of teacher education research that directly addresses desirable pupil and other outcomes and the conditions and contexts within which these outcomes are likely to occur is relatively small and inconclusive" (Cochran-Smith 2005: 5). Although critics cite this inconclusive evidence, they rarely address the exceedingly complex problems of measuring the effects of teacher education programs, especially the effects of the discrete elements of those programs. The range of variables and contexts involved is enormous. In addition, a lack of consensus on appropriate and valid outcome measures further complicates research. Thus, the appeal of the simplistic measurement of schooling outcomes using standardized test scores seems to have clouded the judgment of many teacher education critics, policy makers, and educators who should know better.

Consider, for example, the difficulty in designing research to assess the extent to which the critical, normative, and interpretive perspectives on schooling developed by prospective teachers in social foundations of education courses contribute to changes in structures and processes at the schools where these teachers are eventually employed, which in turn affect student achievement. Another research question related to the social foundations of the education component of a teacher preparation program might involve the assessment of teachers' effectiveness in developing a sense of agency and the knowledge and skills for democratic citizenship in their students. Which measurement instruments would be best for these studies? The complexities of these examples may help explain the complete absence of research related to the philosophy of education, history of education, and democratic goals of public schooling in the AERA report; the terms *democratic, philosophy of education, and history of education* do not appear in the index.

SUPPORTERS OF SOCIAL FOUNDATIONS COURSES

Although the social foundations of education are "not on the radar" for many policy makers or researchers, some prominent scholars in the field do recognize them as valuable. A report by the National Academy of Education (NAE), *A Good Teacher in Every Classroom: Preparing the Highly Qualified Teachers Our Children Deserve*, presents a framework for understanding teaching and learning that acknowledges common topics of social foundations of education courses in teacher education programs: "The vision of professional teaching depicted in the framework... requires that teachers be mindful of what it means to educate students within a democracy so that, as citizens, they can participate fully in political, civic, and economic life" (Darling-Hammond and Baratz-Snowden 2005: 5). In relation to the framework, the NAE committee identified three general areas of knowledge used by effective teachers; one of these is "understanding of the subject matter and skills to be taught in light of the social purposes of education" (2005: 6). This area of knowledge is central to the guiding vision teachers need.

> A "curricular vision"—one that takes into account the social purposes of education in a democracy—is necessary to guide decisions about what to teach and why. This enables teachers to select, adapt, and design materials and lessons so that they can accomplish their goals (Darling-Hammond and Baratz-Snowden 2005: 14).

The National Network for Educational Renewal (NNER) also stresses the need for public schools to prepare democratic citizens. Created by John Goodlad in 1985, NNER's goal is "to improve simultaneously the quality of P-12 education for thoughtful and informed participation in a democracy and the quality of preparation of educators for our school." NNER appears to be the only major national reform effort in teacher education concerned with strengthening democratic citizenship.

The American Association of State Colleges and Universities (AASCU) called for changes to the undergraduate curriculum "to encourage students to become more informed and engaged citizens" (AASCU 2007: 1). For undergraduates to benefit fully from such changes, the AASCU contends that education for democratic citizenship must begin in elementary and secondary schools.

> teacher candidates must be prepared to teach the content of civic preparation; knowledge of the history of the country and principles of democracy; development of civic skills; civic experiences both on and off campus; and reflection, placing all of this work in a framework for citizenship preparation. (AASCU 2007: 1)

While the goal of social justice in public education is consistent with values and ideals held by many democratic-minded citizens, several influential conservative groups want to eliminate social justice from preservice teacher education. Among these is the American Council of Trustees and Alumni, founded in 1995 by Lynne Cheney, wife of former Vice President Dick Cheney. Another group is the National Association of Scholars, whose governing board includes such prominent conservatives as John R. Silber, former president of Boston University, and Chester E. Finn Jr., senior fellow at the

Hoover Institute. The Foundation for Individual Rights in Education (FIRE) also has criticized schools of teacher education for "improperly attempting to dictate the values and ideals that teachers must possess in order to educate students," specifically the values and ideals embedded in the concept of social justice (2006).

In 2006, these three groups used a hearing of the U.S. Department of Education's National Advisory Committee on Institutional Quality and Integrity to pressure the National Council for Accreditation of Teacher Education (NCATE) to remove a recommendation in its accreditation standards that teacher candidates' "dispositions" should be "guided by beliefs and attitudes such as caring, fairness, honesty and responsibility, and social justice." NCATE was aware of the testimony the groups planned to present at the hearing to contest renewal of its recognition by the Department of Education. NCATE President Arthur E. Wise obviated the groups' need to testify by announcing at the hearing that the phrase "social justice" would be removed from the council's guidelines, which resulted in the committee passing a motion to renew recognition for the accreditation organization for five more years (Wasley 2006). While removal of two words from an accreditation document may seem inconsequential, teacher educators and citizens alike should think long and hard about the phrase these conservative groups want stricken from teacher preparation.

CONCLUSION

Courses in the social foundations of education expose students to competing educational goals, and they foster the dispositions and develop strategies for balancing goals in professional practice. In social foundations courses, students learn about the history of public schooling and the centrality of this institution to our democratic society. Courses on instructional methods and planning do not address these ideas.

Social foundations courses encourage educators to contemplate their role as transformative intellectuals in the eradication of injustice and advancement of democratic ideals. They urge teachers to think deeply and seriously about the wisdom of such philosophers as John Dewey who illuminate the connection between schooling and democratic community. And they provide teachers with the perspective to challenge dictates that define the purpose of education as production of human capital for the economy.

Prospects for the social foundations of education in teacher preparation programs do not look good. If all that's expected of educators is to produce high levels of student academic achievement to serve the needs of industry, then much of what is taught in social foundations may be of little benefit. However, if teachers are perceived as professionals who are expected to participate in an ongoing process of renewal in the schools where they work, if they're expected to teach their subjects with a vision of the social purposes of education in a democratic society, then those who form the policies on teacher preparation need to address the indispensability of the social foundations of education.

REFERENCES

American Association of State Colleges and Universities (AASCU). *Democracy & Civic Engagement: Implications for Teacher Preparation and a National Agenda for Inquiry.* Washington, D.C.: AASCU, 2007.

Butin, Dan W. "Is Anyone Listening? Educational Policy Perspectives on the Social Foundations of Education." *Educational Studies* 38, no. 3 (December 2005): 286–297.

Cochran-Smith, Marilyn, and Kenneth M. Zeichner, eds. *Studying Teacher Education: The Report of the AERA Panel on Research and Teacher Education.* Mahwah, N.J.: Lawrence Erlbaum, 2005.

Council of Learned Societies in Education (CLSE). *Standards for Academic and Professional Instruction in Foundations of Education, Educational Studies, and Educational Policy Studies.* Chicago, Ill.: Council for Social Foundations of Education, 2004. www.uic.edu/educ/csfe/standard.htm.

Darling-Hammond, Linda, and Joan Baratz-Snowden, eds. *A Good Teacher in Every Classroom: Preparing the Highly Qualified Teachers Our Children Deserve.* San Francisco: Jossey-Bass, 2005.

Foundation for Individual Rights in Education (FIRE). "FIRE Statement on NCATE's Encouragement of Political Litmus Tests in Higher Education." June 5, 2006. www.thefire.org/index.php/article/7079.html.

Labaree, David. *The Trouble with Ed Schools*, New Haven, Conn.: Yale University Press, 2004.

Levine, Arthur E. *Educating School Teachers.* Washington, D.C.: Education Schools Project, 2006.

National Council for Accreditation of Teacher Education (NCATE). *Unit Standards.* Washington, D.C.: NCATE, 2007. www.ncate.org/public/standards.asp.

National Network for Educational Renewal. www.nnerpartnerships.org/index.html.

Teaching Commission. *Teaching at Risk: Progress and Potholes.* New York: Teaching Commission, 2006.

U.S. Department of Education. *Meeting the Highly Qualified Teachers Challenge: The Secretary's Annual Report on Teacher Quality.* Washington, D.C.: U.S. Department of Education, Office of Postsecondary Education, 2002.

Teachers College Accreditation Team. *Conceptual Framework.* New York: Teachers College, Columbia University, 2003. www.tc.edu/administration/oaa/PDF_DOC/Conceptual_Framework.pdf.

Wasley, Paula. "Accreditor of Education Schools Drops Controversial 'Social Justice' Language." *Chronicle of Higher Education*, June 16, 2006: A13.

Educational Dilemmas

By Ian Winchester

Are there genuine educational dilemmas? There appear to be a number of kinds of dilemma that a teacher might face, some of which might be characterized as (a) teaching and learning dilemmas, (b) emotional dilemmas, (c) practical social dilemmas, (d) moral dilemmas, and even (e) legal dilemmas. There may be many others.

The sort of things I have in mind might be illustrated by a number of examples:

The following situation is the one that might easily obtain in a classroom. There are a number of children who have learning difficulties of an identifiable kind that require careful personal attention, the majority of those in the classroom appear to be normal learners, and a few of the children appear to be especially quick learners, some with special powers or abilities. And further suppose there is no extra help for either those with difficulties or those specially gifted. How ought a teacher to devote her or his time over the course of the days, weeks, months, or year(s)?

The following strategies might easily come to mind: (a) devote extra time to those with learning difficulties and assume that, given the days assignments, the others will manage perfectly well to learn what they ought; or (b) devote extra time to both those with learning difficulties and those with special gifts, and assume that the normal will manage the days assignments as they ought without further ado; or (c) spend no special time with those with learning difficulties and no special time with those who learn quickly or have special gifts, instead, spend all of the time seeing that each one of the majority of the class, the normal learners, learns what they ought so that the class can move on as a group with these learners satisfied; or (d) devote no special time either to those with learning difficulties or the normal group, but rather spend a lot of extra time with those with special gifts who are quick learners. The problem with each and every one of these solutions is that it poses both a moral and practical dilemma for a teacher.

The above scenario has many possible emotional counterparts. For example, one might imagine a class in which most of the children have no difficulties at home, come to school well fed or happy, and are not in fear and trembling either of the teacher or of other children. But some of the children may have enormous emotional difficulties both at home and therefore derivatively in the classroom setting. This sort of thing was anticipated by the 19th century school promoters in England, in the

United States, and in Canada who saw the common school as a refuge from the vagaries and difficulties of many homes. Their banner was the wiping out of crime, poverty, and ignorance via the safe haven of the common school. Again the dilemma facing a teacher is whether to spend a disproportionate amount of her or his time with the emotionally troubled children helping them to cope and in doing so get on with their learning, or to relatively neglect the emotionally stable majority who may have other learning difficulties.

The general form of such dilemmas is always the same for a teacher who works with a class full of children as opposed to a tutor who works with one, namely, how am I best to devote my energies given the limited time I have and the multiple children needing my attention? Such dilemmas are always practical dilemmas, for a teacher is always faced with the difficulties faced by the children at the moment. And the solution to such dilemmas is always in the form of a choice here and now by a teacher to work with just this child on this problem or to work with some other or others or to work entirely with the class as a whole, neglecting the individual difficulties faced by some.

There are of course other kinds of dilemmas that a teacher may face. For example there is what one might call social dilemmas relating to the teacher's response to her or his knowledge of how a child might be being treated at home or in that child's community. It can come to the attention of a teacher that a child is being physically abused out of school, the teacher suspects it is parental abuse of the children, and yet fears if the powers of the social system are called into play, the child's learning may suffer more than it does in the status quo. What is the teacher to do? Should she or he report the suspected abuse? Should she or he comfort the child and give the child a safe haven at least for the time the child is in the school? Again a teacher will face the dilemma the only way that she or he can, by making a difficult choice, by taking some difficult action.

There are, of course, much less troubling dilemmas that a teacher must face all the time. Here I am thinking of matters of pedagogical detail, the "how to present" questions that fill a teacher's day. Should I use just this illustration or that one? If in a mathematics class is this form of proof more easily grasped, more helpful, sounder? And on what basis ought I to choose? Should I introduce the grammatical detail now, or wait until the children understand some more, or have had a chance to delight in the poem, the play, the essay? Or should the teacher proceed as if there are no standard provincial, state, or other general examinations faced by the children because she or he believes this is pedagogically sound while facing the possibility that the details of such an examination may bypass the children's learning without her or his direct intervention?

Such dilemmas are not commonly discussed in the literature. I would like to encourage those who find dilemmas in their work as educators and how they have tackled them, to write up some of their thoughts and send them in, perhaps to JET, for others to think about and perhaps comment on.

Ian Winchester
Editor

Section II

History and Philosophy of Education

Race, Knowledge Construction, and Education in the U.S.A: Lessons from History

By James A. Banks

ABSTRACT: The article uses examples of research, books, and reports on race and ethnic groups published between 1911 and 2000 to document how the knowledge created by social scientists, historians, and public intellectuals reflects their social and cultural contexts as well as their political and economic interests. Because of variations in their socialization and epistemological communities, researchers develop competing paradigms and explanations in each historical period. Most of those that become institutionalized reinforce a society's prevailing ideologies and social arrangements. Transformative knowledge usually originates within racial and cultural communities outside the mainstream. Although it is often marginalized and made invisible within the dominant society, transformative knowledge—when combined with action—helps to democratize society and its institutions. Consequently, it is an essential part of the curriculum in the schools, colleges, and universities in democratic, pluralistic nation states.

The *Studies in the Historical Foundations of Multicultural Education Series* (hereafter *Series*) was initiated by the Center for Multicultural Education at the University of Washington in 1992. The purpose of this research project is to uncover the roots of multicultural education, to identify the ways in which it is connected to its historical antecedents, and to gain insights from the past that can inform school reform efforts today related to race and ethnic diversity (Banks, 1996a).

Another aim of the *Series* is to identify the ways in which the knowledge constructed within a society reflects the social, political, and economic contexts in which it is created as well as the subsocieties and personal biographies of historians and social scientists (Banks, 1998). Studies in the *Series* identify important ways in which theory, research, and ideology in multicultural education are both linked to and divergent from past educational reform movements related to race and ethnic diversity (J. A. Banks, 1995, 1996a, 1996b, 1998; C. A. M. Banks, 1996, in progress; Hillis, 1996; Roche, 1996).

This article extends the ongoing work of the Series by examining the historical and social contexts from 1911 to 2000 to identify ways in which the research and knowledge constructed about race and ethnic groups mirrored and perpetuated these contexts. This historical survey will of necessity be highly abbreviated and condensed. Race relations research on both adults and children will be discussed and related to the social, historical, and political contexts in which it was conducted. In this article, I describe research that supports the claims I made in an earlier article in the Series project (Banks, 1998).

- The cultural communities in which individuals are socialized are also epistemological communities that have shared beliefs, perspectives, and knowledge.
- Social science and historical research are influenced in complex ways by the life experiences, values, personal biographies, and epistemological communities of researchers.
- Knowledge created by social scientists, historians, and public intellectuals reflects and perpetuates their epistemological communities, experiences, goals, and interests.
- How individual social scientists interpret their cultural experiences is mediated by the interaction of a complex set of status variables, such as gender, social class, age, political affiliation, religion, and region. (p. 5)

THE RISE OF NATIVISM IN THE EARLY 1900s

In the early decades of the last century—1900 to 1924—the U.S.A experienced massive immigration from southern, central, and eastern Europe. Europeans were leaving their homelands in massive numbers because of economic dislocations in Europe and the power and promise of the American dream. The American dream and its promises were conveyed across the Atlantic to potential newcomers by letters from European immigrants already in America and by steamship companies. The companies were anxious to profit from the 'huddled masses' from Europe described in Emma Lazarus's (1886/1968) poem that is inscribed on the base of the Statue of Liberty.

The 'old' European immigrants—who had come largely from northern and western Europe—considered themselves 'native Americans' by the turn of century. They became alarmed by the large number of immigrants from southern, eastern, and central Europe who were settling in the U.S.A (Higham, 1972) because, they believed, these immigrants differed from themselves in several important ways. A large percentage of the new immigrants were Catholics, and most spoke languages different from those spoken by the 'native Americans.' Also, the 'old' immigrants believed that the 'new' immigrants were easy pawns for city politicians because they exchanged their votes for patronage. Consequently, argued individuals who spoke for the old immigrants, the new immigrants threatened democracy in America. They were also a threat to U.S. democracy because of the possibility of a papal takeover in the U.S.A

(Higham). This belief developed because of the large percentage of the new immigrants who were Catholic. A significant percentage were also Jews; some also came from China—and, after 1882, Japan.

The nativists were also alarmed about the new immigrants because they considered the immigrants—such as Jews, Italians and Poles—to be members of races that were separate from and inferior to the descendants of northern and western Europeans (Jacobson, 1998). Madison Grant (1923) argued that the mixing of these inferior races with the northern and western European groups would result in the emergence of a lower type of civilization in the U.S.A. His book had the evocative title, *The Passing of the Great Race.*

THE CONSTRUCTION OF KNOWLEDGE ABOUT RACE IN THE EARLY 1900s

As is usually the case during a particular historical period, conflicting and oppositional paradigms were constructed about the southern, central, and eastern European immigrants during the early decades of the twentieth century. One was a *nativist paradigm*, which was given voice and legitimacy by a number of influential books and other publications. Researchers and writers who embraced this paradigm documented ways in which the new immigrants differed from the northern and western Europeans and how they were a threat to American democracy and to the survival of the Anglo-Saxon 'race.'

Researchers and writers such as Madison Grant (1923) and T. Lothrop Stoddard (1920) documented the ways in which southern, central, and eastern Europeans were genetically inferior to northern and western Europeans by using findings from craniometry, the method and science of measuring skull sizes (Gould, 1996). This research indicated that southern, central, and eastern Europeans had smaller skulls than those of northern and western Europeans and consequently were genetically inferior. Jews and Blacks, both regarded as inferior to northern and western Europeans, were also targets of the nativists. Jews were targets because they were considered a distinct race from Whites in the early 1900s and made up a significant percentage of the new immigrants (Brodkin, 1998; Jacobson, 1998). African-Americans had been in America since 1619 and made up a substantial percentage of the nation's population, especially in the Southern states. In 1790, for example, African-Americans made up approximately 19.2% of the U.S. population (Bailey, 1961, p. 67).

An Oppositional Paradigm Emerges

A group of social scientists and philosophers within marginalized ethnic communities—primarily Jewish and African-American scholars—created a *transformative paradigm* that challenged nativist theories (Banks, 1993a). They included the anthropologist Franz Boas (1910) and the philosophers Horce Kallen (1924) and Randolph Bourne (1916). Boas (1938/1963) rejected genetic explanations of racial differences and argued that human behavior could best be explained by the interaction of genetic characteristics with the environment. In response to calls for the forced and rapid assimilation of the new immigrants by educators and policy-makers, Kallen and Bourne argued that the new immigrants were entitled to 'cultural democracy' in America, which was an extension of the political democracy guaranteed by the Constitution. Kallen and Bourne argued that the new immigrants had the right to maintain important aspects of their ethnic cultures and identities as they became Americans. Gordon (1964), summarizing Kallen's work writes:

> A second theme that highlights Kallen's development of the cultural pluralism position is that his position is entirely in harmony with the traditional ideals of American political and social life, and that, indeed, any attempt to impose Anglo-Saxon conformity constitutes a violation of those ideals. (p. 145)

NATIVISM TRIUMPHS

The nativistic sentiments directed against the southern, central, and eastern European immigrants gave rise to the influential and inflammatory nativistic Know-Nothing movement (Bennett, 1988), whose aim was to rid the U.S.A of foreign influences. In 1911, the Dillingham Commission—a Congressional Committee created in 1907 to investigate immigration—issued a report that validated and reinforced the views of the nativists. The Commission concluded that the new and the old immigrants were different in significant ways. Historical research today indicates that the two groups of immigrants were more alike than different (Higham, 1972; Bennett, 1988).

The Dillingham Commission, which was appointed by members of Congress who represented and identified with powerful groups in America, created knowledge and findings that reinforced the dominant prejudices, sentiments, and perceptions of mainstream groups in the U.S.A. The Commission, in the words of Manning Marable (1996), did not 'speak truth to power.' Rather, it reinforced and legitimized mainstream popular knowledge and the groups that exercised the most power in society rather than challenged prevailing conceptions and the people who benefited from them.

The nativists won several major Congressional victories that eventually curtailed the flow of southern, eastern, and central European immigrants to the U.S.A and completely stopped immigration from China. These victories included the Chinese Exclusion Act of 1882—the first immigration act directed toward a specific nationality group. The Immigration Act of 1917 required immigrants to pass a literacy test in their native language. The era of massive immigration to the U.S.A was ended by the Immigration Act of 1924, which discriminated blatantly against the southern, central, and eastern European immigrants.

The nativists and the assimilationists were victorious in part because most of the immigrants themselves surrendered their ethnic cultures and languages to gain full inclusion into American society. This was a possibility for White European immigrants, but not for people of color such as Native Americans, Mexican-Americans, and African-Americans. Even when people of color became highly culturally assimilated, they were still denied structural inclusion into American society. This is to a large extent still true today, although it is mediated and made more complex by social class factors (Wilson, 1978). In the U.S.A today, in large part because of opportunities that resulted from the civil rights movement of the 1960s and 1970s, there is a significant group of middle-class African-Americans. Although middle-class Blacks are able to enjoy most of the material benefits that middle-class Whites experience, they encounter racism in both their personal and professional lives (Feagin & Sikes, 1994).

KNOWLEDGE, POWER, AND TRANSFORMATIVE KNOWLEDGE

A significant finding of the Series is that individuals and groups on the margins often challenge mainstream and established paradigms that violate human rights and American democratic ideals (Banks, 1996a). Boas, Kallen, and Bourne were immigrant Jews. African-American social scientists such as W. E. B. DuBois (Aptheker, 1983; Lewis, 1995), Carter G. Woodson (1933), and Kelly Miller (1908) also challenged the prevailing theories about race and intelligence during the early decades of the twentieth century. As Okihiro (1994) has perceptively argued, it is 'outsiders' and groups and individuals in the margins who frequently keep democratic ideals and practices alive in democratic nation states because they are among the first people to take actions to defend these ideals when they are most seriously challenged.

Social scientists and philosophers such as Boas, Bourne, Kallen, DuBois, Woodson, and Miller created oppositional knowledge—which I call *transformative knowledge*—because of their socialization and experiences within marginalized communities (Banks, 1993a). These communities enable individuals to acquire unique ways to conceptualize the world and an epistemology that differs in significant ways from mainstream assumptions, conceptions, values, and epistemology. Knowledge is in important ways related to power. Groups with the most power within society often construct—perhaps unconsciously—knowledge that maintains their power and protects their interests. Scholars and public intellectuals who are outside the mainstream often construct transformative knowledge that challenges the existing and institutionalized metanarrative (C. A. M. Banks, 1996).

The *Series'* hypotheses about the relationship between knowledge and power are influenced by the work of transformative scholars such as Mannheim (1936), Clark (1965), Myrdal (1969), Ladner (1973), Code (1991), Harding (1991), and Collins (2000). These scholars have described the ways in which knowledge is not neutral but is highly related to the social, economic, and political contexts in which it is created. Code, the feminist epistemologist, writes, 'Knowledge does not transcend, but is rooted in and shaped by, specific interests and social arrangements' (p. 68).

Scholars and researchers less centered in the mainstream tend to have different epistemologies, in part because change and reform, rather than maintenance of the status quo, more frequently serves their social, cultural, political, and economic interests. The epistemological communities in which researchers on the margins are socialized provide them with a unique standpoint or cultural eye that Patricia Hill Collins, the African-American sociologist, calls the 'outsider/within' perspective.

Despite the oppositional knowledge created by scholars such as Boas, Bourne, and Kallen, the nativists were destined to win the battle to stop the massive influx of immigrants from southern, eastern, and central Europe, to culturally assimilate the immigrants, and to maintain Anglo-Saxon cultural and political hegemony. The nativists won the battle for several reasons. Although the knowledge and arguments created by scholars such as Boas, Bourne, and Kallen were incisive and cogent, they largely fell on deaf ears. The political and economic power was on the side of the nativists. Knowledge, no matter how thoughtful and logical, usually fades when it goes against powerful political and economic forces. *Knowledge is viewed as most influential when it reinforces the beliefs, ideologies, and assumptions of the people who exercise the most political and economic power within a society.* Neither the knowledge created by nativist scholars nor that created by transformative scholars such as Boas, Kallen, and Bourne was the decisive factor that resulted in the victory of the nativists. Political and economic factors, rather than knowledge, were the most significant factors in their triumph.

THE INTERCULTURAL AND INTERGROUP EDUCATION MOVEMENTS

The Intercultural Education Movement

The assimilationist and pluralist paradigms that emerged within the larger society were mirrored in the nation's schools, colleges, and universities. In the 1930s, an educational movement emerged in the U.S.A to help immigrant students adapt to American life, to maintain aspects of their ethnic heritages and identity, and to become effective citizens of the commonwealth. This movement was called the *intercultural education movement* (Montalto, 1982). New York City, where most of the European immigrants arrived when they came to the U.S.A, became one of the most important sites for the intercultural education movement.

Rachel Davis DuBois, one of the leaders of the intercultural education movement, initiated ethnic assemblies in schools that celebrated the cultures of the immigrants (C. A. M. Banks, 1996). An important aim of the assemblies was to teach immigrant youths ethnic pride and to help mainstream students appreciate the cultures of immigrant youths.

The Intergroup Education Movement

When World War II began, most African-Americans lived in the Southern states, such as Arkansas, Mississippi, and South Carolina. Blacks were heavily concentrated in the Southern states because as captive workers they most frequently worked in cotton and tobacco fields. African-Americans began the Great Migration to northern, middle western, and western cities when the war began (Lemann, 1991). They rushed to cities such as St. Louis, Chicago, New York, and Los Angeles. Like the southern, central, and eastern European immigrants, African-American migrants were searching for better economic opportunities and for the elusive American dream. They also left the South in large numbers to escape the institutionalized racism and discrimination that became pernicious and rampant in the decades after the Civil War (Logan, 1954/1997).

When they arrived in northern and western cities, African-Americans discovered that these regions were not promised lands. They experienced discrimination in housing, employment, and in public accommodation. Racial tensions developed and erupted in a series of race riots that destroyed many lives and millions of dollars' worth of property. In 1943, riots occurred in Los Angeles, Detroit, and New York City. The Detroit riot lasted more than 30 hours. When it was over, 25 African-Americans and nine Whites had been killed and millions of dollars in property had been destroyed.

The racial riots and incidents in the nation's cities, as well as Nazi anti-Semitism in Europe, provided a new emphasis for intercultural educators. By this time, they frequently referred to themselves as inter-group educators (C. A. M. Banks, in progress). During the 1940s, the intergroup education movement in the nation's schools, colleges, and universities gave birth to a new era of research in race relations and intergroup relations. Like intercultural education, the aims of intergroup education were to minimize ethnic cultures and affiliations, to help students become mainstream Americans and effective citizens, and to teach racial and ethnic tolerance (Taba *et al.*, 1952).

RESEARCH DURING THE INTERGROUP EDUCATION ERA: 1940–54

The intergroup education period in the U.S.A, from about 1940 to 1954, was one of the nation's most prodigious periods for interracial and intergroup research, theory development, and activities. Although the nation's schools, as well as most of its other institutions—especially in the South—were tightly segregated along racial lines, a group of the nation's social scientists, educators, civil rights organizations, and foundations focused on what Myrdal (1944) called the 'American Dilemma.' Most of this research, theory development, and activities originated within ethnic communities that were rather separate and apart from mainstream institutions. Jewish American and African-American schol-ars and civil rights organizations provided much of the leadership in the intergroup and ethnic studies developments during the years that preceded and followed World War II.

Three seminal studies marked this period: *An American Dilemma* (Myrdal, 1944), *The Authoritarian Personality* (Adorno *et al.*, 1950), and *The Nature of Prejudice* (Allport, 1954). Each of these studies was designed to provide knowledge and insights that would improve race relations and contribute to the development of theory and research in the social sciences.

An American Dilemma, funded by the Carnegie Corporation of New York, is the most comprehen-sive single study of race relations in the U.S.A (Myrdal, 1944). Gunnar Myrdal, a Swedish economist, led the research team that gathered the data for this ambitious study and authored the book that resulted from it. One of Myrdal's key findings was that the discrepancy between American democratic ideals and institutionalized racism and discrimination created an 'American dilemma' that had the potential to lead to the reform of race relations in the U.S.A. He believed that most Americans had internalized American Creed values such as equality and justice, and that a dilemma was created for Americans because of the gap between their ideals and realities. Effective leaders, he argued, could bring about reform in race relations by making this dilemma visible to Americans and appealing to their basic democratic beliefs.

The leaders at the Carnegie Foundation who funded the study, who identified with America's power elite, were surprised and embarrassed by Myrdal's candid criticism of racism and discrimination in the

American South. They responded to the study with benign neglect. The major findings of the study challenged the status quo in the South. Although *An American Dilemma* was destined to attain the status of a classic within the American academic community, it received a chilly response in the foundation and corporate worlds (Southern, 1987). One consequence of its publication and reception was a drying up of foundation support for race relations research. Substantial funds for race relations research in the U.S.A would not become available again until the civil rights era of the 1960s and 1970s.

The Authoritarian Personality (Adorno *et al.*, 1950) was another path-breaking research study during the intergroup education period in the U.S.A. Supported and sponsored by the American Jewish Committee as a volume in its *Studies in Prejudice Series*, it was created in the aftermath of Nazi anti-Semitism. It was designed to reveal the personality and social conditions that caused individuals to become anti-Semitic. The first author of the study, Theodor W. Adorno, was a founder of the Frankfurt School in Germany. He was considered Jewish by the Nazi authorities; his father was an assimilated Jew and his mother was a Catholic (Jarvis, 1998; O'Connor, 2000). Adorno immigrated to the U.S.A to escape anti-Semitism in Germany and to find work.

Adorno (1950) and his colleagues concluded that family socialization practices were a major factor that caused individuals to develop authoritarian personalities and consequently to become anti-Semitic. Their research indicated that certain individuals, because of their early childhood experiences, have insecure personalities and need to dominate and to feel superior to other individuals. These individuals, concluded the authors, have an authoritarian personality which is manifested not only in their anti-Semitism but also in their religious and political views. Although Adorno and his colleagues overemphasized personality variables as a cause of prejudice and underestimated structural factors, their theory is an important one. It made substantial contributions to methodology and to theory development in race relations research.

Gordon Allport's (1954) book, *The Nature of Prejudice*, has had a major influence on intergroup education theory and research since its publication. Allport presented his now famous contact hypothesis in this book. He stated that contact between groups will improve intergroup relations if the contact is characterized by these conditions: (1) equal status; (2) cooperation rather than competition; (3) sanctioned by authorities; and (4) characterized by interpersonal interactions in which people become acquainted as individuals.

Most of the research on cooperative learning and interracial contact that has been conducted within the last three decades is based on Allport's (1954) contact hypothesis. This research lends considerable support to the postulate that cooperative interracial contact situations in schools, if the conditions stated by Allport are present in the contact situations, have positive effects on both student interracial behavior and student academic achievement (Aronson & Gonzalez, 1988; Slavin, 1979, 2001).

African-American Scholarship During the Intergroup Education Period

The books by Myrdal (1944), Adorno *et al.* (1950), and Allport (1954) received notable attention, discussion, and reviews in mainstream academic publications and discourse. However, the mainstream intellectual and popular communities largely ignored most of the research, work and publications written by African-American scholars during this period. An exception was *The Souls of Black Folk* by W. E. B. DuBois (1953/1973), which was widely reviewed and sold briskly. DuBois was the most prolific African-American scholar during this period (Lewis, 1995). Although he was a historian and sociologist of first rank, DuBois found it difficult to secure funds to support his research and was unable to obtain a teaching position at a predominantly White university.

Carter G. Woodson, an African-American historian who obtained his doctorate from Harvard, produced a long list of distinguished scholarly works. He also wrote textbooks for students in the elementary and high schools. Woodson's publications, like that of other African-American historians—such as John Hope Franklin and Rayford Logan—were widely used in predominantly Black schools, colleges and universities. Woodson probably had more influence on the teaching of African-American history in the nation's schools and colleges from the turn of the century until his death in 1950 than any other scholar (Banks, 1996b). With others, he founded the Association for the Study of Negro Life and History in 1912. He established the *Journal of Negro History* in 1916.

A number of other publications and research studies by African-American scholars published during this period also became very influential in predominantly Black colleges and universities, including John Hope Franklin's *From Slavery to Freedom: a history of Black Americans*, first published in 1947, and Rayford Logan's (1954/ 1997) *The Betrayal of the Negro*, a study of the post-Reconstruction period. Oliver C. Cox's (1948) important study, *Caste, Class, and Race: a study in social dynamics*, never became influential in the mainstream academic community. Cox, an African-American sociologist who taught at Lincoln University—a historically Black college—gave a Marxist interpretation of race and class.

Research on Children's Racial Attitudes During the Intergroup Education Period

The pace of research on children's racial attitudes quickened during the intergroup education period and attempts to modify their racial attitudes with experimental interventions began. Scholars within the Jewish and African-American communities did most of this research. Research on children's racial attitudes had begun as early as 1929 with the publication of *Race Attitudes in Children* by Bruno Lasker. Eugene and Ruth Horowitz (1938) and Kenneth and Mamie Clark (1939) conducted other early studies of children's racial attitudes in the 1930s. This early research was designed to describe, and not to modify, children's racial attitudes.

The early research on children's racial attitudes by researchers such as Horowitz and Horowitz, Clark and Clark, and Goodman (1946) indicates that very young children are aware of racial differences, that their racial attitudes mirror those of adults that are institutionalized within mainstream society, and that both African-Americans and White children express a white bias. This early research established a paradigm in race relations research that is still highly influential. It states that the preference that African-American children express for white indicates self-rejection or self-hate. More recent research by Spencer (1982) and Cross (1991) confirms the early findings that both White and Black young children express a white bias. However, they interpret the findings quite differently. Spencer distinguishes *personal identity* and *group identity*. Her research indicates that children can have a high personal self-concept and yet express a bias against their ethnic group. She concludes that the white bias often expressed by young African-American children indicates an accurate understanding of the status of Blacks and Whites in American society rather than a rejection of self.

Intervention Studies During the Intergroup Education Years

During the intergroup education period of the 1940s and 1950s, a number of curriculum interventions were conducted by researchers to determine the effects of teaching units, lessons, multicultural materials, role-playing activities, and other kinds of simulated experiences on the racial attitudes of students. Jackson (1944) and Agnes (1947) found that curriculum materials about African-Americans had a positive effect on the racial attitudes of students. Trager and Yarrow (1952) found that a democratic curriculum helped students to develop more positive racial attitudes. They titled their study, *They Learn What They Live*. A variety of curriculum interventions helped students to acquire more positive racial attitudes in a study conducted by Haynes and Conklin (1953). Collectively, these studies indicate that curriculum interventions can help student develop more positive racial attitudes if certain conditions exist in the interventions.

THE AMERICAN CIVIL RIGHTS MOVEMENT

When a group of African-American college students sat down at a lunch counter reserved for Whites in a Woolworth's store in Greensboro, North Carolina on February 1, 1960 and refused to leave until they were served, the civil rights movement had begun (Halberstam, 1998). Race relations in the U.S.A were destined to be transformed. A series of events had given rise to the civil rights movement, including the desegregation of the public universities in the Southern and Border States, and the desegregation of the armed forces by President Truman with Executive Order 9981 in 1948. The *Brown vs. Board of Education* Supreme Court decision, which declared *de jure* school segregation unconstitutional in 1954, was also an important procurer of the civil rights movement of the 1960s and 1970s. The movement had a profound influence on most of the nation's institutions—including schools, colleges, and universities—as well as on research and theory in the social sciences and education.

The National Advisory Commission on Civil Disorders (1968) was established by President Johnson to identify the causes of the urban race riots that had raged in many American cities in the late 1960s. Many people had died and millions of dollars' worth of property had been destroyed in this series of riots. The Commission's report set the tone for much of the research, publications, and public declarations of this period. The Commission—which issued its report in 1968—concluded that institutionalized racism was the root cause of the riots and that America was moving toward two societies—one Black and one White. The Commission called upon the nation to act decisively to heal its racial wounds. It wrote:

> This is our basic conclusion: our Nation is moving toward two societies, one black, one white—separate and unequal ... What white Americans have never fully understood—but

what the Negro can never forget—is that white society is deeply implicated in the ghetto. White institutions created it, white institutions maintain it, and white society condones it. (vol. 1, p. 1)

This was also the period in which Michael Harrington (1962) published *The Other America*, President Lyndon B. Johnson initiated affirmative action with Executive Order 11246 (in 1971), and the nation began its war on poverty. There was a widespread belief within the nation, which was often voiced by its leaders, that by harnessing its tremendous human resources the U.S.A could eliminate racism and poverty. These ideals were publicly expressed by influential leaders such as John F. Kennedy, Martin Luther King, Jr. and Lyndon B. Johnson. In a message to Congress in 1964 in which he declared a war on poverty in America, President Johnson said:

The path forward has not been an easy one. But we have never lost sight of our goal—an America in which every citizen shares all the opportunities of his society, in which every man has a chance to advance his welfare to the limit of his capacities. We have come a long way toward this goal. We still have a long way to go.

The distance which remains is the measure of the great unfinished work of our society. To finish that work I have called for a national war on poverty. Our objective: total victory. (p. 212)

The American civil rights movement, initiated and led by African-Americans, played a major role in the democratization and humanization of American society. As a direct result of action by African-Americans and their supporters in the civil rights movement, Congress passed the Civil Rights Act of 1964. Franklin and Moss (1988) call it 'the most far-reaching and comprehensive law in support of racial equality ever enacted by Congress' (p. 449). As a result of the legal, political, and human rights precedent set by the Civil Rights Act of 1964, equal rights were extended to many other groups in American society, including women, people with disabilities, and groups immigrating to the U.S.A. Related legislation that Congress passed after it enacted the Civil Rights Act of 1964 included Title IX of the Elementary and Secondary Education Act in 1972, which made sex bias in education illegal, and Public Law 94–142 in 1975—The Education for All Handicapped Children Act—which requires free public education for and non-discrimination for all students with disabilities.

The Immigration Reform Act of 1965 was also an extension of the ideas embodied by the civil rights movement and the Civil Rights Act of 1964. This act abolished the highly discriminatory national origins quota system and made it possible for immigrants from nations in Asia and Latin America to enter the U.S.A in significant numbers for the first time in U.S. history. The tremendous demographic changes now taking place in American society are a direct result of this act, and consequently the civil rights movement. Because of its passage, massive numbers of immigrants from nations in Asia and Latin America are now entering the U.S.A. The U.S. Census Bureau projects that people of color will make up 47% of the U.S. population by 2050. In that year, the U.S. population is projected to be 53%

White, 25% Hispanic, 14% African-American, 8% Asian-Pacific-American, and 1% American Indian and Alaska Native (Franklin, 1998).

RESEARCH DURING THE CIVIL RIGHTS ERA

Much of the research and publications during the 1960s and 1970s reflected the social and political ethos of possibility, hope, and the quest for knowledge that would help to eliminate poverty, create equality, and eradicate racism in the U.S.A. People of color—such as African-Americans, Mexican-Americans, and Puerto Rican-Americans—entered predominantly White colleges and universities in significant numbers for the first time in U.S. history as both students and professors. They established ethnic studies programs, conducted research within their communities, and published a score of academic publications that described their histories and cultures from 'insider' perspectives (Gutierrez, 2001; Rodriguez, 2001).

Scholars of color published critiques of much of the previous research that had been done on their histories and cultures by White scholars. They argued that much of this research presented inaccurate and distorted views of their experiences, histories and cultures (Ladner, 1973; Acuha, 1981). They revealed ways in which many White scholars described their histories and cultures from deficit perspectives (Rodriguez, 2001). These scholars developed and published a group of studies that presented their histories and cultures from 'insider' perspectives that were more accurate, complex, and compassionate (Acuha, 1981; Gates, 1988; Rodriguez, 1989; Takaki, 1993; Collins, 2000).

Research on Children's Racial Attitudes: 1960 Through the 1980s

The hope that the civil rights movement ushered in resulted in federal and foundation funds for research on children's racial attitudes and on ways to intervene to help students to acquire more democratic racial attitudes and values. I will discuss only the intervention research studies in this article, although much descriptive research was also published during the 1970s and 1980s (Aboud, 1988; Stephan, 1999). I will use a Weberian-like typology to classify this research into four types of studies: (1) reinforcement studies; (2) perceptual differentiation studies; (3) curriculum intervention studies; and (4) cooperative activities and contact studies (Banks, 1993b). Although these categories overlap, they highlight the important ways in which the four groups of studies differ.

Reinforcement studies. In the late 1960s, John E. Williams and his colleagues at Wake Forest University conducted a series of studies with pre-school children that were designed to modify their attitudes toward the colors black and white and to determine whether a reduction of white bias toward animals and objects would generalize to people (Williams & Edwards, 1969). Using reinforcement techniques, the researchers were able to reduce—but not to eliminate—white bias in pre-school children. This reduction in bias was generalizable to people. Williams and Morland (1976) summarize this work in their book.

Perceptual studies. In a series of trenchant and innovative studies, Katz (1973) and Katz and her colleagues (Katz et al., 1975; Katz & Zalk, 1978) were able to help pre-school White and African-American children acquire more positive racial attitudes by teaching them to perceptually differentiate the faces of outgroup members. Katz and Zalk (1978) also investigated the effects of perceptual differentiation, vicarious interracial contact, direct interracial contact, and reinforcement of the color black on the racial attitudes of second- and fifth-grade children. They found that each of these interventions resulted in a short-term reduction of prejudice.

Curriculum intervention studies. A number of researchers investigated the effects of curriculum interventions such as teaching units and lessons, multiethnic materials, role-playing, and simulation on children's racial attitudes between 1969 and 1980. These investigators included Litcher and Johnson (1969), Weiner and Wright (1973), and Yawkey and Blackwell (1974). In general, these studies indicate that curriculum interventions can modify student racial attitudes if certain conditions exist in the experimental situations. Highly focused interventions of sufficient duration are more likely to modify the racial attitudes of students than those that lack these characteristics. The younger students are, the more likely interventions will be successful. It becomes increasingly more difficult to modify the racial attitudes of students as they grow older.

Cooperative learning and interracial contact studies. During the 1970s and 1980s, a group of investigators accumulated an impressive body of research on the effects of cooperative learning groups and activities on students' racial attitudes, friendship choices, and academic achievement. Most of this research is based on the contact hypothesis of intergroup relations formulated by Allport (1954). Investigators such as Aronson and his colleagues (Aronson & Bridgeman, 1979; Aronson & Gonzalez, 1988), Cohen (Cohen, 1972, Cohen & Roper, 1972), Johnson & Johnson (1981), and Slavin (1979) have conducted much of this research. It strongly supports the postulate that cooperative interracial contact situations in schools, if the conditions stated by Allport exist in the contact situations, have positive effects on both student interracial behavior and student academic achievement.

Very few studies on children's racial attitudes were published during the 1990s (Van Ausdale & Feagin, 2001). Several factors may explain the paucity of studies during this decade. These include the rise of conservatism in the U.S.A during this decade, the shifting of the nation's priorities to other research areas, and the view held by some leaders that the nation had focused enough energy and attention on the problems of minority groups and race. Many Americans also believed that the nation's racial problems had been solved during the civil rights period of the 1960s and 1970s (Schuman *et al.*, 1997).

A ray of hope in race relations research on children developed when the Carnegie Corporation of New York funded 16 studies that investigated ways to improve race relations among adolescents in the late 1990s (National Research Council and Institute of Medicine, 2000). This group of studies produced important findings and provided essential support for scholars doing race relations research in schools. The National Research Council sponsored a workshop that focused on these studies. However, funding for this project was discontinued when the new leadership at the Carnegie Corporation formulated its priorities for the late 1990s and early 2000s.

THE LOSS OF HOPE AND THE FADING DREAM

By the beginning of the 1980s, hope about the possibility of America eliminating poverty and racism had began to fade, a culture of narcissism was on the rise, and conservative politicians were gaining increasing power in the states and in the federal government. The election of Ronald Reagan—the conservative Republican governor of California—to the presidency in November 1980 epitomized the political mood of the nation. Write Franklin and Moss (1988):

> Ronald Reagan had said during his campaign—and he repeated if after his election—that government handouts made people 'government dependent, rather than independent,' and he wanted to put a stop to that. In office he pushed through Congress a number of programs in keeping with his views. His first budget as well as subsequent ones reduced the number of people eligible to participate in federal social programs such as food stamps, Medicaid, student loans, unemployment compensation, child nutrition assistance, and Aid to Families with Dependent Children. (p. 475)

A group of neo-conservative scholars, such as Edward Banfield and Charles Murray—in books and articles—argued that the federal government should reduce help to the poor because it made people dependent. Murray's book, *Losing Ground: American social policy* 1950–1980, published in 1984, marked the birth of a new paradigm that attacked the poor and argued for little government intervention. Just as Michael Harrington's 1962 book signaled the beginning of the war on poverty, Murray's book marked the beginning of 'the war against the poor,' the apt title of Herbert J. Gans's (1995) incisive book. The 'war against the poor' experienced a major victory when the Welfare Reform Act of 1996 was enacted by both houses of Congress and signed by President Clinton. This bill drastically reduced welfare benefits and institutionalized the idea that many low-income people were 'the undeserving poor' (Katz, 1989).

THE COEXISTENCE OF CONSERVATIVE AND PROGRESSIVE POLITICAL FORCES IN U.S. SOCIETY

The neo-conservative movement in the U.S.A that began in the post-civil rights years is characterized by attacks on the poor, affirmative action (Edley, 1996), ethnic studies programs (D'Souza, 1991), and bilingual education (Epstein, 1977). However, the period from 1980 to 2000 was marked by contradictions and competing forces in U.S. society. Both progressive and neo-conservative forces competed to shape a new American identity and to influence research, policy, and educational practice.

Two political developments of the 1990s indicate the extent to which both progressive and conservative forces are influencing American society. Proposition 209, which prohibits affirmative action in state government and universities, was passed by the voters in California in November 1996. However, President Clinton, who opposed the initiative, received the electoral votes for the state, which helped him to win re-election. President Clinton's 'Mend it, but don't end it' position on affirmative action epitomizes the extent to which both progressive and conservative forces are competing to influence public policy in the U.S.A.

The inability of conservative candidate George W. Bush to win a plurality of the popular votes in the 2000 Presidential election and the remarkable showing of Green Party candidate Ralph Nader in several Western states also indicate the extent to which conservative and progressive forces coexist in the U.S.A. The strong negative reaction by many American citizens to the U.S. Supreme Court making a decision that resulted in Bush becoming the winner of the disputed election of 2000 is another indication of the political divisions and competing political forces in U.S. society.

Neo-conservative and progressive forces and movements are both influencing research, curriculum, and teaching in U.S. society today. Books that attack diversity, such as Arthur M. Schlesinger, Jr.'s (1991) *The Disuniting of America* and Dinesh D'Souza's (1991) *Illiberal Education*, became best sellers and were widely discussed and influential within the academic and popular communities. *The Bell Curve* by Herrnstein and Murray (1994)—which argues that poor people and African-Americans have less intellectual ability than middle-class Whites—was on the *New York Times* best seller list for a number of weeks. It echoed and gave academic legitimacy to many of the institutionalized beliefs about poor people and African-Americans within American society.

At the same time that books which attacked ethnic studies and multicultural education—and supported inequality—were enjoying a wide public reception, seminal research was being conducted and published in ethnic studies and in multicultural education. The years from 1980 to 2000 were one of the most prolific and productive periods in the development of ethnic studies scholarship and curriculum reform in the U.S.A. Seminal and important works published in ethnic studies during this period include *The Signifying Monkey: a theory of African-American literacy criticism* by Henry Louis Gates, Jr. (1988), *Black Feminist Thought* by Patricia Hill Collins (2000), *A Different Mirror: a history of multicultural America* by Ronald Takaki (1993), *Black Women in America: an historical encyclopedia* by Darlene Clark Hine (1993, 2 volumes), and the *Handbook of Research on Multicultural Education*, edited by James A. Banks and Cherry A. McGee Banks (1995/2001). Each of these titles has enjoyed remarkable sales and warm receptions within the academic community.

The work by multicultural scholars has not been as successful at reaching the popular market as has the work of conservative scholars. There are a few notable exceptions, such as works by African-American public intellectuals like bell hooks, Henry Louis Gates, and Cornell West. West's (1993) *Race Matters* was on the *New York Times* best seller list for many weeks. hooks has written a score of popular books that enjoy wide sales and high visibility among the public. Gates has published several popular books that have been widely disseminated. He also frequently contributes editorials to popular newspapers and magazines such as the *New York Times* and the *New York Times Book Review*. The reception of works by public intellectuals such as West, hooks and Gates—and the success of the books by conservatives such as Schlesinger and D'Souza—indicate that the American public is as divided in its views as the academic community.

LESSONS FROM HISTORY: TRANSFORMATIVE KNOWLEDGE AND HUMAN FREEDOM

The studies that I have examined in this article indicate that the knowledge which scholars and public intellectuals create reflects the epistemological communities in which they are socialized, their social, political, economic, and cultural interests, and the times in which they live. This review also indicates that in every historical period, competing paradigms and forms of knowledge coexist: some reinforce the status quo and others challenge it. The groups who exercise the most power within a society heavily influence what knowledge becomes legitimized and widely disseminated.

Scholars and public intellectuals in marginalized communities create knowledge that challenges the status quo and the dominant paradigms and explanations within a society. However, this knowledge is often marginalized within the mainstream academic community and remains largely invisible to the larger public. The knowledge that emanates from marginalized epistemological communities often contests existing political, economic, and educational practices and calls for fundamental change and reform. It often reveals the inconsistency between the democratic ideals within a society and its social arrangements and educational practices.

By revealing and articulating the inconsistency between the democratic ideals within a society and its practices, transformative knowledge becomes a potential source for substantial change. When combined with political and social action that reinforces its major claims, assumptions and tenets, transformative knowledge can become an important factor in social, political and educational change that promotes human rights and other democratic values.

The ethnic studies and multicultural education movements in the U.S.A—which grew out of and reinforced the civil rights movement of the 1960s and 1970s—have created transformative knowledge that has brought many benefits to American intellectual and scholarly life. It has not only facilitated the process of democratization in the U.S.A, but has deeply influenced mainstream academic knowledge by helping to make it more truthful and more consistent with the realities of American life. It has also helped to liberate American students from many national myths and misconceptions and consequently given them more human freedom—which includes having the capacity to choose, the power to act to attain one's purposes, and the ability to help transform a world lived in common with others (Greene, 1988).

ACKNOWLEDGMENT

I am grateful to Cherry A. McGee Banks for her insightful and encouraging comments on an earlier draft of this article. I especially appreciate her keen observations about my discussion of the intercultural and intergroup education movements.

NOTE

1. This paper was presented when the author received the Jean Dresden Grambs Distinguished Career Research in Social Studies Award at the 81ˢᵗ Annual Conference of the National Council for the Social Studies, November 16–18, 2001, Washington, D.C..

REFERENCES

Aboud, F. (1988) *Children and Prejudice* (Cambridge, MA, Blackwell).

Acuña, R. (1981) *Occupied America: a history of Chicanos*, 2nd edn (New York, Harper & Row).

Adorno, T.W., Frenkel-Brunswik, E., Levinson, D.J. & Sanford, R.N. (1950) *The Authoritarian Personality* (New York, Norton).

Agnes, M. (1947) Influences of reading on the racial attitudes of adolescent girls, *Catholic Educational Review*, 45, pp. 415–420.

Allport, G.W. (1954) *The Nature of Prejudice* (Reading, MA, Addison-Wesley).

Aptheker, H. (Ed.) (1983) *The Complete Published Works of W. E. B. DuBois: writings in periodicals edited by W. E. B. DuBois, Selections from the Crisis (vol. 1, 1911–1925)* (Millwood, NY, Kraus-Thomson Organization).

Aronson, E. & Bridgeman, D. (1979) Jigsaw groups and the desegregated classroom: in pursuit of common goals, *Personality and Social Psychology Bulletin*, 5, pp. 438-446.

Aronson, E. & Gonzalez, A. (1988) Desegregation, jigsaw, and the Mexican-American experience, in: P. A. Katz & D. A. Taylor (Eds) *Eliminating Racism: profiles in controversy*, pp. 301–314 (New York, Plenum Press).

Bailey, T.A. (1961) *The American Pageant: a history of the republic* (Boston, MA, D.C. Heath and Company).

Banks, C. A. M. (1996) The intergroup education movement, in: J. A. Banks (Ed.) *Multicultural Education, Transformative Knowledge*, and Action, pp. 251–277 (New York, Teachers College Press).

Banks, C. A. M. (in progress) *The Intergroup Education Movement: insights from the past, lessons for the present and future* (New York, Teachers College Press).

Banks, J. A. (1993a) The canon debate, knowledge construction, and multicultural education, *Educational Researcher*, 22(5), pp. 4–14.

Banks, J. A. (1993b) Multicultural education for young children: racial and ethnic attitudes and their modification, in: B. Spodek (Ed.) *Handbook of Research on the Education of Young Children*, pp. 236–250 (New York, Macmillan).

Banks, J. A. (1995) The historical reconstruction of knowledge about race: implications for transformative teaching, *Educational Researcher*, 24(2), pp. 15–25.

Banks, J. A. (1996a) *Multicultural Education, Transformative Knowledge, and Action: historical and contemporary perspectives* (New York, Teachers College Press).

Banks, J. A. (1996b) The African American roots of multicultural education, in: J. A. Banks (Ed.) *Multicultural Education, Transformative Knowledge, and Action: historical and contemporary perspectives*, pp. 30–45 (New York, Teachers College Press).

Banks, J. A. (1998) The lives and values of researchers: implications for educating citizens in a multicultural society, *Educational Researcher*, 27(7), pp. 4-17.

Banks, J. A. &Banks, C. A. M. (Eds) (1995/2001) *Handbook of Research on Multicultural Education* (San Francisco, CA, Jossey-Bass).

Bennett, D.H. (1988) *The Party of Fear: from nativist movements to the new right in American history* (Chapel Hill, NC, University of North Carolina Press).

Boas, F. (1910) The real racial problem, *Crisis*, 1(2), pp. 22–15.

Boas, F. (1938/1963) *The Mind of Primitive Man*, revised edn (New York, The Free Press; original work published 1938).

Bourne, R.S. (1916) Trans-national America, *Atlantic Monthly*, 18 (July), p. 95.

Brodkin, K. (1998) *How the Jews Became White Folks and What That Says About Race in America* (New Brunswick, NJ, Rutgers University Press).

Clark, K.B. (1965) *Dark Ghetto: dilemmas of social power* (New York, Harper & Row).

Clark, K.B. & Clark, M.P. (1939) The development of consciousness of self and the emergence of racial identification in Negro preschool children, *Journal of Social Psychology*, 10, pp. 591–599.

Cohen, E. (1972) Interracial interaction disability, Human Relations, 25, pp. 9–24.

Cohen, E.G. & Roper, S.S. (1972) Modification of interracial interaction disability: an application of status characteristic theory, *American Sociological Review*, 37, pp. 643–657.

Code, L. (1991) *What Can She Know? Feminist Theory and the Construction of Knowledge* (Ithaca, NY, Cornell University Press).

Collins, P.H. (2000) *Black Feminist Thought: knowledge, consciousness, and the politics of empowerment,* revised edn (New York, Routledge).

Cox, O.C. (1948) *Caste, Class and Race: a study in social dynamics* (New York, Monthly Review Press).

Cross, W.E. Jr. (1991) *Shades of Black: diversity in African-American identity* (Philadelphia, PA, Temple University Press).

D'Souza, D. (1991) *Illiberal Education: the politics of race and sex on campus* (New York, The Free Press).

DuBois, W. E. B. (1953/1973) *The Souls of Black Folk: essays and sketches* (Millwood, NY, Kraus-Thompson Organization; original work published 1953).

Edley, C. (1996) *Not All Black and White: affirmative action, race and American values* (New York, Hill & Wang).

Epstein, N. (1977) *Language, Ethnicity, and the Schools* (Washington, D.C., Institute for Educational Leadership, George Washington University).

Feagin, J.R. & Sikes, M.P. (1994) *Living with Racism: the Black middle-class experience* (Boston, MA, Beacon Press).

Franklin, J.H. (1947) *From Slavery to Freedom: a history of Negro Americans* (New York, Knopf).

Franklin, J.H. (Chairman) (1998) *One America in the 21ˢᵗ Century: forging a new future. The President's Initiative on Race, The Advisory Board's Report to the President* (Washington, D.C., U.S. Government Printing Office).

Franklin, J.H. & Moss, A.A. Jr. (1988) *From Slavery to Freedom: a history of Negro Americans* (New York, McGraw-Hill).

Gans, H.J. (1995) *The War Against the Poor: the underclass and antipoverty policy* (New York, Basic Books).

Gates, H.L. Jr. (1988) *The Signifying Monkey: a theory of African-American literary criticism* (New York, Oxford University Press).

Goodman, M.E. (1946) Evidence concerning the genesis of interracial attitudes, *American Anthropologist*, 48, pp. 624–630.

Gordon, M.M. (1964) *Assimilation in American Life* (New York, Oxford University Press).

Gould, S.J. (1996) *The Mismeasure of Man*, revised and expanded edn (New York, Norton).

Grant, M. (1923) *The Passing of the Great Race* (New York, Charles Scribner's).

Greene, M. (1988) *The Dialectic of Freedom* (New York, Teachers College Press).

Gutierrez, R.A. (2001) Historical and social science research on Mexican Americans, in: J. A. Banks & C. A. M. Banks (Eds) *Handbook of Research on Multicultural Education*, pp. 203–222 (San Francisco, CA, Jossey-Bass).

Halberstam, D. (1998) *The Children* (New York, Random House).

Harding, S. (1991) *Whose Knowledge? Whose Science? Thinking from Women's Lives* (Ithaca, NY, Cornell University Press).

Harrington, M. (1962) *The Other America* (New York, Macmillan).

Haynes, M.L. & Conklin, M.E. (1953) Intergroup attitudes and experimental change, *Journal of Experimental Education*, 22, pp. 19–36.

Herrnstein, R.J. & Murray, C. (1994) *The Bell Curve: intelligence and class structure in American life* (New York, Free Press).

Higham, J. (1972) *Strangers in the Land: patterns of American nativism 1860–1925* (New York, Atheneum).

Hillis, M.R. (1996) Research on racial attitudes: historical perspectives, in: J. A. Banks (Ed.) *Multicultural Education, Transformative Knowledge, and Action: historical and contemporary perspectives*, pp. 278–293 (New York, Teachers College Press).

Hine, D.C. (Ed.) (1993) *Black Women in America: an historical encyclopedia*, 2 vols (Brooklyn, NY, Carlson).

Horowitz, E.L. & Horowitz, R.E. (1938) Development of social attitudes in children, *Sociometry*, 1, pp. 301—338.

Jackson, E.P. (1944) Effects of reading upon attitudes toward the Negro race, *Library Quarterly*, 14, pp. 47–54.

Jacobson, M.F. (1998) *Whiteness of a Different Color: European immigrants and the alchemy of race* (Cambridge, MA, Harvard University Press).

Jarvis, S. (1998) *Adorno: a critical introduction* (New York, Routledge).

Johnson, D.W. & Johnson, R.T. (1981) Effects of cooperative and individualistic learning experiences on interethnic interaction, *Journal of Educational Psychology*, 73, pp. 444–449.

Johnson, L.B. (1964) The war on poverty, in: *The Annals of America*, vol. 18, pp. 212–216 (Chicago, IL, Encyclopaedia Britannica).

Kallen, H. (1924) *Culture and Democracy in the United States* (New York, Boni & Liveright).

Katz, M.B. (1989) *The Undeserving Poor: from the war on poverty to the war on welfare* (New York, Pantheon).

Katz, P.A. (1973) Perception of racial cues in preschool children: a new look, *Developmental Psychology*, 8, pp. 295–299.

Katz, P.A. & Zalk, S.R. (1978) Modification of children's racial attitudes, *Developmental Psychology*, 14, pp. 447–461.

Katz, P., Sohn, M. & Zalk, S. (1975) Perceptual concomitants of racial attitudes in urban grade school children, *Developmental Psychology*, 11, pp. 135–144.

Ladner, J. (1973) *The Death of White Sociology* (New York, Vintage).

Lasker, G. (1929) *Race Attitudes in Children* (New York, Henry Holt).

Lazarus, E. (1968) The new colossus, in: *The Annals of America*, vol. 11, p. 108 (Chicago, IL, Encyclopaedia Britannica; original work published 1886).

Lemann, N. (1991) *The Promised Land: the great Black migration and how it changed America* (New York, Alfred A. Knopf).

Lewis, D.L. (Ed.) (1995) *W. E. B. DuBois: a reader* (New York, Henry Holt).

Litcher, J.H. & Johnson, D.W. (1969) Changes in attitudes toward Negroes of White elementary school students after use of multiethnic readers, *Journal of Educational Psychology*, 60, pp. 148–152.

Logan, R.W. (1954/1997) *The Betrayal of the Negro: from Rutherford B. Hayes to Woodrow Wilson* (New York, Da Capo Press; original work published 1954).

Mannheim, K. (1936) *Ideology and Utopia: an introduction to the sociology of knowledge* (New York, Harper).

Marable, M. (1996) *Speaking Truth to Power: essays on race, resistance, and radicalism* (Boulder, CO, Westview Press).

Miller, K. (1908) *Race Adjustment: essays on the Negro in America* (New York, Neale).

Montalto, N.V. (1982) *A History of the Intercultural Education Movement 1924–1941* (New York, Garland).

Murray, C. (1984) *Losing Ground: American social policy, 1950–1980* (New York, Basic Books).

Myrdal, G. (1944) *An American Dilemma: the Negro problem and modern democracy* (New York, Harper & Row).

Myrdal, G. (1969) *Objectivity in Social Research* (Middletown, CT, Wesleyan University Press).

National Advisory Commission on Civil Disorders (1968) *Report of the National Advisory Commission on Civil Disorders*, 2 vols (Washington, D.C., U.S. Government Printing Office).

National Research Council and Institute of Medicine (2000) *Improving Intergroup Relations among Youth: summary of a workshop* (Washington, D.C., National Academy Press).

O'Connor, B. (Ed.) (2000) *The Adorno Reader* (Malden, MA, Blackwell).

Okihiro, G.Y. (1994) *Margins and Mainstreams: Asians in American history and culture* (Seattle, WA, University of Washington Press).

Roche, A.M. (1996) Carter G. Woodson and the development of transformative scholarship, in: J. A. Banks (Ed.) *Multicultural Education, Transformative Knowledge and Action: historical and contemporary perspectives*, pp. 91–114 (New York, Teachers College Press).

Rodriguez, C.E. (1989) *Puerto Ricans Born in the U.S.A* (Boston, MA, Unwin Hyman).

Rodriguez, C.E. (2001) Puerto Ricans in historical and social science research, in: J. A. Banks & C. A. M. Banks (Eds) *Handbook of Research on Multicultural Education*, pp. 223–244 (San Francisco, CA, Jossey-Bass).

Schlesinger, A.M. Jr. (1991) *The Disuniting of America: reflections on a multicultural society* (Knoxville, TN, Whittle Direct Books).

Schuman, H., Steeh, C., Bobo, L. & Krysan, M. (1997) *Racial Attitudes in America*, revised edn (Cambridge, MA, Harvard University Press).

Slavin, R.E. (1979) Effects of biracial learning teams on cross-racial friendships, *Journal of Educational Psychology*, 71, pp. 381–387.

Slavin, R.E. (2001) Cooperative learning and intergroup relations, in: J. A. Banks & C. A. M. Banks (Eds) *Handbook of Research on Multicultural Education*, pp. 628–634 (San Francisco, CA, Jossey-Bass).

Southern, D.W. (1987) *Gunnar Myrdal and Black-White Relations: the use and abuse of an American dilemma* (Baton Rouge, LA, Louisiana State University Press).

Spencer, M.B. (1982) Personal and group identity of black children: an alternative synthesis, *Genetic Psychology Monographs*, 106, pp. 59–84.

Stephan, W. (1999) *Reducing Prejudice and Stereotyping in Schools* (New York, Teachers College Press).

Stoddard, T.L. (1920) *The Rising Tide of Color against White World Supremacy* (New York, Charles Scribner's).

Taba, H., Brady, E. & Robinson, J. (1952) *Intergroup Education in Public Schools* (Washington, D.C., American Council on Education).

Takaki, R. (1993) *A Different Mirror: a history of multicultural America* (New York, Little Brown).

Trager, H.G. & Yarrow, M.R. (1952) *They Learn What They Live: prejudice in young children* (New York, Harper).

United States Census Bureau (2000) *Statistical Abstract of the United States: 2000*, 120th edn (Washington, D.C., U.S. Government Printing Office).

Van Ausdale, D.V. & Feagin, J.R. (2001) *The First R: how children learn race and racism* (New York, Rowman & Littlefield).

Weiner, M.J. & Wright, F.E. (1973) Effects of undergoing arbitrary discrimination upon subsequent attitudes toward a minority group, *Journal of Applied Social Psychology*, 3, pp. 94–102.

West, C. (1993) *Race Matters* (Boston, MA, Beacon Press).

Williams, J.E. & Edwards, C.D. (1969) An exploratory study of the modification of color and racial concept attitudes in preschool children, *Child Development*, 40, pp. 737–750.

Williams, J.E. & Morland, J.K. (1976) *Race, Color, and the Young Child* (Chapel Hill, NC, University of North Carolina Press).

Wilson, W.J. (1978) *The Declining Significance of Race: Blacks and changing American institutions* (Chicago, IL, University of Chicago Press).

Woodson, C.G. (1933) *The Mis-education of the Negro* (Washington, D.C., Associated Publishers).

Yawkey, T.D. & Blackwell, J. (1974) Attitudes of 4 year-old urban Black children toward themselves and Whites based upon multi-ethnic social studies materials and experiences, *Journal of Educational Research*, 67, pp. 373–377.

What Are the Philosophical Foundations of American Education?

By Kevin Ryan and James M. Cooper

Just as the subjects of anatomy and chemistry are essential to the practice of medicine, certain areas of organized knowledge are essential to the practice of education. These areas, called the *foundations of education*, provide the intellectual underpinnings of educational practice. This section covers several of these key areas: school governance, finance, philosophy, and history. Truly professional teachers ground their daily practice in the wisdom gleaned from these; foundational areas. This section concludes with a chapter on recent movements for educational reform, in which all the foundational components come to bear in the effort to improve our schools.

Chapter Preview This chapter examines the role of philosophy, a key foundational discipline in the work of the teacher. First, we describe philosophy; then we discuss four different philosophies and analyze their applications to the classroom.

This chapter emphasizes that:

- Philosophical knowledge has a fundamental role in clarifying questions of education.
- Philosophical thought has distinct characteristics which contribute to the way we know the world. Four branches of philosophy—metaphysics, epistemology, axiology, and logic—relate rather directly to the work of the teacher.
- Four philosophies of education—perennialism, essentialism, romanticism, and progressivism—have many practical implications for the classroom teacher.
- Psychological theories, particularly constructivism, influence modern educational thought.
- Teachers need to have a philosophy to guide their practice, Many develop eclectic personal philosophies that incorporate elements of several major philosophical views.
- Discovering your personal philosophy is a lifelong process, but it should begin now.

A medical student who wants intensely to be a surgeon, has marvelous hands, and displays a high level of technical skill, but does not know how the body functions or what constitutes health can hardly be called a doctor.

Kevin Ryan & James M. Cooper, "Foundations and the Future: What Are the Philosophical Foundations of American Education," *Those Who Can, Teach*, pp. 262-293. Copyright © 2004 by Cengage Learning, Inc. Reprinted with permission.

An aspirant to the ministry who loves to work with people and possesses a marvelous gift of speaking, but has no opinion about humanity's relationship to God or about the purpose of religion can hardly be suited for religious ministry.

And a person who has a great desire to be with young people, wants to live the life of a teacher, and possesses great technical skill, but lacks purpose and direction is hardly a teacher.

These three individuals are like wind-up toys, moving along blindly without a plan or an intellectual compass. And although this image may be somewhat dramatic, there *are* people who prepare for professions without getting to the core meaning of what those professions are all about. Such directionless behavior can cause problems in any occupation or profession, but particularly in teaching. What kind of a teacher can someone be who lacks a view of what people are and a vision of what they can become? Who cannot clearly define right and wrong in human behavior? Who doesn't recognize what is important and what is unimportant or can't distinguish clear thinking from sloppy thinking? The person who would take on the responsibility for educating the young without having seriously wrestled with these questions is, to say the least, dangerous, for he or she is going against the very grain of what it means to be a teacher. In fact, it is safe to say that such a person is not a teacher, but a technician.

This chapter introduces you to philosophy, one of the foundational subjects in education, which, along with history and psychology (and, to some degree, economics, political science, sociology, anthropology, and the law), forms the intellectual underpinning on which the practice of education rests. The study of philosophy helps the teacher systematically to reflect on issues that are central to education, including such basic concepts as *learning, teaching, being educated, knowledge,* and *the good life.*

WHAT IS PHILOSOPHY?

The word **philosophy** is made up of two root words: "love" (*philo*) and "wisdom" (*sophos*). In its most basic sense, then, philosophy is the *love of wisdom.* Although not all people love wisdom in the same way or to the same degree, all humans are questioning beings—seekers of answers. As children, we are preoccupied with such lofty questions as, "How do I get fewer veggies and more dessert?" Then we progress to such questions as, "How does the teacher always know to call on me when I don't have the answers?", and "What do I need to do to get a decent grade in geometry?" Ultimately, we may move to more fundamental levels of questioning: "Who am I?", "What is the purpose of life, and what am I doing here?", "What does it mean to be a really good person?"

Fundamental Questions of Existence

Until about one hundred years ago, most people relied on religion and philosophy for answers to such fundamental questions. Whereas religion is said to represent the revealed word of God, philosophy represents a human attempt to sort real out by reason the fundamental questions of existence. Many of the great thinkers of Western civilization—Plato, Aristotle, St. Thomas Aquinas, Rene Descartes, Jean-Jacques Rousseau, Immanuel Kant, Friedrich Nietzsche, John Locke, John Stuart Mill, William

James, Alfred North Whitehead, and John Dewey—have been philosophers. Because education has always been a central human concern, philosophers have thought and written a great deal about education and the questions surrounding it.

> *The real object of education is to have man in the condition of continually asking questions.*
> —*Bishop Creighton*

Only a few people in our society are professional philosophers who earn their daily bread (usually a rather meager fare)—Bishop Creichton by pursuing answers to the fundamental questions of life. However, all of us who wrestle with such questions as "Who am I?" and "What am I doing with my life?" are engaged in philosophical activity. Although there is a distinction between the few professional philosophers and the our lives great number of us who are amateurs, the questions we ask and the answers we glean usually have a major impact on the practical affairs of our lives and on how we choose to spend our life force.

Sources of Our Philosophy

The very practical decision of whether to become a teacher, a real estate broker, or a professional bungee jumper almost always has its roots in a person's philosophy of life. In developing a philosophy, we draw on many influences: our experiences in life, our religious views, and our reading of literature, history, and current events. A major difference between professionals and amateurs, however, lies in the precision of their methods.

Philosophy is an extremely pure and abstract science. Philosophers work with neither test tubes nor white rats, use neither telescopes nor microscopes, and do not fly off to remote societies to observe the natives. The method or process of philosophers is questioning and reasoning; their product is *thought*.

The Philosophers's Methods and Language

Basically, philosophers are concerned with the meanings of things and how to interpret those meanings. Therefore, they have an intense interest in the real meanings of words. Although some philosophical discussion and writing involves technical language, it generally uses "plain language," the ordinary language of people. However, philosophers try to be extremely clear and careful about their use of terms. They do not want their ultimate goal (meaning) to be lost in a thicket of fuzzy language.

Although philosophy appears to deal with simple issues in simple language, behind the philosophers' questions are raging debates about profound issues that can have far-reaching implications. For example, the question, "What is a human?" leads to other questions, such as "When, if ever, can a fetus be aborted?" and "What rights do severely disabled persons have?" Or "Should humans clone humans?"

Pause and Reflect

Before you go much further in this chapter, you should clarify where you stand today. What are your answers to these philosophical questions:

1. What are the fundamental life questions to which you are seeking answers?
2. What is or are the ends or goals of an education?
3. Should a school lay out what is to be learned, or should the students have a large say in what and how they learn?

THE TERRAIN OF PHILOSOPHY

Philosophy covers a large amount of intellectual turf. The terrain of philosophy is divided into several areas, including four that are particularly important to the teacher: metaphysics, epistemology, axiology, and logic. These four branches of philosophy are central to the educative process and, in fact, speak directly to the work of the teacher.

Metaphysics

Metaphysics involves the attempt to explain the nature of the real world, or the nature of existence. Metaphysics attempts to answer the question "What is real?" without relying on revealed religion, such as the Bible. Further, the metaphysician characteristically believes that it is not possible to address fundamental matters such as the nature of a human being or of the universe, simply by collecting data and formulating statistically significant generalizations. From most metaphysical perspectives, the true nature of a person cannot be captured by measuring or counting alone. A person is more than the sum of his or her height and weight, IQ (intelligence quotient) and SAT scores, and other "vital" statistics.

In probing the nature of reality, the metaphysician asks a whole array of questions: "Does life have meaning?", "Are human beings free or totally determined?", "Is there a purpose to life?", "Is there a set of enduring principles that guide the operation of the universe?", "Can these principles be known?", and "Is there such a thing as stability, or is our world ever-changing?"

Metaphysics and the Curriculum

These abstract questions are ones that the educator cannot dismiss. Ultimately, the purpose of education is to explain reality to the young. The curriculum and how we teach it represent one statement of what that reality is. Although teachers may not actually be meta physicians, they do take a stand on metaphysical questions. If a teacher decides to teach because he or she believes the most important thing in the universe is a human mind, that a career decision is driven by a metaphysical view: the importance of an individual person. The people on school boards also take stands on metaphysical issues. For example, whether a particular school system makes a major investment in educating individuals with severe mental disabilities or emphasizes vocational education depends very much on someone's decision about the nature of the person and the place of work in a person's life.

Epistemology

Epistemology deals with questions regarding knowledge and knowing. The epistemologist, seeking the true nature of knowing, asks such questions as "What is true knowledge (as opposed to false ideas)?" and "Is truth elusive, always changing and always dependent on the truth seeker's particulars of time, place, and angle of vision?" Some people, whom we call skeptics, question our capacity to ever really know the truths of existence. And some, whom we call agnostics, are convinced there are no "truths" and that seeking knowledge of ultimate realities is an empty hope.

Epistemology deals not only with the nature of truth but also with the ways in which we can know reality. Questions, such as "How do we come to know the truth?" and "What are the sources for gaining knowledge?", are part of the conversation. There are a variety of ways by which we can know, and each of these ways has its advocates and detractors. Among the ways of knowing are by divine revelation, by authority, through personal intuition, from our own five senses, from our own powers of reasoning, and through experimentation.

Teaching and Ways of Knowing

Questions concerning knowledge and knowing are, almost by definition, of great concern to the teacher. The epistemological question "How do you know this or that?" goes to the heart of teaching methodology. If a teacher wants her students to have a concept of democracy, how does she proceed? Does she explain the characteristics of different forms of government, such as monarchy and oligarchy, and then the characteristics of democracy? Or does she take a more hands-on approach and have the students do a role-playing exercise during which one student is appointed class dictator and the rest must obey the student-dictator's orders? The student who has only read about democracy "knows" it in an epistemologically different way than a student who has been bullied and harassed for several days by a teacher-appointed dictator.

It is becoming increasingly clear, in fact, that individuals differ in their preferred methods of learning. As discussed more fully in the chapter on "Who Are Today's Students in a Diverse Society?", much of the teacher's work is helping the student find the most effective way of coming to know (or gaining new knowledge).

In some instances, the teacher may find that some people—for example, parents and community members—may have strong opinions regarding these epistemological questions. Many people have strong beliefs about the true origin of humankind and how one knows it. This issue is sometimes called the creationist controversy, and it rests on a sharp and fundamental argument over the questions "Who are we?" and "How did we get here?" One faction insists that the public schools should present the evidence of our origin that is given in the Book of Genesis, which we know by divine revelation. Others insist that the way to know the origin of the human race is through the scientific theory of evolution, grounded in the interpretation of artifactual evidence. So behind this ongoing educational controversy is a fundamental question of epistemology.

Axiology

Axiology focuses on the nature of values. As human beings, we quite naturally search for the correct and most effective way to live. In doing so, we engage questions of values. Of course, when different people look at life, they often come up with very different sets of values. For instance, hedonists believe in seeking pleasure and living for the moment. On the other hand, stoics have an austere way of looking at life and seek to be unaffected by pleasure or pain. Many people regard values from a religious perspective, asserting that unless humanity and the rest of the natural world were originally created by God, existence as we know it is just the meaningless coming together of cosmic dust and debris. In this view, the only genuine values derive from God.

Most people would agree with Socrates that schools have a dual responsibility: to make people smart and to make them good. To the degree that teachers accept the second function, they are grappling with an axiological issue. In fact, teachers are intimately involved with questions of moral values. Young people are seeking ways to live lives that are worthwhile, and teachers traditionally have been expected to help students establish moral values both as individuals and as contributing members of society. (See the chapters entitled "How Should Education Be Reformed?" and "What Are the Ethical and Legal Issues Facing Teachers?" for more discussion of this issue.) Moral values such as honesty, respect for other people, and fairness are necessary if we are to live together in harmony. Despite a large core of values on which a majority of people agree, such as respecting others and avoiding violence in settling disputes, other value issues separate people. Sexual behavior, capital punishment, gun control, and abortion are examples of contemporary social issues that involve a wide range of viewpoints about what is right.

Ethics and Aesthetics

Axiology has two subtopics: ethics and aesthetics. Ethics takes us into the realm of values that relate to "good" and "bad" behavior, examining morality and rules of conduct. At one time, teaching children how to deal with issues of good/bad and right/wrong was the primary purpose of schooling. In recent decades the pendulum has swung the other way, and schools have been more concerned with factual knowledge and skills than with ethical knowledge. There are, however, many signs that schools are being called back to help children deal with ethical issues.

The subject of ethics not only teaches us how we can intellectually ascertain the "right" thing to do, but also is often used to help us establish a particular set of standards, such as a code of ethics. In the chapter entitled "What Are the Ethical and Legal Issues Facing Teachers?", we give particular attention to these issues.

The second subtopic of axiology, **aesthetics**, deals with questions of values regarding beauty and art. Many discussions about the value of a particular film, book, or work of art are attempts to come to some aesthetic judgment on the value of the work. Whether a person "has good taste" is an example of a common aesthetic judgment.

Logic

Logic is the branch of philosophy that deals with reasoning. One of the fundamental qualities that distinguishes human beings from animals is that humans can think. Logic focuses on reasoning and

---

LEADERS IN EDUCATION
SOCRATES (469–399 B.C.)

The ancient Greek philosopher Socrates was condemned to death for supposedly corrupting the youth of Athens. Today we know him primarily through the written "dialogues" of his student Plato. How much Plato's portrayal resembled the actual man is open to debate. Nevertheless, the Socrates of Plato's dialogues has had a deep and lasting influence on both philosophy and education, giving us such common terms as *Socratic teaching, Socratic questioning,* and the *Socratic method.* The following passage explains some of the basic tenets of Socrates' approach.

Socrates expressly denied that he was a teacher in the commonly accepted sense of that term. What he meant by this—at least in part—was that he was not a sophist, a professional pedagogue who, for a fee, would endeavor to transmit some knowledge that he possessed to someone who lacked it. Not only did Socrates charge no fees, he claimed not to have command of any such knowledge.

The learning that Socrates was concerned with simply didn't fit the information-transmission model of education implicit in the Athenian public mind and the teaching profession. Neither did his pioneering focus on virtue and wisdom square well with the popular attachment to honor, fame, and wealth. As he tries to explain at one point to Anytus in Plato's dialogue *Meno,* "[W]e are inquiring whether the good men of today and of the past knew how to pass on to another the virtue they themselves possessed, or whether a man cannot pass it on or receive it from another." Since it was clear that wisdom and virtue could not simply be passed on from one person to another, Socrates sought an alternative way of conceptualizing how such excellences of mind and character were acquired. What was the teacher's role in that acquisition, if not simply being a supplier?

As an alternative to the receiving-knowledge-from-another model, Socrates proposed that learning was "recollection"—that is, a process akin to dredging up knowledge from one's own resources. "Teaching" on this model he later compared to acting as a "midwife"—assisting in the birth of knowledge in another person rather than serving as a supplier of it to another person. This was to be accomplished in conversation, mostly by skillful questioning and cross-examination ("Socratic teaching," "Socratic questioning," and "Socratic method").

Socrates admitted to behaving like a "gadfly" in this dialectical pursuit of truth, goading people into serious thinking about human living. And he also confessed to acting like a benumbing "sting ray" or "torpedo fish," referring to his ability to render people tongue-tied about matters that they thought they already knew perfectly well—but actually didn't. Not until people felt the sting of not really knowing about life's important matters could they be prompted to inquire into them seriously. —*Source: Reprinted by permission of Steven S. Tigner.*

---

modes of arguing that bring us to valid conclusions. The pursuit of logic is an attempt to think clearly and avoid vagueness and contradictions. Certain rules of logic have been identified, and they constitute the core of this branch of philosophy.

Deductive Reasoning

A primary task of the schools is to help children think clearly and communicate logically. Two types of reasoning are commonly taught in schools: deductive and inductive. In **deductive reasoning**, the teacher to presents a general proposition and then illustrates it with a series of particulars. The most highly developed form of this approach is the classic method of the syllogism. In a syllogism, one makes two statements, and a third statement, a conclusion, is *deduced* or drawn from them. For instance:

All human beings are mortal.
I am a human being.
Therefore, I am mortal.

In deductive reasoning, such as in this example, the general proposition, an abstract concept, is followed by a factual statement, which in turn leads to a new factual statement and the creation of new knowledge, at least for the learner.

As another example, imagine that in October, Mrs. Wells, a fifth-grade teacher, writes on the board:

All trees that shed their leaves at the end of a growing season are deciduous trees.

As a two-week project, Mrs. Wells asks her class to observe and record data about the trees that surround their school. For two weeks, the students observe the three dozen maple trees shedding their leaves during the fall. The teacher then writes her earlier sentence on the board again:

All trees that shed their leaves at the end of a growing season are deciduous trees.

And, using their observational data (and a little intellectual nudging from Mrs. Wells), the students complete the syllogism:

Maple trees shed their leaves at the end of the growing season.
Therefore, maple trees are deciduous.

Then the students try to identify other types of trees that fit the deciduous: classification.

Much of what a teacher does in school is helping children both acquire the intellectual habits of deductive thinking and expand their storehouse of knowledge through this process.

Inductive Reasoning

Inductive Reasoning works in the opposite fashion. The teacher sets forth particulars, from which a general proposition is derived or *induced*. For instance, the teacher may wish to lead the students to the discovery that water is essential to plant growth. He gives each child two similar plants (a different type, from weeds to flowers, for each child) and then has each student daily feed one plant with water and leave the other plant without water. After ten days the teacher has the students report the condition of their plants, and from all of these individual reports he leads the students to generalize about the necessity of water to plant life. In fact, they have derived or induced their answer.

While the two forms of reasoning are opposite, both are essential to logical thought and, therefore, need to be developed in learners. Effective teachers sign a variety of learning activities, some of which, like the tree example above, help students think deductively, and others, like the plant example, focus on inductive reasoning.

Logic, however, is not confined to inductive and deductive reasoning. To think logically means to think clearly, in many different ways. Teachers need logic in many aspects of their work, from trying to understand the behavior of a child who seems to have an erratic learning pattern to developing tests that accurately measure what has been taught in a course. Most of all, teachers need to model this clear, logical thinking for students.

Overall, the four branches of philosophy—metaphysics, epistemology, axiology, and logic—address some of the major concerns of the teacher. The answers they suggest to the teacher and the implications they have for actual classroom practice are areas to which we now turn.

Pause and Reflect

1. Which of these four branches of philosophy do you think is of greatest importance to you as a future teacher?

SCHOOLS OF EDUCATIONAL PHILOSOPHY

Answers to the philosophical questions that pepper the preceding section have almost infinite variety. Over the years, however, certain answers by particular philosophers have received more attention and allegiance than others. These more enduring sets of answers or world views represent schools of philosophy. Some started with the early Greek philosophers and have grown and developed through the centuries. Other schools of thought are more recent and offer fresh, new formulations to ultimate questions.

In this section, we describe four philosophies that have had a major impact on American education and demonstrate the variety of ways in which teaching and learning can be conceived. It is important to keep in mind, however, that many important philosophies relevant to education, such as neo-Thomism and classical Eastern thought, or existentialism, are not included here. In addition, there are major educational ideas that do not quite qualify as "philosophies," but are having a big impact on schools.

The four philosophies we have selected for this chapter are perennialism, essentialism, romanticism, and progressivism. Behind these very daunting words are very different ideas of what people are, how we should live our lives, and how we should conduct the education of children. We have selected these philosophies, not because they are our pick of the "Top Four Philosophical Hits," but because of the level of influence each viewpoint has had on American educational thought and practice. We have grouped these philosophies as *subject-centered* or *child-centered*. For each of these philosophies, we present first a brief explanation of its origins and the core ideas it embodies, the implications for teaching and learning, and then a "personal point of view" by a teacher (fictitious) who is committed to that particular philosophy. We have tried to show that these positions are not just windy abstractions or the preoccupations of ivory tower thinkers; rather, they shape what people teach and how they teach it.

The first two schools of philosophy, perennialism and essentialism, stress the importance of subject matter knowledge in education. Both schools of thought show a strong allegiance to the curriculum and both argue that well-educated students should possess a defined body of knowledge.

Perennialism

Perennialism, derived primarily from the writings of Plato, views truth and nature, in particular, human nature, as constant, objective, and unchanging. Beneath the superficial differences from one century or decade to the next, the rules that govern the world and the characteristics that make up human nature stay the same. The purpose of life, according to Plato, was the search for these constant and changeless truths, which reside in the nature of things. This search was achieved through the Socratic dialogue or dialectic, a process in which ideas are debated in a back-and-forth discussion until some recognizable clarity (the light) was reached. Essential to undertaking such a pursuit was mental discipline and rational thought processes.

Perennialism in the School For the perennialist, the purpose of education is to find the changeless "truth," which is best revealed in the enduring classics of Western culture. Classical thought, then, should be emphasized as a subject matter in schools. Perennialists believe that schools should teach disciplined knowledge through the traditional subjects of history, language, mathematics, science, and the arts. Perennialists place particular emphasis on literature and the humanities because these subjects provide the greatest insight into the human condition. Although this view of the curriculum is evident in many areas of education, in its most complete form it is known as the *Great Books approach*, developed by Robert Maynard Hutchins, who was president and chancellor at the University of Chicago throughout the 1930s and 1940s and the recently deceased Mortimer Adler, a professor at the University of Chicago during the same time period. The Great Books, which constitute a shelf of volumes stretching from Homer's *Iliad* to Albert Einstein's *On the Electrodynamics of Moving Bodies*, are a perennialists ideal curriculum.

For perennialists, the development of the intellect is best achieved through a teacher-directed instructional approach in the early years of schooling. Socratic dialogue is then used to help mature learners question and examine their beliefs in order to move closer to the truth.

Since the early 1990s, a controversy has arisen over the content of perennialist literature, history, and philosophy courses. Scholars and students have criticized colleges and high schools for promoting a "Eurocentric" view of knowledge and culture, one that ignores the contributions of all but "dead, white, male writers and thinkers." They urge a more inclusive curriculum, one that gives greater attention to women, minorities, and Eastern, African, and Hispanic cultures. Whereas some take this movement as a direct attack on the perennialist curriculum, others see it as a natural and useful extension of the perennialists' search for the best of the world's wisdom. One perennialist friend of ours, who welcomes this new approach, suggested, "Sure, students should know about Islamic literature and Eastern philosophy, but they should first get to know their own neighborhood, Western culture."

The Paideia Proposal   For the perennialist, then, immersion in these great works helps students reach the perennialist's goal, which is a state of human excellence that the ancients called *paideia*. This is a state not only of enlightenment but also of goodness. As such, it is a goal that perennialists believe all humans should seek.

In the 1980s, Mortimer Adler and a group of educators breathed new life into perennialism with the publication of *The Paideia Proposal* and then a series of supporting books. *The Paideia Proposal* presents this educational philosophy not as an austere, joyless curriculum, but as an exciting, involving intellectual and aesthetic journey. Several of the Paideia Group who worked with Adler in formulating this plan are both minority group members and superintendents of big-city school districts serving a large population of poor and minority students. Much of the appeal of *The Paideia Proposal* is that it asserts that all children, not just the gifted or the privileged children of the rich, should have this classical education. Members of the Paideia Group see it as providing both quality and equality in education. Nevertheless, interest in *The Paideia Proposal* has faded somewhat in recent years, another curricular movement has attracted the interest of educators with perennialist leanings.

Education As Preparation for Life

Education, then, is of great importance to perennialists, but it is an education that is rigorous and demanding. Perennialists hold that education is preparation for life, and should therefore not attempt to imitate life or be lifelike. Students should engage in a rigorous examination of the classics in order to discover the timeless wisdom embodied therein, rather than focusing on knowledge that might seem personally meaningful.

In summary, the perennialists' view is that one learns through disciplined study of the great works and ideas of the past. It is a view that leans heavily on the authority of the collected wisdom of the past and looks to traditional thought to guide us in the present. As such, the curriculum is structured and clearly defined. Further, perennialists see education as protecting and conserving the best thought from the past. In this sense, the perennialist favors a very traditional or conservative ("conservative") as in *conserving* the best of the past) view of education. The following case study presents the point of view of a more or less typical perennialist teacher.

Case Study: A Perennialist Teacher

I came into education twenty-five years ago for two reasons. First, I was bothered by what I thought was all the nonsense in the curriculum and by all the time my friends and I wasted in school. We were allowed to take whatever courses we wanted, the majority of which were electives which seemed to be little more than the teacher's hobby. There were so many discussions—discussions that seemed to go nowhere and seemed only vaguely to touch on the supposed content of the course. I often felt as if we were simply sharing our ignorance. My second reason for becoming a teacher is a more positive one. I am convinced that our society, our culture, has great ideas, ideas that have been behind our progress in the last 2,500 years. We need to share these ideas, to vigorously teach these ideas to the young. Essentially, I see my job as passing on to the next generation, as effectively and forcefully as I can, the important truths: for instance, about human dignity and the capacity of people to do good and evil.

That has always been the teacher's role until recent times, when we seem to have lost our way. I am convinced that a society that doesn't make the great ideas and the great thoughts the foundation of education is bound to fail. Nations and societies do falter and fall. The last fifty years have seen several formerly prominent nations slip to the wayside while other younger, more vigorous countries, like Singapore and South Korea, have risen. I am convinced that most of those failed countries fell because of the inadequate education they provided. I am dedicated to the goal of not letting that happen here.

I think students are just great. In fact, I've given my life to working with them. But I don't think it is fair to them or to me or to our country to allow them to set the rules, to decide what they want to learn, or to tell me how to teach it.

Sure, I listen to them and try to find out where they are, but I make the decisions. My job is to teach; theirs is to learn. And in my classroom, those functions are quite clear. Really, students are too young to know what are the important things to learn. They simply don't know what they need to know. As a teacher, as a representative of the larger culture and of society, that's my responsibility. Turning that responsibility over to students or giving them a huge say in what is taught just strikes me as wrong.

I also believe that students should be pushed. School should be very demanding, because life is very demanding. I'm not worried about students' so called self-esteem. Self-esteem is empty unless it is earned. It will come when they discipline themselves. All of us are lazy when we are young. We would much rather play than work. All of this trying to make school like play is just making it more difficult for students to acquire the self-discipline needed to take control of their lives. What schools are turning out right now—and it pains me to say this—are a lot of self-important, self-indulgent kids. And it's not their fault. It's our fault as teachers and parents.

And the answer is so simple! We just need to go back to the great ideas and achievements of the past and make them the focal point of education. When we achieve this goal, the students don't mind working. The students and the other teachers kid me about being a slave driver. I don't really pay attention to that. But I do pay attention to the large number of students, both college-bound and non-college-bound, who come back two or three years out of high school and tell me how much they value having been pushed, how glad they are that I put them in contact with the very best!

Pause and Reflect

1. Have you seen elements of the perennialist view in your own educational background?
2. How much emphasis on classical enduring works do you hope to include in your own teaching?

Essentialism

Essentialism is a uniquely American philosophy of education which began in the 1930s and 1940s as a reaction to what was seen as an overemphasis on a child-centered approach to education and a concern that students were not gaining appropriate and adequate knowledge in schools.

The Roots of Essentialism   Essentialism has its philosophical origins in two older philosophies and draws something from each. From Plato's *idealism*, it takes the view of the mind as the central tool for understanding an objective and unchanging reality, as well as for learning the essential ideas and knowledge that we need to live well. From Aristotle's *realism*, it takes the tenet that the mind learns through contact with the physical world; therefore, to know reality, we must learn to observe and measure the physical world accurately. From our observations, we use our reasoning ability to gain new knowledge. This contrasts with the perennialist view that reasoning alone can lead to truth.

The essentialists believe that there exists a critical core of information and skill that an educated person must have. Further, essentialists are convinced that the overwhelming number of children can and should learn this core of essential material. The school, then, should be organized to transmit this knowledge and skill as effectively as possible. For the essentialists, then, the methods used to transmit this knowledge and skill are not specifically prescribed. The focus is, instead, on the knowledge that is gained by the students.

Essentialism begins to sound a good deal like perennialism. Although these two views have much in common, some important differences exist between them. For one thing, essentialists do not focus as intently on "truths" as do perennialists. They are less concerned with the classics as being the primary repository of worthwhile knowledge. They search for what will help a person live a productive life today, and if the current realities strongly suggest that students need to graduate from high school with computer literacy, the essentialist will find a place for this training in the curriculum. In this regard, essentialists are very practical. Whereas the perennialist will hold fast to the Great Books, the essentialist will make more room for scientific, technical, and even vocational emphases in the curriculum. Essentialists see themselves as valuing the past but not being captured by it.

The philosophy behind the Core Knowledge program (discussed in the chapter entitled "What Is Taught?"), which speaks out in detail about what students from kindergarten to eighth grade should know, is probably best categorized as essentialist. Based on the book, *Cultural Literacy*, by E.D. Hirsch, Jr., this content-rich curriculum stresses academics and learning of specific knowledge. While its emphasis on important ideas and great works of the past makes it attractive to perennialists, the curriculum's focus on current literature and emphasis on science point more to its alignment with the essentialist movement. Currently the Core Knowledge curriculum is being used in more than 600 schools.

Essentialist Goals and Practices   For essentialists, the aim of education is to teach the young the essentials they need to live well in the modern world. To realize this goal, schools should focus on the established disciplines, which are the "containers" of organized knowledge. The elementary years should concentrate on the basics such as the "three Rs." These and other foundational tools are needed to gain access to the disciplined knowledge with which one begins to come in contact in high school.

Although there is some debate about what is "essential" in the curriculum, essentialists believe this is not a debate to which children can contribute fruitfully. Therefore, the role of the student is simply that of learner. The individual child's interests, motivations, and psychological states are not given much attention. Nor do essentialists hold fast to what they would call a "romantic" view of children as being naturally good. They see the students not as evil, but as deficient and needing discipline and pressure to keep learning. School is viewed as a place where children come to learn what they need to know. Teachers are not guides, but authorities. The student's job is to listen and learn. Given the imperfect state of the students, the teacher must be ingenious in finding ways to engage their imaginations and minds.

One notable essentialist was James Bryan Conant, a Harvard professor and president for much of the first half of the twentieth century. Concerned about disparities in the knowledge and skills that different high school students brought with them to college, Conant argued for standardization of college requirements for high school students. He was also influential in the establishment of the SAT as a measure of essential knowledge a potential college student needs to possess.

The "Back-to-Basics" movement of the 1980s was also an essentialist-driven reaction to schooling in the 1960s and 1970s, during which core academic studies took a back seat to individual self-fulfillment and social equity. The following case study offers the perspective of a representative essentialist teacher.

Case Study: An Essentialist Teacher

In my view the world is filled with real problems, and the young people who leave school have to be ready to take up the challenge to solve those problems. So for me, the watchword in education is *usefulness*. I think everything that is taught has to pass the test of whether or not it is useful. My job as a teacher is to find out what is useful and then to make sure the students learn it.

I believe that school should be relevant to the young. However, my view of what is relevant is very different from the views of lots of other people. For me, relevance is not what is personally "meaningful" or a "do-your-own-thing" approach. What is relevant is what helps the individual live well and what benefits humanity. For that we need to look very carefully at the past and sort out the most valuable learning. That is what should be taught and what should be learned. I find the back-to-the-classics approach quite valuable. However, most advocates go too far in concentrating on classics. They also stress the humanities and the arts a little too much and tend to underplay science and technology. If children are going to function in today's world, and if our world is going to solve all the problems it's confronted with, we have to give more attention to science and technology than we have in the past. But clearly the past is the place to begin our search for the relevant curriculum.

It's not the most pleasing or satisfying image, but I think the concept of the student as an empty jug is the most accurate one. Certainly kids come to school with lots of knowledge and lots of interests. However, the job of school is to teach them what they don't know and to teach these things in a systematic and organized way. It's not to fill their minds with isolated fragments of information but to fill them with systematic knowledge. They need tools to learn, and, as they get older, they need human insights and skills that come from the disciplines.

Given that there is so much to learn, an emphasis on student "interests" and "projects" and "problem solving" is quite wasteful. There is plenty of time for that outside of school or when school is over. Inside the school, the teachers are the authorities, and the students are there to learn what they don't know. The environment should be task oriented and disciplined. It doesn't have to be oppressive or unjust or any of that. I tell my students that learning is not necessarily going to be fun, but that at the end of the year they will have a great sense of accomplishment. I'd take accomplishment over fun anytime. By and large, most students do too.

Pause and Reflect

1. What knowledge do you believe will be essential for the students you teach to learn in order to be effective members of their society?

Child-Centered Philosophies

In contrast to perennialism and essentialism, the next two schools of philosophy, romanticism and progressivism, look first to the learner rather than the curriculum. Both consider the development of the learner to be the main purpose of education. A well-educated person does not necessarily have a definite body of knowledge; rather, a well-educated person is able to function well in society and life.

Romanticism

Romanticism, or naturalism, is based on the writings of Jean Jacques Rousseau, an eighteenth century Swiss-French philosopher. In a condemnation of society and the educational system of the time, Rousseau wrote *Emile*, a novel that details Rousseau's ideas about education through the example of a fictional young boy, Emile.

The Education of Emile   Rousseau believed that children are born good and pure, but once exposed to the evils of society, they become corrupted. To keep children good, they need to be isolated from society for as long as possible. Rousseau describes a serene, yet well-controlled bucolic environment for the ideal education of Emile; he is to be educated by a private tutor at the country manor where he lives. Emile's education begins with his exploration of the world of nature surrounding him. From his observations, he may ask questions about the natural world that the tutor answers. There are no formal lessons, no books to read or facts to memorize, no specific curriculum to learn. Emile decides what he learns about and when. As Emile matures, the tutor helps him develop rational thinking skills, but Emile continues to decide the topics of study. When Emile is around fifteen, he is slowly introduced to certain social situations until he is deemed "ready" by his tutor to resist the evils of society and live a productive life in the social world. By the time he is twenty, Emile is ready to take a mate and make a life for himself.

Implications for Education Unlike the perennialists and essentialists who highlight the importance of educating the individual for society, the romantics consider the individual more important than the needs of society. For the romantics, the purpose of education is individual self-fulfillment, which means that education must help the students develop physically, intellectually, socially, and morally (usually in that order).

Romantics believe that education is a natural process, one that grows out of children's innate curiosity. This curiosity is most obvious during the "why?" phase of young childhood, when nearly every utterance out of the child's mouth is another question: "Why is the dog barking?", "Why is the boy sad?", or "Why is the bird blue?" (Parents often want to ask in return, "Why do you ask so many questions?") Romantics argue that we must let children's interests and curiosity drive their learning. The teacher's job is to respond to the children's questions as they arise and not to impose the learning of subjects that are not of interest to the child. The learner's responsibility is to maintain his or her natural curiosity and desire to learn. Because learning is guided by student interests, there is no set or common curriculum of study for the romantics. Some students may be interested in kayaking while others want to study photography and still others may be fascinated by how a DVD player works. As students pursue their own areas of study, the approach to teaching and learning also becomes individualized. Much of the learning is self-directed and self-guided by the students, with teachers serving as sources of information or resources to help the students satisfy their curiosity rather than as taskmasters or authorities on knowledge.

Romanticism has been especially influential in the early childhood and elementary grades. Many early childhood educators, including such pioneers as Maria Montessori, Frederick Froebel, and Johann Pestalozzi, basically agreed with Rousseau's ideas about humans' innate curiosity and using the child's interests to define the curriculum. Although none proposed as radical a school setting as Rousseau's pastoral manor, they did adopt some of Rousseau's other ideas about education, such as providing young children with extensive opportunities to manipulate wooden blocks and clay and other real materials.

Today, schools like Summerhill in Suffolk, England (http://www.s-hill. demon.co.uk/index.htm), and the Sudbury Valley School in Framingham, Mass., (http://www.sudval.org/svs/startup.html), embody many of the beliefs of the romantics. At these schools, there are no set curricula, no formal classes, and no tests. Students decide what they want to study and in some cases are also expected to take responsibility for their learning.

Case Study: A Romantic Teacher

Have you ever seen the thrill on a young child's face when he or she figures out how to make something work? What about their wonder as they ask another question about why there are rainbows or thunder and lightning? I see these young children, and then I look at some of the students in school today. Their faces are filled with so much dread or disinterest or boredom that I get disheartened. What happened to that enthusiasm, that excitement for learning, I wonder? That schools, which should be places of learning, can turn students off to learning so strongly is the reason I became a teacher. I want my classroom to be a place where students can explore their interests and satisfy their curiosities. I can't make them learn information if it's not something they're interested in.

In my classroom, students decide what they want to study and I help them find the resources. Sometimes we get books from the library, or find Web sites on the Internet. The Internet has been a wonderful resource for my students. Some of them have been able to have online conversations with professionals in fields like aerospace engineering and bioengineering, Sometimes, I set up face-to-face meetings with professionals in a particular field, Last week, we had a computer programmer in to talk to a couple of students who were interested in learning more about writing code. It's so exciting to see students enthusiastic about what they are learning.

I am aware of the criticism about this approach to learning; students have big holes in their knowledge, they don't learn "the hard stuff," they can't pass standardized tests. My students may not do very well on standardized tests (what do they *really* measure, anyway?), but they do learn the hard stuff! I mean, computer programming, aerospace engineering, and bioengineering? Those are not easy topics to understand. It may be that my students don't know a lot of facts in the standardized subjects, but they know well what they learn because they have selected these topics themselves. They *want* to learn about them, so they do.

Pause and Reflect

1. How would teachers in public schools, who are held account-able for students' mastery of curriculum standards, be able to follow a romantic philosophy of letting student interest guide the curriculum?

LEADERS IN EDUCATION

JOHN DEWEY (1859–1952)

John Dewey, the founder of instrumentalism, is widely considered the single most influential figure in the history of American educational thought. At the same time, his ideas and beliefs have been frequently misunderstood and misinterpreted, leading to the misapplication of his theories.

Dewey grew up in Vermont, where he attended public schools and the University of Vermont. As a graduate student in philosophy at Johns Hopkins University, he was deeply influenced by the ideas of Charles S. Pierce and William James, founders of pragmatist philosophy. Dewey recognized the implications for education of Pierce's argument that ideas, or propositions, have worth only if they make a difference in future thoughts or actions. Calling his own philosophy instrumentalism to emphasize the principle that ideas are instruments, Dewey argued that philosophy and education both involve the practical, experimental attempt to improve the human condition, Dewey denounced the public school's classical curriculum in the nineteenth century as totally unsuited to the demands of newly industrialized society of the United States, He claimed that the schools were divorced from life and that they failed to teach children how to use knowledge. Defining education as a "continuous reconstruction of experience," Dewey said that schools should teach children not what to think but how to think. In his 1916 Democracy and Education, Dewey claimed that the schools offered students as future citizens no preparation for the responsibility of citizenship in a democracy. Dewey called for schools to provide a concentrated study of democratic processes and to reflect those processes in the organization of school life, going as far as advocating that students be given the power to make decisions affecting life in the school in a democratic way. Participation in life, rather than preparation for it, he considered the watchword of an effective education.

In 1896, Dewey established the University Laboratory School, an elementary school at the University of Chicago, It was experimental in two senses: in its use of experiment and inquiry as the method by which the children learned and in its role as a laboratory for the transformation of the schools. The activities and occupations of adult life served as the core of the curriculum and the model teaching method. Children began by studying and imitating simple domestic and industrial tasks. In later years they studied the historical development of industry, invention, group living, and nature. Dewey wrote that we must "make each one of our schools an embryonic community life, active with types of occupations that reflect the life of the larger society and permeated with the spirit of art, history, and science."

The late 1920s to the early 1940s, the era of progressive education, saw a massive attempt to implement Dewey's ideas, but the rigid (and often inaccurate) manner in which they were interpreted led to remarkable extravagances in some progressive schools. For instance, some educators considered it useless to teach geography because maps changed so rapidly. The role of subject matter was gradually played down in progressive schools, replaced by a stress on method and process. The rationale was that it was more important to produce a "good citizen" than a person who was "educated" in the classical sense. Well into his nineties, Dewey fought vehemently against these corruptions of his views.

The centrality of John Dewey's thought to American education has waxed and waned over the years. Traditionally more popular in universities than in actual classroom practice, Dewey is often invoked by people attempting to make the schools more humanistic and the curriculum more relevant to the current world. Whether in favor or out, John Dewey represents the United States' most distinctive contribution to educational thought.

Visit the Web site for more information about John Dewey.

Progressivism

Progressivism is a relatively young philosophy of education. It came to prominence in the 1920s, growing out of the progressive political and social movement of the time. It drew from some of the ideas of Rousseau and from the work of John Dewey, the most influential educational philosopher of the twentieth century (see the "Leaders in Education" box in this section).

Progressivism views nature as being in flux, as ever changing. Therefore, knowledge must continually be refined and rediscovered to keep up with that change. Whereas other philosophies see the mind as a jug to be filled with truth, or as a muscle that needs to be exercised and conditioned, the progressive views the mind as a problem solver. Like the romantic, the progressive believes that people are naturally exploring, inquiring entities. When faced with an obstacle, they will try to find a way to overcome it. When faced with a question, they will try to find an answer. For the progressive, education aims to develop this problem-solving ability.

Progressive Education Progressive educators believe that the place to begin an education is with the student rather than with the subject matter. The teacher identifies what the student's interests and concerns are and tries to shape problems around them. The student's motivation to solve the problem is the key and posing problems based on student interests helps heighten their motivation.

The teacher then helps the student develop strategies to solve the problems posed.

Students should start with simple study projects and gradually learn more systematic ways to investigate until they finally master a variety of problem-solving strategies. Rather than being a presenter of knowledge or a taskmaster, the teacher is an intellectual guide, a *facilitator* in the problem-solving process. Students are encouraged to be imaginative and resourceful in solving problems. They are directed to a variety of methods, from reading books and studying the traditional disciplines to performing experiments and analyzing data.

Method is of great importance to the progressive. On the other hand, knowledge—formal, traditional knowledge—is not given the same honored place. For the progressive, there is really no special, sacrosanct knowledge or subject matter which students must learn. The value of knowledge resides in its ability to solve human problems.

Regarding the school curriculum, progressives believe that a student can learn problem-solving skills from electronics just as easily as from Latin, from agronomy just as well as from geometry. The focus for progressive educators is teaching students *how* to think rather than *what* to think. Progressive teachers often use traditional subject matter, but they use it differently from the way it is used in a traditional classroom. Because the problems students are trying to solve are of paramount importance, the subjects contribute primarily through providing contexts for problems students must solve. Subject matter knowledge may also provide information that leads to solutions. The focus for progressive educators is teaching students *how* to think rather than *what* to think. It is the process, not the product, which is of greater importance. Although both romantic and progressive educators start with the student's interests, progressives have more structure behind their teaching and they have goals for their students, to which we turn now.

POLICY MATTERS!
Standards: High Academic Achievement or Test-Driven Classrooms?

What's the Policy?

Back in January 1996, then president Bill Clinton spoke to the nation in these words: "I challenge every community, every school, and every state to adopt national standards of excellence, to measure whether schools are meeting those standards and to hold them accountable for results." A movement in the 1980s and 1990s to establish national standards had failed. However, many states have since developed and adopted their own sets of standards for what students should know and be able to do. However, national standards, or at least national testing, may be experiencing a resurgence. President George W. Bush has made education a priority of his administration and, in 2001, Congress adopted legislation that would require school districts that receive federal funding (nearly all public schools in the United States) to test all students in grades 4, 8, and 12.

How Does It Affect Teachers?

Standards are something of an educational double-edged sword. On the one hand, standards provide clarity. Teachers and students know what they are trying to accomplish, and therefore they can focus instruction and attention on achieving those standards (for instance, "At the end of second grade, students will be able to read at X level of proficiency; at the completion of tenth grade, students will have attained Y level of mathematical proficiency"),

On the other hand, the focus of instruction often narrows, not to the larger concepts behind the standards but to the tests that claim to measure the standards. Scores on these tests become the criteria for students'—and, yes, the teacher's—success or failure. Given that fact of life, teachers may tend to rely on that infamous educational methodology, teaching-to-the-test.

What Are the Pros?

Supporters of educational standards have positive goals. The *standards movement*, as it is called, is driven by the desire of parents and other taxpayers to have the well-educated young adults of the United States help it to maintain its position in the world.

Also, educators and others naturally desire to have clear targets and to know how well we are doing. Further, the standards movement has been energized by widely published reports of international studies of student achievement, studies that show American students' performance ranging from poor to mediocre.

What Are the Cons?

Philosophical disagreements seem to underlie many of the key objections to the use of standards. Standards, with their emphasis on mastering specific bodies of knowledge that experts believe students should know, appear to emanate from perennialist or essentialist concepts of education, Perhaps because of these emphases, standards seem to work against teachers committed to progressive or constructivist methods of teaching. As discussed earlier, when teachers are under pressure to make sure their students meet standards of achievement, creative methods such as cooperative learning and projects often go by the board. Direct instruction becomes the rule, followed by much drill and practice. This may help to accomplish high test scores, but these short-term achievements may make education dull, uninspiring, and ultimately counterproductive. In other words, a legitimate public desire for better education may be fostering quite questionable educational practice with little or no long-term gains.

What Do You Think?
1. What other arguments can you think of to support the standards movement in schools? To oppose the standards movement?
2. Can you think of some effective ways to measure students' problem-solving abilities or the development of their own sense of meaning?
3. How does your philosophy of education influence your views on academic standards?
4. Critics argue that standardized tests measure only factual bits of knowledge rather than deep conceptual knowledge. What should be the measure of student knowledge?

Visit the web site to learn more about this policy.

The School As Training Ground for Democracy   Unlike the romantic educator who may see society as a negative influence on the student, the progressive sees society as an integral aspect of the student's life. Progressives view schools as small societies themselves, places where students are learning as they live life, not simply preparing for life. This gives the progressive school a unique atmosphere, different from a perennialist store house of wisdom or a place with clearly defined roles and authority structures of the essentialists.

Progressive educators believe the school should be democratic in structure so that children can learn to live well in a democracy and become good citizens. They emphasize group activity and group problem solving so that students learn to work with others and help others. This is one reason many teachers who describe themselves as progressive educators are enthusiastic about cooperative learning strategies such as those discussed in the chapter on "What Is Taught?".

Implicit in the progressive approach is the belief that children must not only learn to solve their own problems, but also to solve those of their neighbors. For progressives, one of the main purposes of education is to make society better, which requires people working together to solve problems. It is not uncommon for the problem-solving activities of the progressive school to spill out into the community, and involve students in issues like ecology and poverty. In this way, students learn an important principle of progressive education: knowledge should be used to redesign or improve the world.

One notable progressive educator was William Heard Kilpatrick (1871–1965). who was a professor of philosophy of education at Columbia University in New York. He was a follower of many of Dewey's ideas about education, but differed on the importance of subject matter in a child's educational experience. Rejecting formal curriculum study, he developed the project method of education in which students work in groups on a topic of interest to them. He believed that students learn only what is of interest to them so that they should be the ones to determine topics of study. He also helped to found Bennington College in Vermont, which still embodies the progressive philosophy.

Both progressive and essentialist educators claim their particular approach is the true American philosophy of education. One can make a case that they both are, but each reflects different aspects of the American personality Progressivism represents our antiauthoritarian, experimental, and visionary side; essentialism speaks to our more practical, structured, and task-oriented side. In recent years, many of the tensions and public debates in American education can be traced to struggles between these two philosophies of education. Clearly, though, essentialist educators gained ground on progressive educators in the 1980s and 1990s, Concerns over the country's global economic competitiveness and the perceived "softness" of our schools have created a receptive climate for essentialist views.

To judge your own sympathy for the progressive approach, see what you think of the following representative statement by a progressive educator.

Case Study: A Progressive Educator

I'm a progressive educator and proud of it. I'm not ducking that label just because it is unpopular in many quarters these days, usually among people who don't really understand what it is. Quite honestly, for the life of me, I cannot understand how a teacher can be anything *but* a progressive educator.

I'm dedicated to a few simple and, I believe, obvious principles. For one thing, children come into the world with a very plastic nature, capable of being molded one way or another. We should therefore work to surround them with activities and opportunities that bring them in contact with good things. Also, by their nature, children are curious. Instead of rejecting their curiosities, I believe we should build on them. Schools should be exciting, involving places where students are caught up in interesting activities.

I think that I'm a progressive educator because I have looked at my own experiences. I know I learn best when I'm trying to solve a puzzle or a problem that really interests me. And somehow I've always been able to get much more interested in how we're going to solve the problems of our own society than in the affairs of the Athenians and Spartans. I can get much more involved in a research problem about which DVD player gives the best value for the dollar than about some dry economic problem presented to me by a teacher. And I really don't think I'm different from the overwhelming majority of students.

I see many of my fellow teachers spending all their energy damming up student curiosity and imposing work on their students. And then the teachers wonder why they themselves are so tired or burned out, I'm sure it's quite tiring to try to convert children into file cabinets and to stuff facts into their heads all day.

One of the things that sets me apart is that I'm not so hung up as others are on what I call the "talky" curriculum, I am convinced that students learn most effectively by *doing*, by experiencing events and then reflecting on and making meaning out of what they have experienced, I think more science is learned on a nature walk than from the same time spent reading a textbook or hearing teacher explanations. I think students learn more abstract principles, such as democracy, from trying to set up and maintain a democratic society in their classroom than from a lot of learned lectures and dusty prose on the subject, I'm trying to get to their hearts and their heads. The traditional approach gets to neither place.

To me, life is a matter of solving problems. New times have new problems and demand new knowledge. I don't want my students to be ready for life in the eighteenth century. I want them to be effective, functioning, curious citizens of the twenty-first century. They are going to need to be able to develop solutions to fit new and unique problems. Although much knowledge is important, they need to realize that knowledge is only today's tentative explanation of how things work. Much of what we know now is incorrect and will have to be replaced.

It's not that I think that ideas and content and the traditional subjects are worthless. Far from it, I teach much of the same material as other teachers. However, I get there by a different route. I let the issues and problems emerge and then give the students a chance to get answers and to solve problems. And, as they quickly learn, they have to know a great deal to solve some of the problems. Often they get themselves involved with some very advanced material. The only difference is that now they want to. Now they have the energy. And, boy, once they get going, do they have energy! No, it doesn't always work, I have students who coast, and I've had projects that failed. But I'd put my track record against those of my more traditional colleagues any day.

Pause and Reflect

1. Did any of your teachers take a progressive approach to teaching? If so, how did you, as a student, respond? Do you believe your students would respond well if you chose to implement a progressive approach?

THE INFLUENCE OF PSYCHOLOGICAL THEORIES

Since early in the twentieth century, educational practice has been greatly influenced by the discipline of psychology. Psychology, the scientific study of the mind and human behavior, was a natural influence on the work of teachers, particularly with its focus on how we learn. Over the years, various schools of psychology have emerged, often having roots in particular philosophies. Some of these psychological theories have had a great deal to say to educators. Two in particular have had an impact on our schools: behaviorism and cognitive psychology.

Behaviorism: Conditioning Students or Setting Them Free?

The psychological theory of behavior modification or **behaviorism** is an educational approach that emerged directly from the pioneering research of the late B. F. Skinner (1904–1990), who himself was influenced by the social efficiency movement in education of the 1920s and 1930s. Skinner developed the theory called operant conditioning, which viewed learning as the learner's response to various stimuli (for example, sounds, words, or people) present in the environment. Subscribing to the view that humans learn to act in specific ways based on the response they receive for their actions (generally reward or punishment), the behaviorist teacher believes that learners need incentives, both positive and negative, as motivators to learn. The curriculum is organized in sequenced, discrete segments. Behaviorist teachers will often use objective tests made up predominantly of multiple-choice questions to measure how well students have learned the curriculum and to give prompt feedback to students. In some behaviorist classrooms, students are expected to practice a specific skill until they show a certain level of mastery of the skill. In planning for teaching, the behaviorist (1) uses clear objectives, spelled out in terms of the behaviors to be learned; (2) establishes a learning environment, which will positively reinforce desired behaviors and eliminate undesirable behaviors; and (3) closely monitors and gives the learner feedback on progress until the goal is achieved. Because the same behaviors and knowledge are desirable for all students, standardization of the curriculum and of measuring progress is important.

In the 1960s and 1970s, many educators made behaviorism their dominant, organizing educational theory. However, this education movement was criticized for being teacher dominated and causing teachers to treat students as passive objects to be conditioned. Nevertheless, behaviorism remains a dominant theoretical presence, particularly in the areas of special education and classroom discipline. Many teachers rely on behavior modification practices to get students to be quiet when they see or hear the teacher's signal or to do their best work to get a reward sticker.

Critics argue that a behaviorist teacher exercises too much control over students' learning and focuses on the learning of facts rather than deep conceptual knowledge. In response, behaviorist teachers insist that their goal is to eventually put control of learning in their students' hands once they have learned to respond appropriately to the teacher's prompts.

Cognitive Psychology: Students As Makers of Meaning?

Over the past twenty years, researchers in both medicine and psychology have been investigating the human brain to find out more about its role in human learning and memory. Cognitive psychologists, drawing heavily on the trail-blazing research of Swiss psychologist Jean Piaget (1896–1980), as well as that of the Russian psychologist Lev Vygotsky (1896–1934), and the American psychologist Jerome Bruner (1915–), have discovered a great deal about how people learn to think and solve problems. Their discoveries have led to the development of new theories about learning and cognition that have tremendous implications for how teachers teach. One increasingly popular theory derived from the research findings is that in order for new information to be internalized by the learner, it must be integrated into the learner's pre-existing knowledge base. This process of integration is referred to as **constructivism**.

According to this theory, knowledge cannot be *transmitted* directly from the teacher to the learner, but is *constructed by the learner* and, later, *reconstructed* as new information becomes available. Instead of seeing students as partially full vessels waiting to be filled, teachers should view them as actively engaged in making meaning. Teachers, therefore, need to create learning situations where students can build their own knowledge rather than having students sit and listen to the teachers' lectures. Constructivism has become so influential in education in recent years that we give it particular attention here.

Constructivists view individuals as having an aversion to disorder. They believe that we are all continually trying to sort things out, to find clues and patterns amid our impressions that will help us to make sense of the world around us. When we encounter something new, say, a strange sound in the night, we immediately attempt to fit it into the patterns or structures we already possess (for example, "That's the midnight whistle of the Ole Ninety-Eight headin' down to New Orleans"). But sometimes we encounter new information which leads (or forces) us to realize that our knowledge base as it is currently "constructed" is incorrect or outdated ("Uh-oh! The railroad retired that train two years ago!"). We may respond in a number of ways: we search for new input from our senses, seeking either to reconstruct the knowledge base, developing different patterns and structures so that the information "fits" ("Maybe that noise was from the hot water boiler and it's about to explode," or "Maybe that creepy guy from the apartment down below is on my fire escape," or "Maybe I shouldn't read Stephen King novels before going to bed!"). In some instances, we may be so convinced of our knowledge base that we refuse to make allowances for the new information. ("No, I'm sure that it was a train whistle. They must have put that train back in service.") Students follow the same patterns as they try to make sense of new information they encounter in school.

Cognitive psychologists also suggest that we organize our knowledge in ways that allow us easy access to knowledge we use regularly. These cognitive structures, which are called *schemas* or *schemata*, change constantly and continually as new information is taken in, hypotheses are developed, and theories are tested. These processes of hypothesis development and testing can be done independently or in interaction with others. Thus, real learning for constructivists involves moving from the Trivial Pursuit or Jeopardy type of factual or declarative knowledge to applicable knowledge—in other words, from "knowing what" to "knowing how," To do this, learners must develop cognitive learning strategies for particular kinds of learning tasks; that is, they have to learn how to think through or go about solving problems.

VOICES FROM THE
CLASSROOM

Susan Dougherty writes about her career as a fourth-grade teacher at Bayberry School in Watchung, New Jersey.

Constructivist Philosophy

As I began my career in education I held firm one belief about students: they must be active participants in the classroom. Twelve years later, I hold that same basic belief but have refined what it means for a learner to be active. Early in my career active meant that my students would not sit in rows and spend the day doing seatwork. My first position as a kindergarten teacher quickly revealed that I might strive for something greater than physical activity. Of course, kindergarten students are active—try and keep them from being anything but active! I came to recognize that while active bodies can be important, what I really wanted was to engage the minds of my students. As I taught students at many elementary levels, I learned to ask probing questions that required my students to consider their learning carefully. How do you know to add these two numbers? What kind of person do you think the main character of this story is? How would you explain why oil floats on water to someone who didn't understand? While my students were often physically active, acting out scenes from a novel we were reading, experimenting with magnets or prisms, or using pattern blocks to build models of math problems, they also spent time physically inert, but inwardly engaged in active thought.

Soon, however, I was not satisfied with simply engaging the minds of my students. I wanted to reach their hearts. I wanted to awaken a passion for learning within each student. How might a teacher encourage the awakening of such passion? One key, I think, is to allow and encourage the students to ask and seek the answers to their own questions. In this way, students' minds and hearts become active, leading them on a lifelong journey of inquiry and self-motivated learning.

Visit the web site for more Voices from the Classroom.

Implications of Constructivism for Teachers in the Classroom

The constructivist teacher does four things: (1) actively involves students in real situations, (2) activates students' prior knowledge before presenting new information, (3) uses questions to provoke students' thoughts, and (4) structures learning experiences so that new information is presented in readily accessible forms. At heart, the constructivist teacher behaves more like a coach. Such a teacher is interested primarily in helping the child engage problems and issues, search below the surface, try out various possible solutions or explanations, and finally construct meaning from these experiences. Constructivist classrooms are active places with many opportunities for discovery and experimentation, often a heavy use of cooperative learning, and teachers who are fellow learners rather than fact givers and drill masters.

Critics of constructivism claim that its qualities of student-centered and self-constructed learning have led to declines in both academic achievement and classroom discipline. If this is true, it represents a poor application of constructivist principles, which are making their way into our classrooms. In contrast, we believe that constructivism is the linchpin to truly learning to learn, a key component to the school reform programs discussed in the chapter entitled "I Should Education Be Reformed?".

TABLE 1 Four Philosophies and Their Applications to Education

	Perennialism	Essentialism	Romanticism	Progressivism
Metaphysics: What is real? Does it have meaning?	The meaning of life is the search for unchanging truth found in the collective wisdom of Western culture.	What is relevant is What helps an individual live well and what benefits humanity.	Reality is stable; the meaning of life *is* derived primarily through self-development away from society.	Reality is in flux and ever-changing, so meaning is in the context of the individual, who is a "problem solver."
Epistemology: Knowledge and knowing—what is truth?	Truth and knowledge are changeless, revealed through guided reflection and in classics of Western culture.	Truth exists in the classics *and* modern science. Students must learn process *and* content. Knowledge is gained through the interaction of experiences and rational thought.	Knowledge is gained through sensory experiences and interaction with one's environment.	Knowledge is gained via individual experience: Truth is individually defined so that emphasis is on learning *how* to learn.
Axiology: Values, ethics, aesthetics	Changeless. Determined by the very nature of reality.	Determined by the natural order of things. Values exist in the best of culture.	Determined by the individual.	Determined by each individual in interaction with his or her culture, based on the shared values of the community or culture.
Logic: How we think, deductive and inductive	Rationality, especially deductive thought, is developed by studying classics and through the Socratic dialectic.	Rationality is best developed through interplay of deductive and inductive thinking.	Primarily inductive thought since learning starts with experiences and moves to hypotheses.	Emphasis is on inductive thinking and problem solving.
purpose of Education/Schooling	Educate the intellect; develop in learner rational thought and an understanding of the truths of humankind.	Prepare students to be productive, contributing members of society.	Make learner strong (physically, intellectually, morally) to resist the evils of society.	Helps students become good citizens familiar with the workings of democracy and with good problem-solving skills.
The Teacher	Teacher is expert of content knowledge. Passes on to next generation the accumulated wisdom of the past.	Teacher is expert of content knowledge. Teaches essential knowledge. Maintains task-oriented focus.	Teacher responds to learner's requests for knowledge; does not initiate learning in learner.	Teacher is facilitator of student learning; provides resources for students' problem-solving abilities. Develops students' problem-solving abilities. Helps children do what they want to do.
The Child	Cultivates rational powers through contact with the culture's best and through imitation. For older students, Socratic dialogue is key to uncovering truths found in classics. Is there to learn what is taught.	Avoids methodological frills and soft pedagogy and concentrates on sound, proven instructional methods. Is there to listen and learn.	Creates productive learning environment for learner; individualized approach to learning, depending on student interests. Is naturally good and must be protected from the evils of society.	Stimulates students to plan and carry out activities and research projects using group processes and democratic procedures. Learns by doing and by discovering.
The Curriculum	In younger grades, focus on basic skills to develop mental discipline and rational thought processes. Older learners study materials reflecting universal and recurring themes through which the truths of humanity can be revealed.	Strong emphasis on basic skills in elementary schools and on disciplined knowledge and scholastic achievement in secondary schools.	Dependent on the interests of the learner. No set curriculum, no specific skills to be acquired.	Centered on student's interest in real problems and interdisciplinary solution seeking.

YOUR PHILOSOPHY OF EDUCATION

At this point, you may well be confused and possibly discouraged. To expect to be able to understand and evaluate critically every aspect of each philosophy is to expect of yourself what few professional philosophers are able to do. What you have just finished reading is a precis of some of the major ideas of Western civilization (see Table 8 for a summary). Some of these ideas have been around for centuries, and some are the fruits of twentieth-century thinkers.

Selecting the philosophy by which you will live and by which you will guide your professional activities takes much more investment of time, thought, and energy than reading our short chapter.

Some teachers, like the teacher-philosophers in this chapter, settle on one philosophical view, and that view structures all of their work. Other teachers lean strongly toward a particular philosophy, even if they may not be fully conscious of their position or be able to give it a proper philosophical label. Typically they have a particular view of the learner, of how the learner should be approached, and of what is most worth knowing.

However, few teachers are philosophical purists. Some teachers, recognizing that they draw ideas from various philosophies, label themselves *eclectics*. But what does it really mean to be an eclectic in contemporary education?

Pause and Reflect

1. It is perhaps unfair of us to ask you so soon after having read descriptions of different philosophies and theories of education, but, right now, which one holds the great intellectual appeal to you? Which one holds the least appeal? And, "why" to both questions?

Eclecticism: Not an Excuse for Sloppy Thinking

Eclecticism embodies the idea that truth can be found anywhere and therefore people should select from various doctrines, systems, and sources. The eclectic teacher selects what he or she believes to be the most attractive features of several philosophies. For example, the teacher might take from romanticism the innate curiosity of the learner and from essentialism a curricular viewpoint dominated by the criterion of usefulness.*

Eclecticism is quite popular, but often for the wrong reasons. It sometimes appears as the easy way out of philosophical uncertainty, just taking what you please from the philosophical cafeteria of ideas. ("Let's see now: I think I'll begin with a light salad of romantic individuality and follow that up with a main course of progressive problem-solving projects, but with some hearty perennialist classics as side dishes. And, oh, yes—let's finish with a popular and tasty dessert of essentialist vocational training.") One problem with this approach is the possibility of inconsistency. To take one's view of society from the romantic, who gives primacy to individual freedom, and one's teaching methodology from the progressivist, who stresses group membership and democratic process, is liable to make everyone confused. Selecting eclecticism cannot be an excuse for lazy thinking.

*In the process of writing this chapter, we discovered that we are really traditional but progressive essentialists who are searching for a Great Books Club to join.

On the other hand, most teachers feel quite free and justified in borrowing teaching methodologies and strategies that are associated with various philosophies of education. The ardent perennialist teacher may choose to involve his other sixth-grade students in a "hands-on" project constructing a large topographical map of Odysseus's ten-year journey to his home after the fall of Troy. Conversely, the free-spirited romantic teacher may insist that each student memorize and be able to recite fifty lines of *The Odyssey*. Although this type of eclecticism may, in a narrow sense, seem philosophically inconsistent, at its root is the recognition that no philosophy of education is able to dictate the ideal methodology or learning strategies for all situations or all students trying to learn all subject matter. Related to this is the growing realization, discussed in the chapter entitled "Who Are Today's Students in a Diverse Society?", that different students possess a great range of learning styles and that what works with one student may flop with another. In sum, eclecticism can be a serious philosophical position, and eclecticism in the selection of teaching strategies is quite justified. But, again, the choice to be "eclectic" should not be a substitute for sloppy thought.

Identifying Your Own Philosophical Leanings

Think of your favorite teacher from elementary or secondary school, or a teacher you have admired during your teacher education. On a separate piece of paper, list some of that teacher's practices that you admire most. Include instructional techniques, classroom management strategies, ways of relating to the students—anything you think helped that person be an effective teacher.

Now, on the same piece of paper, write the philosophical outlook that you think may have underlain each practice you admired. This will take some reflection, and you may well find that no single philosophy matches all the teaching characteristics you listed. Use whatever philosophical labels seem most appropriate.

After completing both tasks, what general conclusions can you draw about the philosophy of this teacher you admire? Does your teacher reflect the tenets of a single educational philosophy discussed in this chapter? Or does she or he take an eclectic approach, drawing on different philosophical traditions? Are there ways in which this teacher is too unique to fit any category?

As a final step, reflect on what this tells you about your own philosophical leanings. If you hold this teacher in high regard, presumably you share at least some of his or her philosophical convictions. Is there anything that surprises you about the philosophical beliefs you have deduced? Do they suggest that you are more traditional or more progressive than you supposed? More child-centered or subject-matter-centered? More nicely balanced, or just more muddled? What aspects of your own philosophical base do you need to think about further and clarify?

Philosophy and Liberal Education

We are not suggesting that you sit yourself down, think through all these issues, and come up with a tight set of philosophical answers that will last the rest of your lifetime. Rather, we hope that we have focused—or refocused—your attention on some of life's most critical questions and on some issues that are at the very core of teaching.

One purpose of the general education component of teacher education programs (that is, the courses in the arts and sciences required of the prospective teacher) is to provide a chance for future teachers to think through these fundamental questions of human existence. A primary purpose of the college curriculum is to present the student with a spectrum of society's best thinkers and their attempts to understand their own existence. On the other hand, the infamous college bull sessions may be where the real philosophical inquiry goes on; they are frequently thinly veiled discussions of what really counts in life and what one should try to do with one's life. In effect, then, both the formal apparatus of college and its curriculum and the informal opportunities to meet, talk, and test your ideas with a variety of people should help you discover where you stand on some of these essential human questions.

A FINAL WORD

As we said at the beginning of this chapter, the teacher who will be more than a technician has an obligation to take philosophical issues and questions seriously, Teachers owe it to themselves and to their students to understand where they are going and why they are going there. On the other hand, teachers owe it to themselves to make sure that the schools they work in are hospitable—and certainly not hostile—to their own philosophies of education. It is important, therefore, that you be ready both to discuss your own philosophy of education with prospective employers and to inquire about the district's or school's philosophy. However, do not expect those interviewing you to be able to define their schools precisely according to the particular philosophies described in this chapter. Although educators live out a philosophy of education, we are not always able easily to capture it in words.

KEY TERMS

aesthetics (268) axiology (267) behaviorism (285) constructivism (286) deductive reasoning (270) epistemology (267) essentialism (274) ethics (268) inductive reasoning (270) logic (268) metaphysics (266) perennialism (272) philosophy (264) progressivism (281) romanticism (278)

FOR REFLECTION

At the present time, what beliefs do you have about the following: the role of the teacher, the nature of the learner, the nature of the curriculum, how people learn best? Thinking about these topics will help you to begin to formulate your philosophy of education.
1. What role, if any, does religion play in your philosophy of education?
2. Why do you think that superintendents and principals often ask teaching candidates about their philosophy of education?
3. And now, a really hard question: If you are leaning toward eclecticism, in what areas of teaching and learning would you draw on the various philosophies presented?

FOR FURTHER INFORMATION: PRINT RESOURCES

Gary D. Fenstermacher and Jonas F. Soltis. *Approaches to Teaching* (New York: Teachers College Press, 1986).

This slim volume shows how two philosophers can unpack the term teaching and explain what is behind: several different approaches to instruction.

Jostein Gaarder, *Sophie's World: A Novel About the History of Philosophy* (New York: Farrar, Straus , and Giroux, 1994).

This interesting and innovative book is an excellent introduction to philosophy and the history of ideas. The writer is clearly a marvelous teacher, plus a most engaging writer.

Gerald Gutek, *Historical and Philosophical Foundations of Education: A Biographical Introduction,* 3d ed, (Upper Saddle River, NJ: Prentice-Hall/Merrill, 2000).

This textbook is a comprehensive and up-to-date account of the competing schools of educational philosophy and their application to schooling. It provides thumbnail sketches of key figures and leads the reader in investigating their thought.

Section III

Education, Power, and Hegemony

Power and Culture

By John R. Hall, Mary Jo Neitz, and Marshall Battani

What is the relation of culture to the exercise of power—the subordination of individuals and groups to the will of others or to the constraints of an established social order? Karl Marx once held religion to be the opiate of the people. Granted, Marx's view was more complex than this remark would suggest. But this strong version of class domination through cultural domination remains a useful benchmark by which to examine relationships between culture and power. This reading explores the social and technological forces that shape the conditions under which culture might prove powerful, and then examines various theories of power and culture. These theories are diverse: one view holds that the power of culture is beyond the control of any group or social stratum. Alternatively, the patterns of culture by which people live are seen as shaped in one or another way by the influence of powerful interests.

Questions of power may be addressed in two broad ways: (1) by looking at *power aspects of the established order of culture* and (2) by investigating the *political economy of cultural production*. The latter approach explores how the form and content of cultural objects may be shaped by the economic and political control of cultural production. The former issue, to which we now turn, is about the power implications of a society's cultural patterns.

POWER AND THE ESTABLISHED ORDER OF CULTURE

Sociologists widely recognize the importance of the ability to produce and distribute culture, but there is considerable disagreement about how much, how, and which powerful interests control the content and form of culture for their own benefit. One theoretical possibility is that an overall *established order*—the ongoing institutional arrangements—of cultural production has *functional* consequences for the power of different social groups, independently of any individual's, organization's, or stratum's capacity to control the shape of the established order. For example, although the field of media industries is dominated by a mere handful of organizations, we must also recognize that the overall structure of media production is the product of multiple forces, and that it is thus "relatively autonomous" of any given company's or corporate sector's ability to organize or transform the established cultural order. For example, although certain organizations seek to manipulate the structure of the music recording industry and thus benefit disproportionately from the established order, crucial factors contributing to the shape of that order—the shifting relative importance of verbal, written, printed, and visual communication and the development of digital technologies—are in important ways beyond the control of particular organizations and groups.

The established order of culture thus may be understood in two ways. First, technology and the interplay of a variety of social forces may produce cultural patterns that allocate power. Second, independently of these processes, it is possible to understand the cultural order as a realm of ideas and symbols that powerfully shape society.

Technology, Social Forces, and the Cultural Order

Is there a difference between a culture based largely on print and speech communication and one where people routinely watch television and use DVDs, VCRs, computers, and wireless communication? Do authoritarian societies have different cultural patterns from democratic ones? Posing questions about technology and social forces in such stark terms yields a ready affirmative answer. The more subtle question has to do with whether and how these differences condition the power arrangements of societies.

Technology

Marshall McLuhan's (1964) famous formulation that "the medium is the message" suggests a sort of technological determinism. For McLuhan, the content of what we hear on the radio is not so important as the way that the radio organizes our worlds, both in the capacity to transmit information and entertainment and in the ways we incorporate sounds from beyond our immediate life-worlds into our everyday activities. With radio, patterns of human interaction are changed to the extent that music (and a wide variety of it) becomes accessible to us without much effort—certainly without the need to assemble musicians, attend a concert, or make music ourselves. Other technologies—the automobile, television, the VCR, the computer—also reconfigure the ways we interact with one another.

Joshua Meyrowitz (1985) extended McLuhan's analysis by looking at the information we get through various media. Instead of assuming that information comes into a social world that itself is unchanged by the process, Meyrowitz asks how one or another particular medium shapes social relationships. In his view, print media—books, magazines, newspapers—offer a depth and detail of information that makes each person something of a specialist on the basis of what he or she reads, whether astrophysical theory, home hobby books, or gossip columns. With print, we each get to know a great deal about selected topics, but what we know and what others know can be quite different, because people burrow into many different topics. Television, on the other hand, is oriented to more general audiences, and it lacks the capacity to convey detailed information yet offers its audiences a wide awareness of things previously known only by specialists (rituals of warfare among Pacific island natives, for example). General audiences also become familiar with knowledge previously held largely by people with distinctive status positions; for instance, children can become conversant with the "backstage" worldview of parents.

Technological and economic changes shaping media industries during the 1990s amplified the importance of Meyrowitz's argument. The veritable explosion of cable channels and the internet (and the emerging convergence of the two) rapidly have increased the availability of often highly specialized content. Citizens not only get to read newspaper accounts of politicians' speeches; they get to inspect very intimate details in the life of the president of the United States, as when Bill Clinton's affair with a White House intern became the focus of media attention in the late 1990s, or when George W. Bush lost consciousness, and nearly his life, after choking on a pretzel while alone watching a football game on television in the White House.

For Meyrowitz, such developments blur the distinctions between backstage and frontstage, and between expert and lay person. Thus, frontstage presentations by public figures—how they want to be seen—compete with images about backstage activities. As a variety of commentators have noted, public life obtains the dramatic quality of a soap opera that feeds on previously secret "scandal" or other plots that are easily serialized. In a similar way, the expertise of professionals becomes subject to second-guessing because television offers everyone a patchwork of expert knowledge in diverse fields. Overall, television and streams of information available online have made many people much more sophisticated about "performances," and, possibly for that reason, people sometimes do not easily impress. Ironically, though, awareness of the constructed character of public images brings people to recognize that images do make a difference. For example, in the weeks following the 9/11 attacks in the United States in 2001 considerable television airtime, column inches, and server space were given over to a debate about the appropriate name for the war on terrorism. The original name coined by the Bush administration, "Infinite Justice," was criticized as vengeful, and the administration then chose a new name, "Enduring Freedom," both to reflect better on the motives for war and—importantly—to avoid alienating potential members of the international coalition the administration was forging to prosecute the war (cf. Arundhati 2001; Rosenberg 2001).

Meyrowitz's focus on television can obviously be broadened to include other technologies that followed—the video cassette recording, the compact disc, the digital video disc, electronic computer mail, and so on. Each technology gives rise to a distinctive set of possible relations between individuals and culture, and each shapes social relationships among the people who participate in it. McLuhan grandly imagined a sort of "global village" in which people would be united into one large community by the enveloping web of communication. The worldwide web and the huge audience for events like the World Cup seem like unifying developments, yet the opposite image—of alienation—also seems relevant: people become separated from one another by their ability to select and experience culture individually through technology like MP3, which allows individuals to download and store music from the web on portable hard drive/players, or the "TIVO" and devices like it, which can instantly record and time-shift television programming and even make programming choices in response to the history of a given user's viewing habits. Rapidly changing technologies that alter the web of communication thus may either increase or decrease the degree to which people are connected.

How are these changes related to power? The answer depends on both the nature of culture under various technologies and the relation of technologies to the established order of culture. Participants in what began as the Frankfurt School of critical theory have argued since the 1930s that there can be no single theory of how power operates in societies because every change—even toward freedom—establishes a set of conditions in which new arrangements of domination can take hold. There are dialectical shifts in the exercise of power. For example, a well-established democracy can be subverted by the rise of propaganda. Similarly, free choices in the marketplace can be constrained by the social conditions under which they are made, such that the range of choices cannot be assumed to match buyers' wants and needs.

In the dialectic of power identified by the critical theorists, people interested in minimizing the non-legitimate exercise of power need to identify specific sources of power that operate in their immediate circumstances. Early on, the critical theorists wondered why the working class lacked the revolutionary fervor that Karl Marx had expected. One answer pointed to the new technological possibilities of cultural domination. Already in the 1930s, Walter Benjamin (1969) identified a key divide in culture, noting the increasing prevalence of mechanically reproduced recordings, art prints, films, and so on, distributed on a mass basis. In our era, the mass production and distribution of culture is the central arrangement by which people have access to culture, and this is as true for much of high culture as it is for popular culture (Gans 1974; Halle 1993). Both classical composers and the latest offerings of the pop music industry are available on compact discs and as MP3 files. What, then, was Benjamin's concern? For Benjamin a real cultural object has "authenticity," a special "aura," and a kind of "authority" that are diminished by mass copying. In his view, the shift to mass production—from live to recorded music, from theater to film and TV, from painting to art prints and reproductions—has dire consequences. Art loses its significance as a critical activity when mass reproduction makes it more of a commodity subject to the same forces of manufacturing and marketing as other commodities—cars or laundry detergents, for example. "To an ever greater degree," Benjamin wrote, "the work of art reproduced becomes the work of art designed for reproducibility" (1969, p. 224).

Of course, Benjamin had not seen the half of it. Television and streaming video delivered via the worldwide web may appear to represent the world, but acting, the technologies of animation and editing, and the possibilities of embedding images in a variety of textual and graphic contexts mean that the world as it is depicted on television and via the web need not have any existence beyond the screen, even though, as a Baudrillardian simulacrum, the screen reality paradoxically threatens to overshadow the significance of everyday life. The images brought into our homes by television and the web create a new claim of authenticity. We are dazzled by the experiences made possible by the new technologies: they allow us to see and hear things in ways unavailable in our everyday worlds. Yet for Benjamin our individual responses to the fascinations of mass-produced culture are prefigured in their design. Indeed, the successful producers of popular entertainment and advertising have developed substantial lore about how to use media techniques to create particular effects in mass audiences. Benjamin was not completely opposed to the new developments. He recognized that mechanical reproduction could free art from its "parasitical dependence on ritual," thus contributing to the possibility for autonomous artistic practice (1969, p. 224). But mainly he worried that the mass production of culture heightened the potential for promoting entertainment over critical thought and offered a distraction from the circumstances of actual social life by spreading new kinds of (debased) ritual values—those of mass spectacle—with affinities both to fascist politics and to consumer capitalism.

Overall, technology shapes culture in important ways: it establishes the media of cultural interchange; it may make culture more accessible to some groups and less accessible to others; it can shift our connections to culture and change how we view the world. However, technology itself is an insufficient basis on which to explain the power effects of an established order of culture. In response to the technology argument, critical theorists Max Horkheimer and Theodor Adorno observed in the 1940s: "No mention is made of the fact that the basis on which technology acquires power over society is the power of those whose economic hold over society is greatest" (1982, p. 121).

Social Forces

Despite the significance of technology, empirical sociological research suggests that the established order of culture cannot be reduced to its technological basis. To the contrary, as Benjamin (1969) indicates clearly in the epilogue of his famous essay, technology, artistic schools, and political movements are interrelated. Whatever the consequences of a cultural order for the distribution of power, diverse social forces help shape its emergence.

We might assume, to take one example, that technological innovations in printing brought the modern newspaper into being. But Michael Schudson has argued that it is just the reverse: in the U.S., various social forces of change came to a head in the 1830s, creating demand for a new kind of newspaper, and this demand in turn motivated technological innovations that made printing easier (1978, pp. 31–5). What were these social forces in the nineteenth-century U.S.? Schudson points to three: the emergence of a broadly based market economy, the diffusion of political participation among wider and wider sectors of the population, and the eclipse of small-scale community by a more complex society. When increasing numbers of people become drawn into the market economy, they begin to have an interest in news of commerce that previously was important solely to business people. Similarly, the growing interest in politics could not be adequately served by the party-organ newspapers of the day, which primarily published the views of the political parties without offering what we today think of as "news." Finally, even if in small communities face-to-face conversations could serve as a medium of communication that helped bind people together, a complex society created wider social ties beyond the world of people's immediate neighbors: what happened in another state or country became of interest to people whose horizons were expanding. In the nineteenth century, forces were at work changing the social world and people's ties to it; these changing conditions, Schudson argues, created circumstances in which "news" gained a sufficient audience to fuel the birth of the first modern newspapers.

What about other kinds of societal arrangements, for example of material culture? Let us take the case of the American motel. It would be easy to argue that technology gave rise to the motel. At the end of the nineteenth century, hotels were a form of travel accommodation appropriate to cities and to forms of travel such as trains that served urban places. With the early-twentieth-century advent of the automobile—a technological innovation—motels might be explained as hotels moved out to the highway. But this common sense explanation is drawn into question by Warren Belasco (1979), who shows that motels indeed originated by catering to the motoring public, but not simply as hotels at the edge of town. Instead, the motel form of overnight travel accommodation emerged as a byproduct of status competition between elite vacationers and other people with whom they shared the road. When the grand American spas and resorts began to attract a less elite clientele in the latter part of the nineteenth century, some patrons began to seek out other forms of leisure. Motivated by the desire for a nostalgic return to nature and embracing "the strenuous life" recommended by President Theodore Roosevelt at the turn of the twentieth century, some people used the first automobiles for "auto-camping, " going, as they said, "a gypsying" to escape the constraints of the increasingly industrial, bureaucratized, and urban social landscape. To cater to this trend, city campgrounds gradually became established, and then private ones, which charged a fee, thus excluding vagrants and the migrating poor. By the 1920s entrepreneurs were offering tourist cabins and cottages on campgrounds as more comfortable accommodations for their paying clients. It was at these autocamping/cabin facilities that the first motels were established. Thus, the motel as a business format for lodging was born of changing tastes among automobile tourists engaged in status competition with one another.

The importance of diverse social forces can also be seen in long-term and global developments toward contemporary culture. At the beginning of the twenty-first century, complex interactions between global media technologies, consumer capitalism, international tourism, and migration are reshaping social relationships within and across nation-states, including the very notion of citizenship. People's identifications with communities have become defined less in political terms and more in terms of what cultures they consume and how they become tied to new hybrid cultures that have developed out of increasing social interchange across national boundaries. As Nick Stevenson argues,

> citizenship becomes less about formalized rights and duties and more about the consumption of exotic foods, Hollywood cinema, Brit. pop CDs and Australian wine. To be excluded from these commercial goods is to be excluded from citizenship (that is full membership) in modern western societies. (N. Stevenson 1997, p. 2)

On the flip side of this international consumption dynamic are the emerging imperatives of relations between culture and the market. To be a full member of the global community is to offer up one's images, practices, language, and other cultural artifacts to those with the power and resources to consume them (buy them, watch them, eat them, study them). Thus, to understand globalization it is essential to recognize that mass-mediated communications technologies which make culture available to a wide audience are operating in a globalized social climate of consumer capitalism and tourism. In this globalized circumstance, social relationships to culture increasingly become defined as relationships between performances and audiences. The relationships of individuals and groups to cultures beyond the boundaries of their own societies may have political effects as well. Just as Meyrowitz argues that relations between individuals are reshaped when television makes formerly "expert" knowledge available to lay persons, globalizing media may be transforming the nature of citizenship by making social and cultural resources available that allow individuals to distance themselves from their own official state-centered discourses and connect transnationally with other bases of identity (J.B. Thompson 1994; 1995).

Emergent patterns of culture as diverse as the newspaper, the motel, and globalized identity discourses cannot be explained by technology alone. Cultural developments are shaped by social forces at work in the societies where they appear. We may suspect that further research would show the significance of social forces for diverse kinds of culture—popular music, film, craft fairs, literature, motorcycle gangs, and so on. Yet to explain the origins of an established cultural order by either the influence of technology or social forces does not necessarily explain that order as a basis of social power. This is true for two reasons. First, whatever the origins of a cultural order, once it is established it may have consequences as a set of meanings and objects that inscribe power within society. Second, individuals and groups that own or control key organizations in the established social order may be able to exercise power through cultural production.

The Established Cultural Order As a Medium of Power

Do the institutionalized patterns of culture that inform our actions themselves amount to orders of power? If so, why and how? Sociologists like Durkheim (1995) focus on culture as a force of social integration. Yet this does not deny the power of culture. To the contrary, culture can thereby define the boundary between social integration versus alienation or deviance. At least implicitly, this means that culture is a medium of power: people who operate within the boundaries of a culture are dominated by its categories and meanings; those who deviate from cultural expectations may be subject to sanctions both at the hands of authority and of other people who conform to the established cultural order.

Sigmund Freud confronted the coercive power of culture much more directly than Durkheim. Freud argued the existence of a fundamental conflict between the individual's subconscious desires for sexual pleasure and the demands in a civilized world for the individual to knuckle down to the responsibilities of family and work. The superego, representing normative social demands on the individual, had to be accommodated by the individual ego, or society could not exist. As with Durkheim, the victory of culture over the individual is a functional necessity in any society. For Freud, the persistence of culture requires the repression of individual freedom.

In the view of critical theorists, the "necessity" of cultural domination is organized within contemporary societies by the necessity of channeling social life along lines that gear into capitalist-organized satisfaction of wants that substitute for the freedom to satisfy individual desires. For theorists like Benjamin mass production of culture played into this possibility: production, distribution, and consumption crystallized as an organized complex that gave rise to specifically capitalist styles of life. Some twenty-five years later, Herbert Marcuse argued for the connection between capitalist cultural domination and the lifestyles of specific social strata—working-class youth, suburban professionals, and so on—by suggesting that consumption may be an act of free choice, but the choice is "spurious": it conceals the "universal coordination" of consumers, and it has consequences for all kinds of people, even the affluent.

> The high standard of living in the domain of the great corporations is restrictive in a concrete sociological sense: the goods and services that the individuals buy control their needs and petrify their faculties. In exchange for the commodities that enrich their life, the individuals sell not only their labor but also their free time. (Marcuse 1962, pp. 90–1)

Like Horkheimer and Adorno, Marcuse emphasizes the role of corporate business interests in the structuring of a world organized to surround and envelop consumers. In this view, power is based on the ability to shape the world so that people will freely choose to define their needs, wants, their entire existence, through consumption. Yet this power is hardly total: as can be seen from global ramifications of the Asian market collapse in 1997 and the U.S. U.S. economic slowdown in 2001 and 2002—exacerbated by the terrorist attacks of 9/11 and business scandals—the spending practices of consumers may shift radically from time to time, with dramatic consequences for a capitalist-organized consumer order.

Though critical theory offers mostly interpretation rather than concrete research, its interpretations are not without empirical support. Sociologists who have studied commercial architecture, for example, have found that restaurants and stores often are designed to maximize sales, maintain customer turnover after purchase, and meet other corporate goals, such as appealing to multiple customer values with a strong yet inoffensive "business format." At franchise restaurants, we enter worlds designed as extensions of their advertised images, on the basis of market research (Wright 1985). Similar considerations go into the design of shopping malls, which recreate the civic space of downtown shopping streets, but under totally private auspices, which can maximize control of a thematically integrated environment, excluding nonconforming business activities, the homeless, or political controversy, and thereby sustaining a sense of "mall gentility" in which "nothing unusual is happening" (Jerry Jacobs 1984, pp. 13–14).

The success of shopping malls across the U. S.U.S. came largely at the expense of downtown shopping areas. Efforts in response to revitalize downtown shopping areas—and later to create entire "gate-guarded" communities—have in some sense transferred the ideology of mall gentility into actual civic spaces. The planned community of Celebration, Florida, for example, began selling houses in 1995 amid accusations that its funder—the Walt Disney Corporation—was plotting "to lure unwitting citizens into living in theme parks" (Jerry Adler 1995, p. 44). In 2001, the grand opening of "The Village," a housing development in Northern California, offered prospective homebuyers the opportunity to live in a community entirely modeled after the paintings of Robert Kincade—a highly successful artist roundly criticized for creating mass-produced art sold to the middle classes through a chain of retail galleries in suburban malls.

In the early 1840s, before Karl Marx developed his theory of capitalism, he engaged in a philosophical critique of bourgeois society that warned against a situation in which private interests would come to structure the organization of civic space (1978, p. 33). But Marx could not anticipate the world of the mall and the planned community that so many shoppers—and citizen-consumers—would find so attractive.

The designs of restaurants, stores, malls, and towns are physical manifestations of a culture created by business corporations. Yet this is not the end of the matter. As Robin Leidner (1993) shows through participant-observation research on service workers, human interaction itself, not just physical structure, is constructed and scripted to serve business interests. By studying insurance sales and McDonald's restaurants, Leidner demonstrated the subtle and not so subtle ways that scripted interactions—which are an attempt to control both workers and clients—have consequences for identity and self-image. Corporate scriptings transform the affective display of emotions into work (cf. Hochschild 1983). Routinizing those displays may violate everyday norms of authenticity, autonomy, sincerity, and individuality, but if the practices become commonplace, they routinize a public culture of inauthentic authenticity.

Of course, not everyone responds to any given script enacted by service workers and therefore even for a given material need different products and marketing strategies are required to satisfy a diverse population. Market research is able to identify "clusters" of consumers to "target" with goods, services, and business formats designed specifically for them. Malcolm Gladwell (1997) has described a very sophisticated version of this targeting with respect to the highly lucrative U.S. teen market. He calls it "coolhunting." Coolhunters fancy themselves as anthropologists who observe teen subcultures in order to define newly emerging trends. Coolhunters sell the information they gather to culture-producing firms (a one-year subscription to one of the most well-known sources of cool, Look-Look, runs at $20,000). Perhaps, one could argue, such research procedures are democratically oriented toward insuring that producers respond to the needs and desires of consumers. But, as media critic Mark Crispin Miller (in Goodman and Dretzin 2001) points out, producers are not always interested in giving consumers what they want or need. They are often concerned with devising ways to sell some image that they already control to a very lucrative market whose members like to imagine themselves to be independent of the corporate marketing of culture. After all, what is "cool" often is by definition outside of convention.

In the final analysis, a critical theory of power does not assume the existence of a single, cohesive, powerful group; nor does it depend upon centralized control of communication. Advertising, market research, and capitalist consumer production are significant elements of a wider set of social institutions that includes politics, government bureaucracies, information-processing organizations, planning agencies, and scientific laboratories. The power of these institutions may lie in their diffuse yet pervasive character—in their ability to structure everyday experience. Thus, in the view of the contemporary critical theorist Jurgen Habermas (1987), the social world of everyday life—the "life-world"—has become overshadowed by the "system." In part this change occurs because systematic rationalization of social life has invaded the lifeworld to the point that much of life is overwhelmingly organized via corporate and governmental bureaucratic systems. These systems produce goods, services, and information in ways that affect the environment, the character of cities and towns, what we eat, how we maintain health, how we care for the sick, and so on. Habermas's argument is largely theoretical, but it makes sense when one recognizes, for example, the use of "under-the-radar" techniques of youth marketing like hiring teens to log on to internet chat rooms and surreptitiously promote products or hiring college freshmen to throw parties and pass out promotional materials. The life-world has shifted from once having been the location from which action proceeded to the reverse: the realm of everyday life is now organized increasingly from the outside, by the "system."

The model of power illuminated by critical theory argues that organization of the social world yields a de facto domination of society's members through its cultural arrangements, shaped especially in the arena of large-scale economic and political organizations. Such a theory can be put into sharper focus by asking how cultural arrangements yield such a form of power. The most insightful answer to this question has been provided by Michel Foucault, who moves in a quite different direction from critical theory.

In a fascinating array of studies on prisons, mental illness, and other aspects of social life, Foucault (1965, 1975, 1979, 1978–86) consolidated an important account of the diffuse institutionalized power of culture. Other strands of research already had begun to explore this terrain. Labeling theorists had shown, for example, that "madness" is not simply a psychological fact; it is a shifting social construction of meanings that coordinates institutionalized arrangements designed to identify and deal with people at the fringes of society. The matter of who is at the fringes of society depends on time and place (Goffman 1961; Scheff 1966; Laing 1967; Szasz 1987). Foucault deepened this fundamental insight by positing a time before the emergence of the modern world in which neither "reason" nor "madness" described the average person. In this view, the emergence of modern reason as a category of popular personality at the end of the sixteenth and into the seventeenth and eighteenth centuries had two implications for the social order. In the first place, it allowed reasoning *about* madness. However, for Foucault, the power of reason does not guarantee truth and it has not yet tamed madness. Perhaps this failure stems from the second implication of reason's emergence: that madness was uncommon in an earlier era because reason was uncommon. The birth of reason made possible the delineation of madness, in that reason established a standard of comparison by which madness could be identified.

Because madness and reason are intimately connected with each other, changes in what counts as reason will change what counts as madness too. Foucault's account suggests that we are trapped in the very boxes established by social efforts to create valid categories. The social arrangements for processing people through treatment or incarceration or monitoring have the effect of constructing the specific conditions of madness, from the warehousing of schizophrenics in the back wards of mental hospitals to the "mentally ill" homelessness of today. In other words, institutionalized practices based on reasoned knowledge in the disciplines of psychiatry and psychology, social welfare, and police procedure construct both the life circumstances and the meaningful categories of "madness" (Foucault 1965, 1979). It is this critique of reason itself, and our entrapment in and through its unfolding, that separates Foucault from the social constructionists.

For Foucault, even one of the most intimate aspects of personal life—sexuality—is "deployed" from outside the sites of its practice. But Foucault did not follow Freud in regarding civilized power as an exercise in repressing sexuality. To the contrary, there is a flood of discourses on sexuality—in movies, advertising, in the newspapers and magazines, in therapy groups, and with doctors. These discourses are powerful, not because they offer rules of conduct, but because they establish the web of meanings that embed sexuality within society. Sexual activity, at its core an animalistic behavior, has become imbued with specifically moral attributes. Thus, we do not simply act sexually as animals. Sexual practices carry specific culture freight. Forms of heterosexual, monogamous, marital, homosexual, and other sexual conduct transpire within fields of meaning organized by professional and mass-mediated discourse (Foucault 1978–86). To take but one example, Mark Monteiro (1997) examined discourses of masculinity in the popular Brazilian magazine *Ela Ela: uma revista para ler a dois* ("Him Her: a magazine to be read by the couple"). This magazine was published between 1969 and 1972—a period when Brazil was facing sociohistorical changes associated with the rise of countercultural social movements advocating feminism, gay power, and the entry of women into the once male-dominated workforce. Monteiro finds that the visual and written discourse on men undergoes a shift over the period: there are more pictures of male models, more articles dealing with male vanity, new cosmetics marketed to men, and treatments of male homosexuality. However, a durable undercurrent of male social dominance remains, for social changes are represented as running counter to norms of heterosexual patriarchal power. The image of the "real man" persists as a yardstick against which to measure social change.

For madness, sexuality, and other aspects of social life as well Foucault connects "reason" to disciplines of knowledge, and disciplines of knowledge become the basis of another "discipline," the bodily exercise of power over the subjects of disciplinary knowledge.

Foucault's emphasis on knowledge has informed the work of a wide variety of scholars. Notably, the Subaltern Studies Group that emerged in the 1980s made an effort to rewrite the history of India from the perspective of groups oppressed by colonial rule. This effort required that the group critique the discipline of history itself, in particular for its complicity in extending the discourses of colonialism, nationalism, and modernity. "The inescapable conclusion from [the group's] analyses is that 'history,' authorized by European imperialism and the Indian nation-state, functions as a discipline, empowering certain forms of knowledge while disempowering others" (Prakash 1994, p. 1, 485).

Gayatri Chakravorty Spivak (1988) raised the relevant question: "Can the subaltern speak?" Spivak, who both champions and critiques postcolonial studies, draws from Jacques Derrida to deconstruct the rhetorics and images of colonialism and postcolonialism, and argues that without an explicit critique of the disciplinary bases of knowledge subalterns simply become, once again, subordinated to the discourses of modernism and modernization, and to those who might speak for those discourses—Western intellectuals. Such an argument is particularly disarming because it depicts a cultural domination that operates without conspirators yet reduces the agency of acting subjects to mere reflections of the cultural categories that frame social life. The consequence of such domination, in the case of the subaltern, is that efforts to liberate the dominated subject simply reinscribe the hierarchy of dominant/dominated positions.

Both in subaltern studies and elsewhere, Foucauldian analysis can seem to create an intellectual impasse for the less powerful. We all seem trapped within culturally constructed standpoints that imprison both our reasoning and our selves. For this reason, the efforts of the Subaltern Studies Group have gained importance outside India. Florence E. Mallon (1994), in surveying their influence in Latin American studies, has urged scholars to remain focused on the tension between postmodern discourse analyses and emancipatory politics. Otherwise, there is no privileged standpoint like that asserted for the working class by Marxists, and power and domination eclipse both objective analysis and subjective agency.

Any given societal arrangements rarely benefit everyone equally. Instead, they work to the advantage of particular social classes, ethnic groups, professions, and one gender (almost universally men) over another. How are these inequalities to be explained, and what is the significance of culture? Some theorists emphasize the cultural patterns as products of a capitalist consumer society. Others, like Habermas and Foucault, see the cultural power basis of contemporary society as grounded in a wider set of institutions than purely economic ones. Yet one feature of theories about how culture helps sustain an established order is especially worth noting. Privileged groups that benefit from the cultural matrix do not necessarily achieve this benefit by the direct exercise of power, and people from disprivileged strata are not necessarily excluded from participation in the apparatus. What matters is that a diffuse but pervasive set of meanings, objects, and arrangements establishes a de facto power by the incorporation of culture into our everyday lives.

Insofar as the power of culture is diffuse, as Foucault suspected, political change and even a shift in economic organization would not change the powerful operation of culture in daily life. Indeed, for Foucault, even broad cultural change—a change in sexual mores, the end of colonial rule—seems only to herald a new set of categories that entangle us. Thus, Foucault has been read both as a conservative theorist, pessimistic about the possibilities and benefits of cultural change, and as a new radical who produced a fundamental critique that must be reckoned with if meaningful social change is to occur. If Foucault is right, efforts at social change must be directed toward the categories of culture, their consequences, and the implications of changing their operation in social relations. Only if he is wrong, and the content of culture is connected to specific economic and political interests, does the question of who controls cultural production make very much difference.

THE OWNERSHIP OF CULTURAL PRODUCTION

A venerable tradition in sociology confronts power much more directly than Foucault does. If power is defined as the ability to make people do things whether they want to or not, then power to shape culture can be traced to those people and organizations that produce culture. Obviously culture is directly produced by cultural workers—artists, journalists, film producers, novelists, fashion designers, teachers, and sociologists. The questions then become, whom do cultural workers work for, and how does the ownership of cultural production affect culture?

The close of the twentieth century saw unprecedented growth in media industries brought on by waves of mergers made possible by wide-ranging deregulation. A brief look at the economic value of the biggest media-company mergers that took place between 1980 and 2000 reveals the dimensions of this startling consolidation. In 1983 the largest merger, achieved when Gannet Newspapers bought

Combined Communications (billboards, newspapers, and broadcasting) was worth $581 million (in constant 2000 dollars). Six years later the largest merger created a $19.4 billion company, bringing together Time Incorporated and Warner Communications. Two years after that, AT&T combined with TCI for $56 billion, and when AOL got together with Time Warner in 2000 the deal was worth $166 billion (Croteau and Hoynes 2001). The fourth largest international media conglomerate, with 1998 sales of $12.8 billion, was Rupert Murdoch's News Corporation, which brings together the Fox channels (news, sports, Fx), a string of television stations and newspapers, including the *New York Post*, book publisher HarperCollins, several sports teams, including the Los Angeles Dodgers, and British Sky Broadcasting (Demers 1999).

As Croteau and Hoynes point out, media empires are nothing historically new. What make today's empires different is their enhanced opportunities for media integration. Today they seek to integrate both horizontally, by owning many different types of media products, and vertically, by owning or controlling all phases of the creation, distribution, and marketing of a particular media product. Although "product placement" (placing a product within the story of a film or TV in exchange for an advertiser's money) has been an accepted business practice for some time, the new profit-making strategies almost completely blur the boundary between advertisement and product. Now, for example, internet players of "The Sims Online" video game find a handy McDonald's kiosk where busy cyber-social individuals can stay happy eating fast food. "Synergy" or "cross-promotion"—the new industry buzzwords—is made possible by ownership and business alliance patterns that create what some media critics refer to as the "integrated communications mix."

When the Disney Corporation makes a feature film about a youth hockey team called the "Mighty Ducks," when they actually own part of a National Hockey League team called the Mighty Ducks, and when they own the ESPN cable network that televises hockey games, when they use their ESPN network and Disney stores to sell jerseys (licensed by the League and worn by both fictional players on the film screen and professional players on the TV screen), and when this all somehow gears together nicely with the Disney character Donald Duck, it becomes difficult to tell what is a promotion, what is a product, and what is culture. There might not be any difference. As Douglas Rushkoff puts it:

> Look how Viacom leverages [Howard Stern] across their properties. He is syndicated on 50 of Viacom's Infinity radio stations. His weekly TV show is broadcast on Viacom's CBS. His number one best-selling autobiography was published by Viacom's Simon and Schuster, then released as a major motion picture by Viacom's Paramount Pictures, grossing $40 million domestically and millions more on videos sold at Viacom's Blockbuster Video. (Rushkoff, in Goodman and Dretzin 2001)

Growth and conglomeration of mass-media outlets have contributed to the direct political power of owners and to the consolidation of media under the dominance of large-scale, consumer-oriented corporate capitalism. In turn, the latter development has shaped the content and formats of mass media. This consolidation, of course, has taken place as part of a wider consolidation of corporate capitalism—in food brands, shopping-mall chains, department stores, and so forth. The power entailed is not simply that of direct authority and influence. Instead, it is a power to design, produce, and distribute culture on a mass basis.

DISCUSSION QUESTIONS

1. Discuss the debate surrounding powerful interests and control of the content and form of culture.
2. Discuss how technology shapes culture and its significance for power and culture.
3. What are other elements that exert power over culture?
4. Discuss how the established order influences culture?
5. What are some ways the form and content of cultural objects can be shaped by the economic and political control of cultural production?

REFERENCES

Adler, Jerry. 1995. "Paved paradise." *Newsweek* (May 15): 42–5.

Adorno, Theodore. 1945. "A social critique of radio music." *Kenyon Review* 7: 208–17.

Arundhati, Roy. 2001. "The algebra of infinite justice." *Guardian* [United Kingdom] (September 29). Guardian Unlimited: http://www.guardian.co.uk/Archive/Arti-cle/0,4273,4266289,00. html.

Belasco, Warren J. 1979. *Americans on the Road: From Autocamp to Motel*, 1910–1945. Cambridge, Ma.: MIT Press.

Benjamin, Walter. 1969 (1955). *Illuminations*. New York: Schocken.

Croteau, David, and William Hoynes. 2001. The Business of Media: Corporate Media and the Public Interest. Thousand Oaks, Ca.: Pine Forge Press.

Demers, David P. 1999. Global Media: Menace or Messiah? Cresskill, N.J.: Hampton Press.

Durkheim, Emile. 1995 (1915). The Elementary Forms of Religious Life., translated with an introduction by Karen E. Fields. New York: Free Press.

Foucault, Michel. 1965. Madness and Civilization: A History of Insanity in the Age of Reason. New York: Pantheon.

——. 1975. *The Birth of the Clinic: An Archeology of Medical Perception*. New York: Vintage.

——. 1978–86. *The History of Sexuality*, vols. I–III. New York: Pantheon.

——. 1979 (1975). *Discipline and Punish: The Birth of the Prison*. New York: Vintage.

Gans, Herbert. 1974. *Popular Culture and High Culture*. New York: Basic.

Gladwell, Malcolm. 1997. "The coolhunt." *New Yorker* (March 17): 78–88.

Goffman, Erving. 1961. *Asylums*. Garden City, N.Y.: Anchor.

Goodman, Barak, and Rachel Dretzin, producers. 2001. "Merchants of Cool," program #1911 (February 27). Transcript: http://www.pbs.org/wgbh/pages/frontline/ shows/cool/etc/script.html.

Habermas, Jurgen. 1987. *The Theory of Communicative Action, Vol. II: Lifeworld and System: A Critique of Functionalist Reason*. Boston, Ma.: Beacon Press.

Halle, David. 1993. *Inside Culture: Art and Class in the American Home*. Chicago: University of Chicago Press.

Hochschild, Arlie Russell. 1983. *The Managed Heart: Commercialization of Human Feeling*. Berkeley, Ca.: University of California Press.

Jacobs, Jerry. 1984. *The Mall: An Attempted Escape from Everyday Life*. Prospect Heights, Il.: Waveland.

Laing, R. D. 1967. *The Politics of Experience*. New York: Pantheon.

Leidner, Robin. 1993. *Fast Food, Fast Talk: Service Work and the Routinization of Everyday Life*. Berkeley, Ca.: University of California Press.

Mallon, Florencia E. 1994. "The promise and dilemma of subaltern studies: perspectives from Latin American history." *American Historical Review* 99: 1, 491–515.

Marcuse, Herbert. 1962 (1955). *Eros and Civilization: A Philosophical Inquiry into Freud*. New York: Vintage.

Marx, Karl. 1978 (1843). "On the Jewish question." Pp. 26–52 in Robert C. Tucker, ed., *The Marx-Engels Reader*. New York: W.W. Norton.

McLuhan, Marshall. 1964. *Understanding Media*. New York: McGraw-Hill.

Meyrowitz, Joshua. 1985. *No Sense of Place: The Impact of Electronic Media on Social Behavior*. New York: Oxford University Press.

Monteiro, Mark. 1997. "Him/her: discourses of masculinity in a Brazilian magazine, 1969–1972." *Antropologia*. http://www.artnet.com.br/~marko/him.html.

Prakash. Gyan. 1994. "Subaltern studies as postcolonial criticism." *American Historical Review* 99: 1, 475–90.

Rosenberg, Roy 2001. "Infinite Justice?" Salon. com.

Scheff, Thomas. 1966. *Being Mentally III: A Social Theory*. Chicago: Aldine.

Schudson, Michael. 1978. *Discovering the News: A Social History of American Newspapers*. New York: Basic.

Spivak, Gayatri Chakravorty. 1988. "Can the subaltern speak?" Pp. 299–307 in Cary Nelson and Lawrence Grossberg, eds., *Marxism and the Interpretation of Culture*. Urbana, Il: University of Illinois Press.

Stevenson, Nick. 1997. "Globalization, national cultures, and cultural citizenship." *Sociological Quarterly* 38: 41–66.

Szasz, Thomas. 1987. Insanity: *The Idea and its Consequences*. New York: Wiley.

Thompson, John B. 1994. "Social theory and the media." Pp. 27–49 in David Crowley and David Mitchell, eds., *Communication Theory Today*. Stanford, Ca.: Stanford University Press.

——. 1995. *The Media and Modernity: A Social Theory of the Media*. Cambridge: Polity.

Wright, Eric Olin. 1985. *Classes*. London: New Left.

Hoosiers, Hicks, and Hayseeds
The Controversial Place of Marginalized Ethnic Whites in Multicultural Education

By Elizabeth E. Heilman

Poor white children, often with roots in Appalachia, can present puzzling and intractable challenges for the multicultural educator. These students are not considered in multicultural textbooks, yet they face language and dialect issues, low educational attainment, under-representation in curriculum, and negative cultural stereotypes. This article details the history, language, dialect, and school experiences of marginalized ethnic Whites; explores problems inherent in representation related to race, class, and marginality; and discusses action research on pre-service education intended to strengthen teachers' perception of the special problem of marginalized Whites. This work highlights the importance of problematizing and expanding "basic" categories and terms such as "black," "white," "urban," and "rural" to consider important differences of experience—an imperative in an education profession committed to diversity and social justice.

Educating pre-service teachers around issues of diversity remains a considerable challenge (Banks, 2001; Boyle-Baise, 2002; Rosaen, 2003), but progress in spreading multicultural values has been made. Teachers are increasingly aware of the ways in which ethnically diverse children experience inequality, from unequal school funding patterns to damaging cultural stereotypes. More teachers are becoming aware of the need for culturally responsive teaching that acknowledges inequality and the needs of specific groups of children (Futrell, Gomez, & Bedden, 2003; Gay, 2000; Ladson-Billings, 2000).

Still there are new areas to pursue in theory, research, and education. I have been a teacher educator in the Midwest for a number of years. During multicultural education field experiences, my pre-service teachers and I have routinely struggled with questions about the ways in which culture, ethnicity, economic status, and language influence students, education, and the curriculum. In our region, in urban and rural settings, poor white children with roots in Appalachia have presented the most puzzling and intractable challenges. These students speak with heavy "hoosier" accents, using "ain't" and

Elizabeth E. Heilman, "Hoosiers, Hicks, and Hayseeds: The Controversial Place of Marginalized Ethnic Whites in Multicultural Education," *Equity & Excellence in Education*, vol. 37, issue 1, pp. 67-79. Copyright © 2004 by Taylor & Francis Group LLC. Reprinted with permission.

the word "y'uns" as the third person plural, and they do not appear in our multicultural textbooks as a category of children we need to understand. They are consistently ostracized by successful students and are often objects of scorn and contempt among teachers. One elementary school principal, known for her support for progressive curriculum and multiculturalism quite unselfconsciously reported, "We have a big group of trailer trash in this school," when orienting a new group of pre-service teachers. Similarly, an urban Indianapolis teacher insidiously confided, "These city hillbilly kids are the real bottom of the barrel, if you know what I mean." This article describes marginalized ethnic Whites, explores problems inherent in representation related to race, class, and marginality, and discusses action research on pre-service education intended to strengthen teachers' perception of the special problem of marginalized Whites.

WHO ARE MARGINALIZED ETHNIC WHITES?

History and Geography of the Marginalized Ethnic Whites

Marginalized white student populations in our region include poor people of Scottish Appalachian descent from an identifiable Appalachian region and rural Whites originally from the English under-class, poor urban students of Irish descent, and poor urban students of Eastern and Southern European descent. The Irish and those of Eastern and Southern European descent have tended to settle initially in Northern urban areas; Scottish Appalachians and poor rural Whites of underclass English origin have more commonly lived in the rural South and Midwest. The Irish and those of Eastern and Southern European descent have typically had a stronger sense of collective group determination and have pressed for their rights through the Catholic Church, labor unions, the Democratic Party, and through culturally based organizations. Also, Catholic immigrants from Eastern and Southern Europe gained power through affiliation with longer settled American Catholics (Barrett & Roediger, 1997).

By contrast, Scottish Appalachians and poor southern Whites had a weaker sense of collective ethnic group determination and were less successful in working for rights to education and employment through formal organizations associated with their groups. During the nineteenth and early twentieth century, while the Irish and Eastern and Southern Europeans were typically employed as laborers and in service and manufacturing work, Scottish Appalachians and poor Southern Whites were most often employed in agricultural and mining activities. Rural work is often isolated and involves sharecropping, so that migrant labor and subsistence farming have not easily fostered collective group determination or group solidarity. Furthermore, in Appalachia, wealthy, educated elites and corporations came to control a disproportionate share of the region's wealth and natural resources, especially fossil fuel resources (Billings & Blee, 2000; Drake, 2001) and the long history of violence against union movements further discouraged collective action. As Jensen (2001) describes, "Many such rural areas reflect a two class system in which the "haves" wield their power over jobs and opportunities to maintain their privilege, while subjugating the have-nots, who are desperately poor, socially isolated, and, in fact, a world apart" (p. 145).

Though poor rural Whites may have a Protestant Northern European ethnic heritage, their arrival in North America followed a very different pattern than that of more privileged white groups. It is common in multiculturalism to follow Ogbu's (1978, 1992) distinction between immigrants as "voluntary" and "involuntary," in which voluntary immigrants are described as Whites, while involuntary immigrants are understood to be Black and Native American. Voluntary minorities are immigrants who came to the colonies or the United States of their own free will, while involuntary minorities are those who were enslaved, conquered, or colonized. In fact, some Whites were involuntary immigrants during the colonial period. Early during the colonial era, both Blacks and Whites experienced relatively similar treatment and social status as slaves and indentured servants (Axtell, 1992; Franklin & Moss, 1988) and were held in what Lerone Bennett (1982) calls "equal contempt" (p. 39). In fact, it is estimated that at least half of white colonial immigrants were slaves or indentured servants. Though some of these people willingly entered indenture, many were kidnapped or were convicts, often in prison for debt or poverty-driven petty theft. Whites provided the majority of non-free labor until the late seventeenth century. The recognizably black slave contributed to the dramatic growth of black slave labor over white (Higginbotham, 1980; Omi & Winant, 1994). Nevertheless, in the seventeenth century, white convict laborers still comprised an estimated quarter of all white colonial immigrants (Ekirch, 1987).

Once released from bondage, "the statistical probability for rising to even middle-class position was very slight" (Nash, 1970, p. 220). Freed indentured servants fared better in the North. In the South, for a landless, typically illiterate free laborer in a slave economy, poverty was almost inevitable. Many worked as unskilled laborers or as tenant farmers. Urban and industrial work was much less available in the Southern and Southern-Midwestern agricultural economies. Many of these underclass Whites moved toward what was then the frontier to settle as squatters on unproductive, marginal, or mountainous lands. This is the origin of some of the Appalachian settlers and of some of the white, Southern rural poor often called "white trash." Others were Scotch-Irish and German pioneers. Even during early settlement, land was distributed inequitably. "By 1810 three quarters of the region's acreage was absentee owned, and distant speculators laid out towns, sold or leased farms to settlers, and engrossed areas believed to offer wealth in minerals" (Dunaway, 1995, p. 67). Later, mining, logging and textiles industries encroached upon farm land. Eller (1982) explains that in 1880 the average mountain farm was 187 acres, while in 1930 it was only 76 acres. "The small marginal farm usually associated with the stereotyped picture of Appalachia was in fact a product of modernization—that is, a more recent development not associated with the purported isolation of the region." (p. 6).

Negative social opinion of this group seems to have arisen immediately and has carried on consistently from colonial days to the present. In 1737, the Governor of North Carolina described these people as, "the lowest scum and rabble ... [who] build themselves sorry huts and live in a beastly sort of plenty" (Bailyn, 1988, p. 117, cited by Goad, 1997). They were almost always viewed as morally depraved, "devoted to calumny, lying, and the vilest tricking and cheating; a people into whose heads no means can beat the notion of a public interest or persuade to live like men" (Bailyn, 1988, p. 117, cited in Goad, 1997). The 1860 work, *Social Relations in Our Southern States* features a chapter called "Poor White Trash" (Hundley, 1860, cited in Goad, 1997), which described poor Whites as follows:

They are about the laziest two legged animals that walk erect on the face of the Earth. Even their motions are slow, and their speech a sickening drawl … while their thoughts and ideas seem likewise to creep along at a snail's pace … [They show] a natural stupidity or dullness of intellect that almost surpasses belief (p. 97).

Poor Southern Whites and Appalachian people are still stereotyped as poor, violent, crude, and ignorant (Billings, Norman, & Ledford, 2001), and this stigmatization carries over to cultural interpretations of related poor, rural Midwestern groups. For example, there are many jokes directed at poor rural Whites featuring people from Oklahoma and Kentucky.

Other marginalized white groups, including the Irish and Eastern and Southern Europeans, also were described as intrinsically and irremediably inferior. During the nineteenth century, large numbers of Irish arrived in the United States in the wake of the potato famine after 1848. The Irish had been sophisticated farmers who did not rely on one single crop for sustenance. The British, however, had pushed the Irish onto smaller and smaller parcels of land, seizing the best land for their own purposes and compelling the Irish to labor for them. Many Irish people exclusively grew potatoes on their tiny plots simply because potatoes were the crop with the most caloric yield per square yard. Even before the famine, many Irish were deeply impoverished. When blight struck the potato crop, there was no recourse but emigration or starvation for millions. Throughout the potato famine, the British continued to import large quantities of food from the land they had seized from the Irish (Scalley, 1996) while 1.5 million died and another million were forced to emigrate. By the nineteenth century, to justify 700 years of oppression, the British created a racialized depiction of the Irish as inferior, as the following quotes illustrate, "This is a race of savages: I say again a race of utter savages … all their ways are brutish and unseemly" (Barnard's translation of a twelfth century text by Giraldus Cambrensis, cited in Shanklin, 1994, p. 3). In 1860, British writer Kingsley said of the Irish, "To see White chimpanzees is dreadful; if they were Black one would not feel it so much" (quoted in Cahill, 1995, p. 6) Froud, in 1845, wrote, "[They are] more like squalid apes than human beings" (cited in Shanklin, 1993, p. 4). Even Darwin, writing in 1898 in the widely-read, *The Descent of Man*, referred to Celts as a "less favored race" and wrote, "The careless, squalid, unaspiring Irishman multiplies like rabbits" (Darwin, quoted in Shanklin, 1993, p. 5).

The Irish initially occupied a very low social rung in the Unites States, just above African Americans, and were systematically excluded from all but the lowest occupations. Into the twentieth century, it was not uncommon to find businesses with signs reading, "No Irish, No Dogs." One of the strategies used by the Irish to escape their racial labeling, however, was ostensibly to highlight their whiteness as compared to the black man. A majority of Irish gradually assimilated, abandoning most hallmarks of their Celtic culture (Ignatiev, 1996).

Between 1870 and 1920, almost 26 million people came to the United States. The new immigrant Mexicans, East European Jews, peasant Italians from the Mezzogiorno and Sicilians, Poles, and Slavs were similarly understood to be biologically and racially inferior to white Anglo Saxon Protestants, and were victims of discrimination in employment, education, and law enforcement. The meaning of whiteness was debated because immigrants were valued by industrialists for cheap labor, but this need conflicted with republican and also nativist ideas about who should become citizens (Jacobson, 1998).

> A whole range of evidence—laws; court cases; formal racial ideologies social conventions; popular culture in the form of slang, songs, films, cartoons, ethnic jokes, and popular theater—suggests that the native born and older immigrants often placed these newer immigrants not only above African and Asian Americans, for example, but also below "White" people. Indeed, many of the older immigrants and particularly the Irish had themselves been perceived as "nonWhite" just a generation earlier (Barret & Roediger, 1997, p. 7).

In many urban Northern, Eastern, and Midwestern regions, descendents of Irish, Hungarian, Polish, Slavic, and Italian immigrants remain poor or marginally working-class. They retain the hallmarks of their "in between status." Though the descendants of many of these immigrants, after three to four generations, have achieved social mobility, not everyone has been able to become middle-or upper-class. The lowest status Whites are still typically those who were unable to overcome the inter-generational effects of inferior education, housing, and employment based at least in part on racialized class and cultural prejudices.

Marginalized Ethnic Whites in K-12 Field Classrooms

My pre-service teachers and I first talked about these issues as social class issues alone, but as we began to learn more about these young students, it was clear their experiences were cultural as well as class-based and that their ethnic identity varied depending on location in the state. Large recognized populations of urban Appalachian students exist in Indiana, Ohio, and Kentucky cities and also in suburban and rural areas where they are less recognizable as members of a distinct ethnic group. In some schools in northern Ohio and Indiana (closer to Chicago), similar groups of marginalized students exist with origins in Eastern European and urban Irish cultures. The composition of marginalized ethnic white subgroups varies according to geographic location. For example, in Louisiana, certain French Creole groups qualify as marginalized Whites (Henry & Bankston, 1998). Stereotypes can make it especially hard to identify marginalized ethnic Whites. For example, Russian Jewish immigrants comprise a marginalized ethnic white group in New York. Yet the stereotype of Jews as successful can make such marginalization difficult to recognize.

Marginalized ethnic Whites can be identified by the following common (and interrelated) definable features. Students are descendants of a historically marginalized constituent from a specific ethnic group, though they often may have no sense of being from a distinctive ethnic group (Alba & Logan, 1997). Their social class status is low, either working class or poor. Their speech and writing patterns (Eller, 1987) reflect dialects or accents of English that are associated with poverty and lack of education and sometimes treated as communicative disorders (American Speech-Language-Hearing Association, 1998). Levels of educational attainment among family members are low (Macleod, 1995). Students have generally negative beliefs about school, teachers, themselves, and their job futures (Brantlinger,

1994, Fiene, 1991). Students are also socially and educationally marginalized in schools (Macleod, 1995; McNeal, 1998; Oakes, 1992).

In the classrooms in this study there were large identifiable subgroups represented in the specific Indiana K-12 student populations of the field observation schools where research took place. They included poor people of Scottish Appalachian descent from an identifiable Appalachian region, poor urban students of Irish descent, and poor urban students of Eastern and Southern European descent. Furthermore, each group had been stereotyped as crude, lazy, unintelligent, prone to alcohol abuse and violence, and sexually loose or deviant. Derogatory nicknames included hillbillies, hicks, hayseeds, rednecks, crackers, Oakies, white trash, Micks, Pattys, Polacks, Hunkies, Ginnies,[1] Spics, and Wops.

Beyond historic descent and poverty, the extent to which students and their families have remained in oppressive cultural and economic configurations is significant to understanding marginalized ethnic white students. Some have "mixed" ethnic heritages. Equally important, history and culture are connected to current oppression, and to the symbolic language use, values, and outlooks that define marginalized ethnicity. Status as a marginalized ethnic White is thus not merely an economic label, even when ethnic Whites who have been left behind and remained marginalized do not consider themselves culturally and historically distinctive.

Economics, however, are crucial. Chronic generational poverty is a significant identifying factor. The U.S. Census Bureau (2003) reports that in 2001, among white children (under 18), 13% lived in poverty. Among white female heads of households with children under 18, 22.4% lived in poverty. As the Children's Defense Fund (2003) highlights, "There are more poor White Non-Hispanic children (4.2 million) than poor Black children (3.5 million) or poor Hispanic children (3.6 million), even though the proportion of Black and Hispanic children who are poor is far higher." Also, poor children are more likely to live in suburban and rural areas than in central cities.

MARGINALIZED ETHNIC WHITES AND THE QUESTION OF REPRESENTATION

The research described here argues that marginalized ethnic white students can be an under-recognized population in many seemingly homogeneous communities such as Midwestern urban and rural white working-class communities. They also can be under-recognized in diverse urban settings. Learning how to meet the educational needs of these students is crucially important and also serves the purpose of honing pre-service teachers' multicultural skills in areas where no diversity is said to exist. In seemingly racially homogeneous rural communities, teachers sometimes fail to engage with multicultural issues because they do not see them as relevant to their pre-service field placement settings (Cook & Van Cleaf, 2000) or to their in-service classroom teaching. As Irwin (1999) describes, "Teachers in rural areas may not view multicultural education as seriously as their urban counterparts. They may perceive multicultural education as an urban concern" (p. 42). They miss the chance, therefore, for opportunities to put learning into practice and to experience dispositional change. Yet, there is often unnoticed diversity and oppression.

Many of the issues facing marginalized ethnic white students, such as class stigma, discrimination due to language and dialect use, low educational attainment, under-representation in the curriculum, and negative stereotypes are shared by other marginalized groups. Because of social discrimination, "low class" dialect, and poor education, these marginalized ethnic Whites do not experience higher scores on standardized tests, positive encounters with realtors, shop keepers or the justice system, access to well-funded schools, and an absence of discrimination in hiring patterns. If "race" is understood to be an historical and social construction with no biological reality;[2] and the white "race" is "a historically contingent and socially constructed racial category ... defined by privilege and power rather than by marginalization and domination" (Rodriguez, 1999, p. 21), it can be argued that these students are not fully "white."

The uncertain meaning of whiteness and blackness, of race and marginality, the situated social construction of knowledge and identity, and the resultant challenge of representing the "other" has been increasingly problematized within educational research (Britzman, 1995; Denizin, 1997; Lather, 1991; Luttrell, 2000; Parker & Lynn, 2002) and across the disciplines (Donald & Rattansi, 1992; Hollinger, 1995; Marable, 1992). Such perspectives on race and representation are consistent with postmodern and poststructural explorations of the relationships among power, knowledge, and ways of knowing and being that analyze processes in which subjectivity and identity are constructed through discourses and the discursive practices they help produce and legitimate. The concept of "race" is now understood as a social construct created to rationalize oppression. Scholars in philosophy, literary theory, cultural studies, history, anthropology, and geography have demonstrated how constructions of both "blackness" and "whiteness" are unstable, situated products of particular historical, political, and cultural moments. What it means to be a member of a group is different for each person and differs across time and place. Also, as Hollinger (1995) asserts "Racism is real but races are not" (p. 39). Cornell West (1982) traces how techniques of natural history have been inappropriately applied to people creating a comparative analysis "based on visible, especially physical, characteristics ... [which] permit one to discern identity and difference, equality and inequality, beauty and ugliness among animals and human bodies" (p. 55).

The reification of biological ideas of racial and ethnic category have led to essentializing—the tendency to reduce complex persons, including children in school, to stereotypical racial labels. Though race and racism have an unavoidable cultural reality, identity and oppression are both deeply complex. Patricia Hill Collins (1990) argues that oppression is structured along multiple lines, including race, gender, and social class. Rigid and simplistic discourses of race and marginalization that simplify these issues mask not only the complexity of oppression but also, in some cases, the actual simultaneity of oppression and privilege. Collins notes, "White feminists routinely point with confidence to their oppression as women but resist seeing how much their white skin privileges them" (p. 229).

Since blunt labeling of group membership ignores such subtleties, another way to think about oppression is to consider the way it actually functions in society. Instead of basing oppression on a category of signifier, Iris Marion Young (1990) details the "five faces of oppression" as follows: (1) exploitation that transfers the results of the labor of one social group to benefit another, (2) marginalization that occurs when whole categories of people are expelled from useful participation in social life, (3) powerlessness when persons lack authority or professional status, (4) dynamics of cultural imperialism involving the universalization of a dominant group's experience and culture, and its establishment as the norm, and (5) violence including physical attacks, harassment, intimidation, or degrading ridicule (pp. 47–61). According to Young the experience of marginalized Whites is clearly that of oppression. A single-category mode of analysis such as race alone viewed in isolation from class or other stigmatizing factors obscures the real-world complexity of intersecting multiple-categories of domination or subordination.

A review of the multicultural research and major teacher education textbooks suggests that marginalized ethnic white students are rarely considered in multicultural education courses. An exception is Joel Spring's (1999) text, *The Intersection of Cultures: Multicultural Education in the United States and the Global Economy*, that considers some of these issues in several chapters and was used as one of the resources in the pilot marginalized ethnic white curriculum. Whiteness Studies is a burgeoning field that "attempts to trace the economic and political history behind the invention of 'whiteness,' to attack the privileges given to so-called 'Whites,' and to analyze the cultural practices (in art, music, literature, and popular media) that create and perpetuate the fiction of 'whiteness.'" Although the weakness of monolithic categories of analysis, such as "black" and "white," and critiques of the concept of "whiteness" separated from social class and linguistic issues of accent and usage have gained increasing prominence in history, sociology, and cultural studies, such perspectives have only recently entered research and discourse in education (Giroux, 1997; Kincheloe, 1999). Also, although there are resources describing the historical research on whiteness (Kolchin, 2002), the political evolution of whiteness (Lipsitz, 1998) and particular marginalized white sub-cultures, these most commonly focus on historical experiences (Anbinder, 2002; Billings, Norman, & Ledford, 2001; Brodkin, 1999; Guglielmo, 2003, Ignatiev, 1996; Jacobson, 1999; López, 1996), rather than contemporary experience. Currently, there is no resource that provides systematic and scholarly attention to the education and school experiences of marginalized ethnic Whites. A general acceptance in American culture for the vilification of the poor and those of low socioeconomic status as well as mainstream scholarly perspectives on multiculturalism appear to contribute to a lack of research on or support for this inquiry—a blind spot if there ever was one.

Discussions of whiteness in education focus more on the construction of white privilege rather than white diversity, marginalized Whites, or the difficulties of representing the "other" or the marginalized. For example, in much writing in education there still appears to be a conflation of whiteness with undifferentiated membership in the dominant culture as the following quote illustrates: "Not seeing color blinds White teacher interns to their own dominating culture and behaviors" (Valli, 1995, p. 122).

Also, whiteness is described as a uniform, monolithic category and is most often described as a quality of teachers rather than of students. "In general, Whites stick together on common definitions of issues that involve race relations, and behave accordingly. We live largely with other Whites, socialize mainly with Whites, consume white media, vote for Whites, etc." (Sleeter, 1994, p. 35). Indeed *most* of the literature on whiteness in multicultural education focuses on whiteness as a social construction of power and privilege (McIntyre, 1997; McLaren, 1995; Scheurich, 1993; Sleeter, 1995). Yet, if all

Whites are considered to be "dominant culture," there is no room to consider the existence of marginalized ethnic Whites—that is, Whites who are not dominant. Ann Louise Keating (1995) stresses that to "shift from 'Whiteness' to 'White people' … draws on false generalizations and implies that all human beings classified as 'White' automatically exhibit the traits associated with 'Whiteness'" (p. 907). The question that one pre-service teacher in this study asked, "Could a marginalized ethnic white male Appalachian student have less privilege than an upper middle-class black female?" seems to be taboo.

Importantly, Blacks and other minorities are not considered by sub-groupings that acknowledge comparable privilege or marginalization. Unfortunately, blunt and loose definitions and labeling have contributed to the invisibility of the 40% of Blacks who are middle-class (or higher) and has contributed to the invisibility of marginalized ethnic Whites. It also lends credence to reductionist, intrinsic, or biological ideas of race. As hooks (2000) observes, "Poverty in the White mind is always primarily Black. Even though the White poor are many, living in suburbs and rural areas, they remain invisible" (p. 4). As Elizabeth Ellsworth explains about whiteness:

> I and other white people are never just white. We are also always positioned within gender, language, sexuality, class, ability, size, ethnicity, and age … At some times and in some places, those [white] privileges that come with white skin can be temporarily and problematically overridden by oppressions and discriminations. Whiteness is always more than one thing. And it's never the same thing twice (1997, p. 266).

In educational research, differences among Whites that suggest the presence of a subgroup with significant and different educational needs are not highlighted even when compelling data is available. For example, the study, "Gender and Racial Difference in Mathematics Performance," by Hall and Davis (1999), reports, "White students scored significantly higher than the Black students" and "there were no significant gender differences" as the main findings (p. 677). The authors mention in passing. "Parents' highest level math course and parents' education level were that the least educated subgroup of White parents transferred their negative experience to their children more comprehensively than Black parents" (p. 681). Yet, this finding revealing that a subgroup of white children was doing worse than Blacks was not discussed.

The need for specific educational attention to poor and working class ethnic white students is thus an appropriate focus of study in multicultural education, which argues against oppression and in favor of acquiring cultural knowledge to serve culturally different, oppressed, and marginalized children (Banks & Banks, 1989; Gay, 1994). Multicultural education research indicates that multicultural coursework in both pre-service and in-service education should both build knowledge and address attitudes and beliefs (Banks & Banks, 1989; Cochran-Smith, 1995; McDiarmid & Price, 1993; Pohan, 1996). In addition, McDiarmid and Price and Hollingsworth (1989) have argued that not only do many pre-service teachers need to expand their knowledge and explore their beliefs but they also must have opportunities to put this learning into practice in real classrooms. Classes with seemingly non-ethnic rural and urban white students can potentially serve as real multicultural contexts, which provide such powerful experiences.

This research, however, is somewhat controversial. It can arouse powerful feelings as it may seem inappropriate to research marginalized white students when traditionally recognized minorities of color clearly continue to need the attention of teachers and researchers (Ladson-Billings, 2000). Yet, dominant and non-dominant groups vary by neighborhood and regional geography. In many midwestern rural and urban schools Appalachian ethnic white children occupy a low social rung. And yet these "southern crackers" are not always fully white because they lack the privileges and connotations that this signifier entails. They are oppressed according to Young's delineation. They experience exploitation, marginalization, powerlessness, even cultural imperialism and violence. They are ridiculed and stigmatized. Yet, they cling to whiteness, reject solidarity with other marginal groups and accept their marginalized status with the sole consolation that they are not black. (The implications of this paradox are more fully explored in the conclusion.)

White ethnicity is rarely understood to be composed of numerous groups, and is not often understood as "different" or as "marginalized." "Whiteness" is typically described exclusively as dominant culture in much work on multiculturalism, and social class receives little attention. As hooks (2000) writes "class matters." The research described here has been carried out with commitment to the principle that the purpose of education is to prepare all children to be full, active, critical participants in a democratic society. Similarly, teacher education must be democratic, critical, and courageous and committed to exploring diversity in all its complexity.

METHODOLOGY

As my students increasingly puzzled over issues related to the complexity of race and marginality and whiteness I knew our course, Multiculturalism and Education, needed to adapt to accommodate their inquiry. This responsiveness was imperative to me as a constructivist teacher committed to the integration of theory and practice. The constructivist teaching-learning process honors the social and cultural dimensions of teaching and learning and supports the collaborative construction of knowledge in context and through social negotiation. Our course also was explicitly intended to increase knowledge and understanding of the ways in which students experience the world, both within and outside of school, as it is influenced by ethnicity, language, gender, sexual orientation, and social class, and to use this knowledge for classroom decision making and foster education for a more democratic, just society. With these goals, I identified the following research questions: What is the history, experience, language, cultural status, and education of marginalized ethnic Whites? How can pre-service teacher education help future teachers understand the complexity of representation and the reality of marginalized ethnic Whites in classrooms and society?

This research on my teaching and on students' understandings and beliefs was conducted as critical action research, which reflects both a philosophical commitment to democracy in education and to improved pedagogy (Carr & Kemmis, 1986; Noffke & Stevenson, 1995; qa & Smulyan, 1989; Schuyler & Sitterly, 1995). The research pursued two related lines of inquiry. The first phase involved a literature review of the history, experience, language, cultural status, and education of marginalized ethnic Whites and of the concept of whiteness. I reviewed literature problematizing race, representation, and whiteness, literature on whiteness in education, and literature on the experience, culture, and history of specific marginalized ethnic white groups.

The second line of inquiry was a critical action research case study in which data were gathered in my role of teacher-researcher as I introduced curriculum on marginalized ethnic Whites into two consecutive required sections of Multiculturalism and Education that met three hours a week. As Yin (1984) asserts, when research questions seek to uncover "how" and "why" answers, it is best to use non-experimental methods. Observations are important because, as Carspecken (1996) reminds us, "the significance of a study on … constructs lies in the situated social acts produced by people who hold to the constructs" (p. 39).

Participants and Context

Participants were elementary and secondary pre-service teachers attending a Research I Midwestern university located in a city in Indiana surrounded by rural areas. The pre-service teachers were primarily in their sophomore year at the university and, consistent with national demographic profile of teachers, were mostly white, middle-class females. One class included 26 students, the other 28 students, roughly 65% of who were female. Among the 54 students, 49 were from the Midwest. Only 7 of these pre-service teachers had ethnic backgrounds typically identified with marginalization or minority status. These students had Asian (1), Hispanic (1), African American (3), and Jewish ethnicity (2). With the exception of one student in her thirties, all were 19 to 21 years of age. As the course progressed, two additional students in each class (4) came to identify themselves as marginalized ethnic Whites. All students spent one half day per week engaged in multicultural field experiences in five different schools, including rural, suburban, and urban environments, near the Indiana city in which the university was located. The schools ranged from 77% to 91.4% white and from 14% to 46% free or reduced lunch, an indicator of poverty levels. Pre-service teachers identified marginalized ethnic whites in all five schools (see Table 1).

Qualitative data were gathered from multiple sources including (a) detailed field notes documenting class discussions and activities, (b) field notes during field classroom observation school visits, (c) students' reflective course assignment writings including field experience reports and a Cultural Self-Analysis paper, and (d) students' written in-class responses to course materials and published research. Data collection and analysis took place simultaneously, focusing on understanding students' ideas and developing effective teaching strategies. Thus, the early analyses of students' responses affected the further development of teaching strategies.

Teaching strategies focused on an integrated approach to classroom instruction and curricular concerns for marginalized ethnic white students, consistent with multicultural education strategies for other populations. These included:

1. Factual overviews, including an historical review and historical readings
2. Education on language and dialect issues

Table 1. Field Site School Demographics

Type of school	% white	% free/reduced lunch
Rural high school	91.4	24
Small city high school	81	14
Rural elementary	87	46
Rural/suburban middle school	90.5	26
Small city elementary	77	38

3. Guided field experience observation to consider the educational experiences of marginalized ethnic Whites
4. Consideration of wider social, cultural, and economic factors
5. Narrative and autobiographical readings by marginalized ethnic Whites
6. Personal reflection

The following discussion describes the history, language and dialect, and school experiences of marginalized ethnic Whites, while detailing the ways in which pre-service teachers seem to understand these issues in the two courses. The historical overview is summarized below since it refers to a literature with which some readers may not be familiar. Pre-service teachers began with a broad introductory overview emphasizing that many teachers in the United States will have a significant number of their students from groups that are colloquially referred to as Hoosiers, hicks, homeboys, grits, white trash, seeds, hayseeds, and Oakies.

PRE-SERVICE TEACHERS MAKE CONNECTIONS WITH LOCAL MARGINALIZED ETHNIC WHITE HISTORY

Not one of the pre-service teachers with whom I worked had prior knowledge of the history we studied, and many initially had trouble conceiving of marginalized ethnic white students as a group with compelling educational needs. However, 11 students were able to bring their emerging knowledge of this history into the curriculum of their field placement schools. Eight students introduced this history as part of elementary social studies units in which fourth grade children studied local and family history. These students were in a rural school in which they identified during the course of the family history unit that at least 25% of the children were from marginalized ethnic white families that had migrated out of Appalachia. Three pre-service teachers incorporated this historical information into secondary education; two in history of the Depression Era migration, the other in a literature unit on the origin of stereotypes. As Kelley explained, "When I was able to teach the whole class about discrimination against Southern Europeans, I think it helped Emily and Martin. They both have a Polish background and are not popular or well off kids."

All of the pre-service elementary teachers and just under half of the pre-service secondary teachers thought this historical knowledge would be relevant in their classrooms. The pre-service teachers were more interested in using history as curriculum than as a basis for understanding current students or social divisions. As one future secondary teacher explained, "I will be math teacher so I don't see how this relates." Another interesting result of this focus on history was that in each class students wondered if they might have had ancestors who had experienced ethnic discrimination, asking questions such as, "I'm Irish. Could this have happened to a relative of mine?" Though ultimately only two students (in this class) came to identify as marginalized ethnic Whites, students who thought discrimination was likely to be part of their personal family history began to see discrimination in a new way. They were more likely to see discrimination as a social pathology rather than something related to the characteristics of a specially targeted minority group, targeted, that is, on the basis of social class or accented, idiomatic speech. As Nathan explained, "When society has a cultural value that says some group is inferior they are able to exploit them more easily. It can happen to any group, even white people, but in American history Blacks have been the biggest victims of this kind of thinking."

Language Issues of Marginalized Ethnic Whites

In the K-12 school field placements, students observed that some children, both black and white, used dialects of English. Yet, in the field placement schools there was little recognition among teachers that many marginalized ethnic white children speak a dialect with its own internal consistency and distinct cultural and historical origins. The teachers instead pointed out that many children did not speak "properly." The term "dialect" is commonly used pejoratively to describe a distortion of "real" language, although linguists use the term to describe any consistent functioning variety of a language system (Wolfram & Schilling-Estes 1998). One old joke asserts that "the only difference between a language and a dialect is that a language has an army to back it up," which emphasizes that power, not any internal linguistic feature, is what draws the line. In both school and social settings, the marginalization of certain white groups is reinforced by the students' use of dialects of English (Lippi-Green, 1997). The particular dialect varies by group. For example, Appalachian children have well-recognized and distinctive speech patterns. Yet there are many other dialects in use by marginalized ethnic Whites. For example, in Indiana and Ohio, a "Hoosier" dialect is common among marginalized ethnic Whites. As these pre-service teachers noted, this dialect includes the use of constructions such as "y'uns," originating from "you ones," for a third person plural. Pre-service teachers observed that in one of the more urban high school placements, many marginalized ethnic white students spoke in what is commonly considered to be a black dialect. In class, we discussed patterns in which marginalized white students are bi-dialectic, speaking in Appalachian influenced "hoosier" dialect at home, and in the more "hip" black dialect English at school. In all cases, the dialect is clearly perceived to be low-class and nonstandard, and also marks low levels of education and culture (Wolfram & Schilling-Estes, 1998).

As the teachers in these K-12 schools explained to pre-service teachers, marginalized ethnic white children typically struggle with writing and testing in Standard English. For example, the construction "ain't," a feature of several marginalized ethnic white dialects, is a popular wrong answer on standardized tests. As Lippi-Green (1997) argues, children who speak dialects of English are not using their form of speech as a matter of choice. Their linguistic choices are part of a complete language paradigm and are also a means of identity expression and negotiation. Thus, the expectation that dialect speakers of English should be forced to change their modes of speaking in important contexts such as school is unconscionable, however common the practice. Students who are low literate in "standard" English can be highly literate in other dialects or languages (Heath, 1983).

Linguist Walt Wolfram (1998), reflecting on the controversy and misunderstanding surrounding the Ebonics debate, highlights the recommendations of the American Association for Applied Linguistics (1997). Their publication, *Resolution on the Application of Dialect Knowledge to Education*, suggests actions that can be applied to marginalized ethnic white dialect speakers as well as to other linguistically marked social groups: All students and teachers should learn scientifically-based information about linguistic diversity and the social, political, and educational consequences of differential treatment of dialects and their speakers; teacher education should systematically incorporate information about language variation and its impact on classroom interaction and about the ways of applying that knowledge to enhance the education of all teachers; and research should be undertaken to develop and test methods and materials for teaching about varieties of language and for learning Standard English. Pre-service teachers' field observations suggest that the same types of misunderstandings about African American Vernacular English are often applied to speech by marginalized ethnic Whites.

PRE-SERVICE TEACHERS' UNDERSTANDINGS OF MARGINALIZED ETHNIC WHITE LANGUAGE ISSUES

The pre-service teachers were less successful in making connections to language issues and dialects than they were in making connections with history. Even after field observations and follow-up discussions of the nature of dialect and the types of dialect used by marginalized students, emphasizing that dialects are not intrinsically bad, and showing the need for educational attention, the pre-service teachers in this study, when asked the question in writing, "What do you know about their [marginalized ethnic Whites] speech and writing?" most commonly responded by describing marginalized ethnic Whites' language use as inferior. In addition, although no mention was made in these students' "Multiculturalism and Education" course curriculum of poor ethnic Whites' intrinsic lack of ability, or emotional problems, a number of students (=58%) made such observations. Also, more pre-service teachers commented on educational failure as a fact (17%), rather than the need for support (10%), although educational support was stressed. These poor results may have been influenced by the fact that the teachers in the K-12 field placement schools did not view dialects as different but instead identified them as deficient English. Their comments (total 48) were categorized and calculated to the nearest percent are presented in Table 2. Pre-service teachers sometimes wrote more than one comment.

Table 2. What Do You Know About Their Speech and Writing?

Sample comments	Percentage
Describes MW speech and writing as inferior	= 77%
Describes a specific linguistic feature	= 73%
Describes MW mental or emotional disability/school trouble (in response to the question about only language and speech)	= 58%
Emphasizes variety among MW groups	= 47%
MW speech is stereotyped as inferior	25%
MW students may have trouble in school	= 17%
MW students need educational support related	= 10% to language

MW abbreviates marginalized ethnic white.

PRE-SERVICE TEACHERS LEARN ABOUT MARGINALIZED ETHNIC WHITES' EDUCATIONAL EXPERIENCES

As the pre-service teachers observed, marginalized ethnic white students are typically segregated from other students through grouping and tracking techniques in the school setting. This often begins in the early grades, as students with less experience reading and writing, and less exposure to Standard English, are perceived by their teachers to be less academically competent or talented. In one elementary school, pre-service teachers observed three marginalized white students in the second grade who were tracked into the lowest reading group in spite of average or above reading skills. In the high school setting marginalized white students were typically tracked into the lowest of three tracks. As students learned, this type of disadvantage can be cumulative, as research shows that low-tracked students receive less teacher attention, less challenging and engaging curriculum, and more attention to behavior and discipline (Oakes, 1992).

In addition, these ethnic white students were socially marginalized in school settings (Macleod, 1995; McNeal, 1998). They were perceived as less desirable companions by their middle-class and upper-class classmates and rarely participated in sports and in peer activities by the time they were in high school. According to pre-service teachers' field placement observations among social grouping labels in their particular Midwestern high schools were the terms, Hoosiers, hicks, homeboys, burnouts, hayseeds, and trash. The experience and the label, of course, differ depending on the geographic region and the make-up of the student body. The pre-service teachers in this study were predominantly sophomores, only a year and a half away from their own K-12 school experiences. Thus, in addition to reflecting on their course field site observations, they also wrote about and discussed this issue in light of their own high school education. The following is a sampling of written observations about marginalized ethnic white students' school experiences, based on field observations and recollections.

What are they like in school?

- They are seen as class clowns, attention getters, and disruptive.
- They don't interfere with the clubs and sports and activities that other kids do. They have a separate world within the school.
- They are rebels and they stick together.

How do you think they feel about school, teachers, themselves as learners, and their job future?

- When someone keeps telling you that you are this or that, after a while you start believing it yourself.
- School, etc. is not important, just go back to the farm.
- They feel dumb and they feel like they have no future.
- School is something they must suffer through until they can follow in their parents' footsteps.

These pre-service teachers' observations about marginalized ethnic white students in their field placements are consistent with research on poor and working class students in general. The marginalized K-12 students in the field placements had generally negative beliefs about school, teachers, themselves as learners, and their job future (similar to findings of Brantlinger, 1994, Fiene, 1991). These beliefs were reinforced by their parents and their school and peer environments. Levels of educational attainment among family members were low among marginalized ethnic Whites (Macleod, 1995). The parents of marginalized ethnic white students did not participate in school activities or in advocate for their children at nearly the same rates as middle-class dominant culture parents. Research has shown that white middle-class mothers not only participate more but also they press administrators for additional tracking, which further marginalizes low status populations (McGrath & Kuriloff, 1999). Marginalized ethnic white parents often have negative feelings about education and about their own experiences with education, and these attitudes toward education have a significant effect on their children's educational aspirations (Coleman & Hoffer, 1987; Henderson, 1987; National Center for Education Statistics, 1982).

Marginalized ethnic Whites, like many working-class people, have experienced some of the "hidden injuries of class," (Sennett & Cobb, 1972), resulting in low expectations about their status and chances for success. Rubin (1976, 1994) observed that the working-class families she studied did not have educational role models or access to information concerning college admissions, nor did they try to gain this information because their educated children would be lost to an alien way of life. Also, working-class children and marginalized ethnic Whites as a subgroup consider their chances of upward mobility to be slight and either drop out of school or attend school without engaging it, or attend school while resisting it (Macleod, 1995; Ogbu, 1978; Willis, 1977).

CONCLUSION

Without explicit curriculum that addresses the historical experiences, local culture, language, dialect, learning styles, school experiences, and even popular cultural representations of marginalized ethnic white students, pre-service teachers can easily transmit cultural and social class bias and are at risk of neglecting or misinterpreting the needs of many students. The efforts described here to infuse issues related to marginalized ethnic Whites into curriculum in pre-service "Multicul-turalism and Education" courses were only moderately successful. As the data described above reveals, most pre-service teachers retained stereotypes despite such efforts. Some of these future teachers were from lower-middle-class backgrounds and may have been resistant to the idea of accepting marginalized Whites, because it required an acknowledgment of a "white" groups' earlier racialization, acknowledgment of their own current white privilege, and the need to question ideas of race.

If such efforts are to succeed, these concepts must be wrestled with and issues related to ideas of race and whiteness need to be addressed throughout teacher education, and critically explored in educational policy and research. Since the pre-service teachers in this study had such difficulty with the devaluation of the dialects of students in their field placements, they clearly need to learn more about it. Cultural discourse variations should be carefully addressed in pre-service literacy instruction (Au, 1993; Heath, 1983). This did not occur. The moderate success of the pre-service teachers' history field instruction suggests that subject area methods instructors such as social studies teachers, should consider the ethnic compositions of local areas and become knowledgeable about ways to bring critical thought about history and culture into curriculum.

Also, if, as a range of psychological research (i.e. Brown, 1995; Kleinpenning & Hagendoorn, 1993) suggests, status as a marginalized ethnic white may contribute to the development of racism, careful attention to these specific students as learners and attention to ideology of race and class in the curriculum, may also help prevent adult racism. Fascist white supremacist ideology offered by skinheads and the Aryan brotherhood offers a message that can be appealing to marginalized Whites. Ideally, marginalized Whites should learn to understand how social and economic injustice functions and how specific groups are marginalized. This understanding would instead promote solidarity and social action among different marginalized "races." The alternative is that the reality of marginalized Whites' bad experiences with schooling and employment can be interpreted through a twisted racial logic that is dangerous. The Ku Klux Klan (2003) tells marginalized Whites that:

> Enemies from within are destroying the United Stares of America. An unholy coalition of anti-white, anti-Christian liberals, socialists, feminists, homosexuals, Jews, and militant blacks have managed to seize control of our government and mass media. This gang of criminals and degenerates has declared war on the hard working, tax paying white citizens. White Americans have become second class citizens.

White alienation and marginality is typically avoided by mainstream liberal scholars. The marginalized ethnic White is actually an unlikely research subject for many multiculturalists because the "redneck" is an unsympathetic character in general and may even be the archetypal racist enemy of the multicultural researcher. As Schwarz (1996) points out:

> Among those who would never issue a racial slur or denigrate a foreign people in polite conversation, flaunting one's prejudice against rural Americans is not merely acceptable, it's helpful in establishing one's "progressive" bona fides (p. 28).

Clearly, cultural stereotypes of poor rural Whites as racist and violent people contribute to unsympathetic perspectives on this group. Furthermore, white researchers rarely have any personal experience or understanding of the marginalized ethnic white student because of their typically middle-class status or regional origin. A white urban or suburban middle-class researcher may have no context for understanding rural or urban marginalized ethnic Whites.

This research highlights the importance of problematizing and interweaving the otherwise overly simplistic categories and terms such as "black," "white," "urban," and "rural" to consider their sometimes dramatic, but often neglected, interactions in daily experience. The construction of dominant culture can more effectively be understood as hegemonic, differentiated, and complex rather than as simply "white." This study does not suggest that there are not important relationships between color and dominance, but instead asks researchers, teacher educators, and policy makers to be aware of complexity, and of the dangers of reifying racist categories. When this occurs, we can use theory and research to take an honest look at how children in school are faring, who needs support, and who falls behind in preventable ways. We also can make progress towards preparing our teachers to support the learning of *all* students. The paucity of research in the area of educational policy and marginalized ethnic Whites suggests that more needs to be done. Such research is an imperative in a democratic society and in an education profession committed to diversity and social justice.

NOTES

1. "Guinea" originally referred to Northwest coast Africans, but has been used to describe Greeks, Italians, Portuguese, and Puerto Ricans. Similarly, "Hunky" originally referred to Hungarians, but became a "pan-Slavic slur" (Barret & Roediger, 1997, p. 3).
2. Differences between what we call races are so small that it is inconsequential, less than .012% of DNA (Day, 1998).

REFERENCES

Alba, R., & Logan, J. (1997). White ethnic neighborhoods and assimilation: The greater New York region, 1980–1990. *Social Forces*, 75(3), 883–912.

American Association for Applied Linguistics. (1997, March). *Resolution on the application of dialect knowledge to education*. Paper presented at the annual meeting of AAAL. Orlando, FL.

American Speech-Language-Hearing Association. (1998). Position paper on social dialects. *Journal of English Linguistics*, 26(2), 177–181.

Anbinder, T. (2001). *Five Points*. New York: Free Press.

Au, K. H. (1993). *Literacy instruction in multicultural settings*. Fort Worth, TX: Harcourt Brace Jovanovich.

Axtell, J. (1992). *Beyond 1492: Encounters in colonial North America*. New York: Oxford University Press.

Bailyn, B. (1988). *The peopling of British North America: An introduction*. New York: Vintage Books.

Banks, J. A. (2001). Citizenship education and diversity: Implications for teacher education. *Journal of Teacher Education*, 52(1), 5–16.

Banks, J. A., & Banks, C. A. M. (Eds.). (1989). *Multicultural education: Issues and perspectives*. Boston: Allyn & Bacon.

Barrett, J. R., & Roediger, D. (1997). Inbetween peoples: Race, nationality and the new immigrant working class. *Journal of American Ethnic History*, 16(3), 3–45.

Bennett, L., Jr. (1982). *Before the Mayflower: A history of black America* (5th ed.). New York: Penguin.

Billings, D. B., & Blee, K. M. (2000). *The road to poverty: The making of wealth and hardship in Appalachia*. London: Cambridge University Press.

Billings, D. B., Norman, & Ledford, K. (Eds.) (2001). *Confronting Appalachian stereotypes: Back talk from an American region*. Lexington: The University Press of Kentucky.

Boyle-Baise, M. (2002). *Multicultural service learning: Educating teachers in diverse communities*. New York: Teachers College Press.

Brantlinger, E. A. (1994). The social class embeddedness of middle school students' thinking about teachers. *Theory into Practice*, 33(3), 191–199.

Britzman, D. P. (1995). 'The question of belief': Writing post-structuralist ethnography. *International Journal of Qualitative Studies in Education*, 8(3), 229–238.

Brodkin, K. (1998). *How Jews Became White Folks and What That Says About Race in America* (New Brunswick).

Brown, R. (1995). *Prejudice: Its social psychology*. New York: Basil Blackwell.

Cahill, T. (1995). *How the Irish Saved Civilization: The Untold Story of Ireland's Heroic Role from the Fall of the Roman Empire to the Rise of Medieval Europe*. New York: Talese-Doubleday.

Carr, W., & Kemmis, S. (1986). *Becoming critical: Education, knowledge and action research*. Philadelphia: Falmer.

Carspecken, P. F. (1996). *Critical ethnography in educational research: A theoretical and practical guide*. New York: Routledge.

Children's Defense Fund. (2003). Basic facts on poverty. Retrieved September 1, 2003, from http://www.childrensdefense.org/fs_cpfaq_facts.php.

Cochran-Smith, M. (1995). Color blindness and basket making are not the answers: Confronting the dilemmas of race, culture, and language diversity in teacher education. *American Educational Research Journal*, 32(3), 493–522.

Coleman, J. S., & Hoffer, T. (1987). *Public and private high schools: The impact of communities*. New York: Basic.

Collins, P. H. (1990). *Black feminist thought: Knowledge, consciousness, and the politics of empowerment*. Boston: Unwin Hyman.

Cook, D., & Van Cleaf, D. (2000). Multicultural perceptions of 1st-year elementary teachers' urban, suburban, and rural student teaching placements. *Urban Education*, 35(2), 165–74.

Day, R. (1998). *The mismeasure of man: Reflections on the biology of race. David O. Mckay Lectures.* Retrieved September 2, 2003, from http://w3.byuh.edu/academics/ace/ Speeches/Mckay/R_Day.htm.

Denizen, K. (1997). *Interpretive ethnography: Ethnographic practices for the 21st century.* Thousand Oaks, CA: Sage.

Donald, J., & Rattansi, A. (Eds.). (1992). *"Race," culture & difference.* Newbury Park, CA: Sage.

Drake, R. B. (2001). *A history of Appalachia.* Lexington, KY: University Press of Kentucky.

Dunaway, W. (1995). Speculators and settler capitalists: Unthinking the mythology about Appalachian landholding, 1790–1860. In M. B. Pudup, D. B. Billings, & A. L. Waller (Eds.), *Appalachia in the making: The mountain South in the nineteenth century* (pp. 50–75). Chapel Hill, NL: University of North Carolina Press.

Eller, R. D. (1982). *Miners, millhands, and mountaineers: Industrialization of the Appalachian South,* 1880–1930. Knoxville, TN: University of Tennessee Press.

Eller, R. D. (1987). Dialect effects in Appalachian students' written compositions. In C. Ross (Ed.), *Contemporary Appalachia: In search of a usable past: Proceeding of the Ninth Annual Appalachian Studies Conference* (pp. 28–30). Boone, NC: Appalachian Consortium Press.

Ellsworth, E. (1997). *Teaching Positions: Difference Pedagogy and the Power of Address New York: Teachers College Press.*

Fiene, J. (1991). The construction of self by low-status Appalachian women. *Affilia Journal of Women and Social Work,* 6(2), 45–60.

Franklin, J. H., & Moss, A. A. (1988). *From slavery to freedom: A history of Negro American*s (6th ed.). New York: Knopf.

Futrell, M. H., Gomez, J., & Bedden, D. (2003). *Teaching the children of a new America: The challenge of diversity. Phi Delta Kappan,* 84(5), 381–385.

Gay, G. (1994). *The essence of learning: Multicultural education.* West Lafayette, IN: Kappa Delta Pi.

Gay, G. (2000). *Culturally responsive teaching: Theory, research and practice.* New York: Teachers College Press.

Goad, J. (1997). *The redneck manifesto.* New York: Simon and Schuster.

Guglielmo, J., & Salerno, S. (2003). *Are Italians White?: How Race is Made in America.* New York: Routledge.

Hall, C. W., Davis, N. B., Bolen, L. M., & Chia, R. (1999). Gender and racial differences in mathematical performance. *The Journal of Social Psychology,* 139(6), 677-689.

Heath, S. B. (1983). *Ways with words: Language, life, and work in communities and classrooms.* New York: Cambridge University Press.

Henderson, A. (1987). *The evidence continues to grow: Parent involvement improves student achievement.* Columbia, MD: National Committee for Citizens in Education.

Henry, J. M., & Bankston, C. L., III. (1998). Propositions for a structuralist analysis of Creolism. *Current Anthropology,* 39(4), 558–566.

Higginbotham, A. L. (1980). *In the matter of color: The colonial period.* New York: Oxford University Press.

Hollinger, D. A. (1995). Postethnic America: Beyond multiculturalism. New York: Basic.

hooks, b. (2000). *Where we stand: Class matters.* New York: Routledge.

Ignatiev, N. (1996). *How the Irish became white.* New York: Routledge.

Irwin, L. H. (1999). Do rural and urban elementary teachers differ in their attitudes toward multicultural education in elementary schools? *Contemporary Education,* 70(3), 38–43.

Jacobson. M. F. (1998). *Whiteness of a different color: European immigrants and the alchemy of race.* Cambridge, MA: Harvard University Press.

Jensen, L. (2001). Worlds apart: Why poverty persists in rural America/Working hard and making do: Surviving in small town America. *Rural Sociology*, 66(1), 143–150.

Kleinpenning, G., & Hagendoorn, L. (1993). Forms of racism and the cumulative dimension of ethnic attitudes. *Social Psychology Quarterly*, 56(1), 21–36.

Kolchin, P. (2002). Whiteness Studies: The New History of race in America. *Journal of American History*, 89, 154173.

Ku Klux Klan. (2003). *American Knights platform statement*. Retrieved June 29, 2003, from http://www. texasamericanknights.org/platform.html.

Ladson-Billings, G. (2000). Fighting for our lives: Preparing teachers to teach African American students. *Journal of Teacher Education*, 51(3), 206–214.

Lather, P. (1991). *Getting smart: Feminist research and pedagogy with/in the postmodern*. New York: Routledge

Lippi-Green, R. (1997). *English with an accent: Language, ideology and discrimination in the United States*. New York: Routledge.

Lipsitz, G. (1998). The Possessive Investment in Whiteness: How White People Profit from Identity Politics: Philadelphia.

López, Ian F. Haney. (1996). White By Law: The Legal Construction of Race. New York: New York University Press.

Luttrell, W. (2000). "Good enough" methods for ethnographic research. *Harvard Educational Review*, 70(4), 499–524.

Macleod, J. (1995). *Ain't no making it: Aspirations and attainment in a low-income neighborhood*. Boulder, CO: Westview.

Marable, M. (1992). *The crisis of color and democracy: Essays on race, class and power*. Monroe, ME: Common Courage.

McDiarmid, G. W., & Price, J. N. (1993). Preparing teachers for diversity: A study of student teachers in a multicultural program. In M. O'Hair & S. Odell (Eds.), *Diversity and teaching: Teacher education yearbook I*. (pp. 31–57). Orlando, FL: Harcourt Brace Jovanovich.

McGrath, G., & Kuriloff, P. (1999). They're going to tear the doors off this place: Upper-middle-class parent school involvement and the education of other people's children. *Educational Policy*, 13(5), 603–629.

McIntyre, A. (1997). Making meaning of Whiteness: Exploring racial identity with White teachers. Albany: State University of New York Press.

McNeal, R. B. (1998). High school extracurricular activities: Closed structures and stratifying patterns of participation. *Journal of Educational Research*, 91(3), 183–191.

Nash, G. B. (1970). *Class and society in early America*. Englewood Cliffs, NJ: Prentice Hall.

National Center for Education Statistics. (1982). *High school and beyond*. Washington, D.C.: Author.

Noffke, S. E., & Stevenson, R. B. (Eds.). (1995). *Educational action research. Becoming practically critical*. New York: Teachers College Press.

Oakes, J. (1992). *Educational matchmaking: Academic and vocational tracking in comprehensive high schools. Santa Monica*, CA: Rand.

Ogbu, J. U. (1978). *Minority education and caste: The American system in cross-cultural perspective*. New York: Academic.

Ogbu, J. U. (1992). Understanding cultural diversity and learning. *Educational Researcher*, 21(8), 5–14.

Oja, S. N., & Smulyan, L. (1989). *Collaborative action research: A developmental approach*. Philadelphia: Falmer.

Omi, M., & Winant, H. (1994). *Racial formation in the United States: From the 1960s to the 1990s* (2nd ed.). New York: Routledge.

Parker, L., & Lynn, M. (2002). What's race got to do with it? Critical race theory's conflicts with and connections to qualitative research methodology and epistemology. *Qualitative Inquiry*, 8(1), 7–22.

Pohan, C. A. (1996). Preservice teachers' beliefs about diversity: Uncovering factors leading to multicultural responsiveness. *Equity and Excellence in Education*, 29(3), 62–69.

Rosaen, C. L. (2003). Preparing teachers for diverse classrooms: Creating public and private spaces to explore culture through poetry writing. *Teachers College Record*, 105(8), 1437–1485.

Rubin, L. B. (1976). *Worlds of pain: Life in the working-class family*. New York: Basic.

Rubin, L. (1994). *Families on the fault line: America's working-class speaks about the family, the economy, race, and ethnicity*. New York: HarperCollins.

Scalley, R. J. (1996). *The end of hidden Ireland: Rebellion, famine, and emigration*. New York: Oxford University Press.

Scheurich, J. (1993). Toward a white discource on White racism. *Educational Researcher*, 22(8), 5–10.

Schuyler, P., & Sitterly, D. (1995). Preservice teacher supervision and reflective practice. In S. E. Noffke & R. B. Stevenson (Eds.), *Educational action research: Becoming practically critical* (pp. 43–59). New York: Teachers College Press.

Schwarz, B. (1996). Angry white rural men. *The Nation*, 263(14), 27–30.

Sennett, R., & Cobb, J. (1972). *The hidden injuries of class*. New York: Vintage.

Shanklin, E. (1994). *Anthropology and race*. Belmont, CA: Wadsworth.

Sleeter, C. E. (1994). A multicultural educator views white racism. *The Education Digest*, 59(9), 33–37.

Sleeter, C. E. (1995). White silence and white solidarity. *Race Traitor*, 4, 14–22.

Spring, J. (2000). *The intersection of cultures: Multicultural education in the United States and the global economy* (2nd Ed.). Boston: McGraw Hill.

United States Census Bureau. (2003). *People and families in poverty by selected characteristics*: 2000 and 2001. Retrieved August 23, 2003, from http://www.census. gov/hhes/poverty/poverty01/table1.pdf.

Valli, L. (1995). The dilemma of race: Learning to be color blind and color conscious. *Journal Teacher Education*, 46(2), 120–130.

West, C. (1982). *Prophesy deliverance!: An Afro-American revolutionary Christianity*. Philadelphia: Westminster Press.

Willis, P. E. (1977). *Learning to labor: How working class kids get working class jobs*. New York: Columbia University Press.

Wolfram, W. (1998). Language, ideology and dialect. *Journal of English Linguistics*, 26(2), 108–121.

Wolfram, W., & Schilling-Estes, N. (1998). *American English: Dialects and variation*. Malden, MA: Blackwell.

Yin, R. K. (1984). *Case study research: Design and methods*. Thousand Oaks, CA: Sage.

Young, I. M. (1990). Justice and the Politics of Difference. Princeton, NJ: Princeton University Press.

Elizabeth Heilman is an assistant professor in the Department of Teacher Education at Michigan State University whose research explores the ways in which identity, belief systems, school contexts, and power structures influence the understanding and teaching of curriculum, particularly as it relates to the political and social imagination.

The "Receivement Gap": School Tracking Policies and the Fallacy of the "Achievement Gap"

By Terah Venzant Chambers

Closing the racial achievement gap has been a cornerstone of recent education reform, especially as accountability measures are increasingly relied upon to drive academic performance standards. This article questions the term "achievement gap" and its implication that White students perform better on standardized tests due to greater effort and ability. The term "receivement gap" is offered as an alternative due to its focus on structures, not students, and inputs instead of outputs. Evidence is drawn from a qualitative project using a case study design with seven African American high school students in tracked mathematics and English classes. Results indicated differential treatment by school personnel as early as elementary school that influenced students' later school performance. Accordingly, research supports the recommended term "receivement gap," which is offered in the hope of inspiring a deeper and more nuanced discussion of factors that influence student achievement and distort the achievement of African American students.

Closing the achievement gap has been the focus of both academic and popular dialogues on education reform, argued about in congressional offices and teacher's lounges, discussed on C-SPAN and *Oprah*. Concern about Black-White disparities in academic performance on standardized tests has garnered attention at the highest levels and was even made one of President Bush's primary targets in the 2001 *No Child Left Behind Act* (NCLB, 2002), the largest and most sweeping federal education reform initiative since the 1960s (McGuinn, 2006). The racial achievement gap, defined as the observed gap in academic performance between, usually, White and Asian American students on one hand, and African American and Latino students on the other (Noguera, & Wing, 2006), is an issue that has received increasing attention in recent years (Ladson-Billings, 2006; Orr, 2003; Rothstein, 2004; Thernstrom & Thernstrom, 2003; Thompson, 2007). This has been particularly true as attention in educational circles has turned to accountability measures, including standardized test performance, in the age of NCLB (Gooden, 2005).

Conversations about disparities in achievement between Black and White students, however, are hardly new. Publication of the *Coleman Report* in 1966 jumpstarted the opportunity to discuss gaps in performance between Black and White students, which was often from cultural deficit perspectives (Coleman et al., 1966; Jencks & Phillips, 1998; Ladson-Billings, 2006). For years these concerns were largely encapsulated by the term "test score gap," and were the subject of the seminal book, *The Black-White Test Score Gap* (1998), edited by Christopher Jencks and Meredith Phillips. This issue found audiences in many other publications as well (see, Hedges & Nowell, 1999; Trent, 1997). Interestingly, the term "achievement gap" does not appear in the index to Jencks and Phillips landmark collection of essays, which covers such possible contributions to the gap as "stereotype threat" (Steele & Aronson, 1998) and the burdens of "acting White" (Cook & Ludwig, 1998) to racial bias (Jencks, 1998) and family background (Phillips, Brooks-Gunn, Duncan, Klebanov, & Crane, 1998).

The obvious question, then, is where did the term "achievement gap" originate? The *American Heritage Dictionary* (1993) defines *achievement* as "something accomplished successfully, especially by means of exertion, skill, or perseverance (p. 11)." The definition offered by an online source was similar, suggesting *achievement* was "something accomplished, especially] by superior ability, special effort, great courage, etc.; a great or heroic deed" (www.dictionary.com). Applying these definitions to the term "achievement gap," the obvious insinuation is White students are superior to and more special than Black students, indeed, that they achieve at a higher level by virtue of heroic effort. This much broader and more sweeping conception of disparities in academic performance on standardized tests is a far cry from the simple "test score gap" offered by Jencks and Phillips ten years ago. The connotation seems to imply the problem lies with Black and Latino students' ability to "achieve." Using this term also conveniently sidesteps any possible responsibility on the part of educators, suggesting instead that the entire problem is with the *students*.

These definitions are particularly problematic because the implications run counter to the history and sociology of education and also because of current work on school tracking policies and the institutional/structural barriers to academic success that students of color face in today's school systems. It is with this background that the term "achievement gap" ought to be questioned. The term "receivement gap" perhaps more accurately characterizes the issue, but in more than an attempt to alter terminology this study would serve as a call to refocus and challenge the deficit model of thinking. The term "receivement gap" is useful because it focuses attention on educational *inputs*—what the students receive on their educational journey, instead of *outputs*—their performance on a standardized test. This refocusing also moves attention away from the students as the source of these disparities, and toward the larger structures and forces that play a role in their education and development.

This article takes an expanded approach to the issue of racial achievement gaps to look at the possibility of other contributing factors to the phenomenon. The problem of racial disparities in education is complicated and multifaceted. Jencks and Phillips (1998) understood this dilemma and gathered and highlighted the parallel lines of research relevant to the test score debate. Educators should continue to look for research that adds to the understanding of the problem. This study addresses one such issue, school tracking policies, to show its influence on student achievement. However, it is emphatically noted that there are many other issues that have similar global implications for the achievement gap issue. These include, but are certainly not limited to, school finance disparities, lack of high-quality teachers, residential segregation, access to technology, quality pre-school preparation, and home support. The relevance of these issues merely lends additional support for further reflection on the use of the term.

This article begins with a discussion of related fields that help inform the expanded view of the achievement gap presented here, first with issues within the historiography of African American education, followed by arguments made by scholars using more contemporary analyses. The discussion then moves to the present study, discussing the relevance of findings from African American students in tracked school environments of the receivement gap and the ways the students' experiences help further the understanding of this issue. The discussion closes with general thoughts on larger implications for education.

REVIEW OF LITERATURE: DECONSTRUCTING THE TERM "ACHIEVEMENT GAP"

Historical Considerations

The greatest irony of the term "achievement gap" and the dictionary definitions that imply "great heroism" on the part of White students in their educational accomplishments is that if any group has displayed heroic effort in its educational pursuits, it is unquestionably the African American community. Therefore, an important counter-story to the achievement gap narrative comes from the tradition and history of African American education itself. Much of the African American community valuing academic achievement can be seen in its historical struggle to gain access to education. During slavery, Blacks were prevented from learning to read or write under penalty of death (Anderson, 1988; Litwack, 1999). The sizeable, determined group of Blacks who learned to do so despite the risk to their lives reveals the supreme importance education held in their lives. After emancipation, in the wake of *Plessy v. Ferguson* (1896), African Americans were forced to attend segregated, resource-poor schools, plagued by systemic neglect of monetary and tangible resources to which they were entitled. African American reverence for education was further exemplified by the numbers of Blacks who pooled their own meager resources and were often double-taxed—paying regular government taxes plus making additional monetary donations to their local schools—when their tax money was systematically diverted to White schools (Anderson, 1988). Finally, after the controversial *Brown v. Board of Education* (1954) decision, White hostility to desegregation manifested itself openly in an era of massive resistance. In addition to overt desegregation-avoidant tactics, the advent of desegregation policies in the 1960s and 1970s ushered in an era of increased within-school segregative tactics, including tracking, which were more covert, but served to transfer segregation from the school to the classroom level (Clotfelter, 2004; Dickens, 1996; Donelan, 1994; Meier, Stewart, & England, 1989; Mickelson, 2003). Black and White students may have attended the same "desegregated" schools, but rarely did they share the same classrooms, a condition that continues in many schools with both Black and White students (Mickelson, 2005).

Given the historical background of segregation and desegregation in the Black community, it is not surprising that even as they fought for education, their efforts were dismissed and denigrated. African Americans struggled to obtain access to resources that rightly belonged to them through legislation and were disrespected and met with accusations of Black inferiority by many within the White community. Anderson (2004) outlined the progression of these discussions that sound eerily familiar to current conversations about the achievement gap. He pointed out that the controversy over test score gaps (Jencks & Phillips, 1998) is only the most recent of many educational "epidemics" associated with the African American community—the literacy gap, elementary school attendance gap, and high school completion gap being among the other "crises" that, seen within appropriate historical and political contexts, lose much of their urgent characterization. This is especially true as Anderson documented how each crisis was systematically addressed and the disparities eliminated, so that the vestiges of these gaps exist only in the historical record and our collective memory. He further argued that the test score gap can be similarly eliminated, provided sufficient and appropriate resources are devoted toward its eradication (Anderson, 2004). The historical context of Black struggle for education, paired with characterizations of that struggle by the White community as insufficient and even deficient, provides a strong argument for skepticism about the current crisis over the achievement gap.

Other Voices of Dissent

As conversations increased about the importance of addressing the achievement gap, so have voices questioning the origins of the term. Some scholars have moved away from using the term, choosing "opportunity gap" instead to shift attention to disparate access to quality inputs, such as high-quality teachers (Akiba, LeTendre, & Scribner, 2007; Noguera, Aronson & Mehan, 2004; Oakes, Rogers, Silver, Horng & Goode, 2004; Torre, 2005). Similarly, there are those who have faulted the use of the term to reflect Black–White educational disparities, arguing that discussions about the "achievement gap" have traditionally focused on the differential rates of performance on standardized tests between Whites and Blacks, but not Whites and Asians, where a substantial gap in test score performance exists—with Whites on the lower-performing end (Fryer & Levitt, 2004). Others have criticized the domestic focus, which ignores important international considerations. American students, Black *and* White, still perform below students in many other developed nations (Akiba et al., 2007; Anderson, 2004; Buchmann & Parrado, 2006). However, most of these authors have not used the term "opportunity gap or problematized the use of achievement gap in the way it is being done in this article. Nonetheless, there are other researchers who have made their dissatisfaction with the term more overt. Gloria Ladson-Billings brought international attention to her concerns with the term "achievement gap" in her 2006 presidential address to the annual conference of the American Educational Research Association, which was subsequently published in *Educational Researcher*. Ladson-Billings used this forum to,

[C]all into question the wisdom of focusing on the achievement gap as a way of explaining and understanding the persistent inequality that exists (and has always existed) in our nation's schools. I want to argue that this all-out focus on the "Achievement Gap" moves us toward short-term solutions that are unlikely to address the long-term underlying problem. (Ladson-Billings, 2006, p. 4)

Ladson-Billings suggested that the term fails to take into account the larger, historical factors influencing issues of racial disparities in educational attainment. Instead of focusing on the achievement gap, which she suggested is only the tip of a large iceberg, she urged scholars and the public to understand the problem as one of an "education debt," having accrued over many years and reflecting numerous causes. Her work has moved the thinking forward about the achievement gap, particularly in considering the limitations and short-sighted nature of its use. While this perspective is certainly important, it does not sufficiently problematize the deficit thinking connoted by the term itself.

Tracking and the Achievement Gap

Interestingly, and perhaps not surprisingly, tracking has been associated with the achievement gap in previous research, focusing on the correlation between tracking structure and student achievement (Gamoran, 1992; Gamoran & Mare, 1989; Slavin & Oickle, 1981) and the elimination of the gap through detracking (Burris & Welner, 2005). None of these articles specifically questioned the use of the term "achievement gap," but rather focused on the relationship between tracking and the achievement gap. In response, this article calls for further attention at this point regarding the achievement gap.

METHODS

Design and Procedure

The foundation of this project stemmed from a case study of Highview High School (a pseudonym). Highview is situated in a first-ring, midsized midwestern metropolitan suburb, near the state's capital city. It is located north of sprawling, predominantly White, outer-ring suburbs, but is south of the predominantly minority city school district, placing it in a buffer zone of not-quite suburb and not-quite city. The nearest high school in either the city or the suburb is no more than a few minutes away. Not surprisingly, then, Highview's student population is fairly diverse. The median household income of students in the most affluent area in the district was nearly $140,000, while those in the poorest area came from households earning less than $40,000. A little over 20% of the student body qualified for free or reduced lunch. The demographics of the school are about 73% White, 13% Hispanic, 8% Black, 5% Asian/Pacific Islander, and 1% Native American. By no means resource-poor, Highview was built on a spacious lot with acres of sports fields and green lawn. Although it was renovated recently, it is still no match for the more recently built, state-of-the-art high schools in the surrounding primarily upper-income White suburbs.

A case study design was used for its appropriateness in understanding and maintaining the integrity of real-life occurrences (Yin, 2002). This was particularly the case for Highview, where the intent was to understand the experiences of African American students, specifically with regard to tracking. One primary objective of the project was to highlight and preserve the voices of the student participants in the project, a group that is generally underrepresented in extant research (Cook-Sather, 2002; Dahl, 1995; Fielding, 2001, 2002; Fine, Weis, & Powell et al., 1997; Lincoln, 1995; Mitra, 2004; Raymond, 2001; Rubin & Silva, 2003; Wasley, Hampel, & Clark et al., 1997).

Data were collected over the fall semester of the 2005–2006 school year. Three to four days each week were spent in the school, primarily in the English and mathematics classes of the students in the project. In addition to the classroom observations, document analysis of student handbooks, yearbooks, registration materials, and other relevant documents, as well as individual and focus group interviews, were conducted. Each of the seven selected students (the selection process follows) was interviewed individually three times. After each round of individual interviews, the students from all three tracks were invited to participate in a focus group. Accordingly, three focus groups were held over the course of the project, with three to six students from various track levels attending each focus group. The individual interviews lasted twenty minutes to an hour, while the focus groups lasted between two to three hours each.

The interviews evolved in three stages. Stage One focused on the students' educational trajectories and prior educational experiences as well as their experiences of being tracked. Stage Two focused more specifically on students' thoughts on tracking and the role it played in their career aspirations for the future. In Stage Three, students were asked to think critically about tracking, that is, whether they felt it was an appropriate tool to use in schools, and how it should be revised or abolished to meet students' educational needs. It quickly became clear that while the students spoke directly to the issue of tracking, they also revealed larger structural forces in the school that influenced how tracking decisions were made and, ultimately, how they felt toward school as well.

Highview High School, much like other high schools in the U.S., has no formal tracking policy. Informally, however, three distinct levels, or tracks, can be identified. The Bridge group, housed in an alternative learning center within the main school building, is the most rigidly separated group. Students who are identified as being unsuccessful in a traditional school setting are placed in this program, and are primarily low-income and of color. The two remaining tracks, high-track group and regular track group, are less rigidly defined but have little overlap in the student populations they serve. The high-track group is comprised primarily of students taking Advanced Placement (AP) classes. These students also make up the majority of the school's leadership on the student council and in other extracurricular activities. The regular track students are characterized by their lack of enrollment in any AP math or English courses and their lack of involvement in extracurricular activities in the school, a trait held in common with the Bridge students.

Participants

Students who had attended schools in the district for the bulk of their education were preferred as potential participants. Also, the researcher wanted to get at least one male and one female from each of the three track levels: Bridge, regular and AP. After many hours of classroom observations before students were selected, a few young people stood out based on comments they made or interactions that occurred in class. It was even easier to select the high-track students—the "sample" in this project represents *all* of the African American seniors enrolled in AP courses, a fact verified by course enrollment data provided by the school. One of the students had graduated the year before and was attending an elite private college not far from the city.

Participants were selected from the senior class at Highview High School with one junior and the recent graduate. Seniors were the focus because of the more reflective nature of students who are in their last year of school. These students are older and more mature, and as they prepare to leave high school, they would be more likely to have ideas (and more willing to share them) about their high school experiences. Seven African American students participated in the project: three high track (two females, one male), two regular track (one female, one male) and two students from the Bridge program (one female, one male).

RESULTS

Once the students in the project, especially those in the lower track levels, recounted their stories of routine denials of access to resources they would need to be academically successful, the connection to issues of achievement could not be ignored. Seeing the daily struggle these students had and knowing that the dominant, traditional viewpoint would indirectly blame them for their academic situation seemed to merit further attention.

Some of the students' experiences in school that highlight the disparate attention they faced are shared, revealing the differences in treatment they received at Highview High School that constrained their ability to achieve. These findings mirror those from previous research (Kozol, 1991; 2005; Mickelson, 2003; Nieto; 2000; Oakes, 2005), providing further evidence for reconceptualizing the notion of the achievement gap. The results from study of the African American students at Highview are offered, along with these other studies, to make the argument that the characterization of the achievement gap is unfair and shortsighted. The lower track students in this study encountered teachers, work environments, and classroom management styles that differed significantly from their high-track counterparts' classrooms. Given their experiences, the "achievement gap" label became another obstacle that prevented them from receiving services they needed. The more appropriate label, "receivement gap," refocuses attention where it is due—on the educational institutions, personnel and policies, tracking among them—that create, perpetuate, and exacerbate differences among these students.

After analyzing the data collected throughout the course of the project, certain patterns in the students' discussions began to emerge. Cultivating and expanding these patterns into distinct themes helped create a framework for the stories the students related. One theme identified from that analysis,

Assimilation/Negotiation, is particularly relevant to the discussion of the achievement gap. This theme details a process in which some students were actively encouraged to become part of or assimilate to the school culture through participation in special academic programs with elite teachers and involvement in sports and other extracurricular activities, while other students were discouraged or denied participation in any school-affiliated activities. A few examples from the students' interviews and the classroom observations are provided to elucidate these findings.

Early Experiences with Separation

Much work exists that documents the dominant cultural paradigms in schools that dictate how academically successful students should look, sound, dress, write, work, and prepare; and the proper way for parents to be involved (Barajas & Ronnkvist, 2007; Bourdieu & Passeron, 1990; Carter, 2005; Delpit, 1988; Gewirtz & Cribb, 2003; Giroux, 1983; Lewis, 2003; Nash, 1990; MacLeod, 2004; McCready, 2004; Mickelson, 2003; Nieto, 2000), which makes students who fall outside these parameters feel excluded. This dominant cultural paradigm was found to exist at Highview. Students recalled incidents that showed the paradigm working in early childhood education, normalizing it into their school experiences before they were even able to recognize a problem. Paralleling other studies, evidence of tracking surfaced very early in the students' experiences (Barta & Allen, 1995; George, 1995; Nieto, 2000; Oakes, 1995; Pool & Page, 1995), revealing how this dominant culture manifested itself in decisions about who would belong in the dominant culture.

Ted (all student names are pseudonyms), one of the high-track students, recalled being placed in English as a Second Language (ESL) classes in first grade. This was a common occurrence in this country, given that 3.8 million students receive ELL services (U.S. Department of Education, 2006) but unusual in this case because Ted spoke only English. His mother, who is Mexican American (his father is African American), was often seen with Ted at school since his father was a commercial airline pilot and frequently travelled. As Ted explained, "Well, it was because my mom is Mexican, and so they took it upon themselves to assume that English was my second language." His parents were not notified about the initial placement, and Ted remained in ESL for six months until his parents deciphered from their young son's confusion that something was amiss at school and corrected his placement. Since placement in bilingual education has been linked to lower-track placements (Braddock, 1990; Harklau, 1994; Medina, 1988), this example reveals how decisions, when made inappropriately, can have a significant impact on a student's educational trajectory. In this case, the school made a decision about Ted's fit with the mainstream culture. While there is no further information regarding the circumstances of the placement or the possibility that Ted had other academic difficulties at this age he could not recall, what is clear is that the school placed him incorrectly in ESL and failed to mediate the situation within a reasonable amount of time. Ted's parents, using their social and cultural capital (Bourdieu & Passeron, 1990), were able to advocate for him. This raises the question of what happens when other children (including those who should be high-track) end up in inappropriate placements with no one to speak up for them. Placements like Ted's at an early age have been found to be fairly strong predictors of later track placement (Dickens, 1996; Meier et al, 1989; Oakes, 2005), making his story even more significant.

Normalization of Separation

Another aspect of the tracking process was the normalization of separation that occurred at early ages. While tracking did not seem severe to the students as they discussed these early experiences, the practice was pervasive across all of the participants' experiences. The students seemed to have become comfortable with separations based on "ability," and this set the stage for more entrenched separation in later years. Cortez, a Bridge student, expressed the feelings of most of the group when he said. "I mean, I didn't feel no certain way [about his reading placement in elementary school]. I mean—I wanted to be able to read better, you know, than I did. But, if it was helping me, it was helping me." It became routine to him because "everybody got pulled out at certain times." Darica, another Bridge student, expressed a similar sentiment when she said her placement did not matter because, as she explained,

> I guess, 'cuz I wasn't gonna do it in whichever group I was in. I mean I guess if I could read better, and I liked to read back then. I wouldn't care. But I didn't like to read. I didn't like to do nothing.

But even if she thought her placement did not matter, when asked how her remedial reading placement made her feel she said, "I thought I was dumb." Both Cortez and Darica felt their placements were routine aspects of their school experience, but Darica's statement that she felt it meant she was "dumb" also reveals the feeling she associated with her reading group assignment.

The opinion that the placements were a routine part of the schooling experience was expressed by high track students as well. Katrina, a high-track student, talked about being placed in the fourth grade classroom of an admired teacher in the school. Katrina, along with the other handful of gifted/talented students, was placed in his regular classroom, and he also served as their gifted/talented instructor. Katrina was clearly very proud of being in his class and even many years later looked back fondly on her time in his classroom. She said, "I knew it was because, like, I was smart and that made me feel, like, cool." Like Darica, who inferred from her reading placement something about her intellectual ability (that she was "dumb"), Katrina takes her placement to mean she is "smart." Even at young school ages, these students began associating their ability placement with their intellect.

Interestingly, Cortez, a Bridge student, also had an experience with a reading placement in 4th grade that stood out,

> I had this one teacher, I don't know, I hated her guts, though. She was cool here and there, but I don't know, she used to help me read. She was just basically like somebody on the streets. She used to help me read.

Cortez's recollections about his experience in 4th grade is interesting not only for what he says, but for how he characterizes his help—a woman whom he says came from "the streets." Pairing the experiences Katrina and Cortez had in 4th grade with special reading instruction serves as a helpful illustration of the significance of the normalization of separation that occurred during this age, since both students received special help. What messages, then, do Katrina and Cortez internalize from the differential resources they received? Katrina received one of the best teachers the school had to offer. The support Cortez received, however, did not even come directly from the school. His instructor was brought in from "the streets" to help him read. Katrina's teacher was probably better equipped to help her navigate the unwritten cultural rules and expectations of the school since he was an extension of that environment. These experiences, for better or worse, help to create the foundation on which their future learning would be built.

When the students were interviewed, none of them found the earlier school experiences of separation that had occurred problematic. They felt they deserved the placement they had received and that, by extension, other students deserved their placements. Given this process of normalization, it should not be surprising that in later years, students tended to remain in the same level of classes. The process of normalizing separation in early grades was an important foundation for later stratification in high school.

Compounding Effects Influence Later Placement

The final component of the students' experiences with tracking is the compounding nature of all of the aspects of the students' schooling experiences. Not one factor—school, friends, family—explains the process of assimilation that occurs. Rather, all of these factors influence the students by providing the high-track students with constant reinforcement of their placement and the lower-track students with multiple reminders of their lack of fit. Not surprisingly, the students in the project surrounded themselves with friends who were similarly situated. This meant that all of the students in the advanced placement classes had limited contact with other students of color, while the lower-track students had friend groups that were comprised primarily of students of color. The students talked about the lack of contact they had with each other in the second focus group. In the excerpt Nicole, a high-track student who had graduated the previous year and was attending college, talks about being one of very few Black students. Cortez, a Bridge student, and Trevonne, a regular track student, enter the discussion about the lack of contact between students in different tracks.

Nicole: I think, having been in the higher classes—socially you get really siphoned off from the rest of the world. Particularly coming in as a Black student. I was often one of one—or one of two—Tops, one of three—Black students in my classes. And that—it didn't necessarily bother me because I—I'm strong enough of a person that, you know, I could get my cultural identity from myself and other people around me. But I don't think that everybody necessarily can. And I think that's—particularly as a minority student—I think that's detrimental. And it doesn't help anybody. You know, it's not necessarily that they don't like each other, or they don't understand each other—they don't want to be friends—they just don't try.

Cortez: In the end we're just not around each other to even learn anything about it.

Nicole: Exactly. I maybe saw you thirty seconds while I was walking to one class and you were walking to a different one. But that doesn't mean I ever got to learn your name.

Cortez: I know. Yo, I don't know nobody—except them two now [pointing to Nicole and fed]—in some real high class.

Trevonne: She graduated though.

Cortez: Man, she was here last year?

Before the focus groups for this project, many of the high-track students had not had more than passing interactions with lower-track students since elementary school, if then, as indicated in the excerpt. Even though Nicole had recently graduated from Highview, Cortez had no idea that she had been a student at the school. The excerpt from the focus group shows just how separated the students had been from each other and, in fact, had it not been for this project, they might have never met.

Nicole expanded on the implications of this separation in one of her individual interviews, in which she explained how the reinforcement of track placement occurs. In the excerpt, she sheds light on the myriad factors that can influence whether students align with the dominant culture of the school.

Nicole: I think more White students tend to have a confidence that you can assume stems from whatever you want, or maybe a cultural assumption. Like, you know, at home, "You're going to take advanced classes." And their friends take advanced classes and so it just all kind of falls together that, you know, this group of fifteen people ends up in the same class. People they have grown up with, people they go to church with or they go to synagogue with, and live next to. and ride the bus with, and play soccer with them, and whatever. And so. "You're taking advanced? Sure, I'll take advanced, too." You know, it doesn't seem ... I think it's not as daunting.

Terah: Sure. So, if you're going with that theory then, if you're an African-American student who is not in those circles, it would be very daunting then to be in one of those classes.

Nicole: I think it would be terrifying. I'd never been outside the circle of the White kids in the advanced classes, so it was never a question of whether or not my friends were going to be there. But if I wouldn't have had friends—if all my friends would have been in basic, you know, the regular classes, I probably would have been in regular classes.

Nicole, who is strong academically, still admits that she may have been reticent to take advanced classes had her friends not been in them. She is comfortable with her position in the school and becomes somewhat uneasy with the thought of what would have happened to her had she not been in this social network. It is also important to recognize that she does not see the influence of outside factors, aside from parents and friends, in how things "fall together" for students in the classes that they take. As Nicole suggests, friends can have a critical influence on the courses a student enrolls in, an influence which appears to be hard to escape regardless of how strong that student may be.

While the students provided many examples of the complexity of the school environment and the multitude of factors that influenced their track placement, they are not all recounted here. At the start of the project, students expressed opinions that indicated that they had accepted the invisible processes that influenced their ability group placement. By the end of the project, however, students generally became more critical of their experiences. This can be seen from Nicole's previous comments about the comfort she felt in her upper level courses. Cortez also had a revelation about his educational experiences that shifted his thinking about school. In one of his last interviews he talked about regrets in how he had been treated by the education system.

Cortez: I don't like how they just split us up. They make all people that supposed to be smart, which is mostly Black people—they suppose to not be smart or whatever—they put us in these lower classes, put us in stuff like Bridge. And then they got these people that's in these [advanced] classes and we don't even never get to see 'em or look at 'em, or experience what they take with them. They don't got teachers—at least they can do is give us teachers that one section that we work on is from a higher grade—a higher calc[ulus] or a higher geometry, or somethin'—to see if we know that stuff, or we're capable of doing it.

Having never had the opportunity to interact with students from other track levels, or talk about the issue of track placement, Cortez had only his observations and thoughts on the issue. As the project evolved and he was able to see the larger picture and talk with other students, he became much more critical of his educational experiences.

Outside factors had a profound impact on the students' school experiences. These processes were then normalized so that these students were not even aware when there was anything beyond the routine happening. The high-track African American students were the ones who told stories of being encouraged to achieve, while the lower-track students felt like outsiders throughout their school careers. As they fell further and further behind by virtue of their inferior educational preparation and accompanying feelings that academic achievement was not for them (Daniels, 2003; Gay, 2000), the lower-track students arrived at Highview well behind the few Black students in high-track courses.

DISCUSSION

The stories in the previous section revealed how the presence of a strong majority culture affected the Highview African American students, some who were encouraged to align with this culture, and others who were dissuaded. The students' decisions (or ability) to assimilate had lasting implications that extended to their experiences in high school. The students were able to identify early educational experiences that shaped the direction they moved in according to their enrollment in high-, regular-or alternative-track classes later on. While this project dealt solely with African American students, the implications for the achievement gap and comparisons to White student achievement is clear. Only a small number of Black students were able to negotiate their way into the dominant culture of the school, which had significant impact on their ability to be academically successful. Time after time, when students needed just a little more—time, resources, encouragement—they received less. Considering the earlier point made about the multitude of parallel lines of research that affect this issue: school finance disparities, lack of high-quality teachers, residential segregation, access to technology, quality pre-school preparation, and home support, the problems may appear insurmountable. However, there are some larger points that are relevant to a larger dialogue about the achievement gap.

First, these students' stories and experiences highlight the fact that looking at achievement indicators (test results) alone provides an insufficient picture of their academic performance. For the seven students in this study, many factors affected their performance on these tests. In most cases, those factors had been accruing and compounding over many years, having been initiated at early stages of their educational careers. This is supported by research that showed a considerable racial test-score gap between Black and White students as early as third grade (Fryer & Levitt, 2006) that only becomes greater in the higher grades (Bali & Alvarez, 2004; Fryer & Levitt, 2006; Noguera & Wing, 2006). There are other factors influencing students' preparation for and performance on these tests and tracking is just one of them.

The second point of this research is the lack of control students had over their educational placements. Ted was placed in ESL for six months based on a false assumption made by school personnel. Nothing he did during that time altered his path. It took his parents to find out about the placement and intervene before a change occurred. However, not all parents are physically, emotionally, and financially prepared to advocate for their children in the way expected and valued by the school. Once removed from this classroom Ted was moved into a path that prepared him for high-track classes in high school. The case examples of Cortez and Katrina reinforce the lack of control students have. In 4th grade they both received specialized reading instruction: Katrina received help from a highly respected teacher and Cortez from a woman who was brought in from outside the educational system. Someone decided early on which resources each would receive, but this was not the sole factor leading Katrina to high-track classes and Cortez to the Bridge program. A point of no return was reached in which there was too much distance for Cortez to recover from his relative lack of preparation. Focusing on an "achievement gap" may unconsciously direct attention on intra-student factors that affect test score performance, but the students from this project remind us that there are other important variables to consider.

Third, the current educational climate and focus on test scores in the era of accountability under NCLB make a consideration of other outside variables more difficult. There is more information than ever before about how students, in various subgroups, are performing on standardized tests. With the accessibility of these scores, it is no secret what groups of students are performing better on these tests than others. Determining which students caused a school to "fail" to meet set benchmarks is not difficult, but the focus is already at the end of the process. The question is what can be done to change these scores? The voices of the students from Highview serve as a reminder that a lot can happen before the tests are taken—often many years' worth of tracking and neglect—that influence students' performance. Nonetheless, given the intense focus on these test score gaps required under NCLB, it may be difficult for schools to see this larger perspective.

Finally, damage is done to students when they are held responsible for their academic performance in this way. Ladson-Billings (2006) urged educators to look at the achievement gap as an "education debt," which keeps alive a reminder of the larger historical factors that have been educationally influential. One problem with the focus on standardized tests in this age of accountability under NCLB is that it can send unintentional messages to students. Too many African American children do not know the true history of African American education in this country and the sacrifices made so that they could learn. Therefore, when these children get the message that their school is "failing" because of them, they may think that African Americans are "suppose to not be smart," as Cortez did. If educators are not thoughtful about how they approach subgroup accountability in their schools, and especially if students are not given access to their history, then it should not be surprising that students may feel like Cortez. Changing the terminology to receivement gap will certainly not alter the message, but beginning a conversation about what we are really saying to each other and children when we use the term "achievement gap" at least can begin the process of change.

CONCLUSION

This article began with the premise that the term "achievement gap" fails to accurately portray the debate over test scores, especially as it relates to the performance of African American students on standardized tests, and argues that receivement gap more accurately characterizes the issue. Furthermore, it contends that the use of this term also represents a deficit model of thinking that blames the students for their academic performance. While not discounting the relevance and importance of student agency, this article argued that as the collective attention in the education community has turned to measurable educational outputs—test scores and other accountability measures chief among them—we have neglected to place enough attention on educational inputs such as caring and well-trained teachers, quality educational resources, and policies that promote social justice for all students from the very start of their school careers. In this study, school tracking policies were identified as one mechanism that can thwart student achievement by separating students and normalizing that separation, setting the stage for disparities in performance that both intensifies and solidifies. However, in addition to school tracking policies, there are many other parallel lines of research that also bear on the problem of racial disparities in education.

Some may misconstrue the attempt in this article as minimizing the reality or significance of a gap in test score performance between Black and White students. However, the issue of racial disparities in education is a very real and pressing concern. This research is merely pointing out that the casual use of the term "achievement gap," with no clear basis for its use, hurts more than it helps toward eliminating these disparities. This is a call for all of us to do more, for those who are already working hard to work harder, and for teachers, administrators, and policymakers to make good on a promise to educate all children. We must be mindful of the historic lessons, from the Black sharecroppers in the Jim Crow South, who gave their last nickel to build a school and not for the food, clothes, or tools that were was also desperately needed. This was done because they saw what we must see now, that the future of any society lies in ensuring all of its children receive the very best education it has to offer.

REFERENCES

achievement, (n.d.). *Dictionary.com Unabridged*. Retrieved from http://dictionary.reference.com/browse/achievement.

Akiba, M., LeTendre, G. K., & Scribner, J. P. (2007). Teacher quality, opportunity gap, and national achievement in 46 countries. *Educational Researcher*, 36, 369–387.

American Heritage College Dictionary, 3rd edition. (1993). New York: Houghton Mifflin.

Anderson, J. (1988). *The education of Blacks in the South*, 1860–1935. Chapel Hill: The University of North Carolina Press.

Anderson, J. D. (2004). The historical context for understanding the test score gap. *Journal of Public Management and Social Policy*, 10, 2–22.

Bali, V. A., & Alvarez, R. M. (2004). The race gap in student achievement scores: Longitudinal evidence from a racially diverse school district. *The Policy Studies Journal*, 32, 393–415.

Barajas, H. L., & Ronnkvist, A. (2007). Racialized space: Framing Latino and Latina experience in public schools. *Teachers College Record*, 109, 1517–1538.

Barta, J. J., & Allen, M. G. (1995). The dilemma of tracking and grouping in early childhood and middle grades: are we speaking the same language? In H. Pool & J. A. Page (Eds.), *Beyond tracking: Finding success in inclusive schools* (pp. 95–104). Bloomington, IN: Phi Delta Kappa Educational.

Bourdieu, P., & Passeron, J. C. (1990). *Reproduction in education, society and culture*. Thousand Oaks, CA: Sage.

Braddock, J. H. (1990). *Tracking: implication for student race-ethnic subgroups*. Center for Research on Effective Schooling for Disadvantaged Students Report, 1. Baltimore, MD: Johns Hopkins University. (ERIC Document Reproduction Service No. ED325600)

*Brown v. Board of Education of Topeka Kansa*s 347 U.S. 483 (1954).

Buchmann, C., & Parrado, E. A. (2006). Educational achievement of immigrant-origin and native students: A comparative analysis informed by institutional theory. *International Perspectives on Education and Society*, 7, 335–366.

Burris, C. C.. & Welner, K. G. (2005). Closing the achievement gap by detracking. *Phi Delta Kappan*, 86, 594–598.

Carter, P. (2005). Keepin' it real: School success beyond Black and White. New York: Oxford University Press.

Clotfelter, C.T. (2004). *After Brown: The rise and retreat of school desegregation*. Princeton, NJ: Princeton University Press.

Coleman, J. S, Campbell, E. Q., Hobson, C. J., McPartland, J., Mood, A. M., Weinfeld, F. D., & York, R. L. (1966). *Equality of educational opportunity [The Coleman Report]*, Washington, D.C.: U. S. Government Printing Office.

Cook, P. J., & Ludwig, J. (1998). The burden of "acting "white": Do Black adolescents disparage academic achievement? In C. Jencks & M. Phillips. (Eds.), *The Black-White test score gap* (pp. 375–400). Washington, D.C.: Brookings Institute.

Cook-Sather, A. (2002, May). Authorizing students' perspectives: Toward trust, dialogue, and change in education. *Educational Researcher*, 31, 3–14.

Dahl, K. L. (1995). Challenges in understanding the learner's perspective. *Theory into Practice*, 34, 124–130.

Daniels, B. T. (2003). *"Why are all the Black kids sitting together in the cafeteria?" And other conversations about race* (Rvd. ed.). New York: Basic.

Delpit, L. (1988). The silenced dialogue: Power and pedagogy in educating other people's children. *Harvard Educational Review*, 58, 280–298.

Dickens A. (1996). Revisiting *Brown v. Board of Education*: How tracking has resegregated America's schools. *Columbia Journal of Law and Social Problems*, 29, 469–506.

Donelan R. (1994). The promise of *Brown* and the reality of academic grouping: The tracks of my tears. *The Journal of Negro Education*, 63, 376–387.

Fielding, M. (2001). Beyond the rhetoric of student voice: New departures or new constraints in the transformation of 21st century schooling? FORUM, 43, 100–110.

Fine, M., Weis, L., & Powell, L. C. (1997). Communities of difference: A critical look at desegregated spaces created for and by youth. Harvard Educational Review, 67, 247–284.

Fryer, R. G., & Levitt, S. D. (2004). Understanding the Black-White test score gap in the first two years of school. *The Review of Economics and Statistics*, 86, 447–464.

Gamoran, A., & Mare, R. D. (1989). Secondary school tracking and educational inequity: Compensation, reinforcement, or neutrality. *The American Journal of Sociology*, 94, 1146–1183.

Gamoran, A. (1992). The variable effects of high school tracking. *American Sociological Review*, 57, 812--828.

Gay, G. (2000). *Culturally responsive teaching: Theory, research and practice*. New York: Teachers College Press.

George, P. (1993). What's the truth about tracking and ability grouping really? An explanation for teachers and parents. In J. Bellanca & E. Swartz (Eds.), *The challenge of detracking: A collection* (pp. 255–272). Palatine, IL: IRI/Skylight.

Gewirtz, G., & Cribb, A. (2003). Recent readings on social reproduction: four fundamental problematics. *International Studies in Sociology of Education*, 13, 243–260.

Giroux, H. A. (1983). Theories of reproduction and resistance in the new sociology of education: A critical analysis. *Harvard Educational Review*, 53, 257–293.

Gooden, M. A. (2005). Can NCLB really close the achievement gap? *School Business Affairs*, 71, 6–10.

Harklau, L. (1994). "Jumping tracks": How language-minority students negotiate evaluations of ability. *Anthropology and Education Quarterly*, 25, 347–363.

Hedges, L. V., & Nowell, A. (1999). Changes in the Black-White gap in achievement test scores. *Sociology of Education*, 72, 111–135.

Jencks, C., & Phillips, M. (Eds.) (1998). *The Black-White test score gap*. Washington, D.C.: Brookings Institute.

Jencks, C. (1998). Racial bias in testing. In C. Jencks & M. Phillips (Eds.), The Black-White test score gap (pp. 55–85). Washington, D.C.: Brookings Institute.

Kozol, J. (1991/ *Savage inequalities: Children in America's schools*. New York: Harper Perennial.

Kozol, J. (2005). Shame of the nation: The restoration of apartheid schooling in America. New York: Three Rivers.

Ladson-Billings, G. (2006). From the achievement gap to the education debt: Understanding achievement in U.S. schools. *Educational Researcher, 35,* 3–12.

Lewis, A. E. (2003). *Race in the schoolyard: Negotiating the color line in classrooms and communities*. New Brunswick, NJ: Rutgers University Press.

Lincoln, Y. S. (1995). In search of students' voices. *Theory Into Practice*, 34, 88–93.

Litwack, L. (1999). *Trouble in mind: Black southerners in the age of Jim Crow*. New York: Vintage.

MacLeod, J. (2004). *Ain't no makin' it: Aspirations and attainment in a low-income neighborhood*. Boulder, CO: Westview.

McCready, L. T. (2004). Understanding the marginalization of gay and gender nonconforming Black male students. *Theory Into Practice*, 43, 136–143.

McGuinn, P. J. (2003). No Child Left Behind *and the transformation of federal education policy, 1965–2005*. Lawrence: University of Kansas Press.

Medina, M. (1988). Hispanic apartheid in American public education. *Educational Administration Quarterly*, 24, 336–349.

Meier, K. J., Stewart Jr., J., & England, R. E. (1989). *Race, class, and education: The politics of second-generation discrimination*. Madison: The University of Wisconsin Press.

Mickelson, R. A. (2003). When are racial disparities in education the result of racial discrimination? A social science perspective. *Teachers College Record*, 105, 1052–1086.

Mickelson, R .A. (2005). How tracking undermines race equity in desegregated schools. In J. Petrovich & A. Wells (Eds.), *Bringing equity back: Research for a new era in American educational policy* (pp. 49–76). New York: Teachers College Press.

Mitra, D. L. (2004). The significance of students: Can increasing "student voice" in schools lead to gains in youth development? *Teachers College Record*, 106, 651–688.

Nash, R. (1990). Bourdieu on education and social and cultural reproduction. *British Journal of Sociology of Education*, 11, 431–447.

Nieto, S. (2000). *Affirming diversity: The sociopolitical context of multicultural education* (3rd ed.). New York: Addison Wesley Longman.

No Child Left Behind Act of 2001, Pub. L. No. 107–110, Stat. 1425 (2002).

Noguera, P. A., & Wing, J. Y. (2006). *Unfinished business: Closing the racial achievement gap in our schools*. San Francisco, CA: Jossey-Bass.

Noguera, P. A., Aronson, J., & Mehan, H. (2004). Closing the Black-White opportunity gap. *Contexts*, 3, 4.

Oakes, J. (1995). More than meets the eye: Links between tracking and the culture of schools. In H. Pool & J. Page (Eds.), *Beyond tracking: Finding success in inclusive schools* (pp. 59–70). Bloomington, IN: Phi Delta Kappa Educational.

Oakes, J. (2005). *Keeping track: How schools structure inequality*, Second Edition. New Haven: Yale University Press.

Oakes, J., Rogers, J., Silver, D., Horng, E., & Goode, J. (2004). Separate and unequal 50 years after Brown: California's racial "opportunity gap." Retrieved from http://www.idea.gseis. ucla.edu/publications/idea/images/brownsu2. pdf.

Orr, A. J. (2003). Black-White differences in achievement: The importance of wealth. *Sociology of Education*, 76, 281-304.

Phillips, M., Brooks-Gunn, J., Duncan, G. J., Klebanov, P., & Crane, J. (1998). Family background, parenting practices, and the Black-White test score gap. In C. Jencks & M. Phillips (Eds.), *The Black-White test score gap* (pp. 103-148). Washington, D.C.: Brookings Institute.

Plessy v. Ferguson, 163 U.S. 537 (1896).

Pool, H., & Page, J., (Eds.). (1995). *Beyond tracking: Finding success in inclusive schools*. Bloomington, IN: Phi Delta Kappa Educational.

Raymond, L. (2001). Student involvement in school improvement: From data source to significant voice. *FORUM*, 43, 58–61.

Rothstein, R. (2004). *Class and schools: Using social, economic, and educational reform to close the Black-White achievement gap*. Washington, D.C.: Economic Policy Institute.

Rubin, B. C., & Silva, E. M. (Eds.). (2003). *Critical voices in school reform: Students living through change*. New York: RoutledgeFalmer.

Slavin, R. E., & Oickle, E. (1981). Effects of cooperative learning teams on student achievement and race relations: Treatment by race interactions. *Sociology of Education*, 54, 174–180.

Steele, C., & Aronson, J. (1998). Stereotype threat and the test performance of academically successful African Americans. In C. Jencks & M. Phillips (Eds.), *The Black-White test score gap* (pp. 401–430). Washington, D.C.: Brookings Institute.

Taylor, S., & Bogdan, R. (1998). *Introduction to qualitative research methods: A guidebook and resource*. New York: John Wiley.

Thernstrom, A., & Thernstrom, S. (2003). *No excuses: Closing the racial gap in learning*. New York: Simon and Schuster.

Thompson, G. (2007). The truth about students of color and standardized tests. *Leadership*, 36, 22–38.

Torre, M. E. (2005). The alchemy of integrated spaces: Youth participation in research collectives of difference. In M. Fine& L. Weis (Eds.), *Beyond silenced voices: Class, race and gender in the United States* (pp. 251–266). Albany: SUNY Press.

Trent, W. T. (1997). Why the gap between Black and White performance in school?: A report on the effects of race on student achievement in the St. Louis public schools. *The Journal of Negro Education*, 66, 320–329.

Wasley, P. A., Hampel, R. L., & Clark, R. W. (1997). *Kids and school reform*. San Francisco: Jossey-Bass.

Yin, R. K. (2002). *Case study design: Design and methods*, (3rd ed.). Thousand Oaks, CA: Sage.

Miseducating Teachers About the Poor: A Critical Analysis of Ruby Payne's Claims About Poverty

By Randy Bomer, Joel E. Dworin, Laura May, and Peggy Semingson

Background/Context: *This is the first research study to examine the content basis of Payne's in-service teacher education program, A Framework for Understanding Poverty, though others who have reviewed the book have agreed with our analysis. The study took place within a policy context in which the federal government, with the passage of the No Child Left Behind Act (2002), created a new category of students (economically disadvantaged) whose test scores would be monitored by officials in the U.S. Department of Education. This law ensures that the improvement of poor children's test scores becomes a major concern of every public school in the country. These federal requirements have fueled the demand for professional development programs such as that offered by Ruby Payne and her Aha! Process, Inc.*

Purpose: *This article reports on an examination of the content of Ruby Payne's professional development offerings, as represented in A Framework for Understanding Poverty. Given the immense popularity of the program, an assessment of its representations of poor people is warranted and significant. We analyzed the relationship between Payne's claims and the existing research about low-income individuals and families. This study of Payne's work provides administrators and teachers with an evaluation of the reliability of Payne's claims. It also provides scholars in education, anthropology, sociology, and related fields with a description and critique of one of the more common conversations that is engaging teachers about the nature of the lives of many of their students, and the struggle to identify directions in which to improve schooling for the most vulnerable students in the education system.*

Research Design: *This is a qualitative research study whose data were derived from an analysis of A Framework for Understanding Poverty.*

Conclusions/Recommendations: *Our critical analysis of Payne's characterizations of people living in poverty indicates that her work represents a classic example of what has been identified as deficit thinking. We found that her truth claims, offered without any supporting evidence, are contradicted by anthropological, sociological and other research on poverty. We have demonstrated through our analysis that teachers may be*

Randy Bomer, Joel E. Dworin, Laura May, Peggy Semingson, "Miseducating Teachers about the Poor: A Critical Analysis of Ruby Payne's Claims about Poverty," *Teachers College Record*, vol. 110, no. 12, pp. 2497-2531. Copyright © 2008 by Teachers College Record. Reprinted with permission.

misinformed by Payne's claims. As a consequence of low teacher expectations, poor students are more likely to be in lower tracks or lower ability groups and their educational experience more often dominated by rote drill and practice.

When the U.S. Congress determined that economically disadvantaged students would be a subgroup whose test scores would contribute to a school's "adequate yearly progress" (No Child Left Behind, 2002), they made a claim about reality. They claimed that poor children are members of a legitimate category and that those children share features that are related to their experience in school. The making of the category *children of poverty* and the positioning of the people within that category as problems for the education system certainly is not new (Deschenes, Cuban, & Tyack, 2001; Katz, 1990, 1995; Patterson, 2000; Title I, Elementary and Secondary Education Act, 1965). However, the federal law makes sure that the improvement of poor childrens' test scores becomes a major focus of every school in the country.

What happens when a category of student is constructed, through language, as a uniform group in need of improvement? How can administrators and teachers cope with such a demand as that which Congress has placed on them? A category has been created, and along with it, a charge to change the members of that category. Schools look for help. Principals and superintendents ask their neighboring counterparts for advice. The easiest answer is to bring in a program, especially one that will not overly drain already depleted budgets, one that does not ask too much of already overworked teachers. An affordable program is identified, and its language begins to form ways of thinking for the teachers in their interactions with the children from the identified group. The program's language creates representations (Holquist, 1997; Mehan, 1993; Rabinow, 1986; Said, 1979), frames for thinking about "these kids." Policy occasions conceptual and linguistic representations of people, and then it moves those linguistic representations into material school buildings. What at first seems like so many words has real effects on human beings.

Federal requirements to raise the test scores of children from economically disadvantaged families have fueled the demand for professional development such as that offered by Aha! Process, Inc., and its founder, Ruby K. Payne. Payne's professional development offerings are immensely popular with school districts. In her work, Payne discusses differences among students who come from poverty, middle class, and wealthy backgrounds, and she makes recommendations about how teachers can better educate children from poverty. We have confirmed that the program is central to district professional development offerings in thirty-eight states. Suburban districts such as Orange County in California require teachers to attend the program, as do Native American tribal schools, urban districts such as Buffalo, and many rural districts. Several Canadian provinces have used Payne's work, and she has spoken a number of times in Australia. One of Payne's books, *A Framework for Understanding Poverty* (2005), was recently number 360 on Amazon's sales rankings (an unusually high rank for a book about education; Amazon.com, September 14, 2005), and the book cover states that the volume has sold more than 800,000 copies. It has been translated into Spanish as *Un Marco Para Entender La Pobreza*. Because many educators who work with vulnerable populations are exposed to Payne's writings in two-day workshops based upon the book, an assessment of the quality of her claims is of educational and ethical significance. This article reports a systematic examination of the content of Ruby Payne's professional development offerings, as represented in *A Framework for Understanding Poverty*. Ours is the first study to examine the content basis of Payne's in-service teacher education program, though others who have reviewed the book have been in accord with our analysis (see Gorski, 2006; Ng & Rury, 2006; Osei-Kofi, 2005) in viewing Payne's work as unsubstantiated and built upon a deficit perspective. Payne's text paints a portrait of economically disadvantaged people, a portrait many teachers are using to inform their relationships to students. We wanted to analyze whether this representation was accurate, fair, and likely to have advantageous consequences for students. We systematically analyzed the relationship between Payne's claims and some of the existing research about individuals, families, and communities that could be described as "in poverty." This analysis provides district and school administrators and teachers with an evaluation of the reliability of Payne's claims and the beginnings of an alternative perspective from which to consider the lives of students from poor families. At the same time, it provides scholars in education, anthropology, sociology, and related fields a description and critique of one of the more common conversations engaging teachers about the nature of the lives of many of their students and the struggle to identify directions in which to improve schooling for the most vulnerable students in the education system.

When we first became acquainted with Payne's work, it seemed to us that her "framework" included negative stereotypes that drew from a longstanding U.S. tradition of viewing the poor from a deficit perspective. If that is the case, many schools and teachers may be reinforcing ways of thinking and talking about children in poverty that are false, prejudiced, or at the very least, limited. In her book, Payne refers to her claims as "data" (1; page references to *Framework* are in parentheses), although she has conducted no actual research. She cites few sources, and when she does cite, the source is often not a research study or does not say what she says it does. We have a broad view of research and acknowledge many valid ways of knowing that are not research. But claims to have data and research to support generalizations about a population should be possible to confirm. Schools are, after all, academic communities, and one should apply at least minimal standards of academic convention to information and perspective exchanged among education professionals. Furthermore, Payne does not write as a practitioner, embedding her claims in narratives of her own practice. She writes in generalities, as if her claims were founded upon research data.

In an era in which there are calls for teaching to be scientifically-based or evidence-based, we wish to make a distinction. We are not persuaded that research can prove a particular instructional intervention or system to be best for all populations in all situations, and so we do not intend to subject the instructional strategies Payne recommends to that kind of scrutiny. However, educators should have accurate, evidence-based pictures of what their students' lives are like, what competencies and understandings they might bring to school if school were ready to receive them, and what social and cultural contexts have a bearing upon the interactions that occur in classrooms. Since much of Payne's book is concerned with just such questions, it is appropriate to apply rigorous standards of research and evidence. Attempts to describe reality, especially the reality of the lives of a vulnerable population such as poor children, should be based on careful study and accurate evidence, and they should take into account the perspectives of the people of whom they speak. Our research questions, therefore, were these: What patterns are detectable in Ruby Payne's truth claims about children's lives in poverty? To what extent are those truth claims supported by existing research?

METHODS OF INVESTIGATION

Teachers who had been through the Ruby Payne workshops at their schools, including two of the authors, confirmed that *A Framework for Understanding Poverty* provided the central content of the professional development program, so we determined that we would take that book as our data corpus. We did not simply read and review the book, however, because we wanted to examine the text's claims more closely and systematically. We treated the book as qualitative data, moving through it sentence by sentence in order to extract propositional content from individual truth claims.

We limited our attention to language that made specific claims about reality, ignoring speculative comments such as those about things "schools can do." Many sentences contained a single truth claim, such as "Often the attitude in generational poverty is that society owes one a living" (47). Other sentences contained multiple truth claims, such as "The use of formal register, on the other hand, allows one to score well on tests and do well in school and higher education" (28). We recorded three truth claims from that sentence, that "The use of formal register allows one to score well on tests;" "The use of formal register allows one to do well in school;" and "The use of formal register allows one to do well in higher education." In order to construct explicit truth claims in many cases, we had to rely on text cohesion to put pronouns with antecedents and otherwise reassemble meanings that had been distributed among sentences.

Many times, truth claims were not directly stated in the text, and they had to be inferred. For example, Payne has a quiz in the book, called "Could you survive in poverty?" which consists of a checklist whereby the reader can self-assess whether they have knowledge and characteristics Payne deems necessary for survival in poverty. One item on this list, for example, is "I know which grocery stores' garbage bins can be accessed for thrown-away food." We recorded this as a truth claim that, "In order to survive in poverty, one must know which grocery stores' garbage bins can be accessed for thrown-away food" (38). In our judgment, the language here was categorical enough to warrant being identified as a truth claim. There were borderline cases where we did not take the language as containing propositional content. For example, Payne provides nine fictional scenarios or case studies. Though these are clearly intended to be taken as paradigmatic cases of people living in poverty, we did not interpret truth claims from them, because interpreting narratives would have involved a different analytic method than the one we used in the rest of the book. We also did not take as truth claims Payne's accounts of others' theoretical frameworks that did not relate to poverty or social class.

In all, we extracted 607 truth claims, which we entered into a database program called Tinderbox (Eastgate Systems, 2005). We chose this program because it allowed flexibility in coding and grouping the data and permitted us to view our data as an outline, a map, a tree diagram, or as a hierarchy. Such multi-modal flexibility facilitated category development. We coded each truth claim, remaining for

Table 1.

Super-ordinate category	Category	Code	Truth claims: $n =$
Immediate environment of poor children	Families	Communication	6
		Divorce	2
		Family	21
		Home	38
		Men	30
		Mothers	5
		Parent income	3
		Parents	6
		Punishment	14
		Women	5
	Resources	Relationships	106
		Resources	70
		Support structure	20
	Material Dailiness	Entertainment	9
		Disorganization	21
		Health	14
		Materials	12
		Money	31
		Noise	3
		Property	7
		Trade	21
		Transportation	2
		Work	21

first-level codes as close as possible to the language of the book. We almost always assigned more than one code to a truth claim and sometimes assigned as many as seven, with the rule being that we should tag as much of its propositional content as possible. As our list of codes grew, we employed established codes as often as possible. By the time we finished coding all the data, we had identified 102 codes. We collapsed these codes into fifteen categories, and then further collapsed them to four super-ordinate categories: *social structures, daily life, language,* and *characteristics of individuals.* These categories serve to structure our findings. Table 1 illustrates how one of the super-ordinate categories can be broken down. In the pages to follow, we outline key claims in each of the above four major categories, comparing Payne's claims to existing research evidence as we go. After that, we provide a discussion of our findings across the categories and the significance of those findings.

SOCIAL STRUCTURES

To write about large sociological concepts such as social class and poverty, one must develop definitions of some notoriously difficult terms. In this section, we analyze Payne's conceptions of class and poverty, as well as her treatment of race and gender and her crucial construct of "hidden rules" that define class membership. Categories for this section were "class," which included seven codes drawn from 389 truth claims, and "larger social structures," which contained seven codes and 53 truth claims. By "larger social structures," we refer to social realities beyond the everyday, material circumstances we deal with in another section, and in this category, we included codes for social categories such as race as well as bureaucratic/governmental categories such as immigration.

Class

Payne asserts that there are three socioeconomic classes: the poor, the middle class, and the wealthy (3, 42–43). She does not elaborate further on this thinking, nor does she offer an explanation of how these three classes relate to one another or how each of the classes may encompass varying types of socioeconomic status. In Payne's world, most people are middle class, the poor make up about 12% of the population, and a smaller percentage (she estimates about 6%) are wealthy (2). Contrary to Payne's neat division, many scholars who have done work in social class have discussed multiple classes and substrata within those as comprising the class structure in the U.S. (Bendix & Lipset, 1966; Brantlinger, 2003; Compton, 1998; Foley, 1997; Giddens, 1973; Gilbert, 2003; Grusky, 2001). For example, sociologist Dennis Gilbert provides a class analysis of the U.S. in which approximately 12% are "underclass," 13% are working poor, 30% of the population is categorized as working class, another 30% are middle class, 14% are in the upper middle class, and 1% are considered capitalist class. Significantly, Payne's claim that there are three classes does not account for about 40% of the U.S. population, those traditionally viewed as working class (Gilbert, 2003). We do not know of a single sociologist who claims that there are exactly three classes in the U.S.A (Bendix & Lipset, 1966; Brantlinger, 2003; Compton, 1998; Foley, 1997; Giddens, 1973; Gilbert, 2003; Grusky, 2001).

Poverty

Payne categorizes people as being in poverty regardless of whether their incomes are below the poverty line; rather, Payne suggests that the "poverty" category applies to anyone who carries the "mindset" of the "poverty culture" (61). Payne states that, while the income of an individual may increase, "patterns of thought, social interaction, cognitive strategies, etc., remain" (3). Students from households with incomes above the poverty line still may exhibit behaviors, attitudes, and beliefs that Payne claims are associated with those from poverty. Payne argues that, though financial resources are important, they do not "explain the differences in the success with which "individuals leave poverty nor the reasons that many stay in poverty," (8) and that "the ability to leave poverty is more dependent upon other re-sources" (8) than financial ones (see Resources, below). However, the word "poverty" is not a metaphor here, and by definition, it means lack of money. It is a material condition, not an ethical or behavioral one, but Payne's claims obscure this self-evident fact. This is important to note because contrary to Payne's assertions, one "leaves poverty" when one has obtained sufficient financial resources. As we shall see, defining poverty to mean something other than material disadvantage is the crux of Payne's case.

Culture of Poverty

Payne describes the poor as a homogenous group, with the same ways of using language, interacting with others, and employing strategies to survive in the "culture of poverty" (27-28, 38, 41-42, 44-45, 51, 54–59). This notion of a culture of poverty permits Payne to view the poor as belonging to a single category. The quoted source for Payne's use of "culture of poverty" is an excerpt from Oscar Lewis's 1961 book *The Children of Sanchez*, an ethnography of a poor neighborhood in Mexico City. The concept of *the culture of poverty*, in brief, is that poor people, regardless of their race, ethnicity, or geographical location, all live within a definable culture. This culture includes a self-perpetuating dynamic in which a poor individual re-creates his/her social position as a member of a family so that subsequent generations remain "in poverty." The concept was controversial almost as soon as Lewis introduced it. Many proponents of a deficit perspective historically based on heredity shifted from a genetic pathology explanation and appropriated Lewis's theory to explain the persistence of poverty (Foley, 1997). Many other anthropologists and sociologists were very critical of the concept (Ginsburg, 1972; Keddie, 1973; Leacock, 1971; Liebow, 1967/2003), either on ethical grounds, that it blamed victims of structural inequality, or on scientific grounds, that there were problems either with the data or its interpretation. This and similar concepts of the time were critiqued as well by educators, such as Yetta Goodman (1969/1996). In actual fact, much of Oscar Lewis's work was a Marxist analysis of economic power relations and a call for solidarity and collective action among the poor, but Payne seems unaware of those elements of Lewis's work and only takes up the concept of *culture of poverty*.

Payne's appropriation of the *culture of poverty* (58, 77) allows her to portray the poor as belonging to a single group with specific negative traits. These traits are not neutral and lead Payne to advocate the remediation of the poor. Describing the notion of a culture of poverty, Foley writes:

> Lewis's list of 'cultural traits' of the poor evokes a powerful negative image of poor people as a lazy, fatalistic, hedonistic, violent, distrustful, people living in common law unions, as well as in dysfunctional, female-centered, authoritarian families who are chronically unemployed and rarely participate in local civic activities, vote, or trust the police and political leaders. … For anyone wanting to indict the poor, the culture of poverty theory is a powerful metaphor that spawns a sweeping, holistic image. It provides public policy makers and the general public with a relatively nontechnical, yet 'scientific' way to categorize and characterize all poor people. (1997)

Although Foley is describing Lewis's earlier theory, his words well describe Payne's work, as we shall see in the rest of our analysis. Payne introduces her "culture of poverty" concept through a quote from Lewis, and the characteristics she lists for economically disadvantaged family are identical to those that Foley lists here, as we demonstrate in what follows.

Race, Ethnicity, and Gender

Payne's explicit truth claims do not address or discuss the relationship of poverty to race, ethnicity, and gender. However, in the fictional case studies (which we did not include in our analysis, because they were not truth claims) and in the examples she chooses to place in lists (such as green cards and deportation), Payne enlists the reader's own associations about these social categories. Obviously, casting people of color in six out of the nine "case studies" racializes the representation of poverty, but in the vast majority of the truth claims, she does not address race or ethnicity at all. Racializing the representations of poverty means that Payne is portraying poor people as people of color, rather than acknowledging the fact that most poor people in the U.S. are white (Roberts, 2004). By doing so, Payne is perpetuating negative stereotypes by equating poverty with people of color. Although there is a correlation between race and class, this does not justify her use of racialized "case studies."

Payne's audience of teachers is primarily white, female, and middle class, so their probable shared perspective makes it likely that such signals will be understood as racial. Given that the truth claims do not explicitly address the relationships between poverty, race, ethnicity, and gender, we are merely pointing out the absence of such considerations from Payne's work. They are significant in our data by virtue of their absence, though our fidelity to the data does not permit us to discuss them at length. However, many scholars have shown that race and class are inextricably bound together in U.S. education (Anyon, 2005; Lareau, 2003; McCarthy, 1990; McCarthy & Apple, 1988; Weis, 1988; Weis & Fine, 1993) and that an understanding of gender is crucial to an analysis of families in conditions of poverty (Hays, 2004; Johnson, 2002).

Hidden Rules

According to Payne, people in poverty are mostly identifiable by their adherence to the "hidden rules of poverty" (9, 38, 41, 42, 44). Payne defines hidden rules as "the unspoken cues and habits of a group. Distinct cueing systems exist between and among groups and economic classes."(37). She provides examples of three hidden rules in poverty, informing us that: "The noise level is high (the TV is always on and everyone may talk at once), the most important information is non-verbal, and one of the main values of an individual to the group is an ability to entertain" (9). Payne offers no citations for any statements about hidden rules. She does not inform the reader how these hidden rules came to be revealed to her, nor does she explain the means by which they are supposed to be hidden, or from whom. This "hidden rules" approach is central to Payne's perspective and an area in which she claims special expertise. However, Payne has not conducted any research regarding hidden rules nor does she offer any evidence to support them.

Payne contrasts hidden rules amongst people living in poverty and those living in the middle class. According to Payne, poor people view money as something to be spent, while to people in the middle class, money is something to be managed. For the poor, "{m}oney is seen as an expression of personality and is used for entertainment and relationships. The notion of using money for security is truly grounded in the middle and wealthy classes" (44). Personality for the poor is "for entertainment" (42) and a "sense of humor is highly valued," (42) while for those in the middle class, personality "is for acquisition and stability" (43) and "achievement is highly valued" (43). Views of time are also quite different, where, Payne tells us, those in poverty view the "present most important" (sic) (42) and "decisions are made for moment based on feelings or survival" (sic) (42), while for the middle class, "future most important" (sic) (43) and "decisions made against future ramifications" (sic) (43). Education is "valued and revered as abstract but not as reality" (42) by the poor, while for those in the middle class, it is "crucial for climbing success ladder and making money" (sic) (43). Payne claims that one of the biggest differences among the classes is how the world is viewed. "Middle class tends to see the world in terms of a national picture, while poverty sees the world in its immediate locale" (44). As far as we can tell, these descriptions of the attitudes of both the poor and the middle class are completely baseless. We trust that we may be excused from providing evidence that many middle class people enjoy entertainment and have a sense of humor, or that many people who live in serious financial insecurity think often about their futures.

Payne's purpose in leading teachers to an understanding of hidden rules is so that the rules of the middle class can be taught explicitly to students, (45). The teaching of middle-class norms is necessary, according to Payne, because these rules are important in schools and businesses (3). Payne offers another possible explanation of hidden rules' importance when she writes, "An understanding of the culture and values of poverty will lessen the anger and frustration that educators may periodically feel when dealing with these students and parents " (45). Payne seems to be saying that once teachers and other educators comprehend the ways of the poor by knowing their hidden rules, they will feel less frustrated with them because it is in their essential nature to have values and behavior different from those in the middle class. It is through her conception of *hidden rules* that Payne places the onus on the children and their families, characterizing them as deficient. Though she uses the term "culture," our examination of her truth claims reveals that, in every instance, she pathologizes the "culture" or "rules" of the poor and valorizes the "culture" or "rules" of the middle class. She never considers the alternative, that social, economic and political structures—not their own behaviors and attitudes—have provided barriers to success in schools for poor children. As Tozer (2000) has written:

> The knowledge, language, and practices of one class are dominant and valued; those of the other classes are subordinate and devalued. Instead of a cultural deficit explanation for persistent school failure of low SES children, we can see the possibility of a cultural subordination explanation that is grounded in relations of domination and subordination in the economic and political order of society (p. 157).

Payne does not examine the ways in which schools and society have been structured in the interests of dominant classes. Those who may not fit neatly into the dominant groups' ways of being are defective, lacking in ability, and in need of being re-made so as to better resemble those from the dominant classes.

It is because of this deprecation of every characteristic she falsely and without basis attributes to the poor that we claim Payne's book represents a "deficit perspective." Individuals who subscribe to deficit perspectives do not actually use the term to describe their views. It is an analytic category that can be applied when certain conditions are met, and we think that Payne meets those conditions. Our critique of Payne's deficit perspectives is also supported by others who have written about her work (see Gorski, 2006; Ng & Rury, 2006; Osei-Kofi, 2005).

THE IMMEDIATE ENVIRONMENT OF POOR CHILDREN

Throughout much of *A Framework for Understanding Poverty*, we found assertions about the immediate, everyday environment of individuals and families in poverty. Though Payne is never completely explicit about why she believes teachers need to learn the things she tells them about poor people's ordinary lives, there are many suggestions that, because the lives of the poor are so different from those of teachers, teachers will be at a loss to communicate effectively with their students or parents of their students without explicit descriptions of students' and parents' everyday experiences. They will fail to classify many observable student behaviors as arising from their participation in a *culture of poverty*. Such a failure to classify would, presumably, result in corrections of behaviors such as loudness or lateness in terms that do not explicitly invoke the difference between the student's culture of origin (poverty) and that of the middle class, or school. Teachers are called upon, then, to narrativize and envision the lives of poor children in the way that Payne suggests, so that they can have certain kinds of ideas about those children and use particular language in speaking to them and their parents. The message to teachers is that the daily lives of students from poor families are different, almost exotic, compared to the teacher's own and require explanation from an expert. An objectifying distance is necessary in order to interpret and respond to the behavior of these Others. Within the broad category of "immediate environment," we included Payne's claims about material dailiness, resources, and families, as illustrated in Table 1 and discussed in the next section.

Material Dailiness

In order to impress upon teachers the degree to which life in poverty is alien to those in the middle class, Payne asserts dozens of truth claims regarding the material, daily conditions of poor people's existence. Two of the more well-known elements of the book are a "quiz" designed for teachers to self-assess whether or not they could "survive in poverty" (38) and a separate "IQ Test" designed to measure the "acquired information" of people in poverty (87). Through the questions she places on these tests, Payne asserts that poor people, more than those in middle class, know the following: how to get guns, how to get someone out of jail, and how to function at laundromats. She asserts that the poor get food from grocery store garbage bins, move often, have common law marriages, use "gray tape," and get green cards more than those from the middle class. According to Payne, the poor are more likely to know certain words, such as *roach, dissed,* and *deportation.* Her point is that the poor know these things because the material world is vastly different for people in poverty than it is for people in the middle class. Because so many of Payne's truth claims about the details of material dailiness are fabrications, it is difficult to test them against other sources of evidence. That is, her claims are not based on research, she does not offer any evidence for them, they are not accurate, and it appears that she made them up. We cannot show evidence that middle (and upper) class people know what a roach is, but we are confident that they do. If Payne means duct tape when she says "gray tape," the presence of ample inventory in middle-class home improvement stores would seem to suggest that the poor are not the only people acquainted with it. While it is true that approximately 11% of the U.S. population suffers food insecurity and go hungry at times (Nord, M., Andrews, M., Carlson, S., 2006), we find no evidence that families or individuals living below the poverty line acquire food from grocery store dumpsters. It is difficult to check and Payne provides no support for this claim. It is easy to determine that the poor do not know more about getting guns than do those in the middle class, since most guns are owned by people with college educations (Glaeser & Glendon, 1998; National Institute of Justice, 1997). There is no evidence, therefore, that the poor know better how to get them. The poor do indeed move often, though we could find no statistics comparing the frequency of moves to the middle class. They probably do move for different reasons than do those in the middle class, but because the category "poverty" includes everything from the homeless to the working class, it is not valid to generalize in this way. Seventy-eight percent of children of immigrants live above the poverty line, so the notion that deportation and green cards would be more familiar to individuals in poverty is incorrect (Capps, Fix, & Reardon-Anderson, 2003). The poor use laundromats, as do people who live in apartments, people who are traveling, those who live in urban areas and have little space for machinery, college students, other young people, and people who move frequently. Since only a few states recognize any form of "common-law marriage," knowledge about that topic is more likely to be distributed geographically than by social class. In sum, Payne's truth claims about the everyday lives of people living in poverty cannot be validated by consulting existing research, and she does not provide any evidentiary support for these claims. Later in the article, we present research findings that offer more promising informa-tion for educators.

Many of Payne's representations of the daily lives of the poor emphasize depravity, perversity, or criminality. For example, Payne provides us with three reasons why jail is part of life for many people living in poverty. First, if one is in generational poverty, there is a distrust of, and even distaste for "organized society," so crossing the line into illegal activity is something the poor often do. Second, a lack of resources means that poor individuals spend time in jail because they do not have the resources to avoid it. And finally, the poor "simply see jail as a part of life and not necessarily always bad {because} local jails provide food and shelter and as a general rule, are not as violent or dangerous as state incarceration" (22–23). So Payne believes that the poor do not really mind arrest or incarceration in local jails and simply view it as a part of their lives. Payne does not discuss the fact that many poor youth and adults, especially African-Americans, are given prison sentences for non-violent crimes, not simply time in local jails (Western, 2004). Nor does she consider the fact that, once someone has been incarcerated, it is probable that s/he will be poor for the rest of her/his life (Western, 2002). According to Payne, "Fighting and physical violence are a part of poverty" and "People living in poverty need to be able to defend themselves physically or they need someone to be their protector" (23–24). Payne repeatedly selects elements of daily life that represent the lives of the poor as characterized by violence, depravity, and criminality. Payne's selective representations are negative stereotypes that essentialize poor people as immoral, violent, and socially deficient. These representations do not account for the majority of low-income people, who work hard, obey the law, and do not exhibit the behaviors and attitudes that Payne has described.

Resources

Payne employs the concept of "resources" to label diverse ways in which an individual, family, or community can be endowed or deprived. In fact, she defines poverty as "'the extent to which an individual does without resources'" (7). She identifies eight categories of resources: financial resources, emotional resources, mental resources, spiritual resources, physical resources, support systems, relationships/role models, and knowledge of hidden rules (7). The function of Payne's descriptions is to permit educators to believe that they have some influence on their students' future poverty status. Individuals will be able to overcome their economic status if they learn to overcome a scarcity of resources, such as emotional stability and the right kind of friendships and acquaintances. On the other hand, failure to develop these other resources, Payne asserts (22), is likely to land one in jail, because one is not acquainted with the appropriate limits to behavior. Resources are understood as being available to the individual, if the individual chooses to avail herself of them by drawing from her immediate environment. As Payne wrote, "[T]he resources that individuals have may vary significantly from situation to situation. Poverty is more about resources than it is about money." (25). Payne's conceptualization of resources thus permits her to move poverty out of a material realm and into a behavioral one.

Poor Families

Payne goes to great lengths to represent the nature of poor families. Her defining class concept of generational poverty is rooted in families, since generations are familial by definition. Poverty is handed from parents to children through a kind of cultural heritability that is the responsibility of the school to break. In Payne's view of poor families, people see themselves as holding one another as property, and she states repeatedly that people are owned, or that when one is in poverty, people are one's only possessions (23, 42, 51–52, 59). She describes a family structure unique to poverty, wherein "the mother is always at the center, though she may have multiple sexual relationships," (54). Although Payne does not actually cite Moynihan (1965), her depictions are very similar to his famous report, which has been critiqued by many (Biddle, 2001; Leacock, 1971; Ryan, 1971).

Payne employs diagrams to differentiate the stable, orderly, patrilineal progression of middle-class families, contrasted to a sprawling, web-like structure (including mention of a same-sex lover) extending from a large circle labeled Jolyn," a matriarch in poverty (55). Payne claims that, when men leave their wives in such a structure, as they frequently do, they always stay with mothers or girlfriends, because men are not stable or central in the family (56). People are often in multiple relationships, and the home is full of comings and goings. If disorder characterizes the family structure, it is also present in the home environment, which Payne portrays as disorganized, noisy, violent, and nonverbal. These sorts of generalizations about homes and families of the poor have been long complicated by research that presents a more thorough, empirically based representation of poor households. (Compton-Lilly, 2003; Lareau & Horvat, 1999; Leichter, 1978; Moll, Amanti, Neff, & Gonzalez, 1992; Skilton-Sylvester, 2002; Taylor & Dorsey-Gaines, 1988; Varenne & McDermott, 1986).

In contrast to Ruby Payne's attempt to generalize a single exotic model of a family in poverty on the basis of no research data, Taylor and Dorsey-Gaines (1988) conducted extensive ethnographies of poor, urban families. They found more differences among the families than similarities, and discovered that generalizations were actually very difficult to make, since people, even when they are poor, are different from one another. But they did identify certain similarities: a belief in their own abilities; the determination to raise healthy children; the provision of loving environments; caring for children with tenderness and affection; structured home environments; a concern for children's safety and well-being; and a valuing of children's independence and competence (194). Other studies have reported similar findings, that low-income families are attentive to their children's success in school and provide them with a home environment supportive of learning as well as materials for intellectual growth and schoolwork (Compton-Lilly, 2003; Lareau & Horvat, 1999; Leichter, 1978; Moll, Amanti, Neff, & Gonzalez, 1992; Skilton-Sylvester, 2002; Varenne & McDermott, 1986), but Payne does not consider these sources. If there is evidence to support Payne's claims about the daily lives of economically disadvantaged children, she does not tell us what that evidence might be. We suspect none exists, because we find ample evidence that contradicts her claims.

THE LANGUAGE OF POOR CHILDREN

Payne gives considerable attention to the language of the children of poverty. Language in poverty, according to her analysis, has the following characteristics: a limited vocabulary and reliance on nonverbal signs; circumlocution and indirection; more audience involvement; and a casual register that is not valued in school or work (28–31). These categories fall under the super-ordinate category of "language," and we coded 200 truth claims in these categories. These claims, all of which Payne names as maladies school must help students overcome, constitute deficits. Nonverbal cues are taken as replacing language and limiting the explicitness of disadvantaged people's speech, and "to be asked to communicate in writing without the non-verbal assists is an overwhelming and formidable task, which most of them try to avoid" (28). Casual register is understood as a limitation, something that keeps "poverty" students from appropriating school language, because formal register is "a hidden rule of the middle class" (28) and "to get a well-paying job, it is expected that one will be able to use formal register" (28). Circumlocution she views as a failure to get to the point, and states that "educators become frustrated with the tendency of these students to meander almost endlessly through a topic" (28). Audience involvement is interruptive of a continuous narrative stream and also, according to Payne, causes students to make mistakes in school-like turn taking and results in a failure to develop logical thinking (34). Stating "there is such a direct link between achievement and language" (34) Payne argues that the speech of the poor has stable, identifiable characteristics that present problems for teachers, and that speech prevents them from leaving poverty or experiencing success in school or work.

Payne does not consider the fact that differences in language or culture might be more significant to linguistic variation than socioeconomic status. She does not stipulate that she is talking only about native speakers of English, so we must assume that she means these linguistic descriptions to apply equally to students whose first language is Spanish, African-American English, Navajo, Arabic, Hawaiian, Chinese, Appalachian English, Haitian Creole, Yupik, among others—the kaleidoscope of languages teachers encounter, though, in the U.S., all these groups are disproportionately likely to live in poverty. Keeping such wide variation in language in mind, it is difficult to make sense of a claim like: "For students who have no access to formal register, educators become frustrated with the tendency of these students to meander almost endlessly through a topic" (28). In her claims, she appears to mix things some linguists have said about African-Americans, a misunderstanding of one article contrasting Mexican nationals and U.S. students, some class-based deficit theory from England, with a radically simplified account of registers. She argues, working from this mixture of disparate sources, that it is poverty that creates the speech styles of African-Americans, Mexican-Americans, and many other groups that are disproportionately poor in the U.S. (27–35). This conclusion is out of sync with linguistic and educational research on these groups, which finds, among other things, that language patterns are rooted in traditions of people's origins and in continuous innovations through which group members signal their affiliation with one another (for example, Nieto, 1999; Smitherman, 1977).

Restricted Language

Payne does not explain how the language of people in poverty is both restricted by limited vocabulary and "nonverbal assists," (28) and is also characterized by circumlocution, taking the longest route to get to the point. In other words, the speech of disadvantaged students is both terse and verbose. If Payne means that individuals employ both speech styles, depending upon the sociolinguistic context, she does not say so, and nothing in her characterization of the language of the poor suggests that kind of sophisticated flexibility. Both verbosity and lack of language are described as faults in the speech of students and their families.

As to the first part of the claim, the notion that economic poverty corresponds to a kind of linguistic poverty, a language with fewer words, was common in the twentieth century, and has been researched extensively. Payne has conducted no research herself and cites none with respect to this claim. By and large, linguists have rejected the notion that any group can be thought of as having an impoverished language. The notion is sociolinguistically meaningless, since every group uses language that is adequate to its social needs. Most linguistic researchers critiqued the methods by which language samples were collected from poor individuals, because subjects, usually children, were asked to produce language in unfamiliar and threatening speech situations. Labov found that changing the situation in which the language was elicited—by bringing in another child, sitting on the floor, supplying potato chips, or introducing taboo words—altered the appearance of competence in the performance. He wrote, "the social situation is the most powerful determinant of verbal behavior and … an adult must enter into the right social relation with a child if he wants to find out what a child can do: this is just what many teachers cannot do" (1972, 191). Furthermore, none of the studies on which the linguistic deficit theory was based found that individuals in poverty never produced complex or elaborated syntax or vocabulary; only that they did so less often than middle-class counterparts. Therefore, the issue was not one of competence, but performance; it was something in the speech situation that kept subjects from producing the expected language sample more often. Several linguists (Dittmar, 1976; A. D. Edwards, 1976; J. R. Edwards, 1979; Trudgill, 1974) have examined the claims and counter-claims regarding the restricted language of children from economically disadvantaged backgrounds, and the consensus is that perceived linguistic deficits are invariably due to differences in interpreting aspects of the context. The poor do not have less language than the middle class or wealthy.

Circumlocution and Indirection

In describing what she calls "discourse patterns," (30) Payne asserts that parents and children from poverty "need to beat around the bush" (30) before getting to the point. This circumlocution, she claims, results in miscommunication between teachers committed to getting to the point and parents more used to circumlocution. It is also an impediment to the literacy development of students, because, she says, school writing values getting to the point, whereas children from poverty "circle the mulberry bush" (30). It is true that Smitherman demonstrated that circumlocution and indirection are characteristics of African-American language (Smitherman, 1977), but that is because they are characteristics of African language, not a function of poverty. Michaels (1981) likewise found that some African-American students may have a different understanding of what it means to stay on a topic than do their white teachers, but in Michaels' writing, the failure is not in the student, but in the teacher's lack of recognition of the legitimacy of the student's speech norms. Labov, contrary to Payne's assertion, found that a black young person living in poverty had a much more direct style, with fewer hedges and less circumlocution than a middle-class African-American (1972). Labov's findings indicate that, in fact, lower social class might account for directness, rather than indirectness. There is, in other words, no research-based reason to state that people in poverty, as a class, talk around the topic more than do people in the middle class.

Audience Involvement

Payne also describes the oral storytelling of people in poverty as composed of disorganized episodes with audience participation interspersed (31). High audience involvement, with overlaps, interjections, and interruptions, is a conversational style that characterizes many cultures and subcultures (Tannen, 1981, 1985). The performative dimension of speech, wherein a storyteller is concerned more with the interaction with people in the room than with the clarity of verbal message is often associated with African-American speech styles (Dyson, 1993; Gee, 1990; Grace, 2004; Michaels, 1981; Smitherman, 1977). However, a sense of craft in storytelling is connected to findings that demonstrate the rich potential for meaning and verbal art of various groups, irrespective of economic status (Bauman, 1986). There is no evidence that social class or poverty/wealth distinctions are formative in such oral genres or styles, nor is there evidence that different linguistic and cultural groups that share conditions of poverty have any family resemblance simply as a result of their poverty.

Register

Payne places particular emphasis on the distinction between casual and formal register (27–35). She cites Joos (1962) as her source and outlines his continuum of five different registers, using only two of these—formal and informal—and drawing a sharp line between the two. Joos's book is not based upon empirical research; rather it is simply an assertion that there are degrees of formality in human interaction. Joos does not claim that the formal register is the language of school and work, as Payne does; in fact, his description of what he calls consultative register is much nearer to school discourse, and work language takes many different registers, depending upon the relationships among interlocutors (Joos, 1962). Payne's explicit claim is that there exist two distinct varieties of English—one formal and one informal. She states that "[poor] students cannot use formal register" (28), and she represents poor students as trapped within a barely-verbal casual register. Her approach to the continuum is so binary that it is nearly a claim that English is composed of a diglossia (Ferguson, 1972, 1991)—two separate languages, one formal and one informal. Though there are languages that have such a diglossia, English does not. Some scholars have considered the possibility that African-Americans participate in a diglossic language system between AAE and classroom English, but most have rejected that possibility because the two are not sufficiently distinct when compared with the diglossias of cultures where the language for royalty, for instance, has a completely separate lexicon and grammar. Payne's contention that there are two registers and that their use is bound to social class is not supported by any linguistic or sociolinguistic research we can identify. Everyone uses varied registers in appropriate social situations, and the variation among language groups that might live in poverty is much greater than the similarities.

As her source for her claims about the registers employed by people in poverty, Payne cites a study by Montano-Harmon (Montano-Harmon, 1991) as the basis for the statement that "… the majority … of minority students and poor students do not have access to formal register at home. As a matter of fact, these students cannot use formal register" (28). In fact, Montano-Harmon's study does not investigate poverty effects. The students she studied were "working class," from four linguistic groups: Mexican national speakers of Spanish; ESL students in the U.S., immigrants from Mexico who were native speakers of Spanish; Anglo students in the U.S. who were native speakers of English; and Mexican-American/Chicano students who were native speakers of English. The study investigates contrasting text features (rhetorical strategies) in the writing of ninth-grade students in Mexican schools compared with students in U.S. schools, and considers no data related to speech. Register is not an analytic category in the study at all, and neither is poverty. Montano-Harmon does mention in passing that Chicano students who spoke English and not Spanish had more trouble in school, for reasons of a mismatch between the form of English they usually speak and the form usually valued by the school, but the Chicano students were not poorer than the other students studied. In fact, this study, the only one Payne cites, contradicts her assertion that students in poverty have particular language features in common, and especially that they have a particular register in which they are trapped.

If it matters at all that teachers understand the language patterns that their students bring to school, then surely they should understand them accurately. Payne's poorly delineated summary of language patterns is worse than no help at all, since it prepares teachers to blur distinctions among groups whose language is completely different and who need different forms of support from their teachers. Moreover, by characterizing students' language as deficient and prescribing an approach of "direct teaching" of supposedly middle-class language patterns, Payne positions teachers to look for errors and to correct them. Such a disposition runs counter to the findings and recommendations of many researchers on language development, such as Halliday (1975), Lindfors (1980), Rice (1996), and Nelson (1996), all of whom emphasize that language is learned through meaning, shared attention, and through building on the competence of the learner, rather than aiming for the remediation of deficiencies.

INDIVIDUALS IN POVERTY

The fourth super-ordinate category into which we grouped Payne's truth claims concerns individuals living in poverty. Truth claims in this group dealt with characteristics of individual persons' characters, minds, attitudes, and behaviors. Payne's overall perspective is individualistic, focusing on individuals' choices and habits as defining their identities as poor people as well as the cause of their material poverty. She does not entertain alternative views (see Biddle, 2001) that low-income students' problems in education are attributable to material disadvantages, to discrimination within the education system, to inadequate funding of poor schools, and to careful resource management by the rich and powerful that favors children from their own class backgrounds. We focus here on what Payne does claim in her book and the basis for her claims. We organize our discussion under the categories of cognition (10 codes from 176 truth claims), worldview (27 codes, 302 truth claims), and men and women (four codes, 51 truth claims).

Cognition

Payne claims that, because of various deficiencies, students from low-income households lack cognitive strategies (90). Drawing from Feuerstein (1980), she asserts that poor students have blurred and sweeping perceptions related to the randomly episodic structure in their storytelling; that they see only half of what is on a page; that they have impaired spatial and temporal orientation; that they do not have concepts or vocabulary for directions, location, object size, or object shape, nor can they keep the memory of an object constant; and that they cannot hold two objects or sources in mind to compare them (92–93). The assertions range from perceptual problems to deficiencies in judgment. Here we will provide just one example, quoting Payne, leaving the features of her text as she has them in the book:

> If an individual depends upon a random, episodic story structure for memory patterns, lives in an unpredictable environment, and **has not developed the ability to plan**, then …
> If an individual cannot plan, he/she **cannot predict**.
> I If an individual cannot predict, he/she **cannot identify cause and effect**.
> If an individual cannot identify cause and effect, he/she **cannot identify consequence**.
> If an individual cannot identify consequence, he/she **cannot control impulsivity**.
> If an individual cannot control impulsivity, he/she **has an inclination toward criminal behavior** (bold in original) (90).

Payne makes her way from a narrative style (which she has incorrectly described as random among people in poverty) all the way to criminality. The initial assumptions are incorrect, about the chaotic lives, random narrative style, and inability to plan among low-income citizens. The studies cited earlier demonstrate that lives at the edge of economic stability are often carefully ordered and planned, even if they do not mesh well with the structures of some social institutions. Moreover, the notion that people "cannot plan" is an indefensible assertion of a cognitive deficit. Economic hardship does not make planning impossible as a mental act; it makes the realization of plans difficult, as a material outcome. Furthermore, even if it were true that a particular individual "cannot plan," it is an unwarranted leap in logic to assert that such a condition precludes predicting or identifying consequence. And none of these deficiencies, if they existed, leads to criminality, which is obviously dependent on morality and receptivity to social influences, not just the prediction of particular consequences. Payne's assertions again characterize the poor, without evidence, as deeply flawed human beings, whose personal failings make continued poverty—or worse conditions—inevitable.

Worldview

Payne characterizes the worldview shared among people living in poverty as being chaotic, living from moment to moment, valuing entertainment more than anything else, and disregarding the consequences of one's actions. The households of people in poverty lack order and organization and many of them "are unkempt and cluttered. Devices for organization (files, planners, etc.) don't exist" (53).

Payne claims that poor people live only in the present and that, for the poor, the future does not exist, "except as a word" (52). She asserts that time is flexible for the poor, not measured, and that poor people live in the moment without any consideration for "future ramifications" (52); "Being proactive, setting goals, and planning ahead are not a part of generational poverty. Most of what occurs is reactive and in the moment. Future implications of present actions are seldom considered" (53). Payne's stereotype of the time orientation of low-income people is hardly new and has been familiar since Lewis (1961), if not before.

Payne informs us that the poor have a more sensual and kinesthetic approach to life than the middle class. In fact, she claims that the "mating dance" (52) is a characteristic of people in generational poverty, where the body is used in a sexual way that accentuates parts of the body, through both verbal and non-verbal means: "If you have few financial resources, the way you sexually attract someone is with your body" (52). Once again, the claim lacks foundation and pathologizes the poor as hyper-sexed and deviant. Payne is addressing teachers about the poor children in their classrooms, and in this context, she suggests that the adult women in those children's lives are likely to use sex for economic advancement, a claim that echoes a long history of U.S. middle-class worries about the sexual threat posed by poor people who are assumed to be sexually immoral (Katz, 1995). Meanwhile, Payne implies that middle-class people attract one another sexually by means of financial resources.

Poor people are fatalistic: they believe that destiny and fate govern their lives and that agency is rarely an option for them, according to Payne (52). The poor leave much to chance and do not believe that they can change the present or future through making choices that might affect their lives, Payne claims. They do not view freedom as part of their lives. Ultimately, Payne claims that the poor choose to stay poor, through their orientation and behaviors.

The poor value entertainment highly, according to Payne. She asserts that, because the poor are simply surviving, respite from stressful conditions is extremely important, and that, "in fact, entertainment brings respite" (51). Given the importance of entertainment, a key personality attribute for the poor is the ability to entertain, tell stories, and have a good sense of humor. Without evidence, Payne makes sure that we know that poor people all have VCRs because of the high value they place on entertainment. America has a large entertainment industry; we assume it is obvious that it is not the poor alone who support it. A desire for entertainment, for distraction, seems to be a contemporary trait across much of the world; it is not unique to poverty.

Men and Women

Payne claims that men in poverty are expected to work hard at physical labor and to be fighters and lovers. Bars and work are their only two social outlets and they tend to avoid other social settings. "A real man is ruggedly good-looking, is a lover, can physically fight, works hard, takes no crap" (59). Men who take on the identities of fighters and lovers cannot have stable lives because, in choosing among the three responses to life, ("to flee, flow or fight" (60)) they can only fight or flee. Men fight when under stress, and then they run away from the police and their families. It seems that Payne is arguing that men must both fight and flee. In any case, she does not offer any evidence to support her assertions about men in poverty, and we find none in the research literature. Furthermore, we consider these made-up claims to be stereotyped. What is clear in anthropological and sociological studies of men in poverty is that their responses are diverse.

Payne makes the following claims about women in poverty: Women socialize with women. Unless they are employed outside of their homes, women with children stay at home and their only friends are other female relatives. Real women take care of their men by feeding them and downplaying their faults (59). Mothers are always at the center of their families, and they have multiple sexual relationships, as do their children. Teenage pregnancy and motherhood is common and accepted as part of the "culture of poverty." Payne also claims that one of the rules in generational poverty for women is that they may need to use their bodies for survival: "After all, that is all that is truly yours. Sex will bring in money and favors. Values are important, but they don't put food on the table—or bring relief from intense pressure" (24–25). In this view, women in generational poverty (as well as those in poverty in general) are prostitutes with little in terms of moral/ethical values that get in the way of providing sustenance for their families. Payne does not provide any evidence to support such claims.

Our analysis reveals that, for Payne, poverty is actually behavior—those who exhibit certain types of behaviors are not, by definition, middle class—and therefore, are viewed as belonging to poverty. Poverty is not, for her, a matter of a lack of income; the meaning of poverty is that certain individuals behave in ways that schools and employers find unacceptable. This conceptualization of poverty as behavior rather than economic means is, quite obviously, wrong. The meta-analyses of Duncan and Brooks-Gunn (1999, 2001) reveal that it is lack of income, most importantly in early childhood, that corresponds to persistent problems in academic learning. Lack of household income during adolescence may also stress a family in ways that produce a variety of emotional and behavioral, and consequently academic, difficulties. Payne cannot accept an explanation based upon income, however, because she has determined that poverty does not equate with financial resources but rather with attitude and behavior.

A significantly different set of understandings about the competence of poor individuals is provided by the research conducted by Luis Moll, Norma Gonzalez and their colleagues (Gonzales, Moll, & Amanti, 2005; Moll, Amanti, Neff, & Gonzales, 1992). In their studies of low-income Mexican-origin families, Moll and his colleagues found that these families had ample intellectual and practical "funds of knowledge," both within their own households, as well as in their family social networks, that were an integral part of surviving in low-income communities. A few examples of the abundant and diverse funds of knowledge that these researchers found in Tucson households include: information about farming and animal husbandry, knowledge about construction and building, contemporary and folk medicine, and knowledge about trade, business and finance on both sides of the U.S.-Mexico border:

> The concept of *funds of knowledge* ... is based on a simple premise: People are competent, they have knowledge, and their life experiences have given them that knowledge. Our claim is that firsthand research experiences with families allow one to document this competence and knowledge. It is this engagement that opened up many possibilities for pedagogical actions (Gonzalez, Moll, & Amanti, 2005: x).

These researchers worked closely with teachers to utilize the multiple funds of knowledge in class-rooms as resources for teaching, drawing on students' knowledge as key tools to mediate thinking and learning, and to reposition them in the classroom as knowers who bring vital intellectual and practical resources from their homes. This approach supports an alternative perspective of poor and working class individuals, one that views them "primarily in terms of their strengths and resources (or funds of knowledge) as their defining characteristic" (x).

Contrary to Payne's deficit perspective on poor adults and children, a funds of knowledge orientation demonstrates that poor and working class children have access to a broad array of social and cultural tools and knowledge that may teachers may tap. Researchers in other areas of the U.S.A have documented funds of knowledge for teaching in low-income households (see e.g., Brendan, 2005; Mercado, 2005). Rather than offering ways to remediate "students of poverty," as Payne does, these educators identify the many ways that students might be supported and encouraged to use their knowledge for learning in the classroom (Gonzales et al., 2005; Moll, 1992; Moll et al., 1992).

DISCUSSION

Our analysis of Payne's truth claims reveals that her characterizations of people living in poverty represent a classic example of deficit thinking (Valencia, 1997). Though Payne herself does not use the term "deficit" explicitly, the analysis we have reported above leads us to conclude that the scholarly literature on deficit perspectives may aptly be applied to her book. The deficit perspective has been advanced for decades by some to explain school failure among low-income and students of color, and is currently experiencing a resurgence in educational theory and practice as educators responding to federal mandates "rediscover the poor" (Patterson, 2000). At its root, deficit thinking holds that students who struggle or fail in school do so because of their own internal deficits or deficiencies. Ryan (1971) called this perspective "blaming the victim." These deficits are evident, according to those holding this view, in limited intellectual abilities, linguistic shortcomings, lack of motivation to learn, and immoral behavior (Valencia, 1997). Proponents of the deficit model do not look to external factors to account for school failure, such as the ways schools are organized, inequalities in school funding and resources, and oppressive policies and practices at both the macro- and micro-levels (Anyon, 2005). The perspective is both essentializing of members of groups, so that all "people in poverty" share characteristics, and is simultaneously individualistic, placing the fault for poverty on the inadequate individual.

There are two basic varieties of deficit thinking. One is genetic, where poor performance of students from low-income households is held to be transmitted through biology. The other perspective, and the one that Payne advocates, is the culture of poverty view, where the self-sustaining cultural models of the poor are thought to be carriers of deficits like school failure and intergenerational poverty. In this variety of deficit thinking, the family and home environmental contexts are identified as the transmitters of pathology (Valencia, 1997). As Valencia (1997) has written:

Deficit thinking is a person-centered explanation of school failure among individuals linked to group membership (typically, the combination of racial/ethnic minority status and economic disadvantagement). The deficit thinking framework holds that poor schooling performance is rooted in students' alleged cognitive and motivational deficits, while institutional structures and inequitable schooling arrangements that exclude students from learning are held exculpatory. Finally, the model is largely based on imputation and little documentation (9).

Given Payne's deficit perspective, it is no wonder that the attributes of the poor that she describes are based in their family structure, orientation, dysfunctionality, violence, lack of morals, and "hidden rules." Her views on the poor lack substantiation in research or any other forms of evidence, conforming precisely to the culture of poverty variant of deficit thinking. Thus, Payne's views are in line with current deficit perspectives and practices in education and ask teachers to adopt negative stereotypes and caricatures of poor adults and children.

Payne's views would simply be the factually inaccurate opinions of a self-published former principal, if so many educators were not influenced by her work. However, reading her book and hearing Payne speak appears to influence the thinking of many teachers, or else one could not account for her popularity. Teachers' thinking is important, because teaching involves the enactment of that thinking. Teachers make decisions on the run about how to respond to their students on the basis of the models they have in mind of student learning, the material to be taught, and the students they teach. They plan lessons, curricula, ongoing classroom routines, and experiences for students based in part on their assumptions about what those students already know and what they are capable of learning. They also carry assumptions about the kinds of language they should use with students and the aspects of life they have in common with their students. Much of the research literature on teachers names the idea we are discussing here as *teacher beliefs* (Pajares, 1992). It is well-established in this literature that teacher beliefs have an impact on the ways they teach and on their students' learning (National Commission on Teaching and America's Future, 1996; Nespor, 1987).

Since teachers do make decisions and plans on the basis of their beliefs or conceptualizations of their students, students' daily lives are strongly affected by the influences on their teachers' thinking. We have demonstrated through our analysis that teachers may be misinformed by Payne's claims. Poverty in Payne's work is marked only as a negative, only as a divergence from a middle-class norm, and students who are "of poverty" need to be fixed. This way of regarding the children of poor parents has predictable and undesirable consequences in U.S. education (Brophy & Good, 1974; Rist, 1970; Rosenthal & Jacobson, 1968). As a consequence of low teacher expectations, poor students are more likely to be in lower tracks or lower ability groups (Ansalone, 2001, 2003; Connor & Boskin, 2001; Gamoran & Berends, 1987; Oakes, 1985), and their educational experience is more often dominated by rote drill and practice (Anyon, 1980, 1997; Dudley-Marling & Paugh, 2005; Moll, 1988; Moll & Ruiz, 2002; Valenzuela, 1999).

Nowhere in her book does Payne state that poverty, rather than the poor, is the problem that must be addressed. She offers no perspective that people should hold elected officials accountable for the number of families in poverty, or the conditions in which people must live when their incomes are low. Although the fourth edition was published almost a decade after welfare reform, A Framework for Understanding Poverty makes no reference to the elimination of Aid to Families with Dependent Children (AFDC). She does not connect the misfortunes of the poor to the fortunes of the middle class and wealthy by examining policies regarding housing, segregation, taxation, or public expenditures. She does not analyze the degree to which wealthy and middle-class families proactively structure advantage for their children at the expense of the children of the less fortunate (Biddle, 2001; Brantlinger, 2003; Cookson, 1994). At no time does she suggest that the hundreds of thousands of educators she addresses might attempt to advocate for the basic needs of the children they teach. Poor children do not only have trouble in school; they are likely to live in substandard housing, eat an inadequate diet, wear threadbare clothes, lack health insurance, and have chronic health and dental problems. Though we know many teachers of poor children who regularly feed their students with their own money, one will not find such priorities in Ruby Payne's work. We believe that to discuss poverty among caring people obligates one to challenge others to do something about poverty itself—to give, to volunteer, to speak out, to hold politicians accountable—in short, to change a system that perpetuates poverty.

Furthermore, nowhere in Payne's work is there a suggestion that students might be taught to think about social class and poverty. There is no hint that people ought to be taught to question the structures that oppress them and others like them systematically (Freire, 1970). We would suggest that a curriculum that addresses class as a significant conceptual lens through which to view people's lives, their society, and the texts they read is essential to the responsible education of all people in a social world divided by class, and it might be especially motivating and liberating to those oppressed by such a system (Bomer & Bomer, 2001; Edelsky, 1999; Fecho & Allen, 2003; Finn, 1999; Hicks, 2002; Macedo, 1994; McLaren, 1989; Shor & Pari, 1999; Swenson, 2003; Yagelski, 2000).

We would also suggest that an ethical education system does not teach students to think of anything that makes one secure in the middle class as an unquestioned good. Transforming one's character in order to climb a social ladder should not be necessary and is not a noble thing to do. Other values are available than simply conforming to the middle class. In fact, it has been demonstrated repeatedly that when people without advantage, social position, or opportunity internalize U.S. middle-class values, those very values cause significantly more damage in their lives than they offer new opportunity (Bourgois, 1995; Foley, 1994; Liebow, 1967/2003; Mahler, 1995; Newman, 2000), partly because by internalizing the views of those who are financially better-off, poor individuals come to blame themselves for their failure to get ahead.

This lack of attention to a critical perspective is consonant with Payne's individualistic, deficit, blame-the-victim perspective. Such a perspective aligns well with right-wing social policy. If the poor are poor simply because they do not know how to behave as if they were not poor, then the middle class and the wealthy should not be taxed to provide public assistance, public health, public schooling, or a public sphere in which the poor might participate. According to such a perspective, neither structural inequality, nor public policy, nor barriers to good jobs, nor lack of money cause the plight of the poor; they just don't have the right story structure, or tone of voice, or register, or cognitive strategies.

As we said at the beginning of this article, Ruby Payne's success with her program on poverty is impressive. Her book is self-published; she earns the royalty as well as the publisher's margin; her only expense is having it printed. If in fact over 800,000 copies have been sold between the 1998 and 2005 editions, as the most recent cover claims, that single book has probably made many millions of dollars. The success of the book and the business to which it is attached is not attributable to entrepreneurship alone. The appeal of the book relies on a set of values—a framework—that exists outside of education, and is pervasive throughout middle-class U.S. society. Policy that constructs poverty as a problem of schools creates a large industry that consists of many more businesses than just Payne's. Her success indicts all of us in education, indeed most of the American public, as it reveals the degree to which we use the education system to protect our own sense of entitlement to privilege.

REFERENCES

Ansalone, G. (2001). Schooling, tracking, and inequality. *Journal of Children and Poverty*, 7(1), 33–47.

Ansalone, G. (2003). Poverty, tracking, and the social construction of failure: International perspectives on tracking. *Journal of Children and Poverty*, 9(1), 3–20.

Anyon, J. (1980). Social class and the hidden curriculum. *Journal of Education*, 162, 67–92.

Anyon, J. (1997). *Ghetto schooling: A political economy of urban educational reform*. New York: Teachers College Press.

Anyon, J. (2005). *Radical possibilities*. New York: Routledge Taylor & Francis Group.

Bauman, R. (1986). *Story, performance, and event*. Cambridge, UK: Cambridge University Press.

Bendix, R., & Lipset, S. M. (Eds.) (1966). *Class, status, and power: Social stratification in comparative perspective* (2 ed.). New York: Free Press.

Biddle, B. J. (2001). Poverty, ethnicity, and achievement in American schools. In B. J. Biddle (Ed.), *Social class, poverty, and education* (pp. 1–30). New York: RoutledgeFalmer.

Bomer, R., & Bomer, K. (2001). *For a better world: Reading and writing for social action*. Portsmouth, NH: Heinemann.

Bourgois, P. (1995). *In search of respect: Selling crack in El Barrio*. New York: Cambridge University Press.

Brantlinger, E. (2003). *Dividing classes: How the middle class negotiates and justifies school advantage*. London: Falmer Press.

Brendan, M. (2005). Funds of knowledge and team ethnography: Reciprocal approaches. In N. Gonzales, L. Moll, & C. Amanti (Eds.), *Funds of knowledge: Theorizing practices in households, communities, and classrooms* (pp. 199–212). Mahwah, NJ: Erlbaum.

Brophy, J. E., & Good, T. L. (1974). *Teacher-student relationships: Causes and consequences*. New York: Holt.

Capps, R., Fix, M. E., & Reardon-Anderson, J. (2003). *Children of immigrants show slight reductions in poverty, hardship*. Washington, D.C.: Urban Institute.

Compton, R. (1998). *Class and stratification: An introduction to current debates* (2 ed.). Cambridge, MA: Polity Press.

Compton-Lilly, C. (2003). *Reading families: The literate lives of urban children*. New York: Teachers College Press.

Connor, M. H., & Boskin, J. (2001). Overrepresentation of bilingual and poor children in special education classes. *Journal of Children and Poverty*, 7, 23–32.

Cookson, P. W. (1994). *School choice: The struggle for the soul of American education*. New Haven, CT: Yale University Press.

Deschenes, S., Cuban, L., & Tyack, D. (2001). Mismatch: Historical perspectives on schools and students who don't fit them. *Teachers College Record*, 103(4), 525–547.

Dittmar, N. (1976). *Sociolinguistics: A critical survey of theory and application* (P. Sand, P. A. M. Seuren & K. Whiteley, Trans.). London: Edward Arnold.

Dudley-Marling, C., & Paugh, P. (2005). The rich get richer; the poor get direct instruction. In B. Altwerger (Ed.), *Reading for profit: How the bottom line leaves kids behind* (pp. 156-171). Portsmouth, NH: Heinemann.

Duncan, G. J., & Brooks-Gunn, J. (1999). Consequences of growing up poor. New York: Russell Sage Foundation.

Duncan, G. J., & Brooks-Gunn, J. (2001). *Poverty, welfare reform, and children's achievement*. In B. J. Biddle (Ed.), Social class, poverty, and education (pp. 49–76). New York: RoutledgeFalmer.

Dyson, A. H. (1993). *Social worlds of children learning to write in an urban primary school*. New York: Teachers College Press.

Eastgate Systems (2005). Tinderbox (Version 2.5) [Computer software].

Edelsky, C. (Ed.). (1999). *Making justice our project: Teachers working toward critical whole language practice*. Urbana, IL: National Council of Teachers of English.

Edwards, A. D. (1976). *Language in culture and class: The sociology of language and education*. London: Heinemann. Edwards, J. R. (1979). Language and disadvantage. New York: Elsevier.

Fecho, B., & Allen, J. (2003). Teacher inquiry into literacy, social justice, and power. In J. Flood, D. Lapp, J. R. Squire, & J. M. Jensen (Eds.), *Handbook of research on teaching the English language arts* (pp. 232–246). Mahwah, NJ: Lawrence Erlbaum.

Ferguson, C. A. (1972). Diglossia. In P. P. Giglioli (Ed.), *Language and social context* (pp. 232–251). London: Penguin.

Ferguson, C. A. (1991). Diglossia Revisited. *Southwest Journal of Linguistics*, 10(1), 214–234.

Finn, P. J. (1999). *Literacy with an attitude: Educating working-class children in their own self-interest*. Albany, NY: State University of New York Press.

Foley, D. E. (1994). *Learning capitalist culture: Deep in the heart of Tejas*. Philadelphia, PA: University of Pennsylvania Press.

Foley, D. E. (1997). Deficit thinking models based on culture: The anthropological protest. In R. Valencia (Ed.), *The evolution of deficit thinking: Educational thought and practice*. London: Falmer.

Freire, P. (1970). *Pedagogy of the oppressed*. New York: Continuum.

Gamoran, A., & Berends, M. (1987). The effects of stratification in secondary schools: Synthesis of survey and ethnographic research, 57, 415–435.

Gee, J. (1990). *Social linguistics and literacies*. London: The Falmer Press.

Giddens, A. (1973). *The class structure of the advanced societies*. New York: Harper & Row.

Gilbert, D. (2003). *The American class structure in an age of growing inequality*. Belmont, CA: Wadsworth/Thompson Learning.

Glaeser, E. L., & Glendon, S. (1998). *Who owns guns? Criminals, victims, and the culture of violence* (No. 1822). Cambridge, MA.

Gonzales, N., Moll, L., & Amanti, C. (Eds.). (2005). *Funds of knowledge: Theorizing practices in households, communities, and classrooms*. Mahwah, NJ: Erlbaum.

Goodman, Y. M. (1969/1996). The culturally deprived child: A study in stereotyping. In S. Wilde (Ed.), *Notes from a Kidwatcher: Selected writings of Yetta M. Goodman* (pp. 17–23). Portsmouth, NH: Heinemann.

Gorski, P. (2006). The classist underpinnings of Ruby Payne's framework. ID Number 12322, *Teachers College Record*. Retrieved June 9, 2007, from http://www.tcrecord.org.

Grace, C. M. (2004). Exploring the African-American oral tradition: Instructional implications for literacy learning. *Language Arts*, 81(6), 481-490.

Grusky, D. (Ed.) (2001). *Social stratification: Class, race, and gender in sociological perspective* (2 ed.). Boulder, CO: Westview.

Halliday, M. A. K. (1975). *Learning how to mean: Explorations in the development of language*. London: Edward Arnold.

Hays, S. (2004). *Flat broke: Women in the age of welfare reform*. New York: Oxford University Press.

Hicks, D. (2002). *Reading lives: Working-class children and literacy learning*. New York: Teachers College Press.

Holquist, M. (1997). The politics of representation. In M. Cole, Y Engestrom, & O. Vasquez (Eds.), *Mind, culture, and activity: Seminal papers from the Laboratory of Comparative Human Cognition* (pp. 389–408). Cambridge, UK: Cambridge University Press.

Johnson, J. (2002). *Getting by on the minimum: The lives of working-class women*. New York: Routledge.

Joos, M. (1962). *The five clocks: Publication 22*. Report number 9683101704. Bloomington, IN: Indiana University Research Center in Anthropology, Folklore, and Linguistics.

Katz, M. B. (1990). *The undeserving poor*. New York: Pantheon.

Katz, M. B. (1995). *Improving poor people: The welfare state, the "underclass," and urban schools as history*. Princeton, NJ: Princeton University Press.

Keddie, N. (Ed.) (1973). *The myth of cultural deprivation*. Middlesex, UK: Penguin.

Labov, W. (1972). The logic of nonstandard English. In P. P. Giglioli (Ed.), *Language and social context* (pp. 179–216). London: Penguin.

Lareau, A. (2003). *Unequal childhoods: Class, race, and family life*. Berkeley, CA: University of California Press.

Lareau, A., & Horvat, E. (1999). Moments of social inclusion and exclusion: Race, class, and cultural capital in family-school relationships. *Sociology of Education*, 72, 37–53.

Leacock, E. B. (Ed.) (1971). *The culture of poverty: A critique*. New York: Simon & Schuster.

Leichter, H. J. (Ed.). (1978). *Families and communities as educators*. New York: Teachers College Press.

Lewis, O. (1961). *The children of Sanchez*. New York: Random House.

Liebow, E. (1967/2003). *Tally's corner: A study of Negro streetcorner men*. Lanham, MD: Rowman & Littlefield.

Lindfors, J. W. (1980). *Children's language and learning*. Englewood Cliffs, N.J.: Prentice-Hall.

Macedo, D. P. (1994). *Literacies of power: What Americans are not allowed to know*. Boulder: Westview Press.

Mahler, S. J. (1995). *American dreaming*. Princeton, NJ: Princeton University Press.

McCarthy, C. (1990). Race and curriculum: Social inequality and the theories and politics of difference in contemporary research on schooling. Philadelphia: Falmer.

McCarthy, C., & Apple, M. (1988). Class, race, and gender in educational research. In L. Weis (Ed.), *Race, class, and gender in American education* (pp. 9–39). Albany, NY: State University of New York Press.

McLaren, P. (1989). *Life in schools: An introduction to critical pedagogy in the foundations of education.* White Plains, NY: Longman.

Mehan, H. (1993). Beneath the skin and between the ears: A case study in the politics of representation. In S. Chaiklin & J. Lave (Eds.), *Understanding practice: Perspectives on activity and context* (pp. 241–268). Cambridge, UK: Cambridge University Press.

Mercado, C. I. (2005). Reflections on the study of households in New York City and Long Island: A different route, a common destination. In N. Gonzales, L. Moll, & C. Amanti (Eds.), *Funds of knowledge: Theorizing practices in households, communities, and classrooms* (pp. 233–255). Mahwah, NJ: Erlbaum.

Michaels, S. (1981). "Sharing time": Children's narrative styles and differential access to literacy. *Language in Society,* 10, 423-441.

Moll, L. (1988). Some key issues in teaching Latino students. *Language Arts,* 65(5), 465–472.

Moll, L. (1992). Bilingual classroom studies and community analysis: Some recent trends. *Educational Researcher,* 21, 20–24.

Moll, L., Amanti, C., Neff, D., & Gonzalez, N. (1992). Funds of knowledge for teaching: Using a qualitative approach to connect homes and classrooms. *Theory Into Practice,* 31(2), 133–141.

Moll, L., & Ruiz, R. (2002). The schooling of Latino students. In M. Suarez-Orozco & M. Paez (Eds.), *Contexts for learning: Sociocultural dynamics in children's development* (pp. 19–42). New York: Oxford.

Montano-Harmon, M. R. (1991). Discourse features of written Mexican Spanish: Current research in contrastive rhetoric and its implications. Hispania, 74(2), 417–425.

Moynihan, D. P. (1965). *The Negro family: The case for national action.* Washington, D.C.: United States Department of Labor.

National Commission on Teaching and America's Future. (1996). *What matters most: Teaching for America's future.* Washington, D.C.: National Commission on Teaching and America's Future.

National Institute of Justice. (1997). *Guns in America: National survey on private ownership and use of firearms.* Washington, D.C.: United States Department of Justice. Retrieved September 15, 2005, from http://www.ncjrs. org/txtfiles/165476.txt.

Nelson, K. (1996). *Language in cognitive development: The emergence of the mediated mind.* Cambridge, UK: Cambridge University Press.

Nespor, J. (1987). The role of beliefs in the practice of teaching. *Journal of Curriculum Studies,* 19(4), 317–328.

Newman, K. S. (2000). *No shame in my game: The working poor in the inner city.* New York: Vintage.

Ng, J. C., & Rury, J. L. (2006). Poverty and education: A critical analysis of the Ruby Payne phenomenon. ID Number: 12596. *Teachers College Record,* Retrieved September 30, 2006, from http://www.tcrecord.org.

Nieto, S. (1999). *The Light in their eyes: Creating multicultural learning communities.* New York: Teachers College Press.

No Child Left Behind Act of 2001. Pub. L. No. 107-110 (2002).

Nord, M., Andrews, M., Carlson, S. (2006). Household food security in the United States, 2005. Washington, D.C.: United States Department of Agriculture. Retrieved August 1, 2007, from http://www.ers.usda.gov/publications/err29/.

Oakes, J. (1985). *Keeping track: How schools structure inequality.* New Haven, CT: Yale University Press.

Osei-Kofi, N. (2005). Pathologizing the poor: A framework for understanding Ruby Payne's work. *Equity and Excellence*, 38(4), 367–375.

Pajares, M. F. (1992). Teachers' beliefs and educational research: Cleaning up a messy construct. *Review of Educational Research*, 62(3), 307–332.

Patterson, J. T. (2000). *America's struggle against poverty in the twentieth century*. Cambridge, MA: Harvard University Press.

Payne, R. K. (1998/2005). *A Framework for understanding poverty* (4th ed.). Highlands, TX: RFT Publishing.

Rabinow, P. (1986). Representations are social facts: Modernity and post-modernity in anthropology. In J. Clifford & G. E. Marcus (Eds.), *Writing culture: The poetics and politics of ethnography* (pp. 234–261). Berkeley, CA: University of California Press.

Rice, M. (1996). Children's language acquisition. In B. M. Power & R. S. Hubbard (Eds.), *Language development: A reader for teachers* (pp. 3–12). Englewood Cliffs, NJ: Merrill.

Rist, R. (1970). Student social class and teacher expectations: The self-fulfilling prophecy in ghetto education. *Harvard Educational Review*, 70, 257–301.

Roberts, S. (2004). *Who we are now: The changing face of America in the twenty-first century*. New York: Times Books.

Rosenthal, R., & Jacobson, L. (1968). *Pygmalion in the classroom: Teacher expectation and pupils' intellectual development*. New York: Holt, Rinehart, & Winston.

Ryan, W. (1971). *Blaming the victim*. New York: Vintage.

Said, E. (1979). *Orientalism*. New York: Vintage.

Shor, I., & Pari, C. (1999). *Education is politics: Critical teaching across differences, K-12*. Portsmouth, NH: Boynton/Cook.

Skilton-Sylvester, E. (2002). Literate at home but not at school: A Cambodian girl's journey from playwright to struggling writer. In G. Hull & K. Schultz (Eds.), *School's out: Bridging out-of-school literacies with classroom practice* (pp. 61–90). New York: Teachers College Press.

Smitherman, G. (1977). *Talkin and testifyin: The language of Black America*. Boston: Houghton Mifflin.

Swenson, J. (2003). Transformative teacher networks, on-line professional development, and the write for your life project. *English Education*, 35(4), 263–321.

Tannen, D. (1981). New York Jewish conversational style. *International Journal of the Sociology of Language*, 30, 133–149.

Tannen, D. (1985). Relative focus on involvement in oral and written discourse. In D. Olson, N. Torrance, & A. Hildyard (Eds.), *Literacy, language, and learning: The nature and consequences of reading and writing* (pp. 124–147). Cambridge, UK: Cambridge University Press.

Taylor, D., & Dorsey-Gaines, C. (1988). *Growing up literate: Learning from inner-city families*. Portsmouth, NH: Heinemann.

Title I. The Elementary and Secondary School Act. Public Law 89-10 (April 11, 1965).

Tozer, S. (2000). Class. In D. A. Gabbard (Ed.), *Knowledge and power in the global economy: Politics and the rhetoric of school reform* (pp. 149–159). Mahwah, NJ: Erlbaum.

Trudgill, P. (1974). *Sociolinguistics*. Reading, UK: Penguin.

Valencia, R. (1997). Conceptualizing the notion of deficit thinking. In R. Valencia (Ed.), *The evolution of deficit thinking: Educational thought and practice*. London: Falmer.

Valenzuela, A. (1999). *Subtractive schooling: U.S.-Mexican youth and the politics of caring*. Albany, NY: State University of New York Press.

Varenne, H., & McDermott, R. P. (1986). "Why" Sheila can read: Structure and indeterminacy in the reproduction of familial literacy. In B. Schieffelin & P. Gilmore (Eds.), *The acquisition of literacy: Ethnographic perspectives* (pp. 188–210). Norwood, NJ: Ablex.

Weis, L. (1988). *Class, race, and gender in American education*. Albany, NY: State University of New York Press.

Weis, L., & Fine, M. (Eds.). (1993). *Beyond silenced voices: Class, race, and gender in United States schools*. Albany, NY: State University of New York Press.

Western, B. (2002). The impact of incarceration on wage mobility and inequality. American Sociological Review, 67, 526–546.

Western, B. (2004). Mass imprisonment and the life course: Race and class inequality in U.S. incarceration. *American Sociological Review*, 69, 151–169.

Teaching Inequality

How Poor and Minority Students Are Shortchanged on Teacher Quality

A Report and Recommendations by the Education Trust

By Heather G. Peske and Kati Haycock

Next month, for the first time, leaders in every state must deliver to the Secretary of Education their plans for ensuring that low-income and minority students in their states are not taught disproportionately by inexperienced, out-of-field, or uncertified teachers.

For many, this process will be the first step in helping the citizens of their states to understand a fundamental, but painful truth: Poor and minority children don't underachieve in school just because they often enter behind; but, also because the schools that are supposed to serve them actually *shortchange* them in the one resource they most need to reach their potential—high-quality teachers. Research has shown that when it comes to the distribution of the best teachers, poor and minority students do not get their fair share.

Two years ago, with support from the Chicago-based Joyce Foundation, three states—Ohio, Illinois ,and Wisconsin—and their three biggest school systems—Cleveland, Chicago, and Milwaukee—set out with the Education Trust to tackle this very problem. Together, teams of stakeholders in each jurisdiction collected data on teacher distribution and identified patterns. In every case, they found large differences between the qualifications of teachers in the highest-poverty and highest-minority schools and teachers serving in schools with few minority and low-income students. The teams then analyzed the information to determine possible reasons for the patterns, and came up with strategies to achieve a fairer distribution.

This report draws from their experiences in an effort to help other states and cities as they prepare their own action plans. The report:

- Describes teacher distribution patterns nationally, along with selected findings in these pilot states and districts;
- Summarizes evidence about how differences in teacher quality affect student achievement, especially among low-income students, students of color and low-achieving students of all races;

- Explains the requirement in No Child Left Behind that all groups of children receive their fair share of strong teachers;
- Shares key lessons from the pilot states and districts that may be useful to other states and districts as they move to address the problem of teacher distribution; and,
- Sets forth a range of strategies that can be used to address this problem—some from the stakeholder groups in the pilot states and districts, and others from the Education Trust.

Not all of these lessons and recommendations will be applicable in every state and district; but together, we hope they will provide a useful foundation for much-needed conversations and action on this problem.

THE DISTRIBUTION OF TEACHER QUALITY IN THE U.S.

Every year, a large number of children enter school substantially behind. Sometimes that's because of poverty. Sometimes it's because they speak a language other than English. Sometimes there are other issues. But regardless of the reason, many children—especially low-income and minority children—are entering the classroom without the knowledge and skills they need to succeed.

Unfortunately, rather than organizing our educational system to pair these children with our most expert teachers, who can help "catch them up" with their more advantaged peers, we actually do just the opposite. The very children who most need strong teachers are assigned, on average, to teachers with less experience, less education, and less skill than those who teach other children.

Certainly, there are fine, dedicated teachers who have devoted their lives to low-income and minority children, but they are the exception. Overall, the patterns are unequivocal. Regardless of how teacher quality is measured, poor and minority children get fewer than their fair share of high-quality teachers.

For example, despite clear evidence that brand-new teachers are not as effective as they will eventually become, students in high-poverty and high-minority schools are disproportionately assigned to teachers who are new to the profession. Children in the highest-poverty schools are assigned to novice teachers almost twice as often as children in low-poverty schools.[1] Similarly, students in high-minority schools are assigned to novice teachers at twice the rate as students in schools without many minority students.[2]

Students in high-poverty and high-minority schools also are shortchanged when it comes to getting teachers with a strong background in the subjects they are teaching. Classes in high-poverty and high-minority secondary schools are more likely to be taught by "out-of-field teachers"—those without a major or minor in the subject they teach. (See Figure 1).

In high-poverty secondary schools, more than one in three core academic classes are taught by out-of-field teachers, compared to about one in five classes in low-poverty schools.[3] When it comes to minority students, the same pattern persists. In secondary schools serving the most minority students, almost one in three classes are assigned to an out-of-field teacher compared to about one in five in

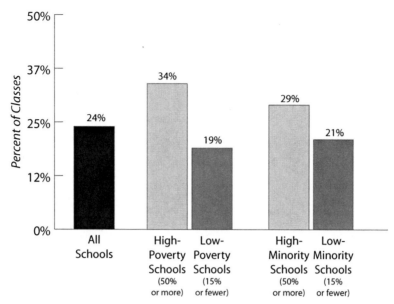

* Teachers lacking a college major or minor in the field. Data for secondary-level core academic classes.

Source: Reported in *All Talk, No Action: Putting an End to Out-of-Field Teaching*, Craig D. Jerald, The Education Trust. 2002.

Figure 1. More Classes in High-Poverty, High-Minority Secondary Schools Are Taught By Out-of-Field Teachers*

low-minority schools. Importantly, these are teachers without a college major or minor—by most accounts, a low-bar in terms of demonstrating knowledge of content (See Figure 2).

Given the importance of math skills to work and citizenship in the 21st century, we might expect to see more attention to ensuring that math teachers have a strong grounding in their subject and that they are fairly distributed. Instead, the opposite is the case; there is more out-of-field teaching overall and more inequality. Nearly half of the math classes in both high-poverty high schools and high-minority high schools are taught by teachers who don't have a college major or minor in math or a math-related field, such as math education, physics, or engineering.[4]

The situation in grades five through eight is even worse. In high-poverty and high-minority middle schools, about 70 percent of math classes—seven out of every 10 classes—are taught by a teacher who does not even have a college *minor* in math or a math-related field.

Of course, teacher quality cannot be measured only by years of experience and knowledge of basic skills and subject matter. At some time in our lives, almost all of us have heard about a brand-new teacher who was remarkable or a veteran teacher who was ineffective. And nobody who has spent much time in higher education would argue that deep knowledge of subject matter necessarily translates into quality teaching.

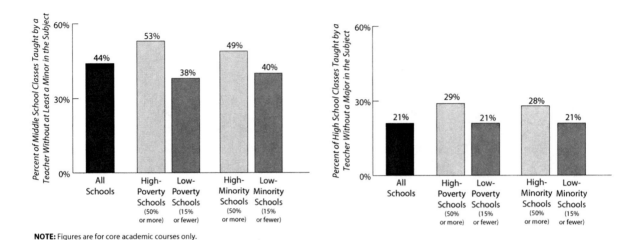

NOTE: Figures are for core academic courses only.

Source: Reported in AH Talk, No Action: Putting an End to Out-of-Field Teaching, Craig D. Jerald, The Education Trust. 2002.

Figure 2.

But substantial bodies of research show that these proxies for teacher effectiveness, though imperfect, do matter to teachers' ability to produce student learning. So when all of the proxies tilt one way—*away* from low-income and minority students—what we have is a system of distributing teacher quality that produces exactly the opposite of what fairness would dictate and what we need to close achievement gaps. This system, quite simply, enlarges achievement gaps.

The Distribution of Teacher Quality: A Look at How These Patterns Play Out in Three States

Three Midwest states (Illinois, Ohio, and Wisconsin) and three school districts (Chicago, Cleveland, and Milwaukee) organized teams, in collaboration with Education Trust, to examine the distribution of teachers in their schools and propose solutions. Teams included state and district officials, plus union representatives, business leaders, researchers, and community groups. Each team used multiple, research-based indicators of teacher quality, depending on available data. The stakeholder teams sought to understand who taught whom in which schools in their districts. Every one of the teams uncovered inequities. The full reports from the teams, with recommendations tailored to each site, will be released

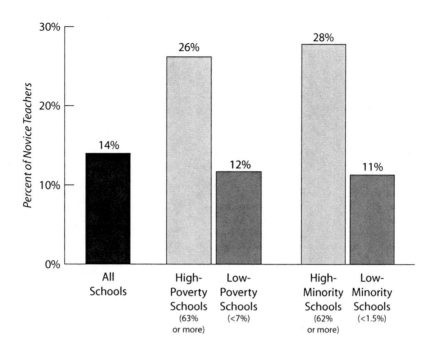

Source: Teacher Distribution Project: Wisconsin. April 5, 2006.

Figure 3. Highest-Poverty and Highest-Minority Schools in Wisconsin Are More Likely to Be Assigned Novice Teachers (<3 Years)

by the states and districts later this summer. Here we highlight some of the selected findings from the research.

How Teacher Experience Is Distributed in Wisconsin

In Wisconsin, just as in the national data, students of color and students growing up in poverty are disproportionately assigned to novice teachers.

Statewide, one in seven teachers (14 percent) had fewer than three years of teaching experience. But in the highest-minority schools,[6] that figure rises to about one in four teachers, compared to about one in 10 in the lowest-minority schools. The imbalances were similar in high- and low-poverty schools (See Figure 3).

When the Wisconsin stakeholder committee expanded its definitions to include teachers with five years of experience or less, the results were even more staggering. Almost one out of every two teachers in the highest-minority schools had less than five years of experience, compared with only one in five in the lowest-minority schools (See Figure 4).

Curious about the relationship between teacher experience and school achievement, the Wisconsin committee also analyzed staffing at schools that are ranked high or low by the state's accountability

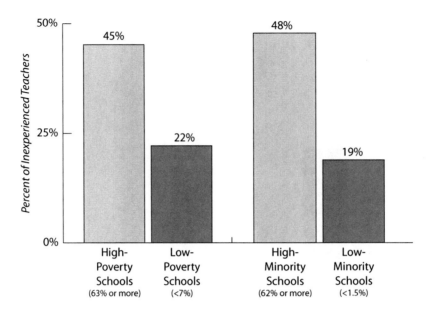

Source: Teacher Distribution Project: Wisconsin. April 5, 2006.

Figure 4. Highest-Poverty and Highest-Minority Schools in Wisconsin Are More Likely to Be Assigned Inexperienced Teachers (<5 Years)

system. The group found significant differences: Schools that were low performers had approximately twice the percentage of novice teachers as high-performing schools (See Figure 5).

In Milwaukee, Wisconsin's largest city, the stakeholder committee conducted an analysis of the distribution of teacher experience *within* the district.

As in the rest of the state, experienced teachers in Milwaukee are more likely to be teaching in schools with fewer low-income and minority students. In the highest-poverty schools in the district, 40 percent of the teachers had five years or fewer of experience, compared to the least-poor schools where 25 percent of the teachers were inexperienced. Similarly, in the schools with the most minority students, teachers who had five years or less of experience made up 40 percent of the faculty, compared to schools with fewer minority students, where 26 percent of the teachers were inexperienced.[7]

Schools serving the most English-language learners also had more inexperienced teachers than other schools. In schools where almost half of the students were English-language learners (45 percent), nearly half of the teachers had five or fewer years of experience, compared to the schools with the fewest English-language learners (15 percent or fewer), where 35 percent had five or fewer years of experience.

How Highly Qualified Status Is Distributed in Ohio

Participating states and districts also looked at other teacher characteristics. For example, the Ohio team looked at the distribution of highly qualified teachers in the state.[8]

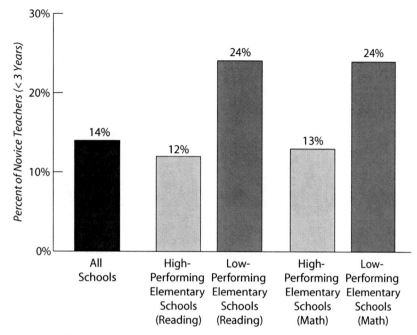

NOTE: Low-performing in reading is 70.2% proficient or lower; high-performing is 96.2% or higher. Low-performing in math is 57% proficient or lower; high-performing is 92.9% or higher.

Source: Teacher Distribution Project: Wisconsin. April 5, 2006.

Figure 5. More Novice Teachers in Low-Performing Wisconsin Elementary Schools

The committee found that highly qualified teachers in Ohio are more likely to be teaching in schools with less poverty, fewer students of color, and in schools with higher achievement. In elementary schools with the highest-minority enrollments, about one in eight teachers is not highly qualified, which may not seem alarming until you see that in low-minority elementary schools only one in 50 teachers is not highly qualified. Similarly, in the highest-poverty elementary schools, one in eight teachers is not highly qualified, while in lowest-poverty elementary schools, only one in 67 doesn't meet the highly qualified criteria.

The problem worsens in Ohio's middle and high schools. In the highest-poverty and highest-minority secondary schools, nearly four out of 10 teachers are not highly qualified, about double the rate for the lowest-poverty and lowest-minority schools (See Figure 6 & 7).

In high school math—one of the most critical content areas for students' academic success—there are large gaps in teacher qualifications. In the highest-poverty high schools, nearly one in four math teachers was not highly qualified, compared to one in 20 in the lowest-poverty high schools. Similarly, in the highest-minority high schools, one in five math teachers was not highly qualified, compared to one in 16 in the lowest-minority schools (See Figure 8).

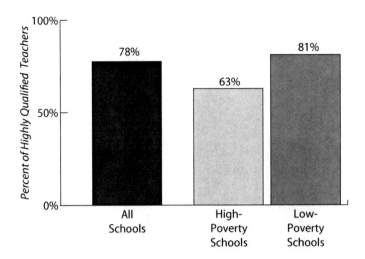

Source: Ohio Department of Education. Key Findings from the Ohio Distribution of Teacher Characteristics Study. September 23, 2005.

Figure 6. High-Poverty Middle Schools in Ohio Have Fewer Highly Qualified Teachers

The stakeholder committee in Ohio, as in Wisconsin, was interested in any relationship between the percentage of highly qualified teachers and school performance in the state's accountability system. Not surprisingly, at all school levels—elementary, middle, and high—where there were proportionally fewer highly qualified teachers, the schools were lower performing. (See Figure 9)

How Teachers' Basic Academic Skills Are Distributed in Chicago

Some of the state and district stakeholder groups were interested in examining measures of teachers' basic skills, especially their verbal skills, because of considerable research that suggests that these are important in teacher effectiveness. But only one district—Chicago—had data that enabled the stakeholder team to get a handle on something close: failure on teacher licensure exams.[9]

In their analysis of this measure, the Chicago team discovered a similar pattern for other measures. In short, teachers in the highest-poverty schools and highest-minority schools in the district were much more likely to have failed the test of basic skills than teachers in the schools serving fewer poor or minority students. In the highest-poverty schools in the district, one in eight teachers had failed the exam at least once—twice the rate of teachers in low-poverty schools.

The *Chicago Sun-Times* identified this same problem in 2001, when it found that in schools with the fewest White students, teachers were five times more likely to have failed at least one test and 23 times more likely to have failed five or more tests than teachers in schools with the most White students.[10]

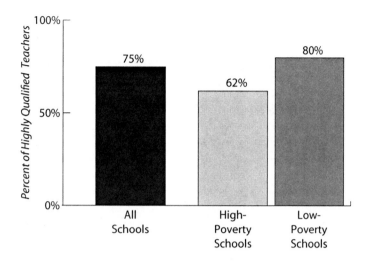

Source: Ohio Department of Education. Key Findings from the Ohio Distribution of Teacher Characteristics Study. September 23, 2005.

Figure 7. High-Poverty High Schools in Ohio Have Fewer Highly Qualified Teachers

Combining Measures for a Look at the Distribution of Teacher Quality in Illinois

Of course, none of these indicators in isolation guarantee teacher quality, much less provide an adequate measure of a teacher's actual ability to take students to needed levels of achievement.

Theoretically, teachers could be weak on one measure, but strong on others, just as schools weak on one measure could be strong on others. Available research suggests otherwise. "Even though it is feasible that some schools have less skilled teachers as measured in one dimension, while others have less skilled teachers as measured by another dimension, this is generally not the case," say Lankford, Loeb, and Wyckoff based on their analysis of teacher distribution in New York.[11]

The Illinois Education Research Council linked multiple measures of teacher quality into an overall "index," called the Teacher Quality Index (TQI), to look at distribution patterns. They found that the multiple measures revealed a similar pattern as single indicators. A large database for all Illinois teachers from 2002–2003 was built that allowed researchers to look at the distribution of all 140,000 teachers in the state using five teacher attributes[12] that have been shown in previous research to be related to student achievement, weighted them appropriately, and assigned each school a TQI rating. Then they lined schools up from top to bottom on their TQI ratings and divided them into quartiles. Schools in the top quartile had teachers who were more experienced, better educated, had stronger academic skills, and the like, than those in schools in the bottom quartile.

Going one step further, they then analyzed patterns of teacher distribution and demographics. They concluded that students in the highest-poverty and highest-minority schools are assigned teachers who are qualitatively different from teachers in other schools.

Schools with the highest concentrations of minority students in the state were particularly affected, with 61 percent of those schools with TQIs in the bottom 10 percent of the state. A full 88 percent of these high-minority schools had TQIs that fell in the bottom 25 percent of the state. In contrast, of

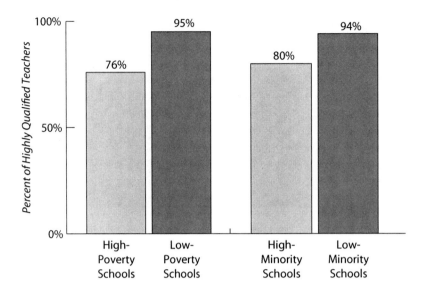

Source: Ohio Department of Education. Key Findings from the Ohio Distribution of Teacher Characteristics Study. September 23, 2005.

Figure 8. High School Math Classes in Ohio

schools that had the fewest minority students, only 11 percent were in the bottom TQI quartile, and only one percent were in the bottom 10 percent (See Figure 10).

The patterns were similar when looking at income. Of the schools with the most low-income students, for example, 84 percent were in the bottom quarter in teacher quality, and more than half (56 percent) of those fell in the very bottom 10 percent for teacher quality. Only 1 percent of the highest-poverty schools had a teacher quality index in the top quarter of the state. That's only three schools in the state. Compare these figures to schools with the fewest low-income students, where almost half (46 percent) of the schools had a teacher quality index in the top quarter and only 5 percent had a teacher quality index in the bottom quarter (See Figure 11).

THE IMPACT OF TEACHER DISTRIBUTION ON STUDENTS ACHIEVEMENT

Repeated research over many years shows that the same measures employed by the state and district stakeholder committees in this project are in fact related—albeit imperfectly—to teachers' abilities to produce gains in student learning.

Following is a brief review of relevant research on the indicators used by the various stakeholder teams.[14]

- **Teachers' Academic Skills and Knowledge** (*e.g., Performance on Assessments*)
  Researchers consistently have found that a teacher's level of literacy, as measured by vocabulary skill and other standardized assessments, is related to student achievement.[15] For example, in

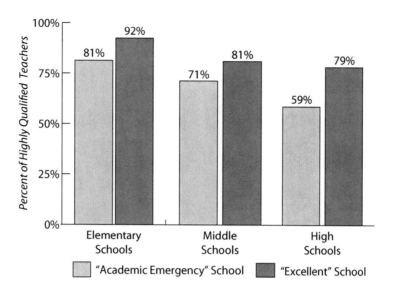

Source: Ohio Department of Education. Key Findings from the Ohio Distribution of Teacher Characteristics Study. September 23, 2005.

Figure 9. Fewer Highly Qualified Teachers in Ohio's Low-Performing Elementary, Middle, and High Schools

a study of teachers in several metropolitan Alabama districts, Ferguson and Ladd found that a significant increase in the test scores of teachers who teach African-American children would produce a substantial decline in the Black/White test-score gap in that state.[16] Two reviews of the research on teacher quality concluded that teachers' levels of literacy accounted for more of the variance in student achievement than any other measured characteristic of teachers.[17] Each study of teachers' academic skills and knowledge uses a slightly different measure, but the findings are so robust and so consistent that there is broad agreement that teachers' academic skills have a considerable impact on student achievement. Indeed, both Whitehurst's[18] 2002 recent review of the literature and Darling-Hammond and Young's critique of that review agree that teachers' academic skills have an important effect on student learning.[19]

- **Mastery of Content** *(e.g., Major or Minor in Field, Passing Tests of Content Knowledge)*
  Not surprisingly, there is also considerable research showing how important teachers' content knowledge is to their effectiveness with students, especially at the middle and high school levels. The data are especially clear in mathematics and science, where teachers with a major in the subject they teach routinely elicit higher student performance than teachers who majored in something else.[20]

  Content knowledge, albeit at a lower standard, can also be demonstrated by a minor in the subject taught or by passing a test in the subject area. A requirement for demonstrating content knowledge is embedded in the "highly qualified" teacher provisions of the *No Child Left Behind Act.*

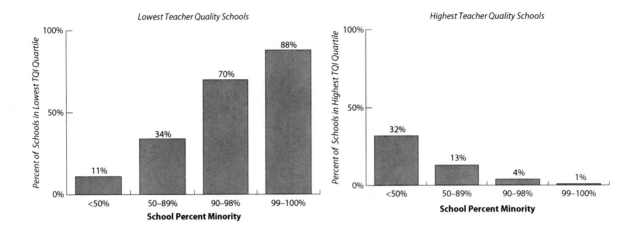

Figure 10. As Minority Enrollment Increases in Illinois, Teacher Quality Decreases

- **Experience**

    The evidence is incontrovertible that experience makes teachers more effective. Most research suggests that teachers are considerably more effective after completing two years on the job. Murnane was one of the first to document the relationship between teacher experience and student achievement; controlling for other factors, teacher effectiveness escalated in the first three years of teaching.[21] Similarly, Rivkin, Hanushek, and Kain reported that, beginning teachers in mathematics and second- and third-year teachers "perform significantly worse than more experienced teachers."[22] In a recent study of teachers in New York City, researchers found that as teachers gained experience in their first three or four years, student performance increased.[23]

- **Pedagogical Skill** *(e.g., Certification, Courses in pedagogy)*

    Clearly, content knowledge is not sufficient for effective teaching. That said, large-scale research is less clear about the value of measurable proxies for teaching knowledge like coursework in pedagogy, advanced education degrees, and scores on exams about pedagogy. Some researchers find a relationship (see, for example, Darling-Hammond and Young's overview); others don't. Teacher licensure has been correlated with some measure of quality, though it is not a very strong predictor of student achievement.

- **Combined Index of Teacher Quality**

    As described earlier, researchers at the Illinois Education Research Council looked at a combination of measures and documented significant differences in the combined characteristics of teachers in high- and low-poverty schools. They also attempted to understand how, if at all, these differences affected student achievement.

Their answer: Teacher quality turns out to matter a lot. In the highest-poverty high schools that had high Teacher Quality Indices, for example, there were about twice as many students meeting state standards as there were in similarly poor high schools that had low TQIs. In elementary and middle

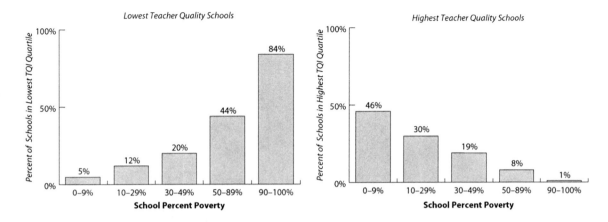

Source: Ohio Department of Education. Key Findings from the Ohio Distribution of Teacher Characteristics Study. September 23, 2005.

Figure 11. As Poverty Increases in Illinois, Teacher Quality Decreases

schools, when the TQI increased, so too, did the percentage of students who met or exceeded state standards, even after controlling for students' background characteristics.[24]

Since Illinois administers the ACT assessment to every 11th-grader, the IERC researchers were also able to evaluate the impact of teacher quality on the college-readiness of students in the class of 2002 who took particular sequences of mathematics courses. Not surprisingly, students who took more advanced mathematics courses in high school generally were more likely to perform at the college-ready level on the ACT. But there were stunning differences in levels of readiness according to the quality of teachers in a school. In schools with just average teacher quality, for example, students who completed Algebra II were more prepared for college than their peers in schools with the lowest teacher quality who had completed calculus[25] (See Figures 12 and 13).

- **Beyond Proxies: Data from Value-Added Research**

  The variation in teachers' impact on children is probably clearest in the research of the statisticians and economists who are studying the relationship between individual teachers and the growth students achieve in their classrooms during the school year. This approach is called "value-added" measurement.

  William L. Sanders, who founded the Value-Added Research and Assessment Center at the University of Tennessee, Knoxville, found that, on average, low-achieving students gained about 14 points each year on the Tennessee state test when taught by the least effective teachers, but more than 53 points when taught by the most effective teachers. Teachers made a difference for middle- and high-achieving students as well.[26]

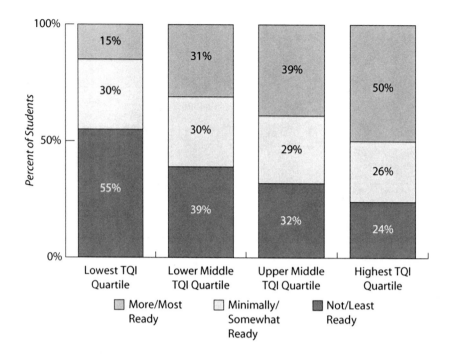

Source: Presley, J. and Gong, Y. (2005). The Demographics and Academics of College Readiness in Illinois. Illinois Research Council.

Figure 12. College Readiness Increases with Teacher Quality

FEDERAL LAW COULD ADDRESS EQUITY MORE DIRECTLY

The federal government, through the Title I program, sends billions of dollars a year to districts specifically to ensure that students from low-income families get extra services and support. Title I presumes that there are equal educational opportunities for all students *before* federal funds are applied, and that the federal money provides "extras" for students growing up in poverty. But the way that teachers are assigned to schools makes the presumption patently untrue.

The schools that have the most low-income children get the most federal Title I money, but they also get the least in terms of teacher talent. High-poverty schools are more likely to have inexperienced teachers and under-qualified teachers. These teachers are paid less than veteran and fully credentialed teachers who are concentrated in more affluent schools. Consequently, school districts actually often spend less money in Title I schools and other high-poverty schools than in other schools, even after the addition of Title I funds.[27]

Title I is supposed to prohibit this kind of inequality, but the law contains a massive loophole. The law ostensibly demands "comparability" in the educational opportunities provided in Title I schools and non-Title I schools. But the law allows districts to ignore disparities in teacher qualifications across different schools, and the resulting disparities in teacher salaries. Any district that has a single-salary

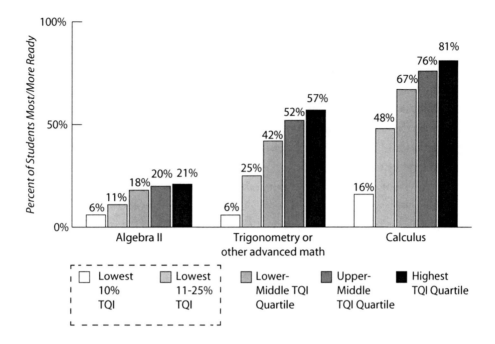

Source: Presley, J. and Gong, Y. (2005). The Demographics and Academics of College Readiness in Illinois. Illinois Research Council.

Figure 13. College Math Readiness Affected by Teacher Quality More than Courses Taken

schedule—that is, that pays all teachers according to the same criteria—is deemed to have established comparability, despite the fact that a single-salary schedule does nothing to ensure equality in how teachers are assigned to schools.[28]

This is a loophole that lets states and districts off the hook for ensuring genuine comparability. In our work in California, we have seen the loophole's effect. Millions of dollars in that state are being directed away from high-poverty schools to subsidize higher teacher salaries in schools with fewer children in poverty.[29]

This is allowed to happen because school districts generally don't tell individual schools how much money they have to spend on salaries, but rather allot the number of teaching positions to be filled. Whether a school hires a teacher who makes $35,000 or $55,000 makes no difference to the school's budget, because the budget process uses only average salaries.

Very few districts set any limits on the concentrations of the highest-or lowest-paid teachers in schools. Principals in more affluent schools don't have to worry about the salary costs of highly experienced teachers—they are free to recruit all of the proven, talented teachers in the district. Principals in high-poverty schools, who often are relegated to hiring mostly novices, get no additional money to train and support their inexperienced, lower-paid staff. This makes the current salary schedule work as a sort of Robin Hood in reverse, robbing the poor to pay for the rich.

There is evidence that some districts actually may be defrauding the Title I program by allotting Title I money based on average teacher salaries for the district rather than the actual salaries for teachers covered by Title I, who may be paid significantly less . Federal officials should investigate whether federal funds meant for high-poverty schools are being spent in those schools and take action against districts that are misdirecting federal funds.[30]

If Congress closed the comparability loophole and stopped looking the other way on blatant in-equality between Title I and non-Title I schools, it would force districts to confront the discriminatory effects of the current system.

In the meantime, school districts should not wait until they are forced by law to end unfair budget practices. Individual school budgets should reflect the needs of the students they serve. By weighting students according to the challenges they present, systems could (1) create incentives to serve the children who need the most help and (2) ensure high-poverty schools (as well as schools with more English-language learners and students with disabilities) have additional resources to compete for teacher talent. School budgets also should reflect the actual salaries that teachers are paid to ensure that funds intended to supplement the education of students growing up in poverty are actually reaching the schools serving these students.

> These teacher effects appear to be cumulative. For example, Tennessee students who have three highly effective teachers in a row score more than 50 percentile points above their counterparts who have three ineffective teachers in a row—even when they started with the same score.[27] An analysis in Dallas found essentially the same pattern.[31]
>
> The cumulative impact of teacher quality is biggest for initially low-achieving students. A recent study in Tennessee suggested that students who fail the state's fourth-grade examination are six times more likely to pass the graduation examination if they have a sequence of highly effective teachers than if they have a sequence of the least effective teachers.[32] In sum, students whose initial achievement levels are comparable have "vastly different academic outcomes as a result of the sequence of teachers to which they are assigned."[33] Differences of this magni-tude—50 percentile points in just three years—are stunning. For an individual child, it means the difference between a "remedial" label and placement in the accelerated or even gifted track. And the difference between entry into a selective college and a lifetime of low-paying, menial work.

Sadly, however, data on actual teacher effectiveness in promoting student learning show much the same teacher maldistribution as other measures. In Tennessee, for example, African-American students are about twice as likely as White students to be assigned to the state's least effective teachers, and considerably less likely than White students to be assigned to the most effective teachers.[34] Data from Dallas, one of the few districts outside of Tennessee to have collected such data over multiple years, show much the same pattern.[35]

No matter which measure we look at, the pattern is basically the same. In state after state, district after district, we take the children who are most dependent upon their teachers for academic learning and assign them to teachers with less of everything. Less experience. Less education. Less knowledge of content. And less actual teaching skill.

FEDERAL LAW REQUIRES EQUITY

Inequalities in educational opportunities have always bedeviled public education. For more than 40 years federal policy has tried to address the problem. Title I is the most significant component of this effort, providing billions of dollars to schools serving concentrations of poor children. The idea behind Title I is simple: Because poor children often enter school behind, they need extra educational services to catch up.

The law's intent, however, is thwarted every day by the fundamental fiction on which it is based—the notion that these are somehow extra dollars on top of an equitable base of state and local resources.

The truth is quite different. Even with the addition of Title I dollars, schools serving concentrations of poor and minority children provide those children with less of the very thing they need the most to catch up with other children: effective teachers.

The maldistribution of teachers has persisted over decades without improvement. Congress, realizing that achievement gaps cannot be closed without closing gaps in teacher quality, in 2002 finally demanded that states address the issue. With the No Child Left Behind Act (NCLB), Congress insisted that states and districts had to commit to identifying and addressing shortages of qualified teachers in high-poverty and high-minority schools if they wanted to continue receiving federal funds to help with the education of disadvantaged students. Every state and district that wanted to participate in Title I had to develop a plan *"to ensure that poor and minority children are not taught at higher rates than other children by inexperienced, unqualified, or out-of-field teachers."*[36]

Those provisions were ignored by the U.S. Department of Education until recently. No regulations were issued to govern the "equity plans" and states were not asked to produce them. But in fall, 2005, the education department began to scrutinize compliance with the teacher-quality provisions of the law and focused attention on the required equity plans.[37]

All states must submit by July 7, 2006 their "equity plans" for ensuring that poor and minority children are not taught by inexperienced, unqualified, or out-of-field teachers at higher rates than other children.[38]

LESSONS LEARNED

Over the course of our work, we have learned some lessons about how to approach teacher-distribution issues. Before offering some recommendations for tackling the substantive issues, we have listed some of the strategies that can help make the process constructive and effective.

- **The Data Dilemma**

  Most states and districts have yet to enter the information age when it comes to data on the distribution of teacher quality. Even when necessary information has been collected, it often is maintained in bureaucratic silos in different formats, so it cannot be connected. For example, data on teacher qualifications from the personnel department needs to be connected to data on school demographics and data on student achievement from the school accountability office. But these typically reside in different departments, and are organized in different and sometimes incompatible formats.

  As education leaders implement more immediate reforms to balance access to teacher talent, they also must lay the foundation for more strategic planning and monitoring in the future. Accurate data collection and compatibility are fundamental to addressing distribution patterns.

- **Non-Educators Need a Seat at the Table**

  Inequality in teacher distribution is a complicated problem that has developed over a long time. It cannot be solved by educators alone, at least in part because they are often "too close" to the problem to see it clearly.

  The solution will require honest conversations with a broad range of stakeholders about equity and about the new, broader goals of public education. Parent representatives, community advocates, and business leaders all have a stake in this issue and deserve to be included in crafting solutions.

- **Single Indicators in Isolation Are Easy to Ignore**

  Any individual measure is by itself inadequate to capture the range of qualities that go into effective teaching. Stakeholders may question whether inexperience or lack of certification represent serious problems when confronted by anecdotes about an inexperienced teacher who was terrific in the classroom right from the start, or the teacher who wasn't yet fully certified but connected with students in powerful ways. But the truth is that, on average, these things matter a lot. The best approach—that is, the best approach short of using actual data on how much students grow in each teacher's classroom—is to look at teacher quality through a number of lenses, including experience, educational background, certification, etc. That said, large inequalities in any one of these indicators should not be dismissed. Aggregating all the proxies into a single measure of quality, like the Teacher Quality Index in Illinois, creates a richer portrait and avoids the pitfalls of single-measure analyses. The combined measure has more power to explain the differences in student outcomes and helps stakeholders understand that the differences in teacher quality have quantifiable, discernable effects on student achievement.

- **From Teacher Qualities to Teacher Quality: Measuring Teacher Effectiveness**

  While combined indices are more powerful than looking at indicators in isolation, we need to move to a more direct measure of teacher quality. What really matters is teachers' effectiveness at growing students' knowledge. With annual assessments, it is possible to determine how much students have grown during their year in an individual teacher's classroom. By controlling for external variables, we can isolate the individual teachers' contribution, or value-added. This method looks at what was taught in a classroom, but doesn't disadvantage teachers who take the toughest assignments.

Now that it is possible to connect gains in student achievement with the teachers who were responsible for them, we can get much more sophisticated in how teachers are educated, assigned, supported, evaluated and compensated. As new data systems are designed, they should connect individual teachers with student achievement over time to get an accurate measure of teacher effectiveness.

- **Respect for Teachers' Abilities and Professionalism Must Be at the Heart**
Although research has been mounting for decades that teachers are the single most important factor in how much students learn, too many people—both inside and outside education—cling to the myth that factors outside of school override anything teachers can do. This myth, which survives because of its appeal to underlying assumptions about race and class, not only demeans the contributions of teachers, but prevents meaningful change by excusing what should not be excused. Education leaders who want to ensure equity in access to teacher quality need to make the case that teachers matter.

- **Talent Is Drawn to Challenge**
Many stakeholders mistakenly believe it is not possible to recruit an adequate supply of qualified teachers into urban districts without first solving big, systemic problems. This belief constantly gets in the way of discussions about the distribution of teacher quality.

Contrary to conventional wisdom, though, many of our biggest and poorest school districts today are attracting more new teachers than they have in decades. Among our participating cities, for example, Chicago has received 13,700 applications for about 1,500 teacher vacancies from candidates applying for the 2006–2007 school year. The district estimates that by the end of the hiring season, they will receive 18,500 applications.

Bureaucracy, closed hiring processes and late hiring have as much to do with the problems of staffing as does applicant interest. Clear-eyed analysis is needed to ensure that our solutions are focused on the real problems.

A PLAN FOR EQUITY

In the coming weeks, states must outline the steps they will take to end the unfair distribution of teacher quality. To help states confront and solve the teacher-distribution problem, we are recommending a range of actions that states should consider in devising their equity plans.

Some of these suggestions will take longer to implement than others, and some will require significant changes to long-standing practices.

This much is clear: States and districts cannot ignore the imbalance in teacher quality any longer. It is a primary cause of the achievement gap in American education, and as long as that inequity persists, so too will the gaps that separate poor and minority students from other young people.

Immediate Steps

Overhaul hiring practices for teachers

Current hiring practices often put schools that serve low-income students, students of color and low-performing students at a disadvantage when it comes to effective and qualified teachers.

- Give principals more authority to choose who teaches in their schools.
- Scale back prerogatives that allow senior teachers to pick their assignments.
- And, finally, take a cue from professional sports and start using a "draft strategy." That is, put high-poverty, struggling schools at the head of the hiring line, allowing them to have the first pick of teaching talent. If we can give struggling sports teams first dibs on talented new players, can't we do the same for low-performing schools and provide these schools a decent shot at giving good teachers to the students who need the most help?

Pay Effective Teachers More in High-Need Schools

Lock-step salary schedules don't recognize great teachers and don't provide incentives for teachers to take on the toughest assignments. School districts need to get more sophisticated about identifying the most effective teachers and pay them more to teach in schools with shortages.

Balance the challenge

Balance the challenge of working in high-poverty schools by giving teachers reduced student loads, so they can have more time with individual students, more time to collaborate with their colleagues and more time for coaching and induction. It's hard to imagine any schools in which these kind of incentives would not be welcome, but the goal is to provide extra support to the teachers who take on the most challenging work. That means focusing first on high-need schools.

Give teachers "a break"

Recognize the toll that teaching in the poorest communities can take on teachers by providing fully paid sabbaticals, enabling teachers to recharge their intellectual and emotional batteries. This would encourage teachers to return to the classrooms where they are most needed and stem the tide of more experienced teachers leaving high-poverty schools.

Rethink tenure

Districts can improve the overall quality of the teaching force by reserving tenure for those teachers who demonstrate effectiveness at producing student learning. At the same time, districts need to help ineffective teachers improve, and encourage those who do not improve to leave the profession.

Place the best principals in the schools that need them the most

After teachers, principals have the biggest effect on school success. Supportive, collaborative principals are hugely important to attracting and holding strong teachers in high-poverty schools. Districts should provide salary incentives to attract high-quality, experienced principals to work in schools that serve high concentrations of poor and minority students. That includes linking principal pay to both improved conditions and improved achievement in their schools.

Ban unfair budgeting practices

District budgeting policies should not allow the most advantaged schools to "buy" more than their share of the most highly paid teachers. Staff budgets should be set at the school level and should be proportionate with student needs.

Improve the supply of teachers in critical areas

The higher-ed world must ramp up the work of supplying teachers in shortage areas, like math, science, special education and bilingual education.

Longer-Term

Build better data systems

To help identify the most effective teachers, we need better data systems that link individual teachers to the academic achievement of their students over time. This information will help administrators identify the unusually effective teachers—and those who need extra help.

That said, states and districts should not wait for better data systems before tackling teacher-distribution issues. They can act on the data that are available to get more effective teachers to low-income students and students of color.

Evaluate Teacher-Prep Programs

More sophisticated data systems about student achievement and teacher effectiveness should be used as a tool to gauge the quality of teacher-preparation programs. Louisiana is one state that holds higher education institutions accountable for the quality of the teachers they prepare. One step that other states and districts can take is to look at the new teachers whose contracts are not renewed by source institution. Institutions that produce large numbers of teachers who are so ineffective that they are let go early on or leave the profession should either be improved or closed.

Eliminate state-level funding gaps

States should make sure that all schools get their fair share of funding. States need to take more responsibility for funding education and target that funding to high-poverty districts. Schools and districts that serve high concentrations of low-income families need more money to reach the same educational goals as more affluent districts. But in most states, these schools and districts actually get less money—hampering their efforts to compete for the best teachers.

Rethink teacher compensation

States and districts need to completely re-evaluate teacher compensation, including paying more to teachers for their effectiveness in growing student learning, the challenge of their teaching assignment, and the roles they play within schools. The current system, which pays teachers based on experience and continuing education, is unrelated to teacher effectiveness and out of step with the goals of education reform.

CONCLUSION

Addressing gaps in access to teacher quality is the most critical element of a successful education reform agenda. But the reality is that many states simply do not know how teacher quality is distributed. And states that have that information will find change difficult because the current inequitable distribution is deeply rooted in tradition—and in politics.

We do not believe that the inequalities that exist today are the result of intentional actions to hurt children. And no purpose is served by pointing fingers of blame, especially at teacher unions. For, while some contract provisions need to be re-considered in light of unintended consequences, it's worth remembering that every teacher contract has been approved by a school district. School districts, not teacher unions, are responsible for balancing competing interests among stakeholders. It would appear that pleasing powerful constituents has sometimes forced equity to take a back seat.

The simple truth is that public education cannot fulfill its mission if students growing up in poverty, students of color, and low-performing students continue to be disproportionately taught by inexperienced, under-qualified teachers.

These manifestly unequal opportunities make a mockery of our commitment to equal opportunity and undermine genuine social mobility. What we have is a caste system of public education that metes out educational opportunity based on wealth and privilege, rather than on student or community needs.

Young people learn as much or more by watching what adults do as they learn from any classroom curriculum. Right now, they are learning that where you are born and how much money your parents make determine educational opportunity. Nowhere is this clearer—or more destructive-than in access to effective teachers.

Education leaders and policymakers must confront this legacy more openly and honestly than ever before. If Americans truly value equality of opportunity, it is time to teach by example.

More sophisticated data systems about student achievement and teacher effectiveness should be used as a tool to gauge the quality of teacher-preparation programs.

NOTES

1. "Novice" in this case refers to teachers with three years or less experience. National Center for Education Statistics, *Monitoring Quality: An Indicators Report*, December 2000.
2. National Center for Education Statistics, *Monitoring Quality: An Indicators Report*, December 2000.
3. *All Talk, No Action: Putting an End to Out-of-Field Teaching*, Craig D. Jerald, The Education Trust, 2002.
4. Ibid.

5. Ibid.

6. Highest-minority schools in Wisconsin serve 61.5 percent or more minority students. Lowest-minority schools serve 1.5 percent or fewer minority students.

7. In Milwaukee, the highest-poverty schools are defined as those in which more than 80 percent of the students receive free or reduced-price lunch. Lowest-poverty schools have fewer than 50 percent of students receiving free and reduced-price lunch. The highest-minority schools enroll 90 percent or more minority students, compared to less than 60 percent in the lowest-minority schools.

8. To be considered highly qualified in Ohio, a teacher must hold a bachelor's degree with a major or 30 coursework hours in the content area he/she is teaching; demonstrate subject-matter knowledge by passing the PRAXIS exam if he/she is new to the profession as of 2002; or successfully complete the HOU.S.SE process (for not-new teachers); and be fully certified by the state. To learn more about the HOU.S.SE provisions in Ohio, see *http:// www.ode.state.oh.us/teaching-profession/PDF/HighlyQualifiedTeachers20Oct.pdf*.

9. Note that the Chicago Public Schools Research Department did not have access to teachers' test results for 30 percent of the teachers, likely because they were veterans who entered teaching before testing was required.

10. Rossi, R., Beaupre, B., and Grossman, K. 2001. "5,243 Illinois teachers failed key exams" in *Failing Teachers: A Sun-Times Investigation*. Chicago Sun-Times. September 6. Available: *http://www.suntimes.com/special_sections/ failing_teacher/*.

11. Lankford, H., Loeb, S., and Wyckoff, J. *Teacher Sorting and the Plight of Urban Schools: A Descriptive Analysis*. Educational Evaluation and Policy Analysis Spring. (2002): Vol. 24, No. 1, 37–62.

12. The five attributes included in the TQI: the percentage of teachers with BA degrees from more-competitive colleges; the percentage of teachers with less than 4 years of teaching experience; the percentage of teachers with emergency or provisional credentials; the percentage of teachers who failed the Basic Skills test on the first attempt; and the average ACT composite score of teachers.

13. DeAngelis, K.J., Presley, J.B., and White, B.R. (2005). *The Distribution of Teacher Quality in Illinois*. Illinois Education Research Council. Policy Research Report: IERC 2005-1. See also: Presley, J.B., White, B.R., and Gong, Y. (2005). *Examining the Distribution and Impact of Teacher Quality in Illinois*. Illinois Education Research Council. Policy Research Report: IERC 2005-2. Available: http://ierc.siue.edu.

14. For a comprehensive review of the available literature on indicators of teacher quality, see Rice, J.K. 2003. "Teacher Quality: Understanding the Effectiveness of Teacher Attributes." Economic Policy Institute.

15. See, for example, Greenwald, R., Hedges, L., & Laine, R. (1996). *The Effect of School Resources on Student Achievement*. Review of Educational Research, 66, pp.361–396.

16. Ferguson and Ladd, *How and Why Money Matters: An Analysis of Alabama Schools*, in Holding Schools Accountable: Performance Based Reform in Education, Brookings Institution: Washington, D.C., 1996.

17. Wayne, A.J., and Youngs, P., 2003. *Teacher Characteristics and Student Achievement Gains: A Review*. Review of Educational Research, Vol.3, No. 1, pp. 89–122; Whitehurst, Grover *Research on Teacher Preparation and Professional Development*, White House Conference on Preparing Tomorrow's Teachers, March 5, 2002.

18. Whitehurst, Grover. *Research on Teacher Preparation and Professional Development*, White House Conference on Preparing Tomorrow's Teachers, March 5, 2002.

19. Darling-Hammond and Youngs, *Defining "Highly Qualified Teachers": What Does "Scientifically-Based Research" Actually Tell Us?*, Educational Researcher, 2002.

20. Goldhaber and Brewer, *Evaluating the Effect of Teacher Degree Level on Educational Performance*, in Developments in School Finance, 1996; *Monk and King, Multilevel Teacher Resource Effects on Pupil Performance in Secondary Mathematics and Science*, in Ronald G. Ehrenberg (ed.), Choices and Consequence. Ithaca, NY: ILR Press, 1994.

21. Murnane, Richard J. *The Impact of School Resources on the Learning of Inner City Children*. Balinger Publishing Company. 1975.

22. Hanushek, E.A., Kain, J.F. & Rivkin, S.G. (2005). Teachers, Schools, and Academic Achievement. Econometrica, Vol. 73, No. 2, 417–458.

23. Boyd, D., Grossman, P., Lankford, H., Loeb, S., Wyckoff, J. 2005. How Changes in Entry Requirements Alter the Teacher Workforce and Affect Student Achievement. Teachers Pathway Project.

24. Jennifer Presley, Bradford R. White, & Yuqin Gong. *Examining the Distribution and Impact of Teacher Quality in Illinois*. Illinois Education Research Council. Policy Research Report: IERC 2005-2, p. 1. Available: http: //ierc.siue.edu.

25. Jennifer Presley and Yuqin Gong. 2006. The Demographics and Academics of College Readiness in Illinois, Illinois Education Research Council, 2005. http://ierc.siue.edu.

26. Sanders and Rivers, *Cumulative and Residual Effects of Teachers on Future Students Academic Achievement*, 1996, p. 9.

27. Roza, M. and Hill, P. "How Within District Funding Inequities Help Some Schools to Fail," Brookings Papers on Education Policy 2004, available online at: http://www.crpe.org/pubs/pdf/InequitiesRozaHillchapter.pdf.

28. NCLB, Section 1120A.

29. See www.hiddengap.org.

30. Roza, M, Miller, L., and Hill, P. "Strengthening Title I to Help High-Poverty Schools: How Title I Funds Fit Into District Allocation Patterns," Center on Reinventing Public Education, 2005. http://www.crpe.org/workingpapers/pdf/TitleI_reportWeb.pdf.

31. Sanders and Rivers, 1996.

32. Jordan, Mendro and Weerasinghe, *Teacher Effects on Longitudinal Student Achievement*, Dallas, TX, 1997, p. 3.

33. Rivers, June. *The Impact of Teacher Effect on Student Math Competency Achievement*, University of Tennessee, Knoxville, TN, 1999.

34. Sanders and Rivers, 1996. p. 9.

35. Sanders and Rivers, 1996.

36. Jordan, Mendro and Weerasinghe. 1997.

37. ESEA Section 1111(b)(8) (C). The analogous provision for school districts can be found at ESEA Section 1112(c)(1)(L).

38. See the October 21, 2005 letter from the Secretary of Education that outlines requirements for states. Available: *http://www. ed.gov/policy/elsec/guid/secletter/051021.html*.

39. These requirements are described in the letter from the Secretary of Education to the Chief State School Officers, March 21, 2006. Available: *http://www.ed.gov/programs/teacherqual/cssoltr.doc*. See, also, letter to the Chief State School Officers, May 12, 2006. Available: *http://www.ed.gov/programs/teacherqual/hqtltr/index.html*

40. Jessica Levin and Meredith Quinn, Missed Opportunities: How We Keep High-Quality Teachers Out of Urban Classrooms, The New Teacher Project, 2003.

41. *The Funding Gap 2005: Low-Income and Minority Students Shortchanged by Most States*. The Education Trust, 2005.

APPENDIX

	STATE REPORTED		FEDERALLY REPORTED	
	Percentage of Secondary Classes in Core Academic Subjects Taught by Teachers Who Are Not Highly Qualified, 2005*		Percentage of Secondary Classes in Core Academic Subjects Taught by Out-of-Field Teachers, 2000**	
State	High-Poverty Schools	Low-Poverty Schools	High-Poverty Schools	Low-Poverty Schools
Alabama	33	16	33	11
Alaska	55	72	54	22
Arizona	9	7	53	32
Arkansas	3	10	43	27
California	39	19	34	30
Colorado	11	5	48	21
Connecticut	3	1	43	28
Delaware	N/A	N/A	N/A	N/A
District of Columbia	31	51	N/A	N/A
Florida	12	7	47	20
Georgia	3	1	43	36
Hawaii	36	32	43	N/A
Idaho	3	1	62	18
Illinois	8	0	52	22
Indiana	N/A	N/A	N/A	23
Iowa	9	6	N/A	22
Kansas	22	8	25	28
Kentucky	7	4	53	N/A
Louisiana	20	8	56	55
Maine	9	6	N/A	25
Maryland	46	17	N/A	20
Massachusetts	14	6	N/A	19
Michigan	N/A	N/A	49	28
Minnesota	5	2	10	8
Mississippi	19	6	40	N/A
Missouri	6	1	51	21
Montana	1	1	40	15
Nebraska	8	3	27	20
Nevada	47	26	N/A	36
New Hampshire	11	1	N/A	17
New Jersey	9	3	N/A	22
	STATE REPORTED		FEDERALLY REPORTED	

State	Percentage of Secondary Classes in Core Academic Subjects Taught by Teachers Who Are Not Highly Qualified, 2005*		Percentage of Secondary Classes in Core Academic Subjects Taught by Out-of-Field Teachers, 2000**	
	High-Poverty Schools	Low-Poverty Schools	High-Poverty Schools	Low-Poverty Schools
North Carolina	11	12	34	13
North Dakota	34	34	31	29
Ohio	23	5	44	29
Oklahoma	1	1	47	43
Oregon	12	6	50	22
Pennsylvania	11	1	36	18
Rhode Island	27	23	N/A	17
South Carolina	43	20	17	18
South Dakota	11	8	43	17
Tennessee	29	19	42	39
Texas	8	6	48	38
Utah	40	25	58	22
Vermont	12	8	N/A	30
Virginia	7	3	42	34
Washington	3	1	48	23
West Virginia	8	6	33	22
Wisconsin	1	0	N/A	15
Wyoming	17	11	N/A	36

NOTE: Not Available (N/A).

* Source: State Consolidated Performance Reports for School Year 2004–2005, submitted to the U.S. Department of Education on March 6, 2006.

** Source: U.S. Department of Education, 1999–2000 Schools and Staffing Survey, analysis by Richard Ingersoll, University of Pennsylvania. Reported in *All Talk, No Action: Putting an End to Out-of-Field Teaching*, Technical Appendix, Craig D. Jerald, The Education Trust, August 2002.

‡ Out-of-field teachers are those without a major in the subject taught.

Definitions:

For Data on Highly Qualified Teachers:

- **Secondary Classes** are defined as all classes in grades 9–12. Grades 6, 7 and 8 are classified as elementary or secondary by the states.
- **High-Poverty Schools** are defined as schools in the top quartile of poverty in the state.
- **Low-Poverty Schools** are defined as schools in the bottom quartile of poverty in the state.

For Data on Classes Taught by Out-of-Field Teachers:

- **Secondary Classes** are defined as all departmentalized classes in grades 7–12.
- **High-Poverty Schools** are defined as schools in which 50 percent or more of the student body is eligible for the federal free or reduced-price lunch program.
- **Low-Poverty Schools** are defined as schools in which 15 percent or less of the student body is eligible for the federal free or reduced-price lunch program.

In the Shadow of Brown

Special Education and Overrepresentation of Students of Color

By Beth A. Ferri and David J. Connor

ABSTRACT: In this first decade of the 21st century, we mark two milestones in education history: the 50th anniversary of the Brown v. Board of Education decision in 2004, and the 30th anniversary of the Individuals with Disabilities Education Act (IDEA) in 2005. Both Brown and IDEA asserted the need for increased educational opportunities for once excluded groups of students and asserted that segregation was inherently harmful and unequal. However, although we might wish to celebrate, there is also a need to critically examine the unfulfilled promise of both these efforts toward integrated education. In this article, we focus on one of the most long-standing critiques of special education practice: the disproportionate placement of students of color in special education programs, referred to in the education literature as overrepresentation. We then trace some of the origins of the current problem of overrepresentation by tracing the tangled relationship of special education and resegregation in the first years following the Brown decision.

In this first decade of the 21st century, we mark two important milestones in education history: the 50th anniversary of the *Brown v. Board of Education* decision in 2004 and the 30th anniversary of what we now know as the Individuals with Disabilities Education Act (IDEA) in 2005. Both of these reforms asserted the need for increased educational opportunities for once excluded groups of students and asserted that segregation was inherently harmful and unequal. As Justice Warren's oft-cited words reveal, segregating students "generates a feeling of inferiority as to their status in the community that may affect their hearts and minds in a way very unlikely ever to be undone" (cited in Williams, 1987, p. 34). Although many last year will have claimed *Brown* as a source of pride and engaged in all manner of ritualized celebrations of Brown's 50th birthday, it might be more honest to commemorate rather than celebrate. As Orfield and Eaton (1996, p. xix) wrote, "slowly, quietly, and without the nation's comprehension, political and legal forces have converged to dismantle one of our greatest constitutional victories." In other words, although we might wish to celebrate, there is also a need to critically examine the unfulfilled promise of both these landmark cases.

For example, we must acknowledge that our schools are as segregated as they ever were, with European American students remaining the most racially segregated of all student groups (Orfield,

Beth A. Ferri & David J. Connor, "In the Shadow of Brown: Special Education and Overrepresentation of Students of Color," *Remedial and Special Education*, vol. 26, no. 2, pp. 93-100. Copyright © 2005 by Sage Publications. Reprinted with permission.

cited in Irons, 2002). Half a century after *Brown*, African American and Hispanic American students now face increasing rather than diminishing school segregation, with most students of color attending schools where the majority of students are economically disadvantaged, creating a situation of concentrated poverty (Orfield & Eaton, 1996). Likewise, students in special education continue to experience a separate existence in schools, despite being ensured a free and appropriate public education in the least restrictive environment (Lipsky & Gartner, 1996). In addition to the individual failings of both *Brown* and IDEA, we must consider what failings are shared or interactive. In thinking about these issues, two questions come to mind: How has special education ignored the intersection of race and disability and, in so doing, contributed to the failure of *Brown*? And how did *Brown* fail to consider disability, and special education more specifically, as mechanisms for resegregating students of color within otherwise desegregated schools?

In this article, we focus on one of the most longstanding critiques of special education practice: the disproportionate placement of students of color in special education programs, referred to in the education literature as *disproportionality* or *overrepresentation*. We then trace the origins of the current problem of overrepresentation to the tangled relationship of special education and resegregation in the first years following the *Brown* decision.

THE PROBLEM OF OVERREPRESENTATION

The United States Office of Civil Rights (OCR) has reported a persistent problem of overrepresentation of minority children in certain disability categories since the 1970s. Thus, the problem of overrepresentation has not gone unnoticed. For example, early on, Dunn (1968) critiqued the overrepresentation of ethnic and racial minorities in special education, particularly in the category of mental retardation. Several landmark legal cases, such as *Diana v. State Board of Education* (1970) and *Larry P. v. Riles* (1971), challenged biases inherent in the standardized testing procedures used to identify students as eligible for special education. In *Diana*, a class action suit was filed on behalf of nine Hispanic children who were forced to take an individually administered IQ test in English and, as a result, were classified as labeled with educable mental retardation (EMR). Interesting enough, when retested by a Spanish-speaking examiner, only one of the nine children was classified as EMR. In a similar suit, *Larry P.*, the overrepresentation of minority children in EMR classes throughout San Francisco was determined to be due to unfair educational practices, including teacher bias. Both cases illuminated the role of school personnel, tests, and testing practices in erroneously labeling students of racial and linguistic minorities with a disability and placing them in restrictive special education classes.

These cases drew attention to the ways that special education labeling and placement decisions reflected stereotypic beliefs about White intellectual superiority. Both *Diana* and *Larry P.* called into question the widespread use of "scientifically" objective measures to gauge intellectual ability. Intelligence, which had been seen as innate, fixed, one-dimensional, and "naturally" distributed along racial and class lines, was now cast in a different light. As a result of these cases, it became increasingly clear that the use of evaluation instruments falsely reinforced presumed intellectual hierarchies among racial and ethnic groups. Although ability tests continue to be seen by many in the fields of educational psychology and special education as relatively neutral and valid, others within education have come to view standardized tests as forms of institutionalized racism. Critics have questioned cultural and linguistic biases within the tests and norms, which were based on the supposedly universal values and experiences of American, White, middle class students.

Moreover, because the special education eligibility process typically begins with teacher referral, the widening racial imbalance between the teaching corps and an ever more diverse population of public school students remains an ever growing concern. Recent reports show that 90% of public school teachers in the United States are White, whereas 40% of U.S. public school students belong to racial or ethnic minorities (Delpit, 1995). Similar imbalances can be seen in the number of individuals who are licensed to administer assessments. Because cultural, social, class, and linguistic biases often influence teacher and examiner perceptions of a student's ability, students from racial and linguistic minorities continue to risk having their differences pathologized when measured against exclusionary, ethnocentric norms and standards. Thus, more than 30 years after Dunn's critique, and despite important legal cases, the problem of overrepresentation has not lessened.

Most troubling is the finding that special education, although conceived as a way to provide support and access for previously excluded students, has paradoxically participated in maintaining rather than minimizing obvious inequities. The most recent government reports reveal that although Black students constitute 14.8% of the school-age population, they represent 20.2% of the students placed in special education (Losen & Orfield, 2002). These same reports document that Black students remain three times as likely to be labeled as having mental retardation (MR) as White students, almost two times as likely to be labeled as having emotional disturbance (ED), and almost one and a half times as likely to be labeled as having learning disabilities (LD). The disability labels associated with the highest levels of disproportionate assignment of students of color are also the most subjective. In other words, the labels that are most reliant on clinical judgment of all of the disability classifications (Parrish, 2002) are also the labels that are overly ascribed to students from racial and linguistic minority backgrounds. Conversely, less subjective categories, such as blindness or deafness, are ascribed proportionately to all student groups. Among these subjective categories, MR, which is one of the most stigmatizing labels, remains most likely to be assigned to Black students. Furthermore, Black students who attend school in wealthier communities are more likely to be labeled as having MR and assigned to segregated classes than those attending predominantly Black, low-income schools (Oswald, Coutinho, & Best, 2002). Depending on context, both social class and racial biases can increase the risk of minority children being labeled and placed in segregated classrooms.

The problem of overrepresentation is complicated and is not confined to African American students alone. In states with high Hispanic or Native American populations, Hispanic and Native American students are also more likely to be overrepresented in special education (Parrish, 2002). Once labeled, students from racial, ethnic, and linguistic minority groups are all more likely to be placed in more restrictive or segregated classrooms than their European American peers (Fierros & Conroy, 2002). Moreover, students from minority groups who attend school in large, urban districts are placed in the most segregated and restrictive of placements (Fierros & Conroy, 2002). Data on

Hispanic students is complicated by the fact that they tend to be underidentified for special education in elementary school, but overidentified in high school (Artiles, Rueda, Salazar, & Higareda, 2002). It is important to note that when we say that Hispanic students are underidentified in special education, we are not saying that these children are likely to be placed in general education classrooms, but rather that they are most likely to be placed in self-contained, bilingual or English as a second language (ESL) classes. These classes, like self-contained special education classes, are overly restrictive and may limit a student's ability to gain access to the general education curriculum or to keep up with their grade-level peers. Students who are English language learners (ELL) or labeled as having limited English proficiency (LEP) are also likely to be placed in ESL or bilingual classes at the elementary level and then disproportionately placed in special education in the upper grades (Artiles et al., 2002). An exception to the minority overrepresentation trend is the underrepresentation of Asian American students (Losen & Orfield, 2002). Stereotyped as the "model minority," Asian American students are far less likely to be placed in the subjective categories of MR, ED, or LD than any other minority group. Further research is needed to determine if there are within-group differences, especially between newly arriving Asian immigrants and refugees and their middle class counterparts. Research is also needed to determine if there are differences in disproportional placements in schools with and without ESL or bilingual classes.

Although the category of MR often receives the most attention, the category of LD has also been deeply implicated in the problem of overrepresentation. Emerging during the 1960s, the category of LD was characterized by average or above-average intelligence, specific rather than generalized deficits, and a cultural or familial background that was unrelated to the academic difficulties that the student experienced in school. This category became associated with White students to such a degree that students of similar levels of achievement were given different labels along racial, ethnic, and class lines. In fact, in the first 10 years following the emergence of the LD category (1963–1973), the vast majority of students labeled LD were White, middle class boys (Sleeter, 1995). Sleeter hypothesized that middle class White parents negotiated this less stigmatizing category to explain their children's difficulties in school. Moreover, because students were placed in separate classrooms according to their label or disability category, special education became as racially segregated as general education. Thus special education, like "ability tracking" (Mickelson, 2001), further reified the racial divisions that *Brown* was designed to dismantle.

It is of no small concern that the inappropriate classification of racial, ethnic, and linguistic minorities for special education leads to lowered achievement and poor postschool outcomes (Wagner, D'Amico, Marder, Newman, & Blackorby, 1992). Students in segregated special education classrooms are denied access to the general education curriculum and to their typically achieving peers. Students who are placed in special education are also more likely to drop out of school than their nonlabeled peers. Moreover, students in special education are more likely to experience lower teacher expectations as a result of being labeled and provided with instruction associated with poor transition outcomes after the student leaves school. These factors combine to negatively affect the academic performance of students of color who are labeled with a disability, who also have higher rates of suspension, face more severe disciplinary actions, and experience a higher dropout rate than their White and nondisabled peers (Losen & Orfield, 2002). Moreover, the failure to obtain a high school diploma further restricts occupational opportunities and leads to the increased likelihood of poverty. Unfortunately, the problem of overrepresentation is starting earlier and earlier, as children from economically poor Black or Hispanic families are increasingly being labeled with the ill-defined "at risk" category even before they enter school (Mutua, 2001).

Although many have suggested that socioeconomic status accounts for some or even all of the racial disparities in special education identification, recent reports have illustrated that the problem cannot be explained by any one factor. There remain large variations from district to district and from state to state in levels of overrepresentation in special education, suggesting that the degree of overrepresentation is affected by many variables and contexts. Southern states, for example, continue to have some of the highest incidence of overrepresentation regardless of social class, suggesting a connection to a longer legacy of racial segregation. Moreover, there are substantial within-group differences in terms of gender and age of diagnosis. Black girls, for example, are less likely to be overidentified than Black boys, but more likely to be labeled than White girls and boys. Again, because we can assume that Black boys and girls share similar social class standing, within-group gender differences in identification rates confound attempts to explain racial differences as primarily due to social class or race. Moreover, when language is taken into consideration, Spanish-speaking students who are learning English are much more likely to experience over-representation than those who are not. Such within-group differences point to an urgent need for more sophisticated research methodologies to fully understand the relationship of race, disability, and special education. In the next section, we highlight some of the ways that school desegregation orders were subverted in the wake of *Brown*, and we argue that special education inadvertently became employed as one such strategy.

STRATEGIES OF RESEGREGRATION

Many factors, including the repeal of judicial oversight and the failure to institute bussing across suburban and urban districts in large metropolitan areas, contributed to the lack of progress in achieving the promise of *Brown*. Furthermore, pupil placement laws instituted in the wake of *Brown* gave school boards the authority to place students according to dubious measures of ability or aptitude (Bullock, 1967). Of course, the goal of such measures was to subvert desegregation orders. Such pupil placement laws, adopted in at least 10 Southern states in the mid- to late 1950s, were

> shrewdly designed statutes that avoided mention of "Negro" or "race." They stipulated that local districts should assign students to schools according to very complicated psychological and "academic" criteria, such as student preparation and aptitude, and the "morals," conduct, health, and personal standards of the pupil. The goal, of course, was to perpetuate segregated schools. (Patterson, 2001, p. 100)

In Virginia, for example, pupil placement boards rejected hundreds of thousands of Black applicants seeking admission to White schools based on questionable criteria, such as health and ability to adapt (Patterson, 2001). In the Richmond *Afro American*, the editor critiqued a pupil placement policy that included criteria such as "aptitude of the child and curriculum adjustment" as well as a catch-all category that included "all other factors considered pertinent, relevant and material affecting either the child or the school" ("They're fooling," 1955, p. 4). The editor wrote,

> In the frantic search for some means to evade the school desegregation decision, members of the Wake County (N.C.) Board of Education have come up with a slick new scheme. It is so slick that other boards are eyeing it with interest, hoping that here, at best, is a way to disobey the court and still stay within the law. The gimmick is both simple and deceptive. … [but] it takes no vivid imagination to envision how these rules would be manipulated to hold that not a single colored child in Wake County could ever be qualified by aptitude, health, welfare, or availability of facilities to sit in classes with white children. ("They're fooling," 1955, p. 4)

Pupil placement boards instituted across the South after *Brown* were only one strategy to circumvent court orders—there were quite a few others. For example, some suggested segregating students on the basis of gender in order to calm Southern fears of miscegenation. Others went as far as proposing to abolish public schools rather than desegregate them. Such plans were suggested in a number of states, including Georgia and Virginia. The Prince Edward County schools in Virginia were actually closed between 1959 and 1964, which meant that two thousand Black children received no formal education in Prince Edward County during these years (Irons, 2002). Of course, White children received state-sponsored tuition grants to attend private academies during these years. In addition to these efforts designed to refuse court orders to desegregate schools, one of the most long-standing ways to maintain segregation was achieved by resegregating students *within* schools.

Ability tracking, which Mickelson (2001) called "second-generation segregation" (p. 215), was one such method used to resegregate within schools after *Brown*. Such practices of sorting students are "grounded in ideologies [of intelligence] that maintain race and class privilege" (Oakes, Wells, & Datnow, 1997, p. 484). Rooted in biological determinism, these notions of ability "provide[d] students from White and wealthy families with considerable advantage, but under the guise of their 'natural' abilities" (p. 486) as opposed to their privileged social status. A teacher remarked, "We all know that [tracking has] been a masquerade sometimes for institutional racism and classism" (cited in Oakes et al., 1997, p. 482). In many instances, tracking was instituted to appease White parents who assumed that integration would result in lower academic standards. Thus, tracking was seen as a strategy to curb the phenomenon of White families enrolling their children in private or suburban schools—a practice that came to be known as *White flight*. However, tracking was not always enough to keep White parents assured of their children's privileged position. As one parent lamented, "we've moved our sixth-grader to parochial school … [because] the whole curriculum's deteriorated" (Morgan, 1980, p. A6). Similar worries about "disrupting" the curriculum would resurface later when students with disabilities were seeking access to the general education classroom. Whether the normative space of the classroom was threatened by desegregation or by the inclusion of students with disabilities, the responses by White families and families of nondisabled children were similar in voicing strong resistance to integration and inclusion.

In addition to tracking, one of the most effective and pernicious means of resisting desegregation has been to over-refer students of color to segregated special education classes. In one example, perhaps to curb the huge tide of White students who were leaving the district, the schools in Washington, D.C., doubled their enrollment of students in special education classes by placing many of their newly admitted Black students in segregated special education classrooms ("Negroes," 1956). In fact, in the D.C. schools between 1955 and 1956, special education classes not only doubled their enrollment, but approximately 77% of students in special education classes 1 year after schools were ordered to desegregate were Black ("Negroes," 1956). Of course, special education is always embedded within the larger education system, in which we continue to find racial disparities in areas such as dropout rates, juvenile infractions, academic tracking, and suspensions (Losen & Orfield, 2002, p. xvi). However, because of its central role in resegregation, the field of special education *in particular* must interrogate the ways that it has participated in the failure of *Brown* (Artiles et al., 2002). Whether we are talking about desegregation, immigration, compulsory attendance laws, or increased referrals to special education in response to statewide testing, special education has always served as a place for students who cannot or will not be assimilated (Heubert, 2002).

Thus, although special education may be seen as benevolently serving students with disabilities, it also serves the needs of the larger education system, which demands conformity, standardization, and homogenization (Hehir, 2002). Such values are often at odds with creating an inclusive school environment that is accepting and welcoming of human difference and diversity. Ironically, history illustrates that at the very moment when difference is on the verge of being integrated or included, new forms of containment emerge to maintain the status quo. Thus, when schools were finally ordered to desegregate, other modes of dividing students by race were instituted. This meant that segregation, which was once achieved by building separate schools, could now be achieved by building separate classrooms. In the first years after *Brown*, racial resegregation was accomplished in large part by placing non-White students in non-academic tracks and in special education. In the next section of this article, we focus on the origins of the current problem of overrepresentation by tracing the tangled relationship of special education and resegregation in the first years following the *Brown* decision.

EARLY REFLECTIONS ON *BROWN*

In the first 2 years following the *Brown* decision, several newspapers reported follow-up stories on schools that had begun to desegregate. What these follow-up stories shared was a hyperfocus on racial difference, which, of course, served to shore up White supremacy at a time when it was being threatened. Many of these follow-up reports listed or charted student comparisons on every dimension imaginable, and "ability" was increasingly enlisted to justify within-school segregation and tracking.

Schools in St. Louis, for example, were followed in the first and second years after integration in the *Southern School News*, a monthly publication financed by the Ford Foundation, which compiled news stories and editorials from across the country to chart the progress of desegregation. The first of these reports was from a previously all-White St. Louis high school, which gained 500 Black students in the first year after *Brown*. The enrollment jumped from 900 to 1,400 that year, and one third of the students in the school were now Black ("First year," 1956, p. 3). Although desegregation in St. Louis schools began before the official court order and proceeded "without a single incident of identifiable racial friction," teachers in the first year reported vast differences between their White and Black students. For example, teachers reported that Black students were "tardier to school, tardier to class, more prone to skip an afternoon's classes, more inclined to absenteeism" (p. 3).

In another report, the principal, Mrs. Compton, noted that although students were getting along "famously," very few of the Black students "are rated by standard tests in the above average group … Most are low average or below average" ("Missouri," 1955, p. 19). Elementary teachers in this school were also interviewed. A sixth-grade teacher stated, "Most of 'them' [Black students] are definitely slow to learn. The Negroes generally are slower physically and mentally" (p. 19). Her colleague, a fourth-grade teacher, agreed, "The scholastic differences are 'dreadful'" (p. 19). She told the reporter that the "individual needs of the very inferior Negro students just cannot be met in a class of this size." She stressed that White and Black students learn differently and Black students "have trouble following detailed instructions" (p. 19). Finally, a first-grade teacher reported, "The five Negroes are all below average, and the lowest in the class" (p. 19).

Teachers and administrators in these reports seemed to have come to a shared consensus that the "biggest problem [posed by integration] is the difference in academic aptitude and achievement" among White and Black students ("Missouri," 1955, p. 19). A common feature of these reports is the documentation of comparisons in various subjects among White and Black students, carefully listed in percentages. In one of these reports, however, the reporter was careful to mention that teachers made these comparisons of students, "without reference to racial prejudice, and attributing the facts solely to differences in cultural, social, and economic background" ("First year," 1956, p. 3). As this statement illustrates, there was a degree of carefulness about the ways in which student differences were explained. We found similar statements about differences in ability or achievement not being racial per se repeated several times in this and other articles. Of course, although teachers were not willing to attribute differences to race, they had no problem pathologizing students' cultural or familial backgrounds.

The following year, in an article entitled, "The Second Year is Harder," St. Louis teachers stated that "now the novelty has worn off" ("The second year," 1956, p. 1). The teachers in the second report stated, "Scholastic disparity remains just as great … [but these differences are] now complicated by feelings of frustration and defensiveness on the part of the Negroes" (p. 1). Of course, the fact that Black students were dealing with the indignity of being called "slow learners" and "below average" in their local paper was not seen as having anything to do with these "feelings of frustration and defensiveness" (p. 1). Again, this year, the principal was careful to say,

> They are not racial differences. ... They are differences of cultural background, family habits, educational level, interest in and capacity for learning, and parental concern and direction, and so on. It is not the color of the skin that makes these differences. ... The fact is we now have in our school one group of youngsters so very different in all these ways that the teaching problem is complicated and the social results in the classroom difficult. ("The second year," 1956, p. 1)

Although she was careful not to attribute differences to race, her words were contradicted by an accompanying chart, which listed the numbers of students who were White and Black and then divided those groups into average, below-average, and above-average achievers ("The second year," 1956, p. 1). The chart did not explain, however, how the school came up with these numbers or what criteria they used to determine these categories. Moreover, on this list only one Black student was rated above average out of a total of 59 Black students (less than 2%), whereas 27% of White students in the school were deemed above average. In fact, more Black students were rated below average (62%) than were included in the average or above-average categories combined! Only 21% of the White students were rated in the below-average range. No text accompanied the chart—the figures were reported simply as fact.

In this second-year report, teachers were again interviewed. One teacher reported that the "majority of Negro pupils in her class are slow learners, need special attention, may ultimately affect the quality of education available to others" ("The second year," 1956, p. 1). She also claimed that absenteeism and tardiness were more of a problem with her Black students. She also found Black parents "uncooperative and unresponsive to suggestions." She concluded from her observations that "Negroes have a poorly developed sense of responsibility, apparently due to neglect at home" ("The second year," 1956, p. 1). Another teacher explained that Black students were experiencing a "conflict between *traditional* standards for middle-class White children and lower standards, which Negroes in a segregated school and at home had been accustomed to" (p. 1, italics added).

Again, in these reports, we found an almost unrelenting focus on differences between White and Black students, although again the differences between White and Black students were not characterized as racial differences. Some of the interviewers went so far as to inquire about differences in "hygiene and cleanliness" ("First year," 1956, p. 3) or "health and sanitation problems" ("Parochial school," 1955, p. 14) between White and Black students. Although teachers did not report any differences in these areas, the fact that hygiene and sanitation would even be questioned reflects an unstated assumption about the depth of presumed differences between these two races.

Teachers in these follow-up reports were often asked to reflect on the impact that increased diversity among students was having on themselves and other teachers. In one report, two teachers gave very different responses to this question. One teacher reflected that "Negroes may benefit from integration, but at this stage the teacher is drained of vitality due to strain of managing differences in academic standards, cultural background, behavior patterns, personality" ("The second year," 1956, p. 1). The reporter contrasted this teacher's experience with another teacher who claimed to have a very different experience. The reporter described,

> one new teacher who had just come out of university, where she studied alongside Negroes in a wholly integrated situation, did not report nearly so many problems and disappointments as some of those who had been teaching for many years in an all-White school. She accepted integration from the start and began her teaching career within that frame of reference. ("The second year," 1956, p. 1)

At least in this one example, we can see some hint that the problem of diversity may lie in the perceptions and attitudes of teachers and administrators, or even of White students and families, as opposed to Black students themselves.

In another report of a parochial school that began integration voluntarily, the principal reported that although everything was going along fine, several complications had arisen from the school's interactions with public schools that had "declined to play them in basketball" because they were an integrated team. A field trip also had to be abandoned because the state-owned park would not admit a Black student ("Parochial school," 1955, p. 14). This is the only example in which the politics of integration takes center stage, although the principal also warned that the "problem of integration becomes [more] difficult as the proportion of Negroes to Whites in a school increases" (p. 14).

Perhaps the most disturbing aspect of any of these reports is the second follow-up report from St. Louis, in which a teacher stated that "segregation within integration" was developing this year, not on racial lines but on those of ability and cultural background ("The second year," 1956, p. 1). Apparently, the same students who a year ago were "getting along famously" were now resegregating themselves in accordance with school-based definitions of ability. The teacher described the students as "voluntarily" segregating themselves. The teacher reported, "Neither group seeks out the other ... [and] each seems to find it more comfortable to be with their own kind" (p. 5). After 2 years, Mrs. Compton agreed with these divisions and said that the most "retarded Negroes should be given special attention in classes for slow children, so that they would not burden the regular classes" (p. 1). This theme of diversity being a burden or drain on the system would surface again with the inclusion of students with disabilities. In both cases, the normative space of the classroom is seen as being under siege.

CONCLUSION

It is important to note what was said and not said in these follow-up reports. In general, nothing was contextualized. For example, we did not find questions about whether the teacher expectations or the measures of aptitude or achievement that were yielding such differences along racial lines might be biased. Nor could we evaluate these measures, as none of them were mentioned. We do not know why students were missing class or to what degree they were late or absent. Nor did we find any mention of shortened school schedules for Black schools, so as to not interfere with White plantation owners' planting and harvesting schedules. We also did not read that many Black schools were forcibly closed in the struggle to resist desegregation orders—or that many Black students were actively denied transportation.

What we *did* read in these reports and others was an increasing cognitive merging of race and ability, which was then used to further justify the impossibility of desegregating schools or to argue for the necessity of resegregating classrooms through tracking or segregated special education placements. For example, in an article entitled "Slow Learner Plan Urged," the commissioner of education advocated "holding back slow learners until they catch up" ("Slow learner," 1956, p. 6). Furthermore, the commissioner argued for revising the school system "to permit the placement of children in accordance with their ability to learn" (p. 6). As another report explained, "there would be no integration this fall and the academic lag between White and Negro schools was given as one reason" ("East Tennessee," 1956, p. 7).

Thus, what emerges from these early reports is the use of perceived academic difference as a justification for racial segregation and exclusion. When segregation could no longer be justified based on the rationale of race, a new way of talking about student difference had to be created. This deficit way of thinking about differences would lead to a burgeoning of ability tracking and special education classes during the years following *Brown*. Thus, of all the many strategies that were employed to resist desegregation—and there were quite a few—one of the most effective was the use of tracking and segregated special education. This is the shameful legacy of the current problem of overrepresentation. Of course, these supposedly non-race-related strategies were recognized early on by African American leaders, such as Mary McLeod Bethune and others, as nothing more than thinly veiled racism. As Preston King (1955) wrote,

> The issue inherent here is, what legal or moral position can Georgia and the South take which would foster upon the Negro a second class citizenship and yet be just? … There is no shred of evidence to indicate that the Negro is racially inferior and unfit. (p. 4)

Mary McLeod Bethune (1955) agreed:

So many of us have heard that there are great "differences" between White people and Negro people. This is what we might call a "half truth." There are great differences between all people, for we are each a unique being, a person. It is the emphasis on the differences, instead of all that we have and all that we are in common, which makes for tension. Emphasis on our similarities, on the ways we are alike, makes for understanding and hence for appreciation of each other. (p. 9)

If we are to learn from the history of *Brown*, we must consider how many of our current educational practices serve as tools of social control and *exclusion* and not, as we might prefer to think, as democratic tools of social transformation. By focusing on technologies of *exclusion* rather than examining strategies that support and justify inclusion, we aim to question traditional progress stories, in which special education is characterized as building on previous civil rights movements and struggles. In other words, we argue that it is time to rethink the origin story of special education and to acknowledge the ways that special education has contributed to the subversion of *Brown*. We hope that by attending to our failures and our complicities, we can, from the shadow of *Brown*, create a different and more inclusive future.

BETH A. FERRI, PhD, is an associate professor in programs in teaching and leadership, cultural foundations of education, and disability studies at Syracuse University. **DAVID J. CONNOR**, MEd, is a doctoral candidate in the Learning dis/Abilities program at Teachers College, Columbia University. Address: Beth A. Ferri, 105 Harpers Court, DeWitt, NY 13214; e-mail: baferri@syr.edu.

AUTHORS' NOTE

We wish to thank Ellen Brantlinger for her careful reading of this article in manuscript.

REFERENCES

Artiles, A. J., Rueda, R., Salazar, J. J., & Higareda, I. (2002). English-language learner representation in special education in California urban school districts. In D. J. Losen & G. Orfield (Eds.), *Racial inequity in special education* (pp. 117–136). Cambridge, MA: Harvard Education Press.

Bethune, M. M. (1955, March 19). Ignorance, root of prejudice, is serious foe of democratic living. *Chicago Defender*, p. 9.

Brown v. Board of Education. (1954). 347 U.S. 483.

Bullock, H. A. (1967) *A history of Negro education in the South: From 1916 to the present*. Cambridge, MA: Harvard University Press.

Delpit, L. (1995). *Other people's children: Cultural conflict in the classroom*. New York: New Press.

Diana v. California State Board of Education (1970). No. C-70, RFT, Dist. Ct. No. Cal.

Dunn, L. M. (1968). Special education for the mildly retarded: Is much of it justifiable? Exceptional Children, 35, 5-22.

East Tennessee views on school issue. (1956, July). *Southern School News*, 3(1), p. 7.

Fierros, E. G., & Conroy, J. W. (2002). Double jeopardy: An exploration of restrictiveness and race in special education. In D. J. Losen & G. Orfield (Eds.), *Racial inequity in special education* (pp. 39–70). Cambridge, MA: Harvard Education Press.

First year of desegregation is analyzed at school. (1956, February). *Southern School News*, 2(8), p. 3.

Hehir, T. (2002). Eliminating ableism in education. *Harvard Education Review*, 72(1), 1–31.

Heubert, J. P. (2002). Disability, race, and high-stakes testing of students. In D. J. Losen & G. Orfield (Eds.), *Racial inequity in special education* (pp. 137–166). Cambridge, MA: Harvard Education Press.

Individuals with Disabilities Education Act (IDEA) of 1990, PL 101-476, 20, U.S.C. 1400 et seq.

Irons, P. (2002). *Jim Crow's children: The broken promise of the Brown decision.* New York: Penguin.

King, P. (1955, August 23). No evidence indicates Negro is inferior. *The Atlanta Journal and Constitution,* p. 4.

Larry P. v. Riles (1979 & 1986). C-71-2270 FRP. Dist. Ct.

Lipsky, D., & Gartner, A. (1996). Inclusive education and school restructuring. In W. Stainback & S. Stainback (Eds.), *Controversial issues confronting special education: Divergent perspectives* (pp. 3–15). Boston: Allyn & Bacon.

Losen, D. J., & Orfield, G. (Eds.). (2002). *Racial inequality in special education.* Cambridge, MA: Harvard Education Press.

Mickelson, R. A. (2001). Subverting Swann: First- and second-generation segregation in the Charlotte-Mechlenburg schools. *American Educational Research Journal,* 38, 215–252.

Missouri. (1955, June). *Southern School News,* p. 19.

Morgan, D. (1980, July 28). Blacks, Whites, critical of Cleveland's desegregation effort. *The Washington Post,* p. A6.

Mutua, K. (2001). Policied identities: Children with disabilities. *Educational Studies,* 32, 289–300.

Negroes make up 68 p.c. of district enrollment. (1956, December). *Southern School News,* p. 16.

Oakes, J., Wells, A. S., & Datnow, A. (1997) Detracking: The social construction of ability, culture, politics, and resistance to reform. *Teachers College Record,* 98, 482–510.

Orfield, G., & Eaton, S. E. (1996). *Dismantling desegregation: The quiet reversal of Brown v. Board of Education.* New York: New Press.

Oswald, D. P., Coutinho, M. J., & Best, A. M. (2002). Community and school predictors of overrepresentation of minority children in special education. In D. Losen & G. Orfield (Eds.), *Racial inequality in special education* (pp. 1–13). Cambridge, MA: Harvard Education Press.

Parochial school report given. (1955, June). *Southern School News,* p. 14.

Parrish, T. (2002). Racial disparities in the identification, funding, and provision of special education. In D. Losen & G. Orfield (Eds.), *Racial inequity in special education* (pp. 15–38). Cambridge, MA: Harvard Education Press.

Patterson, J. T. (2001). *Brown v. Board of Education: A civil rights milestone and its troubled legacy.* New York: Oxford University Press.

The second year is harder: Faculty of Missouri school reviews two years of desegregation. (1956, July). *Southern School News,* p. 1, 5.

Sleeter, C. (1995). Radical structuralist perspectives on the creation and use of learning disabilities. In T. M. Skirtic (Ed.), *Disability and democracy* (pp. 153–165). New York: Teachers College Press.

Slow learner plan urged. (1956, July). *Southern School News,* p. 6.

They're fooling only themselves. (1955, August 13). *The Afro American,* p. 4.

Wagner, M., D'Amico, R., Marder, C., Newman, L., & Blackorby, J. (1992). *What happens next? Trends in postschool outcomes of youth with disabilities* (Second comprehensive report of the National Longitudinal Transition Study of Special Education Students). Menlo Park, CA: SRI International.

Williams, J. (1987). *Eyes on the prize: America's civil rights years, 1954–1965.* New York: Viking Penguin.

White Privilege/White Complicity

Connecting "Benefitting From" to "Contributing To"

By Barbara Applebaum

In a 1945 program to denazify Germany, posters began to appear across occupied Germany illustrated with pictures of concentration camps and an accusatory finger pointed at the reader with the words, "You are guilty."[1] Many ordinary citizens were forced to acknowledge (some for the first time) that the camps really did exist, though denial and indignation were common. "We are innocent! How can we be responsible for these terrible crimes when we did not know that they existed and even if we did know, we could not have done anything?" Can people be responsible for evil they did not directly perpetrate, might not have known about, or might not have been able to affect? Intention, understood as free will, and causality are the hallmarks of responsibility. Yet intention and causality were absent in the case of many ordinary Germans. Nevertheless, Hannah Arendt, who coined the piercing term "the banality of evil" to describe how evil is perpetrated by regular people who uncritically go about their daily lives, intimates that any German who even indirectly supported Nazi ideology was responsible for the Nazi regime's evils.[2]

Recently, critical race theorists have insisted that white people are responsible for and complicit in systemic racism. At least two shifts in understanding race and racism contributed to this claim. First, race is commonly understood not as biologically based, but as a socially constructed category in which racial groups are mutually constituted through normalization processes where one group becomes the measure and all other groups are evaluated as "different" or "deviant." Second, the understanding of racism has shifted from a focus on individual people and prejudiced attitudes to an awareness of institutional and cultural practices that generate and maintain it. Whiteness, as the racial norm, lies at the center of the U.S. problem of race.[3]

Within this framework, the claim that white people are racist is frequently asserted. White people, especially well-intentioned white people, often respond with indignant denials and resistance. In 2007, the discussion topic "all whites are racist" in a mandatory university residential life program led to

Barbara Applebaum, "White Privilege/White Complicity: Connecting 'Benefiting From' to 'Contributing To,'" *Philosophy of Education*, pp. 292-300. Copyright © 2008 by Philosophy of Education Society. Reprinted with permission.

charges of brainwashing and indoctrination, and the university abandoned its antiracist initiative.[4] It is clearly important to understand what people mean when they maintain the claim of white complicity.

One way to elucidate this is by reference to white people's unconscious attitudes and beliefs that come from living in a racist society. Barbara Trepagnier contends that

> No one is immune to the ideas that permeate the culture in which he or she is raised. Silent racism … refers to the unspoken negative thoughts, emotions, and assumptions about black Americans that dwell in the minds of white Americans, including well-meaning whites that care about racial equality.[5]

Larry May connects unconscious racist beliefs to racially motivated harms enacted by others; he contends that even if one did not directly contribute to harms done through racially motivated crimes and discrimination, one can be responsible for them. Although only certain group members directly perpetrate racial violence, May insists that "seemingly innocent" group members are partially responsible if they share racist attitudes or if they fail to challenge these attitudes when exposed to them.[6]

Dwight Boyd, Iris Marion Young, and Peg O'Connor have critiqued May's focus on individualistic factors, such as attitudes, to link people to responsibility for wrongs, thus underestimating the social structures that connect people to injustice.[7] Still, while May is exclusively concerned with negative attitudes and explains how whites are indirectly responsible for overt harms perpetrated by other whites, he neglects how power circulates through all white bodies in ways that make them directly complicit in perpetuating a system they did not, as individuals, create.

The complicity thesis need not be exclusively concerned with unconscious negative beliefs and attitudes toward nonwhite people since complicity is linked to white privilege. White people benefit from the group privileges of racism that simultaneously marginalize people of color. All whites are racist or complicit by virtue of benefiting from these privileges, even though these privileges cannot be voluntarily renounced through individual action.[8]

Sandra Bartky argues that

> most white people in this country are complicit in an unjust system of race relations that bestows unearned advantages on them while denying these advantages to racial Others. Complicity in this system is neither chosen nor, typically, is it acknowledged, because there are both powerful ideological systems in place that serve to reassure whites that the suffering of darker-skinned Others is not of their doing and because the capacity of whites to live in denial of responsibility is very highly developed.[9]

As Bartky puts it, "I am guilty by virtue of simply being who and what I am: a white woman, born into an aspiring middle-class family in a racist and class-ridden society."[10] How is it that well-meaning whites, even anti-racist people, contribute to systemic racism through privileges that adhere to them, even without their will?

This essay explores the link between "benefiting from" an unjust system and "contributing to" its perpetuation. How does being systemically privileged lead to collaboration within an unjust system? How can one be held responsible for such collusion, even when it is unintended or resisted? By expanding and developing the meaning of white privilege, I explore the unique conception of "benefit" presumed in such claims of complicity[11] and then identify systemic white ignorance as a form of privilege. Such ignorance protects the morality of whites and shields unjust systems from interrogation. Finally, I elucidate the link between benefiting from and contributing to, and clarify the ways that whites are responsible for racism. This analysis can help us to understand Fiona Probyn's claim that complicity must be the starting point and the condition of ethics itself.[12]

THE BENEFITS OF WHITE PRIVILEGE

Peggy McIntosh's oft-quoted "knapsack" of privileges has powerfully exposed the ways that whites maneuver more comfortably than those who are not ascribed whiteness.[13] Yet the knapsack metaphor implies that privileges can be taken off or disowned at will and that a nonracial subject is behind the privileges. Also, the metaphor overlooks the unconscious habits and character traits that are manifestations of privileged experiences, and it disregards how experiencing privilege is constitutive of one's very being.[14]

Privilege is not only a matter of receiving benefits but consists also in traits of character, certain outlooks, and ways of moving. Sara Ahmed identifies a phenomenology of whiteness, and illustrates this by the tendency of white people to "take back the center," often without realizing it.[15] Shannon Sullivan also exemplifies white privilege as an unconscious habit of "white expansiveness" or the tendency of whites to assume that they can act and think as if all spaces are or should be at their disposal as they desire.[16] Adrienne Rich refers to "white solipsism" as whites' tendency "to speak, imagine and think as if whiteness described the world," and Alice McIntyre notes the "privileged affect" expressed in whites' exclusive focus on their own need to feel good.[17]

White solipsism is often implicated in white desire to do and be good. Even when well-intentioned whites decide not to live in all white neighborhoods, the very choice assumes and reinforces the "privileged choice" they have.[18] Privilege is something white people tend to assert even as they seek to challenge it. Ahmed draws attention to how white moral agency can be problematic and involves solipsism:

> to respond to accounts of institutional whiteness with the question "what can white people do?" is not only to return to the place of the white subject, but it is also to locate agency in this place. It is also to re-position the white subject somewhere other than implicated in the critique.[19]

White moral agency may function to reinscribe rather than dismantle systems of privilege by presuming that white people are the central agents, and also by implying that the white moral agent's innocence can be preserved.

Benevolent white acts can also illuminate how white privilege and complicity protect systems of oppression from challenge. In some white feminism, for instance, white compassion for the suffering of black women has been self-serving and appropriating. Elizabeth Spelman asks, "At what point or under what conditions does compassion become parasitical upon its suffering host?" This hidden self-centeredness means that people who "enjoy being in the saddle of compassion may have disincentives to cancel the suffering that provides the ride."[20]

The ideology of color-blindness also illustrates how white privilege and complicity can be veiled under the cover of morality. "Black, white, red, purple—all that matters is that we appreciate and celebrate our difference and just get along." Ignoring race is considered to be a virtuous moral position, but in a context where the color of one's skin still makes a difference, this is not a virtue and functions to maintain the invisibility of injustice as well as to sanction white people's privilege in not even having to consider how they might be contributing to the perpetuation of an unjust system.

Ahmed explains how the utterances of white critics of whiteness do something other than what they claim to do.[21] She is not saying that they do not mean what they say; her point is that such assertions do not do what they say. For instance, in declaring "I am racist" or "I am complicit," the white critic of whiteness implies the opposite—"I am not racist" or "I am not complicit." Whereas the person who declares "I am modest" is clearly not a modest person, the one who declares "I am racist" is not declaring his or her goodness directly. Ahmed cautions the white critic of whiteness that assertions that "I am a bad white" can imply that "I am really a good white." Probyn contends that "a white studying whiteness trying not to reinscribe whiteness" is a paradox.[22] Whiteness is the object of the white critic's inquiry but also the subject and the obstacle to his or her project, especially when it obstructs the difficult task of being skeptical of the need to have "arrived somewhere."

Probyn challenges the prevailing focus in critical whiteness studies on unmasking whiteness, of unveiling it, and then proclaiming, "now I see" in "shocks of revelation." She hopes that "it isn't just these shocks that keep the patient alive."[23] "Noble" declarations of whiteness, Probyn insists, must be probed for their desires for purity. Ahmed likewise cautions, "We need to consider the intimacy between privilege and the work we do, even in the work we do on privilege."[24]

It should be clear that a unique type of benefit is connected to systemic privilege, and it involves more than material gains, and even psychological advantages. White privilege also protects a type of moral certainty and arrogance. White privilege is often addressed in terms of gain and considered from the viewpoint of the individual or aggregates of individuals. To understand how all white people are complicit in the perpetuation of systemic injustice, however, requires a shift from understanding benefit in individualist terms to understanding benefit collectively and macroscopically.[25]

Surveys continue to find large differences between the views of U.S. whites and blacks on key measures of race relations; in general, whites minimize the harmful effects of current racism.[26] This may reflect different understandings of harm. Alan David Freeman distinguishes between the harms of racism from the perspective of the victim rather than the perpetrator. From the victim's perspective, racial discrimination involves "those conditions of actual social existence as a member of a perpetual underclass … (and) includes both the objective conditions of life … and the consciousness associated with those objective conditions." This view involves more than asking an individual victim about what the harms consist of; it involves understanding harm within the framework of an unjust system. From the perpetrator's perspective, in contrast, discrimination is understood individualistically, "not as conditions but as actions, or series of actions, inflicted on the victim by the perpetrator. The focus is more on what particular perpetrators have done or are doing to some victims than on the overall life situation of the victim class."[27] Benefit, and not just harm, must be analyzed from the victims' perspective. With this expanded notion of privilege and benefit, I next examine white ignorance.

SYSTEMATIC WHITE IGNORANCE AND RESPONSIBILITY

Cris Mayo argued that "Privilege … gives whites a way to not know that does not even fully recognize the extent to which they do not know that race matters or that their agency is closely connected with their status."[28] Charles Mills asks, "How are white people able to consistently do the wrong thing while thinking that they are doing the right thing?"[29] Some recent research examines the epistemology of ignorance and, in particular, the dynamics of white ignorance.[30] Mills argues that it involves a systemically supported and socially induced pattern of (mis)understanding the world that functions to sustain systemic oppression and privilege.[31] Such ignorance mystifies the consequences of the unjust system so that those who benefit from it do not have to consider their complicity in perpetuating it. Vivian May notes, "there are many things those in dominant groups are taught not to know, encouraged not to see, and the privileged are rewarded for this state of not-knowing."[32] Willful ignorance involves a pattern of assumptions or socially authorized "inscribed habits of (in)attention" that privileges the dominant group and gives license to members of that group "to be ignorant, oblivious, arrogant, and destructive," all the while thinking of themselves "as good."[33]

Well-intentioned whites are often surprised to encounter experiences that compel them to consider what they do not know about systemic racism. Tyron Foreman and Amanda Lewis underscore this in reference to the intense surprise of many U.S. whites after Hurricane Katrina revealed the reality of racial inequality in New Orleans; they attribute this astonishment to a racial apathy consequent to the white ignorance manifested in the ideology of color "ignore-ance."[34] As Mills maintains, one's social positionality influences the questions one believes are important to ask and the problems one believes are valuable to pursue. White ignorance involves not asking (having the privilege not to need to ask) certain questions, and it generates specific types of delusions—wrong ways of perceiving the world that are socially validated by dominant norms.

White ignorance involves not just "not knowing," but also "not knowing what one does not know while believing that one knows." This latter phenomenon, fueled by a refusal to consider one's possible moral complicity, promotes a resistance to knowing. Consequently, concepts "necessary for accurately mapping these realities … will be absent." Mills correctly notes that "the crucial conceptual innovation necessary to map nonideal realities has *not* come from the dominant group."[35] While not only whites are susceptible to white ignorance, whites are particularly susceptible because they have the most to gain from remaining ignorant. Benefit, thus, is related to keeping ignorance in place.

Mills argues that the "recognition problems" that ensue from white ignorance must be acknowledged because "it becomes easier to do the right thing if one knows the wrong things that, to one's group, will typically *seem* like the right thing."[36] Yet it is not easy to get whites to consider their complicity. Scholars have shown that denials of complicity are a characteristic feature of white ignorance.[37] O'Connor offers a resonant illustration, discussing a white student who resists the possibility of a relation between race and securing a mortgage. Shown statistics that demonstrate that people of color are refused mortgages significantly more often than whites, the white student offers a variety of explanations that elide race, focused perhaps on the person's credit history or the nature of the neighborhood and the business obligations of the bank.[38] The point here is not to deny the possibility of the validity of such explanations in particular cases, but rather to note that the white person rejects even considering that race might be a factor, and may even allege that blacks are always "playing the race card."

Whites have a positive interest in remaining ignorant because this serves to sustain their moral self-image.[39] If one denies that race may be related to securing a mortgage, then one does not have to engage the possibility that one's own racial privilege helped one to receive a mortgage. Thus, white ignorance is not only about "not knowing what one does not know," but also involves a "passion for ignorance"[40] when it comes to learning "difficult knowledge" that challenges one's sense of moral self and compels one to seriously engage with one's complicity in systemic injustice.

One way, then, that whites contribute to the perpetuation of systemic racism is through experiencing privilege and a systemically induced ignorance that promote a relentless readiness to deny, ignore, and dismiss what victims of racism are saying, and that thereby enable whites to maintain their moral innocence. Understanding these dynamics helps to illuminate what white people must continually work toward challenging.

CONCLUSION

Connecting systemic privilege to practices of ignorance helps us to understand how systems of oppression are protected from critique and how white people deny their complicity to safeguard their self-understandings of moral goodness. In other words, "benefiting from" results in "contributing to" racism.

The link between "benefiting from" and "contributing to" racism is crucial for understanding the type of vigilance required of whites committed to social justice. White moral responsibility requires that white people be willing to explore the blocks that inhibit the acknowledgment and thoughtful analysis of white complicity. Even those who are committed to acknowledging complicity are not absolved from complicity. No white person is morally innocent. No white person can stand outside of the system.

To understand what this means, I return to what Ahmed writes when she discusses the white person who asks, "but what are white people to do?" She explains that this question is not totally misguided, although it does re-center on white agency, as a hope premised on lack rather than presence. … The impulse towards action is understandable and complicated: it can be both a defense against the "shock" of hearing about racism (and the shock of the complicity revealed by the very "shock"); it can be an impulse to reconciliation as a "re-covering" of the past (the desire to feel better); it can be about making public one's judgment ("what happened was wrong"); or it can be an expression of solidarity ("I am with you"). But the question, in all of these modes of utterance, can work to block hearing; in moving on from the present towards the future, it can also move away from the object of critique, or place the white subject "outside" that critique in the present of the hearing. In other words, the desire to act, to move, or even to move on, can stop the message getting through.[41]

I read Ahmed as recognizing that for whites to join with people of color in alliances to challenge systemic racism, they have to acknowledge white complicity. This means being vigilant about white moral agency, because it can ironically obstruct a genuine engagement with those who are victims of racial oppression. Ahmed cautions white people to examine their desire "to do something," because it can function to protect one's moral innocence and the social system on which it is based. "If we want to know how things can be different *too quickly*," as she argues, "then we might not hear anything at all."[42]

Audrey Thompson exhorts white people to acknowledge uncertainty and engage with what people of color tell them about their experiences in a way that does not just "come to say no."[43] Whites must be willing to risk engaging in the difficult listening that leaves one open and vulnerable. An important insight about being open and vulnerable is suggested by Naomi Scheman when she explains how the privileged must learn from others whose "social locations on the borders of intelligibility equip them precisely for dismantling the structures we may deplore but cannot ourselves see beyond—since they are, for those of us who are intelligible in their terms, the 'limits of our language.'"[44] In response to those who argue, "but how can one be open to everything and everybody?" Scheman astutely responds that how we choose what we give attention to is exactly the issue. She does not advocate "epistemic promiscuity," or being open to every passing argument; she emphasizes that we must examine how we choose which arguments to seriously engage that challenge our beliefs, whose critique we try hard to understand, whom we read, and where we might look for ways that "might shake us up."

Complicity, as Probyn insists, must be the starting point and the condition of ethics itself. This involves understanding what is meant by the benefits of white privilege, as well as the ways in which white ignorance distorts white perception of reality. Damien Riggs suggests that "rather than 'solving racism' by being better white people," whites need "to recognize that belief in the 'goodness' of white people, values and ways of knowing is precisely the foundation of practices of oppression."[45] Acknowledging rather than denying complicity is the first step in creating a shared language and a condition of dialogue.

It is by showing how we are stuck, attending to what is habitual and routine in "the what" of the world, that we can keep open the possibility of habit changes, without using that possibility to displace our attention to the present, and without simply wishing for new tricks.[46]

Not seeking so zealously to "get over" the discomforts of acknowledging complicity and being willing to remain engaged even in the midst of discomfort promotes the possibility of creating alliance identities and is a necessary step in working together to challenge and undermine the unjust system we are currently so deeply embedded in.

NOTES

1. Andrew Schaap, "Guilty Subjects and Political Responsibility: Arendt, Jaspers and the Resonance of the 'German Question' in Politics of Reconciliation," *Political Studies* 49, no. 4 (2001): 749.

2. Hannah Arendt, *Eichmann in Jerusalem: A Report on the Banality of Evil* (London: Faber and Faber, 1963).

3. Barbara Flagg, "Whiteness as Metaprivilege," *Washington University Journal of Law and Policy* 18, no. 1 (2005): 1.

4. Eric Hoover, "U. of Delaware Abandons Sessions on Diversity," *The Chronicle of Higher Education*, November 16, 2007, http://chronicle.com/weekly/v54/i12/12a00103.htm.

5. Barbara Trepagnier, *Silent Racism: How Well-Meaning White People Perpetuate the Racial Divide* (Boulder, Colo.: Paradigm, 2007), 15.

6. Larry May, *Sharing Responsibility* (Chicago: University of Chicago Press, 1992).

7. Dwight Boyd, "The Legacies of Liberalism and Oppressive Relations: Facing a Dilemma for the Subject of Moral Education," *Journal of Moral Education* 33, no. 1 (2004): 3–22; Iris Marion Young, "Responsibility and Global Labor Justice," *Journal of Political Philosophy* 12, no. 4 (2004): 365–88; and Peg O'Connor, *Oppression and Responsibility: A Wittgensteinian Approach to Social Practices and Moral Theory* (University Park: Pennsylvania State University Press, 2002).

8. Beverly Daniel Tatum, *"Why Are All the Black Kids Sitting Together in the Cafeteria?" and Other Conversations About Race* (New York: Basic Books, 1997).

9. Sandra Lee Bartky, "Race, Complicity, and Culpable Ignorance," in *"Sympathy and Solidarity" and Other Essays* (Lanham, Md.: Rowman and Littlefield, 2002), 154.

10. Sandra Lee Bartky, "In Defense of Guilt," in *"Sympathy and Solidarity,"* 142.

11. For a critique of the trope "white privilege," see Lewis Gordon, "Critical Reflections on Three Popular Tropes in the Study of Whiteness," in *What White Looks Like: African-American Philosophers on the Whiteness Question*, ed. George Yancy (New York: Routledge, 2004), 173–94.

12. Fiona Probyn, "Playing Chicken at the Intersection: The White Critic of Whiteness," *Borderlands* 3, no. 2 (2004), http://www.borderlandsejournal.adelaide.edu.au/vol3no2_2004/probyn_playing.htm.

13. Peggy McIntosh, "White Privilege and Male Privilege: A Personal Account of Coming to See Correspondences Through Work in Women's Studies," in *Critical White Studies: Looking Behind the Mirror*, eds. Richard Delgado and Jean Stefancic (Philadelphia, Pa.: Temple University Press, 1997), 291–9.

14. Shannon Sullivan, *Revealing Whiteness: The Unconscious Habits of Racial Privilege* (Indianapolis: Indiana University Press, 2006).

15. Sara Ahmed, "The Phenomenology of Whiteness," *Feminist Theory* 8, no. 2 (2007): 149–68.

16. Sullivan, *Revealing Whiteness*, 10.

17. Adrienne Rich, "Disloyal to Civilization: Feminism, Racism, Gynephobia," in *On Lies, Secrets, and Silence: Selected Prose* 1966–1978 (New York: W.W. Norton, 1979), 299; and Alice McIntyre, *Making Meaning of Whiteness: Exploring Racial Identity with White Teachers* (Albany: State University Press of New York, 1997).

18. Mcintosh, "White Privilege and Male Privilege," 297.

19. Ahmed, "Phenomenology of Whiteness," 165.

20. Elizabeth Spelman, *Fruits of Sorrow: Framing Our Attention to Suffering* (Boston, Mass.: Beacon, 1997), 158–9.

21. Sara Ahmed, "Declarations of Whiteness: The Non-Performativity of Anti-Racism," Borderlands 3, no. 2 (2004), http://www.borderlandsejournal.adelaide.edu.au/vol3no2_2004/ ahmed_declarations.htm.

22. Probyn, "Playing Chicken at the Intersection."

23. Ibid.

24. Ahmed, "Declarations of Whiteness."

25. Marilyn Frye, "Oppression," in *The Politics of Reality: Essays in Feminist Theory* (Trumansburg, N.Y.: Crossing Press, 1983), 1–16.

26. Jack Ludwig, "Perceptions of Black and White Americans Continue to Diverge Widely on Issues of Race Relations in the U.S.," *Gallup*, February 28, 2000, http://www.gallup.com/poll/3193/Perceptions-Black-White-Americans-Continue-Diverge-Widely.aspx.

27. Alan David Freeman, "Legitimizing Racial Discrimination Through Antidiscrimination Law: A Critical Review of Supreme Court Doctrine," in *Critical Race Theory: The Key Writings That Formed the Movement*, eds. Kimberle Crenshaw, Neil Gotanda, Gary Peller, and Kendall Thomas (New York: New Press, 1995), 29.

28. Cris Mayo, "Certain Privilege: Rethinking White Agency," in *Philosophy of Education* 2004, ed. Chris Higgins (Urbana, Ill.: Philosophy of Education Society, 2005), 309.

29. Charles W. Mills, *The Racial Contract* (Ithaca, N.Y.: Cornell University Press, 1997), 94.

30. Shannon Sullivan and Nancy Tuana, eds., *Race and Epistemologies of Ignorance* (Albany: State University of New York Press, 2007).

31. Charles Mills, "White Ignorance," in Race and Epistemologies of Ignorance, eds. Sullivan and Tuana, 13–38.

32. Vivian May, "Trauma in Paradise: Willful and Strategic Ignorance in *Cereus Blooms at Night*," *Hypatia* 21, no. 3 (2006): 113.

33. Mcintosh, "White Privilege and Male Privilege," 295.

34. Tyrone A. Forman and Amanda E. Lewis, "Racial Apathy and Hurricane Katrina: The Social Anatomy of Prejudice in the Post-Civil Rights Era," *DuBois Review* 3, no. 1 (2006): 175–202.

35. Charles W. Mills, "'Ideal Theory' as Ideology," *Hypatia* 20, no. 3 (2005): 175.

36. Charles Mills, *Blackness Visible: Essays on Philosophy and Race* (Ithaca, N.Y.: Cornell University Press, 1998), 149.

37. Kathy Hytten and John Warren, "Engaging Whiteness: How Racial Power Gets Reified in Education," *Qualitative Studies in Education* 16, no. 1 (2003): 65–89.

38. O'Connor, *Oppression and Responsibility*, 123–4.

39. Linda Alcoff, "Epistemologies of Ignorance: Three Types," in *Race and Epistemologies of Ignorance*, eds. Sullivan and Tuana, 39–58.

40. Deborah Britzman, *Lost Subjects, Contested Objects: Toward a Psychoanalytic Inquiry of Learning* (Albany: State University of New York Press, 1998).

41. Ahmed, "Declarations of Whiteness."

42. Ibid (emphasis added).

43. Audrey Thompson, "Listening and Its Asymmetries," *Curriculum Inquiry* 33, no. 1 (2003): 79–100.

44. Naomi Scheman, "Openness, Vulnerability, and Feminist Engagement," *APA Newsletter* 00, no. 2 (2001), http://www.apa.udel.edu/apa/publications/newsletters/v00n2/feminism/11.asp.

45. Damien Riggs, "Benevolence and the Management of Stake: On Being 'Good White People,'" *Philament* 4, http://www.arts.usyd.edu.au/publications/philament/issue4_Critique_Riggs.htm.

46. Ahmed, "Phenomenology of Whiteness," 165.

The 2007 Charles H. Thompson Lecture-Colloquium Presentation

Creating Schools Where Race Does Not Predict Achievement: The Role and Significance of Race in the Racial Achievement Gap

By Pedro A. Noguera

ABSTRACT: This article explores the ways in which race is implicated in efforts to address the achievement gap in U.S. schools. Through an analysis of the theoretical and historical issues that have framed the relationship between race and intellectual ability, the author explains why the effort to close the achievement gap is politically and socially significant. The efforts of two suburban school districts to address the achievement gap is presented to illustrate why some schools are making progress in closing the achievement gap while others are not. These cases are used to make a call for a new discourse about the role of race in student achievement and to clarify how and why race continues to be so controversial and confounding to educators who are working to ensure that all children, regardless of their backgrounds, receive a quality education and have the opportunity to experience academic success.

The effort to find ways to close or at least reduce the achievement gap—the disparities in test scores and academic outcomes that tend to follow well-established race and class patterns—has become a national priority. Since the enactment of No Child Left Behind (NCLB, 2002) and its requirement that schools and students be held accountable for achievement through annual standardized tests, a sense of urgency has developed over the need to improve the educational outcomes of under-performing students. In many communities, this has placed greater focus and attention on the need for strategies to improve academic achievement among children who have traditionally not done well in school, namely, poor and disadvantaged children, students with learning disabilities, recent immigrants and English language learners, and in many communities African Americans, Latinos, and other students of color, generally (Miller, 1995).

Those familiar with American history and the history of American education, in particular, will undoubtedly be struck by the irony and significance of the current national preoccupation with closing

Pedro A. Noguera, "The 2007 Charles H. Thompson Lecture-Colloquium Presentation: Creating Schools Where Race Does Not Predict Achievement: The Role and Significance of Race in the Racial Achievement Gap," *The Journal of Negro Education*, vol. 77, no. 2, pp. 90-103. Copyright © 2008 by Howard University. Reprinted with permission.

the racial achievement gap. Racial gaps in achievement, attainment and measures of intellectual ability are by no means new. In fact, throughout most of American history, racial disparities in educational achievement and performance were attributed to innate genetic differences between population groups, and as such, were regarded as acceptable and understandable "natural" phenomena (Fredrickson, 1981). Intelligence was regarded as an innate human property rooted in the particular genetic endowments of individuals and groups (Duster, 2003), and therefore altering patterns of academic achievement was not regarded as feasible or even desirable.

Given this history, the fact that federal educational policy has made the goal of closing the racial achievement gap a national priority is truly remarkable Although policymakers have not called attention to the fact that the effort to eliminate racial disparities in student achievement represents a repudiation of America's past views on race, educators at the center of this effort cannot help but engage attitudes and beliefs that are associated with the vestiges of racial attitudes from the not so distant past. The notion that children of color are not as intelligent and capable as White children continues to find adherents among educators and the general public. Furthermore, seven years after the adoption of NCLB, it is clear that eliminating racial disparities in academic outcomes will require more than an official renouncement of traditional views about the nature of race. Race continues to be implicated in patterns of student achievement in predictable and disturbing ways, and the persistence and pervasiveness of these patterns compels us to ask why? It also forces us to reconsider what it might take to alter the long-standing relationship between race and achievement since so many efforts to alter racial patterns have been unsuccessful.

This article explores these issues through an examination of the historical and theoretical factors that influence the role of race in educational performance. Additionally, through analysis of empirical research in school districts where efforts to close the racial achievement gap have been undertaken, this author will consider why greater progress has been achieved in some communities as compared to others, and will examine the factors that seem to obstruct further progress in other places. The goal of such an exercise is to clarify how and why race continues to be so controversial and confounding to educators who are working to ensure that all children, regardless of their backgrounds, receive a quality education and have the opportunity to experience academic success.

WHAT'S RACE GOT TO DO WITH IT?

According to the view of intelligence that prevailed throughout most of the 19th and 20th century, non-Whites, particularly Blacks, Native Americans, Hispanics and even some Eastern Europeans, were believed to possess lower levels of intellectual capacity than Caucasians, particularly those that originated in the countries of northwestern Europe (Gould, 1981). Such views about the relationship between race and intelligence had considerable influence on social science research, psychology, and education (Lemann, 2000). Although less overtly pernicious, these views were consistent with beliefs about race held by previous generations; such as beliefs that rationalized slavery, genocide, imperial aggression, Manifest Destiny and later, Jim Crow segregation (Fredrickson, 1981; Takaki, 1989; Zinn,

1980). Early in the twentieth century, advocates of Eugenics—the "science genetic engineering"—propagated the notion that groups and individuals with superior intellect and physical ability, should be encouraged to procreate to strengthen the national gene pool, while inferior groups should be actively discouraged and even prevented from reproducing their progeny (Duster, 2003). Given their views, it is not surprising that many of the Eugenicists were leaders in the effort to devise tests for measuring intelligence (Lemann, 2000). They sought to ensure that intelligence tests and examinations such as the SAT (Scholastic Aptitude Test) would be used to provide an "objective" measure of talent and ability. They also pushed for the results from these standardized tests to be used to determine who should be recruited for top occupations and for enrollment at elite universities (Fischer, 1996).

The history of beliefs about the relationship between race and intelligence in the United States is not irrelevant to current efforts aimed at closing the achievement gap. Although it is increasingly politically incorrect to attribute differences in achievement to genetic differences between racial groups, it is important to remember that, *The Bell Curve* (Herrnstein & Murray, 1994) made precisely this point, and the book received a mix of condemnation and acclaim at the time of its release (Fischer, 1996). Such views have been prevalent in American society for many years even though they have never been supported by research on genetics or advanced by scientists engaged in research linking human biology to intelligence. For example, even though neither of the authors of *The Bell Curve* studied genetics (Herrnstein was a psychologist and Murray is a political scientist), their lack of knowledge about genetics did not stop them or others from making arguments about the genetic basis of intellectual ability or the inferiority of racial minorities. Not long ago, former Harvard University President Lawrence Summers suggested that one of the reasons why women were not well represented in mathematics and science-related fields was due to innate differences in intellectual ability (Bombardieri, 2005). If the President of Harvard University, an economist by training, felt comfortable making remarks about the genetic basis of intelligence, it would not be a stretch of logic to conclude that similar views about the relationship among race, gender, and innate ability continue to be widely held throughout American society.

While it is increasingly less common for arguments about the genetic inferiority of minority groups to be made in public, it would be a mistake to suggest that these discussions have entirely disappeared. In their place, arguments that attribute differences in achievement to differences in broad and undefined notions of culture (McWhorter, 2000; Ogbu, 1987), parental influences (Epstein, 1994) and even rap music (Ferguson, 2002) have been used to serve a similar purpose: rationalizing the lower rates of achievement among Black and Latino students as the result of problems that are inherent to these groups. Unlike biology, culture has been embraced as a less politically distasteful explanation because it is assumed that cultures are not immutable but can be changed over time. Among those advocating this perspective are scholars such as anthropologist John Ogbu (1987; Ogbu & Davis, 2003) who argued that non-voluntary minorities—groups that were incorporated into the United States through conquest, slavery, or force (i.e. Native Americans, African Americans, Puerto Ricans, and Mexican Americans) consistently do less well in school because they adopt an "oppositional culture" in relation to schooling (Ogbu, 1987). According to Ogbu, to the degree that non-voluntary minorities regard schooling as a form of forced assimilation, they are less likely to embrace the behaviors that contribute to school success (e.g., obeying school rules, studying for examinations, speaking standard English, etc.). Ogbu's views have been embraced by many scholars as an effective way to explain why many "voluntary" immigrant minorities (especially Asians) do well in school while many domestic minorities do not.

Similarly, linguist John McWhorter has attributed the lower achievement of many African American students to a "culture of anti-intellectualism," while former English professor Shelby Steele has attributed it to what he calls "victimology": the tendency on the part of Blacks to blame "the White man" for their problems (McWhorter, 2000; Steele, 1990). McWhorter contends that "victimology stems from a lethal combination of this inherited inferiority complex with the privilege of dressing down the former oppressor" and he adds that it "condones weakness and failure" (p. 28). Others such as sociologist Orlando Patterson and journalist Juan Williams (Patterson, 2006; Williams, 2007) have cited the culture of "gangsta rap" with its emphasis on "bling" (flashy jewelry), violence, and disdain for hard work, as producing a culture of failure. Finally, a number of others (such as Ruby Payne whose work has been embraced by a number of school districts) have cited a "culture of poverty," as the reason why poor children of all races often fail to perform well in school (Payne, 2005). Such theories draw on the work of anthropologist Oscar Lewis who argued that inter-generational poverty among Puerto Ricans was reproduced because the poor embraced norms that perpetuate poverty (Lewis, 1966).

Cultural explanations of the achievement gap such as those articulated by Ogbu, Payne, and McWhorter have been widely embraced by researchers, policymakers, and educators (Noguera, 2001, 2003). Even though such explanations of academic performance fail to account for those who deviate from established patterns—poor Black students who excel, middle class White, and Asian students who struggle—but who share a culture with others who conform to these patterns, such theories continue to be embraced by a broad spectrum of researchers and practitioners. An article in the *New York Times* Sunday Magazine (Tough, 2006) put the cultural argument in this way:

> Kids from poor families might be nicer, they might be happier, they might be more polite—but in countless ways, the manner in which they are raised puts them at a disadvantage in the measures that count in contemporary American society, (pp. 16–17)

Recognizing how difficult it will be to achieve the goals of NCLB if cultural differences are at the root of the achievement gap, the Tough goes on to ask, "Can the culture of child-rearing be changed in poor neighborhoods, and if so, is that a project that government or community organizations have the ability, or the right, to take on" (pp. 22–23)?

When asked whether low achievement among African American students might be explained by a fear smart Black children have of being accused of "acting White," or if Asian students are culturally oriented to excel in mathematics, this author points out that such arguments are based on gross generalizations of culture and overlook the powerful role that schools can play in promoting or hindering academic achievement. It could be argued that the success or failure of students cannot be attributed to the amount of culture they do or do not possess. Rather, a close examination of achievement patterns at their schools may reveal conditions within them that play a major role in shaping the academic outcomes of its students.

Ironically, broad generalizations about culture are so widely embraced and deeply imbedded in popular thinking about race and school performance that they manage to exist even when there may be empirical evidence to undermine their validity. For example, Julian Ledesma, at the University of California, Berkeley, tested the strength of the Asian model minority stereotype in a paper (Ledesma, 1995). He surveyed students and teachers at Fremont High School in Oakland about which ethnic group they believed was most academically talented. The vast majority of those he surveyed identified Asian students as the highest performers. This was even true for the Asian students he interviewed who were not doing well in school. Given that Asian students were overrepresented in honors and advanced placement courses at the school, and given that several of the school's valedictorians had been Asian, their responses were hardly surprising. However, in his analysis of student performance data Ledesma showed that although many of the academic standouts at the school were Asian, these students were not representative of Asian students as a whole. In fact, the grade point average for Asian students at the school was a 1.9 on a scale of 4.0. He pointed out that because Asian students were perceived as academically successful; little effort had been expended to provide them with the kind of academic support or special services that had been made available to other students.

An example, such as the one of Ledesma, does not prove that cultural influences are irrelevant to student achievement. At an aggregate level, Asian American students do out-perform other groups in mathematics, White students do achieve at higher levels than Black and Latino students, and middle-class children generally out-perform poor children (Farkas, 2004). Individual exceptions exist, but the patterns cited are fairly consistent (Ferguson, 2007). To some degree these patterns may in fact be attributed at least in part to characteristics that may be loosely associated with culture. However, in order to be helpful in finding ways to ameliorate or at least reduce disparities in achievement, the specific aspects of culture that seem to be most influential must be identified. For example, certain child-rearing practices such as parents reading to children during infancy or posing questions rather than issuing demands when speaking to children are associated with the development of intellectual traits that contribute to school success (Rothstein, 2004). Similarly, parental expectations about grades, homework, and the use of recreational time have been shown to influence adolescent behavior and academic performance (Ferguson, 2007). In his research at the University of California, Uri Treisman found that many Asian American students studied in groups and helped one another to excel while reinforcing norms that contribute to the importance of academic success. In contrast, the African American students he studied were more likely to socialize together but study alone (Treisman, 1992). Whether or not such behaviors can be attributed to culture can be debated, but clearly identifying specific behaviors that seem to positively influence academic achievement is more helpful than making broad generalizations about "oppositional" and "anti-intellectual" cultures because this information can be used to teach others to emulate behaviors that lead to success.

Even when behaviors that appear rooted in culture are identified educators must be careful about relying on cultural explanations to guide their thinking about academic achievement. Such thinking often has the effect of reinforcing inaccurate stereotypes because they fail to account for the high degree of diversity within racial groups. Differences related to socioeconomic status and income, the educational background of parents, the kind of neighborhood a student lives in, and most importantly the quality of school a student attends, significantly affect student achievement (Miller, 1995; Noguera, 2001, 2003). Such factors influence the academic performance of all students, but because of the tendency to over-emphasize the influence of culture on the performance of racial groups, they are often ignored. Consequently, although there are a number of White students who do poorly in school (Jencks & Phillips, 1998), there is substantially less attention paid to this problem than to the issues facing minority students. Academic failure among White students, like the existence of poverty among White people in the United States, are phenomena that are rendered invisible due to the high degree of emphasis placed on race in many aspects of American social policy. Moreover, it is rare to hear "experts" cite culture as an explanation for why some White students do poorly in school.

Given that it is hard to imagine how we might go about changing the culture of individuals who seem to embrace attitudes and norms that undermine possibilities for academic success, it is far more sensible to focus instead on factors that we actually can do something about. There is a lot that our nation could do to reduce poverty and racial segregation, to equalize funding between middle class and poor schools, to lower class size, and to insure that we are hiring teachers who are qualified and competent. These are all factors that research has shown can have a positive effect on student achievement (Noguera, 2001, 2003), and none of them involve trying to figure out how to change a person's culture.

In light of this history, the fact that the effort to close the gap in academic achievement is now at the top of the nation's educational agenda must be seen as a significant and historic departure from the past. It suggests that prevailing beliefs about race in the United States may have dramatically shifted away from the assumption that differences in intellectual ability are rooted in genes—one in which these differences are regarded as the product of social experiences. President Bush's poignant call for educators to "end the soft bigotry of low expectations" goes even a step further for it has placed the onus on schools to devise ways to boost the achievement of all students regardless of their backgrounds (NCLB, 2002). It also serves as the clearest indication that at the highest levels of government there is a prevailing belief that the obstacle to higher achievement for children of color is rooted in educational practices and beliefs that limit student performance, rather than innate ability.

However, despite the significance of the beliefs that buttress the *No Child Left Behind Act*, there is ample evidence that it will take more than exhortations from the President to make these disparities or the beliefs that accompanied them disappear. The persistence of the so-called racial achievement gap and its accompanying predictable patterns—White and Asian students consistently out-performing Black and Latino students on most measures of academic performance—suggests that regardless of how they are explained, the relationship between race and student achievement remains largely intact. Moreover, the persistence of the achievement gap has the effect of reinforcing traditional views about the link between race and intelligence.

TOWARD A NEW UNDERSTANDING OF RACE AND ITS INFLUENCE ON ACADEMIC ACHIEVEMENT

As a result of the amorphous nature of racial categories, scholars have rejected the notion that race should be regarded as a biological concept, or that differences between racial groups can be attributed to essential genetic differences. Instead, scholars have advanced the idea that race should be considered a socially constructed political category (Omi & Winant, 1986). To justify this approach to the study of race these scholars pointed out that throughout U.S. history racial categories have changed over time and even been defined differently by states and regions (Roedigger, 1991). For example, while the so-called "one drop rule" has been used to determine who is Black in America (i.e., one drop of Black blood makes you Black, Omi & Winant, 1986), several states historically used conflicting criteria for how to define Blackness. Whereas in Virginia an individual with one-eighth or more of Black blood was defined as Black, in South Dakota anyone one-sixteenth Black or more was placed in that category. Courts in Louisiana ruled that a person was Black if their genealogical make-up exceeded one-thirty-second (Takaki, 1989).

That a person could literally change their race simply by moving from one state to another is often cited by contemporary race scholars as further evidence of its arbitrariness. Similar points have been made in relation to other groups—Latinos, Asians—because of the high degree of diversity in phenotype and other physical characteristics associated individuals who have been assigned to these groups.

In concurrence with the abovementioned view, this author takes the position that if racial categories are social and not, primarily, biological in nature, then it should be possible to fundamentally alter the predictability of racial patterns related to academic ability and performance, which does not imply that the physical differences associated with race—skin color, hair texture, physical features—are irrelevant, rather that the social significance associated with these differences varies over time. (For a discussion on how phenotype and the physical characteristics associated with race relate to the idea that race can be regarded as a social construct, see Fergus, 2005.) This does not mean that the racial patterns manifest in most academic outcome data can be dismissed as a figment of the collective imagination. Rather, it suggests that while it may be possible to disregard the idea that achievement patterns cannot be changed due to the genetic endowments of children, one can not avoid addressing the social conditions that produce and give meaning to these disparities for they, too, can have a powerful effect on beliefs and behavior. Therefore, in order for schools to produce academic outcomes that demonstrate that race is irrelevant to academic achievement they must address the many ways in which racial identity and racial stereotypes are reinforced and even reproduced within academic settings. The notion that African American, Latino, and Native American children are not as smart or capable as White students, is not only deeply rooted in American history, it is also propagated in the media and popular culture (Massey, 1998). Because schools generally reflect the larger values and beliefs of society, stereotypes about the relationship between race and intelligence are invariably reinforced within the structure and culture of schools, and unless educators make a deliberate and concerted effort to challenge them, these forces can have the same impact as older views about the relationship between race and intellectual ability (Steele, 1997).

Unfortunately, the number of schools where race is not a strong predictor of academic performance and no longer "matters" with respect to its ability to predict academic outcomes are relatively few (Noguera, 2001, 2003). While there are a small number of schools where it is common to find Black students among the highest achievers (Perry, Steele & Hilliard, 2003) and even a number of high-performing high poverty schools (Education Trust, 2002), in most schools in the U.S. the racial achievement gap remains, despite the President's exhortations to eliminate it. (For the purpose of this article the term Black will be used rather than African American to identify students of African descent because Black is meant to include students of African and Caribbean heritage. In many school districts data on student performance do not draw distinctions within racial groups based on immigration status or national origin.)

In order to understand how schools can address the ways in which race continues to be implicated in patterns of student achievement, the remainder of this article presents an analysis of two suburban school districts that have gone to great lengths to address the achievement gap. It has been shown that one district has made significant progress in its efforts to reduce the achievement gap, while the other has not. In presenting these two cases, it is this author's objective that by understanding the factors that contribute to success in one setting and paralysis in another might provide a clearer sense of what it would take to create schools where the race of children have no bearing on their performance in school.

A TALE OF TWO DISTRICTS

Suburban school districts with a disproportionate number of low-performing Black and Latino students are faced with both top-down and bottom-up pressure to find ways to address the achievement gap. NCLB and state level accountability measures force district and school leaders to show evidence of adequate yearly progress (AYP) in the achievement of their historically underachieving students. Simultaneously, district leaders are faced with pressure from parents' groups and community organizations who seek to hold them accountable for the low performance of these students. In the face of such pressures, the leadership in suburban districts can not offer superficial solutions to the challenges facing their low-performing minority students because the parents they serve are generally too savvy and well organized to be easily put off. Instead, suburban districts are compelled to develop new approaches to addressing the achievement gap and to demonstrate real evidence that the strategies they implement are working.

While the factors that contribute to the achievement gap, both those external and internal to schools, are similar across most districts, there are clear differences in the policies and practices that districts have used and in the commitment they have shown to address disparities. Not surprisingly, some have made more progress and shown greater resolve in closing the achievement gap than others. In 2006 and 2007, this author conducted research in two school districts in suburban communities in the New York City metropolitan area. Prior to the research both districts had undertaken a variety of measures to reduce disparities in student achievement. Despite their efforts neither had experienced the level of improvement necessary to meet the demands of NCLB or to assuage the demands of the local community. In an effort to understand why past efforts had failed and concerned that public frustration with their inability to serve the needs of an increasingly diverse student population were growing, the two districts approached me for assistance. Over the course of two years, one year in each district, extensive research was carried out to uncover the factors that contributed to the persistence of racial disparities in student achievement. The findings suggested that while both districts continued to exhibit substantial racial disparities in student achievement, there were clear differences in both the districts' dedication to closing the gap and in the institutionalization of policies and practices that would reduce the disparities.

Gardenville

Gardenville (pseudonym) placed the need to address the achievement gap as a high priority due to political pressure. Long recognized for its cultural, ethnic, and religious diversity, Gardenville was one of the first communities in the United States to voluntarily integrate its public schools. However, in recent years the district's schools experienced considerable White flight. Despite a steady decline in White student enrollment since the 1980s, the district retained a diverse student population from pre-kindergarten through 12th grade. During the 2005–2006 school year the district had 5,500 students. Black students constituted almost half of the student population (48.7%) followed by Latinos (21.2%), Whites (18.8%), and Asians (10.9%). Although the community was relatively affluent, with an average home value exceeding $350,000 and a median family income of $74,903, nearly one in five (19%) students qualified for free and reduced lunch. The presence of such a large number of low-income students was a source of controversy among the district's educators, several of whom suggested that a sizable percentage of these students were illegally attending school in the district by using local addresses of extended family members. Several remarks were made to the researchers that this issue was one of the key causes of the achievement gap in the district.

In addition to controversies related to low student achievement there was considerable pressure in the community over local property taxation. In 2006, per pupil spending in Gardenville was $14,320; one of the highest rates of expenditure in their state. However, approximately 40% of families in the town did not enroll their children in the district's public schools. This was particularly the case for Orthodox Jewish residents who constitute a large and growing presence in the community and on the school board. With a large percentage of voters, particularly those without children enrolled in the public schools and resentful because of the heavy tax burden created by the cost of public education, while still others dissatisfied by low levels of student achievement among Black and Latino students, Gardenville district leaders found themselves in an untenable situation.

Riverview

Riverview (pseudonym) is a small town with a rich history and a racially and ethnically diverse population. Like many suburban communities nationwide, Riverview is experiencing dramatic demographic change. While there was, historically, a significant Black presence in the area, during the past decade there has been a steady increase in the number of Black and Latino families moving into the community. Latinos moving into Riverview came from a variety of national backgrounds, and there is evidence that the population is comprised of both documented and undocumented persons. Finding ways to respond to the needs of its changing student population was the primary reason for the district's interest in examining the factors behind its persistent gaps in student achievement.

Comparable to Gardenville, the Riverview school district has benefited from a high tax base (per pupil spending in 2007 was $19,054). Riverview, however, is far from a monolithic community and median household incomes ranged from $53,549 to $127,274 based on the highly segregated areas within the community. Similar to Gardenville, Riverview voluntarily integrated its schools. The district adopted an integration plan in which children in the district move through each grade together from elementary through high school. The plan was fully implemented in 1981, and the graduating class of 1993 was the first group to complete their entire K-12 schooling experience in integrated classrooms. The district has received national recognition for its academic accomplishments, and its high school has been ranked as one of the top one hundred high schools in the nation. Despite these accolades district leaders were fully aware that not enough of their Black and Latino students were meeting educational standards. Having fully acknowledged the disparities that existed, Riverview made closing the achievement gap a top district priority.

While the data collected from Riverview did not identify it as an unqualified success story, many of the strategies that were used there show promise and are worthy of emulation by other districts interested in addressing the achievement gap. Most importantly, the lessons learned from the relative success of Riverview, especially when juxtaposed to the reform paralysis experienced by Gardenville, may prove instructive to researchers, policymakers, and educational leaders who seek to understand what it takes to begin to narrow gaps in student achievement.

Race and Achievement in School

Not surprisingly, disparities in student achievement are reflected in graduation rates. In 2005, one third of all Gardenville high school graduates received alternate diplomas since they were not able to pass the state's mandatory exit examination. Disproportionately, these students were Black and Latino males. In Riverview, there was a significant difference in the percentage of students among demographic groups graduating within four years. White students had a four-year graduation rate of 97%, while Black students only had a four-year graduation rate of 50% and Latinos fared only slightly better at 60%.

During the 2005–2006 school year, White and Asian students in Gardenville were overrepresented in the 4th grade gifted and talented courses, while Black and Latino students were underrepresented. Nearly twenty percent (17.2%) of White students and 16.7% of Asian students in the 4th grade were placed in gifted and talented compared to 5.7% of Black students and 3.9% of Latino students. Students who were enrolled in advanced or honors courses attained higher achievement and SAT scores, and not surprisingly, these students were also more likely to be admitted to Tier I postsecondary institutions (Owings, Madigan, & Daniel, 1998). Black parents expressed dissatisfaction with the inequitable access to the district's top courses for their children and several parents complained that their students were discouraged from enrolling in the rigorous courses. Although Gardenville offers open enrollment to advanced classes, students of color reported that they felt discouraged from enrolling in honors courses.

The lack of minority students in advanced courses was confirmed by classroom observations and other data on student performance collected during the research. Most students of color were enrolled in general education classes that drew much criticism from parents. One high school parent said "classes [were] rigorous if you're in honors; but if not, the kids [were] not being challenged." This belief combined with the limited access to gifted and talented honors and advanced placement (AP) courses for students of color, added significance to the over-representation of White students in rigorous and accelerated courses.

In Riverview, the students who enrolled in advanced courses also had higher academic outcomes than students who did not take advanced-level courses. The study revealed clear patterns of an achievement gap between students enrolled in AP and non-AP courses. During the 2006–2007 school year, Black and Latino students were the most underrepresented in the advanced mathematics sequence. Black students were nearly 10% and Latino students 13% less likely than White and Asian students to take and pass the mathematics state examination in the 8th or 9th grades after controlling for achievement. While approximately 50% of Black and Latino students reported that they would be attending two- or four-year colleges after graduation, more than 82% of White students and 100% of Asian students made similar assertions. For the high school state mathematics examination, Black and Latino students had mean scores below 70 (out of a maximum 100) while White and Asian students had mean scores in the 80s.

Students in advanced academics tracks made up the largest portion of Riverview's highest-performing high school students. These students were estimated to perform 6% to 16% better on the study's selected achievement measures. They were also estimated to be 48% more likely to pass the examinations required for a diploma with Advanced Designation and 38% more likely to report that they would attend a four-year college upon graduation. In Riverview, the effect of being on the advanced academic track was positive, relatively large, and strongly significant, even after controlling for a student's prior achievement. An examination of all students who were in the 11th grade during 2005–2006, revealed that more than 70% of White students in the grade and all of the Asian students took at least one AP or college course, while only 45% of Latino students and 28% of Black students took one of these courses. Less than half the Black and Latino students passed the examinations required for the Regents diploma compared with 84% of White students. In regards to the Advanced Designation diplomas, 23% of Black students and 11% of Latino students qualified, when compared to 63% of the White students. The finding does not suggest that the students who did not pass at the Regents diploma level were not eligible to graduate because the Local diploma option was available for those students who did not pass the Regents examinations. Students who earned a Regents diploma, however, were more competitive applicants for college admission than students earning Local diplomas.

As a way to address the lack of diversity in the AP courses at the high school, the Riverview district worked with a local college to offer a variety of college credit-earning courses to attract Black and Latino students. Some of the courses focused on African American and Latino history and culture, which were aimed at recruiting Black and Latino students. Additionally, this initiative offered other courses in mathematics, science, foreign language, and history, and consistently, there were more minority students enrolled in these classes than in the high school's AP courses.

Efforts to Close the Achievement Gap

The investigation of the two districts revealed strong connections between the social conditions, academic placement procedures, and the widening of the racial achievement gap. Interestingly, while in Gardenville, there was a distinct tendency to blame students and parents for low minority student achievement among teachers and administrators, in Riverview there was greater willingness to accept responsibility for changing student outcomes. Prior to carrying out research there, the Riverview district had established mentoring programs specifically for Black and Latino students at the middle and high school levels to address some of the social marginalization felt by the students. It had also introduced other reforms, including block scheduling, and advisory groups at the high school that were intended to change the context for teaching and learning, and provide students with a greater degree of personal support. These efforts appeared to have had a positive impact on the achievement of minority students. The measures also contributed to considerable support for the district among minority students and parents. In contrast, data from surveys and focus groups revealed that while Gardenville was mired in a debate over who was to blame for low student achievement, stakeholders in Riverview were working together to find solutions to a problem they believed could be solved.

The Role of District Leadership in Closing the Achievement Gap

The experience of these two suburban school districts should serve as a sobering reminder of why it is difficult to bring about genuine, concrete progress in efforts to close the achievement gap. Despite their stated commitments to educate all students and despite the considerable resources at their disposal, neither Riverview nor Gardenville can be viewed as examples of school districts that are closing the achievement gap. In both districts, wide disparities corresponding to race and class persist, and neither district has shown any clear evidence that these disparities will close in the near future. The lack of success in these school districts that have had success in educating White middle-class students, and where conditions for change are not hampered by a lack of funds or overt racial bias should be seen as a clear indication that changes at a national level will be slow and arduous.

However, while the lack of progress in the two districts is discouraging, there are signs that in Riverview, at least, steps are being taken to reduce disparities in student achievement that may produce change over the long term. Through concrete measures such as increasing access of minority students to rigorous courses, improving the mentoring and counseling for students regarded as "at risk" of failure, and increasing stakeholder involvement in school-related reforms, the district appears to be serious about closing the gap. While these initiatives are unlikely to result in short term changes in academic outcomes, these strategies may result in incremental change and higher rates of achievement for students of color in the future.

In contrast, there is less optimism for change in Gardenville where there has been little effort to make change in the structure or culture of schools. While educators in Riverview have embraced the challenge of closing the achievement gap and they continue to search for ways to improve learning conditions in its schools, in Gardenville there is no such commitment. This is because educational leaders in Gardenville have mostly addressed this issue as a response to political pressure from a community that is increasingly dissatisfied with the quality of its public schools. While Gardenville's leaders may like to reduce the pressure they are under, they lack a clear commitment to address the more complex educational issues that stand in the way of change. The mere fact that so many teachers and administrators continue to blame students and parents of color for low achievement is the clearest sign that they have not yet begun to accept responsibility for addressing their obstacles to achievement. The first step in such a process would be a willingness to ask what they might do differently with respect to the ways in which they are sorting and labeling students, the way they are teaching them, and the way they have organized their schools. Unlike Riverview where this type of introspection and critical analysis is widely embraced, in Gardenville the community appears to remain paralyzed in a debate over who should be blamed. In the face of empirical evidence, which showed how racial disparities are maintained, the leaders in Gardenville were not able to escape this paralysis that characterized their reform efforts.

These two cases suggest that educational efforts to reform schools and raise student achievement cannot be viewed separately from political issues related to race and achievement, and questions of leadership. Several researchers have found that political attitudes toward the presence of minority students and their families influence how these students are treated in school (Lipman, 1998; Meier, Stewart, & England, 1989). In communities where White educators lament demographic change due to "White flight," and complain about the growing presence of students of color, the commitment to serving their educational needs is usually lacking. In contrast, in schools and communities where students of color are embraced and where educational leaders willingly accept the challenge of making sure that all students receive a good education, possibilities for change in student outcomes benefit from broader openness to change.

The experiences of these two school districts also demonstrate why it is important for educational leaders to openly address the highly politicized nature of the relationship between race and student achievement. District leaders must convince their teachers, students, and other community stakeholders that increasing the achievement of Black and Latino students is not only possible, but also necessary. In order to accomplish this, district leaders must move beyond the all too common tendency to perceive efforts to promote educational equity as a situation in which efforts to address the needs of struggling students are perceived as coming at the expense of high-achieving White students. When this occurs, racial polarization and incrimination often stymie efforts to promote change (Noguera & Wing, 2006). In contrast, districts and communities that confront the challenge of racial disparities directly, with a clearly articulated and fully funded strategy, are more likely to experience tangible gains for their students. The ability of educators to promote change will ultimately determine whether or not progress is made in closing the nation's racial achievement gap.

CHANGING THE DISCLOSURE ON THE RELATIONSHIP BETWEEN RACE AND ACHIEVEMENT

In an unusual break from past practice, NCLB has significantly expanded the role of the federal government in the operation of the nation's public schools. With its requirement that states adopt clear academic standards and accountability measures for schools and students, the federal government has extended its influence over public education in ways that break significantly from the tradition of state and local control. Even among his fiercest critics, few have argued that the President's desire to improve public education has not been an important and even laudable goal.

Part of the reason for the controversy surrounding compliance with NCLB can be explained by the fact that for the first time in U.S. history, schools are required to produce evidence that all students are learning. Ironically, even as the Bush administration has opposed affirmative action and rejected the use of race in college admissions, it has required school districts to report student achievement on the basis of race and other so-called subgroups. Many schools and districts are struggling under the new law simply because they have never been expected to educate all children before, and they have experienced difficulty in fulfilling this basic requirement. This appears to be the case in large urban school districts where the majority of students are poor, Black, and Latino, and achievement has historically been low, and it is also the case in affluent suburban communities where the under-performance of a few poor and non-White children who were previously overlooked or simply unrevealed because the majority of White students were relatively successful (Noguera & Wing, 2006). Not surprisingly, much of the opposition to NCLB emerged first in these more affluent communities as a result of NCLB's heavy emphasis on standardized testing and the resentment caused by having some of their schools labeled "failing" because of the performance of children of color.

MOVING BEYOND THE RATIONALIZATIONS OF THE GAP

As previously mentioned, cultural explanations of the achievement gap are often associated with a tendency to rationalize the failure of certain students as a "normal" phenomenon simply because it has been manifest for so long. In schools where race and class are strong predictors of achievement; where few Black or Latino students are enrolled in gifted or honors courses but they are overrepresented in special education and remedial courses; and where the link between race and achievement has been firmly established in the minds of educators, students, parents, and even the broader community, a sense of complacency about student achievement can develop. In such communities, the under-achievement of students of color can become normalized when educators and others accept low performance as the by-product of factors that they cannot control.

Too often, educators can grow comfortable with seeing their minority students under-perform and fail in large numbers. In such schools, students of color may also grow accustomed to receiving failing grades while avoiding academic pursuits or taking challenging courses. Additionally, parents and the broader community can become so conditioned by pervasive and persistent failure among certain groups of students that low test scores, discipline problems, and high drop-out rates generate little outrage or concern.

When failure is normalized and no one is disturbed by low student achievement, it can be nearly impossible for student outcomes or schools to change. Reforms may be implemented—new textbooks and new curricula may be adopted, schools may be reorganized and restructured, principals may be replaced—but unless there is a strategy for countering the normalization of failure, it is unlikely that disparities in achievement will be reduced or that schools will ever change.

The factors that contribute to normalization are often quite real, and should not be dismissed. Student motivation and the attitudes that students display toward learning profoundly affect patterns of achievement. Schools that do not have a strategy for convincing students to become more invested in their education by coming to school on time and prepared, working harder, studying, and generally, caring about learning, are likely to fail to reduce disparities in academic outcomes or raise student achievement. Similarly, parents who are negligent about reinforcing the value of education, who fail to encourage their children to apply themselves, or who do not regard education as an effective means to improve the lives of their children because it did not work that way for them, may engage in behaviors that contribute to the failure of their children. All of these factors can contribute to the normalization of failure and complacency related to racial patterns in achievement. What is needed is a strategy that makes it possible to change the discourse about the relationship between race and achievement from one focused on who's to blame to one in which all of the key stakeholders accept responsibility for their role in raising achievement.

CONCLUSIONS

President Bush has called for the nation to "end the soft bigotry of low expectations," as his way of describing what this author calls the normalization of failure. Similar to other slogans used by the President to further his policy objectives, such phraseology is not useful in helping educators figure out how to approach the challenge of raising achievement for all students.

Our attitudes invariably influence our actions and whenever educators blame low student achievement on some factor they cannot control, there is a strong tendency for them to refuse to accept responsibility for those factors they do control. For this reason, countering the normalization of failure must be seen as the first step in any effort to close or at least reduce the achievement gap.

Closing the racial achievement gap and pursuing greater equity in schools will undoubtedly be a long term, uphill struggle that is fraught with difficulty because historically the education of Whites and non-Whites remains profoundly unequal. Educators must continue to recognize that the sources of inequity typically lie outside of schools—in disparities in income and wealth, in inequity in parent education and access to healthcare, and in access to good paying jobs and vital social services. At this time, there is very little political interest in closing these gaps in the quality of life, but there is at least some discussion about the need to close the achievement gap. Even if many of those who have embraced this call do not truly believe that it can be done, the mere fact that the call has been made provides an opportunity to call for a broader agenda for equity within and among schools. The effort to promote educational equity and close the achievement gap is consistent with the basic promise of American public education that schools should function as the equalizers of opportunity (Jencks, 1972; Sizer, 1984). No matter how difficult and elusive such an effort may be, closing the achievement gap remains a goal that schools must pursue if they are to remain viable as public institutions, and that our society must embrace if we are to avoid greater racial polarization and conflict.

REFERENCES

Bombardieri, M. (2005, January 17). Summers' remarks on women draw fire. *The Boston Globe*, p. A1.

Duster, T. (2003). *Backdoor to Eugenics*. New York: Routledge.

Education Trust. (2002). *Dispelling the Myth revisited: Preliminary findings from a nationwide analysis of high-flying schools*. Washington, D.C.: Author.

Epstein, J. L. (1994). Theory to practice: School and family partnerships lead to school improvement and student success. In C. Fagnano & B. Werber (Eds.), *School, family, and community interaction: A view from the firing lines* (pp. 39–54). Boulder, CO: Westview Press.

Farkas, G. (2004). The Black-White test score gap. *Contexts*, 3, 12–19.

Fergus, E. (2005). *Skin color and identity formation: Perception of opportunity and academic orientation among Mexican and Puerto Rican youth*. New York: Routledge.

Ferguson, R. (2002). *What doesn't meet the eye: Understanding and addressing racial achievement gaps in high achieving suburban schools*. Retrieved January 1, 2008, from http://www.ncrel.org/gap/ferg/.

Ferguson, R. (2007). *Toward excellence with equity*. Cambridge: Harvard University Press.

Fischer, C. (1996). *Inequality by design: Cracking the Bell Curve myth*. Princeton, NJ: Princeton University Press.

Fredrickson, G. (1981). *White supremacy*. Oxford, UK: Oxford University Press.

Gould, S. J. (1981). *The mismeasure of man*. New York: Norton.

Herrnstein, R. J., & Murray, C. A. (1994). *The Bell Curve: Intelligence and class structure in American life*. New York: Free Press.

Jencks, C. (1972). Inequality: *A reassessment of the effect of family and schooling in America*. New York: Basic Books.

Jencks, C., & Philips, M. (Eds.). (1998). *The Black-White test score gap*. Washington, D.C.: Brookings.

Ledesma, J. (1995). *Rethinking the model minority thesis*. Unpublished manuscript, University of California, Berkeley.

Lemann, N. (2000). *The big test: The secret history of the American meritocracy*. New York: Farrar, Straus, and Giroux.

Lewis, O. (1966). *La Vida: A Puerto Rican family in the culture of poverty—San Juan and New York*. New York: Random House.

Lipman, P. (1998). *Race, class, and power in school restructuring*. Albany, NY: SUNY Press.

Massey, D. (1998). America's Apartheid and the urban underclass. In F. Pincus & H. Ehrlich (Eds.), *Race and ethnic conflict: Contending views on prejudice, discrimination, and ethnoviolence* (pp. 125–139). Boulder, CO: Westview Press.

McWhorter J. (2000). *Losing the race: Self-sabotage in Black America*. New York: Free Press.

Meier, K., Stewart, J., & England, R. (1989). *Race, class, and education: The politics of second-generation discrimination.* Madison: University of Wisconsin Press.

Miller, L. S. (1995). *An American Imperative: Accelerating minority educational advancement.* New Haven: Yale University Press.

No Child Left Behind Act of 2001. (2002). Pub. L. No. 107–110, 115 Stat. 1425.

Noguera, P. (2001). *The elusive quest for equity and excellence.* Education and Urban Society, 34, 18–41.

Noguera, P. (2003). *City schools and the American dream: Reclaiming the promise of public education.* New York: Teachers College Press.

Noguera, P., & Wing, J. (2006). Unfinished business: Closing the racial achievement gap in our schools. San Francisco: Jossey-Bass.

Ogbu, J. (1987). Opportunity structure, cultural boundaries, and literacy. In J. Langer (Ed.), *Language, literacy, and culture: Issues of society and schooling* (pp. 265–283). Norwood, NJ: Ablex.

Ogbu, J., & Davis, A. (2003). *Black American students in an affluent suburb: A study of academic disengagement.* Mahwah, NJ: Lawrence Erlbaum.

Omi, M., & Winant, H. (1986). Racial formation in the United States: From the 1960s to the 1980s. New York: Routledge.

Owings, J. Madigan, T., & Daniel, B. (1998). *Who goes to America's highly ranked "national" universities* (NCES 98-095). Washington, D.C.: U.S. Department of Education, Office of Educational Research and Improvement.

Patterson, O. (2006, March 26). A poverty of the mind. *The New York Times,* p. B6.

Payne, R. K. (2005). A framework for understanding poverty. Washington, D.C.: Aha Press.

Perry, T., & Steele, C., Hilliard, A. III. (2004). *Young, gifted, and Black: Promoting high achievement among African American students.* Boston: Beacon Press.

Roedigger, D. (1991). *The wages of Whiteness-. Race and the making of the American working class.* New York: Verso Press.

Rothstein, R. (2004). *Class and school: Using social, economic, and educational reform to close the Black-White achievement gap.* New York: Teacher College Press.

Sizer, T. (1984). *Horace's compromise: The dilemma of the American high school: The first report from a study of high schools, co-sponsored by the National Association of Secondary School Principals and the Commission on Educational Issues of the National Association of Independent Schools.* Boston, MA: Houghton Mifflin.

Steele, C. M. (1997). A threat in the air: How stereotypes shape intellectual identity and performance. *American Psychologist,* 52, 613–629.

Steele, S. (1990). *The content of our character: A new vision of race in America.* New York: St. Martin's Press.

Takaki, R. (1989). *Strangers from a different shore: A history of Asian Americans.* New York: Penguin.

Tough, P. (2006, November 26). What it takes to make a student. *The New York Times* [Sunday Magazine], pp. 16–31.

Treisman, U. (1992). Studying students studying calculus: A look at the lives of minority mathematics students in college. *College Mathematics Journal,* 23, 362–372.

Williams, J. (2007). *Enough: The phony leaders, dead-end movement and culture of failure that are undermining Black America—and what we can do about it.* New York: Kindle Press.

Zinn, H. (1980). *A people's history of the United States.* New York: Harper.

The Gender Income Gap and th of Education

By Donna Bobbitt-Zeher

E ducation is thought to be the pathway to success for disadvantaged groups. Given that young women now match or surpass men's educational achievements on many measures, how do they fare in terms of equal earnings? Would further educational changes matter for closing any existing gap? Analyzing data from the National Educational Longitudinal Survey, the author found that college-educated men in their mid-20s already earn, on average, about $7,000 more per year than do college-educated women. The findings suggest that this gap would still be substantial—about $4,400 per year—if women and men had similar educational credentials, scores on standardized tests, fields of study, and degrees from colleges of similar selectivity. Although women's gains in education may have been central to narrowing the gender gap in income historically, gender differences in fields of study continue to disadvantage women. Moreover, gender differences in work-related factors are more important than are educational differences for understanding contemporary income inequality among young workers.

Given the obvious connection between educational success and labor market outcomes, many consider education to be key to reducing group inequalities. In particular, schooling is thought to play a pivotal role in the success of racial/ethnic groups, such as Asian Americans, and the continuing struggles of others (e.g., blacks, Native Americans, and Hispanics). But what role does education play in lessening gender disparities in the larger society? With women's educational attainment and achievement patterns now matching or surpassing those of men on many measures, are women on their way toward gender equality more broadly?

The literature has documented the unprecedented success of women in the classroom (e.g., National Center for Education Statistics, NCES 2005) and has suggested that education may have played an important role in reducing gender wage gaps over the past few decades (e.g., Gill and Leigh 2000; Loury 1997). Some studies have isolated educational influences on persisting gender wage gaps, most notably gender differences in skills (e.g., Farkas et al. 1997), college majors (e.g., Bradley 2000), and college selectivity (e.g., Davies and Guppy 1997), while others have concentrated on noneducational influences on wage disparities, such as family formation and patterns of labor market participation g., Kilbourne, England, and Beron 1994; Marini and Fan 1997). Yet few studies have systematically analyzed the mediating role of education in gender disparities in earnings, along with the potentially confounding family and employment factors. In addition, little attention has been paid to the current level of gender disparities in earnings among the beneficiaries of these changing patterns of educational accomplishment or to the prospects of education contributing to further reductions in such inequalities should the patterns of women's educational success persist.

This article, drawing from and extending prior work, addresses the role of education in mediating gender inequality in earnings for young college-educated workers today. Such analyses are important because they empirically test both the level of contemporary gender disparities in earnings and the potentially equalizing influence of education among those who are the most likely to benefit from recent educational changes. I begin by discussing changing educational patterns for women and their potential implications for gender inequality in the contemporary labor market. I then turn to the potentially confounding role of family responsibilities and workplace stratification. The analyses, which draw from the National Educational Longitudinal Survey of 1988 (hereafter NELS), assess the degree to which education mediates gender inequality in income for young college-educated workers. I conclude by discussing the implications of the important but limited role of education in reducing earnings inequality for the prospects of broader gender equality.

BACKGROUND

Consequences of Changing Educational Patterns

While scholars in the 1970s and 1980s highlighted ways in which schools shortchanged girls (e.g., Sadker and Sadker 1994), the focus has shifted in the past decade because young women now outperform young men on many indicators of educational achievement (see NCES 2005; Riordan 2003). Not only are women enrolling in college in greater numbers than men, they are also outpacing men in graduating from high school, attending college, and attaining college degrees (NCES 2004; Sum, Fogg, and Harrington 2003). In addition, gender gaps in enrollment and degree attainment favoring women are expected to widen further in the next decade (NCES 2003a:6; Sum et al. 2003).

These dramatic and well-documented educational changes have been fodder for much public debate regarding a "war against boys" (see Riordan 2003); however, the pressing issue that has been overlooked in the literature is the degree to which the educational success of young women today leads to gender equality later in life. In particular, there has been little research on the implications of changing patterns in higher education for gender equality in labor market outcomes. A notable exception is Loury's (1997) work, which suggested that women's educational success had a direct effect on the narrowing gender gap in earnings in the early to mid-1980s. In particular, Loury concluded that gendered changes related to college grades and fields of study explain virtually all the 6-percentage-point decrease in the gender gap in earnings for college graduates from 1979 to 1986.[1]

Such work connecting women's educational accomplishments to the declining gender gap in income suggests an optimistic picture for young, college-educated women at the time of their entry into careers. In particular, the pattern of women's increasing participation in higher education, given the increasing importance of a college education for labor market success (Cappelli et al. 1997; Farley 1995), suggests that young women who are entering careers may be well positioned, finally, for gender equity in pay.

However, to what extent do young college-educated women reap equal returns in the labor market? The weight of the empirical evidence suggests lingering inequality, with women earning about 15 percent less than men early in their careers (e.g., Blau 1998:129; Marini and Fan 1997). Yet other research has suggested no gender gap in wages for young engineers (Morgan 1998). Understanding the degree of gender inequality in earnings in the early years of careers is important because initial income disparities tend to grow over time (see Marini 1989). And for those who are interested in examining the equalizing effects of education, it is during these early years of a career—when differences in employment histories, life experiences, and accumulated skills are minimized—that educational credentials and school experiences are likely to matter the most.

In addition to the need to determine the magnitude of the income differences for college-educated men and women early in their careers, a second question also looms large: Given the changing gendered patterns of educational success, to what extent do educational factors contribute to any gender disparities in earnings for young workers today? I turn now to this question.

Educational Explanations for the Gender Income Gap

The recent focus on women's educational advances, which are both impressive and deserving of scholarly attention, tends to obscure the ways in which women remain disadvantaged on several educational measures. Gender differences on four of these measures, in particular, are implicated in the gender income gap: (1) choice of a college major, (2) skills as measured by standardized tests, (3) amount of education, and (4) selectivity of the college attended.

The most persuasive educational explanation of gender income inequality is that *women major in fields* that lead to jobs that are not rewarded with higher incomes (Bradley 2000; Davies and Guppy 1997; Gerber and Schaefer 2004). Individuals who major in such fields as engineering and computer science tend to earn more than do those who major in education and the humanities (Daymont and Andrisani 1984; Gerber and Schaefer 2004). However, in spite of the trend toward the integration of fields of study, college majors are still quite gender segregated (see Bradley 2000; Charles and Bradley 2002; Jacobs 1995, 1996). For example, women received 20 percent of the engineering degrees and 77 percent of the education degrees in 2000–01 (NCES 2004:78). Given that men are more concentrated in the higher-earning fields and women are more concentrated in the less rewarded ones, gender segregation in fields of study appears to contribute to gender differences in income.

Indeed, studies that have considered fields of study have found that the choice of college majors explains between roughly one-quarter to one-half of the gender gap in wages for college graduates (Brown and Corcoran 1997; Daymont and Andrisani 1984). Bradley (2000) concluded that this horizontal dimension of gender segregation is pivotal in understanding gender inequality in wages globally.

But what is it about some fields that lead to their being better compensated than others? Is it the content of the field or the gender composition that suggests its worth? It is possible that "certain majors and courses may develop more valuable job-related human capital than do other majors and courses" (Brown and Corcoran 1997:432, citing Paglin and Rufolo 1990). In this view, the labor market rewards this investment in human capital with higher earnings. Alternatively, the gender dominance of the major (i.e., percentage female) may be the most salient difference in field of study, since traditionally male fields have been rewarded more than have traditionally female ones. While most studies have tested the impact of fields of study by using dummy variables for majors, making it hard to know what about the majors is leading to the earnings disparities, NCES (1998; see also Joy 2000) considered women's proportional representation in each field. It found that among the college educated, workers with female-dominated majors averaged 20 percent less in annual earnings in the first year after graduation than did workers with male-dominated majors. Such research suggests that the gender composition of fields should not be overlooked when considering why college majors matter for gender disparities in income.

Another education-related explanation for income inequalities concerns *gender differences in cognitive skills*. Measured using standardized test scores, cognitive skills are thought to affect the gender gap directly as well as indirectly through the choice of college major and access to jobs (Farkas et al. 1997; Paglin and Rufolo 1990). Research has suggested that as the U.S. economy has transformed since the 1970s, math and science abilities have become more predictive of salaries (Murnane, Willett, and Levy 1995), and math skills translate into higher earnings for all types of workers (Mitra 2002). Indeed, Mitra's (2002) study found that the gender gap in income disappears among professional men and women with the highest math skills. Thus, the gender income differential is a result of differences in highly valued skills—generally math skills—which lead to lower-paying jobs for women. Although evidence suggests that differences in boys' and girls' performance on standardized math and science tests are shrinking (Willingham and Cole 1997), persistent differences on standardized tests, including the SAT, favoring men (College Board 2003; NCES 2004) may continue to play a role in gender disparities in income, particularly in today's economy, in which skills are increasingly predictive of salaries (Murnane et al. 1995).

While the strongest educational influences on gender disparities in income are likely to be gender segregation in college majors and differences in standardized test scores, two additional schooling-related factors may contribute to these disparities to a lesser extent. The first is the vertical dimension of gender segregation,[2] or the level of degree attainment. Although women now surpass men in undergraduate degrees that are awarded (NCES 2005), gender parity in the highest degrees has yet to be realized. Women receive approximately 45 percent of all professional and doctoral degrees (NCES 2004:82). Although this is not a large difference, the reality that greater educational attainment leads to higher wages for both women and men (Blau 1998; Kilbourne et al. 1994) suggests that men's advantage in receiving the highest degrees may contribute in a small way to women's lower average earnings.

In addition, some scholars have suggested that women's attendance at less selective schools contributes to women's disadvantaged position in the labor market. College prestige has a positive relationship with earnings later in life (Jacobs 1999), and men are significantly more likely to attend selective postsecondary institutions than are women, net of background and academic factors (Davies and Guppy 1997, replicating the findings of Hearn 1991). Women's attendance at less selective postsecondary educational institutions may be the result of institutional bias favoring men, more selective schools tending not to offer traditionally female-dominated programs, and/or parental choices to invest more financially in sons (Davies and Guppy 1997; see also Jacobs 1999). Although there have been declines in gender differences in the selectivity of postsecondary institution attended (see Jacobs 1999; Karen 1991), institutional selectivity remains a potentially salient influence on gender disparities in income for today's college graduates.

With regard to young adults graduating from college and entering the labor market today, these findings suggest that lingering gender differences in schooling (e.g., fields of study, measured cognitive skills, and college selectivity) may explain persistent gender disparities in earnings. With women's postsecondary education rates surpassing men's, participation in higher education is not likely to contribute to earnings disparities, except at the highest levels, where men's degree attainment continues to surpass that of women.

Education's Limited Role in the Gender Income Gap

The literature just discussed has indicated that educational forces contribute to gender disparities in earnings. However, noneducational factors related to family, employment, and aspirations—generally in the periphery of studies on the effects of education on income differentials—also play a part in gender income inequality. The effects of family formation, particularly marriage and parenthood and their impact on participation in paid labor, are implicated in gender income disparities. For example, net of other factors, such as education, women with children make 10 percent to 15 percent less than do women without children (Korenman and Neumark 1992; Waldfogel 1998), and there is a 7 percent wage penalty for each child that a young woman has (Budig and England 2001). The penalty for having children is greater for married women than for nonmarried women (Budig and England 2001:218). The same patterns do not hold for men; fathers experience no comparable wage penalty for their parental status (Waldfogel 1998). Furthermore, married men receive higher pay than do unmarried men, while there is some evidence of a wage disadvantage for married women (Kilbourne et al. 1994; see, however, Budig and England 2001 for evidence challenging a marriage penalty for women).

The impact of family formation on gender differences in earnings appears to operate through women's decreased labor force participation (Korenman and Neumark 1992). Both length of job experience and part-time employment contribute to lower earnings (Budig and England 2001; Shelton and Firestone 1989). And women historically have had less job experience and have engaged in part-time work more often than have men (Blau and Kahn 1997; Rosenfeld and Birkelund 1995).

Indeed, much research has suggested that the conditions of employment for men versus women contribute to income inequality. Perhaps the most thoroughly discussed explanations for the gender income gap are occupational sex segregation and women's concentration in female-dominated occupations (e.g., Blau and Kahn 2000; England 1992; Huffman 2004; Kilbourne et al. 1994; Macpherson and Hirsch 1995). England (1992:181) found that "the sex composition of an occupation affects the pay it offers, such that both men and women earn less if they work in a predominantly female occupation." Given that women are concentrated in traditionally female occupations, the gender gap in wages can be partially explained by women's overrepresentation in jobs that pay less.

Similarly, the content of women's jobs seems to matter, in that women are concentrated in jobs that are devalued as a result of their nurturing character (England 1992; England et al. 1994; Kilbourne et al. 1994). These jobs pay less, and women's greater representation in them contributes to the wage gap (England 1992; Kilbourne et al. 1994). Given the large degree of occupational sex segregation—half the women would have to switch occupations for gender integration to occur (Padavic and Reskin 2002:67)—and that women's jobs tend to pay less and offer fewer other rewards like benefits and promotional opportunities (see Reskin 1993), Tomaskovic-Devey (1993:10) concluded that "employment segregation is currently one of the central rules by which male employment advantage is created and maintained."[3]

In addition to occupational sex segregation, other work-related factors contribute to inequality in earnings. Men tend to have longer tenure with their employers, greater full-time work experience, and more training, all of which contribute to their higher earnings relative to women (Blau and Kahn 1997; Marini 1989; Wellington 1994). Similar trends hold true for young workers: Women's first jobs tend to be of a lesser quality than men's, and women are more likely than men to be employed part time (Joy 2000). While occupations have received the most attention in studies of income disparities, research on wage differentials across sectors (Moulton 1990) and industries (Fields and Wolff 1995; Groshen 1991), along with gendered patterns of labor force participation, suggest the need to consider gender variations at these broader levels when explaining gender differences in income (see Fields and Wolff 1995; Macpherson and Hirsch 1995; Marini 1989).

Furthermore, as a result of gender socialization, young men and women have different values and occupational aspirations, and these gender differences appear to influence the gender income gap via occupational choices (Daymont and Andrisani 1984; Wilson and Boldizar 1990; see also Corcoran and Courant 1985; Reskin 1993; Shu and Marini 1998). By their last year of high school,

> men were more likely than women to feel that making a lot of money is very important in selecting a job or career. Consistent with societal expectations that men be assertive and dominant, they were also more likely to feel the importance of choosing a job or career that provides an opportunity to be a leader. Women, on the other hand, were more likely to feel the importance of opportunities to be helpful to others or to society, and of opportunities to work with people rather than things. (Daymont and Andrisani 1984:414)

These different occupational aspirations affect decisions regarding higher education, which, in turn, affect the occupations that these young adults enter (Wilson and Boldizar 1990).

Taking all these patterns into consideration, then, the question is this: How much do education-related factors—particularly field of study and standardized test scores—contribute to gender disparities in earnings early in young workers' careers, relative to family, work, and aspiration influences? Much of the research on educational contributions to earnings disparities has not rigorously considered work and family factors, while much of the work and family literature has deemphasized the role of education, which makes it difficult to understand the weight of the two sets of influences relative to one another. Also, much of this literature has focused on women as a whole and has offered little insight into women and men in the early years of their careers.

Yet, a focus on young workers is important for understanding the salience of educational, work, and family factors for gender equality in the contemporary social context. Gender differences in family responsibilities, labor market participation, and other human capital-related characteristics that grow over time are greatly minimized for this group of workers. However, little empirical work has examined the impact of such factors specifically on young workers.

The most compelling research on workers at their entry into adult careers comes from Marini and Fan (1997). Using data from the National Longitudinal Survey of Youth (NLSY), Marini and Fan found that on entry into careers, women earn 84 percent of what men earn. Their findings suggest little reason to believe that differences in educational characteristics drive gender inequality in income for workers at career entry. Years of education and field of study explain only 2.8 percent of this gender wage differential and other educational factors have only "negligible effects" (p. 600).[4]

Marini and Fan (1997) found greater explanatory power in factors that are related to work and aspirations. Indeed, they concluded that 22 percent of the gender wage gap is attributable to differences in men's and women's occupations, and another 28 percent is due to differences in industrial placement. Part-time employment experience explains 9 percent of the gender wage gap, while gender differences in occupational aspirations account for 10 percent. At career entry, family obligations do not seem to affect the gender wage gap directly.

Building on the lessons learned from this past research, this study extends this line of inquiry by overcoming some of the data limitations of past studies and by giving greater consideration to academic factors that are thought to influence the gender gap in earnings for young workers. While Marini and Fan (1997) focused on early career entry, their design used data on first jobs begun at various times over a period of 12 years. Although this approach has the advantage of capturing the gender wage gap for younger workers at a similar place in their career development, it has the disadvantage of including workers at various ages and in different periods. This trade-off makes it hard to know if the patterns are consistent across age cohorts and over time. By following a cohort of young adults through their educational and early labor market experiences, as my study does, I can speak more specifically to the gender income gap for young workers who are experiencing the same historical labor market conditions.

Furthermore, because of the expansive set of indicators of educational characteristics available in NELS, this study is well positioned to provide a more comprehensive assessment of the educational factors that shape the gender gap in earnings. Although Marini and Fan (1997) explored the effects of several academic characteristics on income disparities, their analysis was limited by the data. For example, they considered broad fields of study but did not explicitly test the gender composition of the field, which other research has suggested is important. They also had no measure of level of education or school selectivity and limited indicators of math and reading skills. With better measures of all these educational factors, the study design I used can provide a more in-depth assessment of the importance of educational characteristics (i.e., college major, skills as captured by standardized test scores, graduate and professional education, and institutional selectivity) for income equality at the point in one's career when education is likely to matter most.

Moreover, given the remarkable report that young female engineers now enjoy no gender wage gap (Morgan 1998), a fresh look at the factors that influence the gender income gap is merited with more recent data for workers in all types of academic fields. As we move toward a more highly educated society with fewer educational factors disadvantaging young women, assessing claims about the educational arena's impact on the gender income gap with contemporary young workers provides an especially compelling test.

DATA AND METHODS

Data

NELS offers a rich database for exploring the relationships between educational factors and the earnings gap between young working men and women. It followed students who were eighth graders in 1988 through high school and into their early adult lives.[5] The baseline data are nationally representative, based on a sample of almost 25,000 students from 1,052 public and private schools. The 2000 data contain interviews with 12,144 of these individuals.[6]

This data set is particularly well suited for addressing my research question because it includes information from the students' transcripts for both secondary schools and any postsecondary institutions attended, family formation history, and labor market participation and earnings.[7] NELS offers the opportunity to explore potential explanations for a gender gap in income in the early years of men's and women's careers, since the respondents had been out of high school for approximately eight years, had often completed bachelor's degrees and some graduate degrees as well, and were frequently in the labor force by the fourth follow-up in 2000.

For comparison with national data from the Current Population Survey on the gender wage gap and to avoid part-time and inconsistent workers from biasing the analysis, I limited my analysis to college graduates who were full-time, year-round workers (that is, those with four-year degrees who were working 35 or more hours per week for all 52 weeks in 1999) and had annual income data available for 1999 ($N = 1,946$).[8] I focused on college graduates for two reasons. First, post-secondary educational attainment is one area in which women have made the greatest gains. Given the relationship between post-secondary educational success and labor market outcomes, it is especially important to know to what degree college-educated women enjoy income equity with their male counterparts. Second, many educational characteristics, such as institutional selectivity, are meaningful or applicable only to the college educated. In supplementary analyses, I found that the gender gap in income is larger among those without a college degree.[9] By focusing on college graduates, therefore, I deliberately concentrated on a group for which educational characteristics arguably have the greatest chance of explaining gender gaps in earnings.[10] Missing values were handled through multiple imputation[11] (Allison 2002).

Measures

In all the analyses, the dependent variable is *income*, measured by the respondent's reported annual income in 1999.[12] This variable captures the respondents' answers to the following question: "Including all of the wages, salaries, and commissions you earned in 1999, about how much did you earn from employment before taxes and all other deductions?"

Education-Related Variables   The independent variables correspond to the possible causal factors discussed in the literature review. As a measure of cognitive skills, I used *standardized test scores* from the students' college entrance examinations. This measure of the composite SAT score captures math and verbal scores on the SAT, as well as scores on the ACT, converted to the same scale as the SAT. As an alternate measure of skills,[13] I also tested undergraduate grade point average (*GPA*) a self-reported measure of the student's GPA.

Factors related to educational field, degree, and institution were also considered. *College major* was measured in two ways. First, consistent with Marini and Fan (1997), the general field of study is captured with four dummy variables for the type of major: business; math, natural science, and engineering; social sciences and humanities; and education (with education majors the reference category).[14] Second, to test gender composition effects specifically, I measured the percentage female of each field in a manner that was consistent with NCES (1998). I calculated the percentage female for each major in the data set using national data on the percentage of degrees awarded in each field of study to men versus women.[15]

Although the sample was limited to those with four-year degrees, I also considered *graduate and professional degrees*. Three dummy variables captured the highest degree attained—bachelor's degree, master's degree, and doctoral or professional degree (with the bachelor's degree as the reference category).

In addition, I included measures of the selectivity of the higher education institution attended. The NCES, using methodology from the Cooperative Institutional Research Project (see NCES 2003b:72 for further information on this classification scheme) ranked each institution that the NELS respondents' attended. Selectivity was measured in an interval fashion ranging from not selective (1) to highly selective (4).

Background, Family, Work, and Values Variables   While my primary interest was to understand the contribution of educational factors to the gender gap in earnings for young workers, I also considered nonacademic characteristics suggested in the literature. In regard to family formation characteristics, the variables included marital status, single-parent status, and the number of hours worked per week. Three dummy variables—married, divorced, and single—were used to capture a respondent's *marital status* (the reference group was those who are single). I also considered *single-parent status*, a dummy variable (1 = a single parent, 0 = not a single parent) and the number of *dependents who are children*, measured in a continuous fashion. *Number of hours worked* was a continuous variable capturing the total number of hours the respondent worked at all jobs in an average week in 1999, which was also the year for the income variable.

I used several job characteristics in the analysis. A dummy variable for *for-profit sector* gauged the type of employer for whom the respondent worked at a private, for-profit company. Not-for-profit, governmental, and military employers were the reference category for sector. The NELS data also contain codes for the *industry* in which the respondent was employed in 1999. I created dichotomous dummy variables for each of the 17 industries represented in the sample. See the Appendix for the list of industries. Retail trades is the reference category in all the analyses.

To capture the respondents' *occupations*, NELS aggregated the subjects' responses to the question of their current or previous job title into broad occupational categories. I then created dichotomous dummy variables for each of the 31 occupational categories that were represented in the sample. By sample design, all unemployed persons were excluded. See the Appendix for a list of all the occupations. The regression models used the criminal justice/military category as the reference group.

To gain a better understanding of the relationship between job quality and income equality noted by Reskin (1993) and Wellington (1994), I included job training and job autonomy in the analysis. Job training is a dichotomous variable in which 1 indicates that the respondent received *job training* in the previous 12 months and 0 indicates that the respondent received none. *Job autonomy* measures the level of autonomy the respondents perceived they had on their jobs, with values of 1 to 4; higher values signify higher levels of autonomy.

Furthermore, corresponding to Daymont and Andrisani's (1984) study, I used a measure of values, the *importance of having lots of money*. This is an ordinal variable with ranges of 1 (not important) to 3 (very important) that was measured during the students' 12th-grade year.

In addition to these theoretically guided independent variables, I included measures of the *socioeconomic status of the family of origin* (SES) and the respondent's race as controls. SES is NELS's socioeconomic composite score, constructed from information on parents' education, income, and occupation. Race is measured with dichotomous dummy variables for white, black, Latino, Asian American, and other race; the reference category in all the analyses is white.

ANALYTIC STRATEGY AND RESULTS

I used two regression strategies in the analysis. First, I used estimated generalized least-squares (EGLS) regression to ascertain the effects of the independent variables of interest on income. Because of NELS's clustered sampling design, EGLS is an appropriate analytic approach to correct for estimates of standard errors.[16] In these equations, the interest for interpretative purposes is on the coefficient for the binary variable *female* (1 = female, 0 = male) in each model. This coefficient represents the effect of being female versus being male on income, net of the other variables in the model. A negative coefficient for female indicates an income gap advantaging men. The coefficient for female in the bivariate baseline model may be compared with the coefficient for female in each additional model. I was especially interested in the extent to which the coefficient for female changed across the various model specifications, which allowed me to assess the extent to which each of the possible explanations offered earlier contributes to an understanding of the gender income gap. I began by testing the individual effects of the education-related variables of interest. These individual tests suggest which educational variables merit further consideration. I then tested a series of additive models that capture young workers' typical life course trajectory—moving from ascriptive qualities of race and social class through socialization of values and higher education to the formation of families and entry into careers.

Second, I used regression decompositions to enhance my capacity to capture the influence of each individual factor in the comprehensive regression model. A standard technique among scholars of wage inequality, regression decomposition suggests the amount of the total gender income gap that can be attributed to a given variable. The technique does so by partitioning the influence of gender differences in the characteristics (i.e., the mean differences between men and women on each independent variable) while considering the return for a one-unit increase in that characteristic (i.e., the slope for the independent variable for women and men) (see, e.g., England 1992). To get the necessary information, I ran the equation from the best regression model separately for women and men in the sample. I calculated the decompositions using, alternatively, men's and women's coefficients as the standard, since the choice of standard may influence the effects that are found (see, e.g., Daymont and Andrisani 1984; Marini and Fan 1997). Following Marini and Fan, I took the average of the estimates from these alternate specifications. The amount of the income gap not explained by the attributes of the gender differences in observed characteristics is considered the unexplained portion of the income gap. The gender income differential, then, can be represented by the following formula:

using the male standard,

$$\bar{X}_{mi} - \bar{X}_{fi} = \sum b_m (\bar{X}_m - \bar{X}_f) + \epsilon;$$

using the female standard,

$$\bar{X}_{mi} - \bar{X}_{fi} = \sum b_f (\bar{X}_m - \bar{X}_f) + \epsilon;$$

where the left-hand side represents the mean difference in income between men and women and the right-hand side captures the difference in men's and women's means multiplied by the slope from the male (b_m) or female (b_f) model, respectively, plus the differences in income left unexplained.

Table 1 presents descriptive statistics for income and educational measures for men and women. As expected, the patterns suggest some gender differences in educational outcomes, with women generally garnering better grades and men scoring better on standardized tests in math and science. While patterns of course taking in high school suggest some statistically significant gender differences, these gaps are small in magnitude. However, at the collegiate level, there are significant differences in the majors that men and women choose. Men are significantly more likely to major in business, math, natural science, and engineering, whereas women are significantly more likely to major in social sciences, humanities, and education. The average college major for women is 63 percent female, while the average college major for men is 48 percent female.

These patterns suggest considerable gender segregation of college majors; yet, it is also clear that a large number of men and women choose fields that are neither male- nor female dominated. Although few men and women have completed graduate or professional degrees (8 percent of the sample), women are significantly more likely to have attained a master's, doctorate, or professional degree. There are no significant gender differences in the selectivity of the bachelor's degree institutions that women and men attend.

The Appendix presents descriptive statistics for noneducational conditions and suggests several significant differences by gender. Women, on average, are more likely than are men to be married or in a marriagelike relationship and to be single parents. Although all the workers are full-time employees, men average more hours worked in a typical week. Also, men and women are going into different occupations and industries, and women are significantly more likely to work in the public sector.[17]

By the time these college graduates were working full time in 1999, there were sizable gender differences in average income. In fact, the women earned $6,938 less than similarly aged, college-educated male workers. Stated another way, in the years immediately following college graduation, full-time working women with a bachelor's degree earn, on average, 83 percent of what their male counterparts earn. This pattern is in line with national data on the earnings' ratios of young adults (U.S. Department of Labor, Bureau of Labor Statistics 2004) and suggests a substantial gender gap in income in contemporary American society among young workers with college degrees.

Given that women are making significantly less money than are men, I now turn to regression analysis to explore which factors explain the gender income gap for young college graduates. Table 2 presents the results of EGLS regressions of income on the various education-related independent variables.[18] The baseline model (1) shows that women average $6,938 less than do men per year when no factors are controlled. Given that gender, race, and social class are all ascribed statuses that significantly influence income, I use controls for race and parental SES in all the models, although race and background SES have little direct influence on the gender gap in earnings[19] (see Model 2).

The additional models suggest that the gender composition of college majors is the primary educational influence on gender disparities in earnings. When general fields are measured (Model 3), the income gap decreases 22 percent. More robust, however, is the measure of the gender composition of fields of study; the percentage female of the major accounts for 39 percent of the income differential between men and women when race and background SES are controlled.

The other educational factors considered—cognitive skills, higher degrees, and college selectivity—have modest or little effect on the gender gap in income. When men and women have the same SAT/ACT scores (Model 5), the female coefficient is reduced to -$6,247, suggesting that differences in cognitive skills explain 10 percent of the income gap among the college educated.[20] An alternate measure of skills, undergraduate GPA (Model 6), accounts for none of the gender income gap and suggests that women's higher grades suppress the gap from being even larger than it is. Selectivity of the bachelor's degree institution (Model 7) has a small effect on the income gap, explaining 4 percent when only race and background SES are controlled. Most important, when college-educated workers have the same fields of study, same test scores, and same levels of graduate education and attend the same types of educational institutions, women still earn *$4,436* less per year than their male counterparts do.

Table 1. Means for Income and Education Variables, Including Significance Tests of the Means for Women versus Men, from Imputation 3

Variable	Sample Mean (N = 1,946)	Women's Mean (N = 1,053)	Men's Mean (N = 893)	t-Test of Mean Difference
Income in 1999	36,137	32,953	39,891	11.08***
Standardized Test Scores				
Reading (12th grade)	55.98	56.98	54.81	-5.83***
Math (12th grade)	58.17	57.30	59.19	5.52***
Science (12th grade)	56.14	54.48	58.11	9.47***
SAT math	510.03	492.42	530.80	7 69***
SAT verbal	445.10	445.18	445.01	-0.04
SAT/ACT combined	974.93	956.52	996.63	4.36***
Grades				
English (12th grade)	8.04	8.48	7.53	11 07***
Math (12th grade)	7.30	7.40	7.17	-2.18*
Science (12th grade)	7.62	7.74	7.49	-2.49*
Undergraduate GPA	2.99	3.06	2.91	-7.05***
Course Work (High School)				
Units in English	4.20	4.27	4.11	-4.38***
Units in math	3.75	3.71	3.81	2.99**
Units in science	3.47	3.41	3.53	2.54*
College Major				
Business major	.22	.20	.24	1.99*
Math, natural science, or engineering major	.28	.22	.36	6.89***
Social science or humanities major	.42	.48	.36	-5.15***
Education major	.07	.10	.04	-5.53***
Percentage female of major	56.09	62.98	47.96	-17.66***
Highest Degree				
Bachelor's degree	.92	.90	.94	3.25**
Master's degree	.07	.09	.06	-2.63**
Professional or doctoral degree	.01	.01	.00	-2.62**
Institutional Selectivity	2.29	2.28	2.31	0.84

* *p* < .05, ** *p* < .01, *** *p* < .001 (two-tailed tests).

Table 2. EGLS Regression Coefficients for Female and Percentage of the Gender Income Gap Explained with Alternate Models, including Education[a]

Model Number	Model Description	Income Gap (b_{female})	Percentage of Gap Explained
1	Female	-6,938	—
2	Female, background	-6,643	4.2
3	Female, background, field of college major	-5,418	21.9
4	Female, background, percentage female of college major	-4,244	38.8
5	Female, background, SAT/ACT score	-6,247	10.0
6	Female, background, undergraduate GPA	-7,215	u
7	Female, background, graduate degree	-6,815	1.8
8	Female, background, college selectivity	-6,634	4.4
9	Female, background, percentage female of college major, SAT/ACT score, graduate degree, college selectivity	-4,436	36.1

[a] Background factors are controls for race and parental SES.

Although this look at the individual, direct influences of education on the gender gap in income suggests a substantial effect of schooling on earnings' inequality, these models do not consider confounding influences of values, family formation, and work. Table 3 begins with the average difference in income between men and women and adds clusters of independent variables, following the general life-course sequence. These findings suggest that when schooling is considered alongside background factors and values regarding the importance of earning lots of money expressed during junior high school (Model 4), the gender earnings gap decreases 44 percent. The addition of family-formation factors yields little reduction in the income gap (Model 5); however, consideration of work factors appears to add greatly to an understanding of the income disparities. This best model (Model 6) explains 69 percent of the total gap in earnings.

Given that this best model explains more than two-thirds of the income disparity between these young men and women, I performed a regression decomposition on this model. Presented in Table 4, the regression decomposition suggests how much of the total difference in men's and women's earnings can be attributed to differences in the characteristics of the two groups. The contribution of the educational qualities is substantially smaller than indicated by the regression models that did not control for nonschooling effects. The percentage female of the college major explains 14 percent of the income gap, while scores on standardized tests explain another 5 percent. However, almost half the differences in men's and women's earnings can be attributed to work-related characteristics, especially occupation, sector, industry, and hours worked per week. Values appear to matter only modestly, while family formation has virtually no effect on the income gap for this sample of young workers.

Table 3. EGLS Regression Coefficients for Female and Percentage of the Gender Income Gap Explained with Alternate Models, Including Background, Values, Education, Family Formation, and Work Factors

Model Number	Model Description	Income Gap (b_{female})	Percentage of Gap Explained
1	Female	-6,938	—
2	Female and background	-6,643	4.2
3	Female, background, and values	-6,166	11.1
4	Female, background, values, and education	-3,903	43.7
5	Female, background, values, education, and family formation	-3,854	44.4
6	Female, background, values, education, family formation, and work	-2,132	69.3

NOTE: Background factors are controls for race and parental SES. Values are measured by the importance of having lots of money. Education factors are the percentage female of the field of study, SAT/ACT scores, highest degree earned, and selectivity of degree granting institution. Family formation factors are marital status and single-parent status. Work factors are the number of hours worked per week, occupation, industry, sector, job autonomy, and job training.

Taking into consideration the results from the EGLS regression models presented in Tables 2 and 3, along with the decomposition findings from Table 4, it appears that the gender composition of college majors has a considerable direct effect on the gender gap in earnings. However, employment-related factors are more salient for understanding the income disparities.

DISCUSSION

Girls' success in school is a hot topic among both academics and the general public. Generally absent from this dialogue, however, has been the key question of the consequences of these patterns for the gender equality of young adults as they transition from educational institutions to the workforce. Now that young women's educational performance is so strong relative to men's, how does this newfound "advantage" matter? Given the long-standing debate over the role of education in mediating group inequalities, this discussion is overdue.

The findings of this study suggest that education continues to contribute to gender stratification in a meaningful way despite women's overall success in educational realms. The educational factor that appears to matter most is college major, and college major appears to affect inequality in earnings in two ways. As one may expect, field of study contributes to earnings inequality via occupational choices:

Table 4. Regression Decompositions Showing Contributions of Background, Values, Education, Family Formation, and Work Characteristics to the Gender Income Gap

Characteristic	Men's Slope[a]	Women's Slope[b]	Percentage of Average Slope	Total Gap Explained	Rank of Influence
Background SES and Race	124	33	78	1.1	9
Importance of Having Lots of Money	472	294	383	5.5	6
Education Related SAT/ACT scores	434	226	330	4.8	7
Percentage female of college major	1,087	842	964	13.9	2
Institutional selectivity	18	59	39	0.6	10
Graduate/professional degree	57	-244	-93	-1.3	12
Family Formation	15	3	9	0.1	11
Work Related Hours worked per week	613	816	715	10.3	3
Occupation	1,544	1,319	1,431	20.6	1
Industry	497	492	495	7.1	5
Sector	770	453	611	8.8	4
Other work factors	145	135	140	2.0	8
Total Explained with These Factors	5,776	4,428	5,102	73.5	
Total Unexplained	1,162	2,510	1,836	26.5	
Total Income Gap	6,938	6,938	6,938		

[a] $\sum b_m (\bar{X}_m - \bar{X}_f)$.

[b] $\sum b_f (\bar{X}_m - \bar{X}_f)$.

People tend to work in jobs that are related to their fields of study, and some occupations are better rewarded than are others. Yet, the regression decomposition presented here suggests that college majors play a meaningful role in women's lesser income *independent* of later work factors. Indeed, even when work-, family-, and values-related factors are considered alongside education, 14 percent of the gender gap in income is still attributable to field of study.

What is it about college majors, and why do they matter for the gender gap in earnings beyond their relationship to occupations? It is often argued that some fields are more highly compensated because they develop skills that are more valued in the labor market. Although the content of the field of study seems to have an important relationship with earnings inequality, the gender composition of the field appears to be much more salient[21] (see Table 2). This devaluation of majors associated with women is consistent with the finding of a general devaluation of jobs associated with women (see, e.g., England 1992). And it appears that the lesser value assigned to majors in which women are more heavily concentrated continues to affect one's earnings even when young workers enter comparable occupations. This pattern indicates that educational sex segregation by field of study continues to be an impediment to gender equality beyond its relationship to occupational sex segregation and will have to be addressed directly if gender disparities are to be eliminated.

While the analysis suggests that segregation of college majors plays an important role in earnings inequality early in young workers' careers, its contribution should not be overstated. In their mid-20s, college-educated women make about $4,400 less per year than do men even when they have the same level of education, college major, cognitive skills, and selectivity of the college from which they graduated. The regression decomposition shows that work-related factors explain about half the contemporary gender difference in earnings. Here, it seems that gender differences in types of employment—occupations, industries, and sectors—are especially important.[22] For this group of workers, aspirations for earning lots of money appear to matter only modestly for the income gap, and family formation matters not much at all.[23]

Research on contemporary gender stratification provides a useful framework for understanding these findings and their implications for gender equity (see Charles and Bradley 2002; Charles and Grusky 2004). The denial of opportunities for women to attend college and attain a degree on the basis of their sex is inconsistent with the contemporary gender ideology of equality of opportunity. Yet, as this vertical dimension of segregation has declined, fields of study—the horizontal dimension—remain resistant to integration.

Because gender differences in college majors are viewed more as differences than as inequality, the segregation of fields of study can persist despite a more egalitarian gender ideology and the decline of vertical segregation (Charles and Bradley 2002). Thus, the overall positive picture of women's educational patterns can mask lingering gender differences that have important consequences for gender inequality later in life. Similarly, occupational sex segregation persists and may increase despite the greater presence of women in the labor market (Charles and Grusky 2004).

Unfortunately, the ongoing debate over women's growing "advantage" in schooling has, by and large, overlooked the consequences of these patterns of educational attainment and performance. A look at one important outcome—the earnings of young women and men—should temper the optimism that is generally generated by trends toward girls' educational success. On the whole, the findings of this study suggest little reason to be optimistic that further educational changes will lead to large declines in gender inequality in income. If women maintain their current trajectory of improving their educational credentials relative to men, they will still face the barrier of sex segregation in college majors. And while the integration of majors could generate important reductions in the gender gap in income, research has found a general stagnation of integration of fields of study since the mid-1980s (see Jacobs 1995). Even larger barriers to income equity are related to gendered patterns of employment, and today's young college-educated adults continue to confront these obstacles. Indeed, in spite of women's educational progress, the gendered organization of both higher education and employment remain substantial impediments to equality in earnings.

NOTES

1. Gill and Leigh (2000) also considered the effect of changes in participation in higher education on declines in the gender gap in wages in the late 1980s and early to mid-1990s. Although they did not consider educational performance (i.e., grades), they concluded that gendered changes related to field of study played a part in the reduction of the gender gap in wages.

2. For a discussion of horizontal and vertical gender segregation in higher education, see Charles and Grusky (2004) or Gerber and Schaefer (2004).

3. See England (1992), Jacobs (2001), Reskin (1993), and Tomaskovic-Devey (1993) for a more thorough overview of occupational sex segregation and its causes and consequences.

4. Note that Marini and Fan (1997) considered the following education-related factors: years of education and field of study (considered together), high school GPA, score on the Armed Forces Qualifications Test as a measure of verbal and math skills, and parents' education.

5. Waves of data were collected in 1988, 1990, 1994, and 2000, providing information on these young adults from roughly age 14 to age 26.

6. Patterns of sample attrition between 1988 and 2000 resulted in a more socioeconomically privileged group of young adults than would be found at random. However, a preliminary analysis of attrition patterns did not suggest large gender differences in continuation in NELS.

7. NELS includes information from the students, as well as supplemental information from their parents, teachers, and school administrators. See NCES (2002) for further information on this data set.

8. To correct for skew, I eliminated respondents whose income was four or more standard deviations above the mean ($N = 13$) for fulltime, year-round workers. I also eliminated those who reported $2,000 or less in earnings that year ($N = 5$), since it is illogical that working full time for the entire year would yield earnings that low. Including these workers would suggest a slightly larger gender income gap.

9. While some scholars (e.g., Blau 1998) have found a similar pattern of larger wage gaps among those with less education, there is not a clear consensus on this issue.

10. Limiting the sample as I did to college graduates who were full-time, nonseasonal workers captured the most privileged workers. For example, these workers tended to come from families with higher SES scores, to have performed better in school, and to have fewer children of their own than did the general sample of NELS participants. Accordingly, I limit the generalizability of these findings to full-time college-educated workers. In a supplemental analysis noted in the Discussion section and discussed in note 23, I discuss the gender income gap among those with less education.

11. Using multiple imputation allows the analyst to retain cases that have missing values on some variables. By using information on the relationships among the variables in the data set, multiple imputation creates estimates of what the missing values would most likely be if they were not missing. The imputation process is repeated multiple times at random to allow for the correction of estimates of standard errors. Thus, instead of dropping cases with missing values, as in listwise deletion, multiple imputation preserves for analysis cases with useful information, thereby reducing potential biases that would result from systematic differences in complete cases and cases with missing information. Furthermore, this method of handing missing data "produces estimates that are consistent, asymptotically efficient, and asymptotically normal when the data are [missing at random]" (Allison 2002:27). A supplemental analysis of the missing data suggested that these assumptions are valid with these data, and the findings reported here were not substantially altered when I used listwise deletion of missing cases.

12. As I noted in the Data section, I handled potential skewing by excluding extreme cases (those more than 4 standard deviations above the mean). Doing so eliminated the need to transform the income variable by eliminating skew at the highest income levels and allowed for a more intuitive presentation of results.

13. Loury (1997) suggested that grades influence wage gaps, and the use of GPA is consistent with the approach of Marini and Fan (1997), who tested high school GPA.

14. In a supplemental analysis, I tested a more nuanced measure of field of studies using 18 dummy variables for the various fields represented in the data. I found that the gender gap in income was consistent whether I used this more refined measure or the more general four-category classification. See note 21 for the same issue.

15. The NCES Integrated Postsecondary Education Data System (IPEDS) Completions Survey provides data on the number of degrees awarded by gender and field of study in 2000–01. The national data on degrees aligns rather consistently with the categories used to code majors in the NELS data.

16. NELS used a two-stage, stratified sampling design, sampling on schools (by type, region, and size of enrollment) and then individuals in schools. The complex sample design leads to less variation than a simple random sample would produce (i.e., students in the same schools are more similar than would be expected if students were sampled randomly from the population at large). To adjust for this sampling issue, I used EGLS regression because EGLS yields unbiased estimates of the standard errors in such instances (see NCES 2002: 97).

17. While on the whole, the gender patterns found here are consistent with general patterns in education and employment, the findings related to work experience and graduate degrees suggest that the women in this sample were likely the more privileged workers—perhaps a bit more so than the male workers. This gendered pattern in the sample, then, would suggest a smaller income gap than would be expected if the respondents' work-history patterns and graduate or professional school participation matched the national averages. However, given that the earnings differential found here is consistent with that found with federal data, as well as the one found by Marini and Fan (1997) in their study of young workers in their first jobs, I do not consider that these patterns reflect large biases in the sampling design.

18. For brevity, the results of all models are not shown. Full results are available on request.

19. In supplemental analyses, I tested for interaction effects of race and gender and found no significant interactions. Therefore, the models presented here treat race and gender as additive rather than interactive.

20. I tested 12th-grade math and reading scores as well. Reading scores explain none of the earnings gap, while math scores have an effect similar to that of the SAT/ACT scores.

21. Given that the percentage female of the field is a much more refined measure than is the four-category classification of majors by content area, I also tested a much more nuanced measure of content areas using 18 dummy variables for fields of study. The regression results differed only negligibly. This finding supports the contention made here that the most important difference in fields of study is gender composition.

22. The study attempted to understand gender inequality in income among full-time, year-round workers with bachelor's degrees. Whether the explanatory factors studied here operate similarly among those who work fewer hours per week and/or seasonally remains to be seen. Arguably, full-time, year-round workers are the most advantaged financially and experience less gender inequality in income, given that past research indicated that part-time and intermittent work contributes to the gender gap in wages (see Budig and England 2001). Further research should consider the prevalence, causes, and consequences of gender differences in earnings for workers with various degrees of employment (e.g., workers who are employed full time, part time voluntarily, or underemployed).

23. In these analyses, I focused on individuals with college degrees because I wanted to explore characteristics of education that are applicable only to this group (e.g., field of study, selectivity of institution, and graduate degrees). But, what about those without college degrees? My supplemental analysis of workers with less than a four-year degree suggests that these workers in their mid-20s endure an even larger gender gap in income: Women who work full time earn about 75 percent of what their male counterparts make. The results suggest that education will matter even less for workers without a college degree: Educational factors (e.g., highest level of education, scores on standardized tests in high school, and grades in high school) explain virtually none of the gender gap in earnings for this group. As with those with college degrees, a big part of the gender gap-in-income puzzle is understood in

terms of work characteristics. Gendered patterns of occupational and industrial placement and number of hours worked per week seem critical. However, unlike the situation for college graduates, family-formation factors, particularly being a single parent, appear to explain more of the gender gap in earnings. Furthermore, it is harder to pinpoint the root of the earnings differential for this group, since my best model explains only about half the income disparity for these workers.

APPENDIX

Means for Background, Values, Family, and Work Variables, including Significance Tests of Women's versus Men's Means, from Imputation 3

Variable	Sample Mean (N = 1,946)	Women's Mean (N = 1,053)	Men's Mean (N = 893)	t-Test of Mean Difference
Income in 1999	36,137	32,953	39,891	11.08***
SES of Family of Origin	0.35	0.30	0.40	3.15**
Race of Respondent				
White	0.76	0.74	0.79	2.30*
Black	0.06	0.07	0.05	-1.40
Latino	0.07	0.08	0.06	-1.24
Asian American	0.09	0.09	0.08	-0.93
Other race	0.02	0.02	0.02	-0.46
Importance of Having Lots of Money	2.24	2.14	2.36	8.40***
Family Characteristics				
Single	0.63	0.59	0.68	4 13***
Married or marriage-like relationship	0.35	0.38	0.31	-3.64***
Divorced	0.02	0.02	0.01	-1.97*
Single parent	0.01	0.02	0.01	-1.74
Number of children	0.12	0.11	0.14	1.20
Number of Hours Worked, Typical Week	45.78	44.37	47.46	7.95***
Sector				
For profit	0.70	0.63	0.78	7.28***
Not for profit, government, military	0.30	0.37	0.22	-7.28***
Industry				
Agriculture, forestry, fisheries, mining	0.01	0.00	0.02	2.92**
Construction and allied	0.03	0.01	0.05	5.36***
Manufacturing: Durable goods	0.07	0.06	0.09	2.69**
Manufacturing: Nondurable goods	0.03	0.02	0.04	1.30
Utilities	0.01	0.01	0.01	1.59
Wholesale distribution	0.01	0.00	0.02	3.59***
Retail trades	0.06	0.07	0.05	-1.35
Finance, insurance, real estate	0.13	0.10	0.17	4 17***
Business, personal services	0.08	0.07	0.08	0.81
Entertainment, recreation	0.02	0.01	0.02	0.50
Professional services	0.17	0.18	0.15	-1.45
Public administration, safety, military	0.04	0.03	0.05	2.47*
Health care	0.11	0.15	0.06	-7.35***

Appendix (cont.)

Variable	Sample Mean (*N* = 1,946)	Women's Mean (*N* = 1,053)	Men's Mean (*N* = 893)	*t*-Test of Mean Difference
Industry				
Communications	0.06	0.06	0.07	0.45
Transportation	0.01	0.01	0.02	1.79
Hospitality	0.01	0.01	0.02	0.75
Education	0.14	0.19	0.08	-7 37***
Occupation				
Secretary, receptionist	0.01	0.02	0.00	-3.75***
Cashier, teller, clerk, data entry	0.00	0.00	0.00	-0.68
Other clerical	0.01	0.02	0.01	-1.91
Farmer, forester, farm laborer	0.00	0.00	0.01	3 21**
Personal service, cook, chef, baker	0.01	0.01	0.00	-2.94**
Nonfarm laborer	0.01	0.00	0.02	3.54***
Mechanic, repairer, service technician	0.00	0.00	0.01	1.71
Craftsman, skilled operative	0.01	0.01	0.01	1.69
Protective service, criminal justice, military	0.04	0.03	0.05	2.80**
Business and financial support services	0.06	0.07	0.05	-1.73
Financial service professional	0.11	0.09	0.13	2.42*
Sales, purchasing	0.10	0.10	0.10	-0.33
Customer service	0.01	0.02	0.00	-2.88**
Legal support	0.00	0.00	0.00	-0.42
Medical practice professional, services	0.02	0.03	0.01	-3.35***
Medical licensed professional	0.04	0.06	0.02	-4.55***
Educators (K-12 teachers)	0.09	0.12	0.04	-6.60***
Educators, instructors (non-K-12)	0.03	0.04	0.02	-2.88**
Human service professional	0.03	0.05	0.02	-4 13***
Engineer, architect, software engineer	0.07	0.03	0.11	7 33***
Scientist, statistician professional	0.01	0.01	0.01	-0.89
Research assistant, lab technician	0.01	0.02	0.01	-0.94
Technical, professional worker	0.02	0.02	0.03	1.82
Computer systems, related professional	0.07	0.04	0.10	5 79***
Computer programmer, other computer	0.02	0.02	0.04	2 79**
Editor, writer, reporter	0.03	0.04	0.02	-1.74
Performer, artist	0.01	0.01	0.01	1.01
Manager, executive	0.01	0.01	0.02	1.96
Manager, midlevel	0.04	0.03	0.05	2.36*
Manager, supervisory, office	0.10	0.11	0.08	-2.21*
Health, recreational services	0.01	0.01	0.01	0.30

Job Training	0.76	0.75	0.78	1.35
Job Autonomy	2.78	2.76	2.81	1.45
Work Experience—Full Time in 1998	0.87	0.86	0.87	0.61
Work Experience—Part Time in 1998	0.10	0.10	0.09	-0.92

* $p < .05$, ** $p < .01$, *** $p < .001$ (two-tailed tests).

REFERENCES

Allison, Paul D. 2002. *Missing Data*. Thousand Oaks, CA: Sage.

Blau, Francine D. 1998. "Trends in the Well-Being of American Women, 1970–1995." *Journal of Economic Literature* 36:112-65.

Blau, Francine D., and Lawrence M. Kahn. 1997. "Swimming Upstream: Trends in the Gender Wage Differential in the 1980s." *Journal of Labor Economics* 15:1–42.

Bradley, Karen. 2000. "The Incorporation of Women into Higher Education: Paradoxical Outcomes" *Sociology of Education* 73:1–18.

Brown, Charles, and Mary Corcoran. 1997. "Sex-Based Differences in School Content and the Male-Female Wage Gap." *Journal of Labor Economics* 15:431–65.

Budig, Michelle J., and Paula England. 2001. "The Wage Penalty for Motherhood." *American Sociological Review* 66:204–25.

Cappelli, Peter, Laurie Bassi, Harry Katz, David Knoke, Paul Osterman, and Michael Useem. 1997. *Change at Work*. New York: Oxford University Press.

Charles, Maria, and Karen Bradley. 2002. "Equal but Separate? A Cross-National Study of Sex Segregation in Higher Education." *American Sociological Review* 67:573–99.

Charles, Maria, and David B. Grusky. 2004. *Occupational Ghettos: The Worldwide Segregation of Women and Men*. Stanford, CA: Stanford University Press.

College Board. 2003, August 26. "SAT Verbal and Math Scores Up Significantly As a Record-Breading Number of Students Take the Test: Average Math Score at Highest Level in More than 35 Years." Press release. Available online at http://www.collegeboard.com/press/article/0,,26858,00.html.

Corcoran, Mary E., and Paul N. Courant. 1985. "Sex Role Socialization and Labor Market Outcomes." *American Economic Review* 75:275–78.

Davies, Scott, and Neil Guppy. 1997. "Fields of Study, College Selectivity, and Student Inequalities in Higher Education." *Social Forces* 75:1417–38.

Daymont, Thomas N., and Paul J. Andrisani. 1984. "Job Preferences, College Major, and the Gender Gap in Earnings." *Journal of Human Resources* 19:408–28.

England, Paula. 1992. *Comparable Worth: Theories and Evidence*. New York: Aldine De Gruyter.

England, Paula, Melissa S. Herbert, Barbara Stanek Kilbourne, Lori L. Reid, and Lori McCreary Megdal. 1994. "The Gendered Valuation of Occupations and Skills: Earnings in 1980 Census Occupations." *Social Forces* 73:65–100.

Farkas, George, Paula England, Keven Vicknair, and Barbara Stanek Kilbourne. 1997. "Cognitive Skill, Skill Demands of Jobs, and Earnings Among Young European American, African American, and Mexican American Workers." *Social Forces,* 75:913–38.

Farley, Reynolds. 1995. *State of the Union: America in the 1990s: Volume One. Economic Trends.* New York: Russell Sage Foundation.

Fields, Judith, and Edward N. Wolff. 1995. "Interindustry Wage Differentials and the Gender Wage Gap." *Industrial and Labor Relations Review*, 49(1):105–120.

Gerber, Theodore P., and David R. Schaefer. 2004. "Horizontal Stratification of Higher Education in Russia: Trends, Gender Differences, and Labor Market Outcomes." *Sociology of Education* 77:32–59.

Gill, Andrew M., and Duane E. Leigh. 2000. "Community College Enrollment, College Major, and the Gender Wage Gap." *Industrial and Labor Relations Review* 54:163–81.

Groshen, Erica L. 1991. "The Structure of the Female/Male Wage Differential: Is It Who You Are, What You Do, or Where You Work?" *Journal of Human Resources* 23:457–72.

Hearn, James C. 1991. "Academic and Nonacademic Influences on College Destinations of 1980 High School Graduates." *Sociology of Education* 64:158–71.

Huffman, Matt L. 2004. "Gender Inequality Across Local Wage Hierarchies." *Work and Occupations* 31:323–44.

Jacobs, Jerry. 1995. "Gender and Academic Specialties: Trends Among College Degree Recipients During the 1980s. *Sociology of Education* 68:81–98.

———. 1996. "Gender Inequality and Higher Education." *Annual Review of Sociology* 22:153–85.

———. 1999. "Gender and the Stratification of Colleges." *The Journal of Higher Education* 70:161–87.

———. 2001. "Evolving Patterns of Sex Segregation." Pp. 535–50 in *Sourcebook of Labor Markets: Evolving Structures and Processes*, edited by Ivar Berg and Arne L. Kalleberg. New York: Kluwer Academic/Plenum.

Joy, Lois. 2000. "Do Colleges Shortchange Women? Gender Differences in the Transition from College to Work." *American Economic Review* 90:471–75.

Karen, David. 1991. "The Politics of Class, Race, and Gender: Access to Higher Education in the United States, 1960–1986." *American Journal of Education* 99:208–37.

Kilbourne, Barbara, Paula England, and Kurt Beron. 1994. "Effects of Individual, Occupational, and Industrial Characteristics on Earnings: Intersections of Race and Gender." *Social Forces* 72:1149–76.

Korenman, Sanders, and David Neumark. 1992. "Marriage, Motherhood, and Wages." *Journal of Human Resources* 27:233–55.

Loury, Linda Datcher. 1997. "The Gender Earnings Gap Among College-Educated Workers." *Industrial and Labor Relations Review* 50:580–93.

Macpherson, David A., and Barry T. Hirsch. 1995. "Wages and Gender Composition: Why Do Women's Jobs Pay Less?" *Journal of Labor Economics* 13:426–71.

Marini, Margaret Mooney. 1989. "Sex Differences in Earnings in the United States." *Annual Review of Sociology* 15:343–80.

Marini, Margaret Mooney, and Pi-Ling Fan. 1997. "The Gender Gap in Earnings at Career Entry." *American Sociological Review* 62:588–604.

Mitra, Aparna. 2002. "Mathematics Skill and Male-Female Wages." *Journal of Socio-Economics* 31:443–56.

Morgan, Laurie A. 1998. "The Earnings Gap for Women Engineers, 1982 to 1989." *American Sociological Review* 63:479–93.

Moulton, Brent R. 1990. "A Reexamination of the Federal-Private Wage Differential in the United States." *Journal of Labor Economics* 8:270–93.

Murnane, Richard J., John B. Willett, and Frank Levy. 1995. "The Growing Importance of Cognitive Skills in Wage Determination." *Review of Economics and Statistics* 77:251–66.

National Center for Education Statistics. 1998. *Gender Differences in Earnings Among Young Adults Entering the Labor Market (NCES 98086)*. By Suzanne B. Clery, John B. Lee, and Laura G. Knapp. Washington, D.C.: U.S. Government Printing Office.

———. 2002. *National Education Longitudinal Study of 1988: Base-Year to Fourth Follow-Up Data File User's Manuel (NCES 2002-323)*. By Thomas R. Curtin, Steven J. Ingels, Shiying Wu, and Ruth Heuer. Washington, D.C.: U.S. Government Printing Office.

———. 2003a. *The Condition of Education 2003 in Brief (NCES 2003-068)*. By Andrea Livingston and John Wirt. Washington, D.C.: U.S. Government Printing Office.

———. 2003b. *Postsecondary Attainment, Attendance, Curriculum, and Performance: Selected Results from the NELS:88/2000 Postsecondary Education Transcript Study (PETS), 2000 (NCES 2003-394)*. By Clifford Adelman, Bruce Daniel, Ilona Berkovits. Washington, D.C.: U.S. Government Printing Office.

———. 2004. *Trends in Educational Equity of Girls and Women: 2004* (NCES 2005-016). By Catherine E. Freeman. Washington, D.C.: U.S. Government Printing Office.

———. 2005. *Gender Differences in Participation and Completion of Undergraduate Education and How They Have Changed Over Time*. NCES 2005-169 by Katharin Peter and Laura Horn. Washington D.C.: U.S. Government Printing Office.

Padavic, Irene, and Barbara Reskin. 2002. *Women and Men at Work* (2nd ed.) Thousand Oaks, CA: Pine Forge Press.

Paglin, Morton, and Anthony M. Rufolo. 1990. "Heterogeneous Human Capital, Occupational Choice, and Male-Female Earnings Differences." *Journal of Labor Economics* 8:123–44.

Reskin, Barbara. 1993. "Sex Segregation in the Workplace." *Annual Review of Sociology* 19:241–70.

Riordan, Cornelius. 2003. "Failing in School? Yes; Victims of War? No." *Sociology of Education* 76:369–72.

Rosenfeld, Rachel A., and Gunn Elisabeth Birkelund. 1995. "Women's Part-Time Work: A Cross-National Comparison." *European Sociological Review* 11:111–34.

Sadker, Myra, and David Sadker. 1994. *Failing at Fairness: How Our Schools Cheat Girls*. New York: Simon & Schuster.

Shelton, Beth Anne, and Juanita Firestone. 1989. "Household Labor Time and the Gender Gap in Earnings." *Gender and Society* 3:105–12.

Shu, Xiaoling, and Margaret Mooney Marini. 1998. "Gender Related Change in Occupational Aspirations." *Sociology of Education* 71:43–67.

Sum, Andrew, Neeta Fogg, and Paul Harrington with Ishwar Khatiwada, Shelia Palma, Nathan Pond, and Paulo Tobar. 2003. "The Growing Gender Gaps in College Enrollment and Degree Attainment in the U.S. and Their Potential Economic and Social Consequences." Prepared for the Business Roundtable, Washington, D.C.. Boston: Center for Labor Market Studies. Available online at http://www.brtable.org/pdf/943.pdf.

Tomaskovic-Devey, Donald. 1993. *Gender and Racial Inequality at Work: The Sources and Consequences of Job Segregation.* Ithaca, NY: ILR Press.

U.S. Department of Labor, Bureau of Labor Statistics. 2004, September. *Highlights of Women's Earnings in 2003.* Report 978. Available online at http://www.bls.gov/cps/cpswom2003.pdf.

Waldfogel, Jane. 1998. "Understanding the 'Family Gap' in Pay for Women with Children." *Journal of Economic Perspectives* 12:137–56.

Wellington, Alison J. 1994. "Accounting for the Male/Female Wage Gap Among Whites: 1976 and 1985." *American Sociological Review* 59:839–48.

Willingham, Warren W., and Nancy S. Cole. 1997. Gender and Fair Assessment. Mahwah, NJ: Lawrence Erlbaum. Wilson, Kenneth L., Janet P. Boldizar. 1990. "Gender Segregation in Higher Education: Effects of Aspirations, Mathematics Achievement, and Income." *Sociology of Education* 63:62–74.

Gender Bias Lives, for Both Sexes

By David Sadker and Karen Zittleman

For the last few years, little attention has been paid to gender barriers, in part because so many educators considered gender to mean only girls. Since girls outscore boys on most standardized achievement tests, receive better report card grades, and are much less likely to be behavior problems, the conclusion seemed obvious: gender was not a problem.

In reality, gender bias is very much an issue for both boys and girls, an issue too many educators fail to see. For example, can you imagine a teacher organizing a spelling bee by matching black students against white students? Certainly not in today's society.

But consider the same teacher organizing the same activity by gender, boys against girls. That's a practice so common that it has become an acceptable, unquestioned part of school life. But why? We have yet to come across a single study showing that gender segregation and competition serve any positive educational, social, or psychological purpose. Still, we see some schools separating girls and boys in lunchrooms, class lines, playgrounds, and school buses.

Gender bias is difficult to detect because it affects girls and boys in different ways. In school, it is the boys who may be expected to "act out" and rebel at school work, while the girls are expected to be docile, conforming, and willing to work hard.

As different as those behaviors appear, they both reflect gender stereotyping. While there has been some progress in breaking down this stereotyping in recent decades—more girls taking math and science courses, more boys exploring careers in teaching and nursing—new gender challenges have arisen.

FACING NEW GENDER CHALLENGES

What are the many faces of gender bias? For decades, boys have consistently lagged behind girls in reading and writing performance, a reality highlighted by standardized tests such as those dictated by the No Child Left Behind Act. Some attribute this to developmental or learning style differences, an anti-school culture felt by boys, or even brain differences. Boys often regard reading and writing as "feminine" subjects, and report that reading threatens their masculinity.

David Sadker & Karen Zittleman, "Closing the Gender Gap—Again!" *Principal*, vol. 84, no. 4, pp. 18-22. Copyright © 2005 by the National Association of Elementary School Principals. Reprinted with permission.

Although boys and girls like and do well in math and science in elementary school, girls become less positive and do less well in higher grades. By third grade, 51% of boys and 37% of girls have used a microscope in class. Boys also receive more math- and science-related toys than girls do.

Girls rate themselves considerably lower than boys on technological ability and are less likely to use computers outside school. Current software products are more likely to reinforce gender stereotypes and bias than reduce them. Girls are five times less likely than boys to consider a technology-related career.

Girls receive higher report card grades throughout their schooling career. Boys outscore girls on most high-stakes tests, including both the verbal and math sections of the SATs.

Girls in grades 6 and 7 rate popularity more important than academic competence or independence. Boys are expected to follow a "boy code," a kind of swaggering posture that hides their vulnerabilities and suppresses dependency while leaving them feeling emotionally isolated.

Verbal and physical sexual harassment begins in elementary school. Four out of five girls, and almost as many boys, experience some form of sexual harassment. Some 30% of students are bullied. Boys are both more likely to bully others and to be victims of physical bullying, while girls frequently experience verbal and psychological bullying.

About 9% of the nation's elementary school teachers are men, down from about 18% in 1981. Almost half of elementary school principals are male.

The No Child Left Behind Act includes a problematic proposal to change Title IX, the federal law prohibiting sex discrimination in education, by encouraging the establishment of public single-sex schools and classes for girls and boys. There are real danger signs in this proposal.

Some educators point out that many existing single-sex schools are not particularly effective and attribute the academic successes of others less to single gender and more to smaller classes, engaged parents, well-trained teachers, and strong academic emphasis. Other educators believe that single-sex schools work less well for boys than girls, while still others believe that such schools intensify gender stereotypes and homophobia.

A California experiment in single-sex education for boys a few years ago was a case study for what can go wrong. The schools turned out to be dumping grounds for boys with behavior problems, with no funds for teacher training and no specific programs or curricula. Their failure to achieve promised improved academic achievement was not surprising.

Nevertheless, the federal government is considering doing the same thing on a national scale. Worse yet, the federal plan speaks of "comparable," not "equal," single-sex schools and classes. Would a gifted science class for boys and a practical science course for girls be considered "comparable" under the NCLB definition? We don't know.

What educators do know is that student test scores are critical in determining a school's Adequate Yearly Progress under NCLB. But while test score data are considered for many different groups, gender is not one of them. This seems strange indeed, considering that an elementary school plagued by bullying and sexual harassment may very well find these gender issues driving down student achievement and test scores. Although gender plays a critical role in the nation's public schools, NCLB basically ignores gender issues except for promoting segregation of students by sex.

Here are some indicators to consider in addressing old and new gender gaps:

Teacher bias. Although most teachers want to teach till children equitably, boys and girls often receive different treatment. Teachers call on boys more often than girls, wait longer for boys' answers, and provide more precise feedback to boys. But they also punish boys more than girls, even when their behavior is similar. Girls are more likely to be quiet in class and be praised for neatness. In their classroom visits, principals need to observe how teachers interact with students and to note whether there is a persistent pattern of gender differentiation. When teachers are made aware of their unintentional bias, they will usually make an effort to be more equitable.

Student beliefs. Boys and girls frequently interpret their successes and failures in very different ways. Boys typically attribute success to intelligence and failure to bad luck or insufficient effort. Girls are more likely to attribute success to good luck and failure to inability. This belief creates a harmful, self-fulfilling prophecy for girls: trying harder or risking a new approach won't make much difference because you're simply not smart enough. Teachers too often feed into this misconception, for example attributing boys' success in technology to talent while dismissing girls' success as luck or diligence. Principals need to establish equally high expectations for all students.

Learned helplessness. Teachers often encourage boys to persist with and solve difficult problems, while assisting girls who ask for help. Girls should be encouraged to do for themselves. Yet, one study showed boys taking active roles in student-led science demonstrations, while girls were far more likely to be group note-takers.

Self-imposed stereotyping. Many girls believe they will be unpopular if perceived as "brains" and may avoid "boy stuff" (e.g., math and science), while boys shun "female subjects," like art, music, and even reading. Schools can change this kind of thinking. Find girls who love to set up and use science and technology equipment, and create more options for boys that negate self-imposed stereotypes.

Displays and exhibits. What are the displays and exhibits in your school saying? Are male or female accomplishments more likely to be recognized? Make sure gender is equally represented.

Sexual harassment and bullying. Make certain your district is following Title IX and has a policy on these issues that is communicated to teachers, students, and parents. Learning communities do not flourish where intimidation thrives or inequities are tolerated.

The gender gap is the one demographic that challenges educators at all schools, urban and rural, wealthy and poor. How strange that for many it has become so difficult to see'.

The History of Silencing Children

By Otto Santa Ana

Those who steal the words of others develop a deep doubt in the abilities of the others and consider them incompetent. Each time they say their word without hearing the word of those whom they have forbidden to speak, they grow more accustomed to power and acquire a taste for guiding, ordering, and commanding. They can no longer live without having someone to give orders to. Under these circumstances, dialogue is impossible.

—*Paulo Freire[1]*

I know that it is not the English language that hurts me, but what the oppressors do with it, how they shape it to become a territory that limits and defines, how they make it a weapon that can shame, humiliate, colonize.

—*bell hooks*

CHRONOLOGY OF EVENTS, COURT DECISIONS, AND LEGISLATION AFFECTING LANGUAGE MINORITY CHILDREN IN AMERICAN PUBLIC EDUCATION

This chronology summarizes key historical events for the three major groups of language minority students who continue to be negatively affected by the legacy of U.S. public school policy decisions.

The first group, American Indians, had various systems of education in place when the Europeans arrived. For instance, attendance at the Telpuchcalli 'houses of youth' was mandatory for all Aztec males under the age of fifteen. After the fall of Tenochtitlan, Spanish priests reorganized another educational institution, the Calmecac, or school of the Aztec elite, for missionizing purposes. Nahuatl speakers began attending such Catholic schools as early as 1529. The Aztec elite had previously used their own writing system. With the Contact, their youth learned to read in Latin and to use a new writing system, the ABCs, or Roman alphabet. They then appropriated this alphabet to continue to document their lives in Nahuatl,[2] as well as using Spanish for other officially sanctioned purposes. From this time until the present day, whites have sought to educate Indians. By and large, European and later Anglo-American missionaries endeavored to employ the languages of the Indians as a means to offer their allegedly superior spiritual instruction. Their teaching method can be considered a bilingual approach. It is notable that their technique compares favorably to the standard U.S. procedure, English-only teaching, which was used for 250 years to force the Indians to adopt the Anglo-American way of life. The federal government considered off-reservation boarding schools the host place to socialize very young Indian children in the white men's world-view, by separating them from their parents and the "primitive" worldview of their communities. For whites, Indian education was described as a "civilizing" formula to "raise" the aborigine up toward their level. From the Indian point of view, these policies of linguistic decimation and cultural "domestication" were designed to complete the eradication of the first Americans. A brief period of Indian progressive education finally began in 1934, but the government regressed to past practices in the 1940s. A second fleeting moment of progressive education emerged in the 1960s, but it was cut short during the Reagan era. In the twenty-first century, English-only teaching still dominated Indian education.

The second group of language minority students is the descendants of Africans who were enslaved and brought forcibly to the Americas. For over three hundred years, whites considered African Americans to be mere chattel and systematically denied that they were human beings. As slaves, African Americans were treated as subhuman commodities. Whites granted them less dignity than draft animals. In the South, formal education was systematically denied to them. It was illegal in most Southern states to teach a slave to read. Those who sought formal learning did so under the risk of physical peril. Until after World War I, nine-tenths of all African Americans lived in the Southern states. Freeborn African Americans who resided in the Northern states had a better life, although they were burdened by the prevailing American view that they were a lower scale of humanity than the Americans who were the progeny of Europeans. The few public schools that were set up for African-American children were, in all cases, less well funded and well structured than white schools. In this setting, African Americans struggled for an education as individuals, as well as in organized ways. During the nineteenth century, nearly one hundred court cases challenged segregation or racial discrimination in schools. African Americans won a majority of those cases in Northern states. As early as 1855, Massachusetts prohibited public school segregation.[3] In the South, the road to desegregated schooling would require one hundred more years of court battles. The battle for equal schooling continues.

The third and largest group of language minority students is Latinos. In this summary, the focus will be on Puerto Rican and Chicano history. The 1848 Treaty of Guadalupe Hidalgo is the first important legal document concerning Chicanos. The treaty was designed to protect the property and civil rights of Mexicans living in the Southwest at the end of the war between the United States and Mexico. In particular it declared that all Mexican citizens (mestizos and American Indians) living in what had been northern Mexico "shall be admitted to the enjoyment of all the rights of citizens of the United States, according to the principles of the Constitution" and shall be "protected in the free enjoyment of their liberty and property, and secured in the free exercise of their religion without restriction."

Over thirty-five years before the treaty, Mexico had recognized the full citizenship and equal rights of American Indians and had outlawed its race-based caste system. However, the U.S. Congress weakened the Treaty of Guadalupe Hidalgo before its ratification, by revising article 9, which deals with citizenship rights. In the ensuing years, Anglo-America disregarded the treaty entirely, considering Mexican Americans a conquered people to be subjugated, rather than a group of fellow citizens to embrace. In Texas and elsewhere, Mexicans were denied the right to vote. California's state constitutional convention passed resolutions that ignored the U.S. citizenship of Mexicans. Each state passed retaliatory laws, called "Greaser Laws" in California, to further marginalize Mexicans. Everywhere, they were victims of violence. In short order, Mexican Americans became foreigners in their native land.[4] As Martha Menchaca has convincingly argued, the U.S. legal system, from 1848 to 1947, had accorded privilege to whites and, in the conquered Southwest, instituted new racial restriction policies that violated "the civil rights of Mexicans because under U.S. laws, Indians and 'half-breed Indians' were not considered U.S. citizens." In institutions such as public education, "the inferior treatment of racial minorities" was legitimated.[5] However, as will be shown, the history of Mexican American education in the United States does not end here, as Chicanos and American Indians resisted this onslaught.

Nestled in ostensively tranquil seas, for five hundred years Puerto Ricans have suffered as a colony of two great empires, the Spanish and the American. After Spain ceded the island in 1898, many Puerto Ricans looked with hope to the "Colossal of the North." The Americans, however, viewed Puerto Rico as an island resource to reap profits from, rather than a people to bring into their fold. Given their perspective, it is not surprising that for Anglo-Americans, public education on the island was sustained on a negligible budget and with similar expectations. The colonizers' only passion was Americanizing the native and, in particular, making English the lingua franca, to simplify their administrative concerns. The arrogance of empire is apparent in most Puerto Rican educational relations. Anglo-American attitudes toward Spanish ranged from dismissive to hostile, which was most clearly evidenced in the classroom. English instruction of all educational content was mandated, and by 1907 over four-fifths of all schools held classes in English alone.

Deprivation on the island precipitated the substantial migrations of Puerto Ricans to the Northeastern mainland cities in midcentury. Anglo-American colonialist values did not change once these nominal citizens arrived on the mainland, Puerto Ricans in New York and elsewhere were economic refugees in their own country, and their children attended schools that attested to this. In every U.S. city, these schools were the most severely overcrowded, least resourced, and most poorly staffed, with double sessions, no special classes, and other warehouselike conditions. The empire viewed its colonialized groups, deluding Puerto Ricans, as less talented, less intelligent, and unmotivated. As Meyer Weinstein notes, the teachers of these children often viewed them with paternalism, antagonism,* or indifference: "As time went on, I would always take notes and kept a very neat book and pretended to know what was going 011 in class. ... The fact that I had not learned anything didn't mean too much to that teacher; she passed me anyway because I was sweet and cooperative."[6] Extremely low rates of academic achievement and correspondingly high dropout levels followed on this self-fulfilling prophecy.

The most salient aspect in the northeastern cities of the American empire was its shibboleth: To be a real U.S. citizen required speaking English without a trace of a Spanish accent. Puerto Rican teachers, no matter how excellent, were systematically denied permanent positions if they spoke with their community dialect of English. Rather than advancement, the educational issue in the public's mind regarding Puerto Ricans was their so-called language problem. One 1969 report pointed out that the "question of what a non-native speaking child is also a problem. For some, it is anyone whose last name sounds Spanish. For others, it is any pupil who is rated D, E, or F [on a scale] and for still others, it is any pupil who is rated other than A on the scale." The accentedness scale conflates native English ethnic dialect features with features used by second-language learners, since A was characterized as "speaks English, for his age-level, like a native—with no foreign accent or hesitancy due to a foreign language," while F meant "speaks no English."[7]

This appalling attitude was exactly what the 1968 Bilingual Education Act was designed to address. In the ensuing thirty-four years, the structural problems of colonization have not changed, but the act brought about a partial transformation of the way Puerto Rican children and other language minority children across the country were taught. However, in 2002 a new English-first-and-only language federal policy was enacted. This legislation, the "No Child Left Behind" Act, represents a 180-degree policy turn: the word *bilingual* has been completely expunged from federal policy. This act portends grim times for our nation's language minority school children.

1663 Reverend John Eliot publishes the New Testament in the Massachusetts language, with the help of Indian translators and printers.

1775 The U.S. Continental Congress appropriates five hundred dollars to establish Dartmouth College in New Hampshire for the education of Indian children.

1778–1871 The U.S. enters into over 370 treaties with various American Indian nations. More than one hundred include specific provisions for educational facilities.

1819 Congress earmarks ten thousand dollars for religious missions dedicated to Indian education. U.S. efforts for Indian education provide financial support to Protestant and Catholic church missions for several decades.

1839 Stephen R. Riggs finds teaching English to the Sioux "to be very difficult and not producing much apparent fruit," due not to the students' lack of ability, but rather a lack of interest. "Teaching [the Sioux language] Dakota was a different thing. It was their own language." Riggs and a colleague named Pond write a Dakota primer. Pond is convinced that Anglo-American authority over Indians "would depend very much on the correctness and facility" with which their white teachers speak the Indians' languages. Pond noted that "it has often been represented by persons having a superficial knowledge of Indian languages that they are imperfect and defective, and can be made to express but a very limited range of ideas" but that this claim was patently false for the American Indian language with which Pond was most familiar, Dakota.

1849 California Constitution, Article 2, Section 1; New Mexico Organic Law Act, Section 6 (1850); Organic Act of Arizona Constitution (1863) All three states formally restrict citizenship to

*See Maria Mazziotti Gillan's "Learning Silence," part I.

whites. Indians were prohibited from obtaining citizenship. Consequently, all Mexicans, whether of partial or full Indian descent, are also denied citizenship.

1850 Spain opens public schools in Puerto Rico for children who cannot afford the fees charged by private schools. They are immediately filled to overcapacity.

1860 Bureau of Indian Affairs opens its first school on the Yakima Indian Reservation. The school was partial payment in exchange for one-third of Washington State.

1868 Fourteenth Amendment to U.S. Constitution creates a uniform citizenship law, granting all citizens the enjoyment of all rights, including the right to vote. It rescinds the rights of states to establish citizenship eligibility. However, Indians, and hence Mexican Americans, are specifically excluded from its protection.

1868 President Grant appoints Peace Commissioners to attempt to bring the Indian wars to an end. The commission concludes that language differences led to misunderstandings and that: "Now, by educating the children of these tribes in the English language these differences would have disappeared, and civilization would have followed at once. … Through sameness of language is produced sameness of sentiment, and thought; customs and habits are molded and assimilated in the same way, and thus in time the differences producing trouble would have been gradually obliterated. … In the difference of language today lies two-thirds of our trouble. … Schools should be established, which [Indian] children should be required to attend; their barbarous dialect should be blotted out and the English language substituted."

1870 *People of California v. de la Guerra* Having been charged with "illegally acting" like a citizen, Pablo de la Guerra, who had previously served as a Santa Barbara district judge, disputes this insult. He appeals his case to the California Supreme Court. By claiming to be white, not Indian, he wins his case. However, other Mexican Americans are not recognized to have this same right.

1871 In a missionary report, a white teacher's experiences in Nebraska are described: "She went on for a year teaching these [Indian student] scholars, which the agent, her especial friend, secured, almost compelling them to attend, and at the end of the year these scholars could read English beautifully, could spell English beautifully, and could write English beautifully, and they did not understand the first word of English."

1872 An Indian agent from Tahlequah, Indian Territory, reports that "The children … go to school, and with great labor learn to read and write English, but without understanding the meaning of the words they read and write." On the other hand, because the Cherokee employ their own language, "almost the whole of those Cherokees who do not speak English can read and write the Cherokee by using the characters invented by [the celebrated Cherokee linguist] Sequoyah."

1873 A Quaker named Janney reports on a string of educational successes using Indian languages. Talking about the consequences of developing an orthography for Dakota, Janney writes: "A very small portion of the tribe, so far as I could discover, speak or write the English language, but a large number speak and write their own, and are able to hold correspondence with those who are in Minnesota and Wisconsin." In the same report: "Theirs is a phonetic language, and a smart boy will learn it in three or four weeks; and we have found it far better to instruct them in their own language, and also to teach them English as fast as we can."

1879 Colonel R. H. Pratt launches the infamous Carlisle (Pennsylvania) Boarding School, based on a military regimen. Its inductees are young Indian children who are separated from their parents. Pratt compels complete assimilation and cultural repression. Indian languages are forbidden. An Anglo name is imposed on these children.* They are required to wear military uniforms and to cut their hair as whites do. Expressions of time-honored Indian religious and ceremonial culture, as well as traditional foods, are banned.

1880 A correspondent traveling with the U.S. Secretary of the Interior Carl Schurz reports, "Mr. [Stephen R.] Riggs is of the opinion that first teaching the children to read and write in their own language enables them to master English with more ease when they take up that study; and he thinks, also, that a child beginning a four years' course with the study of Dakota would be further advanced in English at the end of the term than one who had not been instructed in Dakota."

1880 *In re Camille* Naturalization Court declares that "half-breed Indians" are not eligible to become naturalized citizens.

1880 The Indian Bureau issues regulations that "all instruction must be in English" in both religious and government schools under threat of loss of government funding.

1881 Missionaries start a newspaper written mostly in the Dakota language named *Iapi Oaye* 'The Word Carrier'. In an editorial it declares: "It is sheer laziness in the teacher to berate his Indian scholars for not understanding English, when he does not understand enough Indian to tell them the meaning of a single one of the sentences he is trying to make them understand properly, though they have no idea of the sense. The teacher with his superior mind, should be able to learn half a dozen languages while these children of darkness are learning one. Even though the teacher's object were only to have them master English, he had better teach it to them in Indian, so they may understand what they are learning."

1884 *Elk v. Wilkens* U.S. Supreme Court rules that Indians were not U.S. citizens.

1885 J. D. C. Atkins, Commissioner of Indian Affairs, states that the languages of American Indian students are a "barbarous dialect" and that "to teach Indian school children their native tongue is practically to exclude English, and to prevent them from acquiring it."

1886 *Iapi Oaye* prospers and expands. It brings out two issues, an all-Dakota edition, and an all-English language edition.

1887 Commissioner Adkins bears further witness: "Every nation is jealous of its own language, and no nation ought to be more so than ours, which approaches nearer than any other nationality to the perfect protection of its people. True Americans all feel that the Constitution, laws, and institutions of the United States, in their adaptation to the wants and requirements of man, are superior to those of any other country; and they should understand that by the spread of the English language will these laws and institutions be more firmly established and

*See Phil George's "Name Giveaway," part I.

widely disseminated. Nothing so surely and perfectly stamps upon an individual a national characteristic as language. ... [Because the Indians] are in an English-speaking country, they must be taught the language which they must use in transacting business with the people of this country. No unity or community of feeling can be established among different peoples unless they are brought to speak the same language, and thus become imbued with like ideas of duty."

1897 *United States v. Wong Kim Ark* Rules that all U.S. born individuals shall be accorded full rights as citizens—with the explicit exception of American Indians. As a result, this U.S. Supreme Court ruling also indirectly denies U.S. citizenship to Mexican Americans.

1897 *In re Rodríguez* In naturalization court, prosecutors argue that Ricardo Rodríguez cannot apply for citizenship, because by "appearance," he is "of pure Aztec or Indian race." He wins by arguing he was neither Spanish nor Indian.

1890s Observers in the field report that successful missionary teachers learn the tribal language so that they can understand the children and the children can understand them. A Sioux and former Carlisle student, Luther Standing Bear reports: "At that time, teaching amounted to very little. It really did not require a well-educated person to teach on the reservation. The main thing was to teach the children to write their names in English, then came learning the alphabet and how to count. I liked this work very well, and the children were doing splendidly. The first reading books we used had a great many little pictures in them. I would have the children read a line of English, and if they did not understand all they had read, I would explain it to them in Sioux. This made the studies very interesting."

1891 *Iapi Oaye* reprints an article from *The School Journal* declaring the "chief difference between English-speaking and Indian children [is] the need of grinding, drilling, and driving English into them." In the same year in an *Education Review* article, Indian school education is similarly criticized: "Four fifths, if not nine tenths, of the work done is purely mechanical drill. ... The child reads by rote, he memorizes the combinations in arithmetic, he copies letters and forms, he imitates the actions of his teacher."

1896 *Plessy v. Ferguson* Upholds an 1890 Louisiana law requiring railroads to provide "equal but separate accommodations for the white, and colored races." It thereby sanctions state-imposed segregation. If segregation is seen as "a badge of inferiority," the U.S. Supreme Court holds, that is only because "a race chooses to put that construction upon it. The ruling becomes the legal foundation of racial segregation in the public schools.

1898 Rules for Indian schools: "All instruction shall be in the English language. Pupils shall be required to converse with employees and each other in English. All school employees must be able to speak English fluently."

1898 The United States prosecutes the Spanish–American War, a month-long conflict against Spain. It acquires territories in the western Pacific and Latin America. Puerto Rico becomes its colony.

1899 *Cumming v. Richmond County Board of Education* The Supreme Court ejects a bid by blacks to force the Augusta Georgia schools to end secondary education for whites until the district restores it for blacks. The ruling, the first school segregation case to reach the U.S. Supreme

Court, allows wide disparities in the quality of education provided to blacks and whites in the South.

1901–1928 United States government administers Puerto Rico through a commissioner based in Washington. It provides very limited funding for Puerto Rican public schools while promoting Americanization programs in these schools, and an English-only policy.

1901 Estelle Brown takes the Civil Service Examination expecting "to be tested on my fitness to teach children of a savage race to whom the word education was unknown and who were without knowledge of a written language. No such test was given." She expects questions on tribal history and reservation conditions; she is not even told the tribe she was to teach. In effect, this exam (not unlike contemporary tests for teacher competence) is designed for teachers of mainstream students. This cultural bias excludes many potential Indian teachers, while admitting teachers with little or no knowledge of Indians and Indian education. Low government salaries, plus the rural setting of many Indian schools, means that the Indian school teaching is often the last resort for teachers who cannot find employment elsewhere.

1908 *Berea College v. Kentucky* Upholds Kentucky law prohibiting integrated classes for blacks and whites, in a case brought by a private college with a mixed-race education.

1913 *United States v. Sandoval* New Mexico Supreme Court rules that the Pueblo Indians are savages and therefore have no claim to U.S. citizenship under the Treaty of Guadalupe Hidalgo.

1917 Puerto Rico becomes a U.S. territory, "organized but unincorporated." Puerto Ricans can elect their own legislature and join the United States Army. The commissioner retains power.

1923 Puerto Rico Commissioner Huyle forbids Spanish-only public school newspapers. Only school newspapers that are at least 50 percent English text are permitted.

1926 The progressive Meriam Report on American Indian education recommends the following: ending the curriculum that stresses only Anglo-American cultural values; limiting attendance of nonreservation boarding schools to older children; having younger children attend community schools near home; and the Indian Service's providing youth and parents with tools to adapt both to the white and to the Indian world.

1927 *Gong Lum v. Rice* Affirms a Mississippi school district's right to require a Chinese-American girl to attend a segregated black school, rejecting her bid to attend the school for whites.

1927 California attorney general submits his opinion that Mexican American students are Indians and should be placed under the mandate of de jure segregation from white students.

1929 Navajo Indian children are literally lassoed from horseback and kidnapped by federal officials to be sent to boarding schools where they are forbidden to practice their own traditions or to speak their own language, on pain of whippings or going without food.*

1929 Charles Rhoades, first American Indian to become Commissioner of Indian Affairs, begins to put Meriam Report proposals into practice.

1930 *Independent School District v. Salvatierm* Desegregationists win a partial victory. A Texas judge rules that not all Mexican American students are Indians. Some are "Spanish." The latter group cannot be subject to de jure segregation. The judge does not force the school to desegregate. Moreover, he rules that it is legal to segregate Mexican Americans—on the basis of language.

1930s Beginning of migration of Puerto Ricans to U.S. mainland, mainly to New York City, initiated by professionals and the upper class.

1931 *Alvarez v. Lemon Grove School District*   This is the first successful desegregation case won by Mexican Americans. As a local (California) case it cannot be used as a precedent for other statewide or national cases, but it provides the model for the subsequent national education claims to argue that separate classrooms inherently are unequal classrooms. At this time, 90 percent of Texas schools and 85 percent of California schools are segregated by race.

1933 Franklin Roosevelt appoints a longtime Indian-rights advocate, John Collier, as Commissioner of Indian Affairs. Collier promotes sweeping liberalization of Indian education.

1934 Progressive Indian education begins in earnest during the New Deal period. Children are taught through the medium of their own cultural values while becoming aware of the values of white civilization. Indian Service teachers are taught to be sensitive to Indian culture and to use methods adapted to the unique characteristics and needs of Indian children. Community day schools increase from 132 to 226 and enrollment triples. Military regimentation in the boarding schools is abandoned. Vocational programs are developed to teach skills that will be of use to students if they return to their reservations. Indian schools introduce Indian history, art, and language. A directive is issued that there be no interference with Indian religious life or ceremonial expression.

1935 California legislature passes bill to segregate nonwhite Mexican American students on grounds they are children of "Mongolian parentage," a code word for Indian.

1938 *Gaines v. Canada*   This is first challenge to racial discrimination in graduate programs to reach the U.S. Supreme Court. It declares Missouri's failure to provide a law school for blacks to be unconstitutional. The Court finds that the legitimacy of segregated institutions "rests wholly upon the equality" that they offer the separated groups.

1940 United States grants citizenship to Puerto Ricans.

1940s Federal policy reverts to forced assimilation of Indian students. Cross cultural training of Indian schoolteachers ends. During World War II, funding for reservations is cut back. Schools are closed. A 1944 report recommends that students should again attend off-reservation boarding schools, as they had at the turn of the century.

Late 1940s–mid 1950s Massive migration, particularly of rural poor and working classes, from Puerto Rico to New York City. Seventy-five percent of children do not speak English. New York and New Jersey schools with high proportions of Puerto Ricans are severely overcrowded, with split sessions, few special classes. Puerto Rican students who speak English become de facto teacher aides. However, an English-only curriculum is enforced, and Spanish is used only for administrative, "housekeeping" purposes.

1946 *Méndez v. Westminster*   De jure segregation is ruled to be illegal. Federal court decision finds that segregating children (not just Mexican Americans) serves no educational purpose.

---

*See Carole Yazzie-Shaw, "Back in Those Days," part I.

1948 *Sipuel p. Board of Regents of the University of Oklahoma*   Citing the *Gaines* ruling, the Supreme Court directs the University of Oklahoma to provide a legal education to a black student who had been denied entry to its all-white law school. In response, to avoid integrating its graduate school, the state slaps together the minimal semblance of a graduate school for blacks. The high court refuses to overturn Oklahoma's actions.

1948 *Delgado et al. v. Bastrop   Independent School District* The Supreme Court rules that segregation of Mexican American students is discriminatory and illegal because it violates the students' Fourteenth Amendment rights.

1940–early 1960s   To alleviate teacher shortages, U.S. schools recruit Puerto Rican teachers from the island. However, those who speak English with a Spanish accent cannot become "licensed," and can only be "substitute auxiliary teachers," that is, nonpermanent positions.

1950 *Sweatt v. Painter*   The U.S. Supreme Court rules that a hastily contrived law school for blacks in Texas is unconstitutionally inferior. It orders the white law school to admit the black plaintiff.

1950 *McLaurin v. Board of Education of the University of Oklahoma*   Strikes down an elaborate set of rules segregating a black student from whites in a graduate education program. Citing harm caused by intangible as well as physical inequalities, the ruling prefigures the end of state-sanctioned segregation.

1952 Puerto Rico becomes a U.S. Commonwealth, a status it retains today.

1954 *Brown v. Board of Education of Topeka*   Unanimously declares that segregating elementary and secondary students by race violates black (and hence all racialized) children's constitutional right to equal protection of the law. The opinion arises from cases in four states (Delaware, Kansas, South Carolina, and Virginia). On the same day, the court invalidates school segregation in the District of Columbia on the grounds that it violated the black students' right to due process. The court defers judgment on implementing its rulings.

1955 *Brown v. Board of Education of Topeka* Orders the districts in the original *Brown* cases to make a "prompt and reasonable start toward full compliance." Known as *Brown II*, the ruling obligates local school authorities to overcome obstacles to desegregation "with all deliberate speed." This vague time frame prompts states and school districts to employ delay tactics. The Court also directs federal district judges to oversee the process. But it also stresses that constitutional principles cannot be sacrificed "simply because of disagreement with them."

1957 Yearly reports criticize U.S. mainland schools for the lack of language-appropriate educational and other diagnostic tests for Puerto Rican students. One report states that the "large backlog of retarded language learners … is chargeable to the lack of adequate tools for assessing the abilities of non-English speaking pupils."

1958 *Cooper v. Aaron* The Supreme Court rejects a bid by the Little Rock, Arkansas, district to delay desegregation because of the turmoil that followed a handful of black students desegregating a high school the year before. The justices unanimously rule, "Law and order are not here to be preserved by depriving the Negro children of their constitutional rights." This is a blow to white Southern resistance.

1963   The first Spanish-speaking Puerto Rican substitute auxiliary teacher receives a mainland-teaching license. The no-Spanish-accent requirement remains in force. By 1967 only 125 have received a teaching license. By and large, non-Puerto Rican teachers provide instruction in mainland schools.

1964   *Griffin v. Board of Education*   The Supreme Court rules that Prince Edward County, Virginia, one of the districts involved in *Brown*, can no longer avoid integration by keeping its public schools closed, as it had done since 1959. Also affirms a decision blocking tax breaks and tuition grants used to subsidize private schools for whites.

1965   The National Advisory Council on Indian Education is formed. This is a presidential ap-pointed advisory council on Indian education established under Title IX of the Elementary and Secondary Education Act of 1965. The council advises the secretary of education and Congress on funding and administration of programs with respect to which the secretary has jurisdiction, that includes Indian children or adults as participants, or that may benefit Indian children or adults. The council also makes recommendations to the secretary for filling the position of director of Indian education.

1968   *Green v. New Kent County School Board*   Declares in a case from Virginia that districts that formerly operated "dual systems" for black and whites have an affirmative duty to eliminate racial discrimination "root and branch." States that districts must promptly dismantle segrega-tion not just in student assignment but also in faculty, staff, transportation, extracurricular activities, and facilities. These become the six "green factors" that are later used by the courts to gauge whether a district has met its obligations to desegregate.

1968   Title VII of the Elementary and Secondary Education Act This legislation, commonly called the Bilingual Education Act, heralds a limited change in the way language-minority children are taught in the United States. It recognizes their needs, promotes greater access to the cur-riculum, trains educators in the skills they need (such as ESL and bilingual education), and fosters achievement among language minority students. Many opponents, who believe that bilingualism has no place in U.S. public education, will contest it.

1969   *Alexander v. Board of Education*   The Supreme Court overturns an appeals court ruling that gave thirty-three Mississippi districts more time to come up with plans to desegregate. The unanimous ruling says districts must end their dual systems for blacks and whites "at once and to operate now and hereafter only unitary schools."

1969   Ralph Nader testifies in Congress that "in any school with Indian students, BIA or public, cultural conflict is inevitable. The student, bringing with him all the values, attitudes, and beliefs that constitute his 'Indianness,' is expected to subordinate that Indianness to the general American standards of the school. The fact that, he, the student, must do all the modifying, all the compromising, seems to say something to him about the relative value of his own culture as opposed to that of the school. … It is estimated that for half of the Indians enrolled in federal schools, English is not the first language learned. Yet, when the child enters school, he is expected to function in a totally English-speaking environment. He muddles along in this educational void until he learns to assign meaning to the sounds the teacher makes. By the time he has begun to learn English, he has already fallen well behind in all the basic skill areas. In fact, it appears that his language handicap increases as he moves through school. And although it is no longer official BIA policy to discourage use of native languages, many report in the hearings indicate the contrary in practice."

1969 *United States v. Montgomery County Board of Education* Upholds the use of numerical quotas to racial balance an Alabama public school faculty.

1969 Senate report 91–501, *Indian Education: A National Tragedy, a National Challenge*, declares: "the dominant policy of the federal government toward the American Indian has been one of coercive assimilation" with "disastrous effects on the education of Indian children."

1970 *Cisneros v. Corpus Cliristi Independent School District* Mexican Americans are ruled to be an ethnically identifiable minority group and, in terms of desegregation, have rights similar to African Americans. This contradicts the finding of *Ross v. Eckels* (1970), a desegregation case that rules that Mexican Americans are not an identifiable minority group for purposes of desegregation.

1970 *Diana v. State Board of Education, Covarrubias v. San Diego Unified School District* (1971), and *Guadalupe v. Tempe Elementary* (1971) These cases lead to major changes in the grade-level promotion of minority students. All three find that overrepresentation of Mexican Americans in classes for mentally retarded students indicates fundamentally unfair treatment.

1971 *Swann v. Charlotte-Mecklenburg Board of Education* Authorizes mandatory busing, redrawn attendance zones, and the limited use of racial-balance quotas as desegregation tools. Holds that individual schools need not reflect the districtwide racial balance, but that districts bear the burden of proving that any schools that are comprised of students of only one race do not result from discrimination. In one of three related rulings issued the same day, the justices strike down a North Carolina antibusing law that prohibited assignment of students on the basis of race.

1972 *Wright v. Emporia City Council and United States v. Scotland Neck Board of Education* In separate rulings issued the same day, the Supreme Court rejects bids to carve out new school districts in Virginia and North Carolina. In both cases, the districts would have had enrollments with a greater ratio of white students than in the desegregated districts they were leaving.

1973 *San Antonio Independent School District v. Rodríguez* The Supreme Court rules that education is not a fundamental constitutional right. Hence school funding systems that are based on local property taxes enabling wealthier districts to provide more funds per student do not violate the Fourteenth Amendment.

1973 A Navaho kindergarten teacher in Arizona is reprimanded on her teacher evaluation for "on several occasions actually having taught Navajo words over the objection of the school's administration." Although her kindergarten students' dominant language is Navajo, Arizona law at that time requires all instruction in public schools to be in English.

1973 *Keyes v. Denver School District No. 1* Three key rulings come out of this case. For the first time, the Court holds a district liable for intentional segregation, even though it had never required separate schools by law. This extends the "affirmative duty" to desegregate to districts beyond the Southern and Mason-Dixon border states. A majority also finds that official discriminatory acts affecting some schools or neighborhoods create a legal presumption that the whole district should desegregate. And the justices hold that Latinos should be counted with blacks in determining whether a school is segregated.

1974 *Milliken v. Bradley*   This is the first major restriction imposed on public school desegregation. The 5–4 ruling strikes down a plan to merge the Detroit schools with fifty-three largely white suburban districts. Citing a lack of evidence that those districts were guilty of intentional segregation, it orders a new plan confined to the city, where enrollment had been more than two-thirds black. It thus becomes much harder for courts to order city/suburban desegregation plans to counteract the concentration of minorities in the cities.

1974 *Lau v. Nichols*   The U.S. Supreme Court rules that when children arrive in school with little or no knowledge of English, the use of English-only instruction in their education is a violation of their civil rights.

1976 *Pasadena City Board of Education v. Spangler*   The U.S. Supreme Court reverses a ruling requiring this California district to adjust attendance zones annually to preserve court-ordered racial status. A lower court had ordered that no school should have a majority of any minority group, a directive with which the district fell out of compliance after one year. On a 6–2 vote, the justices conclude the enrollment shifts stemmed from demographic changes and are not deliberate "segregative acts."

1977 *Milliken v. Bradley*   Authorizes courts to require remedial education programs as an antidote to past segregation, in a decision know as *Milliken II*. Upholds a ruling directing Detroit and Michigan to split the cost of programs in four areas: reading, in-service teacher training, student testing, and counseling. This ruling opens the door to broader use of remedial programs and extra funding for racially isolated schools across the country.

1978 *Regents of the University of California v. Allan Bakke* On the basis of Equal Protection Clause of the Fourteenth Amendment, the U.S. Supreme Court rules that a medical school discriminated against a white applicant on the basis of race. Its decision significantly narrows the use of affirmative action in higher education. Admissions procedures could no longer evaluate disadvantaged candidates on different criteria than nonminority candidates, or establish numerical quotas for disadvantaged students. However, Justice Powell rules that universities have the right to select students on many relevant factors, including race, as long as any individual candidate's Fourteen Amendment rights are not violated.

1979 *Columbus Board of Education v. Penick and Dayton Board of Education v. Brinkman* Upholds mandatory busing in two districts in Ohio, saying school officials had perpetuated segregation to varying degrees by their actions and inaction since the *Brown* decision. In dissent (future chief justice) Rehnquist says the rulings so blur the line between de jure and de facto segregation that the only way urban districts could avoid court-ordered busing, given residential segregation, was to get rid of neighborhood schools.

1980–1990   Self-determination for American Indian schooling is repeatedly threatened by federal attempts to repeal prior legislation.

1982 *Washington v. Seattle School District No. 1* Strikes down a state antibusing initiative passed by voters, after Seattle voluntarily adopted a desegregation plan involving extensive crosstown busing. A majority of the justices concludes the initiative was racially motivated.

1982 *Plyer v. Doe* The U.S. Supreme Court rules that Texas cannot exclude undocumented children from tuition-free enrollment in the state's public schools, as Texas legislators had attempted to do.

1982 *Crawford v. Board of Education* Upholds an amendment to California's constitution that prohibited state judges from ordering busing for integration in the absence of a violation of the U.S. Constitution. The amendment followed a state's Supreme Court order requiring Los Angeles to desegregate on the grounds that it had been obligated under the state constitution to attack de facto segregation.

1991 Puerto Ricans declare Spanish the only official language of the island.

1991 *Board of Education of Oklahoma City v. Dowell* Stressing that court orders to desegregate were designed to be temporary, by a 5–3 vote the Court states that federal judges should lift desegregation decrees if districts have complied in good faith and remedied past discrimination "as far as practicable."

1992 *Freeman v. Pitts* The Court authorizes lower courts to relinquish supervision over some aspects of a district's desegregation-related obligations (such as extracurricular activities), while retaining it in others. Also judges are granted leeway to consider issues beyond the "green factors," such as educational quality, in assessing whether districts should be declared unitary.

1993 Both English and Spanish become official languages of Puerto Rico.

1994 Proposition 187 This referendum is overwhelmingly approved by California voters. It would have denied to undocumented immigrants a range of social services, including public education. The electorate blames immigrants for an economic recession triggered by the end of the Cold War, but the enmity that Prop. 187 unleashed was fueled by the imminent "browning of California," when it had become clear that the politically dominant Anglo-American population would become a numerical minority. It was immediately struck down in court as unconstitutional, but not bringing racial politics front and center here, and across the country.

1995 The federal Office of Indian Education is allocated a total fiscal-year budget of one dollar. Tribal leaders and pan-Indian organization leaders lobby Congress, hold prayer vigils, and call press conferences to argue for continued funding. Finally, President Clinton maintains the BIA and OIE, by vetoing the budget.

1995 *Missouri v. Jenkins* States that an ambitious magnet school plan in Kansas City aimed at luring suburban whites amounts to judicial overreach. The 5–4 ruling states that neither the goal of attracting whites, nor the persistence of substandard test scores in the city, justified the plan, which the state had been subsidizing and wanted to end.

1996 *Hopwood v. State of Texas* The Fifth Circuit Court of Appeals claims that the 1978 *Bakke* decision was in fact not a precedent for affirmative action cases. It ruled that it was illegal to use race, ethnicity, or gender in admissions in higher education institutions. This ruling applied to states within its jurisdiction, including Texas, Louisiana, and Mississippi. Other appellate courts, reading the same law, continue to use the *Bakke* precedent, which upholds affirmative action.

1996 Proposition 209 This California referendum prohibits local and state agencies from granting "preferential treatment" to individuals based on their race, ethnicity, or sex in the areas of state contracting, employment, and education. It signals a further retreat from affirmative action. Higher education is most affected by the referendum, which became part of the California state constitution.

1998 Proposition 227 This referendum, which restricts bilingual education and instruction of the native language in California public schools, passes handily. Over one million schoolchildren are affected. As a result, students who do not speak English when they arrive at school must be placed in English-only classrooms after one school year. Proposition 227 becomes the model for other state referenda. In 2000 and 2002 respectively, Arizona (Proposition 203) and Massachusetts (Question 2) pass similar English-only measures, while Colorado voters reject its anti-bilingual education Amendment 31 in 2002.

2002 The "No Child Left Behind" Act This federal legislation reverses thirty-four years of U.S. language policy in public schools. It ends the Bilingual Education Act (1968). Federal funds will continue to support English language learners (ELLs), but the swift and brief teaching of English takes priority over longer-term bilingual academic skill development. Moreover, schools now must make annual English assessments. "Accountability" provisions, such as yearly school evaluations of the percentage of ELLs who are reclassified as fluent in English, will discourage schools from continuing native-language instruction, because failure to show academic progress in English will lead to the loss of federal funds.

2003 *Grutter v. Bollinger and Granz v. Bollinger* After twenty-five years, the U.S. Supreme Court returns to the issue of affirmative action in higher education. These rulings dismissed the *Hopwood* appellate court decision. The Court also reaffirmed the *Bakke* precedent, and the right of universities to take racial diversity into account in admissions policies. Schools cannot employ simple formulas that mechanically assign a numeric value to each candidate's race, but they can take race into account (among many other factors) in an individualized evaluation process of each person. The divided rulings indicate that the issue will soon be contested again.

NOTES

Quotes were drawn from, and materials adapted from, the following sources. For the history of U.S. public education of American Indians: Jon Reyhner, "American Indian Language Policy and School Success," *The Journal of Educational Issues of Language Minority Students* 12 (Summer 1993): 35–59; Sharon O'Brien, *American Indian Tribal Governments* (Norman: University of Oklahoma Press, 1989), 238–42; and "History and Facts about Indian Education," an American Indian Education Foundation website: www.aiefprograms.org/history_facts/history.html (accessed on October 10, 1998). The editor would like to thank Ralph de Unamuno for his help on this portion of the timeline. For court decisions affecting racial segregation in public education: a sidebar without a byline appearing in *Education*

Week 18, no. 28 (March 24, 1999): 27–28, 30. For nineteenth-century legal cases centering on race and citizenship: Martha Menchaca, "Chicano Indianism: A Historical Account of Racial Repression in the United States," *American Anthropologist* 20, no. 3 (1993): 583–603. For legal and legislative rulings affecting Latino education: Antonia Darder, Rodolfo D. Torres, and Henry Gutiérrez, eds., *Latinos and Education: A Critical Reader* (New York: Routledge, 1997); Guadalupe San Miguel Jr. and Richard R. Valencia, "From the Treaty of Guadalupe Hidalgo to Hopwood: The Educational Plight and Struggle of Mexican Americans in the Southwest," *Harvard Educational Review* 68, no. 3 (Fall 1998): 353–412; Guadalupe San Miguel *"Let All of Them Take Heed": Mexican Americans and the Campaign for Educational Equality in Texas,* 1910–1981 (Austin: University of Texas Press, 1987); James Crawford "Why Is Bilingual Education So Unpopular with the American Public?" *The Education Policy Studies Brief,* no. 8 (epsl-0302-102-lpru, 2003), website: www.language-policy.org (accessed on September 12, 2003). For Puerto Rican educational history, I drew on Meyer Weinberg, *A Chance to Learn: The History of Race and Education in the United States* (New York: Cambridge University Press, 1977).

1. Paulo Freire, *Pedagogy of the Oppressed* (New York: Seabury Press, 1970), 129.
2. James Lockhart, *The Nahuas After the Conquest: A Social and Cultural History of the Indians of Central Mexico, Sixteenth Through Eighteenth Centuries.* (Stanford, CA: Stanford University Press, 1992).
3. Caroline Hendrie, "In Black and White," *Lessons of a Century: A Nation's Schools Come of Age* (Bethesda, MD: Editorial Projects in Education, 2000), 62–79.
4. See, among many other sources, David J. Weber's anthology *Foreigners in Their Native Land: Historical Roots of the Mexican Americans* (Albuquerque: University of New Mexico Press, 1973).
5. Martha Menchaca, "Chicano Indianism: A Historical Account of Racial Repression in the United States," *American Anthropologist* 20, no. 3 (1993): 583–603.
6. Meyer Weinberg, *A Chance to Learn: The History of Race and Education in the United States* (New York: Cambridge University Press, 1977), Chapter 6.
7. Weinberg, *A Chance to Learn*, Chapter 6.
8. James Baldwin, "If Black English Isn't a Language, Then Tell Me, What Is?" Letter to the editor of the *New York Times,* July 29, 1979. Reprinted in *The Price of a Ticket* (St. Martin's Press).

If you want to really hurt me, talk badly about my language. Ethnic identity is twin skin to linguistic identity, I am my language.

—Gloria Anzaldúa

The brutal truth is that the bulk of the white people in America never had any interest in educating Black people, except as this could serve white purposes. It is not the Black child's language that is in question, it is not his language that is despised: It is his experience. A child cannot be taught by anyone who despises him, and a child cannot afford to be fooled.

—James Baldwin[8]

English is an all-devouring language that has moved across North America like the fabulous plagues of locusts that darkened the sky and devoured even the handles of rakes and hoes. Yet the omnivorous nature of a colonial language is a writer's gift. Raised in the English language, I partake of a mongrel feast.

—Louise Erdrich

Pathologizing the Language and Culture of Poor Children

This article will help teachers resist deficit discourses that pathologize the language and culture of children living in poverty.

By Curt Dudley-Marling and Krista Lucas

Caitlin, a fourth-grade teacher in a diverse, underperforming urban school, began the school year by taking stock of the varied socioeconomic and linguistic resources her students brought with them to the classroom. Elena had come to live with relatives in the U.S. only days before and spoke almost no English. Three other ELL students in Caitlin's class possessed varying levels of English mastery. The rest of her students were Black, most of whom spoke African American Vernacular English (AAVE). Almost all of the children qualified for free and reduced lunch, and some of her students' parents received welfare. Nearly all of Caitlin's students performed poorly on the state reading assessment as third graders.

Caitlin's classroom looks like many other classrooms across the country in which teachers are challenged by the diverse linguistic, cultural, and socioeconomic backgrounds of their students. How teachers like Caitlin respond to this diversity will depend on whether they view students' language and cultural experiences as *assets* on which they can draw in support of school learning or *deficiencies* that must be overcome—or "fixed"—before students can succeed academically. Unfortunately, many teachers, administrators, and policy makers have been persuaded to view poor students as culturally and linguistically deficient. The high level of reading failure among children living in poverty, for example, is often linked to the claim that poor children lack the rich and varied vocabulary needed to succeed in school (Blachowicz & Obrochta, 2005; Blachowicz, Fisher, Ogle, & Watts-Taffe, 2006; Labbo, Love, & Ryan, 2007; Neuman & Celano, 2001). These perceived linguistic *deficiencies* tend to be blamed on parents who, presumably, do not provide their children with sufficiently rich language learning environments (Britto, Brooks-Gunn, & Griffin, 2006; Cooter, 2006; Neuman & Celano, 2001).

The primary source for the claim that poor children grow up in linguistically impoverished environments that limit their vocabulary development and, ultimately, their success in school is an enormously influential study of vocabulary development by Betty Hart and Todd Risley (1995). The Hart and Risley study, which examined vocabulary development in families of differing socioeconomic backgrounds, has been described as "groundbreaking work ... essential reading in any course dealing with early literacy skills" (Walsh, Glaser, & Wilcox, 2006, p. 38). Additionally, the Hart and Risley study has been cited in Congressional hearings ("The critical need for evidence-based programs," 2003), in numerous articles in the popular press, and in over 600 articles published in scholarly journals.[1]

In this article, we argue that strong claims about language deficiencies in poor children and their families based on the Hart and Risley study are unwarranted. Further, we argue that the uncritical acceptance of Hart and Risley's findings is emblematic of a trend among some educators, educational policy makers, and educational researchers to readily embrace a deficit stance that pathologizes the language and culture of poor students and their families (Dudley-Marling, 2007; Foley, 1997). We hope that this critique will help teachers resist "research-based" policies that aim to fix the language and culture of poor and minority students with whom they work.

We begin with a description of the Hart and Risley study of vocabulary development.

THE HART AND RISLEY STUDY

Hart and Risley are among those who have argued that federal educational initiatives targeting the educational performance of poor children have been insufficient to interrupt the cycle of intergenerational poverty. As Hart and Risley (1995) put it, "competence as a social problem is still with us. ... Too many [poor] children drop out of school and follow their parents into unemployment or onto welfare, where they raise their children in a culture of poverty" (p. 2). Hart and Risley hypothesized that language *deficiencies* in poor children and their families play a significant role in perpetuating the cycle of poverty. To examine this relationship, they studied the language interactions of parents and children in the homes of 13 upper-SES (1 Black, 12 White), 10 middle-SES (3 Black, 7 White), 13 lower-SES (7 Black, 6 White), and 6 welfare (all Black) families, all from Kansas City. Families were observed for one hour each month over a period of 2½ years, beginning when children were 7–9 months old.

Based on their findings, Hart and Risley concluded that, among the families in their study, there was a significant relationship between the quantity and quality of language used by parents and children and families' socioeconomic status. They found, for example, that children's vocabulary growth at three years of age strongly correlated with families' socioeconomic status. In perhaps the most widely cited finding from their study, Hart and Risley reported that average three-year-olds from the welfare families demonstrated an active vocabulary of around 500 words compared to the average three-year-old from upper-SES, professional families, who demonstrated vocabularies of over 1,000 words. Hart and

Risley reported that these differences persisted after children entered school and were strong predictors of children's vocabulary development and reading comprehension in third grade.

Crucially, Hart and Risley linked differences in children's vocabulary to differences in the language they heard from their parents. According to Hart and Risley, some children knew more words because they heard more words spoken to them by their parents. Based on an extrapolation of their data, Hart and Risley estimated that "by age 3 the children in professional families would have heard more than 30 million words, the children in working-class families 20 million, and the children in welfare families 10 million" (p. 132). Compared to the welfare families, the high-SES, professional parents not only exposed their children to more words, they displayed more words of all kinds to their children—"more multiclause sentences, more past and future verb tenses, more declaratives, and more questions of all kinds" (pp. 123–124).

> **What is particularly striking about Hart and Risley's data analysis is their willingness to make strong, evaluative claims about the quality of the language parents directed to their children.**

What is particularly striking about Hart and Risley's data analysis is their willingness to make strong, evaluative claims about the quality of the language parents directed to their children. Hart and Risley attached particular significance to the tendency of the welfare parents to prefer direct requests ("Pick up the toys") and "corrective or critical" feedback (p. 187) compared to professional parents' tendency toward indirect requests ("Why don't you pick up the toys for me?") and "affirmative" feedback (p. 124). According to Hart and Risley, professional parents' preference for indirect requests is reflective of "upper-SES culture with its care for politeness" (p. 58). For example, the request form *can you?* "suggest[s] parental confidence that small children are willing but have either forgotten or are not yet skilled or mature enough to do 'better.' They prepare children for the important questions to come: "Did you remember to …?' or 'Was that a nice/fair/smart thing to do?'" (p. 105).

The predominance of indirect requests among the upper-SES parents is, according to Hart and Risley, reflective of a range of language practices that prepare their children "to participate in a culture concerned with symbols and analytic problem solving" (p. 133). Conversely, "in the welfare families, the lesser amount of talk with its more frequent parent-initiated topics, imperatives, and prohibitions suggested a culture concerned with established customs" (p. 133). Hart and Risley conclude that the "prevailing negative tone" (p. 177) carried by the welfare parents' propensity to employ direct requests and critical, corrective feedback had such a negative effect on children that it would take "thousands of hours of affirmative feedback even to begin to overcome what [the] child has learned about herself in her first three years" (p. 188).

For those inclined to embrace deficit thinking (Valencia, 1997), Hart and Risley's study of vocabulary development provides a satisfactory explanation to questions about the intractability of intergenerational poverty and the limited success of early intervention programs. Children living in poverty fail in school because their homes are deficient in language. Moreover, the dearth of language opportunities during poor children's first three years of life cannot easily be overcome. In Hart and Risley's words,

... we saw that what parents said and did with their children in the first 3 years of language learning had an enormous impact on how much language their children learned and used (p. 159). ... We could see too why a few hours of intensive intervention at age 4 had so little impact on the magnitude of the differences in cumulative experience that resulted from those first 3 years. (p. 180)

From this perspective, the language practices of poor parents transmit to their children a "culture of poverty" (Hart & Risley, 1995, p. 2) that denies poor children the cognitive and linguistic resources needed to succeed in school. For educators persuaded by this deficit perspective, closing the achievement gap that plagues American schools requires interventions that change how parents living in poverty interact with their children.

The claim that there is a culture of poverty that limits the academic and vocational success of poor people is based on a flawed theory of culture.

A CRITICAL ASSESSMENT OF HART AND RISELY

Hart and Risley's interpretation of their data implicates deficiencies in the language and culture of families living in poverty as the principal cause of poor children's generally low academic performance. This conclusion is undermined, however, by three factors:

- methodological flaws in how Hart and Risley selected their participants and collected their data;
- an ethnocentric bias that takes for granted the normative status of the linguistic and cultural practices of the middle- and upper-income families in their sample;
- the failure to make explicit the theory of language and culture that frames their analysis.

Again, the purpose of this critique is to help teachers resist the deficit thinking that stands behind Hart and Risley's research and other educational reforms that blame the victims of poverty for their academic and economic struggles.

Methodological Limitations

Many educational researchers and policy makers have generalized the findings about the language and culture of the 6 welfare families in Hart and Risley's study to all poor families. Yet, Hart and Risley offer no compelling reason to believe that the poor families they studied have much in common with poor families in other communities, or even in Kansas City for that matter. The primary selection criterion for participation in this study was socioeconomic status; therefore, all the 6 welfare families had in common was income, a willingness to participate in the study, race (all the welfare families were Black), and geography (all lived in the Kansas City area).

Families living in poverty are, however, an ethnically, linguistically, and racially diverse group (U.S. Census Bureau, 2003). Strong claims about the language and culture of families living in poverty based on a sample of 6 Black welfare families living in Kansas City are unwarranted. Nor is there reason to believe that Hart and Risley's welfare families—or other people living in poverty in the United States—share a "culture of poverty," as Hart and Risley and others (see Payne, 2005, for example) assert. The claim that there is a *culture of poverty* that limits the academic and vocational success of poor people is based on a flawed theory of culture that ignores the rich language and experience possessed by children from all cultural and linguistic groups (Foley, 1997; Gonzalez, 2005; Jones & Luo, 1999). Further, assertions about the language and culture of parents and children living in poverty based on a sample of 6 welfare families, all of whom were Black, and 13 professional families, 12 of whom were White, reinforce harmful stereotypes that conflate poverty and race. The reality is that only 25% of the 33 million Americans living below the poverty line are Black (U.S. Census Bureau, 2003).

The persuasiveness of Hart and Risley's findings is further undermined by the means by which they collected their data. To examine the language of professional, working class, and welfare families, trained observers audio-taped the verbal interactions between parents and children one hour per month over a period of 2½ years. Observers were instructed to interact with families as little as possible, to be "a silent, friendly, but not very interesting presence" (p. 35). Hart and Risley concluded that the observers had little effect on the parents and children they observed. In their words, "parents seemed to be quite comfortable with the observer … over time the observer tended to fade into the furniture" (p. 35).

Smagorinsky (1995) notes that "data are social constructs developed through the relationship of researcher, research participants, research context … and the means of data collection" (p. 192). Indeed, there is a substantial body of literature in anthropology, linguistics, and psychology indicating that observers often affect the behavior of the people they are observing (e.g., Baum, Forehand, & Zegiob, 1979; Le Compte & Goetz, 1982; Rabinow, 1977; Zegiob, Arnold, & Forehand, 1975), particularly when observers are viewed as outsiders (Labov, 1970). Zegiob, Arnold, and Forehand (1975), for example, found that the presence of observers had a significant effect on upper-middle-class mothers' interactions with their children. Specifically, mothers were "more positive in their verbal behavior and structured their activities more" (p. 509) when they knew they were being observed. Other research indicates that the age, race, dress, and demeanor of observers can have a dramatic effect on the language of young Black males, for example (Labov, 1970). Hart and Risley failed to acknowledge even the possibility that observers would affect the parents and children they were observing beyond assuring their readers that the observers "tended to fade into the furniture" (p. 35).

The contexts in which Hart and Risley collected their data may also have affected their findings. Various social contexts recruit different language forms, content, and vocabulary (Gee, 1996). Therefore, it is reasonable to expect that Hart and Risley would have made every effort to ensure that the social contexts in which parents and children were observed were comparable across SES groups. This issue takes on particular significance given the small sample sizes. Hart and Risley did report that parents were asked to choose when they were to be observed, and most chose to be observed during routines like mealtimes. It is unclear, however, whether the professional and welfare families engaged in comparable activities while they were being observed. Nor is there any evidence that Hart and Risley considered variation in activities between groups as a possible threat to their interpretation of their data. It is at least possible that upper-SES, professional parents chose to be observed during activities that were richer in language opportunities than when poor families chose to be observed.

> **Hart and Risley failed to acknowledge even the possibility that observers would affect the parents and children they were observing.**

Ethnocentric Bias

Hart and Risley reported qualitative and quantitative differences in the language practices of the middle- and upper-SES, working class, and welfare families they studied. However, by taking the language practices of the middle- and upper-SES families in their sample as the standard, Hart and Risley transformed the linguistic *differences* they found among the welfare families in their study into linguistic *deficiencies*. For instance, the tendency of welfare families to prefer more direct request forms is presented as an illustration of what Hart and Risley deem the "prevailing negative tone" (p. 177) in welfare families that will take "thousand of hours ... to overcome" (p. 188). Yet, Hart and Risley offer no evidence that the children and parents in the welfare families shared this interpretation of directives in their homes. Nor is there any indication that Hart and Risley even considered the possibility that poor parents and their children might have considered these interactions as mainly positive, business-like, honest, or highly involved.

Arguably, Hart and Risley construed the interactions between the upper-SES, professional parents and their children as higher in quality because they reflected their own values (this group included parents who, like Hart and Risley, were college professors). In the upper-SES, professional families, Hart and Risley saw "quality interactions" that came "naturally" to families in which "parents had all the advantages of higher education, challenging jobs, substantial incomes, and broad experience" (p. 91). The language of professional families was "affirmative in tone" (p. 177), encouraged "politeness" (p. 57), promoted "analytic problem solving" (p. 133) and "recall" (p. 101), "organize[d] thinking" (p. 101), and taught children "to take responsibility for social behaviors" (p. 104).

There is an alternative tradition in linguistic research informed by a sociocultural theory of language that "takes seriously the linguistic and sociocultural strengths of members of non-dominant communities in the hope that demonstrations of these strengths could influence schools and the reception and progress of non-mainstream children within them" (Michaels, 2005, p. 137). Labov (1970), Heath (1983), Michaels (1981), Gee (1996), and Gonzalez, Moll, and Amanti (2005) are among the linguistic researchers who have demonstrated the richness, complexity, and rule-governed nature of the language practices of non-dominant groups. Miller, Cho, and Bracey (2005a), for example, recently reviewed a program of research indicating that the lower-SES, working class adults they studied participate "prolifically, avidly, and artfully in personal storytelling in their homes and communities and that they brought children into this valued activity from an early age" (p. 125). Moreover, Miller, Cho, and Bracey found that these working class families valued storytelling more highly and produced far more stories than their middle-class counterparts. Yet, from the perspective of deficit theorists like Hart and Risley, the language of non-dominant groups is rarely considered on its own terms, but rather is seen only in reference to the language of dominant groups. As Miller, Cho, and Bracey (2005a) put it, "Problems of ethnocentric bias, of invidious comparisons, of dichotomizing differences, of minimizing variation within groups [continue] to plague discussions when children from working-class, poor, or minority backgrounds are compared with their 'mainstream' counterparts" (p. 116).

Failing to consider the language of poor families on its own terms is the fatal flaw of the Hart and Risley study. If language is, in part, about enacting identities (Gee, 1999), then an alternative reading of Hart and Risley's study suggests that the most significant difference between the upper- and middle-SES families and the welfare families who participated was their level of success in enacting the linguistic and cultural identities Hart and Risley shared with the upper- and middle-SES families.

Failing to consider the language of poor families on its own terms is the fatal flaw of the Hart and Risley study.

Absence of a Clearly Articulated Theoretical Framework

Arguably, the position on scientifically based research that has emerged in the context of *No Child Left Behind* elevates method over theory, implying that theory may jeopardize the objectivity of the researcher. Research is, however, always undertaken from a point of view, some position on how the physical and social worlds we inhabit operate. The research tools of the physicist, for example, are created on the basis of (theoretical) assumptions about the nature of the universe. Similarly, the meanings physicists make of their observations are constructed on the basis of a general theory of the physical world (Kuhn, 1970). Indeed, data collected by physical and social scientists only have meaning in the context of some theoretical framework. As Dennett (1995) puts it, "there's no such thing as philosophy-free science; there is only science whose philosophical baggage is taken on board without examination" (p. 21).

It is difficult, perhaps impossible, for researchers to see beyond the margins of their theoretical vision. Still, it is the responsibility of researchers to delineate the boundaries of their theoretical framework. Situating research in an explicitly theoretical framework enables other researchers and practitioners to critique the research on its own (theoretical) terms and from the position of alternative perspectives. Hart and Risley, however, fail to situate their study within an explicit theory of language or culture. They offer no theory of language *or* culture to support their presumption that people living in poverty share a common language or culture, for example. Arguably, by taking on board "philosophical baggage … without examination" (Dennett, 1995, p. 21), Hart and Risley engage in "unreflected action and holding magical beliefs … they conduct research without questioning why they do what they do or how their actions are connected to understandings of knowledge, people, or language" (Bloome, Carter, Christian, Otto, & Shuart-Faris, 2005, p. xviii).

Based on their research, Hart and Risley report differences in the language of professional families and families living in poverty, differences that correlate with children's academic success. On the basis of these findings, Hart and Risley conclude that the linguistic *deficiencies* of children living in poverty are the *cause* of their academic failures, necessitating interventions that change the ways poor parents interact with their children. Conflating correlation with causation in this way illustrates the "magical thinking" that emerges when researchers separate theory from method (Bloome et al., 2005). Hart and Risley make causal claims based on the co-occurrence of linguistic and academic variables, but what's missing is an interpretive (theoretical) framework for articulating the relationship between their data and their claims.

Researchers who fail to situate their research in an explicit theoretical framework deny readers of their work a conceptual position from which to assess or debate the research beyond technical discussions of method. The discourse of "scientifically based research," which equates the scientific method with technique, has led to a body of research that is resistant to meaningful (theoretical) critique. Hart and Risley's conclusions about the language practices of families living in poverty, for example, are emblematic of a discourse of language deprivation that

> *seems impervious to counter evidence, stubbornly aligning itself with powerful negative stereotypes of poor and working-class families. It remains the dominant discourse in many arenas, both academic and popular, making it very difficult to see working-class language for what it is … or to be heard to be offering a different perspective.* (Miller, Cho, & Bracey, 2005b, p. 153)

Hart and Risley offer their readers little guidance on the theoretical framework of their analysis, but our reading of Hart and Risley reveals a "tacit" theory (Gee, 1996) of language and culture that informs their interpretation of their data collection and their data analysis. From this perspective, they are establishing a norm thoroughly biased in favor of middle- and upper-middle-class children. This common-sense rendering of the data pathologizes the language and culture of poor families, reflecting harmful, long-standing stereotypes that hold the poor primarily responsible for their economic and academic struggles (Nunberg, 2002).

> **The discourse of "scientifically based research," … has led to a body of research that is resistant to meaningful (theoretical) critique.**

Blaming the poor for their poverty in this way leaves no reason to consider alternative, systemic explanations for poverty or school failure. There is, for example, no reason to wonder how impoverished curricula (Gee, 2004; Kozol, 2005; Oakes, 2006), under-resourced schools (Kozol, 1992), and an insufficiency of "high-quality" teachers in high-poverty schools (Olson, 2006) limit the academic performance of many poor students. Nor is there any reason to consider how the conditions of poverty affect children's physical, emotional, and neurological development and day-to-day performance in school (Books, 2004; Rothstein, 2004). Recent research in neuroscience, for example, indicates that the stresses of living in poverty can impair children's brain development (Noble, McCandliss, & Farah, 2007). But most Americans do not easily embrace systemic explanations for academic failure. In our highly individualistic, meritocratic society, it is generally assumed that academic underachievement is evidence of personal failure (Mills, 1959).

PATHOLOGIZING THE LANGUAGE AND CULTURE OF POOR CHILDREN

There has been a re-emergence of deficit-based explanations for disproportionate school failure among poor Black and Hispanic youth (Foley, 1997; Ladson-Billings, 1999). Popular family literacy programs that aim to fix literacy deficiencies in poor families (Taylor, 1997); the broad acceptance of Ruby Payne's (2005) portrayal of people living in poverty as deficient in the cognitive, emotional, linguistic, and spiritual resources needed to escape poverty; Bill Cosby's widely quoted denunciation of the language of Black youth (Dyson, 2006); and the tremendous influence of Hart and Risley's research on vocabulary and social class exemplify the willingness—even eagerness—of many educators and educational policy makers to accept explanations for academic failure that implicate the language and culture of poor children and their families as the cause of their academic struggles.

Rolstad (2004) laments that "linguistically baseless language prejudices often underlie [even] well-designed, well-conducted studies" (p. 5).

Linguistic research conducted within theoretical and anthropological linguistics and sociolinguistics that demonstrates the language strengths of children from non-dominant groups "has had virtually no impact on language-related research elsewhere" (Rolstad, 2004, p. 5). The deficit-based research of Hart and Risley, with all of its methodological and theoretical shortcomings, has been more persuasive than linguistic research that considers the language of poor families on its own terms (e.g., Labov, 1970; Heath, 1983; Michaels, 1981; Gee; 1996; see also Michaels, 2005), perhaps because Hart and Risley's findings comport with long-standing prejudices about the language of people living in poverty (Nunberg, 2002).

Revealing the flaws of deficit-based studies like Hart and Risley's is insufficient for changing how (some) people think about children and families living in poverty. Ultimately, the fundamental problem of Hart and Risley cannot be remedied by more or better research. Real social change demands reframing the question, i.e., "changing the way the public sees the world ... [by] changing what counts as common sense" (Lakoff, 2004, p. xv). In this case, reframing the question involves transforming the "common sense" that views people in poverty through the lens of deficit thinking. Acknowledging the richness of the language and culture all children bring to school, for example, leads to a very different set of questions, such as *What is it about school that manages to transform children who are good at learning ... regardless of their economic and cultural differences, into children who are not good at learning, if they are poor or members of certain minority groups? (Gee, 2004, p. 10). How can changing the conditions of poverty (e.g., quality health care, nutrition programs, safer neighborhoods, better housing) affect the academic performance of poor students? Instead of "getting the child 'ready' for school," how do we get "the school 'ready' to serve increasingly diverse children?"* (Swadener, 1995, p. 18).

There is no denying, however, that children from poor families experience higher levels of academic failure than their more affluent peers. In the final section of this article, we briefly consider a pedagogical stance that acknowledges and builds on the cultural and linguistic strengths that students from non-dominant groups bring with them to school.

There is little to be gained, however, by pathologizing the language and culture of children living in poverty.

AN ALTERNATIVE TO DEFICIT-BASED LANGUAGE PRACTICES

Children's language plays a crucial role in school success … and school failure. To succeed in school, children must learn the formal language of schooling. There is little to be gained, however, by pathologizing the language and culture of children living in poverty. Arguably, the representation of students' language and culture as *deficient* contributes to student alienation that some see as the root cause of high levels of school failure in non-middle-class communities (McCarthy and Crichlow, 1993). Moreover, when the language of schooling is viewed as a set of social and cultural practices (New London Group, 1996; Gee, 1996), it is clear that school-based language practices must be learned in the context of schooling. Gutierrez, Baquedano-López, and Turner (1997) put it this way:

> *From a sociocultural perspective, children develop, acquire, and are socialized to various literacies, as they actively participate in culturally defined systems of practices such as participating in religious classes, playing sports or games, and participating in formal and non-formal schooling activities.* (p. 369)

From this perspective, the responsibility for teaching students—especially students from non-dominant groups—the language of schooling rests with teachers, not parents.

As a beginning, teachers need to recognize the linguistic, social, and cognitive resources all children bring with them to school. This must go beyond merely acknowledging the language strengths of students from non-dominant groups, however. Michaels (2005) challenges educators "to go beyond claims and documentation of difference (even differences 'on their own terms') and show specifically how these differences can be recruited, in school, as strengths" (p. 137). In classrooms that make space for students' linguistic and cultural experiences, children have more linguistic, social, and cognitive resources to draw on in support of their learning (Dyson, 1993, 2003; Gutierrez, Baquedano-López, & Turner, 1997). The social practices in these classrooms "authenticate, integrate, and connect the classroom literacy practices to the [discourse] practices" of the communities from which students come (Gutiérrez, Baquedano-López, & Turner, 2007, p. 373). In this way, students' language, culture, and background knowledge become tools for learning. The emphasis in such classrooms is on "what can be done with language, rather than what cannot" (Schleppegrell & Go, 2007, p. 530), and children's everyday language is available as the basis for learning the formal language practices valued in school (Gebhard, Harman, & Seger, 2007).

Finally, Hart and Risley draw attention to a real problem that teachers encounter every day in their classrooms: children enter school with more or less of the linguistic, social, and cultural capital required for school success. However, we take exception to the characterization of this situation in terms of linguistic or cultural *deficiencies*. Through the lens of deficit thinking, linguistic differences among poor parents and children are transformed into deficiencies that are the cause of high levels of academic failure among poor children. In this formulation, the ultimate responsibility for this failure lies with parents who pass on to their children inadequate language and flawed culture. But, in our view, the language differences Hart and Risley reported are just that—*differences*. All children come to school with extraordinary linguistic, cultural, and intellectual resources, just not the *same* resources. It is the responsibility of teachers to draw on these resources in support of school learning, including teaching the language practices valued in school. If there are crucial language experiences needed for school success, then teachers must provide them. The remedy for disproportionate levels of failure among children living in poverty is a school curriculum that respects their background knowledge and experience and builds on students' linguistic, cultural and cognitive "funds of knowledge" (González, Moll, & Amanti, 2005) to teach them what they need to achieve success. As Gloria Ladson-Billings's (1994) research reminds us, respect is the key to successful teaching. Ultimately, this is about respect for students' knowledge, who they are, and where they come from.

NOTE

1. The *Social Science Citation Index* (SSCI) allows users to determine how often a particular publication has been cited in the 1700 social science journals included in the SSCI database. The number of times a work has been cited gives some indication of its influence. We found over 600 references to the Hart and Risley study, nearly half of these in the past five years.

REFERENCES

Baum, C. G., Forehand, R., & Zegiob, L. E. (1979). A review of observer reactivity in adult-child interactions. *Journal of Psychopathology and Behavioral Assessment*, 1, 167–178.

Blachowicz, C. L. Z., Fisher, P. J. L., Ogle, D., & Watts-Taffe, S. (2006). *Vocabulary: Questions from the classroom. Reading Research Quarterly*, 41, 524–539.

Blachowicz, C. L. Z., & Obrochta, C. (2005). Vocabulary visits: Virtual field trips for content vocabulary development. *The Reading Teacher*, 59, 262–268.

Bloome, D., Carter, S. P., Christian, B. M., Otto, S., & Shuart-Faris, N. (2005). *Discourse analysis and the study of classroom language and literacy events: A microethnographic perspective.* Mahwah, NJ: Erlbaum.

Books, S. (2004). Poverty and schooling in the U.S.: Contexts and consequences. Mahwah, NJ: Erlbaum.

Britto, P. R., Brooks-Gunn, J., & Griffin, T. (2006). Maternal reading and teaching patterns: Associations with school readiness in low-income, African-American families. *Reading Research Quarterly*, 41, 68–89.

Cooter, K. S. (2006). Issues in urban literacy when mama can't read: Counteracting intergenerational illiteracy. *The Reading Teacher*, 59, 698–702.

The critical need for evidence-based comprehensive and effective early childhood programs: Hearing before the Committee on Health, Education, Labor, and Pensions, U.S. Senate, 108th Cong., (2002). Available from http://olpa.od.nih.gov/hearings/108/session1/testimonies/headstart.asp.

Dennett, D. (1995). *Darwin's dangerous idea: Evolution and the meaning of life.* New York: Touchstone.

Dudley-Marling, C. (2007). Return of the deficit. *Journal of Educational Controversy*, 2(1). Retrieved January 29, 2009, from http://www.wce.wwu.edu/Resources/CEP/eJournal/v002n001/Index.shtml.

Dyson, A. (2003). Popular literacies and "all" children: Rethinking literacy for contemporary childhoods. *Language Arts,* 81, 100–109.

Dyson, A. H. (1993). *Social worlds of children learning to write in an urban primary school.* New York: Teachers College Press.

Dyson, M. E. (2006). Is Bill Cosby right?: Or has the Black middle class lost its mind? *Reading*, MA: Perseus.

Foley, D. E. (1997). Deficit thinking models based on culture: The anthropological protest. In R. R. Valencia (Ed.), *The evolution of deficit thinking* (pp. 113–131). London: Falmer.

Gebhard, M., Harman, R., & Seger, W. (2007). Reclaiming recess: Learning the language of persuasion. *Language Arts*, 84, 419–431.

Gee, J. (1999). Critical issues: Reading and the new literacy studies: Reframing the National Academy of Sciences Report on Reading. *Journal of Literacy Research*, 31, 355–374.

Gee, J. P. (1996). *Social linguistics and literacies: Ideology in discourses* (2nd ed.). Philadelphia, PA: Routledge/Falmer.

Gee, J. P. (2004). *Situated language and learning: A critique of traditional schooling.* New York: Routledge.

González, N. (2005). Beyond culture: The hybridity of funds of knowledge. In N. Gonzalez, L. C. Moll, & C. Amanti (Eds.), *Funds of knowledge: Theorizing practices in households and classrooms* (pp. 29–46). Mahwah, NJ: Erlbaum.

González, N., Moll, L. C., & Amanti, C. (2005). *Funds of knowledge: Theorizing practices in households and classrooms.* Mahwah, NJ: Erlbaum.

Gutiérrez, K., Baquedano-López, P., & Turner, M. G. (1997). Putting language back into language arts: When the radical middle meets the third space. *Language Arts*, 74, 368–378.

Hart, B., & Risley, T. R. (1995). *Meaningful differences in the everyday experiences of young American children.* Baltimore: Brookes.

Heath, S. B. (1983). *Ways with words: Language, life, and work in communities and classrooms.* Cambridge, UK: Cambridge University Press.

Jones, R., & Luo, Y. (1999). The culture of poverty and African American culture: An empirical assessment. *Sociological Perspectives*, 42, 439–458.

Kozol, J. (1992). *Savage inequalities: Children in America's schools.* New York: HarperCollins.

Kozol, J. (2005). *The shame of the nation: The restoration of apartheid schooling in America.* New York: Crown.

Kuhn, T. S. (1970). *The structure of scientific revolutions* (2nd. ed.). Chicago: Univ. of Chicago Press.

Labbo, L. D., Love, M. S., & Ryan, T. (2007). A vocabulary flood: Making words "sticky" with computer-response activities. *The Reading Teacher*, 60, 582–588.

Labov, W. (1970). *The study of nonstandard English*. Urbana, IL: National Council of Teachers of English.

Ladson-Billings, G. (1994). *The dreamkeepers: Successful teachers of African American children*. San Francisco, CA: Jossey-Bass.

Ladson-Billings, G. (1999). Preparing teachers for diverse student populations: A critical race theory perspective. In A. Iran-Nejad & P. D. Pearson (Eds.), *Review of research in education*: Vol. 24 (pp. 211–247). Washington, D.C.: American Educational Research Association.

Lakoff, G. (2004). *Don't think of an elephant! Know your values and frame the debate*. White River Junction, VT: Chelsea Green.

Le Compte, M. D., & Goetz, J. P. (1982). Problems of reliability and validity in ethnographic research. *Review of Educational Research*, 52, 31–60.

McCarthy, C., & Crichlow, W. (1993). Introduction: Theories of identity, theories of representation, theories of race. In C. McCarthy & W. Crichlow (Eds.), *Race, identity, and representation in education* (pp. xii–xxix). New York: Routledge.

Michaels, S. (1981). "Sharing time": Children's narrative styles and differential access to literacy. *Language in Society*, 10, 423–442.

Michaels, S. (2005). Can the intellectual affordances of working-class storytelling be leveraged in school? *Human Development*, 48, 136–145.

Miller, P., Cho, G. E., & Bracey, J. R. (2005a). Working-class children's experience through the prism of personal storytelling. *Human Development*, 48, 115–135.

Miller, P., Cho, G. E., & Bracey, J. R. (2005b). Expanding the angle of vision on working-class children's stories. *Human Development*, 48, 151–154.

Mills, C. W. (1959). *The sociological imagination*. Oxford: Oxford University Press.

Neuman, S. B., & Celano, D. (2001). Access to print in low-income and middle-income communities. *Reading Research Quarterly*, 36, 8–26.

New London Group. (1996). Pedagogy of multiliteracies: Designing social futures. *Harvard Educational Review*, 66, 60–92.

Noble, K. G., McCandliss, B. D., & Farah, M. J. (2007). Socioeconomic gradients predict individual differences in neuro-cognitive abilities. *Developmental Science*, 10, 464–480.

Nunberg, G. (2002). *A loss for words: "Fresh air" commentary*. Retrieved August 25, 2008, from http://people.ischool.berkeley.edu/~nunberg/vocabulary.html.

Oakes, J. (2006, March). Learning power: Urban education and racial justice. *Second Annual Carnegie Address*, Boston College, Chestnut Hill, MA.

Olson, L. (2006, July 6). As deadline looms, report says states showing little progress in addressing teacher quality. *Education Week (Online)*, 25. Retrieved January 29, 2009, from http://www.edweek.org/ew/articles/2006/07/06/42teacherquality_web.h25.html?print=1.

Payne, R. K. (2005). *A framework for understanding poverty* (4th ed.). Highlands, TX: Aha! Process.

Rabinow, P. (1977). *Reflections on fieldwork in Morocco*. Berkeley, CA: University of California Press.

Rolstad, K. (2004, May). Psychological misconstructions of language development. Paper presented at 12th Annual Conference on Reconceptualizing Early Childhood Education: Research, Theory, and Practice, Oslo, Norway. Retrieved January 29, 2009, from www.reconece.org/proceedings/Rolstad.pdf.

Rothstein, R. (2004). *Class and schools: Using social, economic, and educational reform to close the Black-White achievement gap.* Washington, D.C.: Economic Policy Institute.

Schleppegrell, M. J., & Go, A. L. (2007). Analyzing the writing of English learners: A functional approach. *Language Arts*, 84, 529–538.

Smagorinsky, P. (1995). The social construction of data: Methodological problems of investigating learning in the zone of proximal development. *Review of Educational Research*, 65, 191—212.

Swadener, B. B. (1995). Children and families "at promise": Deconstructing the discourse of risk. In B. B. Swadener & S. Lubeck (Eds.), *Children and families "at promise"* (pp. 18–49). Albany, NY: State University of New York Press.

Taylor, D. (1997). *Many families, many literacies: An international declaration of principles.* Portsmouth, NH: Heinemann.

U.S. Census Bureau. (2003). *Current population survey.* Washington, D.C.: Author. Accessed January 9, 2009, from www.census.gov/prod/2003pubs/p60-222.pdf.

Valencia, R. R. (1997). *The evolution of deficit thinking: Educational thought and practice.* New York: RoutledgeFalmer.

Walsh, K., Glaser, D., & Wilcox, D. D. (2006). *What education schools aren't teaching about reading and what elementary teachers aren't learning.* Washington, D.C.: National Council on Teacher Quality.

Zegiob, L. E., Arnold, S., & Forehand, R. (1975). An examination of observer effects in parent-child interactions. *Child Development*, 46, 509–512.

Curt Dudley-Marling is professor in the Lynch School of Education at Boston College. **Krista Lucas** is a doctoral candidate in Curriculum & Instruction in the Lynch School of Education at Boston College.

Research Reports

Standing Up for Diversity: Lesbian Mothers' Suggestions for Teachers

By Laura A. Bower

I ncreased diversity within student populations has led to a deluge of concerns for meeting the needs of all learners (e.g., Banks and McGee-Banks 2004; Darling-Hammond and Bransford 2005). Traditionally, education has defined diversity in terms of students' ethnicity, language, and academic abilities, thus ignoring several important forms of difference (Dilworth and Brown 2001). In today's environment, however, multicultural efforts fall short if they do not also include sexual orientation and family structure within notions of diversity (Kissen 2002; Ray 2005).

Given the limited focus on diverse sexualities and family structures within education, lesbian mothers are a particularly marginalized group in U.S. schools. I wanted to learn more about the nature of interactions between lesbian mothers and their children's schools and teachers. Because this population provides a snapshot of one group of diverse families among many, their experiences may prove instructive for teachers striving to understand how best to serve a variety of minority parents.

Laura A. Bower recently defended her dissertation, entitled "Finding the Other in Mother: Queering Social Scripts for Mothers and Teachers," at the University of Nevada, Las Vegas. Her other research interests include teacher identity and communities of practice.

BACKGROUND

Educators' focus on student diversity tends to eclipse awareness of differences among students' family structures and among parents, guardians, and caretakers and even to discount the impact families can have on student learning (Epstein et al. 2002). Teachers' inability or unwillingness to embrace diverse families, however, undermines students' learning, given that school-sponsored programs designed to help parents support learning at home lead to increased student test scores (Sheldon and Epstein 2005). High parental academic expectations and regular encouragement from parents are associated with high academic achievement among students, regardless of race, socioeconomic status, or parental level of education (Catsambis 2001).

Laura A. Bower, "Standing Up for Diversity: Lesbian Mothers' Suggestions for Teachers," *Kappa Delta Pi Record*, vol. 44, issue 4, pp. 181-183. Copyright © 2008 by Kappa Delta Pi. Reprinted with permission. Provided by ProQuest LLC. All rights reserved.

Despite the importance of involving families in a child's edu¬cation and the nearly 10 million U.S. school children with gay and lesbian parents (Pawelski et al. 2006), teachers receive little prepa¬ration to work with sexual minority parents (Kissen 2002). As a result, parents express feelings of isola-tion in their children's schools (Bos et al. 2004). They note a lack of inclusion of nontraditional families within the curriculum, and they report high levels of bullying of their children (Ray and Gregory 2001; Mercier and Harold 2003). Similarly, many teachers are dissatisfied with this reality and are willing to attend trainings related to improving school practices for gay and lesbian parents and their children (Bliss and Harris 1999).

THE STUDY

Merriam's (1998) framework for qualitative research guided this inquiry. Through social networking at gay and lesbian events, I recruited lesbian mothers of school-aged children to participate in my study. Participants consisted of 12 mothers whose children ranged in age from 10 months to 21 years. Five mothers had biological children; the others had adopted. Eleven participants had partners, and one was a single mother.

I conducted a focus group interview with eight mothers and completed follow-up interviews with seven of these eight. I interviewed four additional women individually. The focus group interview took place at a gay and lesbian center, and individual interviews occurred at each participant's location of choice.

Interviews centered on mothers' best and worst experiences with their children's schools. Participants also reflected on the type of teacher they would want for their children. I analyzed transcripts from each interview to generate lists of desired and detrimental qualities within teachers. I double-checked this analysis with respondents during follow-up interviews.

RESULTS

Participants' interactions with teachers varied from noticeably hostile to overwhelmingly accepting. Comments regarding these interactions ranged from "[the teachers] were not very fond of us" to "the thing I really enjoy about the teachers is that they're so accepting of what the parents' needs are." They identified desired and negative qualities within teachers and offered suggestions.

Desired Qualities within Teachers

Many of the mothers praised their children's teachers, describing them as "truly gifted," "just fantastic," "phenomenal educators," and "the best we could have hoped for." Respondents wanted their children to have teachers with distinct sets of beliefs, practices, and knowledge. The mothers had experienced many of these qualities; others shared a wish list.

Mothers preferred teachers who are open-minded, have progressive political beliefs, and accept diverse sexual orientations. They articulated the importance of teachers having deep knowledge of students and diversity. Further, they appreciated teachers who try new things, think "outside the box," and are energetic.

Respondents wanted teachers to maintain a habit of educating others about diversity, to include all types of diversity, to ask about students' families, to become involved with students' lives, and to provide face time and contact with parents. Par-ticipants emphasized the paramount need for teachers to prevent teasing and bullying.

Negative Qualities within Teachers

Many interviewed had experienced the qualities they desired in their children's teachers. Some, however, had suffered alongside their children through encounters with teachers whom the mothers described as "vicious and venomous" and "a nightmare." One mother related her conversation with a troubling teacher:

> As a parent, I had to go to the teacher and say, 'If I hear one more thing from our child about her being picked on because we're gay, you're not going to like it.' They have an anti-bully [policy]. But teachers mostly look the other way.

Participants objected to teachers who remain unaware of difference and what to do with it—specifically teachers who ignore family structures. They complained about teachers who categorize or label students without knowing them or who judge students according to parents, particularly those who erroneously assume the child is gay if the parents are gay. Mothers also objected to teachers who verbalize anti-gay sentiments and adhere to strict gender norms (for example, boys play sports and girls play house). Above all, lesbian mothers criticized teachers who allow bullying and teasing or fail to intervene when these incidents occur.

Suggestions for Teachers

Participants insisted that they did not expect any special treatment from teachers. One explained:

> *I am just looking for a teacher to be inclusive. I'm not looking for them to pick up the gay flag for me. I'm just looking for them to be inclusive in the curriculum and to be respectful of all families. Not just our family, but all families.*

The mothers offered suggestions for teachers who want to provide a physically and emotionally safe environment for children from diverse families. Participants recommended that teachers ask parents, guardians, and caregivers about students' family structures rather than assume that all students have one mother and one father. Mothers suggested sending home a flyer asking about students' home situations, including the questions "Who is in your family?" and "Who lives with your child?"

Respondents also requested that forms be changed to reflect the diverse nature of families, suggesting permission slips with several blank lines. When one mother in the focus group mentioned altering permission slips to read "Mother" and "Co-Mother," several voices echoed agreement.

Among other suggestions, participants advocated creating spaces for discussions of multiple family structures. Specific recommendations included asking students to create family mosaics to represent the important people in their lives and reading books containing nontraditional families.

In addition, mothers requested that teachers be sensitive in planning for holidays such as Mother's Day and Father's Day. They appreciated teachers who allowed children to complete two projects for these days or who encouraged making items for an important adult rather than specifying a mother or a father as the recipient. Mothers repeatedly asserted that sensitivity to diverse family structures impacts not only their children but also other children with nontraditional families.

DISCUSSION

With their primary focus on diversity, participants called for teachers who embrace difference rather than minimize it. They described these teachers as people who welcome diversity by talking about difference in a nonjudgmental way, who make knowledge of students and their families a priority in their classrooms, and who strive to learn about diversity from multiple sources, including students and their families.

Embracing diversity necessitates strong anti-bullying and teasing policies. This commitment requires classroom practices that create spaces to talk about difference. By welcoming children from all backgrounds, teachers also send parents and guardians a message of safety and acceptance.

CLOSING THOUGHTS

Though preparing teachers to welcome students from diverse families is important, I sampled only one minority family group within this study. Future research must investigate the perspectives of additional minority family structures, including, but not limited to, gay fathers, single parents, and grandparents. Furthermore, I have included only one side of the story in this article: the mothers'. Future research also must consider teachers' reaction to these suggestions and their willingness and ability to respond.

REFERENCES

Banks, J. A., and C. A. McGee-Banks, eds. 2004. *Handbook of research on multicultural education*, 2nd ed. San Francisco: Jossey-Bass.

Bliss, C. K., and M. B. Harris. 1999. Teachers' views of students with gay or lesbian parents. *International journal of Sexuality and Gender Studies* 4(2): 149–71.

Bos, H. M. W., F. van Balen, D. C. van den Boom, and T. C. M. Sandfort. 2004. Minority stress, experience of parenthood and child adjustment in lesbian families, *Journal of Reproductive and Infant Psychology* 22(4): 291–304.

Catsambis, S. 2001. Expanding knowledge of parental involvement in children's secondary education: Connections with high school seniors' academic success. *Social Psychology of Education* 5(2): 149–77.

Darling-Hammond, L., and J. Bransford, eds. 2005. *Preparing teachers for a changing world: What teachers should learn and be able to do.* San Francisco: Jossey-Bass.

Dilworth, M. E., and C. E. Brown. 2001. *Consider the difference: Teaching and learning in culturally rich schools. Handbook of research on teaching,* 4th ed., ed. V. Richardson, 643–67. Washington, D.C.: American Educational Research Association.

Epstein, J. L., M. C. Sanders, B. S. Simon, K. C. Salinas, N. R. Jansorn, and F. L. Van Voorhis. 2002. *School, family, and community partnerships: Your handbook for action,* 2nd ed. Thousand Oaks, CA: Corwin.

Kissen, R. M., ed. 2002. *Getting ready for Benjamin: Preparing teachers for sexual diversity in the classroom.* Lanham, MD: Rowman and Littlefield.

Mercier, L. R., and R. D. Harold. 2003. At the interface: Lesbian-parent families and their children's schools. *Children and Schools* 25(1): 35–47.

Merriam, S. B. 1998. *Qualitative research and case study applications in education,* 2nd ed. San Francisco: Jossey-Bass.

Pawelski, J. G., E. C. Perrin, J. M. Foy, C. E. Allen, J. E. Crawford, M. Del Monte, M. Kaufman, J. D. Klein, K. Smith, S. Springer, J. L. Tanner, and D. L. Vickers. 2006. The effects of marriage, civil union, and domestic partnership laws on the health and well-being of children. *Pediatrics* 118(1): 349–64.

Ray, J. A. 2005. Family-friendly teachers: Tips for working with diverse families. *Kappa Delta Pi Record* 41(2): 72–76.

Ray, V., and Gregory, R. 2001. School experiences of the children of lesbian and gay parents. *Family Matters* (Australian Institute of Family Studies) 59(winter): 28–34.

Sheldon, S. B., and J. L. Epstein. 2005. Involvement counts: Family and community partnerships and mathematics achievement, *Journal of Educational Research* 98(4): 196–206.

Reducing Harassment of Lesbian, Gay, Bisexual, Transgender, and Questioning Youth in Schools

By Mary Henning-Stout, Steve James, and Samantha Macintosh

ABSTRACT: School-based harassment and violence toward students perceived to be lesbian, gay, bisexual or transgender has been successfully confronted in educational systems across the U.S.A sampling of these programs and linked supportive organizations is presented. Three harassment-reduction programs are described in detail. Program-development and evaluation considerations derived from this review are summarized. While some institutional obstacles to such programming remain in these school settings, their models for protecting sexual minority students are supported by ethical, legal, and financial realities.

The incidence of harassment of young women and men who do not fit into pervasive norms for gendered appearance and behavior is both well-documented and disturbing (Kruks, 1991; Merina, 1995; Pilkington & D'Augelli, 1995; Rosario, Rotheram-Borus, & Reid, 1996; Rothblum, 1994; Zera, 1992). Stories of physical and psychological harassment unfold daily in the lives of children at all levels of education. A school psychologist with whom one of the authors has consulted reported one such incident.[1]

A kindergarten teacher sought consultation on how to work with her students and their parents to address an issue of harassment. Two girls had been in the "house and home" center, pulling clothes out of the dress-up box, arranging pretend food on the table. They draped scarves and lace over their heads and around their shoulders. One said to the other, "I know. Let's get married. We'll be lesbians." The two girls stood together with their arms linked as if they were walking down an aisle. Another girl who had been playing nearby jumped up, yanked a scarf from one of the bride's heads and screamed, "You are in trouble—you're

Mary Henning-Stout, Steve James, & Samantha Macintosh, "Reducing Harassment of Lesbian, Gay, Bisexual, Transgender, and Questioning Youth in Schools," *School Psychology Review*, vol. 29, no. 2, pp. 180-191. Copyright © 2000 by the National Association of School Psychologists. Reprinted with permission.

going to burn up or get really sick because people like you are bad, so stop it!" By this time, a few other children had joined in saying things like, "Yeah, that's nasty," or "I'm gonna tell!" One boy ran into the fray to punctuate what had been words up to that time. In a flurry of movement he kicked one of the dressed up girls and slugged the other. All of this occurred in the few moments it took the teacher to disentangle from the yarn and other art materials she was using with a group across the room. She had heard the interaction and called out several times to stop it. She reached the scene in time to prevent the boy's next blow and began the process of de-escalating the conflict and comforting the two girls. The little girl who had first opposed the imaginary marriage stood back from the scene and said to the teacher, "My mama won't let me come here anymore. I'll tell her, too. People who do like them are the baddest. They make other people sick and they kill other people. My daddy said we have to kill them first."

This teacher was faced immediately with the challenge of relating these events to the parents of the girls who were pretending, to the parents of the boy who faced consequences for his physical aggression, and to the parents of the girl who spoke her fear and hostility with such emotion and conviction. The teacher turned for support to the school psychologist who had limited resources upon which to draw to assist this teacher. She had never had a class that addressed or prepared her for the content defining this event. Neither her supervisor nor the counselor in her building had encountered or anticipated this kind of problem. These situations, they had all believed, only happened in the secondary schools.

But, such is not the case. As this school psychologist's story illustrates, issues of homophobia and related expressions of aggression are present throughout schools, throughout communities. Children learn from what their parents and other close adults in their lives teach them—either directly or indirectly. What can easily be seen through a developmental lens as age-appropriate imaginary play can invoke projections of anger and fear.

The seeds of harassment are planted early. The cost is high as is evident in the other articles in this series. School psychologists are in unique positions to influence the cultures of schools through provision of information, support of respect and tolerance, active programming to address the concerns and attitudes of students and teachers, and engagement in both the articulation of policy and its translation into practice.

This article is intended to serve as a resource for such action. It is our judgment that model programs for addressing and reducing harassment serve as the best guides for the creative development of similar initiatives. In the next pages, we will place the harassment of lesbian, gay, bisexual, transgender, and questioning youth in the context of relevant psychological literature, key public events, and recent case law. We will then describe three school-based programs that have been developed to reduce harassment. Finally, we will offer a list of program development suggestions derived from our review of these three programs and the additional programs briefly summarized in tabular form. These program summaries represent the data of this report; they are the evidence of what is occurring in the field. These data provide illustrations of the next steps in practice and research for school psychologists.

HARASSMENT IN CONTEXT

The research literature on lesbian and gay adults indicates that "coming out," the process of disclosing one's sexual orientation to others, is related to developing positive self identity as a sexual minority individual (Miranda & Storms, 1989). However, for adolescents, it carries significant risks of harassment and physical violence in the schools (Hunter, 1990; Telljohann & Price, 1993) and abuse, isolation, or exclusion from the home (Kruks, 1991). Consequently, sexual minority youth are at risk for low self-esteem (Dempsey, 1994; Savin-Williams, 1989), for engaging in self-injurious behaviors (e.g., substance abuse, teen pregnancy, Cabaj, 1996; Rosario, Hunter, & Gwadz, 1997; Rosario, Meyer-Bahlburg, Hunter, & Exner, 1996), for running away and homelessness (Savin-Williams, 1994, Savin-Williams & Cohen, 1996), for HIV infection (American Medical Association Council on Scientific Affairs, 1996), and for suicide (Ramafedi, 1994).

Harassment is defined in *Webster's New World Dictionary of American English* (Neufeldt & Guralnik, 1996) as persistent efforts to tire, worry, or annoy with repeated attacks. It also is defined as laying to waste. For sexual minority youth, these tiring and destructive attacks occur on multiple levels and, as evident in the literature, take a significant social and psychological toll. For the purposes of this discussion, we propose three levels of harassment.

Popular and professional literatures tend to focus most frequently upon what we are calling *interpersonal harassment* (Savin-Williams, 1994) and *group harassment* (Washington Education Association, 1997). Interpersonal harassment involves one or two perpetrators who have some level of familiarity with their victims; that is, some personal, though perhaps casual, familiarity. Such harassment can occur among schoolmates, in neighborhoods, or in families (Savin-Williams, 1995). In some settings, such as large high schools, interpersonal harassment may include a level of anonymity: a perpetrator who verbally, emotionally, or physically harasses a person she or he does not know personally but assumes some familiarity because of shared affiliation (i.e., students in the same school).

Group harassment occurs when more than two people form a perpetrating group. This level of harassment may involve people familiar or anonymous to one another. In cases of anonymity, the perpetrating group functions on assumptions that the persons they are attacking are homosexual. In any situation involving groups, the social-psychological effects of mob mentality, polarization of beliefs, and escalation of aggression are likely to increase the intensity of the harassment (Zahn-Waxier, Cummings, & Iannotti, 1986).

An extreme, illustration of group harassment is seen in the recent murder of Matthew Shepherd (Layco, 1998). Matt's body was found tied to a fence. He had been tortured and left to die in the manner of ranchers who tie coyotes to posts to deter others of their kind (Layco, 1998). Building on this violence a fraternity at Colorado State University created a parade float depicting Shepard, bloodied and tied to a fencepost, as if to mimic the warning (Layco, 1998). Anonymity and extreme behaviors based upon polarized attitudes can carry weight of authority for those most likely to commit violence. In schools and communities, the balance of information and tolerance is vital to stem the growing tide of such destruction.

To take Matt's story as unique or unlikely because it is set in a college or in a rural area would be to miss an urgent warning. As illustrated in the opening vignette, hostilities toward lesbian, gay, bisexual, transgender and questioning youth are possible from the beginning of children's experiences in school. It also would be a mistake to consider Matt's suffering and death as relevant and disturbing only to sexual minority students and their families. Incidents of violent harassment such as that one have an impact on all students who perceive themselves to be vulnerable to harassment. In the context of the actual incidence of harassment among youth in schools, active work to diminish the likelihood of such harm is critical.

More subtle variables maintain the individual and collective thinking that allows discrimination and harassment to continue. These variables define the third level of harassment as sociocultural harassment. *Sociocultural harassment* occurs in the continuous overt and covert messages lesbian, gay, bisexual, transgender, and questioning youth encounter. These messages convey negative and harmful stereotypes about homosexual people. Most obvious are graffiti, vitriolic talk show hosts, and ballot measures restricting civil rights. Less commonly recognized is the invisibility of homosexual people in public positions as leaders or in the media. This invisibility can translate all too easily to schools in which the curriculum ignores the historic and contemporary roles filled by homosexual people (Norris, 1992), and the subject of sexual orientation and youth is taboo (Stover, 1992). The incessant derision or active ignoring of lesbian, gay, bisexual, and transgender people is tiring, worrisome, and annoying for sexual minority youth. The statistics on suicide and stories like that of Matthew Shepard's murder reveals these sociocultural trends have the potential of laying these youth to waste.

The action by the Salt Lake City School Board on February 20, 1996, to ban all non-curricular clubs from district schools is an example of sociocultural harassment. The goal of the school board's decision was to block the formation of a club that would explicitly include gay and lesbian students (Orchard, 1996). A girl with the support of another 20 students had initiated the formation of a Gay/Straight Alliance group in their high school (Sahagun, 1996). The girl began this initiative after she was assaulted for the second time due to her sexual orientation. The result of the school board's response to this initiative was the closure of young men's and women's associations; ethnic clubs; volunteer councils; Kiwanis clubs; human rights groups; and hiking, skiing, rugby, soccer, chess, and environmental clubs. The message to sexual minority youth in that city's schools was clear. They were not welcomed as themselves.

Legal and Professional Guidance

There are ample professional guidelines (American Psychological Association, 1992; National Association of School Psychologists, 1992) to support psychologists' efforts to improve the climate of acceptance and safety for lesbian, gay, bisexual, transgender, and questioning students. In a joint resolution passed in 1993, the National Association of School Psychologists (NASP) and the American Psychological Association (APA) gave decisive support and guidance to the appropriate treatment of sexual minority youth in schools by resolving that these organizations take leadership roles in promoting societal and familial attitudes and behaviors that affirm the dignity and rights, within educational environments, of all lesbian, gay, and bisexual youths, including those with physical or mental disabilities and from all ethnic/racial backgrounds and classes, [and that these organizations] support providing a safe and secure educational atmosphere in which all youths, including lesbian, gay, and bisexual youths, may obtain an education free from discrimination, harassment, violence, and abuse, and which promotes an understanding and acceptance of self. (p. 1)

This resolution was based in the firm ground of the ethical codes of both organizations (APA, 1992; NASP, 1992)—codes that explicitly call for fair, responsive, and respectful service delivery to all people.

With the guidelines of the profession, there also are legal reasons for reducing and eliminating the harassment of sexual minority youth in schools. In 1996, in the only trial to produce case law linked directly with the concerns of sexual minority youth, the U.S. Seventh Circuit Court of Appeals ruled in favor of Jamie Nabozny's claim that his guarantee of equal protection had been violated (*Nabozny v. Podlesny*, 1995/1996). In this case, high school officials did not protect Nabozny, a high school student, from anti-gay harassment and violence, even after repeated complaints to them by Nabozny and his parents. This was particularly problematic in comparison with the protection they provided other students faced with other forms of harassment or abuse (*Nabozny v. Podlesny*, 1995/1996). The defendants (the district, the district administrator, two principals, and an assistant principal) settled with Nabozny for medical expenses and damages, totaling nearly one million dollars (Logue, 1997), a sum that cannot go unnoticed by school personnel, districts, and their insurers.

One of the most important issues for the court seemed to be that the school provided protection for other students but repeatedly ignored or explained away the abuse Nabozny experienced and reported (*Nabozny v. Podlesny*, 1995/1996). In practical terms, this question arises from this case: In responding to abuse and the potential for abuse of lesbian, gay, bisexual, and transgender students, how do schools create a climate of safety (appropriate responses and prevention efforts) equal to those created for female students, students of ethnic and religious minorities, and students of differing physical abilities? The Nabozny case has given clear illustration of the ethical and legal importance of careful attention to this question.

A more recent suit, *Iversen v. Kent School*, which was settled out of court (Safe Schools Coalition of Washington, 1999) involved issues similar to those in the Nabozny case. Iversen's suit alleged that during the course of his years in middle and high school, the district failed to respond to his complaints of being verbally and physically harassed as a result of being perceived to be gay. The court refused to dismiss the case, but the plaintiff settled out of court. Nonetheless, the case can be taken as additional evidence that districts must go beyond the articulation of anti-harassment policies to implementation and enforcement so that healthy and safe learning environments may be provided for all students.

MODEL SCHOOL-BASED PROGRAMS

In the wake of the Nabozny case, school officials have been called to action. Schools and school person-nel are constitutionally required to stop the harassment of gay students. It is important to consider the implications of this case within the context of the daily operations of schools.

The Nabozny case offers an invitation to work within school systems to "minimize district liability" while at the same time "maximizing all students' safety." This situation represents an opportunity for school officials to learn from gay rights activists as they identify positive ways to ensure a safe learning environment for all learners. Activists who may in the past have been perceived as interested in entering schools solely for what critics have termed *recruiting*, may now be seen more accurately as citizens concerned with the well-being of lesbian, gay, bisexual, transgender, and questioning learners.

In the spirit of learning from existing programs, we initiated a search of electronic and print media to identify programs for sexual minority youth. We looked for programs housed in or connected with schools and selected those with demonstrated stability (in existence two years or more) and evidence of positive support (demonstrated involvement of youth, educators, and community members). For this article, we chose to describe three programs in more detail. Each of these three programs has been in place for a minimum of five years and has served a large catchment area. Based upon our review of these programs and those listed in Table 1, we extracted the common elements of successful school-based programs described in a latter section.

The three initiatives of focus—located in California, Massachusetts, and Washington—have broken important ground in addressing harassment of lesbian, gay, bisexual, transgender, and questioning youth in schools. In each of these states notable programs have been established to document and reduce harassment and to respond to the interests and concerns of sexual minority youth (Governor's Commission on Gay and Lesbian Youth, 1993; Safe Schools Coalition of Washington, 1997; Uribe, 1994).

Project 10

In 1984, Dr. Virginia Uribe began Project 10, a program for sexual minority students at Fairfax High School in the Los Angeles Unified School District (Friends of Project 10, 1989). Uribe planned and implemented this initiative in response to the growing frequency of suicide, alcohol/substance abuse, and risk of AIDS among gay and lesbian teenagers. Project 10 is primarily a dropout prevention program that recognizes sexual minority youth at an increased risk for dropout for various reasons that relate to their sexual orientations. Educational workshops, sensitivity counseling, and accurate non-judgmental information are provided for students and staff alike.

Support groups are at the heart of Project 10. The goals of these groups are to improve self-esteem and provide affirmation for students struggling with the effects of stigmatization based upon their sexual orientation. The counselors for these groups address directly issues such as staying off drugs and alcohol, avoiding high-risk sexual behaviors, getting jobs, staying in school, and going to college. Referrals to outside agencies also are given when necessary.

Testimonials from students have indicated that the groups are valuable to them (Uribe, 1994). Success also has been measured by improved attendance and academic performance, by improved relationships with primary family members, and by the number of males who agree to attend AIDS education programs sponsored by local human service organizations.

Project 10 was the first program of its kind and can be used as a model for other schools and districts. Uribe (1994) indicated that the model can be changed to fit a school or district's unique needs, but ideally consists of the following components: (a) a central location in the district for resources on gay, lesbian, bisexual, and transgender issues; (b) a paid program coordinator; (c) ongoing workshops to train counselors, teachers, and other staff members on issues of institutional homophobia and the special needs of sexual minority youth; (d) training and maintenance of on-site teams to whom students may contact for information and support; (e) assistance to librarians in building collections of fiction and nonfiction on gay/lesbian subjects; (f) development and enforcement of nondiscrimination clauses, anti-slur resolutions, or codes of behavior with regard to name calling; (g) advocacy for lesbian, gay, bisexual, and transgender student rights through commissions, task forces, PTAs and community outreach programs; and (h) networking with community agencies, parents, educational organizations, and teachers' unions.

Following the initiation of Project 10 in 1992, the Los Angeles Board of Education approved the establishment of the Gay and Lesbian Education Commission (GLEC) to advise the board regarding the special needs of gay and lesbian students and personnel in the district. The GLEC is the umbrella under which Project 10 now operates. It is concerned with the following: (a) recommending to the board of education ways to monitor and curtail harassment of gay and lesbian students on school campuses; (b) participating in the review of educational materials used in the school district; (c) recommending expansion of supportive services for gay and lesbian youth, parents of gay and lesbian children, and for gay and lesbian parents; (d) recommending ways of addressing staff education on issues of sexual orientation; (e) planning, implementing, and attending parent/community outreach and other special meetings; (f) acting in a consulting capacity as needed; (g) recommending projects and activities designed to improve educational programs as they relate to gay and lesbian issues; (h) assisting in the strengthening communications between the school district and the community as it pertains to gay and lesbian issues; (i) advising the school board of new and proposed legislation affecting gay and lesbian issues; (j) reviewing the accessibility and usability of district facilities as they relate to gay and lesbian students; and (k) networking with other commissions to establish and maintain dialogues on individual and mutual issues.

The GLEC also sponsors an annual youth conference on the campus of Occidental College at Eagle Rock, CA. The conference, entitled *Models of Pride*, provides a setting in which students can learn from and support one another. The board of education in Los Angeles, in conjunction with the GLEC, has instituted policies, offices, and procedures to help to protect gay, lesbian, bisexual, transgender, and questioning students: (a) a *No Name Calling and No Discrimination Policy* that includes sexual orientation, (b) district offices for handling reports of discrimination and harassment, and for providing information and support to students,

Table 1. Model Programs and Other Resources for the Prevention of Harassment to Lesbian, Gay, Bisexual, Transgender, and Questioning Youth in Schools

Program	Focus	Contact Information
Black Gay Lesbian Leadership Forum	Issues facing African Americans who are lesbian, gay, bisexual, transgender or questioning	http://qrd.tcp.com/qrd/www/ orgs/nbgllf/
Children of Lesbians and Gays Everywhere	Advocacy and education by children of lesbian, gay, bisexual, and transgender parents	COLAGE 2300 Market St., #165 San Francisco, CA 94114 colage@colage.org
Gay, Lesbian, Straight Teachers Network	Coalition of teachers locally and nationally addressing issues of heterosexism in schools	GLSTN 121 West 27th St., Suite 804 New York, NY 10001 glstn@glstn.org
Massachusetts Governor's Commission on Gay and Lesbian Youth	Making schools safe for sexual minority and lesbian youth	Governor's Commission State House, Room 111 Boston, MA 02133 617-727-3600, ext. 312
National Advocacy Coalition on Youth and Sexual Orientation	Advocacy and education for sexual minority youth	NACYSN 1711 Connecticut Ave. NW, Suite 206 Washington, D.C. 20009 202-319-75961
National Gay Youth Network	Research, education, and publication on issues facing sexual minority youth	NGYN P.O. Box 846 San Francisco, CA 94101
National Latino/a Lesbian and Gay Organization	Issues facing Latino/as who are lesbian, gay, bisexual, transgender, or questioning	LLEGO 703 G Street SE Washington, D.C. 20003 NatLLEGO@aol.com
National Resource Agency for Transgender Issues	Clearinghouse for resources on transgender issues	AEGIS P.O. Box 33724 Decatur, GA 30033 770-939-2128
Out Proud!	A national coalition for gay, lesbian, and bisexual youth	Out Proud! P.O. Box 24589 San Jose, CA 95154-4589 408-269-6125

Table 1. Model Programs and Other Resources for the Prevention of Harassment to Lesbian, Gay, Bisexual, Transgender, and Questioning Youth in Schools (continued)

Program	Focus	Contact Information
Parents and Friends of Lesbians and Gays	Advocacy, education and peer support, extensive resource network	PFLAG 1101 14th St. NW, Suite 1030 Washington, D.C. 20005 http://www.pflag.org
P.E.R.S.O.N. Project	Public Education Regarding Sexual Orientation Nationally, K-12 directory for educational equity, other resources	The PERSON Project P.O. Box 5313 Berkeley, CA 94705-0313 http://www.youth.org/loco/ PERSONProject/
Project 10	Support to students, training to school staff, active harassment prevention program	Project 10
The International Foundation for Gender Education	Support for transgender people —an advocacy and educational organization	P.O. Box 367 Wayland, MA 01778 IFGE@world.std.com
Safe Schools Coalition of Washington	Documentation of harassment, publication of resource lists and curricular suggestions for use in schools	Safe Schools Coalition c/o AFSC 814 NE 40th St Seattle, WA 98105 800-5B-PROUD

(c)   a district-wide procedure for processing complaints of harassment and discrimination including those of gay and lesbian students, and

(d)   a reporting process that tracks bias-motivated incidents and hate crimes. A protocol has been instituted to respond to incidents in a standardized manner. Staff training has been made mandatory in the Los Angeles Unified School District to increase staff awareness of the protocol for response to incidents, for disciplinary action, and for reporting incidents of harassment. A curriculum also has been instituted that includes family diversity, heroes, and role models (of various backgrounds and orientations), elimination of name calling, and prevention of hate crimes as themes.

Massachusetts Governor's Commission on Gay and Lesbian Youth

On February 10, 1992, the Governor of Massachusetts, William F. Weld, signed an executive order that created the nation's first Governor's Commission on Gay and Lesbian Youth. This creation of this commission was a response to the epidemic rates of suicide by young gay men and lesbians as revealed by Gibson (1989) in the *Federal Report on Youth Suicide*. Abolishing prejudice and discrimination against gay and lesbian youth was a stated goal of the Commission, which operated and continues to operate at the state level. The Commission was empowered to make recommendations to the Governor, state agencies, and private agencies about the creation of programs and policies that would help gay and lesbian youth in Massachusetts.

After its inception in February of 1992, the Commission released its first report in February of 1993, *Making Schools Safe for Gay and Lesbian Youth*. The report addressed the problems faced by gay and lesbian adolescents in the schools after holding five public hearing across the state of Massachusetts. The problems outlined included harassment of gay and lesbian students in school, isolation and suicide, dropout and poor school performance, gay and lesbian youth and their need for adult role models, and families of gay and lesbian youth.

In December of 1993, the Gay and Lesbian Student Rights Bill was passed in Massachusetts. At the same time, the state amended its law pertaining to educational rights for public school students to include consideration for sexual orientation. Massachusetts also has been a leader in helping schools in other states develop safe and productive environments for their lesbian and gay students and staff. Five priorities have been outlined in this process: policies, training, services, curriculum, and community outreach. Specifically, the *Sexual Harassment Policy Implementation Guidelines and Complaint Form* developed by Framingham (Massachusetts) Middle School (1994) has been used as a model for other states.

Washington's Safe Schools Project

The Washington Education Association (WEA) supported the Safe Schools Anti-Violence Documentation Project (a five-year study) in 1994 to examine and understand the phenomenon of anti-gay sexual harassment and violence in the schools (K-12). The WEA, according to staff attorney Jerry Painter (personal communication, February, 1998), does not purport to be an advocate of gay and lesbian youth. According to Painter, the documentation of anti-gay harassment was the project's original focus and represented the sole WEA initiative linked with gay students. In the meantime, however, the project has expanded in scope.

For example, the Safe Schools Anti-Violence Documentation Project's second annual report (Safe Schools Coalition of Washington, 1995) catalogued specific cases of anti-gay harassment and violence with recommendations of auricular resources and issues to discuss in the classroom. The Safe Schools Project also has adopted the Framingham Middle School's *Sexual Harassment Policy Implementation Guidelines and Complaint Form* (1994).

In the project's third annual report (Safe Schools Coalition of Washington, 1996), harassment data were supplemented with the following: (a) harassment incidence data specific to lesbian, gay, bisexual, transgender, and questioning students; (b) strategies for preventing harassment and fostering climates of respect; (c) a harassment-prevention curriculum; and (d) strategies for responding to anti-gay harassment and for ensuring the safety and well-being of sexual minority students. The project's fourth annual report (Safe Schools Coalition of Washington, 1997) included two volumes, one containing a report of harassment data, the second outlining auricular and other classroom strategies with an appended resource guide.

Although the statistics presented in these reports were not summarized to detect trends, careful review of the data suggests there may be a reduction in incidents of harassment as this project continues. In the initial year of the project (1993/94) there were 22 incidents reported to the project office. In the subsequent three years reports totaled (respectively), 27, 28, and 14. The focus of the reported data has been on the nature of the incidents that totaled 91 during the four years (gang rape, 8; physical assault, 19; physical harassment and/or sexual assault short of rape, 14; ongoing verbal and other harassment, 34; one-time, climate-setting incidents, 16; Safe Schools Coalition of Washington, 1997). Also highlighted in these reports has been the evidence that incidents of harassment involve an average of three perpetrators to one victim (Safe Schools Coalition of Washington, 1997).

The data presented in the publications of the Safe Schools Coalition of Washington with the auricular and other classroom strategies provide important resources for school personnel interested in addressing harassment of sexual minority students. The evolution of the Safe Schools Coalition project activities as evident in the reports across its first four years also stands as an important model for ways in which state initiatives for documentation may be expanded into generating materials to address harassment directly, even as its incidence is being monitored.

During the past 10 years, there have been steady increases in the numbers of schools and community organizations addressing the issues facing sexual minority youth (see Table 1). As these efforts have developed to address the safety and well-being of lesbian, gay, bisexual, transgender, and questioning students, similarities across programs have become evident that may serve to guide schools wishing to make learning in safe and congenial environments available to all students and their families.

COMMON ELEMENTS OF SUCCESSFUL SCHOOL PROGRAMS

The individual stories behind the incidence data determine the nature of programs that emerge in schools, districts, and states. It makes sense that programs—certainly the successful ones—will vary greatly across schools. Thus, any identification of elements common to successful programs must necessarily allow room for the broad range of circumstances, understanding, readiness, and culture in any school or community. Successful programs must be grounded in close and ongoing attention to the particular needs and interests of the persons they will serve (cf. Guba & Lincoln, 1989). At the same time, several guiding ideas, specific goals, functional objectives, and specific processes were distilled from our review of school- and community-based programs that address the harassment of sexual minority youth.

Guiding Ideas

First, successful programs respond directly to a school's concern with harassment issues and consider the community's level of awareness, its ways of seeing and knowing (Schmuck, 1997). One program might involve the inclusion of lesbian, gay, and bisexual concerns in the diversity policies or diversity curriculum of a school. Another might provide specific programming for gay youth that could include support groups, activity groups, political action groups—any one of these or some combination. A program might be focused upon training service providers in schools or communities to be responsive to the interests and concerns of lesbian, gay, bisexual, transgender, and questioning youth. A program might center on moving from idea to action—identifying and enforcing basic rules of social respect; for example, authoring the rules as a school, posting those rules, encouraging the modeling (by the adults) of consistent adherence to the rules, articulating consequences for compromising the rules, and establishing clear and functional procedures for registering and resolving grievance situations.

A second idea guiding successful programs is that they are preventive in their approach (Caplan, 1964; McWhirter, McWhirter, McWhirter, & McWhirter, 1998). When an incidence of violence, including harassment or suicide, has occurred, both first and later responses would be tertiary in nature; that is, focused upon preventing future violence. Programs designed specifically to address the interests and concerns of sexual minority youth, youth who are questioning their sexual orientation, or children of lesbian, gay, bisexual, or transgender parents would stand as secondary prevention efforts developed to support youth who are placed at risk by the presence of bias and harassment in contemporary social structures. Finally, programs that address general populations of children, educators, or social service providers would be programs of primary prevention. These programs influence the movement of social structures toward more inclusive, respectful, supportive functioning. Gordon (1992) has described processes for inviting all students in a school to develop empathy by bringing to collective awareness the oppression they experience as children and youth. Primary prevention can be both elegant and profound when links are made between one person's experienced pain and the general experiences and sequelae of oppression.

Goals and Functional Objectives

The two immediate goals of any successful program for reducing harassment of sexual minority youth are to increase safety for all children and youth, and to counter the heterosexism too often seen in school and community cultures. Movement toward these goals is most likely when grounded in the following commitments: (a) to listen to the people involved—those who are targets, those who are perpetrators, and those who move through the environment in which harassment occurs; (b) to identify the people in each group who have referent and legitimate power, who are likely to be trusted and followed, and to engage them in program development, implementation, and maintenance processes; (c) to support the people who hold stakes in the program as they identify what they need; (d) to model and support ongoing dialogue on issues of difference of opinion, belief, understanding—on addressing conflict, fear, hostility in public and private settings; (e) to teach conflict resolution and mediation and maintain ongoing programs to both support these skills and provide space and social structure in which the skills may be practiced; (f) to listen and respond keeping the two primary goals in view, recognizing there are many paths to any solution; and (g) to take systematic note of the impact adherence to these commitments has on the program's ability to achieve the two primary goals of increasing safety and countering bias.

Specific Processes

Five somewhat distinct processes appear to characterize successful programs of harassment reduction in schools. These processes seem to parallel those evident in community-based programs (James, 1998).

Emergence of local issues. Prior to the development of a program, local issues come to the awareness of individuals or groups who then move toward taking action in response. This awareness may follow a single event such as a suicide, murder, assault, or public revelation of the sexual orientation of one or more students or adults. Issues may become apparent more gradually as one or more members of the school community encounters the needs of sexual minority students. Students themselves may articulate issues through existing school groups or by establishing new ones.

Formation of coalitions. Once issues are identified, individuals in the school community who are motivated to take action seek allies. Some form of strategy building occurs and may include sessions focused upon increasing participation and building group cohesion. These sessions also offer opportunities for developing realistic and measurable goals. Emerging coalitions appear to build strength by engaging supportive authorities and/or representatives of other powerful organizations or groups.

Information gathering. As a group moves toward development and implementation of programs, there seems consistently to be an effort at gathering information regarding the history, nature, and incidence of harassment in the school and community. Groups assess the political climates of the community and school and the power and authority structures within the school, district, and community. They review relevant laws and applicable regulations and file copies for reference. Forming groups also identify and review applicable scientific and popular information. Considerations of safety and support also seem to fit in this category. Groups interested in developing school-based programs for reducing harassment of sexual minority students identify and gather potential allies, often engaging them in information sharing and brainstorming to generate action ideas. They also consider the potential for backlash on both group and individual bases. This process includes careful consideration of the vulnerability of each group member and all potential program participants.

Action planning. Successful programs are built upon clearly identified actions that have been considered for their potential consequences. These programs organize their information, evidence, and allied support so they are prepared to present their information or service with confidence.

Implementation. Actions may include presentation of proposals, policy changes, nondiscrimination clauses, curricular supplements, support groups, staff development programs, or community education plans. Many groups contact supportive national organizations to inform them of their actions. Successful groups draw upon their earlier work to meet any opposition with accurate information and retain an emphasis on finding common ground. Finally, although not typical of the programs reviewed here, successful programs are most sustainable with thoughtful and inclusive plans for evaluating and reporting their progress to the school and community (Guba & Lincoln, 1989).

SUMMARY

In the process of reviewing existing school-based or school-linked programs aimed at reducing the harassment of sexual minority youth, we were repeatedly aware of the relative lack of outcome data to indicate the impact of the programs on the lives of learners in schools. The incidental data of program longevity, level of youth participation, school and community support are compelling, but these programs could be strengthened with consultation in support of program evaluation and development. One clear role for school psychologists is the provision of such service to existing programs. A second and related role for school psychologists is direct research into the nature, incidence, and preventive variables linked with school-based harassment. A third and, perhaps, more fundamental role for school psychologists is consistent attention to and interruption of incidents of harassment toward lesbian, gay, bisexual, transgender, and questioning youth in the schools. This active response to harassment in conjunction with advocacy for programs to address these issues are vital for positive change to occur.

Throughout the literature of school psychology there is repeated emphasis on making learning available to all children and youth in schools. Harassment of any kind toward any individual or group in a school interferes with learning. Not only does harassment stand as an obstacle for the immediate victims, the presence of harassment in schools or their larger communities compromises the safety of learning environments for all children and youth.

The programs reviewed in this article represent thoughtful and effective responses to the problem of harassment of lesbian, gay, bisexual, transgender, and questioning youth in schools. While some institutional obstacles to such programming remain in these school systems, these models for protecting sexual minority students are supported by ethical and legal realities. Ethically, school psychologists serve all learners (APA, 1992; NASP, 1992). Legally, refusal of service to any individual or group based upon their suspected or acknowledged sexual minority status bears heavy consequences (*Nabozny v. Podlesny*, 1995/1996). Given there is no excuse for allowing harassment of sexual minority youth in schools, school psychologists have the responsibility to act as leaders in the establishment and support of programs to reduce and to eliminate this form of aggression.

REFERENCES

American Medical Association Council on Scientific Affairs. (1996). Health care needs of gay men and lesbians in the United States. *Journal of the American Medical Association*, 275, 1354–1359.

American Psychological Association. (1992). Ethical principles of psychologists and code of conduct. *American Psychologist*, 47, 1597–1611.

Cabaj, R. P. (1996). Substance abuse in gay men, lesbians, and bisexuals. In R. P. Cabaj & T. S. Stein (Eds.), *Textbook of homosexuality and mental health* (pp. 783–799). Washington, D.C.: American Psychiatric Press.

Caplan, G. (1964). Principles of preventive psychiatry. New York: Basic Books.

Dempsey, C. L. (1994). Health and social issues of gay, lesbian, and bisexual adolescents. *Families in Society*, 75, 160–167.

Friends of Project 10. (1989). *Project 10 Handbook: Addressing lesbian and gay issues in our schools: A resource directory for teachers, guidance counselors, parents and school-based adolescent care providers.* Los Angeles: Author.

Gibson, P. (1989). Gay male and lesbian youth suicide. In M. Feinleib (Ed.), *Report of the Secretary's Task Force on Youth Suicide* (pp. 110–142). Washington, D.C.: U.S. Department of Health and Human Services.

Gordon, L. (1992, May/June). What do we say when we hear "faggot?" *Rethinking Schools*, 6,4.

Governor's Commission on Gay and Lesbian Youth. (1993). *Making schools safe for gay and lesbian youth: Breaking silence in schools and in families.* Boston, MA: Author.

Guba, E. G., & Lincoln, Y. S. (1989). *Fourth generation evaluation.* Newbury Park, CA: Sage.

Hunter, J. (1990). Violence against lesbian and gay male youths. *Journal of Interpersonal Violence*, 5, 295–300.

James, S. (1998). Fulfilling the promise: Community responses to the needs of sexual minority youth and families. *American Journal of Orthopsychiatry*, 68, 447–454.

Kruks, G. (1991). Gay and lesbian homeless/street youth: Special issues and concerns. *Journal of Adolescent Health*, 12, 515-518.

Layco, R. (1998, October 26). The new gay struggle. *Time, 152*(17), 32–36.

Logue, P. M. (1997). Near $1 million settlement raises standard for protection of gay youth. [Online]. Available: http://www.lambdalegal.org/cgi-bin/pages/documents.

McWhirter, J. J., McWhirter, B. T., McWhirter, A. M., & McWhirter, E. H. (1998). *At-risk youth: A comprehensive response.* New York: Brooks/Cole.

Merina, A. (1995, May). A case study in gay bashing. *The NEA Today*, 73(9), 6.

Miranda, J., & Storms, M. (1989). Psychological adjustment of lesbians and gay men. *Journal of Counseling and Development*, 68, 41–45.

Nabozny v. Podlesny. (W. D. Wisconsin, 1995). (7th CirM 1996). [Online]. Available: http://www.kentlaw.edu/7circuit/1996/jul/95-3634.html.

National Association of School Psychologists. (1992). *Principles for professional ethics.* Bethesda, MD: Author.

Neufeldt, V., & Guralnik, D. B. (Eds.). (1996). *Webster's New World Dictionary of American English.* New York: Simon and Schuster.

Norris, W. (1992). Liberal attitudes and homophobic acts: The paradoxes of homosexual experience in a liberal institution. In K. M. Harbeck (Ed.), *Coming out of the classroom closet: Gay and lesbian students, teachers, and curricula* (pp. 81–20). Binghamton, NY: Harrington Park Press.

Orchard, C. (1996). *Salt Lake City school board bans clubs*. Salt Lake City: Utah Human Rights Coalition.

Pilkington, N. W., & D'Augelli, A. R. (1995). Victimization of lesbian, gay, and bisexual youth in community setting. *Journal of Community Psychology*, 23, 34–42.

Ramafedi, G. (Ed.). (1994). *Death by denial: Studies of gay and lesbian youth suicide*. Boston: Alyson.

Rosario, M., Hunter, J., & Gwadz, M. (1997). Exploration of substance use among lesbian, gay, and bisexual youth: Prevalence and correlates. *Journal of Adolescent Research*, 12, 454–476.

Rosario, M., Meyer-Bahlbuig, H. F. L., Hunter, J., & Exner, T. M. (1996). The psychosexual development of urban lesbian, gay, and bisexual youths. *Journal of Sex Research*, 33, 113–126.

Rosario, M., Rotheram-Borus, M. J., & Reid, H. (1996). Gay-related stress and its correlates among gay and bisexual male adolescents of predominantly Black and Hispanic background. *Journal of Community Psychology*, 24, 136–143.

Rothblum, E. D. (1994). "I only read about myself on bathroom walls": The need for research on the mental health of lesbians and gay men. *Journal of Consulting and Clinical Psychology*, 62, 213—220.

Safe Schools Coalition of Washington. (1995). *Safe schools anti-violence documentation project* (Second annual report). Seattle, WA: Author.

Safe Schools Coalition of Washington. (1996). *Safe schools anti-violence documentation project* (Third annual report). Seattle, WA: Author.

Safe Schools Coalition of Washington. (1997). *The fourth annual safe schools report of the violence documentation project*. Seattle, WA: Author.

Safe Schools Coalition of Washington. (1998). *Iversen v. Kent School*. [On-line]. Available: http:// www.safeschools-wa.org/iversen.html.

Sahagun, L. (1996, February 22). Salt Lake City schools forbid all social clubs: Action targets gay and lesbian group. *The Houston Chronicle*, sec. A, p. 9.

Savin-Williams, R. C. (1989). Parental influences on the self-esteem of gay and lesbian youths: A reflected appraisals model. *Journal of Homosexuality*, 17, 93–109.

Savin-Williams, R. C. (1994). Verbal and physical abuse as stressors in the lives of lesbian, gay male, and bisexual youths: Association with school problems, running away, substance abuse, prostitution, and suicide. *Journal of Consulting and Clinical Psychology*, 62, 261–269.

Savin-Williams, R. C. (1995). Lesbian, gay male, and bisexual adolescents. In A. R. D'Augelli & C. J. Patterson (Eds.), Lesbian, gay, and bisexual identities over the lifespan: *Psychological perspectives* (pp. 165–189). New York: Oxford University Press.

Savin-Williams, R. C., & Cohen, K. M. (1996). Psychosocial outcomes of verbal and physical abuse among lesbian, gay, and bisexual youths. In R. C. Savin-Williams & K. M. Cohen (Eds.), *The lives of lesbians, gays, and bisexuals: Children to adults* (pp. 181–200). Fort Worth, TX: Harcourt Brace.

Schmuck, R. A. (1997). *Practical action research for change*. Arlington Heights, IL: Skylight Press.

Stover, D. (1992). The at-risk kids schools ignore: When homosexuality remains a taboo topic, gay students' needs go unmet. *The Executive Educator*, 3, 28–31.

Telljohann, S., & Price, J. (1993). A qualitative examination of adolescent homosexuals' life experiences: Ramifications for secondary school personnel. *Journal of Homosexuality*, 26, 41–56.

Uribe, V. (1994). Project 10: A school-based outreach to gay and lesbian youth, *The High School Journal*, 77, 108–112.

Zahn-Waxler, C., Cummings, E. M., & Iannotti, R. (1986). *Altruism and aggression: Biological and social origins.* New York: Cambridge University Press. Zera, D. (1992). Coming of age in a heterosexist world: The development of gay and lesbian adolescents. Adolescence, 27, 849–854.

Footnote

1. In response to an earlier draft of this article, one reviewer queried the likelihood that two kindergarten girls would say, "We'll be lesbians." This event actually occurred. It occurred in a city in which public discussions of the human rights of lesbian, gay, bisexual, and transgender people have been at the forefront for nearly a decade. These girls could know lesbians, could be related to or be children of lesbians. For them, "lesbian" is not a sexual term but instead a name for women who are in adult pairings with women.

Section IV

Teaching and Learning—a Multicultural and Global Approach

Multicultural Teacher Introspection

By Nitza M. Hidalgo

In our study of culture, we are not simply analyzers of cultures external to us. While teachers must certainly be versed In the culture of the school and of the communities in which the students live, teachers need to have a complex understanding of their own cultural perspectives, hidalgo, a professor at Westfield State College, provides a way for future educators (or anyone!) to begin to analyze their cultural orientations—an activity that is central to the content and work of this course.

Main educators around the country are interested in developing a multicultural approach to their teaching. They find themselves in classrooms with 25 children of varying racial and cultural backgrounds and are looking for ways to connect what they do in the classroom to the cultures represented by their students. Before we can begin to understand others, however, we need to understand ourselves and what we bring to our interactions with others. For this reason, it is important for teachers interested in learning more about other cultural groups to first look inward.

The initial step in the process involves introspection. Teachers need to ask themselves some fundamental questions: What framework do we bring into the classroom? How does our cultural perspective color our view of the world? Posing these questions helps teachers analyze the deep-rooted cultural features of their backgrounds. Teachers may this begin the process of understanding how our beliefs and behaviors are culturally based and how our system of beliefs is similar to or different from our students' beliefs.

Many teachers may not be accustomed to thinking of ourselves as cultural or ethnic. This experience is likely rooted in our training and socialization, both direct and indirect, which have been monocultural in nature. The mainstream perspective presented through schooling is really an Anglo-European perspective. Thus, becoming an educated "American" implicitly means becoming Anglicized.[1]

Until recently, schooling in general did not include much information about the experiences of racial and ethnic groups in the United States. Different perspectives were marginalized, often presented as attachments to the main orientation, especially in the area of curriculum. Most practicing teachers have not been exposed to a multicultural knowledge base.[2] When teachers were presented information about racial or ethnic groups, the mainstream perspective was typically used to evaluate the information. It was the filter through which information about diverse populations was interpreted.

Not only has the framework for interpretation of knowledge been monocultural—that is, Anglo-European—but variations have been judged to be less valuable. When African Americans, Latinos, Native Americans, and Asian Americans were mentioned, the deficit model came into play. That model viewed racial and ethnic differences as deficient, or lacking. Children of color were implicitly judged deficient because they did not bring to school the same majority culture represented in the school and classrooms. Without realizing it, teachers learned mainstream or "whiteness" to be the norm by which all knowledge about others was measured within schooling.

Adoption of this mainstream perspective reinforces a lack of ethnic consciousness among a good many classroom teachers. Thus, schooling does not require us to think of ourselves as ethnic and may, in fact, minimize ethnic awareness in favor of Americanization.

The irony is that each of us has been socialized in some culture, and often more than one culture. Our culture provides a lens through which we view the world and interpret our everyday experiences.[3] Culture informs what we see and understand, as well as what we omit and misconstrue. Many components make up our view of the world: our ethnic and racial identification, the region of the country we come from, the type of neighborhood we live in, our socioeconomic background, our gender, the language(s) we speak, our disabilities, our past experiences, and our life-style. We need to think about the ways in which these parts of us define our perspectives.

We may think about culture as existing on at least three levels: the symbolic, the behavioral, and the concrete.[4] Our values and beliefs lie on the symbolic level. How we ascribe meaning to our experiences depends on the values we hold and the beliefs that we may have. This level is the most abstract and difficult to articulate, yet it is essential to our interpretation of the world.

This level of culture is implicit and shared by others within our reference group. Our values and beliefs help us to interpret our experiences and shape socially appropriate behavior. For example, the definition of family may vary from one cultural group to another, depending on the importance the group places on family cohesiveness. The Puerto Rican concept of family may go beyond the extended family to kinlike relations with friends (compadres/comadres), while the U.S. American definition of family may include only the nuclear family living at home.[5]

The behavioral level refers to how we define our social roles, the language(s) we speak, the rituals we practice, and the form taken by our nonverbal communication. Our behavior reflects our values. The roles we ascribe to women and men within U.S. culture are different from the gender roles of other cultures. Even within our culture, for instance, the role of women has undergone subtle modifications because of the women's movement. These role ascriptions are based on our beliefs, as a society, about the importance of women's work and their contribution to the household. In response, men have also had to redefine their roles within various situations as evidenced by the development of parenting, rather than solely maternity, leave policies. Thus, it is evident that culture is a dynamic, not static, process.

Also on the behavioral level, language mirrors thought; our language reflects our beliefs and values. Think about the associations we make with simple words like black and white. Is it sheer coincidence that we can generate many negative connotations for the word black and many positive connotations for the word white? Regarding language, the feminist movement has worked to eliminate commonplace correlations such as men and girls (versus men and women) because of the inequality inherent in this type of comparison. These are subtle distinctions that have profound effects on our thinking.

Educators often begin to think about multiculturalism at the concrete level, yet movement to a more abstract understanding is needed. The concrete culture is the most visible and tangible level. The products of culture, such as our cultural artifacts, exist at this level. Technology, music, foods, and artistic works and materials are the concrete, visible elements of culture. This is what is most often interpreted as "the culture" of ethnic groups. School festivals highlighting ethnic foods, flag displays from different countries, performance of ethnic music, and playing international games tend to result in a superficial and exotic impression of multiculturalism. This would be comparable to French students expecting to learn about U.S. culture by studying our ritual practices on the Fourth of July. Knowing about barbecues and fireworks displays tells French students little about the meaning Independence Day has in our nation. Foods, holidays, games, and artifacts reveal little about how ethnic groups experience and make meaning of the world.

Given this definition of culture, we can begin to explore how our own cultural perspectives shape our thinking and actions. In order to answer eventually the broad question of how our cultural perspective influences our work in the classroom, we begin with specific introspective information gathering. A preliminary exercise in staff development work with teacher groups requires that we locate ourselves by region, ethnicity, and family system. The exercise requires teachers to respond to the following questions.[6] Where were you born? What language(s) or dialect(s) were spoken in your home? Where did you grow up? Describe your neighborhood. What is your ethnic or racial heritage? Was religion important during your upbringing? If yes, how? Who makes up your family? What traditions does your family follow? What values does your family hold dear? How do the members of your family relate to each other? How is love expressed? How is your culture expressed in your family? These preliminary questions can help teachers begin their introspection by locating themselves in a framework familiar to them—their family background.

The processing of answers derived from this exercise allows us to become located in our personal social constructions. Teachers can thereby reflect on our conceptualization of family and the definition of social roles and behavior within different families. Becoming aware of our definitions may help with the understanding of alternative definitions of family. Meaningful insight comes from having to think about our backgrounds and then sharing this information with others. From sharing, we gain an awareness of the similarities and differences between the various definitions. Derman Sparks[7] recommends that teachers form a support group of colleagues to facilitate the introspection process. In most instances, we learn that despite diversity of meaning, family and community provide us with social safety nets that we can return to when needed for security and connection to others. This kind of exercise, which explores differences and similarities between ethnic and racial groups presents insightful alternative ethnic and cultural interpretations for teachers. We begin to understand our similarities within our diversity.

Once we have thought about the preliminary questions, a deeper level of introspection can occur. After locating ourselves within a particular family and neighborhood, questions related to the individual should be considered. The questions to think about may include: What is our cultural heritage? How does our cultural background influence how we perceive and understand others? What are our values and beliefs? How do our values influence our behavior toward children? How does our socioeconomic class frame our view about children in poverty? What is our definition of normal? How do we think about differences in children, and do we implicitly relate difference to deficiency? Do we believe there are gender differences in certain types of cognitive or physical abilities? Do we think all children can learn?

These questions do not have simple answers. They touch upon main issues that we may not even be able to talk about, specifically, our values. The aforementioned questions are not related to value clarification, but will reveal our implicit cultural and social constructions. Because some aspects of culture are so ingrained, introspection is required to discover how our attitudes, behavior, and interactions are affected.

For example, through introspection, a teacher may discover she believes, like many U.S.-born Americans, that individuals are the basic building blocks of society. As a society, U.S. families rear children to be independent individuals. We hold individualism in high esteem. In contrast, many Puerto Rican patents believe that the family's welfare comes before that of any individual member; the Puerto Rican definition of individualism takes a different form. Puerto Rican children are reared to value interdependency and to hold family obligation in high esteem. These conflicting beliefs may surface in a classroom when a student (especially a female) is absent from school for an extended period to care for younger siblings. Uninformed about the cultural value of interdependency, the teacher may think the child's parents do not value education. In fact, Puerto Rican parents highly value education and encourage their children to succeed academically.[8] The teacher's reaction to this situation may be based on how the ingrained nature of our cultural beliefs interrelate with our learned societal conceptions.

A number of outcomes may result from the introspection process: teachers may sense a lack of true cultural understanding, or they may feel disadvantaged. When asked define themselves ethnically and culturally, some educators have a very difficult time. Many lack an ethnic consciousness. The difficulty often stems from previous schooling and socialization since the Anglo-European perspective in schools defines the average "American" as one White. Although ethnicity and race are distinct social constructions and ethnicity is an essential part of culture, being ethnic in the United States is implicitly defined by some educators today as being non-White. This belies the experiences of many U.S. citizens, such as those of Italian and White ethnics.

Being "American" seems to be cast as a denial of ethnicity; ethnicity is generalized as an exotic, cultural trait. It often seems that to be "American" is to be nonethnic, when in fact it is closer to being a-ethnic, a consciousness related to the melting-pot myth that requires a loss of ethnicity in return for membership in mainstream U.S. Society.

A melting-pot formulation leading to Americanization can be seen as the result of combined ethnicities cancelling each other over the generations into "Americans." The melting-pot theory is not equally accepting of all ethnic and racial groups. While the contributions of ethnic groups are supposed to compose the common core, when one examines the "common culture," the core is primarily Anglo-European values, beliefs, and achievements. For example, as Americans we commemorate holidays such as Thanksgiving, a celebration of ancestral survival (and its underlying values of determination and hard work), but the reduction of Native Americans to second-class status which facilitated ancestral survival is not acknowledged. The subtle message is to become "American" is to be nonethnic.

On occasion, introspective teachers communicate a sense of disadvantage from our own schooling. We sense that past knowledge presented to us has offered only a partial picture of our multicultural heritage. We have received only a partial education because our schooling was monocultural in nature. We feel the loss of a significant part of our history, a loss which denies us a fuller sense of humanity and citizenship because it has distorted the importance of Anglo-European traditions by omitting diverse contributions to our society. We realize that exposure to alternative interpretations of reality may dispel the sense of superiority implicitly taught to mainstream citizenry and may better promote egalitarian social relations between people from different backgrounds. Some teachers decide this blockage to our true humanity is something we, as adults wishing to gain a multicultural awareness, have to break down.

Introspection also creates cognitive dissonance for teachers when we must reconcile differing versions of reality. This experience can be so powerful because teachers realize that the information we trusted and believed in may be only partially true and that varying cultural interpretations demand we accustom ourselves to more ambiguity. The dissonance can cause us to adjust our existing framework of knowledge and certainty. We can no longer be satisfied with easy answers because through introspection and sharing come deeper insights into the complexities of a multicultural society.

Understanding and facing the complexity of a multicultural society, where there is no one way to do things, promotes critical thinking capacity. We begin to think critically about ourselves, our beliefs, and our histories, and, consequently, about how our beliefs are framed by societal constructions. We begin to recognize the implicit power attributions unequally assigned to cultural groups in the United States. We have to move beyond ourselves as individuals because we have been socialized within a particular society that shares a common history. The process of examining our assumptions and beliefs results in a critical awareness of past and present U.S. contexts.

Asking introspective questions can lead to an intellectual awareness of the functions of culture. Teachers need to go beyond a cognitive awareness of the influence of culture to an affective understanding. Knowing something in the abstract is insufficient to the awareness we seek; we have to be able to empathize with the experiences of others. Knowing about inequality in the abstract, believing in the principle of equality, is only a first step toward the multicultural awareness needed in classrooms. We need, for example, to put ourselves "in the shoes" of new immigrants facing institutionalized prejudices to feel their reality. The goal is to complement our intellectual introspections with affective understanding. We need to transcend thinking about differences to achieve an emotional connection. Although we can never know another's cultural experiences in the same way as the person who undergoes those experiences, we can achieve an emotional empathy along with an intellectual awareness.

The understanding we seek goes far beyond learning about traditional holidays and ethnic foods, which are the more concrete levels of culture. Once we understand how culture shapes our perspective, our inquiry shifts to the classroom to examine how our beliefs influence our behavior. The questions to pose can be general, or directed toward a particular topic which arises in classrooms daily, such as discipline or teacher/student interactions.

A general question would be: How are our values expressed in classroom dynamics with children? More specific questions related to the areas of authority and discipline are: How do we perceive authority? Does authority come with an ascribed role? For example, does the role of teacher automatically give teachers respect, as in the U.S. American culture, or must respect be earned through the behavior of the person fulfilling that role? What do we consider appropriate behavior for children when interacting with adults? For example, when being reprimanded, do we expect children to look an adult in the eyes or to look down to show respect, as in many Latino cultures? These classroom dynamics inherently shape teachers' expectations of children, but are rarely examined from a cultural perspective. Having clear definitions of appropriate behavior facilitates problem-solving when differing behavior is encountered because we have information on our cultural interpretations to compare and contrast to other interpretations. A critical awareness of how culture functions in the classroom demands, as a first step, teachers' insight into our own culture.

Teachers' sustained interactions with children affect how children feel about school. To understand how cultural background designates particular forms of verbal and nonverbal interaction teachers may ask: What kinds of verbal and nonverbal interactions would we consider appropriate between children and the teacher? Specifically, how do we use touching behavior in the classroom? For Puerto Ricans, touching behavior exists within most interpersonal communications.[9] Puerto Rican children expect a lot of touching and hugging behavior from adults they trust; touching behavior is interpreted as an expression of liking for children. Each of these questions invites a comparison to the cultural perspective the teacher brings to the classroom. If we begin with our own perspectives and what shapes them, we then have a basis for comparing differences and similarities between our perspectives and those of our students.

The teacher introspective process occurs in different phases; completing each phase moves teachers closer to the next phase. The first phase examines cultural and social values, both on an individual and societal basis. The second phase situates awareness on an affective level. The third phase transposes teachers' values and behavior into the classroom context. Each phase is interactive with the preceding and following phase. At each phase, teachers should work not in isolation, as we do in so many other professional processes, but in support groups or teams. Within the safely of a supportive environment, teachers can more productively examine our cultural values, beliefs and assumptions. We can share our findings with each other and gain wisdom about the power of cultural diversity.

Efforts to infuse multicultural awareness into a professional development program for teachers have expanded in recent years, largely due to the increase of immigrant children and children of color in public schools and to a growing awareness of the significance of multicultural education reform. School should create the environment which fosters teacher development for teachers to be able to replicate multicultural awareness with their students.[10]

Teachers need to become introspective ethnographers in our own classrooms to decipher the cultural meanings that we and our students bring to the group. Once teachers understand our assumptions and beliefs and can appreciate and accept the unique cultural contributions of our students, we can use this knowledge to mediate effectively between the children's culture and the other cultures represented in the school.

ACKNOWLEDGMENT

The author wishes to thank the National Coalition of Advocates for Students, Boston, for their support of the initial version of this paper.

NOTES

1. J. Banks and C. McGee Banks, *Multicultural Education Issues and Perspectives* (Boston, MA: Allyn and 1989). See also J. Banks, Teaching Strakyin of Studies 5th ed. (Boston, MA: Allyn and Bacon. I'M)-
2. C. Grant, "Urban Teachers: Their New Colleagues and Curriculum," Phi Delta Kappan (June, 1989): 764–770.
3. J. Spradley, *The Ethnographic Interview* (New York, NY: Holt, Rinehart & Winston, 1979).
4. M. McGoldrick, J. Pearce, and J. Giodano, eds., *Ethnicity and Family Therapy* (New York, NY: The Guilford Press, 1982).
5. R. Salgado, "The Puerto Rican Family," in *Puerto Ricans in the Mid '80s: An American Challenge* (Alexandria, VA: National Puerto Rican Coalition, Inc, 1985).
6. H. Sheldon and D. Burden-Patmon, *Odyssey Exercise* (Boston, MA: Community Change, Inc., n.d.).
7. L. Derman-Sparks and the A.B.C. Task Force, *Anti-Bias Curriculum* (Washington, D.C.: National Association for the Education of Young Children, 1990).
8. N. Hidalgo, *"i saw puerto rico once:" A Review of the Literature on Puerto Rican Families and School Achievement in the United States,* technical report (Boston, MA: Center on Families, Communities, Schools & Children's Learning, 1992.)
9. J. Nine-Curt, *Puerto Rican Non-Verbal Communication* (Cambridge, MA: National Assessment and Dissemination Center for Bilingual Education, 1978).
10. S. Sarason, *The Predictable Failure of Educational Reform* (San Francisco, CA: Jossey Bass Publishers, 1990).

But That's Just Good Teaching! The Case for Culturally Relevant Pedagogy

By Gloria Ladson-Billings

For the past 6 years I have been engaged in research with excellent teachers of African American students (see, for example, Ladson-Billings, 1990, 1992b, 1992c, 1994). Given the dismal academic performance of many African American students (The College Board, 1985), I am not surprised that various administrators, teachers, and teacher educators have asked me to share and discuss my findings so that they might incorporate them in their work. One usual response to what I share is the comment around which I have based this article, "But, that's just good teaching!" Instead of some "magic bullet" or intricate formula and steps for instruction, some members of my audience are shocked to hear what seems to them like some rather routine teaching strategies that are a part of good teaching. My response is to affirm that, indeed, I am describing good teaching, and to question why so little of it seems to be occurring in the classrooms populated by African American students.

The pedagogical excellence I have studied is good teaching, but it is much more than that. This article is an attempt to describe a pedagogy I have come to identify as "culturally relevant" (Ladson-Billings, 1992a) and to argue for its centrality in the academic success of African American and other children who have not been well served by our nation's public schools. First, I provide some background information about other attempts to look at linkages between school and culture. Next, I discuss the theoretical grounding of culturally relevant teaching in the context of a 3-year study of successful teachers of African American students. I conclude this discussion with further examples of this pedagogy in action.

LINKING SCHOOLING AND CULTURE

Native American educator Cornel Pewewardy (1993) asserts that one of the reasons Indian children experience difficulty in schools is that educators traditionally have attempted to insert culture into the education, instead of inserting education into the culture. This notion is, in all probability, true for many students who are not a part of the White, middle-class mainstream. For almost 15 years, anthropologists have looked at ways to develop a closer fit between students' home culture and the school. This work has had a variety of labels including "culturally appropriate" (Au & Jordan, 1981), "culturally congruent" (Mohatt & Erickson, 1981), "culturally responsive" (Cazden & Leggett, 1981; Erickson & Mohatt, 1982), and "culturally compatible" (Jordan, 1985; Vogt, Jordan, & Tharp, 1987). It has attempted to locate the problem of discontinuity between what students experience at home and what they experience at school in the speech and language interactions of teachers and students. These sociolinguists have suggested that if students' home language is incorporated into the classroom, students are more likely to experience academic success.

Villegas (1988), however, has argued that these micro-ethnographic studies fail to deal adequately with the macro social context in which student failure takes place. A concern I have voiced about studies situated in speech and language interactions is that, in general, few have considered the needs of African American students.[1]

Irvine (1990) dealt with the lack of what she termed "cultural synchronization" between teachers and African American students. Her analysis included the micro-level classroom interactions, the "mid-level" institutional context (i.e., school practices and policies such as tracking and disciplinary practices), and the macro-level societal context. More recently Perry's (1993) analysis has included the historical context of the African American's educational struggle. All of this work—micro through macro level—has contributed to my conception of culturally relevant pedagogy.

WHAT IS CULTURALLY RELEVANT PEDAGOGY

In the current attempts to improve pedagogy, several scholars have advanced well-conceived conceptions of pedagogy. Notable among these scholars are Shulman (1987), whose work conceptualizes pedagogy as consisting of subject matter knowledge, pedagogical knowledge, and pedagogical content knowledge, and Berliner (1988), who doubts the ability of expert pedagogues to relate their expertise to novice practitioners. More recently, Bartolome (1994) has decried the search for the "right" teaching strategies and argued for a "humanizing pedagogy that respects and uses the reality, history, and perspectives of students as an integral part of educational practice" (p. 173).

I have defined culturally relevant teaching as a pedagogy of opposition (1992c) not unlike critical pedagogy but specifically committed to collective, not merely individual, empowerment. Culturally relevant pedagogy rests on three criteria or propositions: (a) Students must experience academic success; (b) students must develop and/or maintain cultural competence; and (c) students must develop a critical consciousness through which they challenge the status quo of the current social order.

Academic Success

Despite the current social inequities and hostile classroom environments, students must develop their academic skills. The way those skills are developed may vary, but all students need literacy, numeracy, technological, social, and political skills in order to be active participants in a democracy. During the 1960s when African Americans were fighting for civil rights, one of the primary battlefronts was the classroom (Morris, 1984). Despite the federal government's failed attempts at adult literacy in the South, civil rights workers such as Septima Clark and Esau Jenkins (Brown, 1990) were able to teach successfully those same adults by ensuring that the students learned that which was most meaningful to them. This approach is similar to that advocated by noted critical pedagogue Paulo Freire (1970).

While much has been written about the need to improve the self-esteem of African American students (see for example, Banks & Grambs, 1972; Branch & Newcombe, 1986; Crooks, 1970), at base students must demonstrate academic competence. This was a clear message given by the eight teachers who participated in my study.[2] All of the teachers demanded, reinforced, and produced academic excellence in their students. Thus, culturally relevant teaching requires that teachers attend to students' academic needs, not merely make them "feel good." The trick of culturally relevant teaching is to get students to "choose" academic excellence.

In one of the classrooms I studied, the teacher, Ann Lewis,[3] focused a great deal of positive attention on the African American boys (who were the numerical majority in her class). Lewis, a White woman, recognized that the African American boys possessed social power. Rather than allow that power to influence their peers in negative ways, Lewis challenged the boys to demonstrate academic power by drawing on issues and ideas they found meaningful. As the boys began to take on academic leadership, other students saw this as a positive trait and developed similar behaviors. Instead of entering into an antagonistic relationship with the boys, Lewis found ways to value their skills and abilities and channel them in academically important ways.

Cultural Competence

Culturally relevant teaching requires that students maintain some cultural integrity as well as academic excellence. In their widely cited article, Fordham and Ogbu (1986) point to a phenomenon called "acting White," where African American students fear being ostracized by their peers for demonstrating interest in and succeeding in academic and other school related tasks. Other scholars (Hollins, 1994; King, 1994) have provided alternate explanations of this behavior.[4] They suggest that for too many African American students, the school remains an alien and hostile place. This hostility is manifest in the "styling" and "posturing" (Majors & Billson, 1992) that the school rejects. Thus, the African American student wearing a hat in class or baggy pants may be sanctioned for clothing choices rather than specific behaviors. School is perceived as a place where African American students cannot "be themselves."

Culturally relevant teachers utilize students' culture as a vehicle for learning. Patricia Hilliard's love of poetry was shared with her students through their own love of rap music. Hilliard is an African American woman who had taught in a variety of schools, both public and private for about 12 years. She came into teaching after having stayed at home for many years to care for her family. The mother of a teenaged son, Hilliard was familiar with the music that permeates African American youth culture. Instead of railing against the supposed evils of rap music, Hilliard allowed her second grade students to bring in samples of lyrics from what both she and the students determined to be non-offensive rap songs.[5] Students were encouraged to perform the songs and the teacher reproduced them on an overhead so that they could discuss literal and figurative meanings as well as technical aspects of poetry such as rhyme scheme, alliteration, and onomatopoeia.

Thus, while the students were comfortable using their music, the teacher used it as a bridge to school learning. Their understanding of poetry far exceeded what either the state department of education or the local school district required. Hilliard's work is an example of how academic achievement and cultural competence can be merged.

Another way teachers can support cultural competence was demonstrated by Gertrude Winston, a White woman who has taught school for 40 years.[6] Winston worked hard to involve parents in her classroom. She created an "artist or craftsperson-in-residence" program so that the students could both learn from each other's parents and affirm cultural knowledge. Winston developed a rapport with parents and invited them to come into the classroom for 1 or 2 hours at a time for a period of 2–4 days. The parents, in consultation with Winston, demonstrated skills upon which Winston later built.

For example, a parent who was known in the community for her delicious sweet potato pies did a 2-day residency in Winston's fifth grade classroom. On the first day, she taught a group of students[7] how to make the pie crust. Winston provided supplies for the pie baking and the students tried their hands at making the crusts. They placed them in the refrigerator overnight and made the filling the following day. The finished pies were served to the entire class.

The students who participated in the "seminar" were required to conduct additional research on various aspects of what they learned. Students from the pie baking seminar did reports on George Washington Carver and his sweet potato research, conducted taste tests, devised a marketing plan for selling pies, and researched the culinary arts to find out what kind of preparation they needed to become cooks and chefs. Everyone in Winston's class was required to write a detailed thank you note to the artist/craftsperson.

Other residencies were done by a carpenter, a former professional basketball player, a licensed practical nurse, and a church musician. All of Winston's guests were parents or relatives of her students. She did not "import" role models with whom the students did not have firsthand experience. She was deliberate in reinforcing that the parents were a knowledgeable and capable resource. Her students came to understand the constructed nature of things such as "art," "excellence," and "knowledge." They also learned that what they had and where they came from was of value.

A third example of maintaining cultural competence was demonstrated by Ann Lewis, a White woman whom I have described as "culturally Black" (Ladson-Billings, 1992b; 1992c). In her sixth grade classroom, Lewis encouraged the students to use their home language while they acquired the secondary discourse (Gee, 1989) of "standard" English. Thus, her students were permitted to express themselves in language (in speaking and writing) with which they were knowledgeable and comfortable. They were then required to "translate" to the standard form. By the end of the year, the students were not only facile at this "code-switching" (Smitherman, 1981) but could better use both languages.

Critical Consciousness

Culturally relevant teaching does not imply that it is enough for students to choose academic excellence and remain culturally grounded if those skills and abilities represent only an individual achievement. Beyond those individual characteristics of academic achievement and cultural competence, students must develop a broader sociopolitical consciousness that allows them to critique the cultural norms, values, mores, and institutions that produce and maintain social inequities. If school is about preparing students for active citizenship, what better citizenship tool than the ability to critically analyze the society?

Freire brought forth the notion of "conscientization," which is "a process that invites learners to engage the world and others critically" (McLaren, 1989, p. 195). However, Freire's work in Brazil was not radically different from work that was being done in the southern United States (Chilcoat & Ligon, 1994) to educate and empower African Americans who were disenfranchised.

In the classrooms of culturally relevant teachers, students are expected to "engage the world and others critically." Rather than merely bemoan the fact that their textbooks were out of date, several of the teachers in the study, in conjunction with their students, critiqued the knowledge represented in the textbooks, and the system of inequitable funding that allowed middle-class students to have newer texts. They wrote letters to the editor of the local newspaper to inform the community of the situation. The teachers also brought in articles and papers that represented counter knowledge to help the students develop multiple perspectives on a variety of social and historical phenomena.

Another example of this kind of teaching was reported in a Dallas newspaper (Robinson, 1993). A group of African American middle school students were involved in what they termed "community problem solving" (see Tate, this issue). The kind of social action curriculum in which the students participated is similar to that advocated by scholars who argue that students need to be "centered" (Asante, 1991; Tate, 1994) or the *subjects* rather than the objects of study.

CULTURALLY RELEVANT TEACHING IN ACTION

As previously mentioned, this article and its theoretical undergirding come from a 3-year study of successful teachers of African American students. The teachers who participated in the study were initially selected by African American parents who believed them to be exceptional. Some of the parents' reasons for selecting the teachers were the enthusiasm their children showed in school and learning while in their classrooms, the consistent level of respect they received from the teachers, and their perception that the teachers understood the need for the students to operate in the dual worlds of their home community and the White community.

In addition to the parents' recommendations, I solicited principals' recommendations. Principals' reasons for recommending teachers were the low number of discipline referrals, the high attendance rates, and standardized test scores.[8] Teachers whose names appeared as both parents' and principals' recommendations were asked to participate in the study. Of the nine teachers' names who appeared on both lists, eight were willing to participate. Their participation required an in-depth ethnographic interview (Spradley, 1979), unannounced classroom visitations, videotaping of their teaching, and participation in a research collective with the other teachers in the study. This study was funded for 2 years. In a third year I did a follow-up study of two of the teachers to investigate their literacy teaching (Ladson-Billings, 1992b; 1992c).

Initially, as I observed the teachers I could not see patterns or similarities in their teaching. Some seemed very structured and regimented, using daily routines and activities. Others seemed more open or unstructured. Learning seemed to emerge from student initiation and suggestions. Still others seemed eclectic—very structured for certain activities and unstructured for others. It seemed to be a researcher's nightmare—no common threads to pull their practice together in order to relate it to others. The thought of their pedagogy as merely idiosyncratic, a product of their personalities and individual perspectives, left me both frustrated and dismayed. However, when I was able to go back over their interviews and later when we met together as a group to discuss their practice, I could see that in order to understand their practice it was necessary to go beyond the surface features of teaching "strategies" (Bartolome, 1994). The philosophical and ideological underpinnings of their practice, i.e. how they thought about themselves as teachers and how they thought about others (their students, the students' parents, and other community members), how they structured social relations within and outside of the classroom, and how they conceived of knowledge, revealed their similarities and points of congruence.[9]

All of the teachers identified strongly with teaching. They were not ashamed or embarrassed about their professions. Each had chosen to teach and, more importantly, had chosen to teach in this low-income, largely African American school district. The teachers saw themselves as a part of the community and teaching as a way to give back to the community. They encouraged their students to do the same. They believed their work was artistry, not a technical task that could be accomplished in a recipe-like fashion. Fundamental to their beliefs about teaching was that all of the students could and must succeed. Consequently, they saw their responsibility as working to guarantee the success of each student. The students who seemed furthest behind received plenty of individual attention and encouragement.

The teachers kept the relations between themselves and their students fluid and equitable. They encouraged the students to act as teachers, and they, themselves, often functioned as learners in the classroom. These fluid relationships extended beyond the classroom and into the community. Thus, it was common for the teachers to be seen attending community functions (e.g., churches, students' sports events) and using community services (e.g., beauty parlors, stores). The teachers attempted to create a bond with all of the students, rather than an idiosyncratic, individualistic connection that might foster an unhealthy competitiveness. This bond was nurtured by the teachers' insistence on creating a community of learners as a priority. They encouraged the students to learn collaboratively, teach each other, and be responsible for each other's learning.

As teachers in the same district, the teachers in this study were responsible for meeting the same state and local curriculum guidelines.[10] However, the way they met and challenged those guidelines helped to define them as culturally relevant teachers. For these teachers, knowledge is continuously recreated, recycled, and shared by the teachers and the students. Thus, they were not dependent on state curriculum frameworks or textbooks to decide what and how to teach.

For example, if the state curriculum framework called for teaching about the "age of exploration," they used this as an opportunity to examine conventional interpretations and introduce alternate ones. The content of the curriculum was always open to critical analysis.

The teachers exhibited a passion about what they were teaching—showing enthusiasm and vitality about what was being taught and learned. When students came to them with skill deficiencies, the teachers worked to help the students build bridges or scaffolding so that they could be proficient in the more challenging work they experienced in these classrooms.

For example, in Margaret Rossi's sixth grade class, all of the students were expected to learn algebra. For those who did not know basic number facts, Rossi provided calculators. She believed that by using particular skills in context (e.g., multiplication and division in the context of solving equations), the students would become more proficient at those skills while acquiring new learning.

IMPLICATIONS FOR FURTHER STUDY

I believe this work has implications for both the research and practice communities. For researchers, I suggest that this kind of study must be replicated again and again. We need to know much more about the practice of successful teachers for African American and other students who have been poorly served by our schools. We need to have an opportunity to explore alternate research paradigms that include the voices of parents and communities in non-exploitative ways.[11]

For practitioners, this research reinforces the fact that the place to find out about classroom practices is the naturalistic setting of the classroom and from the lived experiences of teachers. Teachers need not shy away from conducting their own research about their practice (Zeichner & Tabachnick, 1991). Their unique perspectives and personal investment in good practice must not be overlooked. For both groups—researchers and practitioners alike—this work is designed to challenge us to reconsider what we mean by "good" teaching, to look for it in some unlikely places, and to challenge those who suggest it cannot be made available to all children.

NOTES

1. Some notable exceptions to this failure to consider achievement strategies for African American students are *Ways With Words* (Heath, 1983); "Fostering Early Literacy Through Parent Coaching" (Edwards, 1991); and "Achieving Equal Educational Outcomes for Black Children" (Hale-Benson, 1990).
2. I have written extensively about this study, its methodology, findings, and results elsewhere. For a full discussion of the study, see Ladson-Billings (1994).
3. All study participants' names are pseudonyms.
4. At the 1994 annual meeting of the American Educational Research Association, King and Hollins presented a symposium entitled, "The Burden of Acting White Revisited."

5. The teacher acknowledged the racism, misogyny, and explicit sexuality that is a part of the lyrics of some rap songs. Thus, the students were directed to use only those songs they felt they could "sing to their parents."

6. Winston retired after the first year of the study but continued to participate in the research collaborative throughout the study.

7. Because the residency is more than a demonstration and requires students to work intensely with the artist or craftsperson, students must sign up for a particular artist. The typical group size was 5–6 students.

8. Standardized test scores throughout this district were very low. However, the teachers in the study distinguished themselves because students in their classrooms consistently produced higher test scores than their grade level colleagues.

9. As I describe the teachers I do not mean to suggest that they had no individual personalities or practices. However, what I was looking for in this study were ways to describe the commonalties of their practice. Thus, while this discussion of culturally relevant teaching may appear to infer an essentialized notion of teaching practice, none is intended. Speaking in this categorical manner is a heuristic for research purposes.

10. The eight teachers were spread across four schools in the district and were subjected to the specific administrative styles of four different principals.

11. Two sessions at the 1994 annual meeting of the American Educational Research Association in New Orleans entitled, "Private Lives in Public Conversations: Ethics of Research Across Communities of Color," dealt with concerns for the ethical standards of research in non-White communities.

REFERENCES

Asante, M.K. (1991). The Afrocentric idea in education. *Journal of Negro Education*, 60, 170–180.

Au, K., & Jordan, C. (1981). Teaching reading to Hawaiian children: Finding a culturally appropriate solution. In H. Trueba, G. Guthrie, & K. Au (Eds.), *Culture and the bilingual classroom: Studies in classroom ethnography* (pp. 69–86). Rowley, MA: Newbury House.

Banks, J., & Grambs, J. (Eds.). (1972). *Black self-concept: Implications for educational and social sciences*. New York: McGraw-Hill.

Bartolome, L. (1994). Beyond the methods fetish: Toward a humanizing pedagogy. *Harvard Educational Review*, 64, 173–194.

Berliner, D. (1988, October). Implications of studies of expertise in pedagogy for teacher education and evaluation. *In New directions for teacher assessment* (Invitational conference proceedings). New York: Educational Testing Service.

Branch, C., & Newcombe, N. (1986). Racial attitudes among young Black children as a function of parental attitudes: A longitudinal and cross-sectional study. *Child Development*, 57, 712–721.

Brown, C.S. (Ed.). (1990). *Ready from within: A first person narrative*. Trenton, NJ: Africa World Press.

Cazden, C., & Leggett, E. (1981). Culturally responsive education: Recommendations for achieving Lau remedies II. In H. Trueba, G. Guthrie, & K. Au (Eds.), *Culture and the bilingual classroom: Studies in classroom ethnography* (pp. 69–86). Rowley, MA: Newbury House.

Chilcoat, G.W., & Ligon, J. A. (1994). Developing democratic citizens: The Mississippi Freedom Schools as a model for social studies instruction. *Theory and Research in Social Education*, 22, 128–175.

The College Board. (1985). *Equality and excellence: The educational status of Black Americans*. New York: Author.

Crooks, R. (1970). The effects of an interracial preschool program upon racial preference, knowledge of racial differences, and racial identification. *Journal of Social Issues*, 26, 137–148.

Edwards, P.A. (1991). Fostering early literacy through parent coaching. In E. Hiebert (Ed.), *Literacy for a diverse society: Perspectives, programs, and policies* (pp. 199–213). New York: Teachers College Press.

Erickson, F., & Mohatt, C. (1982). Cultural organization and participation structures in two classrooms of Indian students. In G. Spindler, (Ed.), *Doing the ethnography of schooling* (pp. 131–174). New York: Holt, Rinehart & Winston.

Fordham, S., & Ogbu, J. (1986). Black students' success: Coping with the burden of "acting White." *Urban Review*, 18, 1–31.

Freire, P. (1970). *Pedagogy of the oppressed*. New York: Herder & Herder.

Gee, J.P. (1989). Literacy, discourse, and linguistics: Introduction. *Journal of Education*, 171, 5–17.

Hale-Benson, J. (1990). Achieving equal educational outcomes for Black children. In A. Baron & E.E Garcia (Eds.), *Children at risk: Poverty, minority status, and other issues in educational equity* (pp. 201–215). Washington, D.C.: National Association of School Psychologists.

Heath, S.B. (1983). Ways with words. Cambridge, U.K.: Cambridge University Press.

Hollins, E.R. (1994, April). *The burden of acting White revisited: Planning school success rather than explaining school failure*. Paper presented at the annual meeting of the American Educational Research Association, New Orleans.

Irvine, J.J. (1990). *Black students and school failure*. Westport, CT: Greenwood Press.

Jordan, C. (1985). Translating culture: From ethnographic information to educational program. *Anthropology and Education Quarterly*, 16, 105–123.

King, J. (1994). *The burden of acting White re-examined: Towards a critical genealogy of acting Black*. Paper presented at the annual meeting of the American Educational Research Association, New Orleans.

Ladson-Billings, G. (1990). Like lightning in a bottle: Attempting to capture the pedagogical excellence of successful teachers of Black students. *International Journal of Qualitative Studies in Education*, 3, 335–344.

Ladson-Billings, G. (1992a). Culturally relevant teaching: The key to making multicultural education work. In C.A. Grant (Ed.), *Research and multicultural education* (pp. 106–121). London: Falmer Press.

Ladson-Billings, G. (1992b). Liberatory consequences of literacy: A case of culturally relevant instruction for African-American students. *Journal of Negro Education*, 61, 378–391.

Ladson-Billings, G. (1992c). Reading between the lines and beyond the pages: A culturally relevant approach to literacy teaching. *Theory Into Practice*, 31, 312–320.

Ladson-Billings, G. (1994). *The dreamkeepers: Successful teaching for African-American students*. San Francisco: Jossey-Bass.

McLaren, P. (1989). *Life in schools. White Plains*, NY: Longman.

Majors, R., & Billson, J. (1992). *Cool pose: The dilemmas of Black manhood in America*. New York: Lexington Books.

Mohatt, G., & Erickson, F. (1981). *Cultural differences in teaching styles in an Odawa school: A sociolinguistic approach*. In H. Trueba, G. Guthrie, & K. Au (Eds.), Culture and the bilingual classroom: Studies in classroom ethnography (pp. 105–119). Rowley, MA: Newbury House.

Morris, A. (1984). *The origins of the civil rights movement: Black communities organizing for change*. New York: The Free Press.

Perry, T. (1993). *Toward a theory of African-American student achievement*. Report No. 16. Boston, MA: Center on Families, Communities, Schools and Children's Learning, Wheelock College.

Pewewardy, C. (1993). Culturally responsible pedagogy in action: An American Indian magnet school. In E. Hollins, J. King, & W. Hayman (Eds.), *Teaching diverse populations: Formulating a knowledge base* (pp. 77–92). Albany: State University of New York Press.

Robinson, R. (1993, Feb. 25). P.C. Anderson students try hand at problem-solving. *The Dallas Examiner*, pp. 1, 8.

Shulman, L. (1987). Knowledge and teaching: Foundations of the new reform. *Harvard Educational Review*, 57, 1–22.

Smitherman, G. (1981). *Black English and the education of Black children and youth*. Detroit: Center for Black Studies, Wayne State University.

Spradley, J. (1979). *The ethnographic interview*. New York: Holt, Rinehart & Winston.

Tate, W.F. (1994). Race, retrenchment, and reform of school mathematics. *Phi Delta Kappan*, 75, 477–484.

Villegas, A. (1988). School failure and cultural mismatch: Another view. *The Urban Review*, 20, 253–265.

Vogt, L., Jordan, C., & Tharp, R. (1987). Explaining school failure, producing school success: Two cases. *Anthropology and Education Quarterly*, 18, 276–286.

Zeichner, K.M., & Tabachnick, B.R. (1991). Reflections on reflective teaching. In B.R Tabachnick & K.M. Zeichner (Eds.), *Inquiry-oriented practices in teacher education* (pp. 1–21). London: Falmer Press.

Reproducing and Interrupting Subtractive Schooling in Teacher Education

By Jesse S. Gainer and Clarena Larrotta

But I teach Math. It is not my job to teach English as a second language.

These are the words of one preservice teacher voicing his frustration over the fact that he has been required to take a course focusing on teaching in culturally and linguistically diverse contexts. We can feel his pain because we are two professors who teach such courses and we consistently hear similar complaints from our teacher education students who substitute the word "math" with any number of other content areas which reflect their specialization. Our job is to convince these well-intentioned and idealistic students that it will be *their* job to teach all of their students and in the reality of today's schools they *will* have students who are English language learners (ELLs).

Perhaps it is not surprising that we have encountered such resistance from preservice teachers given the fact that our students, like the majority of preservice teachers in other universities, are White and come from middle-class and monolingual English speaking backgrounds (Villegas & Lucas, 2002). Cochran-Smith, Davis, and Fries (2004) address this issue:

> The strikingly different racial, cultural, and linguistic profiles of the nation's student and teaching populations, coupled with continuing disparities among racial and cultural groups in school achievement and completion rates, poverty levels, and opportunities to learn from qualified teachers, have been highlighted for some time now as pressing—if not the most pressing—issue for teacher preparation research, practice, and policy. (p. 931)

How can we, professors of education, effectively address the needs and the disparities identified by Cochran-Smith, Davis, an Fries in the above quote? In this article, we will describe qualitative

Jesse S. Gainer & Clarena Larrotta, "Reproducing and Interrupting Subtractive Schooling in Teacher Education," *Multicultural Education*, vol. 17, issue 3, pp. 41-47. Copyright © 2010 by Caddo Gap Press. Reprinted with permission. Provided by ProQuest LLC. All rights reserved.

research conducted in the large and diverse states of California and Texas that examine the beliefs and experiences of preservice teachers in relation to issues of cultural and linguistic diversity and education.

Although like others before us who found no easy answers, we have identified spaces of opportunity where students engage in thoughts and actions that counter reproduction of the inequitable status quo based in monocultural hegemony. These spaces are merely moments and do not necessarily reflect major transformations typically called for in research on critical multicultural teacher education. Therefore, we refer to these moments as "interruptions." Though brief, they are filled with potential energy and offer opportunity for teacher educators to tap.

REVIEW OF LITERATURE

Demographic studies confirm that while the number of school-aged children from diverse backgrounds is increasing, the majority of teachers and those in teacher education programs continue to be predominantly White, middle class, and English monolingual speakers (Cho & DeCastro-Ambrosetti, 2005; Gay 2005; Grant & Gillette, 2006; Ladson-Billings, 2005). This is true in the classes that we have taught for preservice teachers. Although there has been a great deal of discussion about the need to diversify the body of teachers serving ELLs, we are still struggling with this reality.

Research points out that Whiteness and racism influence the beliefs of White, monolingual English speaking pre-service teachers about the way they teach ELLs. A study conducted by Marx in 2004 revealed the association of color with deficit thinking mentality. The preservice teachers that participated in Marx's study viewed their Mexican students as having deficits in culture, language, families, intelligence, and esteem. What Marx reports in her study is very likely to happen when preservice teachers have not had exposure to other cultures and languages. This is why we feel compelled to provide these preservice teachers with experiences and learning opportunities to examine their belief system about teaching in general and specifically about teaching ELLs.

Some research studies have attempted to measure and/or demonstrate the type of psychological transformation that should occur in teacher candidates so that they will become more aware of social inequity based on race, class, and gender (Cochran-Smith, Davis, & Fries, 2004; Hollins & Guzman, 2005). This attitudinal transformation then should lead to new ways of addressing curriculum and pedagogy that are more just and inclusive of all students. We are interested in the potential for curriculum and pedagogy in teacher education programs for producing such transformations.

Grant and Gillette (2006) define teacher effectiveness through the punctual description of issues such as culturally responsive teaching, self-knowledge (understanding, acceptance, and willingness to change), a well constructed philosophy of education, pedagogical content knowledge, educational psychology, multicultural knowledge, and making connections to the world outside of the school. When teachers lack preparation to address specific needs of culturally and linguistically diverse (CLD) populations, these students can become curriculum casualties (Mathes & Torgesen, 2000). Thus, it is important to analyze how preservice teachers construct their understanding of learning and teaching this population of students.

One point that is overlooked in many of the studies in this important area of research is the idea that psychological transformation, what could also be termed "true learning," is a process that may take more than one semester (Hill-Jackson, Sewell, & Waters, 2007). This points to a major critique of the superficial way diversity is commonly treated in schools of education.

Villegas and Lucas (2002) highlight the fact that teacher preparation programs often relegate all issues surrounding race, ethnicity, class, and gender to one required "diversity" class. The message that is sent by such a structure is that issues of diversity are secondary in terms of importance and that they are not really connected to content instruction. This framework leads to a ghettoization of multicultural education that allows professors of education to dismiss these issues and most preservice teachers to ignore them. The diversity class is often seen as an uncomfortable obstacle that must be passed in order to move on with the degree plan (Ladson-Billings, 2005).

Villegas and Lucas (2002) call for more coherence around issues of diversity in schooling that would be woven as a central theme into the fabric of all courses. This notion of ideological clarity that centers issues of sociopolitical and economic realities that affect schooling is precisely what Cochran-Smith et al. (2004) are calling for in their quote mentioned earlier in this article. These are not isolated recommendations; in fact many other scholars have made similar calls for wide-scale transformations of teacher preparation programs (Ladson-Billings, 2001; Nieto, 2000; Sleeter & Montecinos, 1999; Smith, Moallem, & Sherrill, 1997).

Apart from *the* required course on diversity that is present in most schools of education, field-based experiences are often highlighted as potentially fertile grounds for preservice teachers to learn about diversity in the context of real schools with actual students. This makes sense given that the public schools where the predominantly White teacher candidates do internships are becoming increasingly diverse in terms of student body.

Smith et al. (1997) suggest that teacher educators go beyond the use of autobiography as a self-reflecting tool. These researchers recommend teacher educators to create spaces for engagement in travel education, personal experiences with discrimination, and exposure to individuals of diverse cultural backgrounds. Through these direct experiences with the reality outside the university classroom, preservice teachers will have opportunity to restructure their way of thinking and they will be given time to reflect on these experiences.

Addressing Disconnections

Ladson-Billings (2005) suggests "the real problems facing teacher education are the disconnections between and among the students, families, and community and teachers and teacher educators. These disconnections emanate from differences in race, cultural background, and socioeconomic status" (p. 229). What we need to do is to examine these issues from within. In other words, we need to examine the way our teacher preparation programs are structured. We also need to explore possibilities for the school, the community, and teacher preparation programs to work together in partnerships. Although many teacher preparation programs make claims of commitment to diversity, many teacher educators expect others to shoulder the responsibility of acting on these commitments (Ladson-Billings, 2005).

Schooling has historically been subtractive of the cultures and languages of children of color. Valenzuela (1999) situates wide-scale achievement problems of minority youth in the U.S. in "school-based relationships and organizational structures and policies designed to erase students' culture" (p. 10). In her ethnographic study of Mexican immigrant and Mexican American high school students' school experiences, she shows how assimilation forces in schooling are subtractive of the cultures of Mexican-origin youth and contribute to student disillusionment, alienation, and failure. Since Valenzuela's classic study, others have documented some of the ways schooling works to subtract resources from culturally and linguistically diverse students (see for example Garza & Crawford, 2005; Worthy, Rodrlguez-Galindo, Assaf, Martinez, & Cuero, 2003).

Subtractive assimilation is due in large part to unconscious discursive practices of primarily White teachers, albeit usually with good intentions. When hegemonic assumptions about the nature of knowledge and learning go unquestioned, schools normalize "Whiteness," thus privileging affluent and middle-class White students. This manifests in prevalent models of education that center around "expert" teachers and transmission styles of instruction. Such models tend to treat school content as politically neutral and ignore real life disparities found in today's schooling and society. Schooling that leaves these forces of assimilation unchecked can contribute to alienation and disillusionment in schooling for children of color.

Schools of education that do little or nothing to help teacher candidates identify and deconstruct the existing socio-cultural and political realities relating to schooling, are by default complicit in reproducing the cycle of subtractive schooling (Valenzuela, 2002). However, even within mainstream education programs spaces exist for critical thinking and unpacking of hegemonic discourse. As teacher educators working within colleges of education in large institutions, we are interested in identifying and tapping such spaces in the hopes of disrupting the forces that lead to wide-scale reproduction of social inequities in schooling.

What we are calling "interruptions" represent small spaces we have identified where there is potential to disrupt the status quo. In this article we provide examples of what we consider interruptions of subtractive schooling that we have found in our work with preservice teachers. Alone, these interruptions are at best just bumps in the road towards more status quo schooling.

However, when identified and analyzed, perhaps these small instances offer promise for transformative learning experiences that teacher candidates will carry with them into classroom teaching. As these interruptions expand, eventually the traditional structure of mainstream subtractive schooling could give way, leading to the possibility of a more equitable system that values the diverse knowledges and experiences students bring to school.

METHOD

This teacher research (Kincheloe, 2003; Loughran, 2000) has emerged from dialogue between two teacher researchers who examine their own practice working with preservice teachers. The data from this article come from universities in California and Texas, two states with large populations of culturally and linguistically diverse students. Both universities in this study have reputations for the quality of their teacher preparation programs.

Setting and Participants

Like many universities across the United States, the two universities connected to this study share certain similarities. First, the students enrolled in the teacher education programs are overwhelmingly White, monolingual speakers of English, and from middle class backgrounds. This is a demographic that is also shared by the majority of the professors these students will encounter during the course of their degree program. In addition, both universities' teacher education programs have recognized a need for coursework to focus on culturally and linguistically diverse students. Both have responded to this need by creating one or two stand-alone courses designed specifically to address educational issues relating to diversity. Finally, both universities put a great deal of import on practical, hands-on, experiences and therefore tie a portion of required coursework to field-based practicum experiences.

The First Setting

The first author, Jesse S. Gainer, teaches field-based literacy classes for students in the Early Childhood-4th grade certification program in a public university in Central Texas. As part of their course requirements, students enroll in a semester long internship where they spend two days a week in elementary classrooms while taking nine hours of credits that include reading and curriculum courses. In addition to teaching the reading methods courses, which are taught in a classroom in the elementary school, Jesse supervises the interns while they are in their field placements.

The elementary school that houses the interns is located in a rural area with a predominantly Latino population. A large percentage of the children in the school are Latino, mostly of Mexican origin, and approximately 30% of the students are from homes where Spanish is the primary language. In addition to monolingual English classrooms and transitional bilingual classrooms, the school has a dual language program that serves students in Kindergarten through fifth grade.

The vast majority of the preservice teachers who enroll in Jesse's field-based courses are White and monolingual speakers of English. For many, the internship will be their first experience in a context where they interact daily with people from cultural and linguistic backgrounds that differ from their own. Since there are a limited number of classrooms available for placements, each semester some interns are placed in bilingual and dual language classrooms even if they are not bilingual.

The Second Setting

The second author, Clarena Larrotta, taught the two required classes on bilingual/multicultural issues to 154 post-baccalaureate students working toward their credential program in a public university in Northern California. The courses are taught in two back-to-back semesters and are given in the setting of a university classroom. The courses are intended to provide teacher education students with necessary frameworks and approaches for successful teaching in linguistically and culturally diverse contexts.

In the first semester, students enrolled in Clarena's course are introduced to issues related to culture and language in schooling. Students engage in readings, class discussion, and projects that build background knowledge about first and second language development, socio-cultural and historical approaches to teaching, culturally responsive pedagogy, and issues of equity and inequity in schooling. In the second semester, students in Clarena's class continue to explore issues related to bilingual and multicultural education. In addition, while in the second semester students participate in a field-based practicum in their certification area. Clarena has students draw on their experiences in the field while dealing with multicultural/bilingual course content.

As is the case in Jesse's classes, students enrolled in Clarena's courses are overwhelmingly White, monolingual English speakers, and from middle-class backgrounds. Also similar to Jesse's students, most students in Clarena's courses have had very limited experiences with people from CLD backgrounds. For many, it is the second semester field experience that represents their first significant encounter with classroom diversity.

Data Sources

The authors collected data from their own teaching contexts. Data included observations, field notes, reflections written by students, interviews, and course evaluations. Different data sources were used in order to inform the different aspects of the study and provide a description of the phenomenon as complete as possible. Methodological triangulation of data collection methods provided a means of enhancing trustworthiness of study findings (Patton, 2002). To analyze the information gathered through the various data sources, we followed the systematic process of analyzing textual data suggested by Tesch (1990).

The results of our analysis indicated that our practices in teacher preparation programs functioned to reproduce subtractive schooling but also contained events that seemed to interrupt the reproduction of school inequities based on assimilation models. Although hundreds of students were observed in the two locations, our synthesis focuses on four illustrative examples that capture the main themes of reproducing and interrupting subtractive schooling in teacher education. These examples provide a strong ethnographic lens for demonstrating how teacher education programs can reproduce and interrupt the cycle of subtractive schooling for minoritized students.

RESULTS AND DISCUSSION

Presented here are four narrative examples to illustrate the complex ways in which White monolingual education students interacted with the diversity issues that arose during their teacher preparation programs. The first two examples (Katie and Sarah, pseudonyms) focus on students in the Texas institution, and the following two (Brian and Melissa, pseudonyms) are from the institution in California. Rather than a complete rejection of tenets of multicultural education on one hand, or a total transformative experience leading to the embracing of multiculturalism on the other, we found students largely fell somewhere in the middle.

Although the structures of the teacher education programs and the mindsets of most students seemed to downplay the importance of diversity pedagogy, evidence showed small ways in which teacher candidates seemed to accommodate multicultural frameworks into their everyday practice. We share some examples to highlight what we mean by "interruptions." We contend that such interruptions of the reproduction of status quo school inequities and subtractive schooling offer potentially powerful springboards for teacher educators working with populations of largely White, monolingual, middle-class preservice teachers.

Narrative One: Elevating Language Status in a "Morning Message" Activity

When Katie started her internship in Ms. Rivera's dual language kindergarten she remembered only a few words from her high school Spanish class. She was pretty sure this would not get her too far with the 5-year-old students who were just beginning to learn English. Though Katie had lived her entire life before college in a suburb of Houston, Texas, she had never had significant personal contact with native Spanish speakers. Based on information she had gleaned from TV, education courses, and church, she did have a rough idea about what to expect. From these sources she learned that the children would likely come to school unprepared and their parents would not be much help when it comes to their education.

When Katie had opportunities to get in front of the class in her dual language placement, she readily obliged. She was there to learn to be a teacher and was eager to get all the experience she could. One day, Ms. Rivera asked Katie if she would like to do *Morning Message. Morning Message* is an activity that is done daily by many teachers of young children. It is a way for the teachers to model writing for the authentic purpose of communication while also teaching early literacy skills such as directionality, phonological awareness, and concepts about print.

The teacher writes a brief message on a dry erase board and the class reads the message together. She might write something like: *Good morning. Today is Thursday February 14, 2009. After lunch we are going to Art. In math we are studying patterns. It is going to be a great day!* This was a moment Katie had been waiting for. She had been rehearsing for this moment in her head each morning while observing the cooperating teacher write her morning message. The activity was already a part of the class' routine so behavior management should not be much of an issue. Then she remembered something: The language of the day was Spanish.

With forty-two little eyes directed at her, Katie walked up to the dry erase board, picked up the blue marker, and addressed the class. "*No sé bien hablar español. Nececito* your help to escribir the message del dia." In a mixture of Spanish and English Katie showed that she had picked up a few words since arriving on the scene only a month ago. More importantly she showed herself to be a learner who valued Spanish and desired to speak better.

The cross-legged children could barely contain themselves from their positions on the carpet. They wiggled and squealed, a sea of little hands waving in the air hoping to be the one who gets to help the teacher with her Spanish. Katie was wise beyond her experience and she knew to call on as many students as possible in this moment. Together, with children sharing the role of "expert" Katie and her students scribed a beautiful morning message in Spanish. When they finished Katie re-read the message to the class as was the custom then she diverged from the "normal" teacher role and she thanked the students for their help.

Perhaps Katie was just being herself, a caring and open person, but what she communicated with her actions as she led the morning activity was a political act and constituted a culturally responsive style of teaching. By relinquishing the role of expert she not only allowed children to construct under-standing of print by helping her write the message, she opened space for them to draw on their funds of knowledge to actually teach the teacher (Gonzalez, Moll, & Amanti, 2005; Vygotsky, 1978). This interrupts the traditional transmission model of instruction (banking model).

In addition, by insisting on abiding with the language of the day even though she could not speak Spanish well, Katie elevated the status of Spanish to one of central importance. This counters the mainstream hegemony of English in U.S. society. She utilized the linguistic resources of the children in this language arts lesson as vehicles for learning (Franquiz & Reyes, 1998). This act of inclusion com-municated to students that in class biliteracy is valued and the language of the students was affirmed. This is summed up nicely by Villegas and Lucas (2002, p. 98) who state:

> To ignore or denigrate a student's language is to ignore or denigrate the student him/herself. Culturally responsive teachers use their knowledge of sociolinguistics and language devel-opment along with what they learn about their students' uses of language ... to draw on language as a resource for learning rather than seeing backgrounds in languages other than English or in varieties other than standard school English as impediments to learning.

Though Katie never explicitly acknowledged that it was her intention to draw on sociolinguistics and purposely create an assets based lesson, this was the consequence of her actions as teacher in that moment.

Narrative Two: Using "Direct Teach" to Subvert Traditional Teacher-Centered Instruction

Sarah grew up in a suburban neighborhood of Austin, Texas. Although she did not speak Spanish proficiently, she recognized that it might be a skill that would be handy in her future career as an elementary teacher. She requested a bilingual classroom and seemed to embrace the opportunity to learn some Spanish while completing her internship.

Sarah chose to teach the skill of note taking for the mandatory direct teach lesson she designed for the fourth grade bilingual classroom where she was placed. Explicit instruction, also known as the Madeline Hunter lesson, is teacher-centered by design. The format of the lesson plan, which is sometimes explained as: "I do, we do, you do," positions the teacher as the expert, the holder of knowledge to be disseminated to the students. Sarah turned this very traditional and teacher-centered lesson format upside down with a creative design that highlighted her expertise in the focus skill of note taking while centering the students' prior knowledge through content.

For the anticipatory set Sarah led a discussion about *My Diary From Here to There* (Pérez, 2002), a book that the class recently read. The book, which deals with a child's experience of moving from Mexico to the U.S., resonated with the experiences of many of the children in the class. After activating students' background knowledge on the topic, she introduced her objective and proceeded to the portion of the lesson where she modeled note taking. At this time Sarah asked her cooperating teacher, Mr. Martinez, to tell about his experiences moving from Mexico to the U.S. as a young child. Sarah took notes on the overhead demonstrating for the students who were spellbound listening to their teacher's history.

For the guided practice that followed, Sarah played an audiotape of her roommate who had moved to this country from Colombia when she was in high school. Students worked in small groups to imitate the note taking strategies they had learned from watching Sarah work on the overhead minutes earlier. The final portion of this lesson, independent practice, allows students to demonstrate their learning of the skill in question. For this portion of the lesson Sarah had invited Mrs. Cantu, the mother of a boy in the class, to come and tell about her experiences moving here from Mexico. Mrs. Cantu spoke very candidly about her reasons for coming, the emotions she felt about leaving family and friends, and the difficulties she has faced as a result of her limited ability to speak English. The children were deeply engaged in note taking while she spoke. When she finished practically every student in the room shot up his/her hand to ask questions.

In this example, Sarah managed to make the most traditional and teacher-centered lesson design a culturally responsive lesson that was based in students' prior knowledge and cultural capital. Sarah noticed the power of tapping into students' funds of knowledge. In a reflection essay she commented:

> [Students] were very engaged throughout the lesson, raising their hands frequently to provide responses or to ask good questions. They really enjoyed listening to different people's experiences and taking notes on them. Many of them wanted to hear their parents' story and even my own so that they could take notes on them.

As the final sentence in her reflection indicates, the students saw the learned skill of note taking as meaningful and wished to continue with it at home and with her. What Sarah did by inviting the cooperating teacher and a parent to share their stories of immigration was to send the potent message to students that the experiences of their families are valued in this class setting and they are integral for school learning. Through lesson design and a humanizing pedagogy (Bartolome, 1994), Sarah interrupted the cycle of subtractive schooling. Rather than ignoring students' backgrounds, or attempting to erase them, Sarah centered her students' experiences in an additive literacy lesson.

Narrative Three: I WILL Teach Mathematics and ELLs

Brian is from a small town in Northern California close to Oregon. He had never been out of his town and his plan was to find a job close by in the San Francisco Bay area. During the first semester, when classes started, Brian was one of the quiet students in the group. As he explained later, he was not timid; he was just not sure about needing instruction on multicultural and bilingual education issues. He had graduated from the Mathematics Department and was getting his credential in that single subject. The following is what Brian wrote in his first class reflection:

> I feel uncomfortable. I don't know what to write about. This is a hard assignment because in Math we never have to write "reflections" and I do not know what to say. I have to turn in this assignment tomorrow and I'm following your advice writing about my thoughts. These topics we discuss in class are not relevant for my teaching, I need to learn how to teach Math …

Brian, like others, believed that his main goal in public education was to teach mathematics and learning about language issues and cultural diversity was not part of his role as a future teacher. Later in the semester, on his second essay, he still resisted the idea of needing to reflect on the student population he was going to be serving in the classroom and the possible challenges he could face in the field when he started his student-teaching portion of the credential program. This is what he noted in his reflection:

> I don't like this class. we talk about lots of touchy-feely topics. That is why I like Math! Numbers are easy.

However, during the second semester when he started his teaching practice his class reflections started to change. When Brian started his practice in the field he realized that not all the students in the math class were monolingual English native speakers, or European-American like him. During class discussion he said that:

> I have seven ELLs in my math class and … I don't know what to do to help them with their problem solving skills because their English is so poor. I never thought I was going to be in this situation.

During the second semester, compelled by the need to reach all students in the classroom, Brian realized that it was important to develop strategies that help him accommodating instruction for the ELLs in his classes. In his last reflection he wrote:

> Teachers should be required to receive pre-service training to be prepared to meet the needs of linguistic minorities. We need to understand about other cultures and be aware that we will have English learners in our classes. Regular classroom teachers should be required to

receive pre-service training to be prepared to meet the needs of linguistic minorities and students that come from other cultures.

These thoughts suggest a shift of attitude from his part toward the importance of receiving multicultural instruction and discussing topics related to teaching ELLs. For most of the students, the second semester doing their teaching practice at the local schools provided them with experiences that made them realize that the readings and discussions we had started in the previous semester made sense.

We consider this an interruption of the cycle of subtractive schooling because through praxis, connecting theory to practice, Brian realized he would need to reach all students, including ELLs, if he hopes to be a successful mathematics teacher. We cannot say Brian is a transformed individual, we have no way of knowing how deeply he has internalized these views, but we can say that he has begun to ask important questions about his own teaching practice in relation to CLD students.

Narrative Four: A Wake Up Call in the Teachers' Lounge

Melissa graduated with a bachelor's degree in Science with a specialization in Biology. Her goal was to obtain a teacher credential and work at the local high school. Similar to Brian, she was also from Northern California and her attitude toward our class and teaching ELLs was similar as well. In her first class reflections she would write comments such as:

> Multicultural education is not my field, I am going to teach biology. I am not going to teach language and I don't know why this class is required for graduation.

However, during the second semester in the credential program, and as a result of her practicum, Melissa realized that the reality outside the university where she dreamed about teaching just biology looked different than what she had pictured. During the third week in her site Melissa overheard a conversation in the teacher's lounge. She reported the following in class:

> There were two teachers talking about the three Latino students they share in their classes. They seemed disappointed and were saying, "*These children are not learning any thing. They are not very intelligent and they are lazy ...*" I couldn't believe they were saying these things in front of me. They are supposed to be experienced teachers and I should be learning from them. To be honest I don't know what to do about their attitude. I don't agree but I don't know what to do. There are only five non-English speakers at the school. why can't we provide for their needs and accommodate instruction to include them? I am very disappointed at these teachers and the school.

Melissa did not understand why school personnel were not making efforts to help these five students progress in their learning. In her monthly reflections, she wrote about school episodes in which she witnessed mistreatment and discrimination against ELLs and students that belonged to other cultures.

She also reported her desire to receive further instruction and practice in the content area to teach ELLs. For example:

> The class was very productive this semester. I feel I learned so much. but I still need to learn more about teaching ELLs. Class was painful sometimes. These issues were hard to discuss and I feel we never finished. There was not enough time to discuss and come up with good answers. Theory and application have been invaluable towards educating me on how to address the many needs of ELLs in my classroom. However I feel incomplete. I am insecure of my ability to do this.

Listening to these teachers and reflecting about the meaning of that conversation was Melissa's wake up call to realize how much these inequities affected her. She could become one of those teachers in the future if she didn't figure out how to reach the ELL students in her Biology class. Melissa's words about feeling incomplete and insecure constitute an interruption of her confidence in her content area knowledge being enough to make her a good teacher. This interruption is not enough to transform her into the Biology teacher she needs to be, but Melissa knows that she has a lot to learn in order to become an effective teacher for all students.

CONCLUSIONS AND IMPLICATIONS

This study examined the ways in which students in two teacher education programs experienced diversity pedagogy and how they enacted their roles as future teachers of culturally and linguistically diverse students. As education professors, we are interested in helping our students gain competence and confidence in their abilities to teach all of their future students. We are also interested in providing opportunities for our students to be able to examine the beliefs they bring to the teacher preparation program because we know that unexamined beliefs can impede new learning. Unfortunately, we are also aware of the fact that our institutions, like many mainstream teacher preparation programs, have not done a good job attracting diverse teacher candidates, nor have we sufficiently structured education programs to help our largely White and monolingual student populations embrace critical multicultural education (Ladson-Billings, 2005).

In fact, the structure of most teacher education programs, ours included, make very little effort to center issues of diversity in the curriculum. By relegating all multiculturalism to one or two stand-alone courses, education programs communicate the message that the issues are separate and of lesser importance than "true" content area knowledge (such as reading and math) and discipline knowledge (such as classroom management). Even when the courses with multicultural content are very good, and we feel sure this is the case in the majority of institutions, one or two semesters is not enough to transform deficit thinking (Ambe, 2006; Cho & DeCastro-Ambrosetti, 2005; Hill-Jackson, et al., 2007).

There is potential for powerful learning when students embark on field-based experiences. Given that teacher education students often report having had little prior experience with diversity, field experiences in diverse contexts seem like a reasonable way to help preservice teachers gain new knowledge in this area. However, just putting students into diverse settings without offering tools for them to critically analyze what they are observing, likely will do nothing but reinforce deficit thinking.

If schools tend to reproduce social inequalities (Apple, 1979), then schools of education function to continue the cycle. Although this probably occurs inadvertently, through the structure of programs failing to challenge inequity, the results are damaging for our society in general, and specifically for many school children experiencing subtractive schooling. As professors of education in mainstream institutions, we recognize our roles in this vicious cycle. Through our participation, we are complicit in the perpetuation of subtractive schooling because we fail to reach significant numbers of our students.

In this research, we have found that even within programs such as ours, which are designed to reproduce the status quo, there are small spaces that can interrupt the mainstream. We have highlighted four examples from our practice that we believe illustrate some potential for change within mainstream teacher preparation programs. However, these interruptions are meaningless if they are not coupled with critical analysis. In order for such interruptions to move beyond isolated and "cute" examples of White teachers voluntarily, or inadvertently, defusing language-power dynamics, teacher candidates must develop clear ideologies based in social justice and critical multiculturalism (Nieto, 1999).

The problem is complex and has many variables. While we resist the urge to reduce findings to "easy answers," we do have hope for change. Change in this case, leading to more equitable schooling for linguistically and culturally marginalized populations, will be a long struggle in need of continuous research and activism. We, as researchers and teachers, must look for many ways to address the problems from within and outside of the mainstream institutions.

A complete restructuring of our programs would likely be the best place to start. A restructuring would place greater emphasis on centering issues of diversity in every aspect of the program to create an ideological and cohesive thread (Villegas & Lucas, 2002). In addition, such a restructuring would make serious efforts to diversify the professoriate and the student populations in colleges of education. In the meantime, those of us who work within teacher preparation programs must examine our practice and look for spaces to implement change, places to create "interruptions."

We contend that "interruptions" exist and offer powerful spaces for teachable moments. If we look for such moments, we can help our students, future teachers, see how their actions are situated in cultural and historical contexts. They can see how their actions can reproduce wide-scale social inequalities and/or represent counter narratives that go against the grain. Expanding the interruptions to significant teaching events will not result in a silver bullet to end racism or subtractive schooling. However, we do believe the interruptions can become little bumps on the status quo superhighway. As the little bumps add up, perhaps the path of subtractive schooling will eventually take a major turn.

REFERENCES

Ambe, E. B. (2006). Fostering multicultural appreciation in pre-service teachers through multicultural curricular transformation. *Teaching & Teacher Education: An International Journal of Research and Studies*, 22(6), 690–699.

Apple, M. (1979). *Ideology and curriculum*. London, UK: Routledge.

Bartolome, L. (1994). Beyond a methods fetish: Toward a humanizing pedagogy. *Harvard Educational Review*, 64(2), 173–194.

Cho, G., & DeCastro-Ambrosetti, D. (2005). Is ignorance bliss? Pre-service teachers' attitudes toward multicultural education. *High School Journal*, 89(2), 24–28.

Cochran-Smith, M., Davis, D., & Fries, K. (2004). Multicultural teacher education: Research, practice, and policy. In J. A. Banks & C. A. McGee Banks (Eds), *Handbook of research on multicultural education* (2nd ed.). San Francisco: Jossey-Bass.

Franquiz, M., & Reyes, M. (1998). Creating inclusive learning communities through English language arts: From chanclas to canicas. *Language Arts*, 75(3), 211–220.

Garza, A., & Crawford, C. (2005). Hegemonic multiculturalism: English immersion, ideology, and subtractive schooling. *Bilingual Research Journal*. 29(3), 599–619.

Gay, G. (2005). Politics of multicultural teacher education. *Journal of Teacher Education*, 56(3), 221–228.

González, N., Moll, L., & Amanti, C. (Eds). (2005). *Funds of knowledge: Theorizing practices in households, communities, and classrooms*. Mahwah, NJ: Lawrence Erlbaum Associates.

Grant, C. A., & Gillette, M. (2006). A candid talk to teacher educators about effectively preparing teachers who can teach everyone's children. *Journal of Teacher Education*, 57(3), 292–300.

Hollins, E. R., & Guzman, M. T. (2005). Research on preparing teachers for diverse populations. In M. Cochran-Smith & K. M. Zeichner (Eds.), *Studying teacher education: The report of the AERA panel on research and teacher education*. Mahwah, NJ: Lawrence Erlbaum Associates.

Hill-Jackson,V., Sewell, K. L., & Waters, C. (2007). Having our say about multicultural education. *Kappa Delta Pi*, 174–181.

Kincheloe, J. L. (2003). *Teachers as researchers: Qualitative inquiry as a path to empowerment*. 2nd ed. London, UK: RoutledgeFalmer.

Ladson-Billings, G. (2001). *Crossing over to canaan: The journey of new teachers in diverse classrooms*. San Francisco: Jossey-Bass.

Ladson-Billings, G. (2005). Is the team all right? Diversity and teacher education. *Journal of teacher education*, 56(3), 229–234.

Loughran, J. (2002). *Improving teacher education practice through self-study*. London, UK: RoutledgeFalmer.

Marx, S. (2004). Exploring and challenging Whiteness and White racism with White pre-service teachers. In V. Lea & J. Helfand (Eds.), *Identifying race and transforming Whiteness in the classroom* (pp. 132–152). New York: Peter Lang.

Mathes, P. G., & Torgesen, J. K. (2000). A call for equity in reading instruction for all students: A response to Allington and Woodside-Jiron. *Educational Researcher*, 29(6), 4–14.

Nieto, S. (1999). *The light in their eyes: Creating multicultural learning communities*. New York: Teachers College Press.

Nieto, S. (2000). Placing equity front and center: Some thoughts on transforming teacher education for a new century. *Journal of Teacher Education*, 51(3), 180–187.

Patton, M. Q. (2002). *Qualitative research & evaluation methods* (3rd Ed.). Thousand Oaks, CA: Sage Publications.

Pérez, A. I. (2002). *My diary from here to there*. San Francisco: Children's Book Press.

Sleeter, C., & Montecinos, C. (1999). Forging partnerships for multicultural teacher education. In S. May (Ed.), *Critical multiculturalism: Rethinking multicultural and antiracist education*. Philadelphia: Falmer Press.

Smith, R., Moallem, M., & Sherrill, D. (1997). How preservice teachers think about cultural diversity: A closer look at factors which influence their beliefs. *Educational Foundations*, 11(2), 41–61.

Tesch, R. (1990). *Qualitative research: Analysis types and software tools*. New York: Falmer Press.

Valenzuela, A. (1999). *Subtractive schooling: U.S.-Mexican youth and the politics of caring*. Albany, NY: State University of New York Press.

Valenzuela, A. (2002). Reflections on the subtractive underpinnings of education research and policy. *Journal of Teacher Education*, 53(3), 235–241.

Vygotsky, L. S. (1978). *Mind in society: The development of higher psychological processes*. Cambridge, MA: Harvard University Press.

Villegas, A. M., & Lucas, T. (2002). *Educating culturally responsive teachers: A coherent approach*. Albany, NY: State University of New York Press.

Worthy, J., Rodriguez-Galindo, A., Assaf, A., Martinez, L. & Cuero, K. (2003). Fifth grade bilingual students and precursors to "Subtractive Schooling." *Bilingual Research Journal*, 27(2), 275–294.

Gender, Racial, and Ethnic Misrepresentation in Children's Books: A Comparative Look

By Hani Morgan

How children's books portray various groups is very important for educators to consider. In many literate cultures, values and attitudes are transmitted through storytelling, often involving the use of children's books (Kortenhaus & Demarest, 1993; Roberts, Dean, & Holland, 2005). Young children usually enjoy having a book read to them.

Unfortunately, children's literature traditionally has not been authentic in representing the experiences of many ethnic and racial minority groups (Nieto, 19%). Research also indicates that children's books do not always portray the female gender equally to the male (Davis & McDaniel, 1999; Kortenhaus & Demarest, 1993). For example, Czaplinski's (1972) study analyzed Caldecott-winning books from 1940 to 1971 and discovered that males outnumbered females in both pictures and text.

It is important to start when children are very young when teaching them to develop a tolerant attitude towards people who are different than they are (Sobol, 1990). Cai and Bishop (1994) use the term "parallel cultures" to describe the desired view of different cultures as equal. Authentic children's books that include a variety of cultures can help future generations view people in different parts of the world, or even those in their own neighborhood, as equal members of society (Tunnel & Jacobs, 2008). Children's literature has been used for many years to develop positive attitudes towards people of different cultures (Hansen-Krening, 1992). Banks (2003) reports children's books to be a powerful tool for teaching concepts involving race, culture, and discrimination to students in the primary grades.

This comparative review of research discusses findings of selected studies concerning gender, racial, and ethnic misrepresentation in children's books. In addition, it offers suggestions for educators on how to deal with this concern. This article will not address all groups, because there is limited research (or none at all) on this subject for certain groups.

GENDER PORTRAYL IN CHILDREN'S BOOKS

In general, the portrayal of various groups in children's books is much better today than ever before, but a few disturbing studies indicate that stereotypical portrayals still occur. A good example is the study by Davis and McDaniel (1999) on gender bias in children's books. This study modeled Czaplinski's (1972) study to examine if any improvements were made in children's books published after 1972. The 1999 study shows that the Caldecott-winning books reviewed from 1972 to 1997 featured 811 male appearances versus 508 female appearances. This study indicates that men represented 61% of the characters and women accounted for only 39%. In Czaplinski's (1972) study, which investigated books dating back to 1940, males represented 63% of appearances, compared to 37% for females.

The results of the study by Davis and McDaniel (1999) indicate that sexism in children's books still exists. It is important to note that this study only focuses on one aspect of gender inequality: the amount of male vs. female representation. It does not emphasize the roles women played in these books. Other studies conclude that females are likely to be portrayed as submissive and dependent (Child, Potter, & Levine, 1946; Jacklin & Mischel, 1973; Purcell & Stewart, 1990). This type of portrayal is stereotypical and not likely to be an accurate representation of many women today.

Kortenhaus and Demarest (1993) suggest that sometimes it is difficult to conclude whether significant changes have been made concerning the portrayal of girls and women, as data can be analyzed in many different ways. Their 1993 study took into consideration the roles that females played in various children's books and found a decrease in sexism.

THE PORTRAYL OF NATIVE AMERICANS

Roberts, Dean, and Holland (2005) suggest that Native Americans may have endured more stereotypes and distorted views about their culture than any other group. Although many Native Americans are highly educated and hold professional positions, many children's books do not represent them this way. Older picture books are more likely to represent Native Americans in a stereotypic way; this is a problem, as some researchers (e.g., Yokota, 1999) report that schools and libraries often keep older books containing stereotypical images and outdated information.

Stereotypical books on Native Americans ignore their cultural heritage and emphasize only a few aspects, such as feathers and animal clothing; consequently, readers may develop inaccurate ideas about the different Native American cultures (Roberts, Dean, & Holland, 2005). Knoeller (2005) argues that schools continue to neglect contemporary Native American authors whose writing reflects tribal cultures and instead choose to use books that portray inaccurate aspects of the cultures. One study done by Lindsay (2003) mentions that books reviewed in 2000–02 about Native Americans were ranked lower in quality than those reviewed in 1989–99, but notes that this decline could be due to the use of higher standards.

There are several reasons as to why inaccurate, offensive, and stereotypical children's books on Native Americans continue to be published. Some authors ignore the latest research (Roberts, Dean,

& Holland 2005). Lindsay (2003) mentions that although some very good children's books, by Native authors and illustrators, have been published recently, publishing houses often have very few reviewers available who are knowledgeable about Native Americans; as a result, they cannot always distinguish good books from bad ones. Reese (1999) discusses how one book published in 1999 was reviewed favorably in leading journals, even though its content offended the Native American community.

Another explanation for this disconnect is that U.S. society generally receives insufficient knowledge about Native Americans and so cannot recognize stereotypical writing and pictures about this group in children's books. Unfortunately, evidence exists showing that many young non-Indian children believe inaccurate concepts about Native Americans (Heller, Cunningham, & Heller, 2003).

THE PORTRAYL OF AFRICAN AMERICANS

African American literature intended for adults and children has had a troubled past (Harris, 1990), partly because schools and libraries have very often omitted this literature from their collections. Harris explains that sanctioned lists created by educators often include only a limited number of texts written by African Americans. In elementary school, for example, children are more likely to read children's books that reflect the values and perspectives of whites, such as *Little House on the Prairie*, rather than those written by African Americans or other people of color. In addition, not many children's books that were published in the recent past focus on black values or feature black major characters (Bishop, 1990).

Various studies have concluded that African Americans are portrayed in stereotypical ways in children's books (Klein, 1985; Sadker & Sadker, 1977). Brown's (1933) study concluded that portrayals of African Americans in early literature suggested that institutionalized racism was justifiable. Harris (1990) states that similar attitudes could be found in children's books and explains that early children's texts were likely to portray African Americans as "dim-witted"; furthermore, few of these books portrayed the horrors of slavery.

The passage of civil rights legislation in the mid-1960s, with the accompanying demands for equality, led to significant improvements in children's literature portraying African Americans and more positive images of blacks (Pescosolido, Grauerholz, & Milkie, 1997). After the civil rights movement, many more children's books began to reflect the cultural traditions of African Americans, including their varied perspectives and experiences. Some of these books discuss the experience of racial discrimination and of other inequalities that blacks had to endure. Harris (1990) reminds educators that these books are not intended to scare children but rather to teach them about people's experiences in historically accurate ways.

Although children's books published since the 1970s depict African Americans more positively than in previous periods, researchers still raise concerns about several issues. Pescosolido et al. (1997) report a lack of stories portraying intimate relationships between African Americans and whites. Other researchers report that stereotypes still persist in children's books, even in those published more recently.

For example, Kalisa (1990) notes that some books on Africa published in the 1980s still contained biases and stereotypes. Examples of these kinds of books include those that only show Africans as poor, malnourished, and primitive.

THE PORTRAYL OF HISPANICS

It can be difficult to describe the way Hispanics have been portrayed in children's books, because of the number of subgroups considered to be Hispanic; these subgroups are sometimes portrayed differently in children's books. The term "Hispanic" has been used to refer to various groups, such as people of Cuban, Mexican, Puerto Rican, and Central or South American origin.

Overall, the portrayal of this group of people has improved in several ways over the past 40 years, but more improvements are necessary (Nilsson, 2005). Rocha and Dowd (1993) found evidence of this improvement while examining the changes in portrayals of Mexican American females in children'sbooks published from 1950 to 1969 and those from 1970 to 1990. This study concludes that the image of females from a Mexican background has dramatically improved, as those books showed a 16% increase in females who are portrayed as strong and enduring. The authors also mention that females are more frequently portrayed as employed and leaders in the community in more recent books.

Some studies (e.g., Nieto, 1982) indicate that certain Hispanic groups can be negatively stereotyped in children's books. Nieto's study concludes that many books written between 1972 and 1982 portrayed Puerto Ricans negatively. Her study consisted of two parts. In the first part, she examined 56 fiction books, and found that many of them describe Puerto Ricans with no sense of diversity (e.g., most live in urban ghettos). In the second part, Nieto examined 29 nonfiction books, and concluded that many of the books are ethnocentric and portray migrants as the cause of their own problems.

Many researchers also note the underrepresentation of Hispanics in books intended for children from preschool to high school (Agosto, Hughes-Hassell, & Gilmore-Clough, 2003; Ayala, 1999; Higgins, 2002; Reimer, 1992). Educators need to regard this oversight as a major issue, as Hispanics have become the largest minority population in the United States (U.S. Census Bureau, 2003).

THE PORTRAYL OF ASIAN AMERICANS

Asian Americans are another fast-growing minority group in the United States. Yokota and Bates (2005) report an increase of over 50% in Asian American school-age children since the 1990 census. Although Cordova (1983) states that Asian Americans have lived in the United States for over 200 years, many American students still tend to view Asian Americans as foreigners (Pang, Colvin, Tran, & Barba, 1992).

Teachers of young children can take advantage of culturally authentic children's literature to change this view. Stereotypical portrayals of Asian Americans include those that repeatedly show them as experts in the martial arts or as overly polite (Pang, 1990). One of the problems in the portrayal of Asians is the limited number of modern realistic stories (MacCann, 1997). Culturally authentic children's books can teach American students to stop viewing Asian Americans as foreigners, as these books often aim to present Asian Americans and other minority groups in U.S. settings rather than overseas.

Lo and Lee (1993) state that educators need to avoid many stereotypical books on Asian Americans, while acknowledging that this is sometimes difficult to do, as many of these books are illustrated attractively or traditionally considered appropriate. Furthermore, teachers often mistakenly believe they are making a good choice when selecting children's books that focus on a particular minority group; they may not realize that the book portrays that group stereotypically (Pang et al., 1992). Lo and Lee (1993) urge educators to examine a book's illustrations to make sure they complement a text and are not simply put in as tokens of the Asian culture. Examples of children's books that misuse illustrations in Asian children's books are those that include too many illustrations of chopsticks and fans. If writing is used to represent a culture, it should be the actual writing of the group and not just any writing made to look foreign (e.g., using a font that mimics Chinese or Japanese characters). Pang et al. (1992) recommend using books that do not rely heavily on illustrations of characters wearing traditional clothing; at the least, the books should clarify that Asian Americans only wear such clothing for special occasions. Illustrations also should show a wide variety of the characters' physical features, such as in the shape of their eyes and body build.

Yokota (1999) states that while many culturally authentic books about Japan have been published in the recent past, some issues have not been resolved. She argues that although cultural details are portrayed more accurately, when "outsiders" write about Asians, they often miss aspects of what is authentic to those who are native to Asia. The author's background should be considered when evaluating the authenticity of any book.

SUGGESTIONS FOR EDUCATORS

The United States has more cultural minorities today than ever before. Teachers can take advantage of culturally authentic children's books to provide a caring and warm environment for these minority students. A curriculum that reflects the backgrounds of diverse students builds self-esteem and helps these students feel appreciated (Gollnick & Chinn, 2006).

Unfortunately, some books with stereotypical elements continue to be published, and many of them that were published years ago remain in circulation. It is important for teachers to avoid these types of books because children's books transmit values and are more than just resources to teach reading. By examining the ways that children's books have misrepresented different groups, teachers can gain insights about how to recognize aspects of books that may be harmful to students, and they can use this knowledge to avoid stereotypic books in the future. Many of the referenced sources listed here provide examples and lists of culturally authentic children's books.

Culturally authentic children's books are important to all students. Mainstream students benefit equally from these books because they teach tolerance toward people of different cultures; this is critical in any society, especially those that are steadily becoming more diverse.

CONCLUSION

Some cultural minority groups are comparatively new to the United States and thus little research exists on them. It is important for future researchers to focus on these groups and to continue exploring the ways the groups discussed in this article are portrayed in children's books. Children develop concepts of race and gender at a very young age. Research has shown that by the age of 5, some students already have developed high levels of racial intolerance (Bigler & Liben, 1993; Doyle & Aboud, 1995). By reaching children in their early years of schooling through the use of culturally authentic children's books, teachers can instill attitudes that foster tolerance and equality towards all.

REFERENCES

Agosto, D. E., Hughes-Hassell, S., & Gilmore-Cough, C. (2003). The all-white world of middle-school genre fiction: Surveying the field for multicultural protagonists. *Children's Literature in Education*, 34, 257–275.

Ayala, E. C. (1999). "Poor little things" and "brave little souls": The portrayal of individuals with disabilities in children's literature. *Reading Research and Instruction*, 39, 103–117.

Banks, J. A. (2003). *Teaching strategies for ethnic studies.* New York: Allyn and Bacon.

Bigler, R.; & Liben, L. (1993). A cognitive development approach to racial stereotyping and reconstructive memory in Euro-American children. *Child Development*, 64, 1507–1519.

Bishop, R. S. (1990). Walk tall in the world: African American literature for today's children. The Journal of Negro Education, 59, 556–565.

Brown, S. (1933). Negro character as seen by white authors. *Journal of Negro Education,* 2, 179–203.

Cai, M., & Bishop, R. (1994). Multicultural literature for children: Towards a clarification of the concept. In A. H. Dyson & G. Genishi (Eds.), The need for story: *Cultural diversity in classroom and community* (pp. 57–71). *Urbana*, IL: National Council of Teachers of English.

Child, I. L., Potter, E. H., & Levine, E. M. (1946). Children's textbooks and personality development: An exploration in the social psychology of education. *Psychological Monographs*, 60, 1–54.

Cordova, F. (1983). *Filipinos: Forgotten Asian Americans.* Dubuque, IA: Kendall/Hunt.

Czaplinski, S. M. (1972). *Sexism in award winning picture books.* Pittsburgh, PA: KNOW, Inc.

Davis, A. P., & McDaniel, T. R. (1999). You've come a long way, baby—or have you? Research evaluating gender portrayal in recent Caldecott-winning books. *The Reading Teacher*, 52, 532–536.

Doyle, A. B., & Aboud, F. E. (1995). A longitudinal study of white children's racial prejudice as a social cognitive development. *Merrill-Palmer Quarterly*, 41, 210–220.

Gollnick, D. M., & Chinn, P. C. (2006). Multicultural education in a pluralistic society. *Upper Saddle River*, NJ: Pearson Prentice Hall.

Hansen-Krening, N. (1992). Authors of color: A multicultural perspective. *Journal of Reading*, 36, 124–129.

Harris, V. H. (1990). African American children's literature: The first one hundred years. *The Journal of Negro Education*, 59, 540–555.

Heller, C., Cunningham, B., & Heller, H. M. (2003). Selecting children's picture books with positive Native American fathers and father figures. *Multicultural Review*, 12(1), 43–48.

Higgins, J. J. (2002). Multicultural children's literature: Creating and applying an evaluation tool in response to the needs of urban educators. *New Horizons for Learning*. Retrieved May 19, 2008, from www.newhorizons.org/strategies/multicultural/higgins.htm

Jacklin, C. N, & Mischel, H. N. (1973). As the twig is bent: Sex role stereotyping in early readers. *School Psychology Digest*, 2, 30–39.

Kalisa, B. G. (1990). Africa in picture books: Portrait or preconception. *School Library Journal*, 36(2), 36–37.

Klein, G. (1985). *Reading into racism: Bias in children's literature and learning materials*. London: Routledge and Kegan Paul.

Knoeller, C. (2005). Not one voice, but many: Reading contemporary Native American writers. In D. L. Henderson & J. P. May (Eds.), Exploring culturally diverse literature for children and adolescents (pp. 22–41). New York: Allyn and Bacon.

Kortenhaus, C.M.,& Demarest, J. (1993). Gender role stereotyping in children's literature: An update. *Sex Roles*, 28, 219–232.

Lindsay, N. (2003). "I" still isn't for Indian: A look at recent publishing about Native Americans. *School Library Journal*, 49(11), 42–43.

Lo, S., & Lee. G. (1993). Asian images in picture books: What stories do we tell our children? *Emergency Librarian*, 20(5), 14–8.

MacCann, D. (1997). Illustrating the point: A commentary on multicultural and stereotypic picture books. In D. Muse (Ed.), *The New Press guide to multicultural resources for young readers* (pp. 62–67). New York: The New Press.

Nieto,S. (1982). Children's literature on Puerto Rican themes. *Interracial Books for Children Bulletin*, 24(1–2), 6–16.

Nieto, S. (1996). Affirming diversity. *White Plains*, NY: Longman.

Nilsson, N. L. (2005). How does Hispanic portrayal in children's books measure up after 40 years? The answer is "It depends." *The Reading Teacher*, 58, 534–548.

Pang, V. O. (1990). Asian-American children: A diverse population. *Educational Forum*, 55, 49–66.

Pang, V. O., Colvin, C., Tran, M., & Barba, R. H. (1992). Beyond chopsticks and dragons: Selecting Asian-American literature for children. *The Reading Teacher*, 46, 216–224.

Pescosolido, B. A., Grauerholz, E., & Milkie, M. A. (1997). Culture and conflict The portrayal of blacks in U.S. children's picture books through the mid- and late-twentieth century. *American Sociological Review*, 62(3), 443–464.

Purcell, P., & Stewart, L. (1990). Dick and Jane in 1989. *Sex Roles*, 22, 177–185.

Reese, D. (1999). Authenticity & sensitivity: Goals for writing and reviewing books with Native American themes. *School Library Journal*, 45(11), 36–37.

Reimer, K. M. (1992). Multiethnic literature: Holding fast to dreams. *Language Arts*, 69, 14–21.

Roberts, L., Dean, E., & Holland, M. (2005). Contemporary American Indian cultures in children's picture books. Retrieved May 15, 2008, from www.journal.naeyc.org/btj/200511/Robertsll05BTJ.asp.

Rocha, O. J., & Dowd, F. S. (1993). Are Mexican-American females portrayed realistically in fiction for grades K-3? A content analysis. *Multicultural Review*, 2(4), 60–69.

Sadker, M. P., & Sadker, D. M. (1977). Now upon a time: A contemporary view of children's literature. New York: Harper and Row.

Sobol, T. (1990). Understanding diversity. *Educational Leadership*, 48, 27—30

Tunnel, M. O., & Jacobs, J. S. (2008). Children's literature briefly. *Upper Saddle River*, NJ: Merrill Prentice Hall.

U.S. Census Bureau. (2003). Hispanic population reaches all-time high of 38.8 million, new Census Bureau estimates show. U.S. Census Bureau News. Retrieved January 8, 2009, from www.census.gov/Press-Release/www/releases/archives/population/011193.html.

Yokota, J. (1999). Japanese and Japanese Americans: Portrayals in recent children's books. *Book Links*, 8(3), 47–53.

Yokota, J., & Bates A. (2005). Asian American literature: Voices and images of authenticity. In D. L. Henderson & J. P. May (Eds.), *Exploring culturally diverse literature for children and adolescents* (pp. 323–335). New York: Allyn and Bacon.

The Problem of School Bullies: What the Research Tells Us

By Lee A. Beaty and Erick B. Alexeyev

ABSTRACT: This article includes an overview of the history of research on school bullying, its nature and prevalence, characteristics of bullies and victims, and teachers' knowledge of and attitudes toward bullying. Also, two model interventions designed to reduce this harmful behavior are examined.

The issue of school bullies and their victims has been a source of much research during recent years. This paper seeks to clarify and elaborate on some of the most salient findings of empirical studies in the United States and other countries. Various interventions have been utilized to deal with students who bully and have also focused on the needs of those who are victimized. The process of bullying can have negative consequences, both for bullies and victims. Psychological profiles of bullies and victims are examined as well as the nature, prevalence, and demographics of bullying.

Several general types of bullying have been identified in the literature (e.g., Donahue, 2004; Owlets, 1993). Among these are (a) *Direct Bullying*: Behaviors such as teasing, taunting, threatening, hitting, and stealing that are initiated by one of more bullies against a victim; (b) *Verbal Bullying*: Taunting, teasing, name calling, spreading rumors; (c) *Physical Bullying*: Hitting, kicking, destroying property, enlisting a friend to assault someone for you; (d) *Verbal (Non-physical) Bullying*: Threatening or obscene gestures, excluding others from a group, manipulating friendships, sending threatening E-mail; (e) *Sexual Harassment*: A form of bullying in which the intent is to demean, embarrass, humiliate, or control another person on the basis of gender or sexual orientation.

Bullying is present in most schools in the country and has been reported to impact (to some extent) as many as 70% of students (Canter, 2005). Students of all ages and grade levels may experience the problems that bullying creates (Acre, 2001; Roberts, 1988). It is all too often symptomatic of the aggressive way in which young people interact with each other in our society (Melton et al., 1998). Every school should recognize the extent of bullying and take steps to stop it. When bullying is ignored or downplayed, students suffer ongoing torment and harassment. It can cause lifelong damage to both victims and those who bully. A school's failure to deal with bullying endangers the safety of all its students by allowing a hostile environment to interfere with learning. There is evidence that school interventions can dramatically reduce the incidence of bullying. We need to know which interventions really work; with this information, school officials can make the appropriate decisions about suitable programs designed to reduce and eliminate this serious problem. Dealing effectively with bullying is one means of improving school climate, maximizing achievement, and curbing the tide of violent behaviors in our schools.

LITERATURE REVIEW

History of Bullying Research

Bullying has received research attention only since the 1980s when Olweus (1991; 1993), a Norwegian researcher, began to study this matter. At that time, a strong societal interest in bully/victim problems, emerged in Scandinavia.

School officials in Scandinavia did not take serious action against bullying until a newspaper report in 1982 revealed that three young adolescent boys from Norway had committed suicide because of severe bullying by peers (Olweus, 1993). This event triggered national interest in bully/victim problems prompting a study in which data were obtained from 140,000 students in 715 schools (Olweus, 1991). The results suggested that 15% of children in Norwegian schools were involved in bullying from time to time or more frequently. About 94% of the students were classified as victims while 6% were classified as bullies (Olweus, 1991).

Nature and Prevalence of Bullying

Following Olweus' (1993, 1991) groundbreaking research in Scandinavia, a number of other researchers studied the prevalence of bullying. In England, Stephenson and Smith (1987) found that 7% of their samples were victims of bullying, 10% were bullies, and 6% were both bullies and victims. Whitney and Smith (1993) reported that 10% of students in their sample were bullied at least once a week. In Australia, Rigby and Slee (1991) asked respondents to identify what percentage of their class was being picked on a lot by other students. The median percent per class was 10.6% for girls and 11% for boys. In another study, Slee (1995) noted that 26% of the sample was bullied once a week or more.

Perry, Kusel, and Perry (1988) observed the rate of peer victimization in the United States to be about 10%. In a Canadian study in Toronto, 8% of respondents reported being bullied weekly or more often (Ziegler & Rosenstein-Manner, 1991). In a recent article, Christie (2005) reported that bullying among 12–18-year-old students had risen from 5% in 1999 to 7% in 2004. Christie also noted that a National Center for Educational Statistics 2000 report indicated that 29% of schools considered bullying to be the single most problematic discipline issue.

Gender of Bullies and Victims

Bullies tend to be boys, either in groups or as individuals (O'Moor & Hillery, 1989; Hazier, Hoover, & Oliver, 1992). Individual boys, groups of boys, and mixed groups seem to be perpetrators of bullying in about equal numbers (Ziegler & Rosenstein-Manner, 1991). Bullying by females should not be dismissed and there is evidence that its frequency is growing (Christie, 2005).

Findings on the gender of victims of bullying are mixed. Some report that the number of boys and girls being victimized by bullies is about the same (Slee, 1995), while others have found that more boys are bullied (Rigby & Slee, 1991). For example, O'Moore and Hillery (1989) observed that 12.5% of boys and 5.6% of girls were frequently bullied. In similar research, boys were reported as victims 73% of the time and girls 27% of the time (Hazier, Hoover, & Oliver, 1992). Thus, various studies support the notion that boys are bullied significantly more often than girls.

Age of Bullies

Bullies most often tend to victimize students who are the same age since they are less often with younger students (Boulton & Underwood, 1992; Whitney & Smith, 1993). Most bullies were in the same grade and same class as the victims, followed by the same grade and a different class and, lastly, in a higher grade. Bullies were generally peers of the victim—they were the same age and in the same grade or class. In general, bullies victimize students with whom they spend time and know well.

Age of Victims

Bullying generally was highest in the youngest age groups included in most samples and declined with age (Rigby & Slee, 1991; Ziegler & Rosenstein-Manner, 1991; Boulton & Underwood, 1992). However, the percentage of bullies at each age remains relatively constant for both genders through-out the age range. Why is this? Is it that older children experience less aggression or have come to terms with it and can cope with it? Sharp and Smith (1994) suggest two main reasons for this developmental observation: (1) the number of older pupils with opportunities to bully at low risk to themselves decreases with age and (2) potential victims become more socially skilled and can thus avoid bullies.

Types of Bullying

The most frequent type of bullying reported is teasing and name calling, followed by hitting and kicking, and threats (Stephenson & Smith, 1989; Sharp & Smith, 1994; Hoover, Oliver, & Hazier, 1992). Borg (1998) observed that boys are generally more violent and destructive in their bullying than are girls, making greater use of physical means of bullying. Girls tend to use more covert and subtle forms of harassment, including rumor-spreading, malicious gossip and manipulation of friendships (e.g., depriving another girl of her best friend). Other research corroborates these findings (Rivers & Smith, 1994; Whitney & Smith, 1993; Siann, Callaghan, Lockhart, & Rawson, 1993).

Where Bullying Occurs

Various authors have noted that there is much more bullying in school than there is on the way to and from school (Olweus, 1993; Ziegler & Rosentstein-Manner, 1991). Within the school itself, the playground is the most common setting for bullying, followed by the hallways, classrooms, lunchrooms, and washrooms (Siann et al., 1993; Whitney & Smith, 1993).

Motivation for Bullying

Hazier, Hoover, and Oliver (1992) reported that the five highest rated items that motivate boys to bully were "didn't fit in," "physically weak," "short-tempered," "who their friends were," and "the clothes they wore," (p. 21). The five items rated highest by girls were "didn't fit in," "facial appearance," "cried/ was emotional," "overweight," and "good grades." Hazier et al. (1992) asked students who were bullied what they believed the reasons were for their victimization. A number of reasons were offered, including favoritism, not being part of the in-group, how they acted, what they said, who their friends were, religion, size, and academic or social shortcomings. Ziegler and Rosenstein-Manner (1991) asked participants in their sample why students (including themselves, if applicable) bully other students. The reason identified most often was the desire to feel powerful, followed by a desire for attention.

Other research points to familial factors. Bullies often come from families where parents use more physical forms of discipline, which may be coupled with parents who are rejecting and hostile or overly permissive (Duncan, 1999). It may be that some school bullies are in fact victims at home. It has also been suggested that bullies are from families with child-parent relationship difficulties, family and marital difficulties, as well as financial and social problems (Nansel et al., 2001; Kumpulainen, Rasanen, & Henttonen, 1998). Familial factors may also predispose children to being bullied. Some victims of bullying come from highly protected backgrounds, making it harder for them to be assertive and causing them to feel more anxious and insecure in their peer relations (Sharp & Smith, 1994).

Bullying and Students with Special Needs

Research indicates that children with special educational needs are overrepresented as victims of bullying, especially on a frequent basis (Whitney, Nabuzoka, & Smith, 1992). The studies noted that while 25% of their sample of mainstream students were bullied, 67% of the special needs students were bullied, and those with moderate difficulties more so than those with mild difficulties. In a sample of adults who stammered as children, 59% reported that they were bullied at least once a week (Mooney & Smith, 1995). Almost all of the respondents indicated that the nature of the bullying was related to their disability.

Profile of Victims

A consistent profile of bullying victims has emerged from the literature. Victims of bullying tend to be physically smaller, more sensitive, unhappy, cautious, anxious, quiet, and withdrawn than other children (Byrne, 1993; Hoover, Oliver, & Hazier, 1992). Most victims of bullying can be termed "passive" or "submissive" victims (Olweus, 1993). They are generally insecure and non-assertive, and react by withdrawing and crying when attacked by other students. In this sense, they are vulnerable to being victimized; bullies know these students will not retaliate (Salmivalli, Karhunen, & Lagerspetz, 1996). A less common profile, the "provocative victim," has also been described. This type of victim exhibits a combination of both anxious and aggressive traits, and sometimes provoke classmates into victimizing them by their overactive and irritating behavior (Olweus, 1993).

Perry, Kusel, and Perry (1988) found that students' victimization scores were negatively correlated with peer acceptance and positively correlated with peer rejection; however, this result does not indicate whether peer rejection preceded victimization, or victimization preceded peer rejection. Craig and Pepler (2000) observed that victims of bullying tended to be victimized repeatedly over time, having established themselves in the role of victim. Being bullied creates a vicious cycle. These students tend to feel badly about themselves which predisposes them to being bullied. This, in turn, makes them feel worse about themselves and thus vulnerable to even more victimization.

Profile of Bullies

Less is known about the profile of the "typical" bully. Bullies are usually loud and assertive, but not necessarily the largest student in the class. Some bullies are more uncontrolled than other students, and may tend not to abide by social rules. In a survey of teachers, Byrne (1993) found that bullies were generally seen as more hostile and aggressive, showing less restraint than other students. However, more recent research has suggested that bullies may actually be the popular and self-confident students—the "cool" kids—and are not necessarily being targeted by intervention programs (Nudo, 2004).

Duncan (1999) discussed two possible conceptualizations of the bully. One is a student who is vicious and uncaring, and may be the child of a dysfunctional family. This type of bully has an aggressive temperament and is hostile in peer relationships (Kaltiala-Heino, Rimpela, & Rimpela, 2000). The second view suggests that some bullies are in fact members of a group that gains strength by harassing vulnerable peers who are not members of their group. The bullying may or may not be malicious in intent, and the members falsely reassure themselves that no real harm is being done.

Responses to Bullying

Boulton and Underwood (1992) asked students how often other students tried to stop bullying, to which the most common response was "sometimes" (41%), "almost never" (16%), "almost always" (12%), and "did not know" (31%) (p. 79). When asked what they themselves did when they saw another student being bullied, the most common response was that they try to help in some way, think they ought to help, or should not get involved. Whitney and Smith (1993) asked participants if other students tried to stop bullying. Half of middle-school pupils and more than one-third of secondary-school pupils indicated that other students did intervene.

For some students, witnessing bullying episodes may encourage them to participate in such activities. For example, Craig and Pepler (200) reported that when students in their sample intervened, it was in an anti-social or aggressive manner. Ziegler and Rosenstein-Manner (1991) reported that one-third of the students surveyed indicated that they might join others in bullying a student they did not like. Thus, witnessing bullying may influence students to imitate bullying behaviors.

Hazier, Hoover, and Oliver (1992) asked participants who saw themselves as victims to rate the responses of school officials to bullying. The majority of victims indicated that officials responded poorly. When students were asked to indicate how frequently teachers intervened to stop bullying, their replies were never to seldom. In other research, a majority of students believed that teachers either sometimes or almost always intervened in bullying (Whitney & Smith, 1993). These results may provide some insight as to why some students do not report incidents of bullying to teachers or other adults. Not only is there concern about the possibility of retaliation, but experience may have taught them that adults are not interested or experience may have taught them that adults are not interested or be inconsistent about their willingness to intervene. On the other hand, it should be noted that teachers may not be responding to bullying because they are unaware of its extent. In particular, verbal and indirect forms of bullying are less obvious and often go undetected by teachers.

Teachers' Perceptions of Bullying

Ziegler and Rosenstein-Manner (1991) observed that teaches were less aware of bullying than were students in terms of its prevalence. They believed that some bullying was in the form of hitting, kicking, or teasing of victims. Teachers saw most bullying taking place on the playground, followed by hallways, classrooms, and lunchrooms, which is similar to their students' perceptions. Teachers indicated that they and other officials intervened often and more than three times as often as did students (Craig & Peplar, 2000).

Siann, Callaghan, Lockhart, and Rawson (1993) and Byrne (1993) found that teachers' description of the prevalence of bullying was similar to that of students, suggesting that 10% of the students in their classes were involved in bully/victim problems. The majority of bullies and victims were boys. Teachers indicated that 27% of the victims and 33% of the bullies were receiving remedial education of one form or other (Siann et al., 1993).

Psychological and Physical Outcomes of Bullying

The tendency to be victimized by bullies has been commonly associated with low self-esteem, shyness, and feelings of isolation (O'Moore & Kirkham, 2001); Rigby & Slee, 1993). A relationship has also been observed between the tendency to bully and depression in both males and females (Seals, 2003; Slee, 1995). Increased fear and anxiety may become an everyday part of the lives of the students who are bullied, as they go to great lengths to avoid bullies and the places they frequent (Seals, 2003); Mooney & Smith, 1995). Other authors have observed that victims of bullying had lower scores on social acceptance, scholastic competence, and global self-worth than non-bullied students (Mouttapa et al., 2004).

In terms of somatic complaints, bullied students were three to four times more likely to experience health issues such as headaches, gastric distress, and insomnia (Salmon & West, 2000; Kumpulainen, Rasanen, & Henttonen, 1998; Nansel et al., 2001). All of these studies support the view that both bullies and their victims are at risk for psychological and physical problems, and that these problems can have long-lasting consequences.

MODEL INTERVENTIONS

Dillon and Lash (2005) describe general strategies for an anti-bullying program. The first step is for the school to administer a student survey to determine which students bully and where they do so. A plan of action can then be developed to address the issue. The plan should include training in social skills to help bullies, victims, and bystanders learn how to combat this problem. In particular, bystanders are usually at a loss as to what to do when they encounter bullying. They also may be afraid of becoming a victim.

Another strategy is for teachers to set aside class time for discussions with students about the problem of bullying. Students need to learn the behavior that is expected of them and understand that they do have choices as to how they behave. For example, bullies can learn how to have their needs met in more positive ways, while victims can learn how to avoid bullying by being more assertive. Students can be taught that it is always appropriate and indeed necessary to report incidents of bullying. Of course, the school should strive to create a climate in which students who do report will not be threatened or face retaliation (Dillon & Lash, 2005). Role play sessions can be used to give students a chance to practice skills for effective bullying controls. It is hoped that students can translate these skills to everyday life situations. What is certain is that bullying will not magically disappear.

In terms of a more systemic approach, Dounay (2005), a policy analyst for the Education Commission of the States, has provided a list of recommendations for developing a comprehensive anti-bullying program. It has been adopted in several states. For example, Vermont House Bill 629 (2005) requires the State Education Commissioner to distribute a model school plan for student discipline. This plan focuses on the following:

(a)   Understand that bullying is a dangerous and disrespectful behavior that will not be tolerated;
(b)   Enable parents or guardians of students to file reports of suspected bullying;
(c)   Enable students to anonymously report acts of bullying to school officials;
(d)   Require teachers who witness acts of bullying to report them to school administrators;
(e)   Require school officials to investigate all reports (written or anonymous) of bullying;
(f)   Include a school intervention plan to deal with bullying;
(g)   prohibit bullying in the student handbook;

(h) Require the school to notify the parent or guardian of a student who bullies about possible responses and consequences;

(i) Require the school to notify the parent or guardian of a bullied victim of the actions taken to prevent further incidents;

(j) require the school to collect data on reported and verified bullying incidents and make this data available to the general public.

The Vermont Model recognizes that bullying is an all too common behavior that, if ignored, can create serious problems. Thus, the real solution to bullying in schools depends on collaborative action from school officials, parents, students, and the community at large. Such actions may be the only effective means of ending this cycle of abuse and violence in our schools.

REFERENCES

Acre, R. (2001). *"Kids rate bullying and teasing as big problem."* Retrieved 10-15-06 from www.cnn.com/2001/U.S./03/08.

Borg, M. G. (1998). The emotional reactions of school bullies and their victims. *Educational Psychology*, 18, 433–435.

Boulton, M. J., & Underwood, K. (1992). Bully/victim problems among middle school children. *British Journal of Educational Psychology*, 62, 73–87.

Byrne, B. (1993). Coping with bullying in schools. *Irish Journal of Psychology*, 12(3), 342.

Canter, A. S. (2005). Bullying at school. *Principal*, 85(2), 42–45.

Christie, K. (2005). Chasing the bullies away. *Phi Delta Kappan*, 86(10), 725–726.

Craig, W., & Pepler, D. (2000). *Making a difference in bullying*. LaMarsh Research Program, Report Series: Report No. 60. LaMarsh Centre for Research on Violence & Conflict Resolution. Toronto: York University.

Dillon, J. C., & Lash, R. M. (2005). Redefining and dealing with bullying. *Momentum*, 36(2), 36–37.

Donahue, M. C. (2004). *Back off, bullies! Current Health*, 30(8), 13–15.

Dounay, J. (2005). *State anti-bullying statutes*. Denver, CO: Education Commission of the States.

Duncan, R. (1999). Maltreatment by parents and peers: The relationship between child abuse, bully victimization, and psychological distress. *Child Maltreatment*, 19, 45–56.

Hazier, R. J., Hoover, J. H., & Oliver, R. (1992). What kids say about bullying. *The Executive Educator*, Nov., 20–22.

Hoover, J. H., Oliver, R. L., & Hazier, R. J. (1992). Bullying: Perceptions of adolescent victims in the Midwestern U.S.A. *School Psychology International*, 13, 5–16.

Kaltiala-Heino, R., Rimpela, M., & Rimpela, R. (2000). Bullying at school: An indicator of adolescents at risk for mental disorders. *Journal of Adolescence*, 23, 661–674.

Kumpulainen, K., Rasanen, E., & Henttonen, I. (1998). Bullying and psychiatric symptoms among elementary school-aged children. *Child Abuse & Neglect*, 22, 705–717.

Melton, G. B., Limber, S., Flerx, V., Cunningham, P., Osgood, D. W., Chambers, J., Henggler, S., & Nation, M. (1998). *Violence among rural youth*. Final report to the Office of Juvenile Justice & Delinquency Prevention.

Mooney, S., & Smith, P. K. (1995). Bullying and the child who stammers. *British Journal of Special Education*, 22(1), 24–27.

Mouttapa, M., Valent, T., Gallaher, P., Rohrbach, L. A., & Unger, J. B. (2004). *Social network predictors of bullying and victimization. Adolescence*, 39, 315–335.

Nansel, T. R., Overpeck, M., Pilla, R. S., Ruan, W. J., Simons-Morton, B., & Scheidt, P. (2001). Bullying behaviors among U.S. youth: Prevalence and association with psychosocial adjustment. *Journal of the American Medical Association*, 285, 2094–2100.

Nudo, L. (2004). Fighting the real bullies. *Prevention*, 56(11), 123–124.

Olweus, D. O. (1991). Bully/victim problems among school children: Basic effects of a school-based intervention program. In D. Pepler & K. Rubin (Eds.), *The development and treatment of childhood aggression* (pp. 411–448). Hillsdale, NJ: Erlbaum.

Olweus, D. O. (1993). Bullying at school. *Maiden*, MA: Blackwell Publishers.

Owlets, D. (1993). *Bullying in schools*. National Association of State Boards of Education Policy Update H-10.

O'Moore, A. M., & Hillery, B. (1989). Bullying in Dublin schools. *Irish Journal of Psychology*, 10, 426–441.

O'Moore, M., & Kirkham, C. (2001). Self-esteem and its relationship to bullying behavior. *Aggressive Behavior*, 27, 269–283.

Pepler, D. J., & Craig, W. M. (1995). About bullying: Understanding this underground activity. *Orbit*, 25(3), 32–34.

Perry, D. G., Kusel, S. J., & Perry, L. C. (1988). Victims of peer aggression. *Developmental Psychology*, 24, 807–814.

Rigby, K., & Slee, P. T. (1991). Bullying among Australian school children: Reported behavior and attitudes to victims. *Journal of Social Psychology*, 13(5), 615–627.

Rivers, I., & Smith, P. K. (1994). Types of bullying behavior and their correlates. *Aggressive Behavior*, 20, 359–368.

Roberts, M. (1988). Schoolyard menace. *Psychology Today*, Feb., 54–56.

Salmivalli, C., Karhunen, J., & Lagerspetz, K. M. J. (1996). How do victims respond to bullying? *Aggressive Behavior*, 22, 99–109.

Salmon, G., & West, A. (2000). Physical and mental health issues related to bullying in schools. *Current Opinion in Psychiatry*, 13, 375–380.

Seals, D. (2003). Bullying and victimization: Prevalence and relationship to gender, grade level, ethnicity, self-esteem, and depression. *Adolescence*, 38, 735–747.

Sharp, S., & Smith, P. (Eds.). (1994). *Tackling bullying in your schools*. New York: Routledge.

Siann, G., Callaghan, M., Lockhart, K., & Rawson, L. (1993). Bullying: Teachers' views and school effects. *Educational Studies*, 19(3), 307–321.

Slee, P. T. (1995). Peer victimization and its relationship to depression among Australian school children. *Personality & Individual Differences*, 18, 57–62.

Smith, P. K., & Thompson, D. A. (1991). *Practical approaches to bullying*. London: David Fulton Conference on Violence in Schools & Public Policies.

Stephenson, P., & Smith, D. (1987). *Practical approaches to bullying*. London: David Fulton Publishers.

Vermont House Bill 629. (2005). *State Commissioner's Model School Plan for Student Discipline*. Retrieved on 10-25-06 from www.leg.state.vt.us/docs/legdoc.cfm?url=/.

Whitney, I., Nabuzoka, D., & Smith, P. K. (1992). Bullying in schools; Mainstream and special needs. *Support for Learning*, 7(1), 3–7.

Whitney, I., & Smith, P. K. (1993). A survey of the nature of bullying in junior/ middle and secondary schools. *Educational Research*, 35(1), 3–25.

Ziegler, S., & Rosenstein-Manner, M. (1991). *Bullying at school: Toronto in an international context*. ERIC Document Reproduction Service (ED No 328848).

Globalization and American Education

By William Merriman and Augustine Nicoletti

ABSTRACT: Globalization is a potent force in today's world. The welfare of the United States is tied to the welfare of other countries by economics, the environment, politics, culture, information, and technology. This paper identifies the implications of globalization for education, presents applications of important aspects of globalization that teachers can use in the classroom, and gives recommendations to promote and improve global education.

How would you like your child to be tutored by someone in Cochin, India? This is the reality of today's world. A 14-year-old student in Chicago is tutored in mathematics via the Internet by an Indian tutor in Cochin who is employed by an India-based tutoring company (George and Irvine 2005). This example shows the direction the world is taking in the 21st century. Some call this movement globalization. According to Baylis and Smith (2001, 7), globalization means "the process of increasing interconnectedness between societies such that events in one part of the world more and more have effects on peoples and societies far away." Albrow (1990) indicated that globalization refers to the processes by which the peoples of the world are incorporated into a single-world society or global society. Friedman (2005) referred to today's world as being flat, without borders, with instant communication, and open financial markets.

Forms of globalization can be linked to earlier times, but the emergence of a dominant and rapidly changing global society can be traced to the end of World War II. Table 1 highlights significant late 20th century events that have contributed to today's globalization.

The topics of globalization and global awareness are important for 21st century education. Many American educators recognize that the purpose of education is to develop good citizens and productive workers for the future. The question for American educators today is, "For what kind of future should American schools prepare students?" The future of the United States seems to be connected to globalization in that the welfare of the United States is tied to the welfare of other countries by economics, the environment, politics, culture, information, and technology. Therefore, a contemporary curriculum in American schools must have a global perspective.

Table 1. Twentieth Century Significant Globalization Events

Year	Technology	Financial	Informational	Political
1945		Wal-Mart® opens its first store.		The formation of the United Nations.
1946	Construction of the first designed computer.			
1950	Expansion of the TV in American households.			
1955		The first McDonald's® restaurant opens.		
1957	Launch of Sputnik.	Issuance of the first Eurocurrency loan.		Advent of intercontinental ballistic missiles.
1962			Launch of the first communication satellite.	
1963		Issuance of the first Eurobond.		
1966			First photograph of the Earth from outer space.	
1969	Creation of the first multisite computer network (ARPANET).			
1971		Establishment of the first wholly electronic stock exchange (NASDAQ).		
1976			Launch of the first direct broadcast satellite.	
1977	The first commercial use of fiber optic cables. Creation of the SWIFT system for electronic interbank fund transfers world wide.			
1989				The collapse of the Berlin Wall.
1991	Introduction of the World Wide Web.			
1995			Netscape® goes public.	

© Scholte. Used with permission.

Global education as part of the curriculum in American schools is not a new idea. Brameld (1970), an educational philosopher who formulated the basic principles of the reconstructionist philosophy of education, called for a close relationship between education and culture to help identify and deal with the problems of society. Thomas (1994, 72) described Brameld's ideas on global education as "fundamental changes [in society and its institutions] that are guided by broad social goals or ends. One such goal is the creation of a new world order. Beyond the present nation states, reconstructionists stand for a new world community of nations. In the present interdependent world, problems must be shared on a global scale. Perhaps Brameld's most important contribution to global education was his recognition of common purposes and strivings among people of every race and nationality."

As Brameld (1970) was to the philosophical underpinning of global education, Lee Anderson (1979) was to the practical aspects of implementing global education in American schools. Anderson, a professor at Northwestern University in the Department of Political Science and the School of Education and Social Policy, wrote extensively between 1960 and 1990 about defining global education and implementing it in the curricula of American schools. In 1979, Anderson published Schooling and *Citizenship in a Global Age: An Exploration of the Meaning and Significance of Global Education*, a work that made a strong argument for globalizing American education.

Based on the ideas of Brameld (1970) and Anderson (1979), educators in the 1980s implemented global education into the school curriculum (Sadker and Sadker 1994). At that time, global education had not been fully embraced and was a low priority because of other demands on school curricula from school reform movements. Global education in the 1980s included topics such as emerging technology, conflict resolution and peace, ecological issues, and cultural tolerance (Sadker and Sadker 1994). New York State's approved global studies curriculum in the 1980s included issues such as terrorism, population, war and peace, human rights, hunger and poverty, world trade and finance, environmental concerns, political and economic refugees, economic growth and development, and determination of political and economic systems (Osborne, Kime, and O'Donnell 1998).

In the 1990s, educators spoke about the need for children to develop global awareness, or the recognition of people's connections to other countries and peoples of the world (McNergney and Herbert 1998). This awareness was believed to be important, according to Tye and Tye (1992), because the welfare of the United States is tied to the welfare of other countries by economics, the environment, politics, culture, and technology. Global education in the 1990s, however, faced many obstacles such as limited teachers' time, disbelief in the importance of a global perspective in education, and a lack of leadership to promote or advance global education (McNergney and Herbert 1998). Global education in the 1990s included topics such as threats to the environment, immigration, reorganization of political alliances, advances in commu¬nication technology, and the growth of nongovernmental organizations (McNergney and Herbert 1998).

Over the past two decades, American educators have begun to think more globally and have encouraged their students to do the same. Curricular changes toward a more global perspective have been slow to evolve, however, because limited classroom time is already devoted to existing curricula, standardized testing, and meeting federal and state mandates. Furthermore, many school districts lack leadership to support and promote global education. The importance of global education, nonetheless, has been given a major boost by Friedman (1999, 2005), a journalist and media commentator, who has written extensively on globalization. Many implications for American education can be derived from Friedman's work and from ideas for global education and awareness from the 1980s and 1990s.

IMPLICATIONS OF GLOBALIZATION ON EDUCATION

Value placed on education in various countries. Friedman (2005) examined countries that are successful in the global marketplace and those that are less successful. Friedman (2005, 332–33) stated, "Another of these intangible things [separating the have and have-not nations] is how much your culture prizes education." Where does the United States stand on how it values education? Comparisons between the United States and other countries on several aspects of education may indicate the worth of education in America's eyes.

In the United States, most school districts require 36 weeks of instruction per year, whereas many other countries, such as the Czech Republic (41 weeks) and Denmark (40.6 weeks), require more (Organization for Economic Co-operation and Development [OECD] 2005a). Salaries for teachers with 15 years of experience are greater in Luxembourg, the Netherlands, Germany, Switzerland, Belgium, and Korea than in the United States (OECD 2005b). Average class sizes in many of these same countries are smaller than in the United States (OECD 2005c). Many countries, such as Sweden, Norway, and New Zealand, spend a higher percentage of their gross domestic product on education than does the United States (OECD 2005d). If the United States wants to maintain its leadership among independent nations, it must reexamine the value of education to its citizens. Factors such as proper funding of all schools (public, private, urban, suburban, and rural), the importance of well-qualified and well-paid teachers, and student learning and performance must be closely monitored.

Mathematics and science proficiency. Friedman (1999) credited globalization for the democratization of three areas: technology, information, and finance. Today's workers must have technological skills and information literacy. Students should receive an education that enables them to gain sufficient levels of reading, mathematical, and scientific literacy. Student performance measures in 29 OECD member countries on combined reading, scientific, and mathematical literacy scales indicated that U.S. students rank 16th on the combined reading literacy scale, 23rd on the mathematics literacy scale, and 19th on the scientific literacy scale (OECD 2003). In *Findings From IEA's Trends in International Mathematics and Science Study of the Fourth and Eighth Grades* (Mullis et al. 2004), mathematics performance assessment for eighth-grade males ranked the United States 8th out of 13 countries and, for eighth-grade females, 7th out of 13 countries. Science performance assessment for eighth-grade males and females ranked the United States 6th out of 13 countries (OECD 2005b).

Has American technological and scientific leadership slipped as we start the 21st century? As many American schools struggle to find new mathematics and science teachers (Keller 2004), our nation must determine what must be done to keep our technological and scientific edge and to improve the mathematics and science performance scores of American schoolchildren. If we do not address these issues, American workers will be less competitive in the global marketplace. This fear has led the National

Academies, a U.S. Congress-created advisory organization, to call for federal initiatives costing $10 billion a year to reverse America's decline in scientific and technological competitiveness—including many initiatives aimed at K-12 schooling (Viadero 2005).

Environmental education. American corporations use raw materials from all over the world to produce their products. To be competitive in the global marketplace, American corporations try to find the cheapest workforce and production facilities, regardless of location. For example, to produce a simple desktop computer, Dell procures nearly 4,500 parts from 300 international suppliers (Lynn 2005). Flextronics, an electronics supplier and manufacturer, has plants at 100 sites in 27 countries (Lynn 2005). This global spread of industrialization brings prosperity to a greater number of countries, but also raises concerns about negative environmental effects in these countries. One major concern is global warming. In an article in *The Wall Street Journal* (2005), global warming was described as follows: "The earth grew warmer by about one degree Fahrenheit in the 20th century. ... Some scientists predict that temperatures will increase by 2.5 to 10.4 degrees over the next 95 years. ... A growing scientific consensus links human activities, such as burning fossil fuels and cutting down trees, to this warming trend." Global warming is causing problematic climate changes leading to extreme weather conditions and drought.

Air pollution due to higher levels of energy consumption and greater automobile use is another major environmental concern. China has repeatedly increased its manufacturing capacity, energy usage, and automobile use (Yardley 2005). Consequently, greenhouse gas emissions, acid rain, and air quality are now important issues in that country. Other important environmental concerns that are related to globalization are depletion of natural resources, reemergence of coal and nuclear energy production, population growth, and food production capacity. These environmental issues are important for all persons on this planet. Consequently, American schoolchildren must study these issues in their classrooms to help them make informed environmental decisions as adults.

Education on global health concerns. As people grow closer due to informational resources and technological advances, they learn of health issues, concerns, and threats that can potentially affect everyone. Today, threats to our food supplies, climate changes causing crop failures and famine, mad cow disease threatening beef sources, and avian bird flu threatening poultry sources and, potentially, human health, exist (Marx 2006). Other global health threats have been and continue to be AIDS, SARS, alcohol and substance abuse, overpopulation leading to hunger and poverty, an increase in obesity in industrialized nations, the inequitable distribution of medications and vaccines, and proper medical care and insurance. Once again, these concerns are vitally important for all persons. American students must examine these health issues in their classrooms because they will affect them at some point in their lives.

Leadership for global education. Reforming American schools by overhauling the nation's educational system is necessary to meet the challenges proposed by globalization (Hart Research Associates and Winston Group 2006). According to Stacey (1992), educational reform must be anchored in reality, linked to action, comprehensive, and embraced by all. Educational reform movements require educational systems that have a fluid, specific, and unique process (Bemis and Nanus 1985). All stakeholders in educational reform must share a vision for the schools that the reform movement will change

(Markham 1999). School leaders are key players in educational reform movements. School reform is effective when a transforming leader with a clear vision has the ability to move a school organization from one cultural mind-set to another (De Pree 1992). A visionary school leader must know when to listen, speak, and learn (Palmer 1998). Changing the mind-set of students and teachers to recognize the importance of globalization requires the efforts of a visionary school leader who is committed to the importance of global education.

The implications of globalization have the potential to cause changes in curricula, and visionary school leaders must know how to appropriately move schools to meet the challenges of globalization. Examples of these challenges include thinking differently about the world situation, gathering information, committing to technology use, and helping teachers recognize the significance of globalization to the classes they teach.

Motivating American students for academic achievement. When the challenges associated with globalization are examined, the readiness of American workers and students to meet these challenges must be determined. Friedman (2005) believed that focus should be placed on the motivation or complacency of American workers and students. Studies by the OECD (2003, 2005b) cited earlier in this paper indicated that American students have fallen behind students from other industrialized nations in reading, mathematics, and science literacy. Astudy conducted by the Center for Education Reform (Hussey and Allen 2006) suggested that American students need to be more highly motivated for academic achievement. Johnson, Duffett, and Ott (2005, 15), in a study conducted for the Public Agenda, stated, "American students know that they could do more. At present, American students perform at the bare minimum to get by." American schools and teachers need to foster greater intrinsic motivation in students so that learners place a greater value on academic achievement and excellence. Do we as a nation and as individuals have the motivation to accept the challenges of our world becoming "flat," or will we be complacent and watch the workers and students of other nations surpass us with new ideas and high academic performance?

Technology needs in a global society. At a time when the world is getting smaller due to technology, American educational leaders must be asked, "Is the United States meeting the technological challenges prompted by globalization?" Some challenges that educators face today in integrating technology include funding, the digital divide among socioeconomic classes, the design and development of quality and effective educational software, and the need for ongoing professional development of the teaching force in technology. For the American educational community to keep up with global trends in technology and information, students and teachers should be abreast of the latest technologies and information sources. Students should keep current on information access, electronic resources, and social software. For teachers, up-to-date computer skills in word processing, record and grade keeping, researching, e-mailing, Internet surfing, distance education, and curriculum sources and development are essential (Parkay and Stanford 2003). With a population of nearly 300 million people in the United States—of which an estimated 68.7 percent are Internet users (United States Department of Commerce 2005)—educators must determine how to channel this Internet usage and knowledge into promoting greater awareness and understanding of globalization and its effects. The applications section of this article serves to answer this question.

America's response to global economics. In an address to members of the International Monetary Fund, deRato (2005) indicated that the United States has been one of the driving forces behind the unprecedented growth of the global marketplace. In that same speech, deRato also noted that India and China's escalating economic growth rates are challenging not only the United States, but also other Western nations, for a larger share of global markets. What does this reconfiguration of the global marketplace mean for future jobs in the United States, particularly given the number of American companies that are outsourcing jobs to subsidiaries in countries such as India and China? For example, computer giant Dell now outsources technical support to Indian companies. Because education and jobs are intrinsically linked, what must the educational system do to approach the outsourcing problem with a proactive attitude? Friedman (2005) unequivocally suggested that the educational system must do a better job in preparing individuals to become specialists in their chosen fields. Educators need to assess and address curricular changes that will maximize students' abilities to compete with students from India and China. Individuals already in the employment ranks must retool themselves to stay ahead of the ongoing and shifting demands created by globalization.

APPLICATIONS OF GLOBALIZATION IN THE CLASSROOM

Aspects of globalization have many applications to K-12 curricula and pedagogy. One way to structure the important aspects of globalization was suggested by Kniep (1989, 538), who recommended four domains of student inquiry:

- *Human values:* Universal values shared by humanity as well as the diverse values of various groups.
- *Global systems:* Emphasis on global systems and an interdependent world, including economy, ecology, politics, and technology.
- *Global issues and problems:* Investigating worldwide concerns and challenges, including peace and security, environmental issues, and human rights.
- *Global history:* The evolution of universal and diverse human values, the history of global systems, and the roots of global problems.

Human values and global peace. In today's global society, peace among nations and promotion of human rights are major concerns. The United Nations (2007), an organization of 192 member nations, promotes peace as affirmed in the preamble to its charter, "We the peoples of the United Nations [are] determined to practice tolerance and live together in peace with one another as good neighbors and to unite our strength to maintain international peace." In addition to the promotion of peace and tolerance, the United Nations' charter also promotes fundamental human rights, the equality of men and women, and justice.

Today's students see threats to peace and human rights in news stories dealing with wars in Iraq and Afghanistan, the mistreatment of prisoners, and the development of nuclear weapons by Iran and North Korea. Students discuss these international conflicts and the abuse of human rights in their classrooms. In addition to acquiring knowledge of these international situations, students must think about the values, attitudes, customs, and cultures of the peoples in the countries involved.

How can teachers teach and demonstrate universal human values to promote global peace and understanding? Teachers can review models of values education such as Kirschenbaum's (1992) Comprehensive Values Education. They can examine Web sites of organizations that promote world peace, such as the United Nations Children's Fund (*www.unicef.org*) and the United Nations Educational, Scientific and Cultural Organization [UNESCO] (*http://portal.unesco.org*) to find material for class discussions. The Global School-Net Foundation (*www.globakchoolnet.org*) promotes collaboration and communication among school-aged children of different cultures and countries. The Southern Poverty Law Center publishes a free, biannual magazine, *Teaching Tolerance* (*www.teachingtolerance.org*), which provides articles to prompt class discussions, lesson ideas, and handouts. The Southern Poverty Law Center also has provided teachers' guides and lesson plans to accompany videos. These videos cover the American Civil Rights Movement, *Mighty Times: The Legacy of Rosa Parks* (2002) and *Mighty Times: The Children's March* (2004); and the *Holocaust, One Survivor Remembers* (1995). Finally, teachers can assign many world literature classics with human values as a central theme for reading and discussion including *Things Fall Apart* (Achebe 1995), *The Death of Ivan Ilyich* (Tolstoy 1989), *To Kill a Mockingbird* (Lee 1999), *Romeo and Juliet* (Shakespeare 2004), and *West Side Story* (Laments 1993).

Global systems: Economy, ecology, politics, and technology. Informed citizens not only need to know about their native lands, but also need information about other nations that impact their countries. For example, Americans need to know about the economy of India because many American jobs are being outsourced to that country. In a constantly changing, interdependent world, a greater emphasis on global systems, such as economics, ecology, politics, and technology, exists. Globalization and the interconnectedness of these global systems are explained well in Friedman's (1999, 2005) books, which are recommended to teachers. Where can teachers get other ideas, themes, and lessons about global systems? Several organizations have been established to foster economic education, particularly at the K-12 level, including the National Center on Education and the Economy (*www.ncee.org*) and the National Council on Economic Education [NCEE] (*www.ncee.net*). The Economic Policy Institute (*www.epinet.org*) also provides useful information on economics education. The NCEE's subgroup, the Global Association of Teachers of Economics [GATE] (*www.ncee.net/gate*), publishes an online journal, Portals, which focuses on global economics education. GATE also offers an online lesson of the month on the NCEE Web site.

American students need to be knowledgeable about global environmental issues. Teachers may want to do some background reading before preparing lessons on these issues. Two books on environmental issues are *Environment* (Raven, Berg, and Aliff 2004) and *Red Sky at Morning: America and the Crisis of the Global Environment* (Speth 2004). Many organizations have been established to foster environmental awareness and to save the planet from potential environmental disasters. Several of these organizations have online resources in English for children and young adults. The United Nations Environment Programme [UNEP] (*www.unep.org*), ENO Environment Online (*http://eno.joensuu.fi*), and the International Coalition for Children and the Environment (*www.internationalcoalition.org*)

are all excellent resources. The UNEP Web site has two sections on global environmental education for children and young adults.

International politics is another area of which American students need to be knowledgeable. Before preparing lessons on global politics, teachers may want to read *International Politics: Enduring Concepts and Contemporary Issues* (Art and Jervis 2004) and Global Politics (Ray and Kaarbo 2004). Sources of information on preparing lessons on global politics include the English-language version of the UNESCO server, *d@dalos (www.dadalos.org)*, a Web site that has a section on teaching politics. The free online magazine, The Globalist, focuses on globalization, the global economy, politics, and culture and has e-learning services for middle and high school students (*www.theglobalist.com*). *Foreign Policy* is another source of information on global politics and the global economy (*www.foreignpolicy.com*). Finally, Political Information is a targeted search engine for politics, policy, and political news (*www. politicalinformation.com*).

American students and teachers need to be skillful and knowledgeable users of technology. The Internet, World Wide Web, search engines, and e-mail have brought worldwide information and communication to anyone with a computer and online access. These technological advances have had a profound impact on international business, national and international politics, and teaching and learning. Friedman (1999, 2005) explained the effects of technology on globalization and global systems. Three books on integrating technology into the classroom and teaching are: *The Digital Classroom: How Technology Is Changing the Way We Teach and Learn* (Gordon 2000), *Integrating Educational Technology Into Teaching* (Roblyer 2004), and *Integrating Computer Technology Into the Classroom* (Morrison and Lowther 2004). An example of integrating technology into the classroom can be found in schools and classrooms that are part of the International Education and Resource Network (*www.iearn.org*), a worldwide program that allows students and teachers to work collaboratively on classroom projects and share basic cultural information through the use of the Internet and other technologies. According to Cavanagh (2006, 10), "The nonprofit global network serves 20,000 schools and youth organizations in 115 countries including 600 schools in the U.S. An estimated 1 million students, ages 5 to 19, take part every day. ... Participants channel their work through Internet forums, e-mail, and other services on the organization's Web site, (*www.iearn.org*)."

Critical global issues. American students find themselves living in a global world, and educators cannot ignore this situation. Educators have a duty and responsibility to present critical global issues that impact the world by fostering awareness in their classrooms. Global issues such as environmental challenges, the ongoing threat of war and terrorism, the discovery of new infectious diseases, the exploitation of workers, and gender discrimination need to be explored by students through creative and effective lessons. Where can teachers get information to create such lessons? Several Web sites can raise student consciousness on many of these critical global issues:

- *www.globalschoolnet.org* helps teachers link with partners in other cultures and countries for e-mail classroom pen pals and other projects.
- *xoww.unicef.org* includes lesson plans based on the State of the World's Children (United National Children's Fund 2005).

- *www.worldwatch.org* broadens people's understanding of environmental and social issues from a global perspective and impact.
- *www.globalization101.org* provides resources for educators who would like to use globalization topics in their classes. Lesson plans on various topics are given.

Several instructional strategies also may be helpful in raising global awareness:

- Create student-sponsored organizations that have as their mission intercultural and international relations.
- Create an ongoing timeline in the classroom that shows environmental milestones, catastrophic events, and scientific breakthroughs.
- Chart the origination of contemporary infectious diseases, such as AIDS and avian bird flu; their impact on victims; the spread of the diseases; and possible government reaction to combat diseases.
- Use children's literature that focuses on human rights and the state of the environment. Dr. Suess stories such as *The Sneetches* (Geisel 1961), which depicts the struggles for diversity and human rights; and *The Lorax* (Geisel 1971), which addresses environmental concerns, are both recommended.

History of global systems. The historical evolution of global systems can be traced to the development of several world cultures that became connected over a period of time through various political, religious, and social systems. Within these systems, many events contributed to the eventual interconnectedness of various cultures. These events include wars; the invention of writing; the evolution of language, the arts, and music; the establishment of trade routes; population shifts; imperialism; the development of governments and laws; and the growth of numerous religions (Halsall 2006).

For teachers of courses such as global studies or world cultures, breaking down the course material into several parts based on time frames would be a good approach. This approach can be facilitated by use of the *Internet History Sourcebooks* (Halsall 2006), located at *www.fordham.edu/halsall*, which divide global history into three periods: ancient, medieval, and modern. Within each period, several cultural pieces are presented, and links to similar Web sites are provided. The historical evolution of world cultures is addressed through categories such as war, migration, and the rise of empires. Another source for understanding the evolution of global systems is the American Forum for Global Education's Web site, *www.globaled.org*. This Web site stresses the importance of including a comprehensive course of study in the American high school social studies curriculum that focuses on cross-cultural understandings.

Teachers need to move away from the more traditional forms of cultural awareness and curricula that include food festivals and ethnic holiday celebrations and focus on global diversity and its effects on current and future American culture. Questions such as "What is culture?" and "Why is it important to learn about other cultures?" should form the basis of a global history course. The importance of studying global systems for teachers and students is to bring an understanding and awareness of how other cultures impact us and affect one another.

RECOMMENDATIONS FOR GLOBAL EDUCATION IN TODAY'S SCHOOLS

Based on the work of Friedman (1999, 2005) and Tye (1999), we believe that the following topics should form the core of global education for today's American students:

- technology and its many uses;
- human rights and tolerance;
- personal and planetary security;
- environmental and ecological concerns;
- population growth and available resources;
- economics; and
- health and wellness.

Though various sources (Sadker and Sadker 1994; McNergney and Herbert 1998; Tye 1999) have focused on the barriers to full implementation of global education, Friedman's (1999, 2005) work has sparked a new interest in understanding globalization and the need for global education. Marx (2006), a futurist who writes about trends that affect education, identified international learning as important. Marx (2006, 7) stated, "International learning [and education], including diplomatic skills, will become basic, as nations vie for understanding and respect in an interdependent world."

Global education is at a crossroads. Some states and school districts have initiated policies that foster greater attention on instruction in world history and culture, foreign language, and the interaction between the United States and other countries (Marx 2006). However, many schools still do not stress global education. To promote and improve global education, the authors recommend these strategies:

- provide greater emphasis on global education in preservice teacher training programs;
- provide more in-service education for teachers in global education;
- encourage more educational research on global education;
- advocate for foreign language requirements for all students and encourage the study of languages (e.g., Arabic, Chinese) that have not traditionally been taught in American schools;
- develop learning communities or networks across nations that enable teachers and students to interact;
- seek the assistance of international corporations and the international business community to promote and strengthen global education;
- infuse global topics in traditional courses that will help students' global awareness where the implementation of global studies is difficult due to logistical concerns.

CONCLUSION

Globalization as described in this paper is a potent force that influences the economic, political, cultural, environmental, and technological systems in the United States. Globalization is also a force to be reckoned with in American schools and classrooms. School leaders and teachers need to come to a common understanding and recognition of the implications of globalization for the classroom and curricula. Many aspects of globalization have application to the classroom, curricula, and pedagogy. As we start the 21st century, an altered mind-set with a focus on globalization is required for all involved in the American educational system to ensure that American students, as potential workers, can compete in an ever-changing, global marketplace. Our students must be prepared for global economics, information and technology, and politics. Isolationism is not viable if the United States and its people are to maintain leadership in the global arena.

REFERENCES

Achebe, C. 1995. *Things fall apart*. New York: Everyman's Library.

Albrow, M. 1990. Introduction. *In Globalization, knowledge and society: Readings from international sociology*, ed. M. Albrow and E. King, 1–5. London: Sage.

Anderson, L. 1979. *Schooling and citizenship in a global age: An exploration of the meaning and significance of global education*. Bloomington, IN: Mid-America Program for Global Perspectives in Education, Social Studies Development Center.

Art, R. J., and R. Jervis. 2004. International politics: Enduring concepts and contemporary issues, 7th ed. New York: Longman.

Baylis, J., and S. Smith. 2001. The globalization of world politics: An introduction to international relations, 2nd ed. New York: Oxford University Press.

Bemis, W., and B. Nanus. 1985. Leaders: *The strategies far taking charge*. New York: Harper & Row.

Brameld, T. 1970. *The climactic decades: Mandate to education*. New York: Praeger.

Cavanagh, S. 2006. Network sponsors worldwide sharing of curricula: Thousands of schools in more than 100 countries are tapping into iEARN. *Education Week*, February 8.

De Free, M. 1992. *Leadership jazz*. New York: Dell.

deRato, R. 2005. Press conference with Rodrigo deRato and Thomas C. Dawson, *International Monetary Fund*, December 14, Washington, D.C..

Friedman, T. L. 1999. The Lexus and the olive tree: *Understanding globalization*. New York: Farrar, Straus & Giroux.

Friedman, T. L. 2005. *The world is flat: A brief history of the twenty-first century*. New York: Farrar, Straus & Giroux.

Geisel, T. S. 1961. *The sneetches and other stories*. New York: Random House.

Geisel, T. S. 1971. *The lorax*. New York: Random House.

George, N., and M. Irvine. 2005. Tutored from afar: With help from India, math and science become a little easier for American high school students. *Trenton Times*, October 23.

Gordon, D. T., ed. 2000. *The digital classroom: How technology is changing the way we teach and learn*. Cambridge, MA: Harvard Education Letter.

Halsall, P. 2006. *Internet history sourcebooks project*. New York: Fordham University. Available at: www.fordham.edu/halsall.

Hart, P. D., Research Associates and Winston Group. 2006. *Keeping our edge: Americans speak on education and competitiveness*. Washington, D.C.: Educational Testing Service.

Hussey, J., and J. Allen. 2006. *The American education diet: Can U.S. students survive on junk food?* Washington, D.C.: The Center for Education Reform.

Johnson, J., A. Duffett, and A. Ott. 2005. *Life after high school: Young people talk about their hopes and prospects*. New York: Public Agenda.

Keller, B. 2004. Slightly higher teacher shortages reported in 2003–2004. *Education Week*, December 8.

Kirschenbaum, H. 1992. A comprehensive model for values education and moral education. *Phi Delta Kappan* 73(10): 771–76.

Kniep, W. M. 1989. Social studies within a global education. *Social Education* 50(7): 538.

Laurents, A. L. 1993. *West side story*. Oxford, England: Heinemann Educational Books.

Lee, H. 1999. *To kill a mockingbird*, 40th anniv. ed. New York: HarperCollins.

Lynn, B. C. 2005. *End of the line: The rise and coming fall of the global corporation*. New York: Doubleday.

Markham, D. J. 1999. *Spiritlinking leadership: Working through resistance to organizational change*. New York: Paulist Press.

Marx, G. 2006. Sixteen trends: Their profound impact on our future. *Alexandria*, VA: Educational Research Service.

McNergney, R. F., and J. M. Herbert 1998. *Foundations of education: The challenge of professional practice*, 2nd ed. Boston: Allyn & Bacon.

Mighty Times: The Children's March. *Southern Poverty Law Center*, 2004.

Mighty Times: The Legacy of Rosa Parks. *Tell the Truth Pictures*, 2002.

Morrison, G. R., and D. L. Lowther. 2004. Integrating computer technology into the classroom, 3rd ed. *Upper Saddle River*, NJ: Prentice Hall.

Mullis, I. V. S., M. O. Martin, E. J. Gonzalez, and S. J. Chrostowski. 2004. *Findings from IEA's Trends in International Mathematics and Science Study of the fourth and eighth grades*. Chestnut Hill, MA: International Study Center, Boston College.

One Survivor Remembers. U.S. Holocaust Memorial Museum Research Institute, 1995.

Organisation for Economic Co-operation and Development. 2003. *Programme for International Student Assessment (PISA) 2003 data se*t. Paris, France: OECD. Available at: http:llpisaweb.acer.edu.auloecd_2003loecd_pisa_data_sl.html.

Organisation for Economic Co-operation and Development. 2005a. Student learning time in and out of school (2003). Chart D1.3. *In Education at a glance 2005*. Paris, France: OECD. Available at: www.oecd.orgldataoecdl0l61l352875U.xls.

Organisation for Economic Co-operation and Development 2005b. Teachers' salaries (2003). Table D3.1. *In Education at a glance 2005*. Paris, France: OECD. Available at: www.oecd.org/dataoecdl0l59/35287577.xls.

Organisation for Economic Co-operation and Development. 2005c. Average class size, by type of institution and level of education (2003). Table D2.1. *In Education at a glance 2005*. Paris, France: OECD. Available at: vnow.oecd.org/dataoecdl0l60l352875i3.xls.

Organisation for Economic Co-operation and Development. 2005d. Expenditure on educational institutions as a percentage of GDP, for all levels of education (1990,1995, and 2002). Chart B2.1a. *In Education at a glance 2005*. Paris, France: OECD. Available at: www.oecd.org/dataoecdl2/ll/35286380.xls.

Osborne, J., S. A. Kime, and R. CDonnell. 1998. *Global studies: A review text*. New York: N and N Publishing.

Palmer, P. J. 1998. *The courage to teach: Exploring the inner landscape of a teacher's life*. San Francisco: Jossey-Bass.

Parkay, F. W., and B. H. Stanford. 2003. *Becoming a teacher*, 6th ed. Boston: Allyn & Bacon.

Raven, P. H., L. R. Berg, and J. V. Aliff. 2004. *Environment*, 4th ed. Somerset, NJ: Wiley.

Ray, J. L., and J. Kaarbo. 2004. *Global politics*, 8th ed. Boston: Houghton Mifflin.

Roblyer, M. D. 2004. Integrating educational technology into teaching, 3rd ed. *Upper Saddle River*, NJ: Prentice Hall.

Sadker, M. P., and D. M. Sadker. 1994. *Teachers, schools, and society*, 3rd ed. New York: McGraw-Hill.

Scholte, J. 2001. The globalization of world politics. In *The globalization of world politics: An introduction to international relations*, 2nd ed., ed. J. Baylis and S. Smith, 13–32, New York: Oxford University Press.

Shakespeare, W. 2004. *Romeo and Juliet*. New York: Washington Square Press.

Speth, J. G. 2004. *Red sky at morning: America and the crisis of the global environment*. New Haven, CT: Yale University Press.

Stacey, R. D. 1992. *Managing the unknowable: Strategic boundaries between order and chaos in organizations*. San Francisco: Jossey-Bass.

Thomas, T. M. 1994. Multicultural education: Reconstructionism coming of age. *Teacher Education Quarterly* 21(4): 71–78.

Tolstoy, L. 1989. *The death of Ivan Ilyich*, reprint ed. New York: Penguin Putnam.

Tye, K. A. 1999. Global education: A worldwide movement. A preview of a study of global education practices in 52 countries. *Issues in Global Education* 150:1–38.

Tye, B. B., and K. A. Tye. 1992. *Global education: A study of school change*. Albany: State University of New York Press.

United National Children's Fund. 2005. *State of the world's children*. New York: UNICEF.

United Nations. 2007. Charter of the United Nations. New York: United Nations. Available at: *www.un.org/aboutun/charter*.

Creating Inclusive Schools for Somali Immigrant Students in Midwestern Region

By Shukri Nur and Mohamed Nur-Awaleh

INTRODUCTION

Amerian public schools face the challenge to effectively educate diverse students that come from various ethnic and socioeconomic backgrounds. It appears that diversity is an ever persisting challenge that teachers and school leaders continue to encounter in terms of educating and dealing with not only diverse American born students, but also immigrant students whose values and cultures are different from those of the American mainstream culture. One challenge of diversity that American born students do not usually have to deal with to the same degree is a language barrier. Unfortunately, research indicates that most teachers are not adequately prepared to work with immigrant students that have language barriers (Nieto, 2000). School districts have tried to respond to the needs of immigrant students by either creating "New Comer" programs or integrating students into the mainstream regular classes, while providing English language instructions (Perkins, 2000).

This chapter will focus on the contact between Somali immigrant students from the war-torn country of Somalia and school principals in a city located in the Midwestern region of United States. Indeed, many Somali parents and their children continue to face challenges that include cultural and communication barriers. For instance, the most difficult issue for the schools is disrupted education due to the civil war. Some of the children grew up in the refugee camps in Kenya and never attended school during the 16 years of the civil war. Another challenge the schools face is the language barrier between the Somali students, teachers and administrators. (Schultz & Hertz, 2006). Because of the factors such as language differences, culture, education, socioeconomic difficulties, and emotional problems caused by the civil war in their country of origin; Somali immigrant parents are struggling to educate their children within the American school system.

But in spite of the serious challenges these Somali students face, they share a great deal in common with other immigrant families. Most every immigrant family experiences "acculturation stress" which involves adopting into the cultural norms of the new country into which they settle; however, some immigrants, such as the Somali students, experience challenges that include psychological traumas related to wars they have encountered in their home countries. Other challenges they face also encompass gender conflicts within the family (parents), language barriers, and economic hardships (Alitolppa-Niitamo, 2002). Somali families are prime examples of immigrants that are experiencing the "acculturation stress" which has contributed to disintegration of some immigrant families. Zhou shows that the success of the immigrant family in the new country depends on the "social capital" of the family which is the family cohesion (Zhou, 1997, p. 993). In other words, without a solid family that is socially grounded in its spirituality and values, it is overwhelmingly difficult for parents to adequately support and educate their children. Even in the cases of solid families with social and spiritual grounding, the family's potency is greatly diminished by the onslaught of the "acculturation stress." For instance, many Somali families both in United States and Europe continue to experience not only acculturation stress, but also psychological traumas and post war traumatic stress disorders. However, Alioppa-Niitamo found that education might be a mitigating factor in some Somali parents' ability to deal with the many stressors they encounter in the new country in which they settle. That is, it depends on parents' level of education, whether they are from a rural or urban background, in terms of trauma experienced and the extent to which the family's cohesion is affected by the acculturation stressor.

Despite the hardships many Somali immigrant families face in the receiving countries, Somali parents continue to emphasize formal education for their children. For instance, according Alitolppa-Niitamo (2002), Somali parents view formal education as a way to "Re-establish a sense of control over one's life and, also, to offset the turmoil of the refugee experience" (p. 279). As such, the parents view that education provides children with the skills and competency to be economically successful and to access to nationwide and international labor markets. I believe that Somali parents culturally value formal education and this even goes back to Somali nomads' emphasis on formal education. For instance, the Somali nomad would send his son or daughter from the village to the cities so that they would live with relatives or other family members in order to acquire formal education.

Given that Somali immigrant parents have the expectation that their children would be educated and retain their Islamic identity; the question then would be what are experiences of the Somali parents and children with the American public school? We believe that whenever new immigrant families settle in large numbers an area, the conventional wisdom requires that school principals and educators first build a relationship with the community and try to understand their lived experiences in order to be able to provide adequate education that meets the educational needs of the children and their parents, but is this assumption warranted?

PURPOSE OF THE CHAPTER

The aim of this chapter to explore how school principals and teachers might seek to create culturally inclusive schools that builds a partnership with Somali families. The following research questions guided this chapter:

(1)To what extent do school principals respond to the changing demographics and promote culturally inclusive school environments that connect/build partnerships between the Somali families and the schools?

(2) What does research show about school leadership responses to educating immigrant students?

METHODOLOGY AND DATA COLLECTION

This qualitative study combined aspects of convenience and purposeful sampling. It was a convenience sample because the participants were chosen from one geographical area of Midwestern region. The sample was also purposeful since personal networks were used in order to identify two to three school principals that were dealing with relatively large Somali immigrant student populations. The criteria for selecting the school principals included the number of years the principals had been dealing with Somali immigrant students, with two years being the minimum period required by the principal to be an administrator in the schools chosen for the sample.

To learn about how the school principals addressed the needs of the Somali immigrant students, and the extent to which they sought to create inclusive schools and build partnerships with the Somali families. We conducted interviews with a sampling of two elementary and one middle school principals from a city of located in the suburb of Midwestern region. We also conducted one semi-structured interview for the duration of approximately one hour with each of the participants. Semi-structured interviews provided to us with the opportunity to probe and ask a follow-up questions. A total of eleven questions were asked the participants. Some parts of the questions focused on the challenges the principals faced in dealing with Somali immigrant students and families whose values, culture and language were different from those of the administrators. The other questions were designed to solicit how the school principals addressed the needs of Somali immigrant students and also whether they created inclusive schools that established partnerships with the families.

AN OVERVIEW OF THE LITERATURE ON SCHOOL LEADERSHIP AND CULTURALLY RESPONSIVE ENVIRONMENT

There is a body of literature in which scholars that include Nieto, 2000; Ladson-Billings, 1994; Katz, 1999 all recommend that schools create a culturally inclusive environment that would in turn create new meanings for all students from diverse backgrounds. However, Riehl (2000) indicates that while 11.5

The literature on school leadership and immigrant students shows that school administrators who lacked an understanding of diversity, student cultures, and backgrounds focused more on maintaining school structures and employed the deficit model. That is, more emphasis was put on student behavior than addressing the educational needs of immigrant students and assisting the students to adjust into the school (Gardiner & Enomoto, 2006; Gitlin, Buendia, Grosland & Doumbia, 2003).

Gardiner and Enomoto (2006) conducted a study that examined six urban school principals' leadership role as multicultural administrators. The research shows that some of the school principals' responses to meeting the educational needs of diverse students involved the deficit thinking model. For instance, one administrator's perspective on educating immigrant students, demonstrates as he put it: "We have some students out of Africa right now that have basically been raised in a tent camp and don't know how to flush a toilet, how to go through a cafeteria line. Our goal is to socialize (the students) to our educational system, as well as teach them some English basic skills" (Gardiner & Enomoto, 2006, p. 570). Children from the refugee camps may not know how to flush a toilet; however, the administrator did not explain what he is doing to help the refugee children to adjust into the new school environment. Instead of focusing on the children not being able to flush the toilet, the discussion should have focused more on ways to support the children and include them. As such, from the administrator's comments, there seems to be lack of awareness of the gravity of the damage that refugee camps do to refugee children. In other words, the administrator's insensitive and culturally fraught commentary did nothing to empathize with the students and address the problem.

Furthermore, school principals that were interviewed by Gardiner and Enomoto were asked whether the curriculum attended to the needs of culturally diverse students. Some of the school principals reported that the teachers have the responsibility for incorporating multiculturalism into the curriculum. Their understanding of creating inclusive school environment (instruction, curriculum, and school symbols) involves pouring culture into the curriculum. Some of the school principals asked for clarification of what "culturally proficient instruction" is (p. 575). If some of the principals were unclear about what constitutes the criteria for culturally proficient instruction, how might the teachers be expected to accomplish this? Worse, some of the school principals interviewed by Gardner and Enomoto showed reluctance to creating a culturally inclusive school environment. School principals such as Sanders stated that multicultural leadership was not her priority, she indicated, "At this school, diversity is pretty limited. The teachers just had limited exposure. Would they be willing to learn? Sure. But I don't think the need has been there" (p. 568).

Gitlin, Buendia, Grosland, and Doumbia (2003) did a qualitative study that examined Kausanar middle school located in a middle class neighborhood. The study investigated approaches to educating immigrant and refugee students that include: Mexican, Bosnians, Somali, and Sudanese. The authors collected data on school assemblies, lunchroom, buses, and discipline policies. Findings of the research show that immigrant students were at once welcomed and marginalized at the same time by school structures and policies. For instance, the approach of the school personnel towards immigrant and refugee students revealed a perception that regarded students' languages and cultures as deficits that students had overcome in order to be successful in an American middle school. School structures that marginalized students included lack of late transportation that would have permitted immigrant children to participate in after-school activities, such as sports clubs and other after school activities.

Moreover, the findings from Gitlin et al. study show that Caucasian students influenced school assemblies. Also, lunchroom monitors ensured segregation by grouping ESL immigrant students into one area of the cafeteria. Immigrant and refugee students were also "marginalized" in school concerts. For instance, ESL students that participated in the choir during the holidays concerts, they sang about a "baby in the manager and gifts from Santa" (p. 104). The data show that the songs were not culturally relevant to the immigrant students' culture and traditions. In other words, the immigrant students were not given the stage in order for them to present some songs or plays about their cultures. The research also found compelling evidence that showed administrators' approach to Mexicans, Bosnians, Somali and Sudanese ESL students was influenced by the deficit thinking method. The approach was to reduce the perceived deficits which regarded students as devoid of social order. As one assistant principal, stated that since some of the ESL kids never attended school in their counties, he uses discipline as a socialization process, as well as, punishing kids for wrong doing. He asserted, "The ESL kids are primarily the kids that I deal with …" (Gitlin et al., p. 108). Also, the authors show that lack of understanding immigrant students complex realities, appears to have contributed to a high suspension rate of the immigrant students 35% compared to the 8% of the Caucasian students at Kausanar (p. 108). The literature points out administrators focused on addressing what they perceived to be student deficits, while neglecting diversity issues and ways to create culturally inclusive schools.

Although there is gap in the literature showing school principals' approach to educating immigrant students, Hertzberg (1998) and Katz (1999) present evidence that demonstrates school principals and teachers who have successfully fostered a caring school environment and managed to build inclusive schools were able to achieve positive student outcomes. Katz's research demonstrates that the educational needs of immigrant students requires from school principals to take an approach that transcends the provision of ESL classes. The author shows an elementary school principal's approach to educating immigrant and low-income students involved in creating "personal linkages between the school and students" (Katz, 1999, p. 498). In this case study, Katz, demonstrates Principal Collins, has successfully managed to personalize the school experience for culturally diverse students and their families. Before Collins became the principal of Rainbow, the school was failing and students engaged in ethnic conflicts. When she became the principal of Rainbow, the author reports that Collins built a healthy school climate and brought changes that included: (a) Restructuring Time and Curriculum to build Connections. Under the Restructuring and Time, Collins created groupings called "families" in which students from Kindergarten until fifth grade stayed with the same families that include the same teachers and students. This has given the students to be part of the same group; (b) to reduce the high suspension rate of students she hired student advisors to mentor students and to reinforce good behavior (Katz, 1999, p. 501).

Further, Katz reports that Collin's approach to student discipline involved "reclaiming" the students instead of resorting to the traditional student discipline such as suspensions. According to Katz, the principal provided opportunities for dialogue with the students, teachers, advisers and the parents, and this enabled them to create solutions to the discipline problems that arose. Katz notes that Collin's leadership is deeply embedded within a social and community activist approach. For instance, to increase parental involvement, she understood the obstacles parents faced and thereby accommodated them by providing them with transportation in order for them to come to the school. She also provided childcare at the school while the parents met with the teachers. Another way Collins connected multiethnic parents to the school was by promoting activities for the parents and students. For example, she created monthly events for parents and children that were tied to specific curriculum, such as family science night and family math activities as well as a literature and an art show featuring students' work. Also, she encouraged teachers to make home visits, since many parents faced economic challenges and had difficulties coming to the school.

In another case study (Senge, Cambron-McCabe, Lucas, Smith, Dutton & Kleiner, 2000), present a school that has utilized the immigrant families as a resource, in order to address certain conditions that have impeded successful student learning from immigrant families trapped in poverty in one of Miami Dade County's neighborhoods. Senge et al. present a classic case of an elementary school where 90% of the students were on free and reduced lunch, and the school was cited as a failing school in the district. The school carried out a pilot project in order to address a health issue of head lice that the children were having. A social worker was assigned to work with the families. Addressing the head lice problem led to a whole range of improvements not only in the school, but also in the community. In fact, parents began to actively become involved in the school as they were hired as paraprofessionals, tutors, and resource support positions. The homework club was managed by the parents since some of the homes did not even have electricity (p. 531). Empowering the immigrant parents had a phenomenal impact on the academic achievement of the students. For instance, there was a reduction in absenteeism and student test scores increased enormously. This case shows that when immigrant and low socioeconomic parents are empowered and provided the opportunity to actively participate in the school, and jointly determine the schooling process with the school and the community, the results can be astronomical. This case informs us that school principals' attempts to improve schools must involve a collective approach from all the stakeholders of the school.

In examining school principals' proficiency in multicultural leadership, Gardner and Enomoto (2006) found that some of the school principals in their study exhibited knowledge about multiculturalism. The authors concluded that they found a strong link between school principals who showed experience with multiculturalism and those who worked well with parents, who were able to build democratic schools, and partnerships between the school and the community. For instance, principal, Kroll, whose school had a large population of low-income students, worked with the district in order to offer high quality all-day kindergarten programs at an affordable rate. The researchers show that Kroll engaged in transformative work by partnering with Operation School Bell to fund school supplies, clothing and books for low income students. The literature demonstrates that principals who have a good understanding of the culture of social class and how socio-economic conditions in the community influence the school context are better able to meet the educational needs of the students.

Hertzberg (1998) did a study on Redwood Elementary School which had a Newcomer program designed for fourth to eighth grade immigrant and refugee students in California. Hertzberg's research involved participant-observation in which she volunteered and observed some of the teachers at Redwood. First, Hertzberg found that organizationally there was recognition of the students' backgrounds and cultures by an incorporation of students' cultural symbols into the school symbols and culture. Second, the curriculum content included students' culture. Third, apart from conducting structured interviews, Hertzberg, observed for a year, Mrs. Sobel's fourth-grade class. The researcher's findings show that the school incorporated "multicultural validation, symbols, content, and practice into the teaching" (p. 400). In addition, she found Mrs. Sobel "actively engaged the children in a cooperative and collective effort of caring. Her actions infused the teaching process with a broad social and political awareness" (Hertzberg, 1998, p. 396). Further, the school's nurturing environment can be seen from how the teacher cares for her students' wellbeing. For example, Mrs. Sobel noticed that one of her students needed dental care, she discussed the matter with the nurse and got him the dental care that the student needed. Also when she found out that another student's glasses were broken she communicated with his parents and persuaded them to get their son another pair of glasses. Mrs. Sobel provided a nurturing environment and attended to the needs of the students thus, attending to the needs of students enabled her students learn successfully.

The neighborhood/home school teachers even praised Redwood school's approach to educating immigrant kids. They advocated for a strong nurturing school environment particularly for newly arrived immigrant students as one of the neighborhood school teacher stated,

> A fourth grader can be a pretty sophisticated creature. This is a kid who may have seen some real pieces of life in his native country. There's going to be a lot of fear. What if you suddenly had to go into a situation where you didn't speak the language or understand what was going on? Well, that's an anxiety-producing situation. So the first thing you have to do is to be able diffuse that business (Hertzberg, p. 397).

In addition, the teachers in the home school indicated that students that come from Redwood often come to the home school prepared and well adjusted to the school. Those students are described to be motivated to learn and focus in class. Also, home school teachers expressed that it is an excellent idea to enroll students at Redwood. However, we wonder if the teachers' perspective is shaped by deficit model or the idea that newcomer students should first be "socialized" and "civilized" into the American way of life.

Hertzberg, indicates that the success of the students at Redwood represents how some public schools could create "positive experiences" that contribute to the educational growth of immigrant students. She contends, that for the fourth graders who move to their neighborhood schools, to sustain their educational success requires "A broader and temporally extended context. The case of Redwood, demonstrates that teachers and students are and can be agents of change ... Positive outcomes, even if occurred in small doses, are the stuff of inspiration and can provide the basis for a groundswell of activism" (p. 410). The author portrays Mrs. Sobel's work as transformative because she addressed the challenges the students faced; as a result, she contributes to an environment that enhances students self esteem and thereby fosters educational success.

PARTICIPANTS OF THE STUDY AND INFORMATION ON SCHOOLS

In this study, a total of three school principals were interviewed. The ethnicity of the three principals is Caucasian. Two of the school principals are female and the third participant is a male. Pseudonyms were used for both the participants and the schools. Lisa Anderson is the principal of North Albion Junior High, (seventh–ninth grade). The total number of students is 800. At North Albion, 70% of the students are Caucasian, 27% of are students of color including: African-Americans, Hispanic, and Somali, with the majority being Somalis. Also, 10% are ESL students, mostly new immigrant students (20% Latino, 25% Somali and 5% Asian). Anderson has been the principal of North Albion for 10 years, her total time as a principal is 30 years. Education degrees include: Masters in Educational Administration, Doctorate in Educational Leadership, Bachelor in Teacher Education, Mathematics, and Social Studies.

Tom Baldwin, is the principal of Hadrawi Elementary Charter School (K–fourth grade) in Minneapolis, Minnesota. The student population is 1200 with an ethnicity of 80% Somali, 10% Oromo (Ethiopia), and the other 10% are students of Middle Eastern origin. Baldwin has been a principal at Hadrawi Elementary for 2 years. He was previously the superintendent of a large district for a number of years. Baldwin's level of education include: Doctorate in Educational Administration, Master of Science in Special Education and Bachelor in Teacher Education.

Nancy Smith is the school principal of Mandela Elementary School in St. Paul, Minnesota. Smith has been principal at Mandela for 10 years. Her qualifications include, Advanced Certificate in Educational Administration, Master of Educational Administration and Bachelor in Teacher Education. Student demographics include: 68% of the African American, with a majority Somali born, and (Somali students are included in the African-American category); 20% are Hmong students, 5% Latino, and 7% Caucasian.

FINDINGS OF THE CHAPTER

To understand the school principals' approaches and the process of addressing Somali immigrant/refugee educational needs, we asked the school principals about the challenges they have encountered when dealing with the Somali immigrant students. All of the school principals reported that the English language barrier was a major challenge for the students and that the students primarily struggled with reading and writing. For instance, Smith stated that she had to create a language academy in each grade from first to the fourth grade levels. The findings show that all the school principals interviewed reported that they emphasized improving language proficiency for the students.

Another challenge the school leaders had to confront was the cultural barrier and lack of understanding and dialogue on the part of the schools and the Somali parents. Anderson indicated, "The initial contact with the Somali kids was difficult because they didn't have anyone to talk to with. They didn't have anyone in their own language to explain to them this is how it works at a public school in United States." Anderson seemed to imply that because of the language barrier, the students may not have had a good understanding of the expectations, the values, and the code of conduct to which the entire school adhered.

Furthermore, Anderson reported that lack of communication between the parents, teachers and students contributed to the hostility between the parents and the teachers. As such, she described the relationship between the school and the Somali parents as "very adversarial." Anderson indicated that the Somali boys were suspended frequently because they engaged in fighting more often than their classmates. The problem was aggravated by the unavailability of Somali interpreters to the parents and the school. She stated that there was anger on the part of the Somali parents and they did not understand on what grounds the school kept on suspending their kids from school. The boys would also get angry and be defiant towards the teachers. The teachers on the other hand felt that the kids had to be suspended because they broke the rules by fighting. It is evident from Anderson's account of how the students were dealt with, that there appears to be cultural dissonance and a lack of understanding on the part of the school of the students' refugee experience. It is also clear from Anderson's statements there was frustration on the part of the school principal and the teachers, and this may have been the result of lack of awareness of the experiences that the Somali children were experiencing in adjusting to American schools. Research shows that immigrant children that have witnessed civil wars experienced psychological stress and traumas not only during the war but also while being in the refugee camps. This causes the children to be distrustful and fearful of people in authority. It could also be that the children were from the refugee camps not used to school and structure, and being defiant and resisting authority may have been adaptive defense mechanisms (McBrien, 2005).

Anderson asserted that the relationship between the school and the Somali parents somewhat began to improve when a Somali community advocate, Layla Hassan intervened and began providing an interpreter to the parents and the teachers. But the school principal also reflected on her approach with the students by reevaluating her perspective and teachers' attitudes towards the Somali boys. For instance, she contended,

> I have to say with pride, that our school I think just stepped back a little bit and said, you know what we need to do! We need to be more patient. We need to figure out why these kids are acting as they do. And we need to provide some support to them so that they don't feel they need to be sort of the tough guy. Over a period of like maybe a year or two years, we worked with the teachers to make them more aware of the situation.

North Albion School demonstrates a classic example of lack of preparedness of school principals in addressing the diversity issue. In other words, Anderson's school depicts a suburban middle school that struggles with immigrant students that have cultures and languages different than the dominant middle class Anglo-Saxon culture in the suburban area.

Another challenge two of the three school principals interviewed indicated they had to confront was involving the Somali parents in the school. For instance, Anderson and Smith reported that they had to embark upon reducing the disconnection between the Somali parents and their schools. They attested that the Somali educational assistants made an enormous impact on bridging the communication gap between the parents and the teachers. Smith indicated that she hired Somali interpreters who made it possible for the parents to be able to communicate with the teachers. Also she stated that she invited a Somali community organization leader who gave workshops to the teachers about Somali culture.

Anderson also conveyed that Hussein and Mubarak (educational assistants) had a positive impact on the communication between the teachers and the parents. That the teachers depended on educational assistants to call the parents and explain to them that the students would bring home homework so that the parents would ensure that the children would do the homework. She added that Hussein and Mubarak would communicate with the families to explain to them about conferences and also provided transportation for some parents that had to attend the conferences.

SCHOOL PRINCIPAL'S APPROACHES TO ADDRESSING THE EDUCATIONAL NEEDS OF SOMALI IMMIGRANT/REFUGEE STUDENTS

The data from the interviews shows that in North Albion and Mandela Elementary School, one of the ways the school principals addressed the educational needs of Somali immigrant students was first overcoming the cultural barriers and lack of communication among stakeholders of the school. In other words, according to Anderson and Smith, once the schools and the Somali parents were on the same level of understanding, then it became possible to focus on the academics.

Furthermore, all of three principals that were interviewed, Anderson, Smith, and Baldwin identified improving the English language as responding to the Somali students' educational needs. Thus, emphasis on students' language acquisition was given a priority. For example, Baldwin explained his approach to addressing the educational needs of Somali immigrant students; he pointed out that his approach to improving English language proficiency for the Somali students involves a very detailed process in which they incorporate English as a second language into the teaching of other subjects. Baldwin explained,

> We have three specialized ESL teachers and we use a model called SAIF sheltered instruction model. We are sending our special ESL teachers to training, and then we do ongoing training with all staff on weekly bases. So we do weekly training English as a second language. We are school of 97% of students are ESL students. So we are focused on every classroom teacher being the person that has to maintain a plan and a focus on accomplishing language proficiency standards in the classroom.

It appears that the priority is given to improving English language proficiency through ESL classes. The principals were asked specific programs they designed for the Somali immigrant and refugee students. For instance, the after school tutoring program is a district program that is offered in North Albion and the two schools. However, Anderson indicated that the Support Group program, which was created by Mubarak, is unique to her school. The program provides Somali ESL students the opportunity to have a conversation about the issues and the difficulties they have with the school.

Anderson described the program as she put it: "The only thing, that I would say we do differently are the opportunity for kids to have someone from Somalia here, and Mubarak actually started to provide what we call a support group. So once or twice a week, she would meet with the boys and then on a different day talk with the girls and just find out how they are feeling about school and how things are going?" Anderson exhibits an understanding of the importance of providing immigrant students a space for conversation where the students are able to voice their concerns. As well, Hussein and Mubarak were also reported to provide support to the Somali ESL students and the teachers. They would do tutoring as they were able to give some directions in Somali language and then help the students figure it out in English.

Moreover, Anderson indicated that she established a grade eight and nine honors program, in which students of color including the Somalis are identified for a gifted program designed for minority students. Students that are placed in the program are kids who have as Anderson described,

> What we call a promise! They have promised to be good leaders, strong students … they have promised to take the advanced placement classes at the high school and to go to college. Many students in the United States that are in what we call the gifted and talented classes, the kids of color or the immigrants not included in those programs because usually it is just by test scores. But four years ago … and now this year too, we have had out of 20 kids that are in the program, we have had anywhere from 2–6 Somali kids in the program, they have just blossomed, especially the girls.

Thus, by facilitating the program and enhancing the number of Somali and other minority students in the gifted program, Anderson demonstrated an awareness of the equity concerns associated with gifted programs by including more culturally and linguistically diverse students in the gifted program.

At the Mandela school, Smith on the other hand pointed out that one of the ways she responded to the needs of Somali immigrant students was by creating programs for both the Somali ESL students and their parents. Programs that include: language academy at each grade level and the SALT program which is an afterschool program. The SALT program focuses on teaching the Somali language to the children. According to Smith, a Somali teacher and educational assistant teach the students every day after-school. Smith discussed that the Somali parents requested for the SALT program. She said, "I think partly was they [parents] didn't want their children to forget their language. And if they were younger children, they may not be even known about reading and writing Somali, this is teaching them that. Because many of the families want their culture to be retained, and so this is one way we could do that." Smith's approach to addressing the educational needs of Somali students involved providing educational services that were needed by the Somali parents and the community. As such, Smith appeared to be empathetic and thereby more receptive to the desires of the Somali parents to maintain their identity and language.

Moreover, for Smith, providing Somali language classes to the students is way of promoting a culturally inclusive school where the diverse cultures of Somali, Hmong and other cultures are equally valued. This is evident from her remarks in which she commented, "I think it is pretty inclusive of everybody, and then constantly changing. Our school has the highest Somali population of all the schools in the district. I think we have a lot more Somali programs here then other schools would have." In addition, Smith's philosophy of educating the ESL students encompassed educating the parents by proving English language classes. She indicated that there are two ESL classes offered during the regular school hours. She explained the benefits of the program to the families, "The Somali parents are learning English, as well as how to apply a job, careers, interviews and becoming a citizen. Right now this year, we have 50 parents of Somali background that are in that class." Smith seemed to use a holistic approach to addressing the needs Somali immigrant students which also involved inviting the parents into the school and proving certain programs that were vital for both of the parents and children.

The school principals were asked about their perspectives on other ways that would have been more successful to address the educational needs of Somali immigrant/refugee students. Anderson stated that she prefers the Newcomer program—specifically designed for ESL immigrant students. She expressed her preference of the Newcomer program, which is very structured and emphasizes more in-depth on teaching English language and math. She indicated that the Newcomer program would have been more appropriate for immigrant students because they would have received six hours of ESL and math instruction, as opposed to three hours of ESL English, which mainly focuses reading and math in her school. In the other three hours ESL students in her school take elective courses that include art and music. She claimed that based on her previous experience of working with other school districts that had the Newcomer program; students that spent 6 hours a day in the Newcomer program developed the beginning language skills and reached a level of conversational English where they are able to understand instruction.

On the contrary, school Principal Baldwin, declared that he found heterogeneous grouping to be a better way of educating the ESL students. He was against homogeneous grouping of ESL students, and noted that it has the tendency to abandon children permanently in one group. He explained that the kids are grouped and then regrouped so that the group is constantly changing, and students are integrated with regular students. He elucidated by saying,

> We do heterogeneous grouping … with regard to language. We also do that with our reading program, SIAF reading program which is a national program …The heterogeneous grouping is based on where children are at with understanding reading. Math, we do less grouping in the math … But the type of grouping that we would do is math concepts, we are teaching math concepts … a Somali educational assistant may take three kids in the back of the classroom and work with the three kids and put them right back in without taking them out of the classroom.

Some research supports Baldwin's reservations with the Newcomer program. His opposition to a Newcomer program partly may have to do with the research that shows the program tends to isolate new immigrant students from the rest of the regular or American born students. Also, Immigrant students that spent years in the Newcomer program did not adequately learn the English language, and the program tends to create inequity in the school (Perkins, 2000). Perhaps it depends on how the Newcomer program is used, that if it is used temporarily until the students are comfortable to understand instruction it could be appropriate. Because there is another research that demonstrates Newcomer program as successful (Kantz, 1995; Hertzberg, 1999).

Smith mentioned that she promoted dialogue between the students and the teachers—which she claimed has enormously reduced the discipline problems in her school. She illustrated,

Our school has 'Responsive Classroom Building.' It is a way of teaching children that we are a community of caring learners for each other. We start out with morning meetings and everyone is in a circle and they talk about various things. They may talk about things that happened in the community or things that happened the evening before or maybe news articles that people are aware off, it depends on the level of the children. But all the classes have the morning meetings, and what that does is it helps some children if they had difficulty in the home, or even on the bus to be able to resolve that through the class meeting before it becomes an issue.

Smith reported that Responsive Classroom Building helped her students to adjust to school, and at the same time provided the entire school the opportunity to have informal conversations and interactions.

CREATING CULTURALLY INCLUSIVE AND PARTNERSHIP BETWEEN THE SCHOOLS AND SOMALI IMMIGRANT FAMILIES

This section of the chapter will focus on the extent to which school principals seek to build partnership with the Somali parents and create culturally inclusive schools. With respect to creating culturally inclusive schools that encourages the Somali families to be part of the school community, two of the three school principals interviewed, Anderson and Smith indicated that they focused on first building a trust and relationship with the Somali immigrant parents. They alluded to creating spaces for a dialogue and understanding. Anderson indicated that she understands the social and economic conditions of the families—that some parents are not able to attend parent teachers' conference because of work schedules. Therefore to foster partnership with the parents, she said, "In the fall, we do conferences at a couple of apartment buildings that had the most Somali families, so that they don't have to drive some place … So we do a little outreach to them because we want them to know that they are important. So in the fall, we hold conferences where they live. It is very comforting because they can talk to someone in their own language. There is just a trust that has been built up in our school." Smith also expressed an awareness of the Somali culture and Islam which had enabled her to understand better the needs and experiences of the Somali students and their parents. As well, Smith's definition of culturally inclusive school meant creating a school community in which the Somali families felt a sense of being part of the school community. For instance, the Somali families utilized the gym in the school for the night prayers during the month of Ramadan. She also provided a quiet place for some sixth grade students that desired to pray during the lunch hour. For Smith providing certain services that are needed by the Somali families enabled her to build a partnership with the Somali families. In addition, Smith pointed out that she works closely with a Somali community leader, who represents the families in the neighborhood. The community leader discussed the needs and concerns with Smith.

When we asked whether teachers are culturally knowledgeable in dealing with the Somali immigrant students, the findings show that at North Albion, the teachers are reported to have multicultural education training; also, the principal and the teachers read articles and books and engage in discussions on certain issues that include poverty, change, the achievement-gap, and the possible reasons students of color are behind. However, Anderson voiced that the curriculum represents the values of the Caucasian middle class. That is, students' diverse cultures are not incorporated into the curriculum, as she put it:

> We don't teach a multicultural education unit, and sometimes I feel bad about that because you know I think it would be a nice feel for Native American kids to be able to have an opportunity to talk in their classes, or African American kids in their math classes to see more African American faces of mathematicians. So our school hasn't gone to that level of the conscious multicultural education that we as a school are going to have a much higher awareness of the different cultures. But, on a level of student to teacher, I think that we are very accepting of different cultures.

Anderson did not show how she would attempt to promote a culturally diverse teachers and curriculum. She left that task to the school district because she said the school follows state curriculum. Creating inclusive school requires from school principals to foster respect for cultural diversity. It is vital that the curriculum reflects the cultures and histories of the immigrant children so that the children and their families are more connected to the schools.

At Mandela school, Smith maintained that the teachers in her school understand students' cultural backgrounds that it was a process that involved learning for her and the teachers. She explained, "Over time it has evolved that way. When I go back and think about the first families that came, we had to have that awareness of the culture." However, Smith acknowledges that she would still like to see more culturally diverse teachers and educational assistants. She said that the obstacle to establishing more diverse faculty is a lack of Somali teachers and educational assistants.

The findings also show that the partnership between the school and the Somali families at North Albion is not strong. Anderson elaborated,

> As far as our partnership, I think we have a long way to go. I think we have opened the door, many of our families and parents do identify Hussein as a person who is from North Albion Junior High School. And they feel comfortable having him contact them. But, we would certainly like the Somali families to be able to be more involved, like for this coming year on our site council, one of the Somali parents, a mother is going to be on our site council.

She added that she would like to do more outreach and involve more Somali parents in site council and other parent advisory positions. For Anderson, the focus has been to bridge the communication gap and understand more about the socio-economic conditions of the Somali families.

Both Anderson and Baldwin also explained the challenges that the Somali immigrant families are going through. For instance, Anderson stated,

> I know there is still a barrier because the Somali families have, as many immigrants do, to figure out about where is the money coming from, where is the job? Many of our families do not have the fathers here, it is only the mother. We have many families who not only have just the mother, but the older children are required to take more responsibility for taking care of the younger kids, and they need to do babysitting. We have some families that the mother is still in Somalia, the father works a lot and may actually be traveling for the work, and then some of the older sisters have to take the responsibility for being the mothers, so they don't finish high school because they take on those roles.

Moreover, the findings of this study show that in the initial contact with the Somali families, the school principals were unaware of the lived experiences of the Somali and other refugees' children. For Anderson, for instance there was an expressed lack of awareness of the experiences of the Somali and Hmong children. She explained,

> Certainly, one of the things I was lacking was just my understanding of what their lives were like in their homeland, what their educational experiences were like in their homeland. Certainly, for the Hmong and for the Somali students I was unaware of how much violence the children saw and how much of an impact it had on them. For some of the kids, no avenue to really talk about some of the deaths they saw. Just that whole general knowledge, understanding sensitivity to what they experienced before they came here is probably the area that I was lacking the most in.

Anderson did not discuss about how she would address the students that have been exposed to violence.

There seems to be a need to look into new ways that provides a caring school environment that attends to and genuinely addresses the psychological wellbeing of the students who are going through posttraumatic disorders, for instance. Thus, it is imperative that these children are provided a psychologically safe place that would enable them to share their stories with school social worker, counselors, and other psychologists that could be solicited from other agencies. To adequately meet the needs of immigrant students requires a different approach that involves being more resourceful in building partnership with other agencies that could provide certain social programs that immigrant students and their families may need.

The research consistently suggests that, in schools that effectively educate ethnically diverse students, the school leaders lead with caring and foster a climate of caring. In other words, it is imperative to lead with an "ethics of caring" and to promote an environment embedded in social justice and a democratic learning community within the schools (Furman, 2000). All three of the school principals showed an understanding of the struggles that the Somali immigrant students are going through; and they are striving to improve the school climate. But, even with a healthy school climate, because of the language barrier, immigrant students might find it difficult to fit in and might feel isolated from the other students. As such, the school principals did not emphasize how they would ensure an empathetic school environment that nurtures immigrant students.

To create culturally inclusive schools, the literature suggests that schools must transform the curriculum into what Ladson-Billings (1994) calls "culturally relevant." Ladson-Billings recommends that educators and teachers adopt and implement culturally relevant knowledge and teaching. According to Ladson-Billings, culturally relevant knowledge is the notion of recognizing the significance and respecting the knowledge that students from different cultural backgrounds bring into the classroom. In addition, culturally relevant teaching also focuses on the teacher facilitating knowledge sharing, preparing students to be critical thinkers, and thereby supporting them to identify the relationships among "community, state, and globe" (p. 49). Even though the school principals—both Anderson and Smith—showed an awareness of the hegemonic curriculum that represents the values of the dominant Caucasian middle-class groups in society, they did not mention ways they could make the curriculum more inclusive of the immigrant students' diverse cultures. For instance, none of the schools principals reported whether they plan to adopt reading literature that represents the Somali, Hmong and Latino/a students' cultural backgrounds.

Furthermore, Gardiner and Enomoto (2006) suggest that, when dealing with ethnically and linguistically diverse school populations, school leaders should engage in transformative work by advocating for marginalized families and providing programs such as ESL classes, day care and hiring parents as cafeteria workers or teacher aides. Such support programs somewhat improve the social and economic conditions of the families and, at the same time, enhance the school/family partnership. Anderson indicated that her school does not have a strong partnership with the Somali families, apart from having conferences in the area where the families are concentrated and having interpreters communicate with the parents when issues arise. Holding parent/teacher conferences at the parents' location is a first step, but this does not constitute real partnership.

CONCLUSIONS AND RECOMMENDATIONS

Meeting the educational needs of all students and creating culturally inclusive schools requires that the school principals first reexamine the schools' visions and address the question of whether the schools' visions represent the educational aspirations of low socioeconomic, immigrant and other minority families. We believe that school visions that were created decades ago no longer represent the values of ethnically and linguistically diverse school communities. Therefore, maintaining and implementing such visions would continue to perpetuate more inequality for minority and immigrant students. Second, building a vision that represents the values of the entire community requires that the principals (Anderson and Smith) promote dialogical relations between ethnically and linguistically diverse communities, including the immigrants and other marginalized groups. Third, the school leaders ought to harness support from the school boards, districts, and the communities. Palmer writes, "The growth of any craft depends on shared practice and honest dialogue among the people who do it" (1998, p. 144). Through dialogue, school visions that represent the collective interest of the entire communities may emerge, and, ultimately, an education viable for educating culturally and linguistically diverse students can be created.

Furthermore, in order for the school principals to turn the schools into learning communities that are culturally inclusive, it is essential to build relationships and trust among the teachers, students, and families—including immigrant parents. Shields and Edwards (2005) suggest the use of a carnival as a "catalyst" to "recreate and rejuvenate dialogue" (p. 141). In addition, they indicate that dialogue can be used not only to build relationships but also to diminish certain organizational factors that perpetuate inequities and hinder a healthy learning community. Therefore, it is imperative that the school principals create nonacademic activities that could provide the opportunities for immigrant families and the teachers to get to know each other on a personal level. Eventually, an approach that involves relationship building could assist the school principals' efforts to create more inclusive school cultures that sustain partnerships with the immigrant families.

With respect to connecting the curriculum to the students' cultures—to create a sense of belonging for the immigrant students and to engage them in learning, the school principals would have to create "personal linkages" to the students' diverse cultures by connecting the curriculum to the students' needs. For instance, school principals and teachers could adopt books for reading that represent and affirm the immigrant students' cultures (Katz, 1999; Hertsberg, 1998). Certainly, such books may have positive influence on students' self-worth and identity.

In addition, to create academically responsive classrooms that are also culturally inclusive would require the school principals to differentiate professional development for teachers (Tomlinson & Allan, 2000) and would also align professional development with the needs of the immigrant students (Fienberg, 2000). For instance, Principals Anderson and Smith talked about educating teachers about the poverty and needs of immigrant students. But there was no indication of aligning professional development with the needs of the immigrant students. Nor did Anderson and Smith discuss adopting professional development that is geared toward educating teachers about refugees and immigrants (some of whom grew up in refugee camps).

To create a genuine school and immigrant family partnership, research recommends that school principals attend to the needs of the parents by providing English language classes, offering full time day-care, creating a site for parents at the school and hiring parents as teacher aides (Gardiner & Enomoto, 2006; Gitlin et al., 2003). Providing such services not only enhance the school/family partnership but also contribute to the advancement of social justice.

The literature shows that certain schools have established programs that made a difference in educating immigrant students. Such school programs concentrated on addressing the psychological, social and academic needs of immigrant students (Feinberg, 2000). Apart from providing ESL and other core subjects, the school principals in this study did not report creating specific programs that dealt with students' psychological needs. Also, the three schools do not have partnerships with social service agencies that could provide counseling to children who have witnessed violence and the trauma of war. For instance, Anderson indicated that her school does not have the capacity to provide counseling to

Somali and Hmong students. It is vital to work with other agencies and social services in order to provide counseling to those children. Immigrant and refugee children—specifically those that witnessed violence—need more than ESL and Somali language classes.

Certainly, the principals and teachers need to take a more activist role in order to attend to the academic and the psychological needs of the children. This is not an easy task, but it is one that is necessary if the children are to adjust well to school and succeed. This would also require that the school principals communicate to the parents the importance of counseling for some of the children who have witnessed the civil war in Somalia. Somali culture regards anyone who attends counseling as mentally ill; there is stigma attached to seeking psychological treatment or counseling. Therefore, the school principals must work with community leaders and explain to the parents the importance of seeking counseling for children in need of psychological services. As I have indicated elsewhere in this paper, research shows that immigrant/refugee children who have witnessed violence tend to have behavior problems and to engage in fights at school. Therefore, if the Somali refugee/immigrant students are to be adequately educated, addressing only language proficiency is not enough. There has to be a holistic approach to addressing the needs of Somali and other immigrant students. There are those who contend school principals should focus on instructional supervision and make sure the curriculum is delivered accordingly. We believe strongly that adequately ensuring successful student learning and teaching first requires an understanding of the factors that influence student learning. Without addressing those factors, it would be unlikely for students to be able to act normally and focus on learning.

In addition, given that the school principals indicated that the Somali parents are struggling to adjust and raise children since some of them work two jobs and also face a language barrier, it is challenging for parents also to help support and improve the literacy of their children. Therefore, it would be beneficial if the school principals were to create and provide summer reading programs for the Somali immigrant students. Kim (2006) studied the effects of a voluntary summer reading intervention on reading performance. He carried out a pretest–posttest, control-group experimental design study that measured the effects of voluntary summer reading intervention on fourth-grade students during the summer. The study was a randomized field trial which involved a sample of 552 students in 10 schools in the Lake County school district. Fourth-grade students received eight books to read at home with their parents or family members. After the summer, standardized tests were carried out to measure whether voluntary reading during the summer increased or improved lower-performing students' performance in reading. The findings of the study show that voluntary summer reading could be a viable option for improving performance in reading for low-performing students, particularly minority students. For instance, the treatment effects on a standardized test of reading achievement (Iowa Test of Basic Skills) show that the effect size was largest for African American students (ES = .22) and Latino students (ES = .14). The study shows that summer reading programs could be employed to increase the reading performance of minority and low-income students. Hence, I suggest that if the schools promote reading programs during the summer, such programs would also be beneficial to immigrant students who might not have the support to read at home during the summer.

Furthermore, establishing mentoring programs in the schools is imperative since the children need positive role models. One or two educational assistants in each school are not able to provide the Somali students the mentoring they need, because the educational assistants not only assist students in the classroom but also interpret for the teachers and parents, as Smith reported. As a result, recruiting Somali professionals who live in the area or Somali students who attend nearby colleges and universities could be advantageous for the children, because mentors could spend some quality time and provide positive guidance to the students.

To successfully meet the needs of Somali immigrant students, the school leaders and teachers need to be the "agents of change" that are committed to the advancement of the values of social justice. This would involve "unpacking" previous approaches and taking a more activist approach to educating immigrant students. Smith demonstrated that taking an active role in providing certain needed services to the families has created a positive relationship between the school and the families. It requires democratic leadership in order to advocate for the voices of immigrant families and other marginalized groups in the schools. This would also involve empowering or helping immigrant parents and community members tap into their energies in order to allow a stronger collective approach to educating the students

REFERENCES

Alitolppa-Niitamo, A. (2002). The generation in-between: Somali youth and schooling in metropolitan Helsinki. *International Education, 13*(3), 275–290.

Feinberg, R. C. (2000). Newcomer schools: Salvation or segregated oblivion for Immigrant students? *Theory into Practice, 39* (4), 220–227.

Hertzberg, M. (1998). Having arrived: Dimensions of educational success in a transitional newcomer school. *Anthropology & Education Quarterly, 29*(4), 391–418.

Gardiner, M. E., Enomoto, E. K. (2006). Urban school principals and their roles as multicultural leaders. *Urban Education, 41*(6), 560–584.

Gitlin, A., Buendia, E., Crosland, K., & Doumbia, F. (2003). The production of margin and center: Welcoming-unwelcoming of immigrant students. *American Educational Research Journal, 40* (1), 91–122.

Katz, A. (1999). Keepin' it real: Personalizing school experience for diverse learners to create harmony and minimize interethnic conflict. *The Journal of Negro Education, 68*(4), 496–510.

Kim, J. S. (2006). Effects of voluntary summer reading intervention on reading achievement: Results for randomized field trail. *Educational Evaluation and Policy Analysis, 28*(4), 335–355.

Ladson-Billings, G. (1994). *The Dream keepers: Successful teachers of African American children*. San Francisco: Jossey-Bass.

McBrien, J. L. (2005). Educational needs and barriers for refugee students in the United States: A review of the literature. *Review of Educational Research, 75*(3), 329–64.

Nieto, S. (2000). *Affirming diversity: The sociopolitical context of multicultural education.* (3rd ed.). New York: Addison Wesley Longman, Inc.

Palmer, P. (1998). *The courage to teach: Exploring the inner landscape of a teacher's life.* San Francisco: Jossey-Bass.

Perkins, M. L. (2000). The new immigrant and education: Challenges and issues. *Educational Horizons, 78*(2), 67–71.

Riehl, C. J. (2000). The principal's role in creating inclusive schools for diverse students: A review of normative, empirical, and critical literature on the practice of educational administration. *Review of Educational Research, 70*(1), 55–81.

Schultz, R., & Hertz, D. (2006). Navigating through high school. *Principal Leadership, 6*(6), 29–32.

Senge, P. M., Cambron-McCabe, N., Lucas, T., Smith, B., Dutton, J., & Kleiner, A. (2000). Schools that learn: *A fifth discipline field book for educators, parents, and everyone who cares about education.* New York: Doubleday.

Shields, C. M., & Edwards, M. M. (2005). *Dialogue is not just talk: A new ground for educational leadership.* New York: Peter Lang.

Tomlinson, C. A., & Allan, S. D. (2000). *Leadership for differentiating schools and classrooms.* Alexandria, Virginia: Association for Supervision and Curriculum Development.

Zhou, Min (1997). Immigrant adaptation and native-born responses in the making of Americans. *International Migration Review, 31*(4), 975–1008.

Implementation of Supportive School Programs for Immigrant Students in the United States

By Szu-Yin Chu

ABSTRACT: *The growing number of immigrant students in the United States continues to affect school programs. First, the author describes the issues that challenge immigrant students, including varying levels of language and academic performance, funding and school resources, and flexibility and accountability. Then, the author discuss what school leaders can do for these students, such as provide supportive school programs and services. In reviewing the characteristics of successful programs, school leaders can better understand how to work effectively with immigrant students. The author concludes with recommendations on evaluating programs and services for immigrants.*

KEYWORDS: *challenging issues, immigrant students, school leader, supportive programs*

The flow of immigrant's changes the demographic character of U.S. elementary and secondary schools. Currently, approximately one in five students in kindergarten through Grade 12 is the child of immigrants. The student makeup includes foreign-born U.S. citizens, native-born children of immigrant parents, and undocumented immigrants (Fix & Passel, 2003). Also, first- and second-generation immigrant students are the fastest growing population in U.S. schools (Capps et al., 2005). Thus, U.S. schools have not only been struggling to serve the existing population of immigrant students but also face a future increase in this population. Immigrant education is a current issue in educational policy circles that educators should address (Gershberg, Danenberg, & Sanchez, 2004).

The Emergency Immigrant Education Assistance (EIEA) Act of 1984 authorized funds to provide needed services for immigrant students. The Emergency Immigrant Education Program (EIEP; Houston Independent School District, 1997) is designed to help immigrant students, those who are born outside the United States and have attended school in the United States for fewer than 3 complete

Szu-Yin Chu, "Implementation of Supportive School Programs for Immigrant Students in the United States," *Preventing School Failure*, vol. 53, no. 2, pp. 67-72. Copyright © 2009 by Taylor & Francis Group LLC. Reprinted with permission.

years (Landerman & Sonnen, 1999). The purpose of the EIEP is to help local education agencies (LEAs) to provide high-quality instruction to immigrant children and youth, help these children and youth with their transition to U.S. society, and meet the same challenging state performance standards that school officials expect of all children and youth.

IMMIGRATION TRENDS AND EFFECTS ON SCHOOLS

The larger trends of immigration reflect the composition of the school population. About 40% of foreign-born immigrants are limited English proficiency (LEP) students. The largest share of foreign-born immigrants is found in middle and high schools rather than in elementary schools (Ruiz-de-Velasco, Fix, & Clewell, 2000). Over 50% of second-generation immigrants are LEP students at the elementary level. Furthermore, most LEP students are native-born students (children of immigrants or children of native-born parents; Capps et al., 2005).

By 2000, the five states with the highest percentage of LEP elementary school students were California, Texas, New York, Florida, and Illinois, which represented 68% of the total number of LEP students in the United States. However, the population of immigrant students is growing the fastest in other states. These growing immigrant student populations are dispersed across all regions of the United States (Capps et al., 2005). The states with the fastest growing numbers of immigrant students also have the fastest growing numbers of LEP students (Fix & Passel, 2003).

Immigrant students are largely served in high-LEP schools, which are located primarily in urban areas. Most LEP students attend schools in which less than 1% of all students are LEP students (Cosentino de Cohen, Deterding, & Clewell, 2005). The new pattern of segregation of LEP students may be emerging because these students in high-LEP schools are isolated from mainstream education (Ruiz-de-Velasco et al., 2000). In addition, the educational services (e.g., quality of school personnel and instructional techniques) of high-LEP schools are different from those of low-LEP schools. For example, high-LEP schools are more likely to have unqualified teachers and substitute teachers. However, in high-LEP schools, native-language instruction is more prevalent (Cosentino de Cohen et al.).

CHALLENGING ISSUES FOR IMMIGRANT STUDENTS

There are three issues related to immigrant students' education in the United States that educators should address, including language and educational achievement, school resources and funding, and flexibility and accountability.

Varying Levels of Language and Educational Achievement

Diversity of students' language proficiency. Immigrant students enter U.S. public schools with different levels of language proficiency and educational achievement. Language proficiency of immigrant students varies with country of origin (e.g., 56% of immigrant students are Hispanic, yet they represent 75% of LEP students; 22% of immigrant students are Asian, yet they represent 13% of LEP students; Ruiz-de-Velasco et al., 2000). Although 25% of immigrants come from countries in which English is the dominant language, this does not mean these students can properly use American English. Educators need to appropriately assess proficiency in the English language among immigrant students prior to enrollment (Beutler, Briggs, Hornibrook-Hehr, & Warren-Sams, 1998).

Academic performance. Because not all immigrant students have been included in national tests, the limited national data on performance (i.e., SATs) of both native- and foreign-born immigrant students makes it difficult to articulate how well they perform. When examining students' school completion, dropout rates vary by immigrant group (e.g., Asian immigrants' dropout rates are lower than those of Mexican immigrants) and different generations (i.e., first-generation students have higher dropout rates than do second generation students1; Ruiz-de-Velasco et al., 2000).

Participation in special education. In addition, recent immigrant students have lower test scores and much lower rates of participation in special education than do native-born students. The rates of participation in special education for recent immigrant students also vary by country of origin (Conger, Schwartz, & Stiefel, 2003). Although the data show that immigrant students have lower rates of participation in special education, educators should still handle not only cultural and linguistic differences but also disabilities. Furthermore, family poverty and personal trauma that immigrant students have experienced may necessitate special education services. Also, educators need to distinguish between a language-learning disability and language difference (Al-Hassan & Gardner, 2002). Therefore, educators should not neglect the effect of immigration on general and special education.

Funding and School Resources for Immigrant Students

On the basis of the concept of equity, educators need to address the relation between school resources and immigrant students (Schwartz & Stiefel, 2004). Educators should focus on how to appropriately apply funds to benefit such students. Furthermore, educators should determine the effect of funding on immigrants, including whether they can access supporting school systems and equalized educational opportunities when students have adequate federal funding (Landerman & Sonnen, 1999).

Although the implementation of supporting school systems must be through resources and funding, there is no specific legislation regarding resources for immigrant students except the federal funding through the EIEP (Schwartz & Stiefel, 2004). In addition, not all immigrant students can receive these funds, because districts (i.e., LEAs) may distribute funds to the specific schools. Immigrant students may not receive funds if they live in LEAs that do not qualify for immigrant funding (i.e., districts with a population that contains fewer than 3% immigrants; Landerman & Sonnen, 1999). Another issue is that federal funds are fixed; not all states can receive the same amount. Some states may get more funding, whereas other states may lose funding (Fix & Passel, 2003).

Schwartz and Stiefel (2004) have indicated that immigrant students are treated inequitably. For example, the nonclassroom expenditures (e.g., counseling and parental outreach) for foreign-born students were fewer than those for other students. However, less spending and large class sizes for immigrants may be compensated by having better qualified teachers. In general, educators need to consider factors that can affect spending on immigrant students, such as enrollment, poverty, limited English proficiency status, and part- and full-time special education status.

Flexibility and Accountability

Not all immigrant students and families are familiar with the U.S. school systems. They frequently face challenging educational experiences, especially regarding flexibility and accountability at the schools, once they enter school systems (Landerman & Sonnen, 1999).

Flexibility. When discussing flexibility, education policymakers aim to determine the effect of funding. LEAs can use the EIEP grants to provide supplemental educational services (e.g., bilingual educational services). The strength of the EIEP is its flexibility in providing support for instructional activities and materials (e.g., field trips) not available through other sources. This process of support can also contribute to students' education outcomes (U.S. Department of Education, 1995). At the same time, many practitioners do not want to specifically tie EIEP funds to student outcomes. Practitioners prefer to flexibly use funds to support other programs (e.g., social services) that may not be funded (Landerman & Sonnen, 1999).

Accountability. The No Child Left Behind (NCLB) Act of 2002 has recently imposed the challenge of new accountability measures for immigrant students (Schwartz & Stiefel, 2004). The NCLB Act emphasizes testing by standardized tests and focuses on English proficiency. Schools may rely less on programs (e.g., bilingual education) that can address the deep needs of building English and native-language skills for immigrant students. Some of these students do not perform well on tests because they may have difficulties in learning English, which create high dropout rates (Capps et al., 2005).

Although school districts provide the resources and services for immigrant students through EIEP funds, accountability data for immigrant students are questionable. There is a limited amount of data regarding immigrant students and their performance that can be shared with teachers. In addition, no specific content standards can guide classroom instruction, and no specific student performance standards can articulate what students are expected to know. Therefore, it is difficult to evaluate whether programs are effective for immigrant students (Ruiz-de-Velasco et al., 2000).

Because of the aforementioned challenges, immigrant students with and without disabilities need effective supporting systems to increase their access and engagement in schools. Educators should answer two key questions: What school systems can best prepare immigrant students for the future? and What school programs can accommodate their needs in limited resources and funding?

IMPLEMENTATION OF SUPPORTING SCHOOL SYSTEMS FOR IMMIGRANT STUDENTS IN THE UNITED STATES

School leaders should provide supportive services for immigrant students to succeed academically and adapt to American society. At the same time, school leaders should consider developing positive learning contexts for immigrants before beginning to design programs, which may include the issues of sociocultural contexts (e.g., discrimination toward immigrant students), structural obstacles of U.S. schools (e.g., departmentalized and fragmented structures), and special education services (because factors, such as personal trauma and poverty, may increase the need for special education services even though some immigrant students are not identified; Al-Hassan & Gardner, 2002; Walqui, 2000). Issues for supportive school programs include program design and implementation, features and components of successful programs, best practices in implementation, and evaluation of effective school programs.

Program Design and Implementation

A school system needs to be well prepared before immigrant students enroll. Promoting the success of these students and of the student community as a whole should be the primary purpose in implementing changes in school systems. School leaders should develop approaches for establishing effective education for immigrant students at elementary- and secondary-level schools (Lucas, 1996). In designing programs, school leaders need to consider the following to meet immigrant students' needs: what approaches or programs should be included, what supporting services should be provided, and what factors school leaders should consider in implementing a program.

Included approaches or programs. Because there is only one federal funding program, EIEP, school leaders should develop alternative approaches (e.g., English as a second language programs, sheltered English content programs, bilingual education programs) and encourage district and state support to serve immigrant students. The importance of such programs is to support these students and their families throughout the school system. When school leaders handle operating programs, they should consider the following: what programs they choose to meet students' needs, what relevant policies may affect students' learning, and how to collaborate with local and state-level government officials.

On the basis of survey data that Gershberg et al. (2004) collected, the primary challenge that immigrant students encounter is English language and academic development in school. In California, schools offer state-funded and administrated programs that help meet immigrant students' needs, including the Community-Based English Tutoring Program, English Language Acquisition Program, and English Language and Intensive Literacy Program. LEAs received funding to initiate these programs that serve not only immigrant students but also English language learners. These programs help students who have language difficulties meet the state's academic and performance standards. Also, LEAs used funding for other student needs, such as transportation services (to and from programs; Gershberg et al.). School leaders need to consider how to spend appropriately on a language acquisition program. A large share of foreign-born immigrant students are in the secondary level (i.e. middle and high schools), but spending on language resources is specifically focusing on the elementary level (Ruiz-de-Velasco et al., 2000).

In addition, newcomer programs are designed to help recent immigrants (those who arrived in the United States fewer than 3 academic years ago) adjust to school and society (Lucas, 1996). Newcomer programs are unlike other programs because they include the comprehensive delivery of services for immigrants. The focus of these programs is on not only academic development, but also supportive services tailored to students' special needs (e.g., survival skills and cross-cultural communication skills). Educators need to consider the following procedures before designing newcomer programs: (a) planning (rationale for the planning program), (b) legal requirements (whether to provide resources to meet students' needs), (c) intake (standardized procedures for identifying students' needs), (d) staff, curriculum, and instruction (school qualification of school personnel and content courses on the basis of district requirement), and (e) evaluation (measurement of students' progress; Chang, 1990; Friedlander, 1991).

Another approach is to develop alternative school programs, especially for immigrant students at the secondary level. These are not temporary programs. School leaders need to consider that some of these students may not attend school at the regular time. Also, school leaders need to provide these students with alternative school programs for studying, such as late-afternoon academic programs (Lucas, 1996).

Last, school leaders cannot ignore the fact that the dropout rate of students with disabilities is twice that of general education students. School leaders should consider supportive services also for immigrant students with disabilities, which include organizing school learning environments to offer quality of instruction and early intervention programs for immigrant students with disabilities, partnering with immigrant parents in designing IEPs and providing parents with comprehensive information, and using fair and equitable assessing procedures to identity students' special needs (Smith-Davis, 2000; Spaulding, Carolino, Amen, & Smith, 2004).

Supportive services. In addition to challenges of language and communication, immigrant students need to face other major challenges, such as fear of legal issues, parental participation and involvement, and general health and social services concerns (Gershberg et al., 2004). Therefore, immigrant students need not only language and academic development, but also comprehensive and supporting systems to help them succeed. School leaders should provide supporting services to work effectively with this group and their families. They should also provide a broad range of supporting services on the basis of students' needs, such as counseling, parent outreach, and career education (Friedlander, 1991).

Factors for implementation. To work effectively with immigrant students, the factors related to program implementation should be addressed, including (a) program location (separate site or not), (b) program structure (what course content should be included), (c) transition to other programs (how long immigrant students stay at a newcomer program before moving to mainstream classes, and (d) registration and placement procedures (students' information from registration procedures used to identify students' needs; Mace-Matluck, Alexander-Kasparik, & Queen, 1998). At the same time, school leaders should decide which program option is better by examining local resources and the previous education experiences of immigrants. The most important goal is to help immigrant students perform well with regular content (Chang, 1990; Lucas, 1996).

Features and Components of a Successful Program

Even though model programs for immigrants could not be replicated, the quality of programs must be based on the concrete features (Mace-Matluck et al., 1998). School leaders should identify the features of schools that promote the success of these students. The features of programs tailored to the needs of immigrant students include the following elements (Adger, 1996; Chang, 1990; Mace-Matluck et al., 1998; Walqui, 2000; Walsh & Prashker, 1991):

1. Build strong leadership at the school sites: All school personnel share a unitary vision of change and believe that change is well worth the time and effort.
2. Provide students a multitude of support services such as group counseling, peer tutoring, and career education.
3. Place high importance on parental involvement.
4. Guide selection of students' courses and programs on the basis of academic preparation for immigrants.
5. Provide access to content and promote engagement by using students' first language in classes.
6. Respond to students' needs through flexible curricula (e.g., individual learning plans) and scheduling (e.g., offer working immigrant students opportunity to attend classes during nontraditional school hours).
7. Adequately train and license qualified teachers.

In addition to learning from the aforementioned features of successful programs, school leaders also need to ensure implementation of programs that involve all learners, school staff, and the whole community in co-constructing achievement for all (Chang, 1990). No two programs are identical, but school leaders should pursue the same goal: to help immigrant students succeed in U.S. schools.

Evaluation of Effective School Programs

According to legal requirements (e.g., EIEA), school leaders must attain the goal of educating immigrant students by maintaining and developing high-quality instructional programs and services (California State Department of Education, 1999; Ruiz-de-Velasco et al., 2000). The guidelines for school leaders and districts are as follows:

1. Establish criteria (for considering the implementation of a program), and document the provided services to determine the effectiveness of the program.

2. Use standards to guide and evaluate language instruction (i.e., how well do immigrants perform on speaking, reading, and writing English) and core curriculum (i.e., how well do immigrant students master the core subjects).
3. Use students' performance data to identify students' grade level and at-risk students.
4. When gathering performance data, consider immigrant students' English language proficiency, progress in learning the core curriculum, and graduation and attendance rates.
5. Organize data and form conclusions on the effectiveness of the program.
6. Improve programs by using data as a guide, and collaborate with teachers and administrators to decide how to improve programs for immigrant students.

CONCLUSION

Immigrant students and families encounter numerous challenges in the majority of U.S. school districts. Many school districts are not appropriately staffed or equipped to provide comprehensive support to help immigrant students (with and without disabilities) in reaching their potential (Smith-Davis, 2000). School leaders should serve as gatekeepers to ensure that competent school personnel work effectively with all immigrant students. Furthermore, school leaders should help immigrant parents understand the issues regarding school practices, such as enrollment procedures, the choices of school and language programs, and the rights to other related educational services (Gershberg et al., 2004; Ruiz-de-Velasco et al., 2000).

Because schools lack valid and reliable measurements to identify ELLs, there is confusion as to whether immigrants should be viewed as ELLs. School leaders should consider how to appropriately address immigrant students' needs (e.g., whether schools should use funding for building language programs). In addition, research data could not explain the correlation between funding and students' outcomes (i.e., whether resources helped students accomplish their academic goals; Landerman & Sonnen, 1999; Schwartz & Stiefel, 2004). However, the most important step school leaders need to take is to ensure that immigrant students receive resources based on educational needs, rather than newcomer status. Also, school leaders need to consider how best to expand the limited resources they have. In addition, they should determine whether additional funds will cover the additional costs of education (e.g., hiring teachers with language credentials) for immigrant students (Gershberg et al., 2004).

Implications for current and future education policy and practice for immigrants should be identified, such as the need to gather information to develop successful practices (or build effective programs), obtain more rigorous evaluation of these programs in and across school districts, and conduct more research to help identify the appropriate program design for a specific group of immigrant students and their educational goals. Educators should be strongly commited: "It is the school's responsibilities to get students on the right track—the track called success" (Schnur, 1999, p. 52).

NOTE

1. First-generation students are foreign-born immigrants; second-generation students are native-born immigrants.

AUTHOR NOTE

Szu-Yin Chu is a doctoral student in the Department of Special Education at the University of Texas at Austin. Her research interests are cultural and linguistic diversities in special education, family-professional collaboration, teacher preparation for diverse students with and without disabilities, and prereferral intervention.

REFERENCES

Adger, C. T. (1996). *Language minority students in school reform: The role of collaboration.* Washington, D.C.: ERIC Clearinghouse on Languages and Linguistics. (ERIC Document Reproduction Service No. ED400681)

Al-Hassan, S., & Gardner, R., III (2002). Involving immigrant parents of students with disabilities in the educational process. *Teaching Exceptional Children*, 34(5), 52–58.

Beutler, M., Briggs, M., Hornibrook-Hehr, D., & Warren-Sams, B. (1998). *Improving education for immigrant students: A guide for K-12 educators in the Northwest and Alaska. Portland*, OR: Northwest Regional Educational Laboratory (ERIC Document Reproduction Service No. ED425893).

California State Department of Education. (1999). *Designing a standards-based accountability system for language minority and immigrant student populations: A guide for school district personnel and program evaluators.* (2nd ed.). Sacramento, CA: Language Policy and Leadership Office and the Language Office Proficiency and Academic Accountability Unit. (ERIC Document Reproduction Service No. ED447159).

Capps, R., Fix, M., Murray, J., Ost, J., Passel, J. S., & Herwantoro, S. (2005). *The new demography of America's schools: Immigration and the No Child Left Behind Act.* Washington, D.C.: The Urban Institute.

Chang, H. N. (1990). *Newcomer programs: Innovative efforts to meet the educational challenges of immigrant students.* San Francisco: California Tomorrow.

Conger, D., Schwartz, A. E., & Stiefel, L. (2003). *Who are our students? A statistical portrait of immigrant students in New York City elementary and middle schools.* New York: New York University.

Cosentino de Cohen, C., Deterding, N., & Clewell, B. C. (2005). Who's left behind? Immigrant children in high and low LEP schools. Washington, D.C.: Urban Institute.

Gershberg, A. I., Danenberg, A., & Sanchez, P. (2004). *Beyond "bilingual" education: New immigrants and public school policies in California.* Washington, D.C.: Urban Institute.

Fix, M., & Passel, J. S. (2003). *U.S. immigration: Trends and implications for schools.* Washington, D.C.: Urban Institute.

Friedlander, M. (1991). *The newcomer program: Helping immigrant students succeed in U.S. schools.* Washington, D.C.: National Clearinghouse for Bilingual Education.

Houston Independent School District. (1997). *Emergency immigrant education program (EIEP), 1996–97: Research report on an educational program*. Houston, TX: Texas Department of Research and Accountability. (ERIC Document Reproduction Service No. ED032845).

Landerman, P. W., & Sonnen, A. M. (1999). *The superintendency and educational research: The emergency immigrant education program*. (ERIC Document Reproduction Service No. ED432815).

Lucas, T. (1996). *Promoting secondary school transitions for immigrant adolescents*. Washington, D.C.: ERIC Clearinghouse on Languages and Linguistics. (ERIC Document Reproduction Service No. ED402786).

Mace-Matluck, B., Alexander-Kasparik, R., & Queen, R. M. (1998). *Qualities of effective programs for immigrant adolescents with limited schooling*. Washington, D.C.: ERIC Clearinghouse on Languages and Linguistics. (ERIC Document Reproduction Service No. ED423667).

Ruiz-de-Velasco, J., Fix, M., & Clewell, B. C. (2000). *Overlooked & underserved: Immigrant students in U.S. secondary schools*. Washington, D.C.: The Urban Institute.

Schnur, B. (1999). *A newcomer's high school*. Educational Leadership, 56(7), 50–52.

Schwartz, A. E., & Stiefel, L. (2004). Immigrants and the distribution of resources within an urban school district. *Educational Evaluation and Policy Analysis*, 26, 303–327.

Smith-Davis, J. (2000). *Immigrant students with disabilities in the U.S. public schools: Preliminary findings of a pilot study*. Retrieved February 15, 2007, from Council for Exceptional Children database.

Spaulding, S., Carolino, B., Amen, K.-A., & Smith, K. B., ed. (2004). *Immigrant students and secondary school reform: Compendium of best practices*. Washington, D.C.: Council of Chief State School Officers.

United States Public Law 103-382, "Title VII-Bilingual Education, Language Enhancement, and Language Acquisition Programs." Oct. 1994.

U.S. Department of Education. (1995). *Biennial evaluation report in fiscal year 1993–1994*. Retrieved March 15, 2007, from http://www.ed.gov/pubs/Biennial/index.html.

Walqui, A. (2000). *Access and engagement: Program design and instructional approaches for immigrant students in secondary school*. Washington, D.C.: Center for Applied Linguistics.

Walsh, C., & Prashker, H. (1991). *Literacy development for bilingual students: A manual for secondary teachers and administrators*. Boston: New England Multifunctional Resource Center for Language and Culture in Education. (ERIC Document Reproduction Service No. ED331319).

CPSIA information can be obtained at www.ICGtesting.com
Printed in the USA
269909BV00003B/11/P